THE OXFORD HANDBOOK OF

THE PSYCHOLOGY
OF APPEARANCE

THE OXFORD HANDBOOK OF

THE

PSYCHOLOGY OF

APPEARANCE

Edited by

NICHOLA RUMSEY

Centre for Appearance Research, Department of Psychology
Faculty of Health and Life Sciences
University of the West of England, Bristol, UK

and

DIANA HARCOURT

Centre for Appearance Research, Department of Psychology
Faculty of Health and Life Sciences
University of the West of England, Bristol, UK

OXFORD
UNIVERSITY PRESS

OXFORD
UNIVERSITY PRESS

Great Clarendon Street, Oxford OX2 6DP
United Kingdom

Oxford University Press is a department of the University of Oxford.
It furthers the University's objective of excellence in research, scholarship,
and education by publishing worldwide. Oxford is a registered trade mark of
Oxford University Press in the UK and in certain other countries

© Oxford University Press, 2012

The moral rights of the authors have been asserted

First Published 2012

Impression: 1

British Library Cataloguing in Publication Data
Data available

Library of Congress Cataloguing in Publication Data
Library of Congress Control Number: 2012937861

ISBN 978-0-19-958052-1

Printed and bound in Great Britain by
CPI Group (UK) Ltd, Croydon, CR0 4YY

Whilst every effort has been made to ensure that the contents of this work
are as complete, accurate and-up-to-date as possible at the date of writing,
Oxford University Press is not able to give any guarantee or assurance that
such is the case. Readers are urged to take appropriately qualified medical
advice in all cases. The information in this work is intended to be useful to the
general reader, but should not be used as a means of self-diagnosis or for the
prescription of medication.

Links to third party websites are provided by Oxford in good faith and
for information only. Oxford disclaims any responsibility for the materials
contained in any third party website referenced in this work.

DEDICATIONS

....

To the Kennedy men; Ian, Alex, and James. Big thanks
for walking through life with me. (NR)

To my Mum and Dad and everyone who asked 'Is the book finished yet?' (DH)

FOREWORD

························

As a graduate student in the early 1970s, I was in search of a meaningful direction for my doctoral dissertation on self-disclosure in the initial acquaintance process. My mentor suggested that I consider how "the physical attractiveness variable" might influence this commencement of interpersonal interactions. Surely, I thought, he must be kidding or testing my foolishness. Why would I risk my doctorate on something so subjective and superficial . . . so unscientific? However, after reading the nascent research on the subject, I followed his advice. At that point and over the subsequent course of my career as a clinical and research psychologist, I came to understand the power, both subtle and profound, of human physical appearance.

Fast forward forty years and here we have this marvelous handbook that thoughtfully educates its readers on the psychology of appearance. This volume draws from decades of various scientific literatures and from emerging applications to assist people affected by appearance-related concerns that challenge the quality of their life experiences. Editors Nichola Rumsey and Diana Harcourt, who are highly esteemed scholars in this interdisciplinary field, have assembled knowledgeable contributors to construct a volume with exceptional breadth and depth.

Their book intelligently incorporates the two core perspectives on physical appearance. The first is the "outside or social-observer view," which pertains to social perceptions of appearance and appearance-based stereotyping and behaviors. Clearly people's lives are affected by how others judge them and treat them us based on their looks. The second perspective is the "inside or self view"—namely, the self-perceptions and attitudes that constitute the contemporary body image concept. Body image strongly affects how people think and feel about themselves, how they behave, and how they relate to others. Regardless of its cause or its focus, a negative body image can greatly undermine self-acceptance, psychosocial functioning, and day-to-day quality of life.

The fifty chapters in *The Oxford Handbook of the Psychology of Appearance* are effectively organized into five sections. The first four sections are helpfully launched by the editors' overview of the ensuing content and are concluded by their summary and synthesis of the preceding chapters. The fifth section and chapter provides the editors' own insightful visions for the field. I commend the editors for sounding their well-spoken voices throughout the volume.

Over the course of this handbook, we come to better understand and genuinely care about how appearance and appearance-altering conditions shape lives within the contexts of culture, gender, human development, familial and interpersonal transactions, and healthcare systems. We learn about the extant theories, methods, and technologies for the study of appearance. We are provided with a critical examination of interventions, both biomedical and psychosocial, intended to enhance the quality of embodied lives. We are invited to consider the need for systemic, societal changes to promote appearance acceptance, whether one's own appearance or that of others. We are always encouraged to identify compassionately with the experiences of persons with visible differences.

This unique compendium is a valuable resource to diverse audiences—researchers, practitioners, social commentators, and policy makers; students and professionals in social and behavioral sciences and those in medical and allied health disciplines; as well as all educated persons who simply wish to expand their awareness of a thought-provoking and influential aspect of the human condition. I extend my gratitude and congratulations to the editors and contributors for this outstanding achievement and advancement of knowledge.

Thomas F. Cash, Ph.D.
Professor Emeritus of Psychology
Old Dominion University
Norfolk, Virginia USA

Contents

SECTION 2 WHO IS AFFECTED BY APPEARANCE CONCERNS, IN WHAT WAY, AND WHY?

SECTION 2.1 APPEARANCE CONCERNS ACROSS THE LIFESPAN

SECTION 2.2 INDIVIDUAL DIFFERENCES IN ADJUSTMENT AND DISTRESS

SECTION 2.3 CONSEQUENCES OF APPEARANCE CONCERNS

SECTION 2.4 EXPERIENCES OF PEOPLE WHO HAVE A VISIBLE DIFFERENCE

SECTION 3 WHAT NEEDS TO CHANGE AND HOW CAN CHANGE BE ACHIEVED?

SECTION 3.1 SOCIETAL INTERVENTIONS

SECTION 3.2 INTERVENTIONS AT AN INDIVIDUAL OR GROUP LEVEL

SECTION 4 RESEARCH ISSUES

SECTION 5 WHERE DO WE GO FROM HERE?

LIST OF CONTRIBUTORS

Lucie Baker
Edith Cowan University,
Perth, Australia

Amanda Bates
University of Kent,
Canterbury, UK

Rebecca Bellew
University of the West of England,
Bristol, UK

Alyson Bessell
University of Plymouth,
Plymouth, UK

Kristin Billaud Feragen
Bredtvet Resource Centre,
Oslo, Norway

Sue Brown
Royal Victoria Infirmary,
Newcastle, UK

Christine Bundy
University of Manchester,
Manchester, UK

Peter E. M. Butler
Royal Free Hospital,
London, UK

James Byron-Daniel
University of the West of England,
Bristol, UK

Julia Cadogan
North Bristol NHS Trust,
Bristol, UK

Alex Clarke
Royal Free Hospital,
London, UK

Neil S. Coulson
University of Nottingham,
Nottingham, UK

Canice E. Crerand
University of Pennsylvania,
Philadelphia, PA, USA

Deirdre Desmond
Trinity College,
Dublin, Ireland

Phillippa C. Diedrichs
University of the West of England,
Bristol, UK

Emma Dures
University of the West of England,
Bristol, UK

Hannah Falvey
The Royal London Hospital,
London, UK

Helen J. Fawkner
Leeds Metropolitan University,
Leeds, UK

Hannah Frith
University of Brighton,
Brighton, UK

Pamela Gallagher
Trinity College,
Dublin, Ireland

Sarah Gaskell
Royal Manchester Children's Hospital,
Manchester, UK

Eyal Gringart
Edith Cowan University,
Perth, Australia

Sarah Grogan
Staffordshire University,
Stoke on Trent, UK

Barrie Gunter
University of Leicester,
Leicester, UK

Emma Halliwell
University of the West of England,
Bristol, UK

Esther L. E. Hansen
Royal Free Hospital,
London, UK

Diana Harcourt
University of the West of England,
Bristol, UK

Nikki Hayfield
University of the West of England,
Bristol, UK

Caroline Huxley
University of Warwick,
Coventry, UK

Elizabeth Jenkinson
University of the West of England,
Bristol, UK

Julie Kent
University of the West of England,
Bristol, UK

Ross Krawczyk
University of South Florida,
Tampa, FL, USA

Victoria Lawson
University College,
London, UK

Valerie Lemaine
Mayo Clinic,
Rochester, MN, USA

Leanne Magee
Children's Hospital of Philadelphia,
Philadelphia, PA, USA

Malcolm MacLachlan
Trinity College,
Dublin, Ireland

Helen Malson
University of the West of England,
Bristol, UK

Daniel Masterson
Staffordshire University,
Stoke-on-Trent, UK

David Mellor
Deakin University,
Melbourne, Australia

Jessie Menzel
University of South Florida,
Tampa, FL, USA

Timothy P. Moss
University of the West of England,
Bristol, UK

Habib Naqvi
NHS Bristol,
Bristol, UK

Grainne Ni Mháille
Trinity College,
Dublin, Ireland

James Partridge
Changing Faces,
London, UK

Martin Persson
University of Bristol,
Bristol, UK

Tom Potokar
Morriston Hospital,
Swansea, UK

Patricia Price
Cardiff University,
Cardiff, UK

Andrea Pusic
Memorial Sloan-Kettering,
New York, USA

Lina A. Ricciardelli
School of Psychology,
Deakin University,
Burwood, Australia

Ben Rosser
University of Bath,
Bath, UK

Nichola Rumsey
University of the West of England,
Bristol, UK

David B. Sarwer
University of Pennsylvania,
Philadelphia, PA, USA

Krysia Saul
Warwick University,
Coventry, UK

Julie Slevec
Flinders University,
Adelaide, Australia

Linda Smolak
School of Psychology,
Deakin University,
Burwood, Australia

Andrew R. Thompson
University of Sheffield,
Sheffield, UK

J. Kevin Thompson
University of South Florida,
Tampa, FL, USA

Marika Tiggemann
Flinders University,
Adelaide, Australia

Irmgard Tischner
University of Worcester,
Worcester, UK

Melissa Wallace
University of Cape Town,
Cape Town, South Africa

Julie Wisely
University Hospital of South
Manchester,
Manchester, UK

Heidi Williamson
University of the West of England,
Bristol, UK

LIST OF ABBREVIATIONS

ARC	Appearance Research Collaboration
ASAPS	American Society for Aesthetic Plastic Surgery
ASPS	American Society of Plastic Surgeons
BAAPS	British Association of Aesthetic Plastic Surgeons
BAPRAS	British Association of Plastic, Reconstructive & Aesthetic Surgeons
BCC	basal cell carcinoma
BDD	body dysmorphic disorder
BHF	British Heart Foundation
BIS-OA	Body Image Scale for Older Adults
BMA	British Medical Association
BMI	body mass index
CAR	Centre for Appearance Research
CBT	cognitive behaviour therapy
CLAPA	Cleft Lip and Palate Association
CQC	Care Quality Commission
CUA	cost–utility analysis
CVD	cardiovascular disease
DAS	Derriford Appearance Scale
DHHS	Department of Health and Human Services
DOL	Department of Labor
ERISA	Employee Retirement Income Security Act
EU	European Union
GMC	General Medical Council
GP	general practitioner
HAART	highly-active antiretroviral therapy
HAES	Health At Every Size
HMO	health maintenance organization
HNC	head and neck cancer
HRQoL	health-related quality of life
IAT	Implicit Association Test
ICU	Intensive Care Unit
IHAS	Independent Healthcare Advisory Services
ISAPS	International Society of Aesthetic Plastic Surgery
LMICs	low- and middle-income countries

NHS	National Health Service
NIMH	National Institute of Mental Health
NICE	National Institute for Health and Clinical Excellence
PPI	patient and public involvement
PRO	patient-reported outcome
PROM	patient-reported outcome measure
PsA	psoriatic arthritis
PTSD	post-traumatic stress disorder
TCD	Tissue and Cell Directive
QALY	quality-adjusted life-year
SCC	squamous cell carcinoma
SDT	self-discrepancy theory
SES	socioeconomic status
SIST	social interaction skills training
SPA	social physique anxiety
UK	United Kingdom
US	United States
WHCRA	Women's Health and Cancer Rights Act
WHO	World Health Organization

INTRODUCTION

NICHOLA RUMSEY

DIANA HARCOURT

THERE has been interest in appearance since records began, but never have 'looks' demanded as much attention, particularly in resource-rich countries, as now. The extent of the preoccupation of many societies with appearance is evidenced through frequent reports of widespread body dissatisfaction amongst young people and adults of all ages, the proportion of airtime devoted to watching makeover shows and music videos and reading magazine articles about how to correct 'faults' in the way we look, and in rises in the rates of appearance-altering practices (including cosmetic surgery and the use of steroids to increase muscularity in men). In a recent survey of 77,000 adults (the largest study into appearance-related concerns to date; Diedrichs et al. (in preparation)), only 16% of women and 27% of men reported liking what they see when they look in the mirror, whilst 46% of women and 62% of men reported feeing ashamed of how they look. More than two-thirds of women (70%) and almost half of men (41%) felt pressure from the media to have a perfect body. The psychological impact of these high levels of dissatisfaction is significant and growing, is affecting self-perceptions and social functioning, and is contributing to the uptake and maintenance of a range of behaviours associated with increased risk for disease (including, for example, smoking and disordered eating as means of managing body size). The need for interventions to support those with appearance-related concerns and for initiatives to promote greater acceptance of diversity in appearance is pressing. In addition, approximately one in five people have a condition which results in an appearance which is different from the 'norm'. Research has demonstrated that having a disfigurement in societies in which appearance is a 'social currency' can be associated with a range of personal and social challenges (Rumsey and Harcourt, 2005). These are amongst the issues that this book sets out to explore.

There have been several significant milestones in this field since we published our last book, *The Psychology of Appearance*, in 2005. Notably, the first full face transplant (which was on the horizon at that time) took place in 2010, and there has been a flurry of media interest in issues related to visible difference, in contrast to the virtual lack of media attention given to this topic in 2005. A number of high-profile campaigns to promote diversity of appearance and body confidence have been launched, and, on a more personal level, the size and focus of the centre in which we both work, the Centre for Appearance Research (CAR), has continued to expand.

Interest in the applied and academic study of the psychology of appearance has increased rapidly in recent years, and bookshelves have started to fill with a growing number of texts on the subject. However, whereas previous texts tend to take a pathologizing stance with a focus on body dissatisfaction and associated problems, we have wanted to offer a more balanced approach, by including research which focuses on psychosocial factors and processes contributing to resilience to appearance concern, by exploring the potential to use people's motivation to enhance appearance as a mechanism to improve health and by examining the factors that influence positive adjustment to an unusual appearance. We have also been keen to include the full spectrum of appearance-related issues rather than focusing solely on 'body image' and its concomitant emphasis on issues relating to weight and shape, and to include disfigurement in this spectrum, rather than treating research and practice on visible difference as a sphere of activity entirely separately from the more 'mainstream' area of body image.

We have also wanted to offer a societal perspective and to give those who are personally affected by appearance issues (both positive and negative) and those working 'at the coal face' (e.g. surgeons, practitioner psychologists, heads of support organizations) the opportunity for their voices to be heard. We have encouraged contributors to include examples from their own work, and quotes from participants/clients wherever appropriate and possible. This reflects the book's applied and interventionist perspective, with a focus on 'knowledge in action' and on the application of research in policy and practice. The majority of contributors are from the UK, but others offer perspectives from the US, Australia, Ireland, and across Europe, and reflections on issues relevant to resource-poor countries.

In drawing together this collection of chapters, we have grouped them into five sections. Firstly, the contributors to Section 1 set the scene for the rest of the book by providing an overview of key research areas and knowledge. Section 2 then asks the big question, 'Who is affected, in what way, and why?', before Section 3 examines what needs to be changed and considers how change could be achieved. Section 4 focuses on issues facing researchers in this field and, finally, in Section 5 we reflect on what still needs to be known, and suggest ways ahead whilst also acknowledging that this book has raised as many questions as it has answered. We introduce each section with an overview of the contributions that follow, and then, in the syntheses, have drawn out what we consider to be key issues cutting across the chapters in each section.

For us, the process of writing does not get easier or quicker as we gain in experience and we were simultaneously flattered and daunted at the prospect of pulling together a volume of this size. As ever, we have snatched pockets of time away from the hurly-burly of CAR. The project was launched as we sat in a cafe next to Sydney Harbour Bridge and completed the task of drawing up a 'wish list' of those we wanted to be involved. We were then delighted when the chapter authors accepted our invitation to contribute. We have known and enjoyed working with many of the contributors for some time. Others we approached by virtue of their reputations in the field, and we are grateful that this book has given us an opportunity to work with them. Their contributions were welcome additions to ours, and it was exciting and rewarding to see their chapters arrive in our overflowing email boxes. We would like to take this opportunity to thank them all for sharing their expertise and enthusiasm for appearance-related research and practice, and for finding the time in their busy lives to work on this book with us.

Over the years, we have developed various coping strategies which have helped us to complete this, and other daunting tasks. One is a bi-annual escape to Cornwall in the South West of England. It was there that we engrossed ourselves in the process of editing this volume, pulling together the framework for the introductions and syntheses on long blustery cliff walks, far away from the day-to-day business of the research centre. Thanks to all at CAR for holding the fort and smiling through gritted teeth when we returned refreshed.

This book is dedicated to all those who have been a part of our working lives over the past few years. In particular, members of CAR both past and present, too numerous to mention individually, who have made it a great place to work; Emma Thomas for keeping us organized, never complaining, and calmly helping us through times of stress; members of the CAR Steering Committee for their support and guidance over the years; Chris Ward for his ceaseless encouragement and faith in all that we aspire to achieve; and to Alex Clarke for her time and energy and enduring commitment to evidence-based practice. Her insights into both research and practice continually leave us in awe. Finally, we are hugely grateful to those who have funded our research and taken such an interest in supporting psychological research into appearance, particularly the Healing Foundation and the Vocational Training Charitable Trust (VTCT).

REFERENCES

Diedrichs, P. C., Rumsey, N., Halliwell, E., & Paraskeva, N. (in preparation). Body image in Britain: The prevalence of appearance concerns among 77630 adults.

Rumsey, N. & Harcourt, D. (2005). *The Psychology of Appearance*. Maidenhead: Open University Press.

SECTION 1

SETTING THE SCENE

CHAPTER 1

SETTING THE SCENE: OVERVIEW

NICHOLA RUMSEY
DIANA HARCOURT

THIS opening section is designed to provide the backdrop for later chapters by introducing readers to a range of contexts, perspectives, and influences contributing to the psychology of appearance. The authors offer insights from a variety of professional backgrounds, including social, clinical, and health psychology, surgery, and sociology. The influence of the private sector is highlighted in relation to messages promulgated by the media, the marketing of new technologies, and in conditions attached to health insurance. Within the public sector, health policies and the prioritization of resources both regionally and nationally limit the current provision of care for those distressed by their appearance. The relative sophistication of the challenges in the United Kingdom (UK) and the United States (US) is brought into sharp relief, however, by a consideration of the issues faced by those working in resource-poor countries.

Hannah Frith's chapter describes what she calls the 'scopic economy'. She explores the role of the media in communicating and reinforcing stereotypes through words and pictures depicting people's outward appearances. Visual and written codes relating to clothing and other aspects of appearance are used to convey information about the status, socioeconomic position, and psychological character of the targets of newspaper and magazine articles, news items, and television (TV) programmes. Hannah's chapter then considers the role of different genres of television make-over programmes in depicting the relationship between physical appearances and the psyche, contrasting approaches revolving around humiliation and mockery compared with friendship and care.

Malcolm MacLachlan, Grainne Ni Mháille, Pamela Gallagher, and Deirdre Desmond describe the concept of embodiment and highlight the need to consider how people sense themselves, both inwardly and from the perspective of being a perceiver, through the medium of their own body. The ways in which experiences are affected by physical, psychological, and social exigencies are discussed through a focus on people with limb amputations and their use of prostheses.

Hannah Falvey argues that the deeper meanings of practices relating to body decoration, modification, adornment, and grooming can only be fully understood from within the cultural context in which they occur. She considers the neglected topic of variation in appearance values and practices in different societies and the extent to which particular cultural norms are adopted by subgroups within the population. The increasing homogeneity in ideals and aspirations across cultures is discussed, as is the increasingly prevalent view that bodies are malleable, rather than the less permeable result of genetic inheritance. The development and proliferation of new technologies for altering appearance and increased access to globalized media are reducing the influence of culture, eroding traditional appearance practices, and narrowing the acceptable range of diversity in appearance.

Esther Hansen and Peter Butler both work in a large regional hospital in London. They make the case that plastic and reconstructive services should not be limited to a focus on altering appearance through surgery and other biomedical technologies. They describe the advantages of an integrated surgical and psychological approach to the provision of care and offer examples of how this has been achieved in their own service. They outline how specialist services are either accessed or denied in the UK and highlight the influence of clinicians' personal assumptions and beliefs—for example, the misguided assumption that the extent and severity of a physical difference in appearance predicts the degree of psychological distress.

Valerie Lemaine and Andrea Pusic then describe ongoing debates relating to the definitions and consequent funding of plastic and reconstructive surgery for people in the US, with a particular focus on whether procedures are considered 'cosmetic' or 'medically necessary'. They highlight challenges associated with providing effective and appropriate psychosocial services and the imperative, fuelled by the current climate of performance metrics, to develop patient-reported outcome measures (PROMs).

Tom Potokar and Patricia Price focus on the considerable challenges inherent in meeting the healthcare and psychosocial needs of people with appearance-related conditions in resource-poor countries across the world. They highlight the relative neglect in countries in which rates of injury are high and where need, particularly for physical and psychological rehabilitation, massively outstrips provision. Local priorities are usually to reduce mortality rates rather than to improve the quality of life of survivors of disease and trauma. Distances to healthcare facilities are often considerable, and once patients are physically healed, they return to communities with no facility for follow-up or ongoing psychosocial support. Tom and Patricia highlight the importance of overseas supporters taking time to assess and respond to local need rather than making their own assumptions about the most appropriate focus for aid and also the desirability of working in collaboration with local clinicians to bring about changes which are sustainable in the long term.

Julie Kent's chapter emphasizes that a social constructivist approach to understanding the impact and consequences of appearance concerns should not be confined to processes affecting the individual, but can also be used to understand the shaping of technologies used to 'correct' abnormalities of appearance and restore the body after trauma or disease. Julie also considers the impact of the marketing and advertising of new technologies, using breast implants and 'living skin' as examples. She explores how these processes can influence people's dissatisfaction with their bodies and their desire for and expectations of treatment.

Finally, Andrew Thompson highlights the multitude of factors influencing appearance concerns and the resulting complexities and challenges of theorizing in this area. He considers several key constructs and theoretical approaches derived from evolutionary, psychological, and sociocultural perspectives which have been proposed to explain how we make judgements concerning appearance both in relation to ourselves and to others. In order to maximize the potential contribution to knowledge, Andrew advocates a pluralist approach to theorizing. He concludes by offering a broad biopsychosocial framework developed from the research of a large collaboration of UK-based researchers and practitioners.

In the synthesis of this section, we consider the emerging themes from this group of chapters, including the influences on changing societal and cultural norms over time, the importance of people's subjective perceptions and experiences of their appearance, the influence of gatekeepers to care, and the implications that the myriad of factors influencing appearance concerns have for theory in this field.

CHAPTER 2

....

APPEARANCE AND SOCIETY

....

HANNAH FRITH

On 4 August 2010, Britain's largest circulation daily tabloid newspaper, *The Sun*, ran a vitriolic front page story about a woman, Teresa Bystram, who had taken her children for a 'nice day out' to the funeral of gunman Raoul Moat (Lazzeri, 2010). Alongside the narrative were photographs of Bystram and a short but evocative description of her physical appearance:

Jobless Bystram, who has never married, was in the same Chelsea soccer shirt she wore to the funeral. She was *swathed* in gold jewellery with a *chunky* ring on every finger and *three heavy* chains around her neck (p. 5, emphasis added).

Focusing on this story rather than those more obviously concerned with appearance (e.g. news coverage of face transplantation, see for example Gilbert 2010) may seem like an odd choice, but it precisely this kind of mundane, routine, and apparently incidental reference to visual appearance that I want to examine since they are so pervasive and powerful. While psychologists have long been interested in the media as a place where societal messages about appearance are circulated and may 'effect' the individual (see, for example, Hargreaves & Tiggemann, 2004; Grabe et al., 2008), sociologists have also been interested in the ways in which the media articulates particular kinds of citizenship and reproduces social divisions through appearance (Skeggs, 2000; Palmer, 2004). Appearance matters, then, since it is implicated not only in the intra- and interpersonal construction of subjectivity, but also in the rearticulation of social divisions and processes of inclusion and exclusion (Skeggs, 1999, 2001; Taylor, 2007). Visual codes simultaneously convey information about status or socioeconomic position and about psychological character, and are central to the processes of classification about the value and worth of ourselves and each other. For example, physical characteristics such as obesity are currently seen as 'aesthetic' markers of social class and as signs of self-indulgence, lack of control, and irresponsibility towards health (Shaw et al., 2003). Skeggs' foundational work on appearance and the reading of it (1997, 1999, 2001) is an important foundation to this chapter. Utilizing Bourdieu's economistic metaphor which describes social life as structured by the distribution of different forms of capital, Skeggs has convincingly argued that physical capital (our appearance) is one way of systematically organizing distinctions through bodily evaluations (based on age, size, hardness, symmetry, beauty, etc.). When combined with the cultural capital (or 'know-how') to present the body through dress, adornment, and other markers of 'taste', individuals can gain exchange value in the 'markets' of marriage, heterosexuality, and work. In this 'scopic economy' appearance is a central mechanism through which we become categorized, known, and placed by others. While individuals may use their embodied and cultural capital to stake a claim in the scopic economy, this claim is always unstable as it relies on being recognized 'as something' by others who may draw on different systems of interpretation and meaning. Skeggs' work speaks to the pain and humiliation of being misrecognized as having little or no value (2001). This chapter explores the dynamics of recognition and misrecognition as these are played out between media texts and their audiences. Firstly, I examine how the brief description of Bystram's appearance positions her as a 'chav'—a figure which circulates through popular cultural representations and has become a pervasive term of abuse for the white poor, evoking mockery and disgust (Tyler, 2008). Secondly, I examine how mockery, disgust, and humiliation are the emotional registers through which makeover television shows engage in symbolic violence against the working classes, before moving on to consider the implications of makeover shows which adopt a different emotional register.

The 'chav' has emerged as a reconfiguration of the familiar notion of the 'underclass' (Hayward & Yar, 2006). Depictions of the working class have always centred on appearance, practices of consumption, and perceived bodily excess since appearance is symbolically linked to a series of supposedly pathological, irresponsible, and immoral lifestyle practices and choices. But while previously the underclass was seen to arise out of a failure to follow long-established norms about engaging in economically or socially productive labour (reflected in moral panics about 'dole scroungers'[1] and 'single mums'), the chav is linked to failures in consumption. It is now unwillingness to consume or consuming in 'vulgar' or tasteless ways which

---

[1] The term 'dole-scrounger' is a pejorative term frequently used in the UK press to refer to someone who is unemployed and unwilling to work and they prefer to claim social security benefits as a way of funding their lifestyle.

mark out class distinctions (Hayward & Yar, 2006), since patterns of consumption have replaced work as a means of establishing and maintaining class-based identities (Bourdieu, 1984; Southerton, 2002). Individuals recognize themselves, and importantly are recognized by others, through their publicly visible consumer choices including the ways these are displayed on and through the body. The appearance of the chav offers visual markers of their abject status and signifies their lamentable lifestyle and morality. For example, the infamous website http://www.chavscum.co.uk claimed one could 'spot them a mile away' by their baseball caps, trainers and branded jackets, and their jewellery:

Thick gold chains: 'Size matters, only count a chain if it is at least 5mm think!'
Don't be put off if it's a rainy day, Chavs will wear their chains outside any garment on full display!'
Sovereign rings: 'The classy piece of hand furniture makes the wearer appear so rich and also comes in handy for giving the missus a back hander!' (cited in Hayward & Yar, 2006, p. 19).

Similarly, journalist Gina Davidson declared 'Call them what you will, identifying them is easy [...] the slack-jawed girls with enough gold or gold plated jewellery to put H Samuel out of business. They are the dole-scroungers, petty criminals, football hooligans and teenage pram-pushers' (cited in Tyler, 2008, p. 21). The 'look' of a chav is a means of identifying those who embody a particular kind of lifestyle marked by excessive sexuality and fertility (teenage pram pushers), a lack of productivity which is burdensome to others (dole-scroungers), and deviance which threatens social cohesion (petty criminals and football hooligans).

It is these processes of coding and recognizing class which are operating in *The Sun*'s description of Bystram, and in the responses to it, which make her identifiable as a 'chav' and an object of class-based abhorrence. It is no accident, for example, that Bystram's jewellery is given particular emphasis and is described as *excessive* (she is 'swathed' in jewellery with 'three heavy' chains around her neck, and a 'chunky' ring on 'every' finger). It is these references which mark her out as recognizable as a chav without the need to make overt reference to this term. In what Lawler (2005) calls 'a kind of join-the-dots pathologization', the reader is left to make the connections by understanding that certain kinds of clothing, accessories, and bodily appearance indicate the deeper, underlying pathology of the chav. Those readers who commented on *The Sun*'s website appeared able to decode the visual clues to reveal the full picture:

You've only got to see the tacky jewellery, rings on each finger, chunky bracelet and those tattoos, couple that with her footie top and it really speaks volumes about how classy this person is. So im not surprised she feels drawn to a thug!
She obviously needs the handouts, her fingers were full of gold rings ... brainless chavs should not be permitted to have children.

Looks like this scumbag only has 1 Chelsea top in her entire dirty wardrobe, along with her chav chunky jewellery, she really is vile.[2]

As well as reiterating the visual codes used in the newspaper the commentaries went on to mock her appearance, describing her as a 'hideous, gormless, tattooed old bag', who 'looks like Hugh Grant in a wig'. Not only are the readers able to recognize and share these visual codes, they also articulate the apparent identities and lifestyles which are presumed to lie beneath—Bystram is constructed as 'stupid', 'vile', 'moronic', or brainless.

Mockery (Raisborough & Adams, 2008) and disgust (Lawler, 2005; Tyler, 2008) such as that exemplified by the descriptions of Bystram's appearance have recently been examined as mechanisms for reconstituting class boundaries. Disgust is evoked by transgressions of taste embodied in and through working class appearance, so Bystram is positioned as disgusting in appearance, behaviour, and taste. As disgust (a sickening feeling of revulsion and nausea) maintains boundaries between *them* and *us*, it is profoundly social. *The Sun* invites a collective response of disgust from its readers explicitly by describing Bystram and her actions as 'sick' and implicitly by placing her at odds with the norms of social responsibility, productive labour, and sexual conservatism characteristic of the middle and 'respectable' working classes. This reaction is collectively given in the commentaries in which individuals present a consensual view of Bystram as sexually repulsive, vile, and dirty. Her appearance is disgusting but this signifies a deeper, pathological subjectivity. This heady mixture of mockery and disgust positions the chav as a figure that we love to hate. Nowhere is this more evident than in media discourse around the 'celebrity' chav where as audiences we are encouraged not to respond with admiration and aspirational desire (as we are to other celebrities) but instead with 'a pleasurable blend of contempt, envy, scepticism and prurience' (Tyler & Bennett, 2010, p. 375). Tyler and Bennett (2010) argue the mockery and derision loaded onto Coleen Rooney (wife of British footballer Wayne Rooney) and Kerry Katona (former pop personality and reality TV star) who are constantly sneered at for being both talentless and tasteless, represents a display of class hatred which would be considered inappropriate if expressed in relation to any other social marginal or disadvantaged group. Arguably, scorning the appearance and poor taste of the celebrity chav offers the pleasures of collective shaming and humiliating which enable 'us' to feel better about ourselves as we affirm that 'I am not that'. It positions 'us', as able to pass judgement on the inferiority, respectability, and morality of those beneath 'us' (Skeggs, 2005; Tyler & Bennett, 2010). Such affective engagement may be central to the lure and popularity of media formats.

---

[2] http://www.thesun.co.uk/sol/homepage/news/3082380/Raoul-Moat-fan-mum-Teresa-Bystrams-33000-benefits.html (accessed 24 August 2010).

There are a number of threads from this illustration which I want to draw together to take forward. The first is the idea that appearance is used as a visual short-cut to displaying and knowing the character and self-hood of individuals and collectivities. Second, this relies on the presentation of these visual codes and their recognition by others/audiences/viewers. Third, taste and distaste are used to construct and police the boundaries between collectivities. And finally, that these processes are infused with emotional appeals and responses. To further explore these ideas I turn away from *The Sun*'s representation of Bystram to consider another proliferating form of cultural representation where appearance and class based antagonisms have come under scrutiny—the makeover show. In particular, I want to compare the dynamics of the UK versions of *What Not to Wear* (WNTW) with that of *How to Look Good Naked* (HTLGN). While both programmes have been widely successful—attracting large audiences, running for a number of series and catapulting their hosts into 'celebrity' status—popular media commentary in the UK has drawn a sharp contrast between the two. While hosts of WNTW Trinny Woodall and Susannah Constantine were once described by Dimbleby as 'two of the cruellest women in the UK' (cited in Palmer, 2004), Gok Wan (presenter of HTLGN) has been described as 'genuinely non-judgemental' and the programme as 'TV's most benign makeover show' (Cooke, 2007).

Television makeover shows have been described as sites for the public denigration of 'women of little or no taste' by 'women of recognized taste' (McRobbie, 2004 p. 99), who are concerned with 'teaching' women how to display and perform the 'right' kind of femininity (McRobbie, 2004; Woods & Skeggs, 2004). They have also been castigated for perpetuating the idea that a woman's worth rests on her appearance, and for exacerbating body image anxieties and normalizing cosmetic surgery (Banet-Weiser & Portwood-Stacer, 2006; Kubic & Chory, 2007). As noted earlier, in consumer societies where the self is created through consumption practices displayed on and through the body, the body becomes a privileged signifier of the inner self. Makeover programmes, then, purport to offer more than simply an altered appearance—by transforming the physical, experts also 'fix' the psyche (Hayes, 2007). They offer the possibility of a new and improved self who embraces and embodies dominant norms of femininity, personal responsibility, self-determination, and class mobility. Drawing on Bourdieu's (1984) analysis of taste as a weapon of distinction, critical work has forcefully argued that makeover shows are highly visible, public sites of class-making (Tyler, 2008). Such work focuses on the ways structurally marginalized groups are re-presented, with careful attention to the ways they are forced to face 'their' shame as the initial stage to transformation, and to the humiliation they experience at the hands of makeover producers, hosts, and experts.

What Not to Wear has received particular scrutiny from academia. Briefly the format of the programme is that an unsuspecting woman, 'volunteered' for the show by friends or relatives who identify her as in need of transformation, is secretly filmed to document her daily fashion 'mistakes'. Hosts Trinny and Susannah offer to tackle the problem. Back in the studio the woman undresses in a cramped 'mirror room' so her body can be scrutinized from all angles. The hosts watch from a distance, giving their own biting critique of her problem areas and poor dress sense. Trinny and Susannah then instruct the woman in the 'rules' for creating a 'tasteful' look suitable for her age and shape, before giving her a sum of money so she can put these newly acquired skills into practice. The hosts watch her progress ready to scornfully intervene when she (inevitably) makes mistakes. Their work is done when the subject no longer needs advice and is able to control and monitor her own consumption of 'tasteful' attire that 'makes the most' of her body shape. Back in the studio the 'big reveal' where professional styling is coupled with new hairstyle and make up makes the transformation complete.

The narrative of the show rests on class distinction. Trinny and Susannah's expertise rests on their cultural capital—their supposed natural good taste as upper middle-class women—rather than on any professional training (Phillips, 2008). This natural taste contrasts with the set of acquired skills which the 'contestants' must learn in order to 'pass' as tasteful. While Trinny and Susannah claim to be 'friends' with their participants, class difference is constantly reiterated. Phillips draws attention the way in which a 'grand house in an unspecified central London location' masquerades as the pair's home or rightful location and is contrasted with their surprised exclamations of 'This is rather nice' when visiting other places such that 'the metropolitan sophistication of the presenters is firmly distanced from the everyday lives of their "out of town" subjects' (Phillips, 2008, p. 123). As Palmer argues (2004, p. 183), 'Trinny and Susannah already have the taste and style that the individual is seen to need. They are signifiers of middle-classness – in manner, accent and bearing'. The good taste of the presenters (and by implication the middle/upper classes more generally) is seen as a cut above the poor taste of the predominantly working-class participants who must learn to emulate their social superiors.

In contrast, the contestants are presented as lacking in taste and as bad subjects who fail to fully take on board the mechanisms of self-improvement and self-presentation which are core to values of social mobility and appropriate femininity. The show represents an active distancing from poor taste towards acceptance of and conformity to 'good' (read middle-class) taste through the consumption of the 'right kind' of consumer goods and deploying appropriate skills and cultural knowledge. If, as Biressi and Nunn (2008) argue, makeover television offers instructional tales about citizenship in late modernity it does so through 'invoking, exposing, shaming and instructing the bad subject' against which the viewers measure themselves (p. 15). Working class subjects are marked out as bad through the spectacle of embarrassment, humiliation, or mockery. This humiliation rests on hierarchical relationships between 'upper-class' experts and 'working-class' participants which manifests in a 'looking down' as part of a 'putting down' of working class taste and values. Surveillance and mockery are two of the key mechanisms through which this humiliation is enacted.

For example, the 'mirror' scene which marks the starting point for this transformation, has been seen by scholars drawing primarily on Foucauldian ideas about governmentality as a pivotal moment for surveillance of the body and the operation of power (Roberts, 2007; Gibbings & Taylor, 2010). Governmentality is useful for understanding how conduct is shaped by non-violent means—how we police ourselves—and how we take action to improve ourselves through means which are apparently freely chosen. The shift from the power of the external gaze through observation or surveillance by others to the internalized gaze in which we learn to police ourselves *as if* we are being observed and learn to see ourselves as others see us is central to this process. The coupling of the intimate surveillance which characterizes lifestyle television in which the audience observes hitherto private areas of life, with the panoptical mirror room and secret filming of the participants, makes *What Not to Wear* a site of governmentality par excellence. In lifestyle television, participants learn to see themselves in new ways, the dramatic narrative of the show is driven by the shock as participants become aware of the mismatch between how they view themselves and how they are viewed by others (Doyle & Karl, 2008; Gibbings & Taylor, 2010). Through these techniques (the mirror room, secret filming, commentaries from friends, relatives, and 'the-man-on-the-street') women are instructed in how to observe their bodies through a normalizing gaze which positions them as 'good' or 'bad'. The bad body is tasteless and is inappropriately cared for or has failed to be improved upon or capitalized upon—the woman has not 'made the best of herself'. Her dress is inappropriate for work—transforming her clothes will result in success in her 'professional' life ('professional' being a class-based euphemism cf. Gibbings and Taylor, 2010), her clothes make her look like a man—she needs to wear dresses and high heels. She should look sexy, but a 'respectable' sexy appropriate for her age. In other words, she learns to see herself through the normalizing gaze of middle-class, feminine, heterosexuality. According to Gill (2007), one of the striking aspects of postfeminist media culture is its obsessive preoccupation with the body in which femininity is defined almost exclusively as a bodily property. Media content is saturated with bodies which are evaluated, scrutinized, and dissected to identify both their successes and (perhaps more often) their failings. These bodies require constant monitoring, surveillance, and discipline in order to meet the demands of normative femininity.

Although surveillance is important, Trinny and Susannah do not simply watch their participants—they also 'giggle and laugh at their mistakes' as the women attempt to abide by 'the rules' in choosing their own outfits and 'guffaw then pounce and stop her' when she gets it wrong (McRobbie, 2004, pp. 105, 99–100). Many commentators have pointed to the mortification of participants as hosts Trinny and Susannah ridicule and poke fun at their apparent lack of taste as being one of the most unpalatable features of the show. But, humiliation and mockery as a *strategic orientation* for doing class distinction through the articulation of taste has received rather less attention (with the exception of Raisborough and Adams, 2008, and Mendible, 2004). That makeover shows have been identified as 'humiliating' for participants is worthy of further attention since humiliation has an interpersonal dimension (Gilbert, 1997). Humiliation is *done to* one person by another— 'humiliation involves being put into a lowly, debased and powerless position by someone who had, at that moment, greater power than oneself' (Miller, 1988, p. 44). The humiliation is *done to* participants by hosts Trinny and Susannah through the mechanisms of insult and mockery and serves to put participants *in their place*, in a position of low-class ignorance and poor taste. Mockery is a way of forcing the women to realize the distaste of her appearance. Raisborough and Adams (2008) have argued that mockery creates spaces for articulating class distinctions which are presented as fun and not-to-be-taken-seriously and simultaneously generate a distancing from these articulations as they are enunciated. As such, this may present a more superficially 'respectable', morally sensitive way of doing class-based distinction than less civil disgust.

These four key features of the show—(1) the naturalized 'taste' of the upper middle-class hosts which is the apparent basis of their expertise; (2) the relative lack of taste apparently exhibited by the targets of the makeover; (3) surveillance and scrutiny as a mechanism for control and governance; and (4) the use of mockery and 'bitchiness' as a mechanism for exerting judgement—are central to the making over of classed and gendered subjects. It is through these mechanisms that lifestyle programmes operate as sites of gross symbolic violence where class antagonisms and other social divisions, are rearticulated (McRobbie, 2004). If this is the case, what can we make of the claim that an alternative makeover show—*How to Look Good Naked*—is benign? In turning to this final point, I want to explore whether humiliation, mockery, and disgust with appearance are the only affective mechanisms at work in lifestyle television and whether these only work to position the audience *at a distance* from the women in the show.

My colleagues and I have argued elsewhere that HTLGN eschews a discourse of humiliation and instead draws on an alternative discourse of benign 'niceness' to propel contestants towards transformation (Frith et al., 2010). The show delights in 'close' relationships based on fun, friendship, and care. This invites us to re-examine the role of hosts/experts in dialogic processes of recognition, and to re-visit the affective dynamics of the programme to explore what is opened up when not viewed solely through the lens of humiliation and class degradation. While HTLGN follows the same basic narrative structure of WNTW—a woman is taught the 'rules' for dressing—there are some important differences. Firstly, host Gok Wan's 'expertise' is not based on 'natural' middle-class taste. Secondly, the problem in HTLGN is not the woman's poor taste or defective body, but her poor self-confidence and lack of body pride. Thirdly, surveillance and the gaze are central elements of the show which are used to praise appearance and as a mechanism for seeing the body positively. Finally, instead of drawing on mockery and humiliation, Gok draws on a discourse of friendship and care. I briefly outline each of these in turn.

Firstly, Gok's status as 'expert' does not arise from a naturalized class-based superiority, but instead (as is the case with other makeover shows such as *Queer Eye for a Straight Guy*) rests on the essentialist idea that gay men know how to dress, have natural good taste (Morrish and O'Mara, 2004; Gorman-Murray, 2006) and are naturally aligned with all things feminine (Maddison, 2000). Gok's sexuality is muted and decidedly asexual and devoid of desire on the show, which serve to render Gok safe and harmless. This 'suspended sexuality' (Frith et al., 2010) gives him a licence to talk about and handle women's bodies in a way which might otherwise be deemed as offensive or inappropriate, and to avoid being positioned as a competitor either in looks and beauty or for the straight male gaze. Instead he takes up the well worn position as the 'gay best friend' (Shugart, 2003). While this may bring its own difficulties, Gok is not positioned as inherently superior to or different from the women on his show in terms of social status.

Secondly, in contrast to Trinny and Susannah who are charged with identifying and labelling the 'problems' of the body and failures in taste which the women themselves do not recognize, in HTLGN women present themselves for transformation. While in WNTW it is the expert eye which hones in on the problems, in HTLGN the problems are in the woman's perception of herself. The 'problem' is not lack of taste and hopeless lack of knowledge about how to dress, rather the problem comes from within and is expressed through the body. This mismatch between the participant's view of her body-as-is and the body-as-seen places the programme firmly in the psychological space of body image. Changing her appearance is presented as a mechanism for provoking a changed relationship between the body and the self. While other shows (such as those based on cosmetic surgery) rely on altering the body so that it matches the person 'on the inside' allowing the 'real' self to be visible to others, in HTLGN the body remains the same and good enough as it is. Clothes are used to reveal the true value of her body to the woman herself. Gok's expertise lies in his ability to coax this new appreciation into being through his styling.

Thirdly, surveillance takes on a different tone in HTLGN. Rather than critiquing her body and dress, in the mirror scene in HTLGN Gok invites the woman to 'tell me what you see'. Standing *alongside* her, looking with her at her image in the mirror, Gok witnesses the woman viewing, scrutinizing, and evaluating her own body, without offering judgement. While the participant, tearful, and ashamed, unfurls a litany of complaints about the apparent flaws and shortcomings of her body, Gok stands silently by. Finally, Gok offers his own assessment of how he 'reads' or sees her body: 'I don't see a freak. I don't see big. I don't see too tall. I see a woman. And it's hugely sexy'.[3] The premise of the show, then, is that the visual

---

[3] All extracts from *How to Look Good Naked* are taken from series 4, show 5 (first broadcast 6 May 2008) unless otherwise stated.

can be read, understood, or evaluated in more than one way. Seeing is not neutral, what we see and recognize depends on the interpretative framework that we bring to making sense of appearance. Unlike WNTW in which other people judge the participant's bodily appearance to be lacking, here others are used to heap praise and admiration on the participant. Her body is exposed to the scrutiny of others in a range of different ways—from over-sized billboards depicting her in her underwear, to being a naked live mannequin in a shop window, or stopping people on the street to ask their opinion. 'The public' are used to confirm Gok's evaluation that her body is 'gorgeous' as it is. For example, as pictures of one woman's body are splashed over the roof and bonnet of her car and displayed to her (female) work colleagues, they make to-be-read-as complementary comments about her 'fantastic boobs', 'lovely skin tone', and 'lovely hair'. They say that she 'should be proud of how she looks, because I would be if I looked like that'. Far from being a 'putting down' of participants, this is a 'building up' of their status and worth. HTLGN draws on a discourse of body affirmation and appreciation in which the contestant is encouraged to see her body as it is, as a beautiful and sexy source of pride. It is not lacking or in need of radical transformation through surgery. The purported aim of the show is not only that she 'learns the rules' of how to dress, but that she learns to love her body—dressed and undressed.

Finally, HTLGN does not draw on strategies of mockery and humiliation. Instead, Gok performs intimacy and friendship through a number of different devices— he uses a variety of pet names and intimate terms of endearment ('angel cake', 'girlfriend', 'darling', 'babes'), he uses informal language (tummies, racks, bangers, bellies), he caresses, strokes, and touches the women who appear on the show, enters into intimate spaces (the changing room or the bedroom), and explicitly positions himself as a friend and supporter:

You've been knocked down time and time again, but this time, you are going to pick yourself up, but you're not going to do it on your own, because I'm going to help you.

The relationship between Gok and the participants is constructed as one governed by warmth, intimacy, and care. Gok's expertise and 'the rules' are less important than how she feels about her body. The relationship is less hierarchical. Gok is not the social 'better'—he has no class-based capital on which to draw or yield. He does not look down on her nor judge her body to be deficient (indeed quite the opposite). Her body is identified as something to be admired rather than an object of revulsion (which typifies her own reaction).

I am not suggesting that HTLGN is not implicated in governmentality, the rearticulation of class-based divisions, or in normalizing heterosexual femininity— it certainly is. But, the mechanisms for propelling women towards these ends are different in WNTW and HTLGN. This raises the question, if the endpoint is the same does it matter if the mechanism is different? It is to this question that I now turn.

Concluding Remarks

This chapter has explored a number of examples of how appearance and the reading of it operate to produce class-based divisions and the different emotional registers which are used to do so—humiliation and mockery versus friendship and care. Mendible (2004) raises two interesting questions for us to consider when trying to make sense of a context in which humiliation is a commodity produced for entertainment. Firstly, if humiliation is a relational process in which the 'victim' is made aware of the fact that they are being humiliated while the 'perpetrator' is aware of the victim's position and derives satisfaction from it, how do we make sense of the fact that contestants willingly submit to their humiliation? Secondly, if gloating by the perpetrator is integral to this process, and if gloating involves thinking of oneself as superior and self-satisfied, then what should we make of the pleasure derived from watching another's humiliation and the fact that the viewers of reality television are predominantly women?

But humiliation is not the only narrative driver in reality television shows. Are we only, or always, watching these programmes as a gleeful opportunity to poke fun at, deride, and feel superior to the women on the screen? While this is undeniably a feature of the current cultural millieu (see Gill, 2007), an alternative set of questions are opened up when we consider care, friendship, and solidarity as alternative motivators for taking part and for watching (and enjoying watching) these programmes. What would it mean if instead of giggling and sniggering, we were moved to tears by these shows? What if the shows invite us to 'get closer' to the participants, instead of looking from a distance? What if we laugh with her as she enjoys her 'new look' and share the joy of transformed self? Are there pleasures to be gained in appearance work which go beyond the pleasure of 'putting down' other women?

Although this chapter has focused on media discourse and representation of appearance and the way this may shape audience readings, we might also consider these dynamics in relation to the interpersonal and intrapsychic dimensions of appearance and recognition. How might these dynamics inform our understanding of the exchange of appearance-based comments between, say, mothers and daughters, between girlfriends, or within ourselves?

References

Banet-Weiser, S. & Portwood-Stacer, L. (2006). 'I just want to be me again!' Beauty pageants, reality television and post-feminism. *Feminist Theory*, 7(2), 255–72.

Biressi, A. & Nunn, H. (2008). Bad citizens: The class politics of lifestyle television. In G. Palmer (ed.) *Exposing Lifestyle Television: The Big Reveal*, pp. 15–24. Ashgate: Aldershot.

Bourdieu, P. (1984). *Distinction: A Social Critique of the Judgement of Taste*. London: Polity Press.

Cooke. R. (2007). In Gok we trust. *The Observer*, 4 November.

Doyle, J. & Karl, I. (2008). Shame on you: Cosmetic surgery and class transformations in *10 Years Younger*. In G. Palmer (ed.) *Exposing Lifestyle Television: The Big Reveal*, pp. 83–97. Ashgate: Aldershot.

Frith, H., Raisborough, J., & Klein, O. (2010). C'mon girlfriend: Sisterhood, sexuality and the space of the benign in makeover TV. *International Journal of Cultural Studies*, 13(3), 1–19.

Gibbings, S. & Taylor, J. (2010). From rags to riches, the policing of fashion and identity: Governmentality and What Not to Wear. *Explorations in Anthropology*, 10(1), 31–47.

Gilbert, P. (1997). The evolution of social attractiveness and its role in shame, humiliation. *British Journal of Medical Psychology*, 70(2), 113–47.

Gilbert, H. (2010). Thank you for my new face. *The Sun*, 26 July. http://www.thesun.co.uk/sol/homepage/news/3069413/Face-transplant-man-thanks-doctors.html (accessed 3 September 2010).

Gill, R. (2007). Postfeminist media culture: elements of a sensibility. *European Journal of Cultural Studies*, 10(2), 147–66.

Gorman-Murray, A. (2006). Queering home or domesticating deviance? Interrogating gay domesticity through lifestyle television. *International Journal of Cultural Studies*, 9(2), 227–47.

Grabe, S., Ward, M. L., & Hyde, J. S. (2008). The role of the media in body image concerns among women: A meta-analysis of experimental and correlational studies. *Psychological Bulletin*, 134(3), 460–76.

Hargreaves, D. A. & Tiggemann, M. (2004). Idealized media images and adolescent body image: 'Comparing' boys and girls. *Body Image*, 1(4), 351–61.

Hayes, C. J. (2007). Cosmetic surgery and the televisual makeover: A Foucauldian feminist reading. *Feminist Media Studies*, 7(1), 17–32.

Hayward, K. & Yar, M. (2006). The 'chav' phenomenon: Consumption, media and the construction of a new underclass. *Crime, Media, Culture*, 2(1), 9–28.

Kubic, K. N. & Chory, R.M. (2007). Exposure to television makeover programs and perceptions of self. *Communication Research Reports*, 24(4), 283–91.

Lawler, S. (2005). Disgusted subjects: the making of middle-class identities. *Sociological Review*, 53(3), 429–46.

Lazzeri, A. (2010). Moat's funeral was better day out for the kids than Legoland. *The Sun*, 4 August, 1, 4, 5.

Lunt, P. & Lewis, T. (2008). Opera.com: Lifestyle expertise and the politics of recognition. *Women and Performance: A Journal of Feminist Theory*, 18(1), 9–24.

Palmer, G. (2004). 'The new you': Class and transformation in lifestyle television. In S. Holmes and D. Jermyn (eds.) *Understanding Reality Television*, pp. 173–90. London: Routledge.

Phillips, D. (2008). What not to buy: Consumption and anxiety in the television makeover. In G. Palmer (ed.) *Exposing Lifestyle Television: The Big Reveal*, pp. 117–28. Ashgate: Aldershot.

Maddison, S. (2000). *Fags, Hags and Queer Sisters*. London: Macmillan Press.

McRobbie, A. (2004). Notes on 'What not to wear' and post-feminist symbolic violence. *The Sociological Review*, 52(2), 97–109.

Mendible, M. (2004). Humiliation, subjectivity and reality TV. *Feminist Media Studies*, 4(3), 335–8.

Miller, S. B. (1988). Humiliation and shame. *Bulletin of Menninger Clinic*, 52(1), 40–51.

Morrish, L. & O'Mara, K. (2004). *Queer Eye for the Straight Guy*: Confirming and confounding masculinity. *Feminist Media Studies*, 4(3), 350–2.

Raisborough, J. & Adams, M. (2008). Mockery and morality in popular cultural representations of the white, working class. *Sociological Research Online*, 13(6), 2.

Roberts, M. (2007). The fashion police: Governing the self in What Not to Wear. In Y. Tasker and D. Negra (eds.) *Interrogating post-feminism: Gender and the politics of popular culture*, pp. 227–48. Durham, NC: Duke University Press.

Shaw, M. Tunstall, H., & Smith, G. D. (2003). Seeing social position: visualizing class in life and death. *International Journal of Epidemiology*, 32(3), 332–5.

Shugart, H. A. (2003). Reinventing privilege: The new (gay) man in contemporary popular media. *Critical Studies in Media Communication*, 20(1), 69–91.

Skeggs, B. (1997). *Formations of Class and Gender: Becoming Respectable*. London: Sage.

Skeggs, B. (1999). Matter out of space: Visibility and sexuality in leisure spaces. *Leisure Studies*, 18, 213–307.

Skeggs, B. (2000). The appearance of class: Challenges in gay space. In S. Munt (ed.) *Cultural Studies and the Working Class: Subject to Change*, pp. 129–250. London: Cassell.

Skeggs, B. (2001). The toilet paper: Femininity, class and misrecognition. *Women's Studies International Forum*, 24(2–3), 295–307.

Skeggs, B. (2005). The making of class and gender through visualising moral subject formation. *Sociology*, 39(5), 965–82.

Southerton, D. (2002). Boundaries of "Us" and "Them": Class, mobility and identification in a new town. *Sociology*, 36(1), 171–93.

Taylor, Y. (2007). 'If your face doesn't fit. . .': The misrecognition of working-class lesbians in social space. *Leisure Studies*, 29(2), 161–78.

Tyler, I. (2008). 'Chav mum chav scum.' Class disgust in contemporary Britain. *Feminist Media Studies*, 8(1), 17–34.

Tyler, I. & Bennett, B. (2010). 'Celebrity chav': Fame, femininity and social class. *European Journal of Cultural Studies*, 13(3), 375–93.

Wood, H. & Skeggs, B. (2004). Notes on ethical scenarios of self on British 'Reality' TV. *Feminist Media Studies*, 4(1), 205–8.

CHAPTER 3

EMBODIMENT AND APPEARANCE

MALCOLM MACLACHLAN

GRAINNE NI MHÁILLE

PAMELA GALLAGHER

DEIRDRE DESMOND

INTRODUCTION

THIS chapter introduces embodiment in relation to the psychology of appearance. We describe the concept of embodiment, its philosophical foundations, and psychological significance. While appearance is often about an 'outer-image', embodiment is concerned with how people sense themselves, both outwardly and inwardly—the experience of how one's body is perceived and, at the same time of being a perceiver, through one's own body. We illustrate the application of an embodiment perspective by focusing on people with physical disability, particularly people with limb amputations and their use of prosthetic technology. We conclude by presenting a framework for thinking about embodiment and appearance.

PHILOSOPHICAL ASPECTS OF EMBODIMENT

The body is 'always there' (James, 1890). Ironically, however, the body has been absent from much metaphysical enquiry. According to philosophers, such as Plato and Descartes, the person is made up of an immaterial mind and a corporeal matter. From this perspective, mind and body are two different substances and it is the mind that conveys a distinct human identity and occupies a super-ordinate position in human life. The embodiment perspective on the other hand, affiliates the person and the mind with corporeality. That is, the body is understood as a critical actor in human experience. Throughout our lifespan, corporeal developments and changes evoke meaningful changes in the social, emotional, and cognitive experiences and capabilities of the person. Embodiment can be defined as 'the identification of an abstract idea with a physical entity' (MacLachlan, 2004). The abstract idea could be the self, a nation, love, or independence and so on. If identified with the flesh, we use the term 'incarnate'—'the devil incarnate'; an expression of the devil, in the *flesh*. The word 'corporality', meaning *of the body*, can also be used to refer to embodied ideas that are incarnate.

PHENOMENOLOGY OF EMBODIMENT

From a phenomenological perspective, embodiment highlights the body as the basis for understanding everyday human experience; the body can be seen as the basis for mind and for an understanding of self. Gallagher (2005) uses the example of neonate proprioceptive awareness and imitative abilities as evidence that newborns have a sense of body and consequently of self. The body immerses us in the world and affords agency, thus conferring a sense of both capabilities and limitations. The boundaries and capabilities of the body allow for the development of a concept of self, which delimits the individual and which is personal. Our visceral experiences provide scope for subjectivity and, consequently, a unique sense of self is differentiated.

Bodily structures, capabilities, and experiences provide the basis and guide for human subjectivity which we create in our everyday lives. For example, Proffitt et al. (2003) found that individuals who were asked to wear heavy backpacks adjudged both hills and distance more severely than those who were not wearing backpacks. Similarly, individuals who were older or inactive saw hills as steeper, than younger or more active participants. Furthermore, emotional bodily states can affect the way individuals process information from the environment. Damasio's somatic marker hypothesis argues that the body and emotional processes guide decision-making in everyday life scenarios, particularly ambiguous situations (Damasio, 1994). Niedenthal and colleagues (2007) also suggested that bodily states influence information processing. They asked participants to rate the funniness of cartoons, whilst holding a pen between their teeth but not touching the lips (facilitating a smile), or conversely holding the pen between their lips but not touching the teeth (preventing a smile). Results revealed that individuals who smiled found the cartoons funnier than their counterparts. Thus, bodily states can facilitate social information processing. Indeed, the manner in which we think about ourselves is bound up with embodied experiences and actions. That is, the body and the person are one and the same and cannot be conceptualized as separate (Laing, 1960).

THE EXPERIENCE OF EMBODIMENT

There are a myriad of different factors and issues that demand an account if we are to appreciate what it means to be embodied. Sense of embodiment is a complex, multilayered experience (Longo et al., 2008). The body operates in a pre-reflective range of consciousness (Gallagher & Meltzoff, 1996) and intuitively supports our actions. We perform inherently complicated actions every day, without conscious reflection upon the required complex embodied performances. The body, an abiding presence in our lives, is also typified by an absence from our moment-to-moment experiences. Nonetheless, our social lives and embodied experiences are intertwined.

Our social identities are heavily influenced by our embodiment. Constraints and possibilities are created for group membership by the corporeal characteristics of age, gender, race, and appearance. The body, therefore, plays a key role in our experience of similarity and difference from other people. Thus, the body informs much of our relationships with others and our experience of social situations. Radley (1991) in referencing Strodtbeck and colleagues (1956) who found that males were more likely than females to be elected jury foremen in artificial juries, exemplifies how bodies differentially create social standings. Bodies can thus be seen as an image of value, or devalue, in society (Douglas, 1999). The appearance of the body is symbolic of important social values and is understood, therefore, as being indicative of a panoply of personal and social identities.

The Lacanian thesis on the *mirror phase* draws our attention to the idea that the body can be, and is, experienced on an objective level as well as a subjective one. Lacan (1935) argued that, during development, the child begins to identify the self with an external 'mirror' image of himself or herself in a mirror or in the image of another child. This forms the foundation of an understanding of the self, both inner and outer, as a private and subjective experience and also a public and mediated experience. Weiss (1999) describes the embodied being as a 'split subject' as the body is experienced, by the individual, as both a subject and an object. The term 'body image' encapsulates our perceptions of bodily form such as bodily size, shape, and characteristics (Cash, 2002). Body image also involves subjective understandings of the body including a conceptual understanding of the body as well as an emotional attitude toward one's own body (Tsakiris et al., 2007). People's perceptions of their body and their physical capabilities bear a close relationship to self-esteem and are important to positive mental health, including happiness (Lindwall & Hassem, 2004).

Perceptions of bodies vary across cultural and historical boundaries (MacLachlan, 2004). Sociocultural discourses can, and do, shape experiences of, beliefs about, and one's relationship with one's body. Decades of research (e.g. Cooper et al., 1987; Strauman & Glenberg, 1994) illustrate that people in modern Western societies display considerable body image dissatisfaction. People consistently over- or underestimate their actual body size and it has been reported that 44% of women feel negatively about their body as a whole, or individual body parts (Fallon & Rozin, 1985; Monteath & McCabe, 1997; Cessin et al., 2008). Men are also increasingly displaying body image dissatisfaction (Mussap, 2008). Society, by delimiting ways that bodies should appear, can give rise to problems for the embodied person. Fredrickson and Roberts (1997) argue that bodies are constantly being looked at and evaluated. This encourages people to objectify their own bodies and regulate their bodies in accordance to this third-person perspective. This identification, with an external perspective, has an alienating effect on one's embodied experiences. Indeed, this process of objectification of the body has been argued to promote feelings of shame in respect of the body (MacLachlan, 2004). For example, identification with the body which is 'different' or 'dysfunctional' may have profound implications for the integrity of the self. The body, therefore, can come to represent negative meaning.

EMBODIMENT AND DISABILITY

Shildrick and Price (1996) recount experiences of the disabled body and argue that, in disability, the body imposes restrictions on the person. Similarly, the body in pain and illness has been argued to be experienced in an objectified sense, which is restrictive and problematic to the self (Leder, 1990; Williams, 1996). Breaches in bodily experiences can effect a radical transformation in the relationship between the body and the self, creating a reassessment of subjectivity. Being a 'disabled' body, therefore, can significantly shape human experiences, not least of which, our sense of value and interpersonal relationships.

Regardless of the physical basis of a disorder, its affects and effects are experienced through a social context, a context that continues to construct the consequences of many disorders as 'invalidity'—literally of being *not a valid person*, because one does not appear to be ordinary/normal/un-interrupted. How to refer to the situation where some people have fewer physical possibilities than others is certainly problematic. Frequently, the term 'impairment' is used to refer to loss of bodily parts or functioning, while 'disability' is understood to describe the societal consequences of such an impairment. These may include cultural and economic disadvantage, oppression of rights, exclusion from society, and so on. Thus, it is society that determines the extent to which an individual is disabled by an impairment, not the intrinsic physical features of the person. However, while the term 'person with a disability' has the advantage of not framing people by their disability (Lupton & Seymour, 2000), it has the disadvantage of possibly overlooking that such a 'disability' is an essential part of the self, and so it may be misleading to talk of an individual self, partitioned from their body (Oliver, 1990).

If one accepts that the human body mediates experiences of the self, and that impaired bodies therefore mediate different experiences of the self and the world, then there is value in recognizing someone's physical status, although not defining them by it alone. In well-functioning 'able-bodied' experience the body is 'absent' (see also, Leder, 1990; MacLachlan, 2004), in a sense it 'dis-appears' from minute-to-minute awareness, but the physically disabled person's body is ever-present—it 'dys-appears', it appears as something it is not. Thus, while 'the person with a disability may not feel ill or be in pain, her or his body is coded as a dysfunctional body. It culturally exists as a transgression, a body that straddles boundaries and, therefore, is anomalous...' (Lupton & Seymour, 2000, p. 1852).

One of our colleagues lives through cerebral palsy and has described how he hates going shopping because he cannot avoid his reflection in large shop windows. This appearance, he feels, is incongruent with his experience of himself: 'that may be what I am, but it's not who I am' he protested, 'I look drunk... like a fool' he said, referring to his lack of coordination, the involuntary movements, the grimacing and unmelodic speaking. As Rousso (1982) suggests, such contrasts may be so stark that to some people with cerebral palsy '...their own gestures and mannerisms may be a source of self-disgust' (p. 84). The ideas embodied by physical experience can thus be stigmatizing and undermining and, for people with significant physical disabilities, they may have to overcome significant prejudice simply because of how they appear to be. Thus, while the disabled body is 'obvious' it should not be definitive. In seeking to distinguish between the disabled body and the able person we seek to *disembody* the person from 'that body'. 'Dys-appearing' the body may help to overcome the stigma sometimes associated with 'being disabled'.

The appearance of a 'disrupted' or 'disabled' body can evoke stigmatizing reactions in others, where the person with a disability is 'reduced in our minds from a whole and usual person to a tainted, discounted one' (Goffman, 1963, p. 12). People without disabilities may ignore those with disabilities for fear of saying the wrong thing, or because they find encounters with them anxiety provoking, and experience unease in their presence (Gething, 1991). The extent to which the disabled physical body can 'frame' an interaction has been illustrated in experimental studies. Kleck, et al. (1966) found that when a person with a simulated amputation conducted an interview with students, the students showed elevated physiological arousal as assessed by their galvanic skin response. Those who expressed discomfort in the presence of a person who had an amputation, also terminated the interview sooner than those who did not express such discomfort.

In Kleck's (1969) subsequent study, students were required to teach Origami (the Japanese art of paper folding) to a confederate either with, or without, a simulated leg amputation. If the confederate had an amputation they were given significantly greater social distance by the students on the first trial, but not on the second. In fact, students in the study formed a more positive impression of the 'disabled' confederate than of the non-disabled confederate. Kleck argued that the formation of a more positive impression might have arisen because of a tendency in society to be kind to 'disadvantaged' individuals. Newell (2000) suggested 'The supposed tendency to kindness may, indeed, be little more than an aspect of establishing our dissimilarity from the disabled person...' (p. 80). In a sense it is almost as though the greater social distance afforded disabled bodies is an implicit statement that 'I am not embodied in (comfortable with) that body'. Kleck et al. quote Davis (1961) in arguing that people with disabilities need to develop techniques that will help them 'move beyond fictional acceptance'. This should, also, be considered in terms of their own self-acceptance, so often mirroring society's 'acceptance'.

Extending our discussion beyond disability, to include disfigurement, it seems that the farther a disfigured body visibly deviates from the desirable 'norm' the less people want to occupy space next to it. Houston and Bull's (1994) study of seat occupancy on a train found that occupancy of the seat next to the confederate was highest when the confederate had no visible defect, next highest when they had bruising, then scarring, and lowest when they had a birthmark. If this 'mirror' that society—possibly unwittingly—holds up to those who are disabled (Taleporos & McCabe, 2002), it is a reflection of discomfort that cannot easily be ignored and may often be internalized. How then do people adapt to a sense of self which is embodied in a different type of body to the one in which their self-image developed?

STRUGGLING WITH EMBODIMENT: A CASE STUDY OF EMBODIMENT AND LIMB AMPUTATION

MacLachlan (2004) described the experience of Colin, a 25-year-old bricklayer's mate, who had his right leg amputated below the knee due to a crush injury. Five months after his accident, Colin described his feelings about his stump and his phantom limb pains:

My stump, as stumps go, is a very ugly stump.

Q: Why do you think so?

Basically, with most stumps you'll just see a scar. Mine has skin grafts, so it's all home-made. That's the bottom of my old foot there, that's the heel. They actually took it off my old foot, and they sewed it on. And that skin's grafted off this leg here…

Q: Do you like to look at it yourself or do you prefer not to look at it?

Sometimes I'm transfixed, nearly. You know, I'll be just staring at it. I can't believe it, like.

Q: You can't believe it's yours?

Yea, yea.

Q: You still don't feel it's part of your body?

Ah, I know it is, but I don't believe it, you know. It's kind of a weird way to phrase it, but in some ways I don't believe that I don't have the leg. You know, I still get shocked if I look down, and it'll take me aback for a second, you know.

Here Colin is finding it difficult to comes to terms, not just with the emotional aspect of his limb loss, but also the 'mechanical' aspect of how 'bits' of him can be moved about to make up the stump. We sense not only disbelief at what is *not* there 'when I look down', but also a sense of disorientation regarding what is there—on his stump. The 'natural' integrity and 'orderliness' of his body has been disturbed, as has his view of himself.

Eight months after his accident Colin was asked about the prosthetic leg he had had fitted in the interim:

I have grown accustomed to wearing it and em, maybe I've eh, I don't know, the word 'relationship' isn't really appropriate… cos I still think of it as like a tool, kind of thing. But em, you know, it's, it's become part of my day, and having to deal with it every day, yea you just get used to I and, but it's still, it's not really, I don't, don't talk to it or nothing, ha. Or make it coffee…

Colin tries to convey to us alternative senses he has of the prosthesis as a 'tool' but, also, as something much more personal, that you might talk to. 'Yea you just get used to I': 'I' and 'it' are interchanged, possibly just in a random slip of speech, or possibly reflecting a struggle with self-identifications. This conversation positions him in a 'meta' perspective, where he is observing himself, commenting on 'himself'.

Colin then goes on to describe his feelings about discovering that his leg had been removed (amputated):

I really wanted it, you know and then, it was almost like em, it wouldn't be near as bad, but it's almost like if you lose a friend, kind of thing, and you do, and you know, it's almost like, if, if a friend, if a friend of yours or a family member works on a boat, and the boat goes down, and they never find the body, you know, and you don't, you can't really go to a funeral, like, you can't eh, you can't say goodbye kind of thing. You know, I never had a chance to say goodbye, like, so it's almost like 'it's still out there', ha, ha 'its hopping its way towards me'. Which is kind of a scary notion, Stephen King kind of thing. But em, yeah, uugh. I, I kind of hated that aspect. I didn't have a chance to do something with it really – whatever.

Fifteen months after his accident Colin was asked if he would agree with some people who describe losing a leg as being like 'experiencing a bereavement'.

Yeah. I lost a friend of mine. You know, and eh, like a friend that you'd call every day, and talk to every day, you know, rain or shine, and eh, then just one day, they're not there any-more. And you still want to call them, and you have to call them, but they're not there. So, you have to talk to a machine instead, kind of, you know. This being the, this being the ma-chine, like [pointing to prosthesis].

These quotes illustrate the process of navigating a passage, between what is 'him' and what is not, and what it is 'reasonable' to have emotions about, 2 years after his leg loss. Colin's experiences show how embodiment and a sense of one's own appearance—inward and outward—are a process of continuous 'negotiation', a process that we probably all experience, but usually in a less dramatic and explicit manner. People with amputations now have an array of assistive or enabling tech-nologies that can help them adapt to 'dis-ablement' and negotiate a new sense of embodiment.

EMBODIMENT AND REHABILITATION

Standal (2010) draws on the works of Merleau-Ponty (1945), Seymour (1998), and Gallagher (2005) to characterize the negotiation of a new sense of embodiment, epitomized in the process of rehabilitation following injury, in terms of *re-embodiment* or the transformation of one's being-in-the-world. In some cases the integration of assistive devices into the newly-(dis)abled body is a key element of this re-embodiment negotiation. Such transformations have been illustrated in accounts of becoming *en-wheeled*, re-embodiment as a wheelchair user after spinal cord injury (Papadimitriou, 2008), in embodied experience of prosthesis use (Desmond & MacLachlan, 2002; Horgan & MacLachlan, 2004; Murray, 2004; Gallagher et al., 2008), and in descriptions of incorporation of a cane as continuance of the blind user's intention in the world (Merleau-Ponty, 2002). Toombs (2001), Standal (2010) and others suggest that, while not always necessary or sufficient, becoming a skilled user of assistive devices can serve to redress the disruption between the body and the world. As Papadimitriou (2008) observes, through rehabilitation the 'I can no longer do' of injured embodiment can become 'I can do again' (p. 696). Achieving this aim necessitates a central focus on understanding the lived-experience of rehabilitation from the perspective of the individual patient with consideration of their individual circumstances, capabilities, preferences, values, priorities, and aspirations. In a recent study, Schaffalitzky et al. (2009) interviewed upper-limb and lower-limb high-tech and conventional prosthetic limb users with the repertory grid technique (RGT), a qualitative technique to explore individual values and preferences regarding specific choices and events. The participants gen-erated distinctive and individualized patterns of personal constructs and ratings regarding prosthetic use and different prosthetic options available. These values regarding different prosthetic options were a critical factor in prosthetic acceptance and ultimate quality of life. User choice is an important factor when matching prosthetic technology to the user. The preference and choice of prosthesis does not always reflect what providers see as the most up to date and cutting edge available. Rehabilitation can, thus, be reinterpreted; rather than the traditional mechanistic and reductionist process of bodily objectification under the medical gaze, rehabilitation can be conceptualized as a process through which strategies for a new way of being-in-the-world emerge (MacLachlan & Gallagher, 2004; Standal, 2010). Papadimitriou (2008) notes an inherent paradox, however, while enabling re-embodiment through the transformation of one's way of being, reconfiguring one's ability to 'do', rehabilitation also serves to subject the individual to public gaze as the accomplishment of re-embodiment 'brings them out in public where they are seen as unable to do' (p. 701).

A FRAMEWORK FOR EMBODIMENT PERSPECTIVES

The 'mind–body problem', as it has been called, has been with us for centuries. We conclude by suggesting that different 'embodiment perspectives', while not constituting 'solutions' per se, do nonetheless identify distinct aspects of just how 'mind' and body are braided together, through a plethora of distinct but related interactions at multiple levels. An embodiment perspective, we feel, should address relationships between the body and the brain, the conscious sense of self, society's view on the body, a person's response to society's view on the body, and how society accommodates different types of bodies.

Cognition embodiment

This relates specifically to the relationship between cerebral functioning and bodily functioning, and the activities of the central and peripheral nervous systems. It relates to the embodiment of social anxiety (blushing), as much as to pre-conscious motor function (returning a tennis serve you hardly saw), and to well-understood psychophysiological conditions such as asthma and poorly understood problems such as phantom limb pain (experiencing pain in an absent limb; Gallagher et al., 2001).

Conscious embodiment

The mind–body aspect relates to the inner experience of being and 'having' your own body. For instance, to make sense of our experience we may need to integrate a feeling of stomach pain with the perfectly usual appearance of our stomach. Alternatively our increased sensory awareness of the weight of a 'dead limb' that has 'gone to sleep', or has 'pins and needles', has to be reconciled with its perfectly usual appearance. Sometimes, such as in Capgras syndrome, the person denies that the body observed is experienced as themself. Thus, conscious embodiment relates in particular to Lacan's mirror phase and the experience of the body, both as an object and as a subject.

Society embodiment

In the sense, described by Mead's 'looking glass self' sense of self, society reflects back to one an image of the self. While accepting that some of the received image may, in fact, be projected from the self, this sense of embodiment encapsulates the image that the person thinks other people have of them and, in particular, of their body—they learn to observe themselves. For instance, people may feel 'bad' because they are 'overweight', or 'good' because they are 'underweight'; in essence, evaluating how they see their own body in terms of how they interpret society's norms about the body. 'Society' here does not, of course, mean 'all' society, but rather the reference group that the perceiver finds most salient, which may change over time or as the person changes their own values.

Minding embodiment

This sense of embodiment relates to what people want to do with their body to achieve certain ends. While people may recognize that their body deviates from norms, they may not want to do anything about it. For others, their body may adhere to established norms, but may not be as 'good' as they wish it to be. Thus, the sense of recognizing difference and trying to change the body are distinct; they recognize quite different aspects of living through the body. How you 'mind your body' in this sense may range from health promoting to health threatening behaviours, for instance, dieting, exercise, purging, anorexia, cosmetic surgery, the use of steroids, and so on.

Civic embodiment

This relates to what sort of provision is made by society to accommodate different types of bodies. Is society organized in ways that assume a 'default' body? Are society's operations situated in certain structures for certain types of bodies? The most obvious example of this would be the accessibility of social institutions—schools, hospitals, libraries, swimming pools, etc.—for people using wheelchairs versus people not using wheelchairs. What sort of body does the society seem to have 'in mind' in the way it is structured and in the way it functions—how accessible is public transport? What reasonable provisions are made to facilitate employment?— (see Swartz & MacLachlan, 2009).

SUMMARY

The embodiment perspective promotes a view of human experience which incorporates existential, cognitive, physical, and social influences. An understanding of embodied experiences can contribute greatly to an understanding of how experiences, such as disability, are jointly shaped by physical, psychological, and social exigencies. From a research and clinical perspective, this approach can assist a non-reductionist understanding of disruption and objectification of self in dysfunction or disability; however, it can also offer opportunities to learn how embodied practices can be involved in the remaking of positive subjectivity and rehabilitation. We hope that the framework of embodiment perspectives, which we offer here, can help orientate researchers and practitioners to the value of an embodiment perspective for appearance.

REFERENCES

Cash, T. F. (2002). Body image: Cognitive behavioral perspectives on body image. In T. F. Cash & T. Pruzinsky (eds.) *Body Images: A Handbook of Theory, Research, and Clinical Practice*, pp. 38–46. New York: Guilford Press.

Cessin, S. E., von Ronson, K. M., & Whiteford, S. (2008). Cognitive processing of body and appearance words as a function of thin ideal internalizations and schematic activation. *Body Image*, 5, 271–8.

Cooper, P. J., Taylor, M. J., Cooper, Z., & Fairbum, C. G. (1987). The development and validation of the body shape questionnaire. *International Journal of Eating Disorders*, 6, 485–94.

Damasio, A. (1994). *Descartes' Error: Emotion, Reason and the Human Brain*. New York: G.P. Putnam's Sons.

Davis, F. (1961). Deviance disavowal: The management of strained interaction by the visibly handicapped. *Social Problems*, 9, 120–32.

Desmond, D. & MacLachlan, M. (2002). Psychosocial issues in the field of prosthetics and orthotics. *Journal of Prosthetics & Orthotics*, 12 (2), 12–24.

Douglas, M. (1999). *Implicit Meanings: Selected Essays in Anthropology*. London: Routledge.

Fallon, A. E. & Rozin, P. (1985). Sex differences in perceptions of desirable body shape. *Journal of Abnormal Psychology*, 94, 102–5.

Fredrickson, B. L. & Roberts, T. A. (1997). Objectification theory: Toward understanding women's lived experiences and mental health risks. *Psychology of Women Quarterly*, 21(2), 173–206.

Gallagher, S. (2005). *How the Body Shapes the Mind.* Buckingham: Open University Press.

Gallagher, S. & Meltzoff, A. (1996). The earliest sense of self and others: Merleau-Ponty and recent developmental studies. *Philosophical Psychology*, 9, 213–36.

Gallagher, P., Allen, D., & MacLachlan, M. (2001). Phantom limb pain and residual limb pain following lower limb amputation: a descriptive analysis. *Disability and Rehabilitation*, 23(12), 522–30.

Gallagher, P., Desmond, D., & MacLachlan, M. (2008). *Psychoprosthetics: The State of the Knowledge.* London: Springer.

Gething, L. (1991). *Interaction with Disabled Persons Scale: Manual and kit.* Sydney: University of Sydney.

Goffman, E. (1963). *Stigma: Notes on the Management of a Spoiled Identity.* Englewood Cliffs, NJ: Prentice-Hall.

Horgan, O. & MacLachlan, M. (2004). Psychosocial adjustment to lower-limb amputation: a review. *Disability & Rehabilitation*, 26, 837–50.

Houston, V. & Bull, R. (1994). Do people avoid sitting next to someone who is facially disfigured? *European Journal of Social Psychology*, 24, 279–84.

James, W. (1890). *The Principles of Psychology* (Vol. 1). New York: Holt.

Kleck, R. (1969). Physical stigma and task oriented interactions. *Human Relations*, 22, 51–60.

Kleck, R., Ono, J., & Hastorf, A. J. (1966). The effects of physical deviance on face-to-face interactions. *Human Relations*, 19, 425–36.

Lacan, J. (1935/1977). *Ecrits: A Selection* (A. Sheridan, transl.). New York: W.W. Norton & Co.

Laing, R. D. (1960). *The Divided Self: An Existential Study in Sanity and Madness.* Harmondsworth: Penguin.

Leder, D. (1990). *The Absent Body.* Chicago, IL: University of Chicago Press.

Lindwall, M. & Hassmen, P. (2004). The role of exercise and gender for physical self-perceptions and importance ratings in Swedish university students. *Scandinavian Journal of Medicine and Science in Sports*, 14, 373–80.

Longo, M. R., Schuur, F., Kammers, M. P., Tsakiris, M., & Haggard, P. (2008). What is embodiment? A psychometric approach. *Cognition*, 107(3), 978–98.

Lupton, D. & Seymour, W. (2000). Technology, selfhood and physical disability. *Social Science & Medicine*, 50, 1851–62.

MacLachlan, M. (2004). *Embodiment: clinical, critical and cultural perspectives on health and illness.* Maidenhead: Open University Press.

MacLachlan, M. & Gallagher, P. (2004). *Enabling Technologies: Body Image and Body Function.* Edinburgh: Churchill Livingstone.

MacLachlan, M. & Swartz, L. (eds.) (2009). *Disability and International Development.* New York: Springer.

Merleau-Ponty, M. (1945). *Phenomenology of perception.* London: Routledge.

Monteath, S. A. & McCabe, M. P. (1997). The influence of societal factors on female body image. *Journal of Social Psychology*, 137(6), 708–27.

Murray, C. D. (2004). An interpretative phenomenological analysis of the embodiment of artificial limbs. *Disability and Rehabilitation*, 26, 963–73.

Mussap, A. J. (2008). Masculine gender role stress and the pursuit of masculinity. *International Journal of Men's Health*, 7, 72–89.

Newell, R. (2000). *Body Image and Disfigurement Care.* New York: Routledge.

Niedenthal, P. M. (2007). Embodying emotion. *Science*, 316, 1002–5.

Oliver, M. (1990). *Politics and language: The need for a new understanding Disability, Citizenship and Empowerment* (K665 Workbook 2 Appendix 4). Milton Keynes: Open University Press.

Papadimitriou, C. (2008). Becoming en-wheeled: The situated accomplishment of re-embodiment as a wheelchair user after spinal cord injury. *Disability & Society*, 23, 691–704.

Proffitt, D. R., Stefanucci, J., Banton, T., & Epstein, W. (2003). The role of effort in perceiving distance. *Psychological Science*, 14, 106–11.

Radley, A. (1991). *The Body and Social Psychology*. New York: Springer.

Rousso, H. (1982). Special considerations in counselling clients with cerebral palsy. *Sexuality & Disability*, 5, 78–88.

Schaffalitzky, E., NiMhurchadha, S., Gallagher, P., Hofkamp, S., MacLachlan, M., & Wegener, S. T. (2009). Identifying the values and preferences of prosthetic users: a case study series using the repertory grid technique. *Prosthetics and Orthotics International*, 33, 157–66.

Seymour, W. (1998). *Remaking the body. Rehabilitation and change*. London: Routledge.

Shildrick, M. & Price, J. (1996). Breaking the boundaries of the broken body. *Body & Society*, 2, 93–113.

Strauman, T. J. & Glenberg, A. M. (1994). Self-concept and body-image disturbance: Which self-beliefs predict body size overestimation? *Cognitive Therapy and Research*, 18, 105–25.

Strodtbeck, F. L., James, R. M., & Hawkins, C. (1956). Sex role differentiation in jury deliberations. *Sociometry*, 19, 3–11.

Swartz, L. & MacLachlan, M. (2009). Disability and international development: The challenges. In M. MacLachlan & L. Swartz (eds.) *Disability & International Development: Towards Inclusive Global Health*, pp. 1–11. New York: Springer.

Taleporos, G. & McCabe, M. P. (2002). The impact of sexual esteem, body esteem and sexual satisfaction on psychological well-being: People with physical disability. *Sexuality & Disability*, 20, 177–83.

Toombs, S. K. (2001). Reflections on bodily change: The lived experience of disability. In S. K. Toombs (ed.) *Handbook of Phenomenology and Medicine*, pp. 247–61. Dordrecht: Kluwer.

Tsakiris, M., Schütz-Bosbach, S., & Gallagher, S. (2007). On agency and body-ownership: Phenomenological and neurocognitive reflections. *Consciousness and Cognition*, 16, 645–60.

Weiss, G. (1999). *Body images: Embodiment as Intercorporeality*. London: Routledge.

Williams, S. J. (1996). The vicissitudes of embodiment across the chronic illness trajectory. *Body & Society*, 2, 23–47.

CHAPTER 4

....

CROSS-CULTURAL DIFFERENCES

....

HANNAH FALVEY

THE purpose of this chapter is to help the reader to gain a broad understanding of culture and cross-cultural psychology as it relates to the field of appearance. The aim is not to be conclusive, but rather to provide rich and varied information from a range of conceptual approaches which will be a robust and helpful platform to provoke creative and productive thought.

HISTORY OF THE STUDY OF CULTURE
....

An interest in studying one's own culture and other, often competing cultures is long-standing. Indeed, today's scientific disciplines of anthropology, the study of culture, evolutionary psychology, and more recently cross-cultural psychology are preceded by the writings of philosophers, missionaries, and travellers dating back thousands of years (Plog & Bates, 1980; Kim et al., 2000). The roots of the term 'culture' have been traced back to German Romanticism. The concept of *Volksgeist* meaning 'spirit of the times' or 'national spirit' was brought into a coherent whole by Herder (1744–1803) who suggested that it represented nations' embodiments of unique sets of cultural characteristics.[1]

---

[1] http://science.jrank.org/pages/8147/Volksgeist.html

Definition of Culture: Appearance As Symbol and As Biology

As definitions have been elaborated, culture can now be described more clearly as referring to the system of shared beliefs, meanings, values, patterns of behaviours, customs, and artefacts with which members of a society identify and use in coping with one another and their world. The assumption of culture is that it is learnt and transmitted via symbols (something verbal or non-verbal which comes to stand for something else due to collective meaning-making). Symbols differ across cultures and are thought to be infinitely flexible, as meanings evolve over time in response to the present generations' adaptations to changing environmental, political, and social landscapes (Plog & Bates, 1980). In this way appearance can be understood as a cultural symbol to which individuals ascribe meanings. Indeed, people from different cultural settings are thought to be influenced by their own standards of appearance and ideal beauty (Yu & Shepard, 1998; Watts, 2004; Jung & Lee, 2006). However, because of the intrinsic links between appearance and biological correlates some evolutionary psychologists suggest that standards of beauty are not arbitrary or infinitely culturally variable because of the connection with mate selection and reproduction (Buss, 2007). Further, patterns of globalization, increased population mobility, cross-cultural communication, and media exposure may have brought about changes for some individuals where traditional values of appearance are being diluted with Western norms (Campbell et al., 2005; Orbach, 2009). These factors may help to explain why while there is much variability across cultures, different cultures also show striking similarities on judgements of attractiveness and sought-after traits (Cunningham et al., 1995; Shaffer et al., 2000).

Differential Uptake of Cultural Norms

In any given culture there is variation in the uptake of the broad cultural norm according to subgroup membership. For example, in the accounts of the contemporary footbinding scholar, Dorothy Ko, she suggests that the cultural practice in China was neither uniform across regions nor attributed with the same core meanings over time (Ko, 1997). Further, there is some suggestion that subcultures may vary in the degree to which they are influenced by the dominant culture. For example, compared to other minority groups, lesbians and gay men are initially socialized within the dominant culture and later within the minority culture (Beren et al., 1997). Also, social class structures both shape meanings and mediate access to cultural norms. Sobal and Stunkard (1989), in their review of studies related to socioeconomic status and obesity, found a significant inverse relationship between a woman's weight and her socioeconomic status in virtually all developed countries studied, whilst a significant relationship in the opposite direction was found in developing countries; men and women of higher status were heavier. The meaning of weight appears to shift with increased weight being a sign of abundance and wealth in developing countries where adequate food and the luxury of reduced physical labour are accessible only by the wealthy. In contrast, decreased weight is desirable, but accessed more commonly by those of higher socioeconomic status who can afford good quality food and gym membership.

ETHNOCENTRIC VERSUS CULTURAL RELATIVIST PERSPECTIVES

The practice of footbinding in China provides an interesting example of how a cultural practice can evoke strong reactions as the meanings behind the practice are debated. On the one hand it is criticized as being a form of body mutilation imposed on women by men for the purpose of providing sexual satisfaction and perpetuating male dominance (Jeffreys, 2005). Conversely, Ko (1997) cautions against ethnocentric interpretations, the tendency to view the customs of other societies through one's own cultural and temporal lens (Kim et al., 2000), suggesting that it can limit understanding and the possibility of uncovering a more complete understanding. Taking a cultural relativist perspective, attempting to view the beliefs and customs of other peoples within the context of time and culture (Plog & Bates (1980), Ko (1997) suggests that contrary to modern perception, footbinding in the 17th century, prior to the intrusion of Euro-American missionaries, was valued as a sign of civility and superiority; a part of female attire or adornment, not a form of bodily mutilation or sign of oppression.

Despite the increased interest in the role of culture, the majority of studies related to appearance and body image have been conducted in Western societies or by researchers from Western societies (Shaffer et al., 2000). The tension exists between applying Western theories to discover universal mechanisms at the expense of reducing cultural differences to superficial manifestations and developing integrated frameworks which combine broader psychological theories with localized indigenous knowledge (Kim et al., 2000). Many questions remain unanswered regarding the role and value of appearance cross-culturally; the universality cross-culturally of valued traits in Western cultures and even the manner in which people of different cultures relate to and experience their bodies.

APPEARANCE

The importance of appearance both as an expression of biological characteristics and determined by culturally specific behavioural practices should be considered.

Broadly speaking, appearance can be said to be that which is viewed by others and the self from 'the outside in'. At a basic level this can refer to the biological make-up of the body in terms of structure and upholstering of the body including each of the individual parts which make up the whole or morphology (body size, frame, skin colour, facial features, etc.). Cross-cultural variation in environment, diet, and gene pool all impact on the biological make-up of the body. Appearance also refers to that which is by design in terms of grooming, styling, decorating, and adorning (Cunningham et al., 1995; DeMello, 2007; Orbach, 2009). Standards of appearance by design are likely to be more culturally variable and reflect learnt patterns of behaviour susceptible to changing meanings over time (symbols). Further, behavioural practices and the standards of 'designed' appearance may drive dissatisfaction with individual biological form and the search for biomedical changes. For example, the application of eye make-up to enhance and enlarge the appearance of women's eyes seems harmless in some populations, but since approximately 75% of Koreans and 50% of all other Asians are born without a double eyelid crease, the value placed on having a larger 'Western' eye has contributed to the rapid growth in Asian eyelid surgery seen in recent years, a surgery which makes the eye rounder (Kobrin, 2004). This is an interesting shift since at one time large eyes in East Asian cultures were considered barbaric (DeMello, 2007). Appearance is also experienced by the individual from 'the inside out'. This refers to the way in which an individual relates to and experiences their appearance, addressed in studies of body image and embodiment (Dumas et al., 2005).

Cross-cultural Differences in Morphology

Race theories were developed in an attempt to categorize the evident diversity in human morphology. The advent of the human genome era brought promise of developing understanding further. The emerging picture confirmed that populations do generally cluster by broad geographical regions which correspond to socially recognized races (Africa, Europe, Asia, Oceania, Americas). The patterns of genetic variation point to single-origin human expansion out of Africa, which followed different pathways of expansion and the accumulation of differences through local selection processes and environmental influences (Tishkoff & Kidd, 2004). Thus races are neither homogeneous nor distinct (Tishkoff & Kidd, 2004).

Lin et al. (2004) studied anthropometric differences of adult males and females among nations of the same race. Their findings are consistent with the suggestions of Tishkoff and Kidd (2004), finding distinct and significant differences between the peoples of the nations of China, Japan, Korea, and Taiwan even though each belongs to the Asian or 'Mongolian' race. They found the tendency for the Chinese to have a narrow torso with moderate limbs; the Japanese to have a wider torso and shorter limbs; the Taiwanese to be wider at the shoulders and narrower at the hip with large hands and long legs; and the Korean to be moderate among the four groups.

Wang et al. (1994), compared anthropometric measurements of body fat between an Asian population (93% Chinese, born in Asia, but living in the US) and a white American population with European origins. They concluded that body mass index (BMI) measurements of body fat resulted in substantial errors when applied to an Asian population since length of trunk and legs relative to height varies significantly by race. The results of the study indicated that the white population were significantly taller, heavier, and had higher BMIs than the Asian population, whilst the Asian population had higher percentage body fat content and thicker subcutaneous fat for a given BMI compared to the white population and in both sexes (percentage body fat compared at BMIs of 15, 25, and 35). Fat percentage increased with greater BMI for males, but reduced with increased BMI for females. Subcutaneous fat distribution also varied by sex and race with the Asian population having greater upper-body fat whilst white females had more lower-body fat (Wang et al., 1994). These findings are highly relevant when thinking about cross-cultural comparisons of body image perceptions and eating disorder pathology since BMI measures alone could result in errors in categorizing comparison groups (Jung & Lee, 2006). Further studies suggest that the Western beauty ideal of 'thinness' for women is not necessarily shared cross-culturally even in those with eating pathology (Jung & Lee, 2006; Jackson & Chen, 2007), and other bodily features can be the focus of dissatisfaction such as facial features in China and Korea (Jackson & Chen, 2007; Jung & Lee, 2006). Whilst people's bodies differ greatly in *appearance* cross-culturally, some fields of literature do suggest elements of universality. In terms of developmental trajectory, for example, all facial and bodily features display a neonate form, such as large eyes, smooth skin, and a small nose, before maturing with age and changes in hormones through puberty to maturity (Cunningham et al., 1995). Further, whilst there is a vast array of differing meanings attributed to appearance cross-culturally, similarities have also been found.

Cross-cultural Differences in Attractiveness Judgements of Physical Appearance

Attractiveness is a value judgement placed on appearance by an individual or group. Some suggest that there are consistencies cross-culturally in terms of the physical features thought to be the most desirable. Cunningham et al. (1995) found that male and female Asian, Hispanic, and white judges (who were international students living in the US for a median time of 4 months) and Taiwanese students studying in Taiwan, were highly consistent in their judgements of attractiveness for

Hispanic, Asian, and white female faces. Higher ratings across all groups and males and females were for *neonate* large eyes, greater distance between the eyes, and small noses; *sexually mature*, narrower female faces with smaller chins; expressive high eyebrows, dilated pupils, larger lower lips, and larger smiles. There was some preference for slightly less sexually mature faces by Asian and Taiwanese judges, but all judges were found to be more similar than different. A further comparison was made between the judgements of black and white American men in response to black and white female faces and their ratings of attractiveness were found to be remarkably similar. Racially regarded features including nostril width and lip size did not affect attractiveness ratings, but there was a same-race affect for the black judges rating black females as more attractive than did white judges. Interestingly, whilst similar judgements existed for the face, there was some evidence that different cultures had different standards for judging the body—black judges indicating greater attraction to heavier figures than white judges including higher ideal weight and larger buttocks. There is further evidence that the role of the face and the body differ in overall judgements of appearance with facial attractiveness being more important than body shape in overall judgements of physical attractiveness for both sexes (Currie & Little, 2009).

In most cultures a stereotype exists which values beauty in women and strength and resource in men (Buss et al., 2000; Jung & Lee, 2006; Buss, 2007). Evolutionary and mate selection models consider that traits which are of evolutionary advantage are likely to influence judgements of attractiveness. For example, physical cues thought to indicate good mate quality and thus linked to more positive judgements of attractiveness for women include cues to youth, health, and fertility, such as full lips, smooth skin, lustrous hair, symmetrical features, absence of sores, and average values of shoulder, waist, and hip widths showing good integration of these three features (Buss, 2007; Donohoe et al., 2009). Masculine physical characteristics in men have been shown to be positively correlated with measures of long-term medical health (Rhodes et al., 2003) and evidence suggests that such features are more important in areas at risk for health difficulties, thus representing a desirable *resource* (DeBruine et al., 2010). DeBruine et al. (2010) found that across 30 different countries, consistent with sexual selection theory, women's average masculinity preference increased as national health decreased and this effect was found to be independent of cross-cultural differences in wealth, or women's mating strategies. Masculinity preferences were related to two-dimensional stimuli of male faces, which were masculinized or feminized in sexually dimorphic aspects of face shape. This is an interesting demonstration of the interaction between environmental context and patterns of attraction to certain physical features for possible adaptive reasons. What constitutes mate resource is likely to vary depending on cultural context and may not always be so closely related to appearance (Buss et al., 2000; Yang et al., 2005).

CROSS-CULTURAL DIFFERENCES IN BODY USE

Temporal, environmental, and sociocultural context also impact on the body in terms of the demands placed on it. Contrary to the focus of the discussion thus far, the body is not just defined by the way that it appears—its appearance is also shaped by the way in which it is used. Compare, for example, the differing demands placed on the body before and after the advent of machinery to aid construction work, factory production lines, and farm labour; the difference in impact on the body of a manual rickshaw driver and a London taxi driver. Add to this the difference in availability and variety of diet and body constitution in terms of muscularity and adipose tissue can vary widely (Campbell et al., 2005). Yet in countries where the physical need for strength in men is decreasing, the cultural emphasis on muscularity has paradoxically increased (Gray & Ginsberg, 2007).

Greater dissatisfaction with degree of muscularity has been found in Western countries than in Third World or traditional cultures (Yang et al., 2005) although there are exceptions to this (Gray & Ginsberg, 2007). Yang et al. (2005) found that men from Taiwan, the US, and Europe would like to be more muscular, but there was a significant difference between the participants from the East and West in terms of the discrepancy between their judgements of their own muscularity and their perception of the preference of women for muscularity. The cultural emphasis on the undressed male body in advertising is significantly less in Taiwanese media than in Western media. The historical valuing of mental strength and intelligence as expressions of masculinity in Taiwan, and greater preservation of the male as household head are thought to contribute to a different emphasis in the expression of masculinity and resource which is less dependent on physical form (Yang et al., 2005). Conversely, there is a suggestion that within cultures in which traditional male roles of breadwinner (i.e. main wage earner) and protector have declined, muscularity has come to be a way of expressing masculinity (Yang et al., 2005; Gray & Ginsberg, 2007). This is an important point since it marks the departure from the body and appearance as defined by biology in relationship with geographical context, diet, and use, to the body which is sculpted and manufactured at will to express dynamic, temporal, and cultural ideals—appearance by design.

APPEARANCE BY DESIGN

Susie Orbach (2009) writes that there has never been a time when bodies were unmarked by cultural practices, and thus there has never been a 'natural body'. The spectacular variability in form of *designed appearance* speaks of the profound and innate human drive for creativity and expression, moving people from the position of being human beings to social beings (DeMello, 2007). Archaeological findings suggest that body painting has been practised since the Palaeolithic era, tattooing since the Neolithic age, and early human graves have yielded jewellery and shown evidence of intentional head shaping (DeMello, 2007). Cultural standards of beauty; the meeting of religious and/or social obligations; the demonstration of professional and/or economic status; the marking of inter-relationships between the individual and society; life phase; age; gender; rite of passage; the spirit world; conflict; ancestry; and the act of stigmatizing and excluding all find form on the human canvas that is the body (Gröning, 2001; Schildkrout, 2004; DeMello, 2007). The deeper meanings of body decoration, modification, adornment, and grooming can only really be understood from within the cultural context since the form is always the expression of a particular culture (Gröning, 2001). However, some generalities can be made, such as the tendency for temporary markings (e.g. body paint) and adornments being used for celebrations, rituals, and to mark transitional status whereas lasting modifications are more commonly used to mark permanent changes in status and both forms reflect cultural beauty ideals (DeMello, 2007).

A review of the differences in designed appearance across cultures would fill several volumes. But by way of introduction to this fascinating area consider for a moment the decorative scars received by Aboriginal novices during religious consecration ceremonies where both body paint and ornamental scars are closely linked to the primeval creator heroes (Gröning, 2001). Imagine the intricate designs made from dotted scars on the girls of the Ga'anda in northern Nigeria known as *Hleeta* which qualify them for marriage (DeMello, 2007). Or more familiar perhaps, the array of powers, creams, concealers, lipsticks, mascaras, eyeliners, whiteners, rouges, and tanning agents used across the globe to promote a youthful and healthy appearance and to differentiate between the sexes (Etcoff, 1999; DeMello, 2007). Compare the motivation for many centuries for black teeth in both Japan and Renaissance Europe (since this was a sign of status, those able to afford sugar which rotted the teeth) with the motivation for white, straight, even teeth in the West and varied practices of tooth filing, sharpening, and evulsion in Bali, Sudan, and Australian Aboriginals respectively (DeMello, 2007).

The practice of tattooing amongst the Maori was to imprint both on the body and mind all the group traditions and philosophies (Levi-Strauss, 1963). Whilst tattooing is not new within the West, contemporary Western tattooing continues to redefine social boundaries (Schildkrout, 2004). Body modifications outside of the norm allow the individual to stand outside of the mainstream social order or express membership to minority subcultures (DeMello, 2007). The neo-primitive or modern primitive movement refers to the adoption by individuals in the West of non-Western beliefs and body art to challenge contemporary social practices (Schildkrout, 2004; DeMello, 2007). Paradoxically, the act of uprooting practices so deeply entrenched in one cultural context and transplanting them into another cultural context divorces the 'art' from the rich source of its original meaning. What was originally a mark of community and connectivity transforms into a mark of separateness and difference, unanchored from its original meaning and purpose (Gell, 1993; Schildkrout, 2004; DeMello, 2007).

Designed appearance displaced from deeper cultural meanings, rituals and community has created a modern movement hungry for whole body transformation to meet an increasingly narrow standard of what is deemed to be acceptable (Orbach, 2009). The possibilities and parameters for designing one's appearance are intrinsically linked with the availability of materials, skills, and technology to effect the changes. As individuals respond to the new frontiers available for designing appearance this in turn alters the norms, values, and behaviours associated with appearance. Increased population mobilization has created an interesting scenario in which individuals are more aware of the many differences in appearance, but are caught in a tension between trying to belong to and operate within a multicultural group whilst not losing touch with their own concept of identity and ethnicity.

The astonishing developments in surgical technique now make the previously unavailable available to those with the means. For example, height has long been valued in China where Chinese diplomats are expected to match the height of their foreign counterparts and those below 5ft 7in (1.70 metres) need not apply to the foreign ministry (Watts, 2004). Leg lengthening is now available in China with the possibility of adding up to 10cm in height (Watts, 2004). Conversely for Scandinavian women who feel they are too tall, leg shortening operations are available (Orbach, 2009). The tension between assimilating to a new cultural context for Asian women living in the US and maintaining a sense of ethnicity has resulted in the report that Asian eyelid surgery is less popular amongst Asian-Americans than amongst those living in Asia where it is one of the most popular procedures for women (Kobrin, 2004; Watts, 2004). Increased exposure to difference through population movement and increased access to Western-dominated media images may give rise to a tension within individuals as to whether to assimilate to an increasingly global culture or to preserve ethnic identity. Since exposure in itself is likely to bring about a shift in perspective which may be implicit, the degree to which people are consciously choosing to become more homogenous may be in question.

Conclusions

This chapter has given an overview of cross-cultural differences in appearance. It is hoped that the ideas presented from a variety of disciplines including evolutionary psychology, cross-cultural psychology, social psychology, anthropology, and women's history have given the reader a rich and varied summary which will be a catalyst for further study and exploration. A review of cross-cultural differences in appearance can bring the reader to a place of wonder due to the incredible variety of appearance expressions and the diverse ways in which it has been designed by and is meaningful to the human race. However, the development of new technologies for altering appearance together with increased access to globalized media is juxta-posed with the erosion of traditional practices which held deep meaning for specific communities, leading to a growing disconnection between appearance expression and cultural identity.

REFERENCES

Beren, S. E., Hayden, H. A., Wilfley, D. E., & Strigel-Moore, R. H. (1997). Body dissatisfac-tion among lesbian college students the conflict of straddling mainstream and lesbian cultures. *Psychology of Women Quarterly*, 21, 431–45.

Buss, D. M. (2007). The evolution of human mating. *Acta Psychologica Sinica*, 39(3), 502–12.

Buss, D. M., Shackelford, T. K., Choe, J., Buunk, B. P., & Dijkstra, P. (2000). Distress about mating rivals. *Personal Relationships*, 7, 235–43.

Campbell, B. C., Pope, H. G., & Filiault, S. (2005). Body image among Ariaal Men from Northern Kenya. *Journal of Cross-Cultural Psychology*, 36, 371–9.

Cunningham, M. R., Roberts, A. R., Barbee, A. P., Druen, P. B., & Wu, C. H. (1995). 'Their ideas of beauty are, on the whole, the same as ours': consistency and variability in the cross-cultural perception of female physical attractiveness. *Journal of Personality and Social Psychology*, 68(2), 261–79.

Currie, T. E. & Little, A. C. (2009). The relative importance of the face and body in judge-ments of human physical attractiveness. *Evolution and Human Behaviour*, 30, 409–16.

DeBruine, L. M., Jones, B. C., Crawford, J. R., Welling, L. L. M., & Little, A. C. (2010). The health of a nation predicts their mate preferences: cross-cultural variation in women's preferences for masculinized male faces. *Proceedings of the Royal Society B: Biological Sciences*, 277, 2405–10.

DeMello, M. (2007). *Encyclopedia of Body Adornment*. Westport, CN: Greenwood Press.

Donohoe, M. L., von Hippel, W., & Brooks, R. C. (2009). Beyond waist-hip ratio: experi-mental multivariate evidence that average women's torsos are most attractive. *Behavioral Ecology*, 20, 716–21.

Dumas, A., Laberge, S., & Straka, S. M., (2005). Older women's relations to bodily appearance: the embodiment of social and biological conditions of existence. *Ageing and Society*, 25, 883–902.

Etcoff, N. (1999). *Survival of the Prettiest*. The Science of Beauty. London: Little, Brown And Company.

Gell, A. (1993). Wrapping in Images: Tattooing in Polynesia. Oxford Studies in Social and Cultural Anthropology. Oxford: Clarendon Press.

Gray, J. J. & Ginsberg, R. L. (2007). Muscle dissatisfaction: an overview of psychological and cultural research and theory. In J. K. Thompson & G. Cafri (eds.) *The Muscular Ideal Psychological, Social, and Medical Perspectives*, pp. 15–39. Washington, DC: American Psychological Association.

Gröning, K. (2001). *Decorated Skin a World Survey of Body Art*. London: Thames and Hudson.

Jackson, T. & Chen, H. (2007). Identifying the eating disorder symptomatic in China: the role of sociocultural factors and culturally defined appearance concerns. *Journal of Psychosomatic Research*, 62, 241–9.

Jeffreys, S. (2005). *Beauty and Misogyny*. Harmful Cultural Practices in the West. London: Routledge.

Jung, J. & Lee, S. H. (2006). Cross-cultural comparisons of appearance self-schema, body image, self-esteem, and dieting behaviour between Korean and U.S. women. *Family and Consumer Sciences Research Journal*, 34, 350–65.

Kim, U., Park, Y. S., & Park, D. (2000). The challenge of cross-cultural psychology: the role of indigenous psychologies. *Journal of Cross-Cultural Psychology*, 31, 63–75.

Ko, D. (1997). The body as attire: the shifting meanings of footbinding in seventeenth-century China. *Journal of Women's History*, 8(4), 8–27.

Kobrin, S. (2004). Asian-Americans criticize eyelid surgery craze. *We News*, 15 August [Online]. http://womensenews.org/story/health/040815/asian-americans-criticize-eyelid-surgery-craze

Levi-Strauss, C. (1963). *Structural Anthropology*. New York: Basic Books.

Lin, Y. C., Wang, M. J., & Wang, E. M. (2004). The comparisons of anthropometric characteristics among four peoples in East Asia. *Applied Ergonomics*, 35, 173–8.

Orbach, S. (2009). *Bodies*. London: Profile Books.

Plog, F. & Bates, D. G. (1980). *Cultural Anthropology* (2nd edn.). New York: Alfred A. Knopf.

Rhodes, G., Chan, J., Zebrowitz, L. A., & Simmons, L. W. (2003). Does sexual dimorphism in human faces signal health? *Proceedings of the Royal Society B: Biological Sciences*, 270, S93–5.

Schildktout, E. (2004). Inscribing the body. *Annual Review of Anthropology*, 33, 319–44.

Shaffer, D. R., Crepaz, N., & Sun, C-R. (2000). Physical attractiveness stereotyping in cross-cultural perspective: similarities and differences between Americans and Taiwanese. *Journal of Cross-Cultural Psychology*, 31(5), 557–82.

Sobal, J. & Stunkard, A. J. (1989). Socioeconomic status and obesity: A review of the literature. *Psychological Bulletin*, 105, 260–75.

Tishkoff, S. A. & Kidd, K. K. (2004). Implications of biogeography of human populations for 'race' and medicine. *Nature Genetics*, 36(11), s21–7.

Wang, J., Thornton, J. C., Russell, M., & Pierson, R. N. (1994). Asians have lower body mass index (BMI) but higher percent body fat than do whites: comparisons of anthropometric measurements. *American Journal of clinical nutrition*, 60, 23–8.

Watts, J. (2004). China's cosmetic surgery craze leg-lengthening operations to fight height prejudice can leave patients crippled. *Lancet*, 363, 358.

Yang, C-F. J., Gray, P., & Pope, H. G. (2005). Male body image in Taiwan versus the west: Yanggang Zhiqi meets the Adonis complex. *American Journal of Psychiatry*, 162, 263–9.

Yu, D. W., & Shepard, G. H. (1998). Is beauty in the eye of the beholder? *Nature*, 396, 321–2.

CHAPTER 5

CHALLENGES IN HEALTHCARE PROVISION IN THE UNITED KINGDOM

ESTHER L. E. HANSEN

PETER E. M. BUTLER

In this chapter, we hope to help the reader understand how appearance concerns are managed within healthcare services in the UK. We (the authors) both work in a large regional plastic and reconstructive surgery unit in London. While our unit provides routine surgical interventions, we also have several national services, including ear reconstruction and facial transplantation. Our unit also has clinical psychologists embedded in the plastic surgery unit, something that is still rather unusual, although the publication by Clarke et al. (2005) outlining a model for a psychological service within plastic and reconstructive surgery units in the UK is facilitating the inclusion of psychologists in surgical services. Esther Hansen is a clinical health psychologist, who conducted research in this area prior to starting her clinical work in this service more than 6 years ago. She strongly believes that psychological interventions (whether with patients or at other levels of the organization) can enhance patient care and satisfaction with outcomes. She is also keen to meet the challenge of producing evidence for these interventions. Peter Butler is a consultant plastic and reconstructive surgeon who is an advocate of integrating psychology services in plastic surgery (not just in burns services) and has worked hard to achieve this in our unit. He believes that interventions, whether surgical or psychological, should be driven by an evidence-based approach.

This chapter will firstly examine how individuals with appearance concerns access help in the community. We will then consider the way in which appearance concerns are treated by medical professionals. This is followed by a consideration of how psychological services can attempt to help individuals manage their appearance concerns. We also discuss the opportunities available for individuals with appearance concerns when these are managed jointly, as is the case in our unit. We will end by inviting readers to consider the importance of interventions beyond those offered to patients by reflecting how engagement in the wider societal context might be achieved, as this often maintains the high level of appearance concerns and investment in appearance amongst people seeking appearance altering surgery.

In the UK, the term 'appearance concerns' is used widely to describe a situation where a person believes their appearance is different to a perceived ideal. It is often accompanied by a degree of anxiety or other forms of psychological distress. Appearance concerns cover a continuum from individuals with a diagnosis of a psychiatric condition (e.g. body dysmorphic disorder, BDD) to those who are not concerned about any aspect of their appearance. The majority of people feel discontented by some aspect of their appearance (normative discontent) and the groups at each end of the continuum are likely to have relatively low numbers (e.g. the incidence of BDD is 0.7% in a community sample (Faravelli et al., 1997; Otto et al., 2001) vs. 13.1% in a psychiatric sample (Grant et al., 2001). Included in the population with appearance concerns are also those with objectively disfiguring conditions, although it is important to note that disfiguring conditions do not necessarily result in concerns about appearance.

While most individuals may feel dissatisfied with an aspect of their appearance, patients in our unit often report that their concerns have been dismissed by both lay and health professionals through statements, such as 'Haven't you got bigger problems to worry about' or 'Don't worry about your [stomach], everybody has something they don't like about their appearance'. They end up feeling that nobody understands their difficulties. However, research and our clinical experience have demonstrated that appearance concerns are not trivial. Appearance concerns can interfere with daily living, lead to a significant negative impact on behaviour, and also be associated with high levels of distress (Clarke et al., 2012).

Elwin, a 34-year-old man black Ghanaian man, attended the surgical clinic asking for help as his lips had changed colour. In his opinion they were an uncharacteristic pink. Other people had picked up on this and asked him questions, such as 'what is wrong with the colour of your lips?' and one family member called him 'pinky'. There was no surgical or medical intervention possible and he was referred to psychology. In my clinic (EH) he reported that he had stopped going out socially and had changed his phone number so he could not be contacted by friends. He said that he was worried all the time about how people would react and would often check his appearance in the mirror. He also reported that all he now did was work, eat and sleep. He had also stopped going fishing, something he previously enjoyed.[1]

In the case of Elwin, it is easy to see how both primary care professionals (e.g. general practitioner (GP) or nurse) could dismiss his 'pink lips' as trivial. However, appearance concerns in many cases like Elwin's lead to avoidance of particular situations and have a negative effect on quality of life. A recent study by the Appearance Research Collaboration (The Healing Foundation, 2008), which investigated factors contributing to positive adjustment to disfiguring conditions, confirms that levels of distress in their community sample (n = 615) were at similar levels to those seen in individuals under the care of secondary services (n = 650). This suggests that a large number of people are not accessing help for their appearance concerns.

APPEARANCE CONCERNS IN THE COMMUNITY

The challenge of providing a service for those with appearance concerns therefore begins in community settings.

People seeking treatment to change their appearance often initially raise their appearance concerns with their GP. Elwin's GP referred him to our service as he recognized the difficulties his patient was experiencing. Unfortunately, individuals' appearance concerns are often trivialized when the 'disfigurement' is deemed minor. In contrast, there is also an assumption that distress is high when the disfigurement is significant.

Jack, a 32-year-old man, was referred as he had acquired a facial palsy and was thought to be 'in need' of some help. In the first and only meeting with the psychologist (EH), he identified that most of the time everybody assumed his life was terrible and that he must be depressed. However, he said that he was doing well and had no difficulties doing all the activities he valued. As a result, we collaboratively decided on the content of my discharge letter that could be shared with many different professionals and also family and friends to spread the news that you can 'live well in spite of having a facial palsy'.

Jack's case illustrates how many professionals and lay people assume that a facial palsy may be a serious challenge to leading a 'normal' life and would necessarily cause distress. However, research has shown that aetiology and severity are not good predictors of adjustment, although the visibility of a difference to others may

---

[1] Identifying factors of this case example (and others in this chapter) have been modified so that patient anonymity and confidentiality is protected.

increase the risk of distress (Robinson, 1997; Thompson & Kent, 2001; Moss & Carr, 2004). This is not well recognized by health professionals and, in our service where psychologists have been present for a number of years, surgeons still occasionally refer individuals writing that *'this person's distress is out of proportion with the [scar] they have'*. The myth that severity predicts distress, shared by both patients and community professionals, is likely to continue to make it easier for Jack to access psychological help than Elwin, who actually experiences a higher degree of distress.

There are other myths around appearance concerns that also shape who is seen as 'in need' of services. It is often assumed that young women are more affected by a difference in appearance than men. However, studies have shown that demographics are poor predictors of distress. Women are not reliably more concerned about their appearance than men (e.g. Cordeiro et al., 2010), and while advanced age is usually associated with lower appearance concerns, this is not an absolute relationship (The Healing Foundation, 2008). A study in our unit with patients who had undergone a split skin graft (a surgical procedure where skin is used from one part of the body to replace an area of the body where skin has been lost or significantly damaged, e.g. following burns) also showed that neither gender nor age can help us reliably predict levels of appearance concerns.

For community services the challenge is to overcome these myths to facilitate access to appropriate care. The National Institute for Health and Clinical Excellence (NICE, 2005) guidelines for BDD emphasize the need for screening and available referral pathways to mental health professionals when symptoms are detected. However, people can experience significant difficulties without meeting the criteria for a diagnosis of BDD. Therefore an awareness that any individual can experience significant distress as a result of appearance concerns is important. Screening that uses subjective evaluations (self-ratings) are more illuminating than objective ratings carried out by clinic staff, as self-evaluations account for the highest degree in variance in levels of distress (Rumsey et al., 2004; Moss, 2005; Ong et al., 2007). Given the high levels of preoccupation and anxiety with appearance found in community samples of people considering themselves to have a disfigurement, we (the authors) would encourage primary care professionals to consider using two screening questions that are likely to identify who would benefit from a referral to either a multidisciplinary hospital department (i.e. dermatology, plastic surgery) or an appropriate psychology service. Through research, two scaling questions have been positively correlated with several measures of adjustment (including the Derriford Appearance Scale (Carr et al., 2000), Hospital Anxiety and Depression Scale (Zigmond & Snaith, 1983)) and could therefore be good indicators of the level of distress (Clarke et al., 2008). These are 'How noticeable is [it] to other people?' and 'How much do you worry about [it]?'.

At present, any onward referral from community services is likely to be to a surgical or medical service, for treatment to 'improve' appearance.

MEDICAL OR SURGICAL MANAGEMENT OF APPEARANCE CONCERNS

Lay beliefs around appearance and managing dissatisfaction shape how primary care health professionals and patients define an appearance problem and the solutions they jointly identify to resolve it. Patients are most likely to derive their knowledge from the media. This is also likely to be the case for GPs who may have, at best, a very limited, or most likely no exposure to plastic surgery training either as a postgraduate or undergraduate (Parikh et al., 2006). Interestingly, the Department of Health advises patients considering plastic surgery to discuss this with their GP. Many surgical services would suggest that this can be unhelpful, as GPs may share the same lay knowledge and promote a skewed view of surgery and its capacity to resolve appearance concerns.

The wider sociocultural context also shapes the inferences made about the consequences of an appearance which is considered to fall short of societal ideals. An attractive appearance is perceived as significantly increasing a person's chance to have success in various aspects of their lives. Despite the lack of research evidence to support these beliefs, the messages that patients and also GPs absorb from the media are:

1 You can resolve appearance concerns with (only) surgery;
2 Surgery is easy (e.g. the 'lunch time boob job'); and
3 Surgery not only changes what you look like, it can also change how you feel.

Thus, many patients attend appointments for surgical or medical services with a skewed understanding about which specialist procedure is appropriate and with unrealistic expectations of the likely outcome.

Fay, a 20-year-old woman, was referred to our unit for significant breast asymmetry. The referral letter stated that 'Fay is ready now to have her breasts corrected by surgery so that she can live a normal life'. In my (EH) meeting with Fay she was horrified to learn that she would be left with permanent scars that could be quite noticeable (e.g. hypertrophic), that she would be in pain postoperatively, need to wear a supportive bra postoperatively, and may struggle to wash her hair for a while (due to pain associated with lifting arms and the need to keep her dressings dry). Through discussion she decided that unilateral breast reduction would substitute one problem (asymmetry) with another as she felt she would continue to be upset looking in the mirror because of the scarring and would continue to feel restricted in her intimate contact. She was upset that she could not have 'normal boobs'.

Fay and her GP both felt that surgery would be a simple and easy solution to her breast asymmetry with surgery enabling her to have a 'normal life'. However, this case illustrates how, in this situation, surgery may not resolve Fay's concerns or help her to achieve her goals and was not the 'quick fix' she had anticipated.

Lay understandings about appearance concerns and their perceived solutions can therefore create a need for medical and surgical services to manage patients' expectations.

Firstly, in our experience, dissatisfaction with surgical outcomes is viewed by patients as 'surgery gone wrong' rather than having any association with their expectations of what would be a likely result of surgery. Many patients in the surgical setting often assume, like Fay above, that surgery will 'fix' their appearance concerns *and* also enable some psychological changes. There is a risk of postoperative dissatisfaction if surgery is carried out on patients who have unrealistic expectations, or if their expectations have not been elicited in a presurgical consultation to ascertain whether surgery is likely to meet them.

Secondly, health professionals working within surgical services may need to help patients understand that sometimes there are no surgical options, or that a different procedure is more appropriate to the one they had assumed. In our experience, patients have responded to this in various ways. Some of the most problematic responses have been *'If I went privately I would be able to get it'* or *'If I go to a better surgeon he will do it'* or *'Because he doesn't like me he doesn't want to do the surgery'*. Patients are often lured in by the promise of surgery and cannot understand that some problems cannot be solved by surgery. In an era where facial transplantation is possible and other pioneering surgeries are offered, patients sometimes find it difficult to understand the limitations of surgery; for example, that they could be left with scars or 'still not have a normal appearance'.

Thirdly, Western medical and surgical services adopt a biomedical approach to address appearance concerns but this may only resolve part of the problem. Different services have different goals, not all of which are solely appearance-related. For example, bariatric services aim to reduce a patient's weight and therefore reduce comorbidity and mortality. Plastic surgery services aim to restore appearance and reduce the noticeability of an altered appearance. Dermatology services aim to reduce symptoms and treat skin disease. However, patients approach their surgical team with concerns that extend beyond biomedical matters. For example, an ongoing bilateral breast reduction study in our unit has shown that women rated psychosocial outcomes (e.g. 'other people will stare less at my breasts') equally as important as a reduction in physical symptoms (e.g. back pain) following surgery. A restricted biomedical view is likely to compromise full understanding of why some patients are dissatisfied following surgery and may prevent the identification of patients who may benefit from preparatory work to reduce any unrealistically high expectations prior to surgery.

These challenges are common to both the private and public health (National Health Service, NHS) sector, but some are distinct to each sector. In the private sector, individuals approach a practitioner directly, having already identified surgery as a solution to their appearance concern. Unfortunately, the private sector is unregulated in the UK, with several professional and regulatory bodies accrediting different levels of expertise. This complicates the potential patient's search for the 'right' professional. Promises made by private clinics often tempt individuals and strong marketing (including financial discounts) can heavily influence a person's decision-making about whether to undergo surgery and, if so, where and when. Increasing numbers of patients are deciding to undergo cosmetic surgery overseas where costs are often considerably cheaper than in the UK. Individuals may be desperate for help and following the advice of a private practitioner may decide to take up the offer of inappropriate treatment. Unfortunately, we (the authors) also meet such individuals in our NHS clinic if they have complications or are unhappy with the result of the surgery. Jeevan and Armstrong (2008) reported that 37% of 203 consultant members of the British Association of Plastic, Reconstructive & Aesthetic Surgeons (BAPRAS) had seen patients in their NHS service who had complications or concerns related to cosmetic procedures undertaken overseas. This figure could be higher if it included patients treated in the private sector in the UK.

Lorraine, a 39-year-old woman, saw me (PB) to discuss ways in which I may be able to help improve her facial appearance. She had had several filler injections to reduce the wrinkles and deeper lines underneath her eyes. However, she felt that she now 'looked worse than ever' as her treatment had resulted in her having 'an uneven facial appearance with some "bulging"' in the area beneath one eye. Lorraine was distraught that I could offer very little to change her appearance and struggled to understand that any further treatment using fillers or other injections would not ameliorate the situation. We (the authors) are aware that she has continued to seek further private treatment and has so far not been able to accept the strong advice from other private practitioners that there are few, if any, options for an improvement in her appearance.

The desperation for Lorraine is clear. There has been a permanent negative change in her facial appearance. While her initial aim was to improve her appearance, she is now seeking treatment to make her look 'more normal'. Partridge (1990) described how appearance concerns can tempt some individuals, like Lorraine, on a 'crusade' to achieve what is an impossible aesthetic result. As a person living with a visible difference, Partridge encourages individuals to consider when and/or whether the surgical journey can have an endpoint and also what indicates that 'enough is enough'. This is often very difficult since it requires the individual to consider how they may live with an appearance they remain dissatisfied with. The inherent disappointment if psychosocial goals have not been achieved with surgery can be significant.

In contrast to the private sector, the challenge facing the NHS in the UK is resource management. Treatment cannot be offered to everyone who wants it and commissioners are therefore obliged to decide what should be available to whom. Although these decisions should be evidence-based, this is currently limited in the emerging field of appearance concerns. There is ample evidence for the aesthetic outcomes of plastic surgery procedures including grafting (e.g. following trauma or

cancer treatment) and other more complex procedures. Evidence of the psychological consequences of surgery is less well researched, particularly for reconstructive procedures (with the exception of reconstruction following breast cancer).
However, the available research to date has shown some improvements in specific
psychological indicators (though not necessarily a generally improved psychological functioning). For example, Cole et al. (1994) found substantial improvements
in quality of life in 92 patients with a variety of 'low-priority' conditions, with the
largest gains amongst those undergoing breast surgery. Improvements in psychosexual indicators (Cerovac et al., 2005), quality of life, and condition-specific difficulties (Shakespeare & Cole, 1997) were evident in women who had breast reduction
surgery. Similarly Cintra et al. (2008) found improved quality of life in patients who
had undergone abdominoplasty following bariatric surgery. Von Soest et al. (2009)
found that cosmetic surgery resulted in increased satisfaction with appearance and
a significant but rather small improvement in self-esteem, although the level of
psychological problems did not change after surgery. Most interesting though is a
study on semi-permanent facial fillers by Ong et al. (2007) which showed that
improvements in psychological well-being are reliant on perceived aesthetic change
highlighting the importance of the patient's perception of the aesthetic outcome in
producing positive psychological outcomes.

One way in which the NHS has attempted to manage resources is through guidelines, stating what can be offered under what circumstances. However, Henderson
(2009) found significant variation in how guidelines were applied and what procedures were funded. Cook et al. (2003) found that guidelines lacked an evidence
base and only referred to certain cosmetic procedures, named specific anatomical
sites and functional or symptomatic reasons for surgery. Most guidelines permitted
surgery 'exceptionally' for psychological reasons. However, there is little explanation of what constitutes 'psychological reasons' or evidence used to suggest who
may benefit psychologically from plastic surgery. Cook et al. (2007) found that
given the ineffectiveness of cosmetic surgery guidelines, plastic surgeons were
resorting to other information (e.g. cost, clinical factors, level of symptoms/
dysfunction, and abnormality of the appearance) in reaching decisions on whether
to offer cosmetic procedures.

There is now emerging evidence that offering treatment purely on the basis of
condition may not be appropriate. A recent study comparing three groups (Cordeiro
et al., 2010), found that levels of distress were lowest among the reconstructive
group (patients with scleroderma, a systemic progressive autoimmune disease
affecting large areas of skin and one or more internal organs) who were most likely
to be offered surgery, while those with the highest distress levels (patients requesting
cosmetic surgery) were the least likely to be offered surgery. Similarly, a comparison of 500 women requesting breast reduction surgery and 500 patients requesting
other cosmetic procedures found that levels of distress were not significantly
different (Clarke et al., 2008) although there are marked inequalities in access to

surgery, with fewer restrictions for breast reduction compared to other cosmetic procedures (Wraight et al., 2007).

The challenge therefore facing the NHS is to demonstrate evidence that plastic surgery procedures are indeed 'psychological surgery' with clear psychosocial benefits for patients in the long term. There is also a need to determine whether levels of distress are a good indicator of whether or not a person is likely to benefit psychologically from surgery. It is clear that decisions based solely on a diagnosis of a particular condition may miss the point in demonstrating the utility of these surgical procedures.

Psychological Management of Appearance Concerns

Implicit in the biomedical approach is the assumption that if appearance is restored or 'improved', then quality of life will also be improved. However it is rarely this simple and surgery can fail to produce any change in appearance concerns. The process of positive adjustment to a change in appearance or visible difference is multifactorial (The Healing Foundation, 2008) so other ways of understanding and managing appearance concerns are necessary.

A large body of evidence, reviewed in other chapters of this book, highlights the fact that a subset of individuals has some difficulties with appearance concerns. In general, they have similar difficulties, with some condition-specific concerns. These may arise from feelings of shame or embarrassment about the appearance (since it is perceived as failing to match their ideal) that then leads to high levels of pre-occupation with appearance and anxiety. This is particularly evident in social (and intimate) interactions. At times, this can lead individuals to avoid particular situations or adopt behaviours that conceal their appearance. These safety behaviours include particular styles of clothing or adopting particular postures. At times, they may also experience feelings of loss or lowered mood, with changes in self-confidence. Interpersonal difficulties are often exacerbated by others' responses if the appearance is unusual. It can invite other people to make comments, ask questions, or stare. This in turn reinforces the person's perceived difference, associated with negative feelings. Individuals can also experience discrimination and bullying.

In spite of the evidence of the effectiveness of psychological interventions (see Chapter 38 for detail) and the lack of a consistent relationship between the severity or nature of the visible difference and psychological distress, the provision of psychological care in the NHS continues to be predominantly driven by the myth that severity of disfigurement predicts distress. Therefore psychological care is often offered to patients according to disease or illness. For example, Clarke et al. (2003)

found that individuals losing an eye (enucleation) had access to psychological care in a leading eye hospital in the UK, whilst those with thyroid eye disease did not, although this group was found to have the highest level of psychological distress. Given the high levels of distress experienced by some plastic surgery patients, it is surprising that not every plastic surgery unit has an established clinical pathway on how to provide access to specialist psychological care. Our telephone survey of all plastic surgery units in the UK found that only 24% of the units providing body contouring surgery had psychological care as part of this clinical pathway (Butler, 2009). Service provision was highly varied: 76% of units had a practitioner with some advanced training as part of their service or could refer to a mental health practitioner within the hospital. Clinical nurse specialists or clinical psychologists were the professionals most likely to be embedded in units, with other professionals, such as psychiatrists, available within the hospital. There was also significant variability in the time offered to plastic surgery patients (ranging from less than half a day per week to a full-time post, though the latter was unusual), with the service sometimes only available to specific groups (e.g. cosmetic surgery, cancer, or burns). This highlights the lack of a national and systematic structure to address the psychological needs of those with appearance concerns in surgical settings.

The challenge therefore is how psychological services can organize themselves to meet the needs of those with appearance-related distress. Effective screening in community settings (as suggested earlier) is already helping to identify those in need of services and this could offer a way of helping shape access to services based on need. A stepped care approach would be the most effective method of determining access to psychological care. All community professionals (level 1) should allow exploration of the person's psychosocial concerns. Professionals in particular fields (e.g. dressing nurses, surgeons, camouflage therapists) should offer information (e.g. websites, leaflets) and advice and discuss concerns (level 2). At level 3, social interaction skills training (SIST) and help with managing social situations could be provided through support groups, or psychological practitioners or occupational therapists in more specialist settings. Cognitive behaviour therapy (CBT) aimed at identifying and modifying unhelpful appearance schemas may be provided at level 4 by those having undergone specialist training.

Level 4 care should be based within general or specialist psychological services (that form part of local mental health services) or provided by psychological practitioners embedded in surgical/medical services. Referrals to generic services can run into the problems outlined earlier if mental health professionals also overestimate the likelihood that surgery can resolve psychological distress and produce 'normal' appearance. Unfortunately, it is impossible to know how many individuals with appearance concerns are offered psychological intervention in a generic service and to ascertain whether any change in distress is similar to that amongst those seen by a professional with specialist training or expertise in appearance concerns.

There is one NHS service in the UK that operates as a stand-alone psychological service offering help to individuals with appearance concerns: *Outlook*. It serves a large geographical area and so relies on individuals and their families travelling to access the service. This suggests they may see a particularly motivated client group that make more use of psychological interventions, particularly as difficulties are more likely to be encountered on discharge from hospital.

In the charitable sector, organizations including *Changing Faces, Saving Faces* or those specific to particular diseases or conditions (e.g. *Lee Spark NF Foundation* for those who have had necrotizing fasciitis) emphasize the psychological impact consequent on a visible difference in appearance. Their work is varied from using an expert-patient model (based on Lorig et al.'s (1985) model) to facilitate support, to running workshops and public campaigns. Approaching a charitable organization or a specialist service like *Outlook* for support has the advantage that problems are framed in a psychological way from the outset so there may be a higher uptake of this service. However, there are also advantages to an embedded service such as the opportunity for informal consultation.

Current economic circumstances within the NHS also mean that appearance-related concerns and their treatment will be under increasing budgetary restriction or threat, as the service is likely to be included within 'low priority treatments'. This view of appearance-related distress as 'low priority' is held not only by the general public but also by the medical profession at large. The challenge for those working in the field of appearance concerns, whether through research, teaching, public health campaigns, or clinical practice, is to produce more evidence of the effectiveness in psychological approaches to resolve appearance concerns. While it is already possible to show commissioners of services that appearance concerns are not trivial, more evidence is required to show that a psychological approach can be effective at treating these concerns. There is also a pressing need for dissemination of information to GPs so that a referral for appearance concerns is no longer necessarily directed to a surgical or medical specialty.

JOINT MANAGEMENT OF APPEARANCE CONCERNS

In the cases presented earlier, Elwin, Jack, and Fay all benefited from meeting with a psychologist. The presence of psychologists within the surgical team has meant that when no procedures are available, as in Elwin's case, patients can still access help to reduce appearance concerns and their impact on day-to-day life. Jack's contact with the psychologist (EH) prevented our service from turning his palsy into a problem. With Fay it helped us to understand why proceeding with surgery (right away) was not appropriate. Unfortunately, in cases similar to that of Lorraine, it can be very difficult to facilitate a psychological understanding of their difficulties as surgical interventions have been so numerous.

The fact that most patients with appearance concerns access services via the surgical route suggest that psychological services embedded in surgical teams may offer many opportunities for patients and also our surgical colleagues. Good care should include consideration of the individual's psychological difficulties in planning treatment.

Clarke et al. (2005) highlight how psychology services could be funded within a plastic surgery department. Our unit has taken more than 7 years to develop an integrated psychological surgical service but the evidence for its effectiveness has taken even longer to produce. Unfortunately, this lack of evidence may become a problem with evidence-based decisions being used to drive future funding.

Being integrated into a plastic surgery team and demonstrating the usefulness of psychologists to clinicians is already a significant challenge. However, rather than viewing treatment as *either* surgery *or* psychology, there are opportunities to formulate joint goals around improving psychological distress and reducing (perceived) visibility of the difference in appearance. Psychological care (apart from reducing appearance concerns) can also help surgeons and patients examine whether surgery alone is sufficient to meet the patient's goals. Psychological involvement prior to surgery can enable a patient to manage their expectations by reducing the psychological impact of appearance concerns (e.g. reducing avoidance behaviours, managing anxiety, learning strategies to deal with questions, comments, and staring). This in turn often enables a person to understand how much change they can achieve and what surgery can realistically alter. Our (the authors') clinical experience suggests that this leads to higher rates of satisfaction with the outcomes of surgery since patients' goals are achieved. This is consistent with work in other surgical areas which demonstrates the importance of meeting patients' goals (often psychosocial) as well as managing the clinical condition (Elkadry et al., 2003, Hudak et al., 2004, Klassen et al., 2009).

Hopefully, as evidence is collated about the effectiveness of psychological interventions, joint management will become easier and more acceptable as illustrated in the following feedback from one of our colleagues: '*Many thanks for your help with the joint care of this patient. I think that between us we have achieved far more for this lady than either of us could have done independently*'.

The other challenge for an embedded service is enabling the uptake of psychological treatment, whether this is alongside surgery or not. Whilst a leaflet about psychological services can result in individuals asking for help, the psychologists in our unit rely on their colleagues to help patients understand the reason for their involvement and also the likely benefits this can offer. This requires psychological practitioners to be clear about their service and its effectiveness in treating difficulties. Unsurprisingly, patients very rarely expect psychological treatment as (part of) their care, and often perceive surgery as a more effective or sole solution. This can be very difficult to manage if they do not understand the limitations of surgery and perceive psychological intervention as a suggestion that their problems are 'in their head' rather than 'real'. Unfortunately, seeing a psychologist when other treatments have failed also implies that it is a second-rate treatment option.

Therefore the skill of the practitioner is essential in enabling the patient to understand how psychological approaches to appearance concerns can make a difference. Presenting research evidence can form an essential part of this process. We have found that when psychologists, surgeons and other multidisciplinary professionals normalize psychological involvement in patient care, this often results in less resistance to the uptake of the service. In redesigning pathways, psychology has also helped the surgical service take into account the psychological aspect of appearance concerns and ensure that patients achieve their goals.

Working at a societal level

This chapter has considered some of the challenges of healthcare provision in the UK for individuals with appearance concerns. However, efforts to address and reduce appearance concerns should also consider working at the societal level.

Professionals need to engage the wider societal context by involving the media and educating referrers (e.g. GPs) through dissemination of high-quality research around appearance concerns. Drawing on the example of bulimia and anorexia (new psychiatric diagnoses in the 1980s), there has been much progress in raising awareness of these problems and their impact. Now there are specialist eating disorder services, a huge body of evidence for various approaches to its treatment (including psychological, dietetics, and psychiatric), and an ability among both the public and healthcare professionals in identifying these types of difficulties. While we (the authors) are not suggesting that appearance concerns warrant a psychiatric diagnosis we feel this is a helpful example of how academic and clinical efforts can result in a shift in the understanding and treatment of difficulties.

Appearance concerns are widespread among the general population with concerns present in both young and old, women and men. Other chapters in this book offer suggestions on how to address appearance concerns through education and public campaigns. Only in reducing the emphasis placed on and invested in appearance generally is there likely to be a reduction in appearance concerns. At present there is little evidence of this happening so that appearance concerns are likely to persist and referrals are likely to increase. This is a great opportunity for psychologists to make a real difference by thinking of how they position themselves to meet this demand.

References

Bulter, P. E. M. (2009) Addressing the funding issues. Presentation at Massive Weight Loss Body Contouring Symposium, The Royal Free Hospital and the Royal Society of Medicine, London, May 2009.

Carr, T., Harris, D., & James, C. (2000). The Derriford Appearance Scale (DAS59): A new scale to measure individual responses to living with problems of appearance. *British Journal of Health Psychology*, 5, 201–15.

Cerovac, S., Ali, F. S., Blizard, R., Lloyd, G., & Butler, P. E. M. (2005). Psychosexual function in women who have undergone reduction mammaplasty. *Plastic and Reconstructive Surgery*, 116(5), 1306–13.

Cintra, W., Modolin, M., Gemperli, R., Gobbi, C., Faintuch, J., & Ferreira, M. (2008). Quality of life after abdominoplasty in women after bariatric surgery. *Obesity Surgery*, 18(6), 728–32.

Clarke, A. & Cooper, C. (2001). Psychological rehabilitation after disfiguring injury or disease: investigating the training needs of specialist nurses. *Journal of Advanced Nursing*, 34(1), 18–26.

Clarke, A., Hansen, E. L. E., White, P. & Butler, P. E. M. (2012). Low priority? A cross sectional study of appearance anxiety in 500 consecutive referrals for cosmetic surgery. *Psychology Health and Medicine*, Feb 28 [Epub ahead of print].

Clarke, A., Rumsey, N., Collin, J. R., & Wyn-Williams, M. (2003). Psychosocial distress associated with disfiguring eye conditions. *Eye*, 17, 35–40.

Clarke, A., Lester, K.J., Withey, S. J., & Butler, P. E. M. (2005). A funding model for a psychological service to plastic and reconstructive surgery in UK practice. *British Journal of Plastic Surgery*, 58, 708–13.

Clarke, A., Hansen, E., White, P., & Butler, P. E. M. (2008) Psychological distress is high and impacts negatively on behaviour: evidence from 1000 cosmetic referrals for cosmetic surgery in the NHS. Presentation at BAPRAS Winter Scientific Meeting, Royal College of Surgeons, London, December 2008.

Cole, R. P., Shakespeare, V., Shakespeare, P., & Hobby, J. A. (1994). Measuring outcome in low-priority plastic surgery patients using quality of life indices. *British Journal of Plastic Surgery*, 47, 117–21.

Cook, S. A., Rosser, R., Meah, S., James, M. I., & Salmon, P. (2003). Clinical decision guidelines for NHS cosmetic surgery: analysis of current limitations and recommendations for future development. *British Journal of Plastic Surgery*, 56(5), 429–36.

Cook, S. A., Rosser, R. J., James, M. I., Kaney, S., & Salmon, P. (2007). Factors influencing surgeons' decisions in elective cosmetic surgery consultations. *Medical Decision Making*, 27(3), 311–20.

Cordeiro, C. N., Clarke, A., White, P., Sivakumar, B., Ong, J. L., & Butler, P. E. M. (2010). A quantitative analysis of psychological and emotional health measures in 360 plastic surgery candidates: is there a difference between aesthetic and reconstructive surgery? *Annals of Plastic Surgery*, 65(3), 349–53.

Elkadry, E. A., Kenton, K. S., Fitzgerald, M. P., Shott, S., & Brubaker, L. (2003). Patient-selected goals: a new perspective on surgical outcomes. *American Journal of Obstetric Gynaecology*, 189(6), 551–8.

Faravelli, C., Salvatori, S., Galassi, F., Aiazzi, L., Drei, C., & Cabras, P. (1997). Epidemiology of somatoform disorders: a community survey in Florence. *Social Psychiatry & Psychiatric Epidemiology*, 32, 24–9.

Frances, J. (2003). *Educating children with a facial disfigurement*. London: Routledge Farmer.

Grant, J. E., Won Kim, S., & Crow, S. J. (2001). Prevalence and clinical features of body dysmorphic disorder in adolescent and adult psychiatric inpatients. *Journal of Clinical Psychiatry*, 62, 517–22.

Henderson, J. (2009). The plastic surgery postcode lottery in England. *International Journal of Plastic Surgery*, 7(6), 550–8.

Hudak, P. L., Hogg-Johnson, S., Bombardier, C., McKeever, P. D., & Wright, J. G. (2004). Testing a new theory of patient satisfaction with treatment outcome. *Medical Care*, 42(8), 726–39.

Jeevan, R. & Armstrong, A. (2008). Cosmetic tourism and the burden on the NHS. *Journal of Plastic, Reconstructive and Aesthetic Surgery*, 61, 1423–24.

Klassen, A. F., Pusic, A. L., Scott, A., Klok, J., & Cano, S. J. (2009). Satisfaction and quality of life in women who undergo breast surgery: A qualitative study. *BMC Women's Health*, 9(11), 1–8.

Kleve, L., Rumsey, N., Wyn-Williams, M., & White, P. (2002). The effectiveness of cognitive-behavioural interventions provided at Outlook: A disfigurement support unit. *Journal of Evaluation in Clinical Practice*, 8, 387–95.

Lorig, K., Lubeck, D., Kraines, R. G., Seleznick, M., & Holman H. R. (1985). Outcomes of self-help education for patients with arthritis. *Arthritis and Rheumatism*, 28(6), 680–5.

Moss, T. & Carr, T. (2004). Understanding adjustment to disfigurement: the role of the self-concept. *Psychology and Health*, 19, 737–48.

Moss, T. P. (2005). The relationship between subjective and objective ratings of disfigurement severity and psychological adjustment. *Body Image*, 2, 151–9.

National Institute for Health and Clinical Excellence (2005). *Obsessive compulsive disorder (OCD) and body dysmorphic disorder (BDD)*. London: NICE.

Newell, R. and Clarke, M. (2000). Evaluation of self-help leaflet in treatment of social difficulties following facial disfigurement. *International Journal of Nursing Studies*, 37, 381–8.

Ong, J., Clarke, A., White, P., Johnson, M., Withey, S., & Butler, P. E. M. (2007). Does severity predict distress? The relationship between subjective and objective measures of appearance and psychological adjustment, during treatment for facial lipoatrophy. *Body Image*, 4(3), 239–48.

Otto, M. W., Wilhelm, S., Cohen, L. S., and Harlow, B. L. (2001). Prevalence of body dysmorphic disorder in a community sample of women. *American Journal of Psychiatry*, 158, 2061–3.

Parikh, A. R., Clarke, A., & Butler, P. E. M. (2006). Plastic surgery and the undergraduate medical school curriculum. *Medical Education*, 40(5), 476–7.

Partridge, J. (1990). *Changing faces: the challenge of facial disfigurement*. London: Penguin Books.

Robinson, E. (1997). Psychological research on visible differences in adults. In R. Landsdown, N. Rumsey, E. Bradbury, A. Carr, and J. Partridge (eds.) *Visibly different: coping with disfigurement*, pp. 102–11. Oxford: Butterworth Heinemann.

Robinson, E., Rumsey, N., & Partridge, J. (1996). An evaluation of the social skills interaction skills workshops for people with disfiguring conditions. *British Journal of Plastic Surgery*, 49, 281–9.

Rumsey, N., Clarke, A., White, P., Wyn-Williams, M., & Garlick, W. (2004). Altered body image: auditing the appearance related concerns of people with visible disfigurement. *Journal of Advanced Nursing*, 48(5), 443–53.

Shakespeare, V. & Cole, R. P. (1997). Measuring patient-based outcomes in a plastic surgery service: breast reduction surgical patients. *British Journal of Plastic Surgery*, 50, 242–8.

The Healing Foundation (2008). *Identifying psychosocial factors and processes contributing to suc-cessful adjustment to disfiguring conditions.* Available at: http://www.thehealingfoundation.org/thf2008/images08/media/ARCFinalReport.pdf (accessed 13 July 2010).

Thompson, A. R. & Kent, G. (2001). Adjusting to disfigurement: processes involved in dealing with being visibly different. *Clinical Psychology Review*, 21, 663–82.

Von Soest, T., Kvalem, I. L., Roald, H. E., & Skolleborg, K. C. (2009). The effects of cosmetic surgery on body image, self-esteem, and psychological problems. *Journal of Plastic, Reconstructive & Aesthetic Surgery*, 62(10), 1238–44.

Wraight, W. M., Tay, S. K., Nduka, C., & Pereira, J. A. (2007). Bilateral breast reduction surgery in England: a postcode lottery. *Journal of Plastic, Reconstructive & Aesthetic Surgery*, 60(9), 1039–44.

Zigmond, A. S. & Snaith, R. P. (1983). The hospital anxiety and depression scale. *Acta Psychiatrica Scandinavica*, 67(6), 361–70.

CHAPTER 6

....

CHALLENGES IN HEALTHCARE PROVISION IN THE UNITED STATES

....

VALERIE LEMAINE

ANDREA PUSIC

By implementing universal healthcare coverage, the current healthcare reform in the US is attempting to improve healthcare provision for millions of American citizens. However, when it comes to reconstructive surgery performed to improve changes in appearance, either following congenital or acquired differences, illness or injury, health insurance providers may continue to deny coverage because they classify such procedures as cosmetic in nature and not medically necessary. In 1989, the American Medical Association adopted the following definition of *cosmetic surgery*: it is 'performed to reshape normal structures of the body to improve a patient's appearance and self esteem' (American Medical Association, 1989). They also defined *reconstructive surgery* as a procedure 'performed on abnormal structures of the body caused by congenital defects, developmental abnormalities, trauma, infection, tumors or disease. It is generally performed to improve function, but may also be done to approximate a normal appearance' (American Medical Association, 1989). This latter definition has been used frequently in the last decade when the Reconstructive Surgery Act was proposed by Democrats in consecutive sessions of the US Congress. This legislation establishes the requirement that health insurance companies in the US provide coverage for any medically necessary and appropriate reconstructive surgery to *improve function* or *restore a patient's normal appearance*, to the extent possible, based on the judgement of the physician performing the surgical procedure. Unfortunately, this federal mandate has failed to become law due to the ongoing overall healthcare debate in the US; currently only a minority of states have such a requirement.

This chapter reviews the current status of healthcare provision in the US with regards to reconstructive surgery affecting physical appearance and suggests future directions for outcomes research and patient advocacy.

CHILDREN BORN WITH CONGENITAL ANOMALIES

Surgical procedures for childhood deformities and congenital defects most commonly denied insurance coverage in the US are associated with primary and secondary cleft lip repair (including associated nasal abnormalities) and correction of craniofacial differences. In 1997, the American Medical Association adopted a resolution declaring that 'the treatment of a child's congenital or developmental deformity or disorder due to trauma or malignant disease should be covered by all insurers'. Multiple bills addressing this issue were unsuccessfully introduced in sessions of Congress. Growing bipartisan support of multiple groups advocating for children with congenital differences helped introduce the 'Children's Access to Reconstructive Evaluation and Surgery Act' (the CARES Act) in the House of Representatives on 5 March 2009. The CARES Act is similar to the Reconstructive Surgery Act, but focuses on providing coverage for the treatment of a child's congenital or developmental differences in appearance. As of July 2010, it was still in the first steps of the legislative process.

At the present time, only 13 states have laws requiring insurance coverage for children born with congenital disorders and craniofacial anomalies. For example, a new law was enacted in California in 1999, prohibiting health insurance companies to deny coverage for reconstructive surgery to correct birth defects and other medical abnormalities such as Poland syndrome (a condition in which the chest muscle is missing and digits are webbed).

BREAST SURGERY

Breast reconstruction following mastectomy

On 21 October 1998, the Women's Health and Cancer Rights Act (WHCRA) (Wilkins & Alderman, 2004; United States Department of Labor, 2010), which amended the Public Health Service Act and the Employee Retirement Income Security Act of 1974 (ERISA), was signed into law by President Bill Clinton. This legislation sets minimum federal standards for, and guaranteed universal coverage of reconstructive surgery following a mastectomy. Administered by the Department of Health and Human Services (DHHS) and the Department of Labor (DOL), WHCRA requires that health insurance companies and self-insured group health plans (i.e. the employer rather than an insurance company or HMO (health maintenance organization) assumes the group's risk) that cover mastectomies also provide benefits for breast and nipple reconstruction. Under WHCRA, important protections for women who elect breast reconstruction following mastectomy are guaranteed, such as coverage of: (1) reconstruction of the breast that was removed by mastectomy; (2) surgical procedures of the contralateral breast to produce a symmetrical appearance; (3) external breast prostheses; and (4) treatment of physical complications following mastectomy, including lymphoedema. WHCRA does not prohibit health plans and insurers to impose deductibles or co-payments for benefits associated with breast reconstruction procedures following mastectomy. Furthermore, state high-risk pools of individuals denied coverage by private insurance companies, and self-insured health plans from employers such as churches, states or local school districts are exempt from WHCRA. As of 2010, 37 states have mandates requiring broader coverage than the minimum requirements under WHCRA (Health Policy Tracking Service, 2008). Although the WHCRA has reduced disparities in insurance coverage for breast reconstruction, utilization remains variable and generally low across the US. According to a recently published survey by Greenberg et al. (2008), nationwide breast reconstruction rates are less than 40% for women undergoing mastectomy. In line with this, in August 2010 the State of New York recently passed a bill requiring that New York hospitals and doctors discuss breast reconstruction options with their patients before performing cancer surgery, to give them information about insurance coverage and to refer them to another hospital, if necessary, for the reconstructive surgery (Health Policy Tracking Service, 2008).

Reduction mammaplasty

Currently in the US, a reduction mammaplasty may be covered by third-party payers if it is considered a reconstructive procedure. Documentation of symptoms related to the weight and size of the breasts usually improves the possibility of obtaining approval by third-party payers. Unfortunately, third-party payers increasingly deny coverage for reduction mammaplasty, basing their decisions on internal medical coverage policies that are not evidence-based (Nguyen et al., 2008). Furthermore, there is a lack of uniformity in the criteria used by health insurance companies to guide their decision to cover this surgical procedure. For example, certain private insurers place a 500 gram-per-breast minimum that must be resected (removed) for the procedure to be covered. Other third-party payers base their coverage decisions on the Schnur Sliding Scale (Schnur et al., 1991), which was developed by a plastic surgeon in an attempt to help determine the minimum amount of breast resection necessary as a criterion for medical necessity for reduction mammaplasty (Schnur et al., 1991). This instrument was developed by plotting the logarithm of the quantity of breast tissue removed (in grams) against body surface area (in metres squared). Based on a survey of plastic surgeons performing reduction mammaplasty, the 22nd percentile line was chosen as a cut off point that would separate women who are undergoing this surgery for medical reasons from those who have cosmetic motivations for choosing this procedure (Schnur et al., 1991). Unfortunately, the Schnur Sliding Scale is often misused by third-party payers (Schnur, 1999). Some private insurers have readjusted the scale to require larger amounts of breast tissue removal, and others misuse this instrument by setting an arbitrary minimum resection of 500 grams of breast tissue per side, regardless of the body surface area (Schnur, 1999).

In 2001, the BRAVO study pioneered the investigation of the impact of breast hypertrophy (excessive and rapid breast growth) on women's quality of life (Kerrigan et al., 2001). One year later, a study evaluating the impact of breast reduction on health-related quality of life (HRQoL) highlighted that weight of breast tissue resection, body weight as well as bra cup size had no significant effect on the demonstrated benefits of breast reduction (Collins et al., 2002). Furthermore, this study also found that the benefits of reduction mammaplasty were found in both heavier and thinner women (Collins et al., 2002). This was followed by the publication of recommended insurance coverage criteria for third-party payers by the American Society of Plastic Surgeons (ASPS), justifying the indication of this procedure to relieve symptomatic macromastia patients, even for reductions of less than 500 grams of breast tissue per side. Prospective data is available to confirm that breast reductions of less than 500 grams per side provide significant improvements of symptoms related to macromastia (enlarged breasts) and overall HRQoL (Spector and Karp, 2007; Spector et al., 2008). Thus, even with a significant body of scientific evidence showing that the removal of a specified amount of breast tissue has not been correlated with alleviation of symptoms of breast hypertrophy, this data has yet to succeed in modifying insurance coverage criteria in the United States.

BODY CONTOURING SURGERY: REDUNDANT SKIN FOLLOWING MASSIVE WEIGHT LOSS

With the increasing prevalence of obesity in the US, bariatric surgery has emerged as an effective method to produce significant weight loss. Because obesity is associated with many debilitating comorbidities such as type II diabetes mellitus, hypertension, dyslipidemia, and osteoarthritis, bariatric surgery is often considered medically necessary, and thus covered by health insurance providers. While the health benefits of massive weight loss are obvious, patients are commonly left with unwanted redundant skin that may result in chronic local skin conditions such as intertrigo, cellulitis, ulcerations, and panniculitis. This excess hanging skin may also interfere with activities of daily living, such as personal hygiene and ambulation. Moreover, body contouring after massive weight loss has been shown to improve quality of life and body image satisfaction (Song et al., 2006; Sarwer et al., 2008). Redundant skin is best treated by surgical excision. In the US, insurance companies usually do not provide coverage for body contouring surgery as it is considered cosmetic. Coverage may be granted by certain insurance providers based on proof of functional deficit due to a severe physical difference or disfigurement resulting from the redundant or excessive skin. Furthermore, both interference with activities of daily living, and photographic evidence of skin disorders (e.g. intertriginous dermatitis, skin ulceration, etc.) have to be documented.

Provision of Psychosocial Services in the United States

Evidence indicates the potential effectiveness of psychosocial services aimed at relieving emotional distress affecting individuals with visible differences and appearance concerns. Presently, some level of psychosocial support is informally provided by various healthcare providers as a part of routine healthcare. For instance, reconstructive surgeons frequently provide informal emotional support to patients, helping them cope with the anxiety and depression often associated with visible difference and surgical treatment. However, when this type of support is insufficient to address a patient's specific needs, more formal psychosocial support services are necessary (Institute of Medicine, 2008).

Available services often come in the form of peer support programmes, and individual or group psychotherapy. Peer support programmes help individuals with similar conditions support each other and share knowledge on effective coping skills. This contributes to enhancing HRQoL by building the person's own self-efficacy, decreasing social isolation, and enhancing confidence, a sense of normalcy, and a sense of control (Barlow and Coren, 2000; Campbell et al., 2004; Ussher et al., 2006). There is a growing body of evidence supporting the possible effectiveness of psychotherapy services for individuals affected by some conditions involving visible differences (Jacobsen and Jim, 2008). However, there is a need to improve the translation of research knowledge on this topic into clinical practice. For example, some studies of psychological interventions for distress in cancer patients have limited ability to inform patient care because of study design (e.g. exclusion of highly distressed patients) (Coyne et al., 2006). Other challenges are present when a clinical practice group has limited resources, or is located in a rural or remote area where few or no psychosocial healthcare resources are available. The only way to provide psychosocial health services on a frequent and timely basis in such instances may be to link patients with remote providers through telephone or Internet access. At the present time, the effectiveness of such interventions has not been thoroughly evaluated (see Chapters 38 and 39). Moreover, patients may be denied financial coverage for psychological support services by private insurers. Overall, the organizational, financial, and size differences among healthcare practices in the US may be considered the main factor influencing the strategies providers use to implement psychosocial support.

FUTURE DIRECTIONS

In the current environment of healthcare industry restriction and performance metrics, measurement of HRQoL outcomes has become increasingly important to healthcare payers, clinical practice, and research (Fitzpatrick et al., 1999; Cano et al., 2004). HRQoL, which encompasses physical, psychological, as well as social functioning, is increasingly used as an outcome metric in decisions regarding insurance coverage of reconstructive procedures. Recently, new condition-specific patient-reported outcome measures (PROMs) have been developed specifically for plastic surgery patients (Cano et al., 2009)—e.g. BREAST-Q® (Pusic et al., 2009), FACE-Q®, (Klassen et al., 2010), and BODY-Q®. Use of these measures may provide valuable insights on patient satisfaction and HRQoL to support patient advocacy and access to treatment. Further emphasis is also being placed on health utilities, which incorporate the change in quality of life (i.e. quality-adjusted life-years or QALYs) conferred by a medical intervention into healthcare cost analyses. In recent years, cost–utility analysis (CUA) has emerged as the preferred method for economic evaluations and value-based medicine in healthcare. CUA can considerably enhance healthcare quality while maximizing the most efficient use of scarce resources (Brown et al., 2000; Thoma et al., 2008; Santerre and Neun, 2010).

In summary, healthcare coverage of reconstructive procedures in the US has various 'grey areas' with some interventions being considered cosmetic in nature, and thus viewed as medically unnecessary. Rigorous quantification of the health burden of conditions altering physical appearance will inform policy decisions regarding access to treatment and insurance coverage. As a central component to comparative effectiveness studies, PROMs and health utilities data will support advocacy and facilitate patient access to procedures that demonstrate a positive impact on their overall health and quality of life.

REFERENCES

American Medical Association Policies of House of Delegates (1989). Definition of 'Cosmetic' and 'Reconstructive' Surgery, H-475.992. In Council Medical services Annual Meeting, Chicago, IL, June 1989.

American Society of Plastic Surgeons. ASPS Positions on Recommended Insurance Coverage Criteria. http://www.plasticsurgery.org/Medical_Professionals/Health_Policy_and_Advocacy/Health_Policy_Resources/Recommended_Insurance_Coverage_Criteria.html (accessed 2 September 2010).

Barlow, J. & Coren, E. (2000). Parent-training programmes for improving maternal psychosocial health. *Cochrane Database of Systematic Reviews*, 4, CD002020.

Brown, G. C., Brown, M. M., & Sharma, S. (2000). Health care in the 21st century: evidence-based medicine, patient preference-based quality, and cost effectiveness. *Quality Management in Health Care*, 9, 23–31.

Campbell, H. S., Phaneuf, M. R., & Deane, K. (2004). Cancer peer support programs – do they work? *Patient Education and Counseling*, 55, 3–15.

Cano, S. J., Browne, J. P., & Lamping, D. L. (2004). Patient-based measures of outcome in plastic surgery: current approaches and future directions. *British journal of plastic surgery*, 57, 1–11.

Cano, S. J., Klassen, A., & Pusic, A. L. (2009). The science behind quality-of-life measurement: a primer for plastic surgeons. *Plastic and reconstructive surgery*, 123, 98e–106e.

Collins, E. D., Kerrigan, C. L., Kim, M., Lowery, J. C., Striplin, D.T., Cunningham, B., *et al.* (2002). The effectiveness of surgical and nonsurgical interventions in relieving the symptoms of macromastia. *Plastic and Reconstructive Surgery*, 109, 1556–66.

Coyne, J. C., Lepore, S. J., & Palmer, S. C. (2006). Efficacy of psychosocial interventions in cancer care: evidence is weaker than it first looks. *Annals of Behavioral Medicine*, 32, 104–10.

Fitzpatrick, R., Jenkinson, C., Klassen, A., & Goodacre, T. (1999). Methods of assessing health-related quality of life and outcome for plastic surgery. *British Journal of Plastic Surgery*, 52, 251–5.

Greenberg, C. C., Schneider, E. C., Lipsitz, S. R., Ko, C. Y., Malin, J. L., Epstein AM *et al.* (2008). Do variations in provider discussions explain socioeconomic disparities in postmastectomy breast reconstruction? *Journal of the American College of Surgeons*, 206, 605–15.

Health Policy Tracking Service (Thomson West) (2008). *Kaiser State Health Facts, State Mandated Benefits, Reconstructive Surgery after Mastectomy.* http://www.statehealthfacts.org/comparemaptable.jsp?ind=490&cat=10 (accessed 21 July 2010).

Institute of Medicine (IOM). (2008). *Cancer care for the whole patient: Meeting psychosocial health needs.* Washington, DC: The National Academies Press.

Jacobsen, P. B. & Jim, H. S. (2008). Psychosocial interventions for anxiety and depression in adult cancer patients: achievements and challenges. *CA: A Cancer Journal for Clinicians*, 58, 214–30.

Kerrigan, C. L., Collins, E. D., Striplin, D., Kim, H. M., Wilkins, E., Cunningham, B., *et al.* (2001). The health burden of breast hypertrophy. *Plastic and Reconstructive Surgery*, 108, 1591–9.

Klassen, A. F., Cano, S. J., Scott, A., Snell, L., & Pusic, A. L. (2010). Measuring patient-reported outcomes in facial aesthetic patients: development of the FACE-Q. *Facial Plastic Surgery*, 26, 303–9.

Nguyen, J. T., Wheatley, M. J., Schnur, P. L., Nguyen, T. A., & Winn, S.R. (2008). Reduction mammaplasty: a review of managed care medical policy coverage criteria. *Plastic and Reconstructive Surgery*, 121, 1092–100.

Pusic, A. L., Klassen, A. F., Scott, A. M., Klok, J. A., Cordeiro, P. G., & Cano, S. J. (2009). Development of a new patient-reported outcome measure for breast surgery: the BREAST-Q. *Plastic and reconstructive surgery*, 124, 345–53.

Santerre, R. E. & Neun, S. P. (2010). *Health Economics—Theories, Insights, and Industry Studies* (5th edn.). Mason, OH: South-Western, Cengage Learning.

Sarwer, D. B., Thompson, J. K., Mitchell, J. E., & Rubin, J. P. (2008). Psychological considerations of the bariatric surgery patient undergoing body contouring surgery. *Plastic and Reconstructive Surgery*, 121, 423e–34e.

Schnur, P. L. (1999). Reduction mammaplasty – the schnur sliding scale revisited. *Annals of Plastic Surgery*, 42, 107–8.

Schnur, P. L., Hoehn, J. G., Ilstrup, D. M., Cahoy, M. J., & Chu, C. P. (1991). Reduction mammaplasty: cosmetic or reconstructive procedure? *Annals of Plastic Surgery*, 27, 232–7.

Song, A. Y., Rubin, J. P., Thomas, V., et al. (2006). Body image and quality of life in post massive weight loss body contouring patients. *Obesity*, 14, 1626–36.

Spector, J. A. & Karp, N. S. (2007). Reduction mammaplasty: a significant improvement at any size. *Plastic and Reconstructive Surgery*, 120, 845–50.

Spector, J. A., Singh, S. P., & Karp, N. S. (2008). Outcomes after breast reduction: does size really matter? *Annals of Plastic Surgery*, 60, 505–9.

Thoma, A., Strumas, N., Rockwell, G., & McKnight, L. (2008). The use of cost-effectiveness analysis in plastic surgery clinical research. *Clinical Plastic Surgery*, 35, 285–96.

United States Department of Labor (2009). *Your Rights After A Mastectomy. Women's Health & Cancer Rights Act of 1998.* http://www.dol.gov/ebsa/publications/whcra.html (accessed 21 July 21 2010).

Ussher, J., Kirsten, L., Butow, P., & Sandoval, M. (2006). What do cancer support groups provide which other supportive relationships do not? The experience of peer support groups for people with cancer. *Social Science & Medicine*, 62, 2565–76.

Wilkins, E. G. & Alderman, A. K. (2004). Breast reconstruction practices in North America: current trends and future priorities. *Seminars in Plastic Surgery*, 18, 149–55.

CHAPTER 7

CHALLENGES IN HEALTHCARE PROVISION IN RESOURCE-POOR COUNTRIES

TOM POTOKAR

PATRICIA PRICE

INTRODUCTION

THIS chapter focuses on the challenges inherent in providing healthcare for patients with disfiguring or appearance-related conditions in resource-poor countries across the world. The clinical and research work of the authors is predominantly related to burns, trauma, and wound healing, so many of the examples come from that area—but the challenges discussed can be extrapolated to cover the provision of care for people with other appearance-related conditions. Both authors are trustees of Interburns (http://www.interburns.org), a charity which was established in 2006 to address the needs of the majority of burns victims and those who treat them in resource-poor countries of the world. Much of the research investigating the psychological consequences of scarring and disfigurement has been undertaken in high-income countries and there is a paucity of information from low-income countries. In preparation for working on this chapter, the authors contacted many of their collaborators and asked them to reflect on the availability of psychological support in their countries. Much of the chapter is therefore based on collaborations with clinicians from these countries, who have worked tirelessly to support their patients and we thank them for their support in informing our awareness of the challenges they face on a daily basis.

Disfigurement can occur as a result of trauma, congenital anomalies (such as cleft lip and palate, club foot, giant pigmented naevi, etc.), neoplasia (such as head and neck cancer), and medical diseases (such as rheumatoid arthritis, lymphoedema, stroke, etc.). The World Health Organization (WHO) estimates that everyday around the world almost 16,000 people die from injuries, and injury accounted for 9% of the world's deaths and 12% of the world's burden of diseases (disability-adjusted life years (DALYs) lost) in 2000 (http://www.searo.who.int/en/Section1174/Section1461.htm). With an ever increasing aged population the incidence of cancer and potentially disfiguring surgery also increases. Those affected are often late presenting for treatment and the extent of the disfigurement can be severe in developing countries. The burden of congenital disfigurements tends to be high in low-income countries with limited prenatal screening and a high rate of malnutrition, and often neglected medical diseases such as noma (a severe destructive ulcerating infection of the face found in malnourished children) and filiariasis (a parasitic infection causing blockage of the lymph system and gross swelling of affected parts) can cause extensive disfigurement and deformity.

In an editorial for the international journal *Burns*, Potokar et al. (2008) questioned why there was a publication bias which focused on high-technology-based developments with little relevance to resource-poor countries, when research to address the majority of injuries worldwide, including how people manage the long-term conditions associated with function and appearance, is rarely published. The reasons for lack of publication mirror many of the challenges that confront colleagues worldwide in providing health services, including resources and infrastructure. However, geography and prioritization are also important influences as well as the profile of appearance-related health provision when in competition for funding relating to life-threatening public health issues, including AIDS and maternal health. These issues will be discussed in turn.

RESOURCES

Resource-poor countries struggle to finance even very limited health services where acute treatment is the priority—whilst work on prevention, education, and awareness-raising take second place, and unfortunately the emphasis is often exclusively on medical, emergency treatment with families and friends left to deal with adjustment and coping issues. Many of the improvements in survival in resource-rich countries have emerged as a result of changes in legislation (particularly health and safety), public awareness (e.g. the important work undertaken by charities such as Changing Faces in working with patients and society to amend stereotypical responses to disfiguring conditions), and safety campaigns (e.g. campaigns around the use of fireworks). This has resulted in a gradual shift in focus from mortality towards quality of life. In the case of trauma, burns, or advanced cancer, the lack of significant improvements in mortality in poorer countries means there are very limited resources to devote to issues of quality of life, particularly outside of large cities. When these resources do exist they tend to focus on the immediate (acute) phase of care and on physical function rather than the psychosocial impact of a condition. For example, burn clinicians from Uganda report that the urgency of resuscitation, pain control, reducing the risk of infection, and establishing adequate nutrition take precedence over considering psychosocial issues. Many international colleagues confirm that psychosocial support is not given high priority; indeed all aspects of rehabilitation and re-enablement only receive a small proportion of available funds—with the majority of available funds spent on the overwhelming demand to treat acute patients. There is also the difficulty of predicting the need for psychological support, as there is little relevant data that can help identify those who should be prioritized for access to the extremely limited resources that may be available—when staff are stretched to the limit, there is little or no time to talk to patients or their families.

It is easy to paint a very negative picture of the work that goes on, and we have both seen examples where the extent of the demand against service delivery is heartbreaking, but there are also pockets of exceptionally good practice—usually led by a dedicated, charismatic individual who is trying to pioneer service development against the odds.

PRIORITIZATION

It is often difficult for resource-poor countries to make the case for the investment of limited funding into appearance-related support or psychosocial interventions. As with many health initiatives in resource-rich countries, the emphasis in resource-poor countries has, historically, been on survival issues or on the management of conditions that pose the biggest public health threat—it is difficult to compete with maternal care/obstetrics or HIV/AIDS when both topics have received a huge amount of national and international publicity, and are the subject of WHO strategic targets.

As an example of this, health professionals from Kenya report that they lose contact with the majority of burn patients once the wounds are 'healed', possibly because patients are aware that there are no further services on offer once the Plastic

Surgery Clinic has dealt with the reconstructive element of care. Most of our international colleagues do not have access to any psychological services whatsoever, although a few are fortunate enough to have access to nursing staff with some counselling experience. Staff from parts of Africa report that they simply do not have the skills, knowledge, or organizational support to offer psychological services, camouflage expertise, or support groups to patients with congenital or acquired differences. Instead, a patient's adjustment to disfigurement is influenced by the perception of the society in which they live—and many integrate into their families and wider social circles very successfully.

PATIENT EXPECTATIONS

Many people who visit resource-poor countries for the first time are confronted with the extreme contrast that exists between the wealthy and the poor—particularly in cities, where luxurious homes and hotels exist in close proximity to families huddled together in makeshift shelters where they live a hand-to-mouth existence. Within such cultural diversity there also exists a wide range of expectations from the healthcare system. Those who have the resources may have access to first-class private hospitals, where the provision is world-class and, in some cases, world-leading. Patients who can afford such provision have high expectations of the service and the demand for cosmetic surgery for a whole host of appearance-related issues is growing. This is in stark contrast to the majority of patients who are pleased just to gain access to the most basic medical facilities where staff are challenged with a lack of physical resources and personnel, such that the emphasis on appearance comes second to issues of survival. At a recent South East Asian burn training event in Bangladesh, representatives from the region highlighted the fact that, particularly, but not exclusively in the government sector, there are extremely limited or a complete lack of resources to address the long-term psychological needs of burns patients and that long-term follow-up of patients is not feasible.

Clinicians from Kenya report that there are very few people with visible differences within their caseload, with a very small minority wanting or needing input from psychological services. This may reflect cultural expectations as most patients simply do not see the need for such interventions, but they would welcome access to material, practical support- particularly related to work opportunities. Colleagues report that support groups exist for people with some health conditions (e.g. breast cancer), but the majority of patients they see with trauma or burn-related injuries come from such poor backgrounds that time away from work to attend support groups would cause financial problems. Furthermore, there is little sense of empowerment to develop such groups in the first place. This does not, however, mean that those patients from poorer backgrounds are necessarily less concerned about their appearance or suffer fewer consequences. Unfortunately there is currently no research addressing these issues, for example, analysing the impact of scarring with respect to financial status or social class in a region such as Africa or Asia.

GEOGRAPHY, INFRASTRUCTURE, AND PATIENT DEMOGRAPHICS

Burn care services in resource-poor countries are not usually centralized, so care takes place in district hospitals and/or outlying health clinics. Away from the main urban areas, patients may be scattered over a vast geographical region. Even in large cities there may be no burn or trauma centre and patients may be cared for in a number of different facilities, often by informal carers or the local healer. To reach specialist services, patients would have to travel—and sometimes walk—for several days in the hope that they can survive long enough to reach specialist help. By the time patients get to the help they need, infection may have taken hold or the window of time for immediate treatment that can improve functional and cosmetic outcomes has already passed. For such patients, issues of functionality take priority over appearance, as manual work is an important source of income. Contracted and scarred limbs can significantly impact on the ability to work, while visible disfigurement can restrict the opportunity to gain any type of employment.

Unfortunately deliberate disfigurement still exists in some parts of the world, where women and/or children are mutilated as a form of punishment. Indeed our colleagues report a number of demographic variables that influence outcomes and/or the demand for support services. Reports from India suggest that females who have a visible disfigurement, poor literacy, and are economically dependent are particularly vulnerable to social exclusion and psychological distress: they need social, psychological, family, and financial support, which unfortunately is rarely available. The only option available may be to introduce them to other women who have had similar experiences. This is often not enough, and young female patients in Pakistan, for instance, often need constant reassurance about finding and keeping lasting and secure relationships. This is a notable problem in a society which is obsessed with marriage: it is difficult to fully comprehend the pressure on the many women who are not educated, since their economic survival is solely dependent on marrying a working man. Cultural norms in many resource-poor countries do not allow couples the opportunity to develop meaningful relationships before marriage, so partnership choices are driven by brief encounters, where appearance plays a major role in impression formation. Males and females do not 'date' or live together for long periods before getting married, so choices are rarely made on the basis of character or personality. In Bangladesh, scarring that is hidden is also a problem, although parents may not seek treatment until the daughter is of an age to marry. Clinicians from Nepal also report greater problems in helping females (and not only those who hope to marry), particularly when the disfigurement is visible—married women fear that their husbands will neglect them, or leave them for other women.

Men in resource-poor countries appear to cope better with their scars, possibly because their spouses are generally very supportive and there is little question of rejection on the basis of looks and, whilst functional impairment may limit the type of employment that is possible, visible disfigurement is less of a problem for them. As a consequence, a visible disfigurement may not impact on the ability to provide for their families. Ironically, clinicians from Nepal report that second marriages among men who have a visible disfigurement are common. This is in stark contrast to women in such situations who, as housewives with few skills suitable for paid employment, have no means of survival if their husbands leave them. In Bangladesh, appearance is not the only reason husbands may abandon their young wives if they are injured after marriage—in a society where treatment has to be paid for by the individual, the costs associated with caring for a badly injured dependent can be prohibitive. However, for both men and women there are still certain occupations and environments (e.g. receptionists and the media) which, just as in resource-rich countries, give undue priority to physical appearance. It is only those who earn substantial salaries that are likely to have access and the ability to pay for reconstructive and/or aesthetic surgery.

In India, children who survive burns injuries or who are disfigured as the result of trauma often face isolation, initially from their peers. There are no school re-entry programmes and they have to deal with challenges of unwanted stares and questioning looks, sometimes over very protracted periods of time and often without support. A number of specialist units may be fortunate enough to have a psychologist as part of the team, but the majority of patients with a visible difference will not be treated in such well-equipped units. Clinicians from Pakistan inform us that bullying and peer pressure are as much a problem there as they are in resource-rich countries. Parents are often very worried, particularly if they have daughters, as they fear for their chances of making a successful marriage and often the anxiety is sufficient to hinder their daughter's development of effective coping skills.

In some countries disfigurement may become an asset, and a way of earning a living: in the streets of Dhaka visitors will see many people with visible differences on the streets, begging in order to live. Whilst this could be seen as an inevitable consequence of rejection, or lack of ability to gain paid employment, local surgeons report that some people with a disfigurement and/or functional limitations are reticent to undergo surgical procedures that could help, for fear of losing the sympathy that results in an income through begging.

On a positive note, anecdotal evidence from both Pakistan and Nepal appears to confirm the research data collected in the UK and elsewhere that those with strong social networks, particularly in the form of supportive family and friends, appear to adjust and manage the demands of visible difference more successfully.

These anecdotal accounts, together with our experiences of working with clinicians in a wide range of resource-poor countries suggest that there are very few opportunities for therapeutic input that can be truly life changing. However, one such example is the Acid Survivors Trust (ASF) in Bangladesh, whose vision is that victims of acid violence (purposeful throwing of acid onto a victim—usually the face, and usually as a result of land or marital disputes) should have access to justice and be full members of society. They have developed a multipronged approach to address the issue of acid violence. As well as working on prevention through education, public awareness, and legislation, they concentrate on the psychological well-being of survivors. ASF's social reintegration services aid survivors in the social and economic reintegration process. In order to help survivors gain economic independence, ASF has formed networks with partner organizations, civil-society organizations, and private companies in order to provide income-generating schemes and job placements. This has meant that in one of the poorest countries in the world, the psychosocial rehabilitation available to a particular subgroup of burns patients, often with severe disfigurement, is exceptional. In addition, due to public awareness campaigns and the use of the media and well-known celebrities, there has been a change in the general perceptions of the public towards people with visible disfigurements, especially women.

INTERBURNS

How can those from resource-rich countries help those in resource-poor regions? To date, there has been a substantial amount of charitable work conducted by a wide range of dedicated, charismatic people who have visited resource-poor countries with the aim of providing practical help or education. The charity Interburns was set up with the aim of addressing the disparity in global burn care between high-income and low- and middle-income countries. It currently consists of a network of burn professionals from around the globe, with the aim of enhancing global burn care through education, training, and research alongside promotion of prevention activities and increasing public awareness of the burden of disease caused by burns. Our activities have principally constituted the development of an Essential Burn Care course (EBC—Interburns) which is a practical and flexible course aimed at personnel treating burns in low- and middle-income countries (LMICs) who have had little or no training. It concentrates on the care of people with mild-to-moderate burns, and on providing practical solutions to local problems.

Our philosophy is rooted in multiprofessional practice, so teams that visit resource-poor countries include a wide range of professions, including psychologists (when possible). Our aim is not to visit, help with treatment, and then leave. Instead, we want to allow those from resource-poor countries to share their experiences of how they have developed excellence within their existing resources, and build strong teams for the future. Our courses therefore include sessions on team building and motivation, as well as emergency first aid, prevention, and therapy. Even our basic training courses include sessions on psychosocial issues as we are keen to ensure that the teams we build for the future include every aspect of care and, whenever possible, we ensure that a local patient (hopefully a success story) can share their experiences and pass on the aspects of their story for the benefit of others. Using local patients who have discovered their own ways of coping with the reactions of others can be a great help when working with patients who are about to face similar problems.

Conclusion

This chapter is based predominantly on the first-hand accounts of those working in resource-poor countries rather than academic research papers, and the issues presented are steeped in experiences that focus on the needs of patients in those particular countries rather than the priorities of a Westernized approach to disfigurement. Evidence of psychosocial need and/or psychological support and interventions is both difficult to collect and evaluate in these countries because health provision is often driven by the priority to maintain life and survival. However, there are examples of excellence in resource-poor countries that demonstrate good practice is not always dependent on funding; although the involvement of committed and passionate individuals appears to be a constant theme. Our experiences have made it clear that we cannot just translate ways of working in resource-rich countries directly to resource-poor countries, as the differences in cultural norms influence every area of practice. In the long term, success must build on the particular cultural norms and/or country-specific health service, where meeting the psychological issues associated with disfigurement are seen as part of usual, comprehensive systems of care.

Reference

Potokar, T., Ali, S., Chamanis, S., Prowse, S., & Whitaker, I. S. (2008). A global overview of burns research highlights the need for forming networks with the developing world. *Burns*, 34(1), 3–5.

CHAPTER 8

....

BIOMEDICAL TECHNOLOGIES AND APPEARANCE

....

JULIE KENT

INTRODUCTION

....

BIOMEDICAL technologies may be used to 'correct' what is perceived as an 'abnormal' physical appearance ('deformity' or 'disfigurement'), or to restore the body following trauma or disease. Increasingly such technologies are also used for enhancement (Hogle, 2005). Contemporary cultural attitudes towards the body increasingly emphasize appearance and body image, shaping patterns of consumption and bodily change. Such cultural shifts have been extensively mapped and criticized, especially by feminist commentators, who draw attention to the gendered consequences of cultural norms which promote patriarchal and sexist values about appearance (Gillman, 1999; Weitz, 2003). Sociologists and anthropologists have investigated how technologies are used to re-shape bodies, for body modification or enhancement and the impacts of this for embodied experience (e.g. see Turner 1994; Nettleton & Watson 1998; Williams & Bendelow 1998). Technologies which alter appearance include the use of prosthetics, tissue transplantation, and most recently new cell- and tissue-based therapies (Kent et al., 2006; Kent, 2012). Following the influential cultural theorist Foucault, biomedical technologies may be seen as having normalizing and disciplinary effects on the body. The body then is a site of political struggle through which sexuality, gender, ethnicity, health and illness are regulated. 'Medical technologies are the medium through which not only clinical but *social* abnormalities or pathologies are contained' (Brown & Webster, 2004, p. 21). In this chapter I briefly explore the social aspects of two technologies which alter appearance. The first is breast implants, the second 'living skin'. In relation to each of these I will discuss the social shaping of the technology, the ways in which risks associated with them are constructed as technical issues, the sociopolitical implications of the technologies, and finally the ethical issues. In so doing my aim is to highlight how embodied experiences of appearance and appearance alteration are constituted at the interface of complex socioeconomic relations.

Technology used to alter appearance is not separate from society but socially embedded—its design, production, use, and impacts are inscribed by culture and politics (Brown & Webster, 2004). So for example asymmetries of power influence both the kinds of technologies which emerge and also how they are distributed or made available, and how they are taken up. The drive to create new markets for innovative products impacts on clinical practice and governance arrangements. From a sociological perspective, the body is not simply a naturalistic, biological entity which is situated within a social context; rather bodies are plastic, unfinished projects, sites for multiple practices, with multiple meanings (Mol, 2005). Commonly individual concerns about appearance are influenced by dominant cultural values and contemporary social attitudes towards 'disfigurement' or bodily difference as these two case studies illustrate.

Gendered Bodies and Breast Implant Technologies

Breasts have considerable social significance both symbolically and materially. A cultural history of breasts reveals how meanings and images have changed over time, how breasts have been represented as sacred, erotic, domestic, political, commercial, and medical objects (Yalom, 1997). The earliest techniques for breast augmentation (enhancement) have been traced to the use of silicone injections in Japan in the 1940s post-war period (with devastating effects on health) and the first silicone-filled breast prosthesis was produced in 1949 (Gilman, 1999). The use of breast implants to enlarge women's breasts has been controversial for many years. As Gilman puts it 'too small breasts, as opposed to missing breasts, which had been surgically removed, were not seen as a significant medical problem that affected the psyche of the patient until after World War II' (p. 238). 'Too small breasts' became a medical problem and breast augmentation became a surgical fix to a psychological problem of 'unhappiness' which could create the new 'body beautiful'. Other women offered breast implants were those who, post-mastectomy, wanted reconstruction, a restored bodily form. Breast implant technology remained relatively simple, a multilayered prosthesis with the outer layer manufactured from different types of biomaterial and a synthetic filler of silicone, or saline. Breast implants became big business and commercial exploitation of the technology and clinical uptake have seen significant increases in the numbers of women being implanted with these medical devices.[1]

Feminist analyses of breast implant surgery and 'breasted experience' highlight how breasts are of critical importance to the gendering of bodies. Breasts are objectified, they are a symbol of femininity and 'a signal of sexuality' and of being a woman (Young, 2003). The embodied experience of those women seeking breast augmentation for cosmetic reasons can be seen, not as the effects of a desire to have a 'beautiful body', but rather a desire to 'be normal', to have a 'normal body'. One study showed that women sometimes sought surgery in response to the critical comments they received about their small breasts and associated with this, the suffering they experienced. For these women elective surgery relieved suffering, was an expression of agency, and a form of empowerment enabling them to reconstruct their identities and renegotiate the relationship between the self and body (Davis, 1995). Others have been critical, arguing that this technology has contributed to the 'colonization' of women's bodies and is a feature of the oppressive effects of a wider 'beauty culture', body fetishization and industrialized biotechnology (Morgan, 2003). The use of this technology (for enhancement) may then be seen as both a practice which normalizes and disciplines women's bodies as part of a type of 'self-surveillance' but may also be liberating and empowering. The effects are contradictory and controversial. For women who have had their breasts removed due to disease (or prevention of disease), the social space to celebrate life, and their bodies without a breast (or two), though contested by visual artists such as Matushka who published photographs of herself after mastectomy surgery, is limited (Davis, 1997; Gilman, 1999). More commonly these women are viewed as having an understandable and legitimate medical 'need' for breast reconstruction to restore their 'damaged' bodies and assist in psychological and physical healing (Harcourt & Rumsey, 2001). While for women who have congenital birth defects (e.g. Poland's syndrome which is associated with asymmetric lack of breast development and chest 'deformity') the pressures to 'become normal' are also likely to lead to breast augmentation.

The contradictory views of breast implant technology have been important in shaping public policy and debates about the risks associated with their use. In the 1990s a vigorous debate erupted on both sides of the Atlantic about the safety of silicone implants and the effects on women's health (Kent, 2003). At the heart of the dispute was whether there were sufficient scientific grounds for removing some types of implant from the market and whether device manufacturers had wilfully

---

[1] For discussion of the use of breast reconstruction post mastectomy see National Mastectomy and Breast Reconstruction Audit, 2009. NHS Information Centre.

(and cynically) exploited women by selling implants which were unsafe. The debate focused both on the technical questions about the safety of silicone in the body, whether fillers from the implant could migrate around the body causing systemic illnesses, and on the credibility of the women who testified about their illness experiences. These women, sometimes described as 'survivors of silicone', gave accounts of silicone invading the body and a consumer movement emerged focused on sharing experiences and information about breast implants, and challenging government regulatory agencies (in the US and Europe) and companies who sold them. Some commentators suggested that campaigners were primarily interested in monetary compensation while others, including myself, argued that the key issue was whether women's voices were being heard and whether their experiences could be regarded as a legitimate basis for knowledge claims (White Stewart, 1998; Zimmerman, 1998; Kent, 2003).

In the US where legal disputes in the courts centred around the testimony of both scientific 'experts' and women who had implants, commercial interests were threatened and juries were seen as favouring complainants (Angell, 1996; Jacobsen, 2000). The US Food and Drug Administration (FDA) regulatory agency, though sometimes accused of conspiring with manufacturers to release these implants onto the market, issued a moratorium on their use in 1992 pending further scientific investigation. Elsewhere in Europe and the UK the silicone-filled implants continued to be in use despite campaigns for them to be banned.[2] Between 1993 and 1998 the UK regulator conducted a series of reviews of the scientific literature and established a breast implant registry but concluded that there were no scientific or clinical grounds to change policy and that the risks to health of silicone implants were unproven. Contrasting ideas about the risks and benefits of breast implants positioned women, regulators, and clinicians within this dispute. Some women were marginalized and regarded as irrational and incapable of understanding the scientific evidence on safety, while other women who supported the use of breast implants 'were represented as having legitimate needs (especially for reconstructive surgery) and asserting citizenship claims' to healthcare (Kent, 2003, p. 410). Technical risk assessment underpinned the scientific assessment and rested on the *absence* of links between silicone in the body and ill health but political expediency shaped the actions of the US regulators (Jacobsen, 2000).

In Europe, in the context of scientific uncertainty and lobbying of the European Parliament on the issue, a commissioned study (Martin-Moreno et al., 2000) accepted that the scientific evidence available provided no conclusive evidence of an association between silicone breast implants and cancer or connective tissue disease but also acknowledged extremely 'strong interests at stake on either side of the issue, both of which may have valid, legitimate claims' (Kent, 2003, p. 412).

---

[2] Interestingly France took a different view and banned these implants until 1995 (Kent, 2003).

The study highlighted areas of weakness in the European Union (EU) regulatory system and protection for women, making a number of recommendations for change. Importantly it was recognized that the quality of information given to women about breast implantation was poor and that there was a need to improve consent procedures, technical standards for implants, clinical guidance and quality assurance processes, marketing control and post-marketing surveillance, and also to strengthen regulation. Breast implants were upgraded to high risk Class III medical devices and in the UK, following a House of Commons Inquiry in 2001, new guidance and information for women was produced. To an extent the claims that women had been exploited and experimented on by the industry were upheld and the subsequent marketing of a new type of implant without clinical trial (Trilucent) and adverse incidents led to their removal from the market and women in the UK being advised to have them explanted, confirming the need for stronger regulation in this area (Kent & Faulkner, 2002). Most recently another alert was issued about the safety of an implant manufactured in France and widely used in the UK (Medicines and Healthcare products Regulatory Agency, 2010).

Regulation is important to secure public trust in the health care system and the role of the UK regulator for medical devices, the Medicines and Healthcare products Regulatory Agency (MHRA)[3] was critically important in rebuilding trust in breast implants. Efforts were made to disseminate improved information about the risks and benefits of breast implants and to promote good clinical practice in the area while the government recognized the difficulties of regulating private cosmetic surgery clinics. In short, the breast implant controversy revealed weaknesses in the regulatory system and in clinical practice and the uncertainties relating to techno-scientific rationality in risk assessment. It also illustrated how commercial and industry interests were mediated through the political process. Ethical issues were highlighted through the focus on poor information for women consenting to surgery and the lack of protection afforded them.

'ENGINEERED LIVING SKIN' AND THE NEW REGENERATIVE MEDICINE

Skin is the outer layer of the body and inextricably linked to appearance. Common clinical problems are burns treatment and wound management following trauma or associated with disease (e.g. diabetic ulcers). Plastic surgeons have since the 19th century been practised in the use of skin grafts (Ang, 2005). Skin may be grafted from one part of the patient's body to another (autograft), or skin may be sourced from a cadaver and stored as split thickness skin or full thickness grafts

---

[3] Previously the Medical Devices Agency until it merged with the Medicines Control Agency in 2003.

(allograft) (Hierner et al., 2005). Techniques for storing and preserving skin have developed and include cryopreservation of 'living skin' and the use of glycerol to preserve 'non-viable' skin (Kearney, 2005). Allografts are used as temporary biological dressings and act as a stimulus for wound healing but do not survive at the transplant site due to immunological response from the recipient body (Snyder, 2005). Fresh skin (from a living body) may be stored in a fridge for up to 14 days, cadaver skin for around 7 days, and preserved non-viable skin for up to 5 years. Until recently it was commonplace for surgeons to store patients' skin on a ward while cadaver skin was stored in a tissue bank. One of the earliest regional tissue banks was set up in Yorkshire and most European tissue banks were established in the 1970s and 1980s to facilitate more effective distribution of tissues (Kearney, 2006). Concerns about the ethics of tissue donation and ensuring the tissue supply was free from contamination underpinned debate about how to effectively regulate this sector (Faulkner et al., 2006; Kent, 2012). Since 2004 all tissue storage comes under the purview of a new European regulation which was developed to set standards for tissue procurement and storage and promote safety (Tissue and Cells Directive 2004/23/EC) (TCD).

While surgical skin transplant techniques are not new, there have been innovations in the development of 'engineered skin'. This entails the use of techniques to grow skin in the laboratory using skin cells sourced from a patient (autologous) or living donor (allogenic). Tissue engineering emerged from the work of Langer and Vacanti in the US in the 1980s (Langer et al., 1995) and while the potential to grow whole organs still seems a long way off, skin has been one of the most successful applications of tissue engineering principles. Organogenesis was a US-based company that first successfully marketed an allogeneic skin product, Apligraf,[4] which used skin cells sourced from the foreskin of baby boys to produce skin on an industrial scale for use in the treatment of venous and diabetic ulcers since 1998 (Kent, 2012). Genzyme was the first global company to introduce an autologous skin product, Epicel, for burns treatment.[5] In the UK other companies such as Intercytex, Celltran, and Smith & Nephew have also used the patient's own skin cells to produce autologous skin patches (e.g. Myskin[6]) (Kent, 2012). However in spite of the perceived advantages of engineered skin especially in supplying 'off the shelf' living skin products or a custom-made skin repair system, the commercial viability and business model for the industry has been seen as highly unstable and vulnerable (Lysaght & Hazlehurst, 2004; Kemp, 2006; Faulkner et al., 2008; Martin et al., 2009).

The commercial exploitation of human tissue has been a focus of heated policy debate and is seen by social scientists as a feature of the capitalization of the biosciences in emergent 'tissue economies' (Waldby & Mitchell, 2006). In Europe, at the

---

[4] http://www.apligraf.com
[5] http://www.genzyme.com
[6] http://www.myskin-info.com

policy level, in the context of developing stricter regulation relating to the procurement and storage of tissue, the potential for generating profit from human body
parts has been ethically controversial (European Group on Ethics, 2004; Kent,
2012). Debate leading to the new TCD centred on developing requirements for free
and voluntary consent in relation to tissue donation, quality standards, and licens-
ing of tissue banks. Additionally the potential for increased risks associated with the
distribution of human tissue products (engineered or otherwise) has become a
growing public health issue while at the same time efforts were being directed
towards promoting the diffusion of technology within Europe (Faulkner et al.,
2006, 2008). These risks have been framed in terms of 'technological safety' including the material risks of cross contamination, uncontrolled cell growth, interspecies
mixing (where human and animal cells come into contact), traceability from donor
to recipient bodies, and the need for quality assurance and good manufacturing
standards. Another perceived risk has been a lack of 'therapeutic efficacy', in other
words evidence that these innovative products afforded clinical benefits has been
disputed (Faulkner et al., 2008). How risks are constructed varies across stakeholder
groups and are highly contestable. They remain the subject of ongoing discussion
within the scientific and regulatory communities, revealing both scientific and
technical uncertainties with respect to these new technologies.

The developments in tissue engineering and most recently stem cell science, provoked lengthy debates about how cell-based therapies should be regulated because
they did not 'fit' within the framework of drugs and devices regulation as it was
developed in the 1990s. While breast implants could be clearly defined as 'medical
devices' and represented a kind of 'old technology' of replacement parts, the newer
types of approaches, such as living skin, which contain living or viable cells and
therefore have a biological component, seemed to be neither device-like nor like
other pharmaceuticals (Faulkner et al., 2003, 2006). New kinds of 'regulatory
objects' therefore emerged in the formulation of a regulatory framework for tissue
and cell based therapies culminating in 2007 with new European regulation of what
have become known as 'advanced therapy medicinal products'.[7] Innovation and
regulation may be seen as closely interconnected and manufacturers have been
politically active in shaping the development of the regulatory framework in order
to facilitate the diffusion and marketing of these new products and therapies.

While much attention has been given to ethical issues relating to tissue donation
there are wider implications of engineered tissues for notions of the body and self
and relations between donors and recipients (Kent et al., 2006). Autologous applications of skin (and other engineered tissues), as part of a wider 'regenerative medicine', are designed to 'regenerate' the body through asexual methods of replication
and repair. The boundaries of the body are rendered unstable and fluid, when cells

---

[7] Regulation (EC) No 1394/2007 Regulation of the EU Parliament and Council on advanced therapy medicinal products and amending Directive 2001/83/EC and Regulation (EC) No 726/2004.

are replicated in the laboratory and returned to the patient as skin, a new form of 'extracorporeality' emerges constructing 'an externalized and extended vision of the self and materiality of the body (Waldby, 2002; Kent et al., 2006). 'These processes of excision, dissection, extraction and manipulation may be read as a threat to bodily integrity only in so far as the body is conceptualized as having a form and boundaries that are distinctive and identifiable' (Kent, 2012). Rather autologous implants may be seen as remaking, or reproducing, the self (Kent et al., 2006) and cell culturing as a technique for the multiplication of life, or generation of surplus (Cooper, 2008). 'Biovalue' is created as patients and their cells are enrolled in a techno-scientific industrial process (Waldby, 2002; Waldby & Mitchell, 2006). While we might usefully contrast autologous and allogeneic products such distinctions may be less clear cut than first appears. Both entail a degree of manipulation, though the extent and divergence of this has been important in regulatory discussions. Both imply a concept of bodies and identities as open and flexible.

The effects of tissue transplants on patients' conceptions of themselves have been relatively unexplored but one study of heart transplant patients points to some interesting findings. Shildrick suggests that disruption to the self is inevitable as patients come to terms with 'bodily hybridity', and 'hosting' the organ of another deceased person and there may be important effects on identity. But, she suggests that this also points to the need to 'embrace concorporeality: the point at which bodies cross over into one another' (Shildrick et al., 2009). This in turn implies a view of identity and subjectivity as more mobile and open, rather than fixed and stable. Recent controversy around the implications of experimental face transplants tend to reinforce a notion of identities as fixed and directly connected to physical characteristics (Royal College of Surgeons, 2006) but a more complex understanding of these connections highlights the productive possibilities of altered form and appearance. Huxtable and Woodley (2005) discuss the ethical issues relating to face transplants and consider that the risks an individual might be willing to take in having this experimental treatment may not be a matter for them to decide alone. They argue that such a decision should not be a question of 'private morality' because such decisions are influenced by wider social values. In relation to skin, Shildrick notes, it no longer makes sense to regard skin as an 'inviolable boundary... a protective layer against the insults of the external world' (Shildrick, 2008, p. 33). While appearance is primarily a concern about the exterior surface of the body, evidently it is not always what it may seem. Engineered skin has recently been considered a potential tool for repairing that surface.

Conclusions

From these two short case examples it is possible to highlight a number of key points about the social aspects of technologies as they relate to appearance. First the design, manufacture, and production of technologies such as breast implants or indeed living skin need to be understood as intimately and inextricably tied to the social dynamics of innovation and economic factors. Breast implant technology emerged as a lucrative business and powerful commercial interests influenced the types of products that were marketed to women. Clinicians were important in the medicalization of 'too small breasts' and in shaping and delivering services for mastectomy and other patient groups in both the public and private sector. Engineered skin has been the most successful tissue engineered product in so far as it has been the most widely marketed for use in burns treatment and wound management. Although commercially its success is limited because it is expensive, and more established methods are cheaper, it has been regarded as clinically useful but has not, so far, become widely available in public health systems such as the UK NHS.

We have also seen that the understandings of risk and approaches to risk management are socially contingent and tied to scientific and technical uncertainties. This was illustrated by the controversy around the evidence of ill health amongst women who had breast implants and also in debate about how the risks of cellular products such as engineered skin might best be regulated. Sociopolitical issues were at stake in both cases, shaping the policy process and positioning different stakeholder groups within it. Ethical issues were also important, for women were not given adequate information about breast implantation and the consent procedures were a subject of criticism. The sourcing, procurement, and commercial use of human tissues have provoked considerable concern across Europe and ethical objections have been raised in response to the increased 'commodification' of the human body associated with these new technologies and the emergent 'tissue economies'.

Finally both cases point to questions about how technologies reconfigure bodies and the relationship between bodies, identity, and subjectivity. Breast implantation, from a feminist perspective, has contradictory effects as it may be a means of normalization; a disciplinary practice (re)constructing idealized gendered bodies. At the same time women may experience breast implantation as liberating and empowering. Tissue and cell transplants, whether a whole face transplant, an organ transplant, or a cellular therapy using donated cells, may appear to threaten identity and have serious psychological consequences. Whether face transplants represent especially difficult challenges to identity or not, I think is an empirical question which has not yet been fully answered. Evidently the recipients of such transplants do not come to resemble the donor even though their own facial appearance is transformed. The transformative effects of such surgery and social significance of *facial* appearance raise important concerns but that is not to say that other, perhaps less spectacular or sensational, technical possibilities for changing appearance or bodily form do not merit attention. As I have tried to highlight here, appearance-altering technologies point to the instability of bodily boundaries, and undermine the very notion that identity or subjectivity is fixed and immutable. Appearance is not simply about the surface of the body, it is socially contingent. Biotechnologies which are deployed to repair, replace, or regenerate the body are themselves socially constituted and have social consequences.

REFERENCES

Ang, G. (2005). History of skin transplantation. *Clinics in Dermatology*, 23, 320–4.

Angell, M. (1996). *Science on Trial: The clash of medical evidence and the law in the breast implant case*. London: Norton.

Brown, N. & Webster, A. (2004). *New Medical Technologies and Society Reordering Life*. Cambridge: Polity Press.

Cooper, M. (2008). *Life as Surplus*. Seattle, WA: University of Washington.

Davis, K. (1995). *Reshaping the Female Body*. London: Routledge.

Davis, K. (1997). 'My body is my art': Cosmetic surgery as feminist utopia? In K. Davis (ed.) *Embodied Practices Feminist Perspectives on the Body*, pp. 168–81. London: Sage.

European Group on Ethics (2004). *Report of European Group on Ethics on The Ethical Aspects of Human Tissue Engineered Products*. http://www.ec.europa.eu

Faulkner, A., Geesink, I., Kent, J., & Fitzpatrick, D. (2008). Tissue- engineered technologies: scientific biomedicine, frames of risk and regulatory regime building in Europe. *Science as Culture*, 17(2), 195–222.

Faulkner, A., Kent, J., Geesink, I., & Fitzpatrick, D. (2006). Purity and the dangers of regenerative medicine: Regulatory innovation of human tissue-engineered technology. *Social Science & Medicine*, 63, 2277–88.

Faulkner, A., Geesink, I., Kent, J., & Fitzpatrick, D. (2003). Human tissue engineered products—drugs or devices? *British Medical Journal*, 326, 1159–60.

Gilman, S. (1999). *Making the Body Beautiful. A Cultural history of aesthetic surgery*. Princetown, NJ: Princetown University Press.

Harcourt, D. & Rumsey, N. (2001). Psychological aspects of breast reconstruction: a review of the literature. *Journal of Advanced Nursing*, 35, 477–87.

Hierner, R., Degreef, H., Vranckx, J., & Garmyn, M.E.A. (2005). Skin grafting and wound healing- the 'dermato-plastic team approach'. *Clinics in Dermatology*, 23, 343–52.

Hogle, L. (2005). Enhancement technologies and the body. *The Annual Review of Anthropology*, 34, 695–719.

Huxtable, R. & Woodley, J. (2005). Gaining face or losing face? Framing the debate on face transplants. *Bioethics*, 19, 505–22.

Jacobsen, N. (2000). *Cleavage: Technology, Controversy and the Ironies of the Man-made Breast*. New Brunswick, NJ: Rutgers Press.

Kearney, J. (2005). Guidelines on processing and clinical use of skin allografts. *Clinics in Dermatology*, 23, 357–64.

Kearney, J. (2006). Yorkshire regional tissue bank—circa 50 years of tissue banking. *Cell Tissue Banking*, 7, 259–64.

Kemp, P. (2006). Cell therapy- back on the up-curve. *Regenerative Medicine*, 1(1), 9–14.

Kent, J. (2003). Lay experts and the politics of breast implants. *Public understanding of science*, 12(4), 403–22.

Kent, J. (2012). *Regenerating Bodies: Tissue and Cell Therapies in the 21st Century*. London: Routledge.

Kent, J. & Faulkner, A. (2002). Regulating human implant technologies in Europe- understanding the new regulatory era in medical device regulation. *Health, Risk & Society*, 4(2), 189–209.

Kent, J., Faulkner, A., Geesink, I., & Fitzpatrick, D. (2006). Culturing cells, reproducing and regulating the self. *Body & Society*, 12(2), 1–24.

Langer, R., Vacanti, J., Vacanti, C., Atala, A., Freed, L.E., & Vunjak-Novakovic, G. (1995). Tissue engineering: biomedical applications. *Tissue Engineering*, 1(2), 151–61.

Lysaght, M. and Hazlehurst, A. (2004). Tissue Engineering: the end of the beginning. *Tissue Engineering*, 10(2), 309–20.

Martin, P., Hawksley, R. & Turner, A. (2009). *The Commercial Development of Cell Therapy—Lessons for the Future? Survey of the Cell Therapy Industry and the Main Products in Use and Development Part 1 Summary of Findings*. Nottingham: University of Nottingham.

Martin-Moreno, J. M., Gorgojo, L., Gonzalez-Enriquez, J., Wisbaum, W. (2000). *Health Risks posed by Silicone Implants in General, with a special attention to Breast Implants: Final Report for the EU Scientific and Technological Options Assessment Unit*. Brussels: STOA.

Medicines and Healthcare Regulatory Agency. (2010). *Device Alert Silicone gel filled breast implants by Poly Implant Prosthese MDA/2010/025 and MDA/2010/078*. London: MHRA.

Mol, A. (2005). *The Body Multiple: Ontology in Medical Practice* (2nd edn.). Durham, NC: Duke University Press.

Morgan, K. (2003). Women and the knife: Cosmetic surgery and the colonization of women's bodies. In R. Weitz (ed.) *The Politics of Women's Bodies: Sexuality Appearance and Behaviour* (2nd edn.), pp. 164–83. Oxford: Oxford University Press.

Nettleton, S. and Watson, J. (1998). *The Body Everyday Life*. London: Routledge.

Royal College of Surgeons (2006). *Facial Transplantation: Working Party Report* (2nd edn.). London: Royal College of Surgeons.

Shildrick, M., McKeever, P., Abbey, S., Poole, J., & Ross, H. (2009). Troubling dimensions of heart transplantation. *Medical Humanities*, 35(1), 35–8.

Shildrick, M. (2008). Corporeal cuts: Surgery and the psycho-social. *Body & Society*, 14(1), 31–46.

Snyder, R. (2005). Treatment of nonhealing ulcers with allografts. *Clinics in Dermatology*, 23, 388–95.

Turner, B. (1994). *Regulating Bodies: Essays in Medical Sociology* (2nd edn.). London: Routledge.

Waldby, C. (2002). Stem cells, tissue cultures and the production of biovalue. *Health: An Interdisciplinary Journal for the Social Study of Health, Illness and Medicine*, 6(3), 305–23.

Waldby, C. & Mitchell, R. (2006). *Tissue Economies: Blood, Organs and Cell Lines in Late Capitalism*. Durham, NC: Duke University Press.

Weitz, R. (2003). *The Politics of Women's Bodies Sexuality, Appearance and Behaviour* (2nd edn.). Oxford: Oxford University Press.

White Stewart, M. (1998). *Silicone Spills: Breast Implants on Trial*. London: Praeger.

Williams, S. & Bendelow, G. (1998). *The Lived Body Sociological Themes, Embodied Issues*. London: Routledge.

Yalom, M. (1997). *A History of the Breast*. New York: Harper Collins.

Young, I. (2003). Breasted experience: The look and the feeling. In R. Weitz (ed.) *The Politics of Women's Bodies: Sexuality, Appearance and Behaviour* (2nd edn.), pp. 152–63. Oxford: Oxford University Press.

Zimmerman, S. (1998). *Silicone Survivors: Women's Experiences with Breast Implants.* Philadelphia, PA: Temple University.

CHAPTER 9

RESEARCHING APPEARANCE: MODELS, THEORIES, AND FRAMEWORKS

ANDREW R. THOMPSON

THERE has been a deepening appreciation of the importance of understanding the psychology of appearance in relationship to the role it plays in wider health and well-being. Certainly, appearance concern within the general population is ubiquitous and appears to have increased over the last three decades with cross-sectional surveys and meta-analyses consistently showing slightly higher levels of dissatisfaction for women than men (e.g. Feingold & Mazzella, 1998; Cash et al., 2004). For example, in the UK Harris and Carr (2001) reported dissatisfaction in just over 60% of women surveyed compared with just over a third of male participants.

The obsession with bodies and the role played by commerce and the media in this phenomenon has been the subject of increasing debate and research, and as we shall see, the importance of sociocultural factors cannot be minimized (see Chapters 2 and 4). Recently, Susie Orbach has posited that in the postmodern age individuals are 'manufacturing their bodies', seeking to shape themselves into a stereotypical image so as to conform to an 'international brand'. As such, Orbach attributes the pressures behind this trend as resulting partly from commercial manipulation (Orbach, 2009; Science Weekly, 2010).

Interestingly, the prevalence of dissatisfaction with appearance amongst individuals living with visible differences or disfigurements has had little attention from researchers although some studies have included consideration of this by using appearance-specific measures (e.g. Rumsey et al., 2004). Instead, studies in the area of disfigurement have focused on levels of psychopathology, such as anxiety, social anxiety, avoidance, and depression. Generally such studies have reported the presence of higher than average levels of psychological distress (Thompson & Kent, 2001; Rumsey & Harcourt, 2004). In addition, recent research suggests that a significant number of people living with appearance-altering conditions report the typical (weight and shape) appearance concerns as found in the general population, which may be anatomically unrelated to their visible difference (Rumsey et al., under review).

There has been an increase in qualitative research highlighting the difficulties that can be faced by individuals with or without visible differences in relation to their appearance-related concerns. For example, Grogan (1999) in her book, included quotes from men, women, and children and in the following extract a young woman discusses the areas of her body about which she is most concerned:

All my bottom part. From my knees upwards and from my chest downwards. My um, my what's it called, trunk. The whole of my trunk I am dissatisfied with (female aged 35, cited in Grogan, 1999, p. 33).

The content of such quotes will not surprise readers and whilst there is still some debate about the degree to which such commonly occurring dissatisfaction is 'normative' and actually affects quality of life and well-being, we should not underestimate its potential to do so for a significant number of people.

Qualitative studies also testify to the significance that living with an altered appearance may have. For example, Uttjek et al., (2007) interviewed people with severe psoriasis and one of the four themes that emerged was 'marked by visibility', as the following quote demonstrates:

The worst thing with psoriasis is that it is visible and I cannot make it disappear. I feel restricted to loneliness, neither starting a new relation with a man, nor looking for a new job (Uttjek et al., 2007, p. 367).

Clearly, understanding individual appearance concern and the way appearance satisfaction (and dissatisfaction) are shaped by society and culture is important, and several theoretical approaches have been proposed to underpin research in this area.

Models, Theories, and Frameworks

Theoretical interest in appearance has lagged behind everyday societal interest in this area, perhaps because as Rumsey and Harcourt (2005) have speculated, the subject matter has in the past been seen as somewhat frivolous and associated with vanity. Indeed, such concerns are still apparent in the general population and have been reported to affect response rates in even relatively recent research. For example, in one study of cosmetic camouflage users (that ironically sought to test a model of disfigurement in which fear of negative evaluation played a central role), a significant minority of potential participants stated that they did not wish to participate for fear of being seen to be too occupied with their appearance (Kent, 2002). I shall return to the concepts of fear of negative evaluation and the related concept of shame later, as they are some of the key constructs that have the potential to guide further research and practice (Thompson & Kent, 2001).

Appearance has been found to play a role in how we judge both others (Langlois et al., 2000) and ourselves (Grogan, 1999), and as such has an impact on individual well-being and social interaction at almost every level, although to a much lesser extent than is usually assumed (see Bull & Rumsey, 1988; Rumsey & Harcourt, 2005). Therefore, perhaps unsurprisingly, over the last 50 years or so there has been an explosion of theoretical interest in appearance and its closely related synonym of body image.

In this chapter, I will describe a number of key theories that broadly focus on (or across) evolutionary, psychological, or sociocultural perspectives. I will discuss how evolutionary theory is useful in understanding some of the underlying commonalities in this area giving a starting point for answering the question as to 'Why is appearance an issue?'. However, I will go on to argue that a focus on evolutionary theory alone is unhelpful, as it has considerable limitations in being able to account for individual variation in our actual experience of our appearance, or how our appearance and our concerns about it exist and operate within a sociocultural context. I will also describe a variety of psychosocial models and argue that it is psychosociocultural factors that are emerging as being crucial in accounting for the nuances associated with answering the bigger questions such as 'Who is affected, how, and in what ways?' (Cash, 2005).

I will conclude by presenting a broad biopsychosocial research framework that draws together some of the key constructs discussed earlier in the chapter. This framework is derived from the work of a large group of UK-based researchers and clinical practitioners (the Appearance Research Collaboration, ARC: Rumsey et al., under review) who came together with the support of The Healing Foundation, a charity championing for people living with disfigurement (see http://www.thehealingfoundation.org).

The need for models, theories, and frameworks

So what is meant in the social sciences by the terms 'model', 'theory', and 'framework'? Such terms are usually used to refer to a simplified description of a system or process and are essentially attempts to lay out an explanation that accounts for a specific phenomenon or set of related phenomena such as some of the 'big questions' dealt with in this handbook. For example, 'Why is appearance an issue?',

'How does it influence individual well-being?', 'How does it influence social inter-action?' and 'How can we explain differences between individuals in how they are affected by appearance related concerns?'.

Theory, method, and practice usually go hand in hand in social sciences, with theory making clear assumptions that lend themselves to being translated into testable hypotheses or predictions. The results of research then allow researchers to further develop theory. In addition, theory should be used to guide practice, as is the case with the interventions designed to change social or individual reactions described in Section 3 of this handbook. For example, Veale et al.'s (2009) self-help guide aims to assist people in overcoming body image issues and is influenced by techniques taken from cognitive behavioural therapy.

Whilst the terms 'theory', 'framework', and 'model' are often used interchange-ably, Brannon and Feist (2007) in their introductory text to health psychology suggest that the term model is more appropriately used early on in the develop-ment of understanding within a given area, when only a small number of observa-tions, or perhaps only a specific phenomenon, are being explained. They go on to suggest that a theory usually aims to have a broader coverage in being able to account for a greater number of observations, such as the theory of implementa-tion intentions that seems to have predicative power across a range of behaviours where motivation is required to effect change (Gollwitzer & Sheeran, 2006; see Palayiwa et al., 2010, for an example of application of this theory to appearance research).

The term 'framework' has less of a pedigree in psychology, and is usually used to describe a more loosely defined collection of theories or conceptual factors in an area in which no one particular theory or model has been demonstrated as having dominance. This was the approach taken by the ARC group in exploring the factors that account for differences in adjustment to disfigurement.

Essentially models, theories, and frameworks can be thought of as conceptual maps. As such, they will always be inherently limited in comprehensively account-ing for the full complexity of experience, particularly in an area such as appearance as it covers so many inter-related phenomena. Arguably by far the most important factor for theories, models, and frameworks in this field, is that *a good one will have real translational value*—in helping to plan interventions to promote appearance-related well-being, or to reduce the distress that may be associated with changes in appearance.

One model or theory is not enough in appearance research

As already described, appearance research covers activity in a range of related areas, including, *body image, attractiveness, disfigurement, and identity*, and it is consequently naïve (and undesirable) to expect that any one model or theory will account for all aspects of human experience across these areas (a point previously made by others, including Cash & Pruzinsky, 1990; Grogan, 1999; Newell, 2000; Price, 1990, 1999; and Rumsey & Harcourt, 2005). Despite the complexities of appearance research, the application of theory to research in this area is desirable and is beginning to result in real advancements in practice. Before going on to discuss some of the theories in detail I will first discuss a couple of caveats in relation to the use of any theory.

A warning about typologies and positionality in appearance research

I would like to make the case for the advantages of pluralism and the need for practitioners to take an idiographic person-centred focus—always considering the individual's unique circumstances and history when considering how extant theory might inform practice. The majority of the existing appearance research has taken a categorical and positional approach to appearance, assuming that there is a difference between the appearance concerns of those with and without various objective appearance-affecting conditions, and interpreting the issues from purely a sociocultural, psychological, or biological position.

Research has tended to focus on trying to explain the appearance concerns of specific groups such as those with eating disorders; or general appearance dissatisfaction. Consequently, many of the extant models and theories attempt to account for phenomenon of specific groups such as those living with an objective disfigurement (e.g. see Newell, 2000; Kent & Thompson, 2002) or those living with body dysmorphic disorder (e.g. see Veale, 2004).

However, applied psychologists and those providing psychological services should strive to achieve an individually tailored understanding or 'formulation' of a specific individual's presenting issues, which may draw on a range of theories which focus on psychosocial processes and outcomes rather than biomedical pathology (Harvey, 2009).

The tension of remaining focused on the psychological processes common to all those with appearance concerns yet keeping in mind the unique consequences of a particular condition, has been previously commented upon by Rumsey and Harcourt (2005) in their book on the psychology of appearance where they stated:

The challenge facing researchers is how best to investigate the nature and impact of appearance issues among those with or without a visible difference [or specific 'psychological' condition] in a way that preserves the uniqueness of their situation without ignoring the commonality (p. 29).

Acknowledging positive adjustment and pride in appearance research

Much of the literature on appearance has been overly focused upon negative functioning. This has served to highlight the difficulties people can experience, but may have unwittingly contributed to a continued sense of marginalization of those affected by appearance concern (Thompson, 2011).

Although large numbers of people are distressed by appearance-related issues, many are satisfied with their appearance and cope well with the consequences of appearance-altering illnesses (Rumsey et al., under review). When done sensitively, providing people who have experienced a change in their appearance as a result of acquiring an illness with positive accounts about adjustment can be empowering (Thompson, 2011).

The following individuals have written about their personal journeys of living with disfiguring conditions and have emphasized the message that positive adjustment and pride in one's appearance is possible. James Partridge, founder of the charity Changing Faces (see http://www.changingfaces.org.uk/Home; and Chapter 33, this volume) who acquired burn injuries as a young man has been a strong advocate of pro-social adjustment strategies and of placing emphasis on the role society has had in contributing to the difficulties faced by people living with a visible difference or disfigurement. He has described his own experience in some depth and largely in terms of post change growth:

Above all, my face has opened new doors in my understanding of life and people (Partridge, 1990 pp. x–xi).

Only recently has research started to actively explore factors that might predict positive adjustment or to rigorously explore the experience of people who manage well, largely unaffected by appearance concern. Meyerson (2001), for example, interviewed people with a condition associated with facial paralysis and found several psychosocial factors including, humour and faith, as being associated with adjustment. Thompson et al., (2002) interviewed women living with vitiligo and found that they had spontaneously developed coping skills akin to the sorts of strategies promoted in psychological therapy, although it should be noted that their participants reported that maintaining stability was effortful. It is still relatively unusual to see detailed qualitative studies focussing on the experience of men. Lobeck et al.'s (2005) qualitative study of men who had had a stroke reported that although the participants initially felt different as a result of the visible change in their bodies, they described developing a range of strategies including humour to manage this. Further, Saradijian et al. (2008) found that men who had lost an arm as a result of trauma or disease were coping well and were using a range of active strategies (including humour) to do this. Both Lobeck et al. and Saradijian et al. found a strong influence of working class male culture in the 'matter of fact' and functional coping styles described by their participants.

Recently Thompson and Broom (2009) and Egan et al. (2011) have reported similar findings when purposively recruiting people who identify themselves as coping well. Thompson and Broom (2009) conducted individual interviews with men and women living with a range of visible disfigurements and reported that the value participants placed on appearance had a significant influence on adjustment:

I make certain choices about what to get sort of worked up about and right now I'm far more concerned that intellectually I have a long way to go, than I do sort of physically to meet some sort of physical perfection… It's amazing, I mean people really think that happiness… equals… appearance (Thompson & Broom, 2009, p. 175).

I conclude this section with an excerpt from Marc Crank writing about his experience of living with the medical condition neurofibromatosis in which he neatly demonstrates the sense of having to consciously invest in other aspects of self:

My looks have shaped me into the person I am today, perhaps giving me greater character, compassion and the vital sense of humour that I may not have otherwise developed. It is not just the actual 'looking different' that has shaped me, but the experiences I have had and the decisions I have had to make. One of the important choices I have had to make was whether to fight for what I really wanted in my life or take what society decided I should have. I have my mother to thank for this determination; she has always refused to accept second best for me (Marc C. Crank, in Lansdown et al., 1997, p. 29).

The implications from this body of research is that positive adjustment may come about with the use of active coping strategies that require ongoing resources and that successful adjustment may be partly achieved by conscious investment in other aspects of the self. However, there is also the suggestion of the role played by valuing the influence that visible difference has had in shaping the self.

Theoretical Approaches

Evolutionary theory and appearance models

Dion et al.'s (1972) seminal study found that people attribute positive characteristics to those deemed to be attractive. The 'what is beautiful is good' stereotype has now been reliably replicated across time and cultures. Although the effect is moderate there is clear evidence that people generally agree on who is attractive and make some degree of personality judgement about them on this basis, at least initially (Eagly et al., 1991; Langois et al., 2000).

Bull and Rumsey (1988) in their review of the area suggested that much early research was based on simplistic cross-sectional studies, which, for example, lacked ecological validity, as there was reliance on undergraduate participants in experimental designs deploying two-dimensional photographs (see also Rumsey & Harcourt, 2005). Nevertheless, there is evidence that people do react differently to people on the basis of their appearance. For example, Grandfield et al. (2005) used photographs showing clear skin or skin affected by dermatological conditions, and measured the explicit and implicit attitudes of their participants. The Implicit Association Test (IAT) was used to measure implicit attitudes. The IAT allows the relative strengths of association between perceived positive and negative concepts to be measured by examining reaction times, and in doing so may reveal biases which might otherwise be moderated by social desirability. Grandfield et al.'s findings suggested that there was an implicit preference for clear skin and that there was not a correlation between the explicit and implicit measures. The findings might be explained by automatic biologically derived reactions or/and activation of internalized stereotypes.

Nonetheless, recent meta-analyses have offered some support for averageness, symmetry, and sexual dimorphism (maleness/femaleness) being used as reliable parameters upon which appearance is evaluated at least in initial encounters. For example, Scott et al. (2008) examined preferences and attribution of traits for 'masculinized and feminized faces' in association with the interaction of contextual factors such as the relationship and physical health status of participants in a small Malaysian sample. They reported that gender preferences were predicted by physical health quality, which they suggested meant that preferences were constrained by 'mate competition' as would be predicted by an evolutionary model. The study has a number of limitations not least its lack of ecological validity, as it uses two-dimensional photographs and a cross-sectional design (as did the Grandfield et al. (2005) study). Nevertheless, evolutionary psychologists have taken such studies to argue that it is largely selection pressures that have shaped our perceptions of attractiveness (see Etcoff, 1999; Rhodes, 2006).

Many evolutionary psychologists like Paul Gilbert (1997, 2002) take a wider perspective that acknowledges the role of social factors. Gilbert suggests that 'social attractiveness' is valued highly by humans as it confers rank, which in turn confers access to resources. Gilbert uses the term 'social attractiveness' to refer not just to appearance but also to behaviours (such as occupational success) that are used to distinguish comparative status. He argues that it is avoidance of group rejection and/or competition for connectedness that drives psychological processes such as social comparison and self-criticism, and it is these processes that can be modified in therapy (see also Gilbert et al., 1995).

Whilst evolutionary theorists have made predictions about the nature of attractiveness and our associated reactions, some of which have been tested (see Rhodes, 2006), extreme caution is needed in drawing simplistic conclusions. Simplistic evolutionary theories that attempt to explain everything by selection pressures fit with current cultural common sense and consequently run the risk of confirming underlying stereotypes and many scholarly reviews of the area advocate taking a wider view that places emphasis on sociocultural factors (Cash, 2005; Rumsey & Harcourt, 2005).

Models of stigma and objectification

Erving Goffman's (1963) work on stigma posits that visible markings designate an affected person as 'spoiled' and consequently less valued by others. Scrambler and Hopkins (1986) proposed the distinction between 'enacted' and 'felt' stigma, which they initially applied in relation to epilepsy. Enacted stigma refers to *actual* rejection and contrasts with felt stigma, which refers to an individual's expectation of stigmatization. This model is particularly useful in explaining avoidance and concealment coping often reported by people with appearance concerns (Kent & Thompson, 2002).

Receiving stigmatizing appearance-focused comments, particularly early in life, has been increasingly recognized in the development of later appearance concern (see Thompson et al., 1999b, for a review). For example, negative reactions from others have been associated with the development of eating difficulties (Taylor et al., 2006; Reddy & Crowther, 2007) and have been shown to immediately lower mood and concentration (Furman & Thompson, 2002; Kiefer & Sekaquaptewa, 2006). Mills and Miller (2007) reported those female participants in their study who received negative comments about weight felt fatter, more anxious, and had higher levels of appearance concern.

Experiences of stigmatization (and sometimes outright discrimination) are also described by those living with a visible difference. For instance, Thompson et al. (2002, 2010) have used qualitative methods to explore the experience of women living with vitiligo. They found instances of stigmatization, bullying, and negative comments, were not unusual:

Everyone in physical education used to say 'What is that on you?' and people calling you names like 'jig saw skin'. It definitely did hurt me (Thompson et al., 2002, p. 217).

I think there is a [Punjabi] slang term for it… Asian society is a lot based on looks and status and to have vitiligo obviously puts you down, it's a stigma, if you don't fit in then you kind of like, no matter if you're really smart or like, you have to try that little bit harder (Thompson et al., 2010, p. 482).

The second quote demonstrates how the experience of stigmatization may be associated with subtle cultural values related to appearance, status, gender roles, and cultural practices.

Another force that might lead to stigmatization is that of *objectification*, which is essentially the process of others reacting to someone as an object (or body), to the exclusion of their other characteristics. It is this process that has been argued as operating within the media, with the promulgation of the stereotypical beautiful body, as previously discussed. Objectification theory arose largely from within a feminist position (Fredrickson & Roberts, 1997) which suggests that through a process of internalization *self-objectification* occurs, where-by appearance becomes of central importance to the self-concept, which in turn then drives self-monitoring of outward appearance.

As with other constructs discussed in this chapter, objectification theory has led to the development of specific measures (e.g. The Sociocultural Attitudes towards Appearance Questionnaire, Heinberg, Thompson, & Stomer, 1995; The Objectified Body Consciousness Scale, McKinley & Hyde, 1996). A variety of studies, predominately examining eating disorders, use measures and report findings that support this model. For example, Tiggemann (2006) found a relationship between media exposure and appearance concern (also see Stice et al., 1994). Tiggemann and Kuring (2004) and Slater and Tiggemann (2010) have also reported correlations between body shame and appearance anxiety and body surveillance and disordered eating, which, whilst discussed by the authors in relation to objectification theory, also leads to a more detailed consideration of the role that shame may play in appearance concern and adjustment.

Body shame and social anxiety models

Goffman (1963) described shame as central to the experience of stigma. Gilbert (1997) has argued that humans have an innate drive to be perceived as attractive by others, and feelings of shame and humiliation arise in relation to beliefs about whether perceived negative reactions from others are felt to be deserved or undeserved. Kent and Thompson have posited that shame is likely to play a crucial role in adjustment to disfigurement and have developed a model that describes how this might operate (Thompson & Kent, 2001; Kent, 2002; Kent & Thompson, 2002). The model suggests that repeated experiences of social exclusion/rejection which are attributed to appearance can lead to the development of specific appearance concern. The model acknowledges the role played by the family and society in this process and suggests that shame and anxiety stemming from such experiences drives cognitive processes akin to those found in social anxiety.

Veale (2004) has described a similar model that focuses on explaining the maintenance of body dysmorphic disorder. He places emphasis within the model upon 'processing of self as an aesthetic object' and discusses how this activates other cognitive processes such as 'selective attention' and 'rumination'. There is a similarity here with Objectification Theory in terms of the important role played by the processing of the self as an aesthetic object. However, Veale's model places greater emphasis on how the processing itself maintains distress, as opposed to Objectification Theory's focus on the external mechanisms by which the self becomes an aesthetic object in the first place.

It has been argued that social anxiety might be thought of as an 'overarching notion' that has 'common connections' with shame and appearance concern (Thompson & Kent, 2001 p. 672). In both appearance concern and social anxiety there is a focus upon self-evaluation and a relationship between this and cognitive processing and behavioural coping styles. Indeed, there is evidence for specific types of cognitive processing playing a substantive role in social anxiety (e.g. Bar-Haim et al., 2007). There is less evidence as yet for the role such processing plays in appearance concern (see Chapter 21). There is evidence from within the eating disorders literature that body dissatisfaction increases the amount of attention paid to appearance-related information (Trampe et al., 2007), and also attentional bias to negative weight-related information has been shown to be associated with body dissatisfaction (Smith & Rieger, 2006; Shafran et al., 2007). There is emerging evidence that similar attentional biases may be present in relation to general appearance concern. For example, Rosser et al. (2010) examined whether processing differences were operating in association with appearance concern, and found that participants who scored more highly on a measure of appearance concern tended to be more likely to rate ambiguous words as appearance related and as negative (an interpretative bias). They also found (using a dot-probe paradigm) that there was an attentional bias operating for those with an interpretative bias. Although this study only demonstrated a small–medium effect size for the attentional bias and was conducted with a largely female student population, it does suggest that interventions aimed at tackling processing biases may be useful for those distressed by general appearance concern.

An Inclusive Framework for Guiding Appearance Research and Appearance-Related Interventions

I have discussed how much of the existing research in this area has been categorical and medically driven in terms of placing people into typologies and being overly focused on negative reactions. I have described some of the key theoretical approaches and models that have the potential to inform psychosocial interventions. However, there is a need for an inclusive and integrative framework that captures the significant theory in this area. The 'biopsychosociocultural' framework shown in Fig. 9.2 is an attempt to do this. It is adapted from a research framework developed by the ARC collaboration (see Fig. 9.1 a: Rumsey & Harcourt, 2005; Rumsey et al., under review) and is by no means a complete representation of all the extant theory, but it does make clear suggestions for future research and practice, and synthesizes the plethora of theories that exist in this area.

The conceptual framework shown in Fig. 9.1 is inclusive in that it encompasses much of the research, clinical findings and trends in this area of research, including

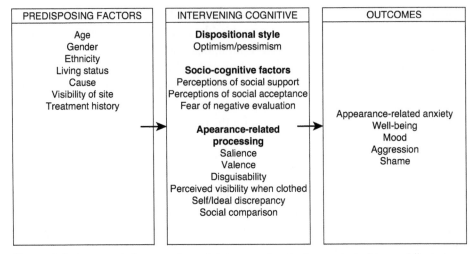

Figure 9.1 A research framework containing constructs demonstrated to contribute to appearance well-being. Adapted from Rumsey, N., Charlton, R., Clarke, A., Harcourt, D., James, H., Jenkinson, E., et al., Factors associated with distress and positive adjustment in people with disfigurement: Evidence from a large multi-centred study. *Journal of Consulting & Clinical Psychology* © 2012 The American Psychological Association.

significant aspects of previous models, most notably the models of Cash (2002), Gilbert (2002), and Kent and Thompson (2002) and takes an integrative stance as described by Pruzinsky and Cash (1990). Initially ARC conceived a framework designed to drive a research programme. This framework was formulated to be broad enough to capture the range of experiences across the spectrum of appearance concern, and yet specific enough to allow for predictions about susceptibility to distress to be made. The original framework includes constructs measured in the ARC programme of research with an emphasis on psychosocial factors which are amenable to change, as the aim of the ARC research programme was to inform the development of interventions. The first element comprises predisposing and historical factors such as demographic characteristics, sociocultural historical factors, and physical appearance factors. Whilst this element of the original ARC framework shown in Fig. 9.1 refers to physical attributes and demographic factors, emphasis is also needed upon the role played by early experiences (and this is made explicit in the reiteration of the model shown in Fig. 9.2).

The second element of the framework focuses upon individual difference factors believed to drive psychological processing and is broadly derived from a social cognitive perspective, which suggests that there are appearance-related beliefs or schema and associated cognitive processing styles as discussed earlier. The framework has at its centre that appearance can be more or less 'salient' in relation to its importance in defining self-concept (Moss & Carr, 2004). In addition, the framework suggests that individuals vary in the extent to which they positively or

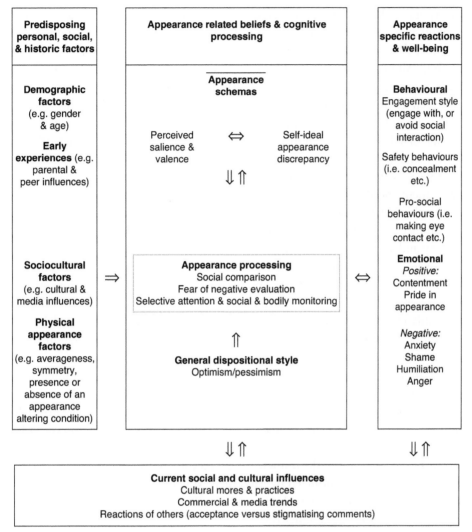

Figure 9.2 A conceptual framework containing additional constructs which may contribute to appearance well-being. Adapted from Rumsey, N., Charlton, R., Clarke, A., Harcourt, D., James, H., Jenkinson, E., et al., Factors associated with distress and positive adjustment in people with disfigurement: Evidence from a large multi-centred study. *Journal of Consulting & Clinical Psychology* © 2012 The American Psychological Association.

negatively evaluate their appearance, referred to as 'valence'. Salience and valence have aspects in common with Cash's (2002, 2005) conceptualization of 'body image evaluation' and 'body image investment'. For Cash, body image investment is broken down into two types—motivational salience and self-evaluative salience. The former concerns the degree of investment in maintaining appearance and the latter concerns the degree to which appearance is central to self-worth. The framework incorporates Altabe and Thompson's (1996) findings that appearance schemas contain access to internalized models of actual and ideal appearance, and that discrepancies between cultural ideals and perceived actual appearance also drive processing (Altabe & Thompson, 1996). This also fits with Price's (1990) model of body image in which contrasts between attitudinal body ideals and body reality are also seen as central. In the framework shown in Fig. 9.1, if appearance is more salient, negatively valenced, and discrepant when compared with ideals, processing occurs that leads to appearance concern. This element of the framework also includes reference to more stable dispositional variables, specifically *optimism and pessimism*, which may moderate the effects of the other schematic variables on adjustment and distress.

The third element of the model is the observable and experienced impact of appearance concerns. Existing work has demonstrated that elevated levels of social anxiety and social avoidance are common in those distressed by their appearance (for reviews, see Rumsey & Harcourt, 2004; Thompson & Kent, 2001). Shame and hostility may also result (Kent & Thompson, 2002). Behavioural factors such as self-presentation and strategies for managing the reactions of others are contained with this element of the framework. Although they are conceptualized here as outcomes, these constructs also serve a maintenance function in relation to the cognitive processes in stage two.

The fourth element (which has been added to the original ARC framework is shown in Fig. 9.2) draws attention to 'cultural mores and practices', 'commercial and media trends', and the 'behaviour of others', and is an attempt to acknowledge how the cultural context can influence (and be influenced by) other aspects within the framework.

The original version of the framework has recently been used to guide a number of connected studies conducted by ARC suggesting it does have utility in directing future work and intervention (Hughes et al., 2009; Thompson et al., 2010; Egan et al., 2011; Rumsey et al., under review).

CONCLUSIONS

This chapter has touched upon the complexities inherent in researching appearance. Whilst there is some evidence for an underlying evolutionary explanation for the value appearance may have to humans (see Etcoff, 1999; Langois et al., 2000; Rhodes, 2006), the mechanisms and nuances by which this operates to generate appearance concern is dependent on a large number of individual difference and psychosociocultural factors (Rumsey & Harcourt, 2005). As Tom Cash, a leading researcher and theorist in the related area of body image, has commented: 'All people are embodied, and their lives are powerfully shaped by the personal and cultural meanings of their physical appearance' (Cash, 2005, p. 440).

Appearance concern is clearly multifactorial and individual appearance well-being is predicted more strongly by dispositional factors including optimism and appearance specific cognitions including salience, valence, and appearance-related self-discrepancies, rather than by demographic or physical/biological factors (Rumsey et al., under review). In addition there is emerging evidence of discrepancies between participant accounts and the results of studies using standardized measures. For example, Thompson et al. (in preparation) report a disparity between participant subjective accounts of their adjustment over time compared with objective measures. It is not sufficient, and may even be misleading, to rely solely on psychometric measures to advance understanding in this field.

Many of the variables proposed by different groups of researchers as playing a part in appearance concern are conceptually closely related. More work is needed to refine the extant constructs in the field and this is likely to require collaboration and debate amongst research groups. There is a need to build and test specific pathways and to identify the precise relationships between the predictor variables. There is also a need to understand in more detail how interventions can influence such processing.

Finally, research is still needed that expands the evidence base beyond the current emphasis on white Western cultures and female participants and which incorporate a consideration of current social and cultural influences.

References

Altabe, M. & Thompson, J.K. (1996). Body image: a cognitive self-schema construct. *Cognitive Therapy & Research*, 20, 171–93.

Bar-Haim, Y., Lamy, D., Pergamin, L., Bakermans-Kranenburg, M. J., & van IJzendoorn, M. H. (2007). Threat-related attentional bias in anxious and nonanxious individuals: A meta-analytic study. *Psychological Bulletin*, 133, 1–24.

Brannon, L. & Feist, J. (2007). *Health psychology: An introduction to behavior and health* (7th edn.). Belmont, CA: Wadsworth Cengage Learning.

British Association of Aesthetic Surgeons (2010). *Annual audit: Britons over the moob: male breast reduction nearly doubles in 2009.* http://www.baaps.org.uk/about-us/audit (accessed 20 December, 2010).

Bull, R. & Rumsey, N. (1988). *The social psychology of facial appearance.* London: Springer-Verlag.

Cafri, G., Yamamiya, Y., Brannick, M., & Thompson, J. K. (2005). The influence of sociocultural factors on body image: A meta-analysis. *Clinical Psychology: Science & Practice*, 12, 421–33.

Cash, T. F. (2002). Cognitive behavioural perspectives on body image. In T. Cash & T. Pruzinsky (eds.) *Body image: A handbook of theory, research and clinical practice*, pp. 38–46. London: The Guildford Press.

Cash, T. F. (2005). The influence of sociocultural factors on body image: searching for constructs. *Clinical Psychology: Science & Practice*, 12, 438–42.

Cash, T. F. & Pruzinsky, T. (1990). *Body images: Development, deviance, and change.* New York: The Guildford Press.

Cash, T. F., Morrow, J. A., Hrabosky, J. I., & Perry, A. A. (2004). How has body image changed? A cross-sectional investigation of college women and men from 1983 to 2001. *Journal of Consulting and Clinical Psychology*, 72, 1081–9.

Dion, K. K., Berscheid, E., & Walster, E. (1972). What is beautiful is good. *Journal of Personality and Social Psychology*, 24, 285–90.

Eagly, A. H., Ashmore, R. D., Makhijani, M. G., & Longo, L. C. (1991). What is beautiful is good, but…: A meta-analytic review of research on the physical attractiveness stereotype. *Psychological Bulletin*, 110, 109–28.

Egan, K., Harcourt, D., Rumsey, N., & The Appearance Research Collaboration. (2011). A qualitative study of the experiences of people who identify themselves as having adjusted positively to a visible difference. *Journal of Health Psychology*, 16, 739–49.

Etcoff, N. (1999). *Survival of the prettiest: The science of beauty.* London: Little, Brown and Co.

Feingold, A. & Mazella, R. (1998). Gender differences in body image are increasing. *Psychological Science*, 9, 190–5.

Friedrickson, B. L. & Roberts, T. A. (1997). Objectification theory: Toward understanding women's lived experiences and mental health risks. *Psychology of Women Quarterly*, 21, 173–206.

Furman, K. & Thompson, J. K. (2002). Body image, teasing, and mood alterations: An experimental study of exposure to negative verbal commentary. *International Journal of Eating Disorders*, 32, 449–57.

Gilbert, P. (1997). The evolution of social attractiveness and its role in shame, humiliation, guilt and therapy. *British Journal of Medical Psychology*, 70, 113–47.

Gilbert, P., Price, J. S., & Allan, S. (1995). Social comparison, social attractiveness and evolution: How might they be related? *New Ideas in Psychology*, 13, 149–65.

Gilbert, P. (2002). Body shame: A biopsychosocial conceptualisation and overview, with treatment implications. In P. Gilbert & J. Miles (eds.) *Body shame: Conceptualisation, research & treatment*, pp. 3–54. Hove: Brunner-Routledge.

Gilbert, P. & Miles, J. (eds.) (2002). *Body shame: Conceptualisation, research & treatment.* Hove: Brunner-Routledge.

Goffman, E. (1963). *Stigma: Notes on the Management of the Spoiled Identity.* Englewood Cliffs, NJ: Prentice-Hall.

Gollwitzer, P. M. & Sheeran, P. (2006). Implementation intentions and goal achievement: A meta-analysis of effects and processes. *Advances in Experimental Social Psychology*, 38, 69–119.

Grandfield, T., Thompson, A. R., & Turpin, G. (2005). An attitudinal study of responses to dermatitis using the implicit association test. *Journal of Health Psychology*, 10, 821–9.

Grogan, S. (1999). *Body image: Understanding body dissatisfaction in men, women and children.* London: Routledge.

Harris, D. & Carr, A. (2001). Prevalence of concern about physical appearance in the general population. *British Journal of Plastic Surgery*, 54, 223–6.

Harvey, P. (2009). From behavioural medicine to health psychology. *Clinical Psychology Forum*, 199, 12–17.

Heinberg, L. J., Thompson, J. K., & Stomer, S. (1995). Development and validation of the Sociocultural Attitudes towards Appearance Questionnaire. *International Journal of Eating Disorders*, 17, 81–89.

Hughes, J., Naqvi, H., Saul, K., Williamson, H., Johnson, M. R. D., Rumsey, N., *et al.* (2009). South Asian community views about individuals with a disfigurement. *Diversity in Health & Care*, 6, 241–53.

Kent, G. (2002). Testing a model of disfigurement: Effects of a skin camouflage service on well-being and appearance anxiety. *Psychology & Health*, 17, 377–86.

Kent, G. & Thompson, A. R. (2002). Models of disfigurement: Implications for treatment. In P. Gilbert & J. Miles (eds.) *Understanding body shame*, pp. 106–16. Hove: Brunner-Routledge.

Kiefer, A., Sekaquaptewa D., & Barczyk, A. (2006). When appearance concerns make women look bad: Solo status and body image concerns diminish women's academic performance. *Journal of Experimental Social Psychology*, 42, 78–86.

Lansdown, R., Rumsey, N., Bradbury, E., Carr, T., Partridge, J. (1997). *Visibly different: Coping with disfigurement*. Oxford: Butterworth-Heinemann.

Langlois, J. H, Kalakanis, L., Rubenstein, A. J., Larson, A., Hallam, M., & Smoot, M. (2000). Maxims or myths of beauty? A mata-anaytic and theoretical review. *Psychological Bulletin*, 126, 390–423.

Lobeck, M., Thompson, A. R., and Shankland, M. C. (2005). The importance of social context in adjustment: an exploration of the experience of stroke for men in retirement transition. *Qualitative Health Research*, 15, 1022–36.

Meyerson, M.D. (2001). Resiliency and success in adults with Moebius syndrome. *Cleft Palate Craniofacial Journal*, 38, 231–5.

McKinley, N. M. & Hyde, J. S. (1996). The objectified body consciousness scale: Development and validation. *Psychology of Women Quarterly*, 20, 181–215.

Mills, J. & Miller, J. (2007). Experimental effects of receiving negative weight-related feedback: A weight guessing study. *Body Image*, 4, 309–16.

Moss, T. & Carr, T. (2004). Understanding adjustment in disfigurement: the role of the self-concept. *Psychology & Health*, 19, 737–48.

Newell, R. J. (2000). *Body Image and Disfigurement Care*. London: Routledge.

Orbach, S. (2009). *Bodies*. London: Profile Books Ltd.

Palayiwa, A., Sheeran, P., & Thompson, A. R. (2010). 'Words will never hurt me': Implementation intentions regulate attention to stigmatising comments about appearance. *Journal of Social & Clinical Psychology*, 29, 575–98.

Partridge, J. (1990). *Changing Faces: The Challenge of Facial Disfigurement*. London: Penguin.

Price, B. (1999). *Altered body image*. Nursing Times Monographs No. 29. London: NT Books.

Price, R. (1990). A model for body image care. *Journal of Advanced Nursing*, 15, 585–93.

Pruzinsky, T. & Cash, T. F. (1990). Integrative themes in body-image development, deviance, and change. In T. F. Cash & T. Pruzinsky (eds.) *Body images: Development, deviance, and change*, pp. 337–49. New York: The Guildford Press.

Reddy, S. D. & Crowther, J. H. (2007). Teasing, acculturation, and cultural conflict: Psychosocial correlates of body image and eating attitudes among south Asian women. *Cultural Diversity & Ethnic Minority Psychology*, 13, 45–53.

Rhodes, G. (2006). The evolutionary psychology of facial beauty. *Annual Review of Psychology*, 57, 199–226.

Rosser, B. A., Moss, T. P., & Rumsey, N. (2010). Attentional and interpretative biases in appearance concern: An investigation of biases in appearance-related information processing. *Body Image*, 7, 251–4.

Rumsey, N. & Harcourt, D. (2004). Body image and disfigurement: Issues and interventions. *Body Image*, 1, 83–97.

Rumsey, N. & Harcourt, D. (2005). *The psychology of appearance.* Maidenhead: Open University Press.

Rumsey, N., Clarke, A., White, P., Wyn-Williams, M., & Garlick, W. (2004). Altered body image: appearance-related concerns of people with visible disfigurement. *Journal of Advanced Nursing*, 48, 443–53.

Rumsey, N., Charlton, R., Clarke, A., Harcourt, D., James, H., Jenkinson, E., *et al.* (under review). Factors associated with distress and positive adjustment in people with disfigurement: Evidence from a large multi-centred study.

Saradjian, A., Thompson, A. R., & Datta, D. (2008). 'The experience of men using an upper limb prosthesis following amputation: Positive coping and minimizing feeling different'. *Disability & Rehabilitation*, 30, 871–83.

Sarwer, D. B., Wadden, T. A., & Whitaker, L. A. (2002). An investigation of changes in body image following cosmetic surgery. *Plastic & Reconstructive Surgery*, 109, 363–9.

Science Weekly (2010). Science weekly: Changing our bodies, 17 May. http://www.guardian.co.uk/science/blog/audio/2010/may/17/science-weekly-podcast-changing-bodies-susie-orbach (accessed 8 August, 2010).

Scott, I., Swami, V., Josephson, S. C., & Penton-Voak, I. S. (2008). Context-dependent preferences for facial sexual dimorphism in a rural Malaysian population. *Evolution and Human Behavior*, 29, 289–96.

Scrambler, G. & Hopkins, A. (1986). Being epileptic: coming to terms with stigma. *Sociology of Health and Illness*, 8, 26–43.

Shafran, R., Lee, M., Cooper, Z., Palmer, R., & Fairburn, C. (2007). Attentional bias in eating disorders. *International Journal of Eating Disorders*, 40, 369–80.

Slater, A. & Tiggemann, M. (2010). Body image and disordered eating in adolescent girls and boys: A test of objectification theory. *Sex Roles*, 63, 42–9.

Smith, E. & Rieger, E. (2006). The effect of attentional bias toward shape- and weight-related information on body dissatisfaction. *International Journal of Eating Disorders*, 39, 509–15.

Stice, E., Schupak-Neuberg, E., Shaw, H. E., & Stein, R. I. (1994). Relation of media exposure to eating disorder symptomatology: An examination of mediating mechanisms. *Journal of Abnormal Psychology*, 103, 836–40.

Taylor, C. B., Bryson, S., Doyle, C., Luce, K. H., Cunning, D., Abascal, L. B., *et al.* (2006). The adverse effect of negative comments about weight and shape from family and siblings on women at high risk for eating disorders. *Pediatrics*, 118, 731–8.

Tiggemann, M. (2006). The role of media exposure in adolescent girls' body dissatisfaction and drive for thinness: Prospective results. *Journal of Social & Clinical Psychology*, 25, 522–40.

Tiggemann, M. & Kuring, J. K. (2004). The role of body objectification in disordered eating and depressed mood. *British Journal of Clinical Psychology*, 43, 299–311.

Thompson, A. R. & Kent, G. (2001). Adjusting to disfigurement: processes involved in dealing with being visibly different. *Clinical Psychology Review*, 21, 663–82.

Thompson, A. R. & Broom, L. (2009). Positively managing intrusive reactions to disfigurement: An interpretative phenomenological analysis of naturalistic coping. *Diversity in Health & Care*, 6, 171–80.

Thompson, A. R., Kent, G., & Smith, J. A. (2002). Living with vitiligo: Dealing with difference. *British Journal of Health Psychology*, 7, 213–25.

Thompson, A. R., Clarke, S. A., Newell, R., Gawkrodger, G., & The Appearance Research Collaboration. (2010). Vitiligo linked to stigmatisation in British South Asian women: A qualitative study of the experiences of living with vitiligo. *The British Journal of Dermatology*, 163, 481–6.

Thompson, A. R. (2011). Adaptation in long-term conditions: the role of stigma particularly in conditions that affect appearance. In S. Randall & H. Ford (eds.) *The Textbook of Long-term Conditions*, pp. 121–137. London: Wiley.

Thompson, A. R., Newell, R., Clarke, S. A., Jenkinson, E., James, H., & The Appearance Research Collaboration. (in preparation). A qualitative investigation of change and stability in psychological adjustment to appearance altering conditions.

Thompson, K. J., Heinberg, L. J., Altabe, M., & Tantleff-Dunn, S. (eds.) (1999a). *Exacting beauty: Theory, assessment, and treatment of body image disturbance*. Washington, DC: American Psychological Association.

Thompson, K. J., Heinberg, L. J., Altabe, M., & Tantleff-Dunn, S. (1999b). Appearance-related feedback. In K. J. Thompson., L. J. Heinberg., M. Altable., & S. Tantleff-Dunn. *Extracting beauty: Theory, assessment, and treatment of body image*, pp. 151–74. Washington, DC: American Psychological Association.

Trampe, D., Stapel, D. A., & Siero, F. W. (2007). On models and vases: Body dissatisfaction and proneness to social comparison effects. *Journal of Personality and Social Psychology*, 92, 106–18.

Uttjek, M., Nygren, L., Stenberg, B., & Dufaker, M. (2007). Marked by visibility of psoriasis in everyday life. *Qualitative Health Research*, 17, 364–72.

Veale, D. (2004). Advances in a cognitive behavioural model of body dysmorphic disorder. *Body Image*, 1, 113–25.

Veale, D., Willson, R., & Clarke, A. (2009). *Overcoming body image problems, Including body dysmorphic disorder: A self-help guide using cognitive behavioural techniques*. London: Constable & Robinson Ltd.

CHAPTER 10

SETTING THE SCENE: SUMMARY AND SYNTHESIS

DIANA HARCOURT

NICHOLA RUMSEY

THE contributors to this section have a variety of applied and academic backgrounds, training, and experience, and employ a range of epistemological and theoretical perspectives in relation to appearance and body image. Yet despite this variety, their chapters capture a number of overlapping and complementary themes that will echo throughout the rest of this book. Specifically, issues relating to the social currency of appearance over time, the disparity between subjective and objective perspectives, the role of gatekeepers in the provision of care, the impact of the media, and challenges for theory have been highlighted throughout this section, and these are briefly considered here.

Firstly, these chapters draw our attention to the dynamic and changing nature of appearance. Hannah Falvey illustrates how appearance ideals have changed within and across cultures and societies over time. Appearance-altering practices such as footbinding and tattooing, for example, must be considered in the context of both culture and history if we are to truly understand their influence and significance. Malcolm MacLachlan and his co-authors draw on accounts of the psychosocial impact of amputation to demonstrate how people's experiences of their bodies can change suddenly and unexpectedly, necessitating a process of adjustment, whilst

Andrew Thompson's chapter reflects on the utility of existing theories and frameworks in explaining adjustment to appearance. The ability of these theories to predict and account for short- and longer-term fluctuations in adjustment over time and for responses to sudden changes to appearance still needs to be thoroughly tested. We consider the challenges of the use of theory in this field in more detail in Section 5, but at this point we raise the question 'Is the "holy grail" of developing a single theory that accounts for the complexities of body image and appearance satisfaction feasible and to what extent should the efforts of researchers be devoted to this?'.

Hannah Frith's chapter includes an examination of TV makeover programmes—a medium through which changes to an individual's appearance over a short, intense period of time are presented for entertainment, albeit in the guise of a supportive intervention. Whilst these programmes present a heavily edited snapshot of the short-term results of appearance changes resulting from surgery, dental work, clothing, make-up, and hairstyling, the longer-term effects on participants and viewers of these programmes are unknown. Are the benefits and happiness highlighted in the final 'reveal' maintained beyond the presence of the cameras and the attention of professionals and supportive TV presenters? How does the message that 'life will be so much better with improved looks' influence the beliefs and subsequent behaviours of viewers?

Secondly, these chapters emphasize the importance of focusing on subjective rather than objective approaches to appearance. Malcolm MacLachlan and colleagues highlight the importance of understanding a person's embodied experience of their physical appearance. Esther Hansen and Peter Butler consider how the provision of care for people with appearance concerns is all too often determined on the basis of objective criteria such as a clinical diagnosis or the measurable extent of any visible difference, which can ignore the individual, personal impact on those affected. These approaches effectively buy in to the myth that psychological distress and well-being are directly associated with an objective assessment of appearance. This is typified by the common assumption that people living with a disfigurement will be troubled by their 'difference', and that this dominates any other concerns they may have about their appearance. In contrast, research and clinical experience demonstrate that people who have a visible difference also report appearance concerns which are not necessarily associated with their visible difference, for example, concerns relating to their weight and shape. This emphasizes the danger of making assumptions about the nature or extent of a person's appearance-related distress, or lack of it, without asking them directly and explicitly for their own views.

These chapters also highlight how people's experiences of their appearance and the provision of care and interventions for those troubled by appearance-related concerns are influenced by a variety of gatekeepers. Family doctors in the UK, insurance companies in the US, and governments managing limited budgets in resource-poor countries determine which interventions are accessible, and to whom. For poorer nations, life-saving procedures may be prioritized, but funds are not available for subsequent rehabilitation. In the US and UK, resource allocation is frequently driven by the belief that the severity or extent of an 'abnormal' appearance is associated with the extent of psychological distress and that biomedical (often surgical) interventions are the solution. While the greater resources in richer countries may provide access to appropriate services for some, equal access for all is by no means assured. The provision of care is not uniform within either the UK or the US and statutes and guidelines that are intended to promote equality of access do not always achieve their goals. Julie Kent's chapter demonstrates how legislation and marketing (for example, around breast implants) also influences individuals' experiences of their bodies. Appearance is experienced and influenced on multiple levels, all of which can be seen as being socially constructed. Marketing, for example, simultaneously creates a problem for individuals by laying the foundations for poor self-image and offering a solution by way of beauty, diet, and surgical products. The message that worldwide, psychological services should be made available alongside medical, surgical, and societal interventions is clear and consistent, and is highlighted again in later chapters.

Any detailed consideration of the psychology of appearance would be lacking if it did not pay attention to the influence of the media and so it is not surprising that this emerges as a common theme in several of the chapters both here and in the sections that follow. Both Hannah Falvey and Hannah Frith examine how media portrayals of appearance promote socially and culturally accepted appearance ideals, which shape the use of stereotypes to characterize and judge people on the basis of aspects such as age, class, or occupation. Magazines and newer media, in particular through the Internet and proliferation of TV channels, increase the opportunities to promote appearance ideals. Large segments of these media are dominated by the cult of celebrity, fixated on the latest images of a relatively small pool of well-known and high-profile individuals whose appearance is consequently acclaimed and derided, often in quick succession. This is demonstrated in a poem performed by the organization Body Gossip (http://www.bodygossip.org) who produce theatrical pieces based on writings submitted to them by members of the public. In the following extract, a celebrity despairs at the pressure of the media's surveillance of her appearance:

What, I get slagged for being fat, and for being thin?
  Well I give up, I don't know how to win

   (from 'Mocha Chocca Latte', by Elizabeth Caproni written for the Body Gossip positive
                                     body image campaign, http://www.bodygossip.org).

Appearance-focused media can have a number of consequences. For example they may encourage appearance-related conversations (including 'fat talk') amongst viewers and readers and within families and between friends. These may promote solidarity and create ties, but may also encourage viewers to poke fun at, humiliate, or denigrate one another or those being observed. To what extent are appearance concerns being used purely as a form of entertainment, acceptable voyeurism, or titillation for others, drawing parallels with the 'freak shows' of days gone by? Whilst some media producers, presenters, and journalists may claim to be promoting acceptance of diversity of appearance and helping people to challenge the impact of appearance ideals, there is an irony associated with viewers typically being exposed to advertisements (for example, those promoting rejuvenating face creams, age-defying hair dyes, and cosmetic procedures) that continue to promote appearance ideals in programme breaks and on magazine pages. Advertisers target consumers of these media, assuming that they have a heightened interest in appearance, and hoping they are a potentially lucrative market for their products. The advertising and media coverage of new technologies, such as living skin, breast implants, and face transplants highlighted in Julie Kent's chapter, actively promotes an expanding range of ways to modify appearance. The limitations of these appearance-altering technologies (for example, the shelf-life of breast implants, or the need for lifetime immunosuppression in the case of a face transplant) bring with them a myriad of ethical and psychosocial dilemmas, yet these are often downplayed, and rarely receive much media exposure.

Finally, this section has highlighted a number of theories that have been developed in appearance research. Whilst others are introduced later in this book, the chapters in this section have already raised questions relating to the extent to which theories can adequately explain psychosocial adjustment and distress in relation to appearance, and the extent to which research can and should be theory driven. Andrew Thompson has highlighted the advantages of linking theory to interventions and we, too, are more persuaded by theories which have a clear use in practice. This focus on application continues within the rest of this volume and has underpinned our own work for several years.

In summary, this section has introduced readers to issues relating to embodiment, theory, culture, society, the provision of care, and development of new technologies, all of which have a critical bearing on individuals' experiences of their bodies and appearance. Having established that such a wide range of influences have a part to play, the question remains 'who is affected by appearance concerns, in what way and why?'. These questions are now examined in detail, in Section 2.

SECTION 2

WHO IS AFFECTED BY APPEARANCE CONCERNS, IN WHAT WAY, AND WHY?

CHAPTER 11

WHO IS AFFECTED BY APPEARANCE CONCERNS, IN WHAT WAY, AND WHY?: OVERVIEW

DIANA HARCOURT

NICHOLA RUMSEY

SECTION 2 explores the nature and consequences of appearance-related concerns. In a recent online questionnaire study of more than 800 young people from the UK, aged 11–18 years, 34% of boys and 49% of girls had been on a diet to change their body shape (Diedrichs et al., in preparation) and more than 50% of 1200 girls and young women aged 16–21 years report that they would consider undergoing cosmetic surgery to change their appearance (Girlguiding UK, 2010). Whilst these figures suggest that dissatisfaction is endemic, a sizeable proportion of respondents nevertheless reported being satisfied with and, in many instances, proud of the way they look. The chapters in this section examine a wealth of factors that play a part in determining this variation in levels of appearance-related satisfaction and adjustment.

The first three chapters (Section 2.1) consider appearance issues over the lifespan. Firstly, Linda Smolak describes the emergence and development of appearance preferences in early childhood and adolescence, and the impact of these on self-perceptions, social functioning, and mental well-being. She discusses techniques used by children and young people in their efforts to achieve an appearance with which they are happy, and which is consistent with their favoured ideals. Marika Tiggeman and Julie Slevec then examine stability and change across adulthood, and how multifactorial combinations of psychological, sociocultural, and biological factors contribute to stability and change in levels of satisfaction with appearance and the importance placed upon it during this lifestage. Lucie Baker and Eyal Gringart then highlight the relative dearth of research into older peoples' experiences of appearance and body image, and present an overview of their research, together with a framework and a measure for body image in older adults.

The next seven contributions (Section 2.2) explore individual differences in adjustment and distress, and ways in which the effects are manifested. Helen Fawkner considers the role of gender and shows how, contrary to some commonly held assumptions, both men and women are affected by appearance concerns, although the precise nature of these concerns differs. Caroline Huxley and Nikki Hayfield then examine appearance norms amongst lesbian, gay, and bisexual groups and illustrate how appearance is manipulated to ascertain and express identity and membership with a group. Habib Naqvi and Krysia Saul consider appearance through the lens of culture and ethnicity, with a focus on how different physical attributes are considered desirable in different parts of the world. Drawing on one of the few studies in this area, a qualitative study of a South Asian community's views of visible difference, Habib and Krysia demonstrate how religious and cultural beliefs relating to appearance can influence attitudes, affect social lives and influence expectations of marriage, particularly amongst women.

Whilst previous chapters have already alluded to the role of the media in this field, Emma Halliwell and Phillippa Diedrichs focus specifically on the empirical evidence and psychosocial theories that attempt to explain the media's influence on levels of appearance concerns. They consider how unrealistic ideals are over-represented, whilst people with a visible difference are rarely portrayed, and highlight how and why some people are more vulnerable to the effects of the media than others.

Rebecca Bellew examines the unique contribution that families make to individuals' experiences of appearance through information, support, verbal and non-verbal cues, modelling, criticism, and attachment. She highlights how guidance in interpreting the social world can be especially pertinent for family members living with a visible difference. The multiple, complex role of friends and peers (including peer pressure, teasing, social comparison, and cultural differences and influences) are examined by Lina Ricciardelli and David Mellor. Whilst most research focuses on predictors of negative body image and appearance concerns, their chapter also considers how peers may exert a positive influence and be instrumental in promoting body satisfaction.

Timothy Moss and Ben Rosser provide a clear guide to the complex world of the cognitive processes implicated in appearance-related adjustment and distress.

They examine a range of coping styles, personality variables and cognitive under-pinnings involved in this processing, including constructions of the self and biases in attention, memory and in the interpretation of ambiguous information. They also challenge some common assumptions around the influencing role of the phys-ical characteristics of a disfigurement (e.g. location, visibility, and severity) on adjustment in those affected, explaining that this relationship is more complex than is often presumed.

The third part of this section moves on to examine some of the consequences of appearance concerns. Specifically, James Byron-Daniel highlights how appearance may act as a motivator or a barrier to engaging in exercise and physical activity. James considers the potential for exercise-based interventions to influence body satisfaction and the role of the physical and social environment in which exercise takes place. Two chapters then focus on eating behaviour. Firstly, Irmgard Tischner and Helen Malson offer a critical perspective on culturally dominant views of peo-ple deemed 'too fat' or 'too thin' and consider how societal views towards body weight can lead people to feel denigrated and pathologized. They call for a shift in society's approach towards diets and weight loss in favour of a focus on health rather than body size. Victoria Lawson then explores the role of appearance con-cerns and body size perceptions in the substantial numbers of people who engage in disordered eating, yet who do not reach the threshold of a clinical diagnosis of an eating disorder. She discusses the dilemma of how to raise awareness of possible health risks associated with weight without fuelling appearance concerns or pro-moting stigmatizing and stereotypical views around body size.

Increases in the demand for cosmetic surgery are a further consequence of appearance dissatisfaction. Canice Crerand, Leanne Magee, and David Sarwer examine research into the psychosocial impact of cosmetic procedures and ask whether surgical 'quick fixes' are effective at reducing psychological distress and body dissatisfaction. They also consider the efficacy of cosmetic surgery for people with eating disorders and body dysmorphic disorder.

Chapters in Section 2.4 examine the experiences of people with an appearance which is visibly different as a result of a congenital or acquired condition and/or medical treatment. Kristin Billaud Feragen uses the examples of cleft lip and/or palate and neurofibromatosis to explore the particular issues facing those with a congenital condition that affects one or more aspects of physical appearance. Her illustrative use of participant voices highlights the need to counter the tendency to pathologize the experiences of children and young people through a focus on problems and difficulties, and instead to adopt a more normalizing, developmental perspective in understanding their worlds. In keeping with her own advice, Kristin highlights positive aspects and protective factors as well as challenges, and considers the need for appropriate psychosocial interventions for those experiencing difficul-ties. The psychosocial impact of an altered appearance after traumatic injury is the topic of Julie Wisely and Sarah Gaskell's chapter. They focus particularly on burn injuries and, again, their inclusion of participant voices illustrates both positive and negative outcomes and adds to the call for interventions, highlighting the particular challenges that are presented when a person leaves the confines of a hospital environment and starts to reintegrate into community and society. Many of the impacts of changes to appearance due to disease are epitomized by the challenges inherent in coping with skin conditions. These are reviewed in Christine Bundy's chapter. Finally, Heidi Williamson and Melissa Wallace explore the impact of surgical and medical treatments (specifically amputation, cancer treatment and highly active antiretroviral therapy (HAART) medication for people affected by HIV/AIDS) that alter appearance. Once again, both positive and negative outcomes are identified and factors that may explain differences in experiences and the challenges associated with developing and providing appropriate interventions are examined. Heidi and Melissa's chapter reminds us that issues around intimacy can be especially challenging and are in need of further consideration by researchers and practitioners alike. Uniquely, this chapter also considers how external changes to appearance can be an indication to others of the person's health status, and the potential issues that this kind of 'disclosure' can present.

The synthesis at the end of this section considers the importance of appearance for males and females of all ages, and the role of psychological, social, and cultural influences in determining levels of body (dis)satisfaction. We also identify areas in need of further research attention.

References

Diedrichs, P. C., Paraskeva, N., & New, A. (in preparation). Quick fixes and appearance concerns among young people in Britain.

Girlguiding UK (2010). www.girlguiding.org.uk/girlsattitudes

APPEARANCE CONCERNS ACROSS THE LIFESPAN

CHAPTER 12

APPEARANCE IN CHILDHOOD AND ADOLESCENCE

LINDA SMOLAK

By adolescence, girls and boys are sufficiently concerned about their appearance to undergo cosmetic surgery (Sarwer et al., 2009), use food supplements or steroids to increase muscularity (Smolak & Stein, 2010), and engage in dieting and other behaviours to lose weight (French et al., 1997). These behaviours are typically assumed to be responses to internalized sociocultural appearance ideals (Thompson et al., 1999).

This chapter has four goals: (1) describe the development of appearance preferences during childhood and adolescence; (2) identify influences on the development of these preferences; (3) consider the effects of these preferences on self-development and social interactions; and (4) discuss techniques that children and adolescents use to achieve an appearance that is consistent with their preferences. While there are numerous components of appearance, the research concerning children and adolescents has focused primarily on facial attractiveness and body shape, particularly weight and shape.

Facial Attractiveness

Preferences

Two- to three-day-old infants prefer to look at attractive rather than unattractive white female faces (Slater et al., 2000). These findings raise the possibility that a preference for attractive faces, at least attractive female faces, is innate. However, a study with even younger infants failed to find a similar preference for attractive female faces (Hoss & Langlois, 2003). Thus, the preference doesn't seem to be inborn. Nonetheless, the Slater et al., data indicate an early developing mechanism that results in the attractiveness bias. This process cannot, of course, depend on media exposure. Nor is it likely that babies are only exposed to attractive women.

One possible explanation is that infants form a prototype of an ideal female face, one that reflects an averaged face (Hoss & Langlois, 2003). Among adults, attractive faces represent a grouping of average features, although the end result is more attractive than average. Rubenstein et al., (1999) tested 6-month-old infants to assess whether averaged attractive faces, which the infants had never seen before, were treated as familiar by the babies. The averaged face was digitally created based on a series of attractive faces that the children were shown. If they treated these averaged faces as familiar, by staring at a 'novel' unfamiliar attractive face, then it would indicate that the infants 'recognize' averaged attractive faces. Infants indeed treated the averaged face as familiar although it was actually novel. Research with younger infants is still needed to ensure that they, too, average across faces. At this time, however, the cognitive averaging explanation is the best fit with the data.

Infants' preference for attractiveness is not restricted to white women's faces. Six–month-olds also show the attractiveness bias when looking at white male, black female, and infant faces (Hoss & Langlois, 2003). However, attractive male faces are frequently not perceived as more masculine though attractive female faces are perceived as more feminine. Thus, among young children (4–5 years), attractiveness moderates identification of a face as female but not as male (Hoss et al., 2005).

Preferences and stereotypes

There is a stereotype, at least among Americans, that 'beauty is good'. There is a general expectation that people who are more attractive are nicer, smarter, and more capable than people who are unattractive. This stereotype emerges by about 3 years of age (Dion, 1973), with children preferring attractive over unattractive playmates. When, and how, might the infant preference for attractive faces transform into the 'beauty is good' stereotype?

By 6 months of age, infants can categorize faces as attractive or not attractive (Ramsey et al., 2004). This is an important step in developing the 'beauty is good' stereotype. At 12 months old, but not at 9 months, infants appear to associate positive auditory stimuli, such as laughter, with attractive faces while associating unattractive faces with crying or negative vocal tones (Hoss & Langlois, 2003). By 36 months, but not at 30 months, children expect that attractive peers will be nice and they are more likely to want to play with attractive children. However, these 36-month-olds did not yet associate unattractiveness with being mean, as is true of slightly older preschoolers (Hoss & Langlois, 2003). Thus, the 'beauty is good' stereotype emerges during infancy and is refined and expanded throughout the preschool years.

Five-year-olds demonstrate the apparent use of 'beauty is good' cognitive schema (Ramsey & Langlois, 2002). Children showed better memory for stories about female characters when the story was consistent with the 'beauty is good' stereotype than when the story was inconsistent with the stereotype. Interestingly, the stereotype did not function in remembering stories about male characters. This schema, then, may function to maintain the stereotype of 'beauty is good' for girls and women but not for boys and men. Thus, a perceptual preference that started as more important in perceiving women's faces has apparently evolved into a cognitive process that operates more strongly in evaluating women. Why the stereotype is more applicable to women remains unclear and is a question deserving of more research.

Influences on stereotype development

The association between attractiveness and positive, desirable characteristics is likely reinforced by the environment (Ramsey et al., 2004). These influences may come from parents and media, though the data are limited. For example, an analysis of books and videos aimed at 4–8-year-olds indicated that most of the videos (72%) associated physical attractiveness with being loved. It is common, for example, to fall in love with female characters based only on the female's looks. They typically do not even know about the personality or interests of the girl/woman (Herbozo et al., 2004). Furthermore, in 84% of the videos, physical attractiveness is associated with positive characteristics, such as happiness or kindness, in the female characters. Thus, there is a gendered message concerning the beauty is good stereotype that might contribute to the finding that children use attractiveness to categorize women's faces more than men's (Hoss et al., 2005).

Parents are concerned about their children's appearance, though they are generally quite satisfied with it (Striegel-Moore & Kearney-Cooke, 1994; McCabe et al., 2007). For example, mothers routinely claim that they make only positive appearance-related comments to their pre-school age daughters. The mothers further report that the young girls and boys themselves emphasize their hair and clothes (McCabe et al., 2007).

Thus, even young children get messages from media and parents about what constitutes an attractive appearance. They receive positive feedback on their appearance, including their 'pretty' faces, from their parents. Nonetheless, this is commentary and information about what it means to have an attractive face as well as the importance of being 'pretty'.

Self and social relationships

Self

Infants and preschool age children do not typically engage in much social comparison. They can, therefore, easily accept the praise of their parents and be quite satisfied with their appearance. Indeed, very young children typically have unrealistically high self-esteem and self-appraisal (Marsh et al., 1998). Beginning in elementary school and increasing at least into adolescence, children engage in social comparison. This process of social comparison to peers and media, as well as direct comments from parents and peers, likely transforms the beliefs and stereotypes about attractiveness into self-evaluation concerning appearance.

Acne is a relatively common skin condition that interferes with attaining the 'perfect' face. Studies frequently find that 10–20% of teens self-report that they suffer from current acne (e.g. Kornblau et al., 2007; Dalgard et al., 2008) with up to 80% suffering at least some acne at some time (Sarwer et al., 2009). Most teens reporting acne also indicate that it has negatively impacted their daily lives (Sarwer et al., 2009). Acne has been associated with lowered self-worth among late adolescent girls, even after statistical adjustments for body mass index (BMI) and depressive symptoms (Dalgard et al., 2008). Late adolescent girls suffering from acne also demonstrate lower body esteem and higher rates of depressive symptoms including suicidal ideation (e.g. Kornblau et al., 2007; Dalgard et al., 2008).

The lowered sense of self-esteem may be at least partly attributable to peer teasing (Magin et al., 2008). In a qualitative study of Australian adolescents and adults, Magin and his colleagues (2008) found that teasing was a common experience of people suffering from acne and other skin diseases (e.g. psoriasis). This teasing was intentionally hurtful rather than playful or inadvertent. Furthermore, at least some of the teasing came from friends and was intended to exclude the person from social interactions. The sense of embarrassment and hurt from such teasing was particularly pronounced during childhood and adolescence.

Social relationships

Over 30 years of research has established that children and adolescents prefer attractive peers as playmates, friends, and even as partners for an academic project (e.g. Dion, 1973; Langlois & Downs, 1979; Boyatzis et al., 1998). This phenomenon is present after 3 years of age. It is true of both boys and girls, and regardless of whether the research employs drawings of typical or atypical unattractive faces or simply verbal descriptions of attractiveness.

Adolescents also believe that attractive teens will be more popular (Boyatzis et al., 1998). This belief likely reflects both the 'beauty is good' stereotype and real-life experiences, since popular teens are rated as more attractive. Indeed, Clark and Ayers (1988) reported that middle-school children rated attractiveness as a more important criterion than academic achievement for friendship.

Appearance-altering techniques

Given its impact on social success as well as the 'beauty is good' stereotype that they have embraced since early childhood, teens seem quite concerned with their appearance. Girls may be more concerned than boys are, though both spend a substantial amount of their own money on clothing, presumably to try to achieve a certain 'look' (magazine.org, 2004). Girls read appearance-oriented teen magazines, with about 60% of middle-school girls reading them two to five times a month (Field et al., 1999a). Girls who are heavy readers of such magazines are particularly likely to buy cosmetics to improve their appearance (magazine.org, 2004).

More dramatically, adolescents do consider and actually undergo cosmetic surgery in order to alter their facial appearance. Adolescents may feel pressure from their parents, especially if the parent has had cosmetic surgery, to improve their appearance. Media images of perfect faces may also influence an adolescent's desire for cosmetic surgery (Sarwer et al., 2009). The most common form of cosmetic surgery among adolescents is rhinoplasty, with nearly 35,000 such procedures performed in 2009 (American Society of Plastic Surgeons, 2010). Otoplasty, used to 'correct' prominent ears, is the third most common (American Society of Plastic Surgeons, 2010). This procedure is often done to try to reduce a child's experience with teasing. Indeed, research suggests improved psychosocial functioning among children undergoing otoplasty (Sarwer et al., 2009).

Cosmetic surgical treatment of acne and acne scars is also fairly common. Over 2,700 teens underwent dermabrasion in 2009 with an additional 9,500 undergoing microdermabrasion, and over 16,000 using laser skin resurfacing (American Society of Plastic Surgeons, 2010). This underscores the importance of clear skin to adolescents. Such treatments do appear to reduce some of the psychosocial distress associated with acne, although they do not eliminate all of the negative outcomes (Sarwer et al., 2009).

Conclusion

Even very young infants prefer attractive faces. This is likely because averaging across faces yields a face that is perceived as attractive. This is especially true of women's faces. As children get older, but again beginning in infancy, they associate other positive characteristics with an attractive face. By the time children are 5 years old, they have developed a cognitive schema for the 'beauty is good' stereotype and use it to interpret information.

Not surprisingly, then, not being sufficiently attractive results in negative self-image and depressive symptoms. Similarly, it should not be surprising that children judge attractive peers more positively and prefer them as friends. Given this as well as pressure from parents, peers, media, girls especially will work to improve the appearance of their faces by adolescence. They frequently use make-up and other beauty products. Many teens take more extreme measures, using cosmetic surgery to improve the appearance of their noses, ears, and skin.

More research is needed to understand what pressures increase the investment in facial appearance to the point that it interferes with psychosocial functioning. Researchers should also consider factors that increase the self-esteem and social skills of children and adolescents who are less attractive than desirable. Furthermore, although we all learn that 'beauty is only skin deep', greater efforts are needed to understand how to help children accept a wider range of appearances.

BODY SHAPE CONCERNS

Preferences

By 3 years old, children routinely hold negative attitudes about obesity (Cramer & Steinwert, 1998; Holub, 2008). Young children think that their overweight peers possess more negative personality characteristics than do other children. For example, in a study of 4–6-year-olds, Musher-Eizenman and her colleagues (2004) found that children rated thin or average figures as nicer, smarter, more popular, neater, cuter, and quieter than chubby figures. Children selected the thin figures as friends 39% of the time while they selected average figures 45% of the time and chubby figures only 16% of the time (Musher-Eizenman et al., 2004). Other studies have found that this anti-fat attitude is independent of the child's own weight (Sigelman et al., 1986). However, children who perceive themselves as heavier, a perception that is not strongly correlated with actual weight at this age, may hold fewer anti-fat attitudes (Holub, 2008).

Interestingly, preschool children also appear to believe that body weight is somewhat controllable. However, the more controllable children believe weight is, the more likely they are to ascribe negative personality characteristics to the chubby figure (Musher-Eizenman et al., 2004). By early elementary school, children will judge a female, but not a male, peer more negatively if they are simply near an overweight peer (Penny & Haddock, 2007). This underscores the strength of the anti-fat prejudice among children. It is reasonable to expect that children also apply this anti-fat attitude to themselves.

Research indicates that these preschoolers do not necessarily experience body dissatisfaction (Davison et al., 2000; Lowes & Tiggemann, 2003). However, by 6 or 7 years old, girls do express a desire to be thinner (Dohnt & Tiggemann, 2004). By age 8, children's self-image has differentiated sufficiently to include a physical appearance component (Harter, 2003). Furthermore, research typically demonstrates that about 40–50% of elementary school children are dissatisfied with some aspect of their body. For girls, this tends to be fears that they are or will become overweight while boys worry both about being too heavy and about being too small (Ricciardelli et al., 2009; Wertheim et al., 2009; Smolak, 2011). For example, Lowes and Tiggemann (2003) reported that 59% of 5–8-year-old girls wanted to be thinner, while 17% wanted to be bigger and 24% were satisfied with their body size. Boys, on the other hand, divided into these groups more equally, with 35% wanting to be bigger, 35% wishing to be thinner, and 30% satisfied with their bodies. Additional analyses showed that it was only girls aged 6 and older who wished to be thinner in significant numbers.

By adolescence, perhaps 70% of girls want to be thinner. Typically, studies report that fewer than 10% of adolescent girls wish to be heavier and most of these girls actually are underweight. Girls associate thinness with being happier, healthier, better looking, and more successful with boys (Wertheim et al., 2009). These girls have clearly internalized the socially sanctioned thin ideal. It is noteworthy that in the US, the desire for thinness and its associated body dissatisfaction is significantly less common among African American girls than any other ethnic group (Franko & Edwards-George, 2009). Indeed, African American adolescents endorse a larger ideal body size than do other American ethnic groups. It is also important to recognize that although the thin ideal is present in various cultures and is commonly adopted by adolescent girls in countries ranging from Australia to Korea to Argentina, it is not a universal phenomenon. Indeed, there is substantial evidence that girls' preference for thinness is culturally influenced (Anderson-Fye, 2009).

The research concerning boys is more limited. Preference for muscularity may increase throughout childhood into adolescence. Studies often show that up to about 45% of boys would like to be larger with a somewhat lower percentage wanting to be thinner. It may be that among children and preadolescents more boys want to be thinner than larger (Ricciardelli et al., 2009). We can, however, draw at least two conclusions about boys' body preference. First, more boys than girls are interested in being bigger and more muscular. Second, boys are concerned both about being too fat and about being too small or non-muscular. They are aiming for a slim, lean, muscled body, particularly once they reach adolescence. However, it is noteworthy that at least one study found that drive for thinness is a more important predictor of body dissatisfaction than investment in the muscular ideal is (Jones et al., 2008).

BMI is a particularly consistent predictor of body dissatisfaction related to thinness in both boys and girls (Smolak, 2011) with higher BMI resulting in greater body dissatisfaction. This may reflect the anti-fat bias that children first show as pre-schoolers. It is not body fat per se that results in the body dissatisfaction. Indeed, body dissatisfaction among obese children is higher among those who have developed weight and shape concerns (Allen, et al., 2006). BMI is not a 'biological' influence. It is the cultural vilification of fat that creates the relationship. In fact, there are cultures in which a heavier body is valued and hence increased BMI is not associated with body dissatisfaction (Anderson-Fye, 2009). Interestingly, BMI is not consistently linked to muscularity concerns or investment (e.g. Smolak & Stein, 2006).

Most theorists employ sociocultural perspectives in explaining preferences for thinness and muscularity (e.g. Cafri et al., 2005; Thompson et al., 1999). Influences such as media, parents, and peers are seen as shaping and enforcing a societal standard. Substantial research supports this approach, particularly for girls' drive for thinness.

Influences on body shape preferences and body dissatisfaction

It is common to measure body dissatisfaction as the difference between an ideal body shape/size and perceived own body shape/size. Thus, body dissatisfaction often includes the internalized ideal. Furthermore, idealization of the media based thin ideal (as measured, for example, by the Sociocultural Attitudes toward Appearance Questionnaire (Thompson et al., 2004)) is frequently related to both investment in thinness and in muscularity (Smolak & Stein, 2006, 2010; Grabe et al., 2008). Thus, body dissatisfaction, drive for thinness, and drive for muscularity are all assumed to reflect the culturally sanctioned ideal body types and preferences for those body types.

Media

Media have received substantial research attention as an influence on muscularity and thinness ideals and on body dissatisfaction. First, it is evident that media, including television and magazines, portray these ideals (e.g. Pope et al., 2000; Herbozo et al., 2004; Harrison & Hefner, 2008; Stankiewicz & Rosselli, 2008). Second, even elementary school children, perhaps particularly girls, are aware of these images and are interested in adopting them (Murnen et al., 2003). Third, media have been related to body image concerns among girls and boys in correlational, experimental, and meta-analytic research (Barlett et al., 2008; Grabe et al., 2008).

Analysing over 90 different effect sizes, Grabe et al., (2008) found a small to moderate relationship between media exposure and body dissatisfaction in girls and women. These 90 studies covered a range of ages and media types and included both experimental and correlational studies. The effect size was homogeneous, i.e. was the same across all types of studies. Grabe and her colleagues also reported a moderate relationship between internationalization of the thin ideal and media exposure. Again, this applied across all ages and media types.

For boys and men, exposure to the media's muscular ideal is related to lower body satisfaction (Barlett et al., 2008). This relationship was stronger for adults than for adolescents. This meta-analysis did not, however, examine the effects of media on boys' interest in being thinner. More research on the influence of media on both muscularity and thinness concerns among boys is warranted.

However, the youngest children in the studies included in the Grabe meta-analysis were 10 and in the Barlett analysis were 12, so it remains unclear whether younger children will show the same effects. Dohnt and Tiggemann (2006) found that 5–8-year-old girls' media use was not related to body dissatisfaction though it was related to dieting awareness and appearance satisfaction. Murnen and colleagues (2003) found that media awareness and internalization were related to body esteem in both elementary school age boys and girls, although the relationships were stronger for girls. On the other hand, Ricciardelli et al., (2006) found that perceived media pressure to achieve a muscular body did not predict body dissatisfaction among 8–11-year-old boys. While it seems possible that there will be media–body image relationships among younger children, the specifics remain unclear.

Parents

Parents may influence children's ideas about the ideal body shape as well as their body images in a variety of ways. First, parents may model beliefs and behaviours related to weight and shape. For example, children's perceptions of their mothers' body dissatisfaction influence the children's own body dissatisfaction (e.g. Lowes & Tiggemann, 2003). Even mothers of preschoolers prefer thinner shapes for children (Musher-Eizenman et al., 2004) and may inadvertently convey this message to the children. Parents might also make direct comments to their children concerning the child's shape or potential shape. Although mothers of preschoolers deny making such comments (e.g. McCabe et al., 2007), research repeatedly indicates that comments from parents about their child's body shape negatively impact the child's body satisfaction (e.g. Smolak et al., 1999; Wertheim et al., 2002). This may be particularly true for maternal comments to their daughters.

Parents may also influence their children's eating habits by the foods they provide and forbid. Parental rules about eating may be an attempt to control a child's weight from an early age (Costanzo & Woody, 1985). Studies indicate that parental attempts to intrusively control children's eating are associated with increased risk for obesity, lower levels of ability to self-regulate eating, and lower self-esteem (Fisher et al., 2009). These negative effects on body image and eating begin to appear during the pre-school years. These rules may send messages to the children about the ideal body shape and the best ways to obtain it.

Peers

Peers, too, can either model an investment in the thin or muscular ideal or they can make direct comments to each other. Even among young girls, perceptions of peers' body dissatisfaction is related to the girl's own body dissatisfaction (Dohnt & Tiggemann, 2006). 'Fat talk', in which girls talk about and criticize the unattractive aspects of their bodies (Nichter, 2000), also provides a model of body ideals and the unacceptability of one's current body. In fact, peer conversations about weight and shape may generally be related to girls' body esteem (Jones, 2004). During early adolescence, having a friend who is dieting predicts the development of body size concerns (Paxton et al., 2006). Thus, there are several ways in which peers can model body ideals, concerns, and dissatisfaction impacting on individual girl's body image.

In addition to modelling, peers also make direct comments to each other about weight and shape. There are at least two forms of this direct commentary: teasing and sexual harassment. In a recent meta-analysis, a moderate–large relationship was found between teasing and body dissatisfaction. This relationship was stronger in children & adolescents than in studies with adult samples (Menzel et al., 2010). Obese children and adolescents are particularly likely to be teased and experience lower body esteem as a result (Neumark-Sztainer, 2011).

Sexual harassment is also associated with lower body esteem among girls. Sexual harassment is quite common and by high school the vast majority of high school girls have experienced it (Leaper & Brown, 2008). In elementary school, cross-gender sexual harassment is related to lower weight-shape esteem in girls but not boys (Murnen & Smolak, 2000). Both qualitative (Larkin, 1994) and quantitative (Harned, 2000) data have related sexual harassment to body dissatisfaction among adolescent girls. Furthermore, sexual harassment may be part of the broader sexualization and objectification of girls (American Psychological Association, Task Force on the Sexualization of Girls, 2007; Smolak, 2009). This means that girls may interpret sexual harassment within a different context than boys do. Prospective data are, therefore, desperately needed to better understand the extent and nature of these relationships, including the gendered context within which sexual harassment is interpreted (Smolak, 2010).

Neurochemistry and genetics

Although most theory and research concerning children's and adolescents' body ideals and body image focuses on sociocultural factors, there are increasing calls for consideration of genetic and neurochemical influences (Kaye et al., 2009; Suisman & Klump, 2011). Although research has suggested some neurochemical correlates of body image disturbances and disordered eating, there are no data from children or adolescents assessing these relationships. This omission has at least two important implications (Smolak, 2009, 2011). First, it means that we can say little about neurochemical correlates of body dissatisfaction in children or adolescents. It is not clear that adult correlates will also apply to children. Second, neuroscientists argue that the brain is a self-organizing system that is deeply affected and shaped by experiences and environment (Cichetti & Curtis, 2006). Indeed, even the problematic body image or disordered eating itself could create neurological 'scar effects', yielding brain differences that are outcomes rather than causes of the problems (Lilenfeld et al., 2006). This is a challenging and crucial area for future research.

Limited research on genetic influences indicates that there is no genetic influence on weight and shape concerns among preadolescent girls. While there is a moderate genetic effect for body dissatisfaction in preadolescent girls, it was smaller than among adolescent girls (Klump et al., 2010). These findings may indicate a role of pubertal hormones in the development of a genetic component of body image/eating problems (Suisman & Klump, 2011).

Self and social relationships

Self

By mid-elementary school, body esteem is part of self-esteem (Harter, 2003). How much body esteem influences general self-esteem is still a debated question as is the direction of the body esteem–self-esteem relationship. For example, cross-sectional data indicate that low self-esteem is related to girls' higher belief in the importance of thinness (Durkin et al., 2007). Longitudinal data, however, are inconsistent in documenting a relationship (Wertheim et al., 2009). Similarly, the data relating self-esteem and body dissatisfaction in boys paint an inconsistent picture (Ricciardelli et al., 2009).

There is, however, convincing prospective evidence that negative body esteem predicts depressive symptomology, at least among adolescent girls (e.g. Stice et al., 2000; Stice & Bearman, 2001). Indeed, Stice and Bearman (2001) suggested that gender differences in body dissatisfaction may at least partly account for the well-established gender differences in depression.

Finally, body dissatisfaction in early adolescence predicts the development of eating pathology. This relationship has been documented in over a dozen studies (Wertheim et al., 2009). While there are many components to disordered eating, there is little doubt that it involves serious, even life-threatening, disturbances of self.

Social relations

Adolescents spend a considerable amount of time engaging in appearance-related conversations, including 'fat talk' (Jones, 2004; Nichter, 2000). Girls participate in such discussions more than boys do. Such interactions are related to poorer body image in both boys and girls (Jones, 2004).

Girls who are concerned with being thin believe that losing weight will help their social relationships, especially with boys (Paxton et al., 1991). They also change their eating patterns, eating less in front of boys than when they eat with others for example, with their families. These eating patterns are associated with disordered eating (McKnight Investigators, 2003). Thus, body image concerns do affect how girls interact with their peers.

Appearance-altering techniques

Dieting

Even fairly young children are trying to control their weight. Elementary school children are aware of dieting as a weight loss technique (Lowes & Tiggemann, 2003; Murnen et al., 2003). Girls as young as 9 are trying to lose weight, frequently by dieting (Field et al., 1999b). Among White, Hispanic, and American Indian adolescent girls, more than 20% may be engaging in calorie restrictive dieting. A smaller percentage of black and Asian American girls are dieting (French, et al., 1997). Boys, too, engage in dieting to lose weight (Ricciardelli et al., 2003).

This dieting is neither healthy nor risk-free. For example, teenage girls who engage in self-imposed, calorie-restrictive dieting are more likely to actually gain weight over the next few years (Stice et al., 1999; Neumark-Sztainer et al., 2006) though teenage boys may not face the same risk (Field et al., 2003). Furthermore, dieting is implicated in the development of disordered eating and eating disorders (Spear, 2006). For example, adolescent boys and girls who diet have been found to engage in more binge eating five years later; girls also purge (Neumark-Sztainer et al., 2006). Such findings concerning purging underscore that adolescents also use more extreme weight-loss techniques in response to negative body image. Such techniques include fasting, crash dieting, and purging via vomiting or laxative abuse (Wertheim et al., 2009).

Muscle-building

A variety of muscle-building techniques are available. Boys especially are likely to engage in exercise, weight lifting, eating more, and using food supplements and steroids in order to build muscles (Ricciardelli et al., 2003; Smolak & Stein, 2010). For example, Smolak and Stein (2010) reported that among 7th and 8th grade white boys, 87.3% exercised, 83.6% lifted weights, 40.8% ate more, 20.7% used food supplements, and 3.5% took steroids at least occasionally during the past year in order to build muscle. Again, these techniques do carry risks, including permanent injury, growth stunting, heart irregularities, and death (Cafri et al., 2005). At least with older teens, prevention programmes can reduce the likelihood of the use of steroids and food supplements (Goldberg & Elliot, 2000).

Cosmetic surgery

There are several types of body reshaping cosmetic surgeries used by adolescents. Liposuction was the fourth most frequently used cosmetic surgery among adolescents.

This is at best a temporary solution for obesity or overweight; indeed, people rarely lose significant amounts of weight as an outcome of liposuction (Sarwer et al., 2009). This, of course, is not consistent with what anorexic or bulimic girls believe when they undergo the procedure. This unrealistic expectation can contribute to a worsening of symptoms post-surgically. Late adolescent women (18–19 years old) also undergo breast enhancement, with over 10,000 procedures in 2007 (Sarwer et al., 2009). As with cosmetic surgery to alter facial appearance, these procedures carry risks of infection and even death from haemorrhaging or anaesthesia errors. Research is desperately needed to help guide physicians' evaluation of and advice to adolescents seeking these surgeries.

CONCLUSIONS

This chapter has demonstrated that appearance preferences, focusing on facial attractiveness as well as on weight and shape, are evident in boys and girls during the preschool years. By elementary school, children are actually concerned about their appearance and begin to take steps to alter it. The appearance concerns may impact self and social functioning as well as mental health. As such, these are serious issues, worthy of both research and public policy attention.

The public policy attention should include programmes to facilitate the acceptance of a wider range of appearances. Without such prevention efforts, both girls and boys are at risk of developing health-endangering behaviours such as dieting, disordered eating, and steroid abuse. Successful prevention programmes are available to combat body dissatisfaction in children and adolescents (Levine & Smolak, 2006, 2009) although more research is needed to improve their efficacy and to expand their applicability to various ethnic and age groups, as well as to boys.

A substantial amount of research has investigated contributors to appearance beliefs and concerns. It is evident that sociocultural factors play an important role. Yet, more research is needed. In particular, we need much more research on the body concerns of boys and of children from ethnic minority groups. We also need to better understand how broad social factors, such as gender roles or social class, form the backdrop for the interpretation of social messages about appearance. Such information will help us more effectively tailor prevention programmes.

REFERENCES

Allen, K. L., Byrne, S. M., Blair, E. M., & Davis, E. A. (2006). Why do some overweight children experience psychological problems? The role of weight and shape concerns. *International Journal of Pediatric Obesity*, 1, 238–47.

American Psychological Association, Task Force on the Sexualization of Girls. (2007). *Report of the APA Task Force on the Sexualization of Girls.* Washington, DC: APA.

American Psychological Association. (2007). *Sexualization of Girls.* www.apa.org/pi/wpo/sexualization.html.

American Society of Plastic Surgeons (2010). *2010 report of the 2009 statistics: National Clearinghouse of plastic surgery statistics.* http://www.plasticsurgery.org/News-and-Resources/2009-Statistics.html

Anderson-Fye, E. (2009). Cross-cultural issues in body image among children and adolescents. In L. Smolak & J. K. Thompson (eds.) *Body image, eating disorders, and obesity in youth: Assessment, prevention, and treatment* (2nd edn.), pp. 113–34. Washington, DC: American Psychological Association.

Barlett, C. P., Vowels, C. L., & Saucier, D. A. (2008). Meta-analyses of the effects of media images on men's body-image concerns. *Journal of Social and Clinical Psychology, 27,* 279–310.

Boyatzis, C., Baloff, P., & Durieux, C. (1998). Effects of perceived attractiveness and academic success on early adolescent peer popularity. *Journal of Genetic Psychology, 159,* 337–44.

Cafri, G., Thompson, J.K., Ricciardelli, L., McCabe, M., Smolak, L., & Yesalis, C. (2005). Pursuit of the muscular ideal: Physical and psychological consequences and putative risk factors. *Clinical Psychology Review, 25,* 215–39.

Cichetti, D. & Curtis, W. J. (2006). The developing brain and neural plasticity: Implications for normality, psychopathology, and resilience. In D. Cicchetti & D. Cohen (eds.) *Developmental psychopathology* (2nd edn.), *Volume Two: Developmental Neuroscience,* pp. 1–64. New York: Wiley.

Clark, M. & Ayers, M. (1988). The role of reciprocity and proximity in junior high school friendships. *Journal of Youth and Adolescence, 17,* 403–11.

Costanzo, P. R. & Woody, E. Z. (1985). Domain-specific parenting styles and their impact on the child's development of particular deviance: The example of obesity proneness. *Journal of Social and Clinical Psychology, 3,* 425–45.

Cramer, P. & Steinwet, T. (1998). Thin is good, fat is bad: How early does it begin? *Journal of Applied Development Psychology, 19,* 429–51.

Dalgard, F., Gieler, U., Holm, J., Bjertness, E., & Hauser, S. (2008). Self-esteem and body satisfaction among late adolescents with acne: Results from a population study. *Journal of the American Academy of Dermatology, 59,* 746–51.

Davison, K., Markey, C., & Birch, L.L. (2000). Etiology of body dissatisfaction and weight concerns among 5-year-old girls. *Appetite, 35,* 143–51.

Dion, K. K. (1973). Young children's stereotyping of facial attractiveness. *Developmental Psychology, 9,* 183–8.

Dohnt, H. K. & Tiggemann, M. (2004). The development of perceived body size and dieting awareness in young girls. *Perceptual and Motor Skills, 99,* 790–2.

Dohnt, H. K. & Tiggemann, M. (2006). Body image concerns in young girls: The role of peers and media prior to adolescence. *Journal of Youth and Adolescence, 35,* 141–51.

Durkin, S., Paxton, S., & Sorbello, M. (2007). Mediators of the impact of exposure to idealized female images on adolescent girls' body satisfaction: An integrative model. *Journal of Applied Social Psychology, 37,* 1092–117.

Field, A., Cheung, L., Wolf, A., Herzog, D., Gortmaker, S., & Colditz, G. (1999a). Exposure to the mass media and weight concerns among girls. *Pediatrics, 103,* e36.

Field, A., Camargo, C., Taylor, C., Berkey, C., Frazier, L., Gillman, M., & Colditz, G. (1999b). Overweight, weight concerns, and bulimic behaviors among girls and boys. *Journal of the American Academy of Child and Adolescent Psychiatry*, 38, 754–60.

Field, A. E., Austin, S. B., Taylor, C. B., Malspeis, S., Rosner, B., Rockett, H. R., *et al.*, (2003). Relation between dieting and weight change among preadolescents and adolescents. *Pediatrics*, 112, 900–6.

Fisher, J. O., Sinton, M. M., & Birch, L. L. (2009). Early parental influence and risk for the emergence of disordered eating. In L. Smolak & J. K. Thompson (eds.) *Body image, eating disorders, and obesity in youth: Assessment, prevention, and treatment* (2nd edn.), pp. 17–34. Washington, DC: American Psychological Association.

Franko, D. L. & Edwards George, J. B. (2009). Overweight, eating behaviors, and body image in ethnically diverse youth. In L. Smolak & J. K. Thompson (eds.) *Body image, eating disorders, and obesity in youth: Assessment, prevention, and treatment* (2nd edn.), pp. 97–112. Washington, DC: American Psychological Association.

French, S., Story, M., Neumark-Sztainer, D., Downes, B., Resnick, M., & Blum, R. (1997). Ethnic differences in psychosocial and health behavior correlates of dieting, purging, and binge eating in a population-based sample of adolescent females. *International Journal of Eating Disorders*, 22, 315–22.

Goldberg, L. & Elliot, D. (2000). Prevention of anabolic steroid use. In L. Goldberg & D. Elliot (eds.) *Anabolic steroids in sports and exercise* (2nd edn.), pp. 117–35. Champaign IL: Human Kinetics.

Grabe, S., Ward, L. M., & Hyde, J. S. (2008). The role of the media in body image concerns among women: A meta-analysis of experimental and correlational studies. *Psychological Bulletin*, 134, 460–6.

Harned, M. (2000). Harassed bodies: An examination of the relationships among women's experiences of sexual harassment, body image, and eating disturbances. *Psychology of Women Quarterly*, 24, 336–48.

Harrison, K. & Hefner, V. (2008). Body image and eating disorders. In S. L. Calvert & B. J. Wilson (eds.) *Handbook of child development and the media*, pp. 645–89. Malden, MA: Blackwell.

Harter, S. (2003). The development of self-representations during childhood and adolescence. In M. R. Leary & J. P. Tangney (eds.) *Handbook of self and identity*, pp. 610–42. New York: Guilford.

Herbozo, S., Tantleff-Dunn, S., Gokee-Larose, J., & Thompson, J. K. (2004). Beauty and thinness messages in children's media: A content analysis. *Eating Disorders*, 12, 21–34.

Holub, S. C. (2008). Individual differences in the anti-fat attitudes of preschool-children: The importance of perceived body size. *Body Image*, 5, 317–21.

Hoss, R. A. & Langlois, J. H. (2003). Infants prefer attractive faces. In O. Pascalis & A. Slater (eds.) *The development of face processing in infancy and early childhood: Current perspectives*, pp. 27–38. New York: Nova Science.

Hoss, R. A., Ramsey, J. L., Griffin, A. M., & Langlois, J. H. (2005). The role of facial attractiveness and facial masculinity/femininity in sex classification of faces. *Perception*, 34, 1459–74.

Jones, D. C. (2004). Body image among adolescent girls and boys: A longitudinal study. *Developmental Psychology*, 40, 823–35.

Jones, D. C., Bain, N., & King, S. (2008). Weight and muscularity concerns as longitudinal predictors of body image among early adolescent boys: A test of the dual pathways model. *Body Image*, 5, 195–204.

Kaye, W., Fudge, J., & Paulus, M. (2009). New insights into symptoms and neurocircuit function of anorexia nervosa. *Nature Reviews Neuroscience*, 10, 573–84.

Klump, K., Burt, S. A., Spanos, A., McGue, M., Iacono, W., & Wade, T. (2010). Age differences in genetic and environmental influences on weight and shape concerns. *International Journal of Eating Disorders*, 43, 679–88.

Kornblau, I., Pearson, H., & Breitkopf, C. R. (2007). Demographic, behavioral, and physical correlates of body esteem among low-income female adolescents. *Journal of Adolescent Health*, 41, 566–70.

Langlois, J. H. & Downs, A. C. (1979). Peer relations as a function of physical attractiveness: The eye of the beholder or behavioral reality. *Child Development*, 50, 409–418.

Larkin, J. (1994). *Sexual harassment: High school girls speak out*. Kensington MD: Second Story Press.

Leaper, C. & Brown, C. (2008). Perceived experiences with sexism among adolescent girls. *Child Development*, 79, 685–704.

Levine, M. P. & Smolak, L. (2006). *The prevention of eating problems and eating disorders: Theory, research, and practice*. Mahwah, NJ: Lawrence Erlbaum Associates.

Levine, M. P. & Smolak, L. (2009). Recent developments and promising directions in the prevention of negative body image and disordered eating in children and adolescents. In L. Smolak & J. K. Thompson (eds.) *Body image, eating disorders, and obesity in youth: Assessment, prevention, and treatment* (2nd edn.), pp. 215–40. Washington, DC: American Psychological Association.

Lilenfeld, L., Wonderlich, S., Riso, L., Crosby, R., & Mitchell, J. (2006). Eating disorders and personality: A methodological and empirical review. *Clinical Psychology Review*, 26, 299–320.

Lowes, J. & Tiggemann, M. (2003). Body dissatisfaction, dieting awareness and the impact of parental influence in young children. *British Journal of Health Psychology*, 8, 135–47.

Magazine.org (2004). *Teen market profile*. Magazine Publishers of America. Available at http://www.magazine.org/content/files/teenprofile04.pdf (accessed on August 26, 2010)

Magin, P., Adams, J., Heading, G., Pond, D., & Smith, W. (2008). Experiences of appearance- related teasing and bullying in skin diseases and their psychological sequelae: Results of a qualitative study. *Scandinavian Journal of Caring Sciences*, 22, 430–6.

Marsh, H. W., Craven, R., & Debus, R. (1998). Structure, stability, and development of young children's self-concepts: A muticohort-multioccasion study. *Child Development*, 69, 1030–53.

McCabe, M. P., Ricciardelli, L. A., Stanford, J., Holt, K., Keegan, S., & Miller, L. (2007). Where is all the pressure coming from? Messages from mothers and teachers about preschool children's appearance, diet and exercise. *European Eating Disorders Review*, 15, 221–30.

McKnight Investigators (2003). Risk factors for the onset of eating disorders in adolescent girls: Results of the McKnight longitudinal risk factor study. *American Journal of Psychiatry*, 160, 248–54.

Menzel, J., Schaefer, L., Burke, N., Mayhew, L., Brannick, M., & Thompson, J.K. (2010). Appearance-related teasing, body dissatisfaction, and disordered eating: A meta-analysis. *Body Image*, 7, 261–70.

Murnen, S. K. & Smolak, L. (2000). The experience of sexual harassment among grade-school students: Early socialization of female subordination? *Sex Roles*, 43, 1–17.

Murnen, S. K., Smolak, L., Mills, J. A., & Good, L. (2003). Thin, sexy women and strong muscular men: Grade-school children's responses to objectified images of women and men. *Sex Roles*, 49, 427–37.

Musher-Eizenman, D. R., Holub, S. C., Barnhart Miller, A., Goldstein, S. E., & Edwards-Leeper, L. (2004). Body size stigmatization in preschool children: The role of control attributions. *Journal of Pediatric Psychology*, 29, 615–20.

Neumark-Sztainer, D. (2011). Obesity and body images in youth. In T. F. Cash & L. Smolak (eds.) *Body image: A handbook of science, practice, and prevention* (2nd edn.), pp. 180–8. New York: Guilford.

Neumark-Sztainer, D., Wall, M., Guo, J., Story, M., Haines, J., & Eisenberg, M. (2006). Obesity, disordered eating and eating disorders in a longitudinal study of adolescents: How do dieters fare 5 years later? *Journal of the American Dietetic Association*, 106, 559–68.

Nichter, M. (2000). *Fat talk: What girls and their parents say about dieting*. Cambridge, MA: Harvard University Press.

Paxton, S., Eisenberg, M., & Neumark-Sztainer, D. (2006). Prospective predictors of body dissatisfaction in adolescent girls and boys: A five-year longitudinal study. *Developmental Psychology*, 42, 888–99.

Paxton, S., Wertheim, E., Gibbons, K., Szmukler, G., Hillier, L., & Petrovich, J. (1991). Body image satisfaction, dieting beliefs and weight loss behaviors in adolescent girls and boys. *Journal of Youth and Adolescence*, 20, 361–79.

Penny, H. & Haddock, G. (2007). Anti-fat prejudice among children: The 'mere proximity' effect in 5–10 year olds. *Journal of Experimental Social Psychology*, 43, 678–83.

Pope, H., Phillips, K., & Olivardia, R. (2000). *The Adonis complex: The secret crisis of male body obsession*. New York: The Free Press.

Ramsey, J. L. & Langlois, J. H. (2002). Effects of the 'beauty is good' stereotype on children's information processing. *Journal of Experimental Child Psychology*, 81, 320–40.

Ramsey, J. L., Langlois, J. H., Hoss, R. A., Rubenstein, A. J., & Griffin, A. M. (2004). Origins of a stereotype: Categorization of facial attractiveness by 6-month-old infants. *Developmental Science*, 7, 201–11.

Ricciardelli, L., McCabe, M., Holt, K., & Finemore, J. (2003). A biopsychosocial model for understanding body image and body change strategies among children. *Journal of Applied Developmental Psychology*, 24, 475–95.

Ricciardelli, L., McCabe, M., Lillis, J., & Thomas, K. (2006). A longitudinal investigation of the development of weight and muscle concerns among pre-adolescent boys. *Journal of Youth and Adolescence*, 35, 177–87.

Ricciardelli, L. A., McCabe, M. P., Mussap, A. J., & Holt, K. E. (2009). Body image in pre-adolescent boys. In L. Smolak & J. K. Thompson (eds.) *Body image, eating disorders, and obesity in youth: Assessment, prevention, and treatment* (2nd edn.), pp. 77–96. Washington DC: American Psychological Association.

Rubenstein, A., Kalakanis, L., & Langlois, J. (1999). Infant preferences for attractive faces: A cognitive explanation. *Developmental Psychology*, 35, 848–55.

Sarwer, D. B., Infeld, A. L., & Crerand, C. E. (2009). Plastic surgery for children and adolescents. In L. Smolak & J. K. Thompson (eds.), *Body image, eating disorders, and obesity in youth: Assessment, prevention, and treatment* (2nd edn.), pp. 303–26. Washington DC: American Psychological Association.

Shaw, W. C. (1981). The influence of dentofacial appearance on their social attractiveness as judged by peers and lay adults. *American Journal of Orthodontics*, 79, 399–415.

Sigelman, C., Miller, T., & Whitworth, L. (1986). The early development of stigmatizing reactions to physical differences. *Journal of Applied Developmental Psychology*, 7, 17–32.

Slater, A., Quinn, P. C., Hayes, R., & Brown, E. (2000). Newborn infants' preference for attractive faces: The role of internal and external facial features. *Infancy*, 1, 265–74.

Smolak, L. (2009). Risk factors in the development of body image, eating problems, and obesity. In L. Smolak & J. K. Thompson (eds.) *Body image, eating disorders, and obesity in youth: Assessment, prevention, and treatment* (2nd edn.), pp. 135–56. Washington DC: American Psychological Association.

Smolak, L. (2010). Gender as culture: The meanings of self-silencing in women and men. In D. C. Jack & A. Ali (eds.) *Silencing the self across cultures: Depression and gender in the social world*, pp. 129–46. New York: Oxford.

Smolak, L. (2011). Body image development in children. In T. F. Cash & L. Smolak (eds.), *Body image: A handbook of science, practice, and prevention* (2nd edn.), pp. 67–75. New York: Guilford.

Smolak, L., Levine, M.P., & Schermer, F. (1999). Parental input and weight concerns among elementary school children. *International Journal of Eating Disorders*, 25, 263–71.

Smolak, L. & Stein, J. A. (2006). The relationship of drive for muscularity to sociocultural factors, self-esteem, physical attributes gender role, and social comparison in middle school boys. *Body Image*, 3, 121–29.

Smolak, L. & Stein, J.A. (2010). A longitudinal investigation of gender role and muscle building in adolescent boys. *Sex Roles*, 63, 738–46.

Spear, B. (2006). Does dieting increase the risk for obesity and eating disorders? *Journal of the American Dietetic Association*, 106, 523–25.

Stankiewicz, J. M. & Rosselli, F. (2008). Women as sex objects and victims in print advertisements. *Sex Roles*, 58, 579–89.

Stice, E., & Bearman, S.K. (2001). Body-image and eting disturbances prospectively predict increases in depressive symptoms in adolescent girls: A growth curve analysis. *Developmental Psychology*, 37, 597–607.

Stice, E., Cameron, R., Hayward, C., Taylor, C. B., & Killen, J. (1999). Naturalistic weight-reduction efforts prospectively predict growth in relative weight and onset among female adolescents. *Journal of Consulting and Clinical Psychology*, 67, 967–74.

Stice, E., Hayward, C., Cameron, R. P., Killen, J. D., & Taylor, C.B. (2000). Body-image and eating disturbances predict onset of depression among female adolescents: A longitudinal study. *Journal of Abnormal Psychology*, 109, 438–44.

Striegel-Moore, R. & Kearney-Cooke, A. (1994). Exploring parents' attitudes and behaviors about their children's physical appearance. *International Journal of Eating Disorders*, 15, 377–85.

Suisman, J. & Klump, K. (2011). Genetic and neuroscientific perspectives on body image. In T.F. Cash & L. Smolak (eds.), *Body image: A handbook of science, practice, and prevention* (2nd edn.), pp. 29–38. New York: Guilford.

Thompson, J. K., Heinberg, L., Altabe, M., & Tantleff-Dunn, S. (1999). *Exacting beauty: Theory, assessment, and treatment of body image disturbance.* Washington, DC: American Psychological Association.

Thompson, J.K., van den Berg, P., Roehrig, M., Guarda, S., & Heinberg, L.J. (2004). The sociocultural attitudes towards appearance scale-3 (SATAQ-3): Development and validation. *International Journal of Eating Disorders*, 35, 293–304.

Wertheim, E. H., Martin, G., Prior, M., Sanson, A., & Smart, D. (2002). Parent influences in the transmission of eating and weight related values and behaviors. *Eating Disorders: The Journal of Treatment and Prevention*, 10, 321–34.

Wertheim, E. H., Paxton, S. J., & Blaney, S. (2009). Body image in girls. In L. Smolak & J. K. Thompson (eds.) *Body image, eating disorders, and obesity in youth: Assessment, prevention, and treatment* (2nd edn.), pp. 47–76. Washington, DC: American Psychological Association.

CHAPTER 13

APPEARANCE IN ADULTHOOD

MARIKA TIGGEMANN
JULIE SLEVEC

INTRODUCTION

APPEARANCE has become a very important part of contemporary life in Western societies. This focus can be clearly seen on billboards, in shop windows, in any magazine, in the ordinary conversations of individuals, and in the amount of money, time, and effort invested in the pursuit of beauty through clothes, hair, dieting, and other everyday grooming practices. While there are many individual attributes that make up an individual's appearance, much of the research has focused on body shape and weight. This is not surprising when current societal standards for beauty particularly emphasize size and shape, prescribing an inordinately thin ideal for women, and a muscular v-shaped ideal for men. Although these ideals are impossible for most men and women to achieve by healthy means, they are nevertheless adopted by many, to almost invariably result in dissatisfaction. Indeed, there is a great deal of evidence that many women and girls are dissatisfied with their bodies, particularly with their body size and weight and wish to be thinner. There is also evidence that men and boys are beginning to experience increasing levels of body dissatisfaction.

However, by far the majority of studies investigating appearance concerns have used samples drawn from student populations, either adolescents in high school or young adults at university. Consequently, the latter have been restricted to a narrow age range of between about 18–25 years (Grogan, 2008), as well as restricted in terms of ethnicity, socioeconomic status, and education level. Thus they provide little insight into appearance concerns in mid-adulthood or across the lifespan. This chapter sets out to review the findings from empirical research with adults older than the typical university student. Two major research questions are addressed. First, are there age changes in appearance concern across adulthood? Second, what factors are associated with appearance concern in adulthood?

AGE CHANGES ACROSS ADULTHOOD

Age changes in appearance

There is no doubt that changes in physical appearance present a challenge in middle adulthood. As people typically put on weight through the lifespan, every year is likely to take them further away from the thin (or muscular) body ideal. In addition, for women, all the biological milestones of puberty, pregnancy, and menopause have the potential to increase fat deposition through the operation of sex hormones (Rodin et al., 1985). For example, women typically put on 25–35 pounds (11–16 kilograms) across the pregnancy, some of which is retained after delivery (Heinberg & Guarda, 2002). Similarly, weight typically becomes redistributed during menopause (usually around age of 50), resulting in larger waist and more rounded shape.

In addition to these changes in body weight and shape, there are (undesirable) alterations in skin elasticity and hair quality that accompany ageing. People develop wrinkles and their hair thins and turns grey—all tangible signs of ageing in the context of contemporary society where youthfulness is valued. Again, these normal age-related changes are likely to be particularly problematic for women, in that women gain status and value through appearance (Wilcox, 1997), and thus are more concerned than men about the visible effects of ageing (Gupta & Schork, 1993). Such concern is justified, in that a number of authors (e.g. Wilcox, 1997) point to a 'double standard of aging', whereby older women are judged much more harshly than older men.

Age differences in satisfaction with appearance

Like their younger counterparts, body dissatisfaction is commonly reported in samples of middle-aged women. Typically, somewhere between 55–75% of women express dissatisfaction with their bodies, most notably with their weight, their waist, stomach, hips, buttocks, and thighs. For example, Allaz et al. (1998) found that in a representative sample of over 1000 women aged 30–74 years in Geneva, Switzerland, 71% wanted to be thinner, most of whom (73%) were of normal weight.

A number of studies have set out specifically to investigate age effects on body dissatisfaction by comparing the figure preference ratings of middle-aged adults with young adults, usually college students (e.g. Rozin & Fallon, 1988; Tiggemann, 1992; Altabe & Thompson, 1993; Demarest & Allen, 2000). These have uniformly found greater body dissatisfaction (measured as the discrepancy between current and ideal ratings) for women than men, and with no effect of age on women's body dissatisfaction. In the main, these findings have been replicated with other measures of appearance or body dissatisfaction. For women, desire to be thinner does not appear to differ between age groups (Allaz et al., 1998). Nor does body esteem (e.g. McKinley, 1999; Tiggemann & Lynch, 2001; Webster & Tiggemann, 2003), satisfaction with appearance (Gupta & Schork, 1993; Wilcox, 1997; Thompson et al., 1998; Paxton & Phythian, 1999; Algars et al., 2009), or satisfaction with body parts (Cash & Henry, 1995; Wilcox, 1997; Deeks & McCabe, 2001).

On the basis of the available research evidence, most commentators (e.g. Tiggemann, 2004a; Grogan, 2008) have reasonably concluded that women's dissatisfaction with their bodies and appearance appears quite stable across the adult life span, at least until they have become quite elderly. There are a number of potential reasons for this somewhat surprising (given the clear changes in physical appearance described earlier) result. Grogan (2008) has speculated that women may shift their body comparisons to age-appropriate peers as they age, rather than to the thin and youthful ideals portrayed in the media. Tiggemann (2004a) has suggested that adult women may also have more realistic expectations about what is possible for them. They may also have a wider range of experience with 'real' men, who actually prefer a larger female figure than the ideal figure generally chosen by women (e.g. Rozin & Fallon, 1988; Markey et al., 2004). In support, Demarest and Allen (2000) found that participants over 30 years were much more accurate than younger participants in their assessment of what the opposite sex found most attractive.

Of these studies which have included men in their sampling, nearly all demonstrate strong gender differences whereby women report more body dissatisfaction than do men (Rozin & Fallon, 1988; Tiggemann, 1992; Altabe & Thompson, 1993; Paxton & Phythian, 1999; Demarest & Allen, 2000; Algars et al., 2009). However, adult men typically also display some level of body dissatisfaction (Rozin & Fallon, 1988; Paxton & Phythian, 1999; Algars et al., 2009). A review of men's body image across the lifespan by McCabe and Ricciardelli (2004) suggested that body dissatisfaction among adult men is not as straightforward as it is among adult women. The authors concluded that while adolescent boys and young adult men are primarily focused on increasing muscle size, adult men are more focused on both losing weight and increasing muscle tone, particularly as they get older. More recently, Tiggemann et al. (2007) have confirmed that the majority of men (both heterosexual and homosexual) across the age range 18–60 years want to be both more muscular and less fat. Age was related to increased dissatisfaction with level of adiposity (fatness) but not muscularity.

Age differences in dieting, disordered eating, and cosmetic surgery

One response to the seemingly pervasive wish to be thinner among women is to diet to lose weight, and reported rates of dieting remain high among adult women. For example, Allaz et al. (1998) found that 42% of their sample of 30–74-year-old women had dieted in the last 5 years. More recently, Gravener et al. (2008) reported that 11% of middle-aged women in a large epidemiological study were 'usually' or 'always' dieting. In addition, although eating disorders are generally considered to be disorders of adolescence or young adulthood, in recent years there has been growing recognition that these disorders may also occur during midlife (Forman & Davis, 2005; Midlarsky & Nitzburg, 2008). Certainly more broadly defined mal-adaptive eating attitudes and behaviours are common during midlife (Procopio et al., 2006; Marcus et al., 2007; Keel et al., 2010). For example, in a community sample, 14.8% of middle-aged women were classified as having disordered eating as assessed by the Eating Attitudes Test (Midlarsky & Nitzburg, 2008).

The research examining age differences in dieting or disordered eating has produced mixed results. On the one hand, McKinley (1999) reported similar rates of dieting and restricted eating among undergraduate women and their mothers. Similarly, Bennett and Stevens (1996), Stokes and Frederick-Recascino (2003), and Perez et al. (2007) found no difference in disordered eating symptoms across their age groups, and Tiggemann (2004b) found no longitudinal change in dietary restraint over 8 years. In contrast, Tiggemann and Lynch (2001) reported decreases in dietary restraint and disordered eating with age across their 20–85-year age range of women. Similarly, Patrick and Stahl (2009) also reported decreases with age in dieting and disordered eating. Two longitudinal studies following up samples who were initially college students (Heatherton et al., 1997; McKinley, 2006a) also found a decline in dieting frequency and disordered eating attitudes and behaviours in women over 10 years. Nevertheless, chronic dieting appears to remain a problem for a substantial number of adult women.

Another increasingly available option in response to appearance dissatisfaction is cosmetic surgery. No longer the preserve of the rich and famous or psychologically disturbed, nearly 10 million cosmetic procedures (of a surgical and non-surgical nature) were performed in 2009 in the US alone (American Society for Aesthetic Plastic Surgery [ASAPS], 2010). And by far the major consumer group is middle-aged women (ASAPS, 2010). It appears that for this group in particular, cosmetic surgery has opened up a new and attractive method of body manipulation, aimed at meeting unrealistic societal standards of beauty (Sarwer & Crerand, 2004).

In 2009, the top five procedures sought by 35–64-year-old women were liposuction, breast augmentation, blepharoplasty (i.e. eyelid surgery), abdominoplasty (i.e. tummy tuck), and facelift (ASAPS, 2010), procedures largely targeted at reducing fat and maintaining a youthful appearance.

Age differences in appearance investment

Cash and colleagues (e.g. Cash et al., 2004) have drawn an important distinction between evaluation of appearance (dissatisfaction) and investment in appearance. The latter refers to the level of cognitive, behavioural and emotional investment in appearance, that is, its importance to self-worth.

A number of research studies have now documented that, in contrast to dissatisfaction, the importance attached to physical appearance tends to decrease with age. Two of the earliest studies of men and women across the life span (Cash et al., 1986; Pliner et al., 1990) reported a steady decline in interest in and importance of appearance with age, until at least age 60. Similarly Thompson et al. (1998) found a decrease in rated importance of appearance and a greater acceptance of age-related changes in appearance. Webster and Tiggemann (2003) likewise found older women reported greater 'cognitive control' (reappraisal and lowering of expectations) over their bodies than younger women. More recently, Tiggemann and Lacey (2009) found age to be negatively related to a specific measure of appearance investment in their sample of 18–55-year-old women. A number of other studies also indicate that habitual body monitoring (a manifestation of investment in appearance) is lower in middle-aged women than in young adult women (McKinley, 1999; Tiggemann and Lynch, 2001; Augustus-Horvath & Tylka, 2009; Crawford et al., 2009), and in a longitudinal study, McKinley (2006b) found that women's body monitoring decreased over 10 years.

Taken together, the results suggest that as women (and perhaps men) age, they place less emphasis on the importance of the body's appearance. This allows a greater acceptance of the otherwise socially undesirable and uncontrollable age-related changes in appearance. Nevertheless, other indicators like the increase in cosmetic surgery and multi-billion dollar 'anti-ageing' cosmetic industries (Huang & Miller, 2007), show that many middle-aged women continue to place a great deal of importance on appearance.

PREDICTORS OF APPEARANCE CONCERNS IN ADULTHOOD

More recent work has begun the attempt to identify factors associated with body dissatisfaction among middle-aged adults. Some factors are the same as those identified in younger samples, but some are more specific to adult women. They span biological, psychological, and sociocultural factors.

Biological factors

Body mass index (BMI)

Among adult women, BMI has been the most consistently observed correlate of both body dissatisfaction (Forbes et al., 2005; Algars et al., 2009; Tiggemann & Lacey, 2009; Dunkel et al., 2010; McLean et al., 2010) and disordered eating (Marcus et al., 2007; McLean et al., 2010). Studies that have included men indicate that BMI is not as reliable a predictor of men's body dissatisfaction (Algars et al., 2009). In addition, in female shoppers, BMI has been associated with increased use of clothing for camouflage and a less enjoyable shopping experience (Tiggemann & Lacey, 2009). Indeed, being able to fit into clothes is a main motivator for women of all ages (Grogan, 2008).

The evidence suggests that higher BMI may be a genuine risk factor (as opposed to a correlate) for body dissatisfaction and disordered eating. In one prospective study of a birth cohort of 933 British women at age 54 (all these women were born in one particular week in 1946, and then followed-up at regular intervals), McLaren et al. (2003) found that mid-life body dissatisfaction was related not only to higher current BMI, but also to being heavier at age 7, as well as a steeper increase in BMI throughout life. Another recent prospective study of female adult fitness centre members also provided evidence for the temporal precedence of BMI, whereby initial BMI predicted increases in bulimic symptoms over a 12-month period (McCabe et al., 2007).

Pregnancy

In pregnancy a woman's body undergoes rapid physical changes in many ways, but most notably in weight and shape. Women typically put on 25–35 pounds (11–16 kilograms) across the pregnancy with marked changes in body shape, skin and hair quality (Heinberg & Guarda, 2002). In his Psychology Today survey results, Garner (1997) commented that pregnancy is increasingly seen as a problem for body image with some women choosing not to have children for this reason. On the other hand, studies of pregnant women show that while the considerable weight and shape changes can be distressing for some women, for others they can be neutral or even liberating. Thus, on balance, body image seems relatively stable across pregnancy (e.g. Duncombe et al., 2008).

Although there is also variation in the postpartum period, here body image is generally more negative (Rallis et al., 2007). The body rarely returns immediately to its pre-pregnancy shape and many women struggle to lose the weight they have put on. As a consequence, many women are dissatisfied with their weight and shape after having a baby and there is an increase in eating disorder pathology (Baker et al., 1999). One possible reason for disappointment is that women (especially primiparous women) expect that their bodies will return to their pre-pregnancy weight and shape shortly after the birth of their child (Jenkin & Tiggemann, 1997). Increasing media attention to the 'yummy mummy' can only fuel this largely erroneous expectation.

Menopause

Another biological factor closely interrelated with both age and BMI is menopausal status. During menopause (12 consecutive months absence of menses) and peri-menopause (a minimum of 3 but less than 12 months of amenorrhea, or increasingly irregular periods), women experience a change in hormone levels and a decreased metabolic rate, which are associated with weight gain, a redistribution of weight from the lower body to the waist and hips (Voda et al., 1991) and a doubling of the percentage of body fat (Rodin et al., 1985). Nevertheless, surprisingly little research has investigated the body image consequences of menopause.

One qualitative study (Dillaway, 2005) found that women's concerns with menopausal bodies were indeed about 'looking good', which most often equated to maintaining an unchanged appearance over time. The most problematic physical changes nominated included weight gain, skin changes, including growth of hair in unwanted places, loss of skin tone, dryness and discolouring, and sagging breasts. The majority of women attributed these changes directly to menopausal life stage. In support, Deeks and McCabe (2001) found menopausal women to be less positive about their appearance and fitness than pre-menopausal women. On the other hand, Koch et al. (2005) found that women's perceptions of their current attractiveness did not differ on the basis of menopausal status. Similarly, McKinley and Lyon (2008) found body esteem did not differ as a function of menopausal status, although across the board, more positive attitudes toward menopause were related to higher body esteem in their 50–68-year-old women.

However, the extent to which menopausal status, as opposed to BMI or age, accounts for the above findings is not clear. McLaren et al. (2003) were able to separate these effects in their birth cohort study of middle-aged (54-year-old) women. They found that postmenopausal women (and women who had started taking hormone replacement therapy (HRT) before menopause) actually felt more satisfied with their weight than did the pre-menopausal group. Only in the case of HRT users was the effect partly due to these women being thinner. One potential explanation for this result is that women who are pre-menopausal at age 54 are very aware of the imminent transition and thus may feel more anxious about their bodies, compared to those who have finished the transition and are perhaps experiencing fewer symptoms. Alternatively, menopause might mark a point when physical appearance and body image cease to be so important. Future longitudinal studies of women across the menopausal transition are required to investigate these possibilities.

Psychological factors

Internalization of ideals

Internalization refers to the extent to which an individual cognitively 'buys into' and attempts to approximate culturally prescribed beauty ideals of attractiveness (Thompson & Stice, 2001). For younger women, there is strong support for thin-ideal internalization as a risk factor for body image disturbance and disordered eating (see Stice, 2002, for a review). A small number of cross-sectional studies have now also found a positive relationship between internalization and body dissatisfaction (Matz et al., 2002; Forbes et al., 2005) or disordered eating (Share & Mintz, 2002) in middle-aged women. A prospective study of female fitness centre attendees (McCabe et al., 2007) found that internalization of thin ideals predicted preoccupation with eating and alteration of eating habits over a 12-month period.

Importance of appearance

In young women, the importance of, or investment in, appearance has been consistently associated with higher rates of both body dissatisfaction and disordered eating (Cash et al., 2004). This has largely been replicated for middle-aged samples. Tiggemann and Lacey (2009) and Slevec and Tiggemann (2011) found a positive correlation between appearance investment and body dissatisfaction, while McLean et al. (2010) found the importance of appearance to be a unique predictor of both weight and shape concern. Although Slevec and Tiggemann (2010) failed to find a relationship between appearance investment and body dissatisfaction in their sample of middle-aged women, they did find a relationship between appearance investment and positive attitudes and intentions towards cosmetic surgery. Overall, it seems that a decreased emphasis on appearance may afford ageing women some protection against poor body image and appearance concerns (Thompson et al., 1998).

Ageing anxiety

It is hardly surprising that many middle-aged women in Western societies experience anxiety about the ageing process (Barrett & Robbins, 2008). Current media present thin and youthful-looking middle-aged celebrities, combined with a barrage of 'anti-ageing' cosmetic advertisements, to send a powerful message that thinness and youthfulness are idealized, achievable, and most importantly, expected during mid-life. The equation of a thin body with youthful looks may fuel body dissatisfaction and drive middle-aged women to engage in unhealthy methods of weight control. Indeed, there is now considerable cross-sectional support for a positive relationship between ageing anxiety (or fear of ageing) and body dissatisfaction (Gupta & Schork, 1993; Lewis & Cachelin, 2001; McKinley & Lyon, 2008; Midlarsky & Nitzburg, 2008; Slevec & Tiggemann, 2011) and body shame (McKinley & Lyon, 2008). There is also evidence for a link between ageing anxiety and disordered eating during midlife (Gupta & Schork, 1993; Lewis & Cachelin, 2001; Midlarsky & Nitzburg, 2008; Slevec &

Tiggemann, 2011). In addition, Slevec and Tiggemann (2010) found a relationship between ageing anxiety and consideration of cosmetic surgery.

Negative affect

Negative affect (encompassing mood states, such as depression, anxiety, stress, and helplessness) is considered a risk factor for eating pathology among younger women (see Stice, 2002, for a review). Such negative affect is commonly experienced by middle-aged women (Bromberger & Lanza di Scalea, 2009), and there is now cross-sectional support for a relationship between negative affect and body dissatisfaction in a diverse range of middle-aged women (McLaren et al., 2004; Hrabosky & Grilo, 2007; Midlarsky & Nitzburg, 2008; Dunkley et al., 2010). There is also evidence for a link between negative affect and disordered eating in middle-aged clinical and non-clinical samples (Forman & Davis, 2005; Marcus et al., 2007; Perez et al., 2007; Midlarsky & Nitzburg, 2008). In a prospective study of middle-aged women, Procopio et al. (2006) found that while depression and anxiety symptoms were significantly related to bulimic symptoms, only anxiety predicted increase in bulimic symptoms 2.5 years later, suggesting it may be an important prognostic indicator in this population.

Self-esteem

A number of studies show that global self-esteem is related to evaluation of appearance or body image satisfaction in samples of both men and women across the adult lifespan (Pliner et al., 1990; Wilcox, 1997; Paxton & Phythian, 1999; Green & Pritchard, 2003). In the main, research with more restricted samples of specifically middle-aged women has largely confirmed this relationship, whereby higher self-esteem is related to better body satisfaction (Tiggemann, 1992; Paa & Larson, 1998; Wardle et al., 2002). Nevertheless, there is some evidence that this relationship becomes weaker as women age (Tiggemann & Stevens, 1999; Webster & Tiggemann, 2003), suggesting that the self and appearance may become less closely aligned. In adult men, Tiggemann et al. (2007) found low self-esteem to be related to dissatisfaction with adiposity (fatness) but not dissatisfaction with muscularity.

Social comparison

Social comparison is thought to be prompted by the basic human drive for self-evaluation (Festinger, 1954) and hence is most often made with individuals who are similar along self-relevant dimensions, such as gender and age. As few women are able to meet the societally prescribed ideals of beauty, such comparison with media figures or peers almost invariably results in the woman finding herself lacking. Indeed, numerous studies in adolescent and young women show social comparison to be related to poorer body satisfaction (e.g. Tiggemann & McGill, 2004). As might be expected given the typical (young) age of fashion models, Kozar and Damhorst (2009) found that on average women over 30 'rarely' compared themselves to fashion models on the attributes of height, face, weight, shape, hair, attractiveness, or style, with the likelihood of doing so decreasing with age. However, across age, the extent of comparison was related to appearance dissatisfaction. The more participants compared themselves to fashion models, the less satisfied they were with their appearance. Similarly, we (Slevec & Tiggemann, 2011) have found the trait tendency for social comparison to be correlated with both body dissatisfaction and disordered eating in middle-aged women.

Sociocultural factors

One of the most generally accepted theoretical accounts for body dissatisfaction and disordered eating is provided by sociocultural theory (e.g. Thompson et al., 1999). This account proposes that societal beauty ideals are primarily reinforced and transmitted by sociocultural influences, most notably the family, peers, and the media. Although a great deal of work has documented the influential role of these sociocultural factors in the development of body dissatisfaction and disordered eating among younger women and adolescent girls, very little has investigated their role in more mature samples.

The media

The media are arguably the most potent sociocultural transmitter of societal beauty ideals. Abundant correlational and experimental evidence confirms a clear link between media and body dissatisfaction or disordered eating in young women and girls (see Levine & Murnen, 2009, for a review). But historically, the media have been seen as having little influence on older women. For example, in 1999, women in their 40s rarely nominated media figures as body image role models (Grogan, 2008), a finding Grogan attributed to a lack of age-appropriate comparison targets in a highly youth-focused media. However, in the decade since that study, the number of middle-aged women featured in magazines and on television has undoubtedly increased. Beautiful (thin and youthful) middle-aged celebrities (e.g. Elle McPherson, Elizabeth Hurley, Michelle Pfeiffer, Madonna) now appear in movies, commercials and video clips, and have served to create a new and unrealistic ideal of mid-life physique. In support, in a more recent study of middle-aged women's body image ideals (Slevec & Tiggemann, 2011), women most commonly aspired ('If you could look like anyone who would it be?') to look like actresses (e.g. Jennifer Aniston, Angelina Jolie, Elizabeth Hurley). With one exception, all actresses nominated were middle-aged (35–55 years).

A few studies have investigated media influence in adult samples. Green and Pritchard (2003) found media influence to predict body dissatisfaction in adult women but not adult men. Similarly, Midlarsky and Nitzburg (2008) found sociocultural pressure to be thin (including media influence) to be associated with body dissatisfaction and eating pathology among middle-aged women. In their prospective study of female fitness centre attendees, McCabe et al. (2007) found media influence to lose weight predicted increases in bulimic symptoms and drive for thinness over 12 months. However, these preceding studies have investigated only *perceived* media influence. Only one study (Slevec & Tiggemann, 2011) has investigated relationships with actual media exposure. We found that media exposure, especially television, was positively correlated with both body dissatisfaction and disordered eating in middle-aged women. This is an important finding, as it suggests that middle-aged women may indeed be increasingly vulnerable to the negative effects of media so well-documented in younger women.

Peer and family influence

Not surprisingly, a great deal of research has shown peer influences to play a major role in the body image of adolescent and young women. In particular, teasing on the basis of weight or shape (by peers or family) has been identified as a risk factor for body dissatisfaction in these age groups (Wertheim et al., 2004). These are complemented by studies of middle-aged women that indicate that childhood teasing is still associated with body dissatisfaction and disordered eating in mid-life (Wardle et al., 2002; McLaren et al., 2004; Hrabosky & Grilo, 2007). These latter findings suggest that weight-related teasing in childhood may have an enduring adverse impact on body image and eating practices across the lifespan, a possibility that requires confirmation by longitudinal studies.

Very few studies have investigated concurrent (adult) peer or family influence. Green and Pritchard (2003) found that perceived pressure from family members was associated with body dissatisfaction in both adult women and men. Similarly, Gravener et al. (2008) found moderate to large effect sizes for the relationship between perceived dieting among same-sex peers and drive for thinness in adults of both sexes. While women's drive for thinness was related only to perceived dieting among female friends, men's drive for thinness was related to perceived dieting among both female and male friends. With respect to teasing, Matz et al. (2002) found that adult, but not childhood, teasing was associated with body dissatisfaction in a sample of middle-aged overweight women. Finally, in their cohort of 54-year-old women, McLaren et al. (2004) found that comments made by partners impacted on body esteem; negative partner comments were associated with poorer body esteem, and positive comments were associated with better body esteem, regardless of body size (BMI).

LIMITATIONS AND UNANSWERED RESEARCH QUESTIONS

There are a number of methodological and conceptual limitations in the research discussed here. First, with few exceptions, the samples investigating appearance concerns in adulthood have been composed primarily of white women. Thus the course of body image across the life span for people of different ethnicity has not yet been systematically investigated.

Second, although body dissatisfaction has been well-documented in adult women, the picture is much less clear for men. Emerging research indicates that adult men also suffer body dissatisfaction, but of a different form (primarily with muscularity, in addition to fatness). In this, research has been severely hampered by the unthinking adoption of measures designed for women. Future research should investigate body dissatisfaction across men's lifespan using gender-appropriate measures. In particular, there may be other aspects of bodies which are important to men. For example, Tiggemann et al. (2008) recently found that men were dissatisfied with their head hair, body hair, height, and penis size, in addition to body weight and muscularity.

Relatedly, investigations of adult women's appearance concerns across the lifespan may also have been hampered by generalization from young women. While the findings indicate that many of the factors associated with body dissatisfaction and disordered eating in midlife are similar to those found in younger women, there are particular concerns associated with age-related changes to appearance, such as increased weight gain, menopause, and the ageing of physical features, specific to this population. In generalizing from young women, it is possible that we may be missing the specific predictors of most relevance for middle-aged women. For example, some commentators (e.g. Tiggemann, 2004a; Tiggemann & Lacey, 2009) have argued that clothing and everyday grooming take on greater importance as women age. More generally, future research should attempt to identify factors that may protect middle-aged women against the development of body dissatisfaction and disordered eating and, more importantly, those that actually contribute to positive body experience.

Undoubtedly the major methodological limitation is that most of the studies have been cross-sectional in design. Thus studies of age effects have investigated age *differences*, rather than age *changes*. This renders them subject to cohort effects, which arise because, by definition, any one age group (cohort) will be the same age at the same point in time. Thus age differences are inexorably confounded with historical events and the particular cultural ideals of that time. Similarly, the studies seeking to identify predictors of appearance concerns have been correlational in nature, and thereby unable to speak to temporal or causal sequencing of variables. They have identified correlates, rather than predictors. Longitudinal studies are required that trace developmental changes in both potential predictors and appearance concerns in the same individuals over a considerable period of time.

The major conceptual inadequacy is the lack of any underlying unifying framework. The research has been conducted piecemeal, with each study investigating individual relationships. Only one study (Slevec & Tiggemann, 2011) has attempted to test a comprehensive sociocultural model of body dissatisfaction and disordered eating in middle-aged women, as has been investigated in younger women and girls (e.g. Keery et al., 2004). Other theoretical approaches, in particular lifespan approaches which include the specific challenges faced by men and women as they age (Lerner & Jovanovic, 1990), warrant consideration.

Finally, one of the difficulties in researching topics like appearance concerns that are clearly set in a sociocultural context is that there is always a time lag in dissemination of results. Thus these may quickly become outdated in a society experiencing a considerable rate of change. For example, the unprecedented increase in the advertising and uptake of cosmetic surgery in middle-aged women (and increasingly men (APSP, 2010)), is literally changing the face of middle age. A number of authors (e.g. Bordo, 2003) argue that cosmetic surgery has shifted cultural expectations as to how women are expected to look in their 40s, 50s, and 60s (e.g. 'Fifty is the new forty'), to create a new set of ideals and norms, and a new set of pressures on middle-aged women. Other changes in media content (e.g. the advent of reality makeover television shows) or information technology (e.g. social networking sites like Facebook) may likewise impact on adult appearance concerns.

Conclusions

It has now been well established that dissatisfaction with appearance and associated dieting and disordered eating behaviours remain at high levels in women across adulthood (Tiggemann, 2004a). For men, the picture is less clear because there are fewer studies with less appropriate measures. Nevertheless, it does appear that adult men also experience body dissatisfaction. As women (and perhaps men) age, however, they place less emphasis on the importance of physical appearance; it no longer plays such a central role in who they are. This allows a greater acceptance of the age-related changes in appearance that take them ever further from the thin and youthful ideal.

The research on predictors of adult appearance concerns clearly shows that the majority of associated factors are similar to those found in younger women. However, some (like menopause and ageing anxiety) are specific to middle age. These latter might present particular targets for intervention strategies with this age group. Future research should use longitudinal research designs and conceptually more sophisticated theoretical frameworks to advance our understanding of appearance issues in adulthood.

References

Algars, M., Santtila, P., Varjonen, M., Witting, K., Johansson, A., Jern, P., *et al.* (2009). The adult body: How age, gender, and body mass index are related to body image. *Journal of Aging and Health*, 21, 1112–32.

Allaz, A.-F., Bernstein, M., Rouget, P., Archinard, M., & Morabia, A. (1998). Body weight preoccupation in middle-age and ageing women: A general population survey. *International Journal of Eating Disorders*, 23, 287–94.

Altabe, M. & Thompson, J. K. (1993). Body image changes during early adulthood. *International Journal of Eating Disorders*, 13, 323–8.

American Society for Aesthetic Plastic Surgery. (2010). *2009 ASAPS Statistics*. http://www.plasticsurgery.org/News-and-Resources/2009-Statistics.html

Augustus-Horvath, C. L., & Tylka, T. L. (2009). A test and extension of objectification theory as it predicts disordered eating: Does women's age matter? *Journal of Counseling Psychology*, 56, 253–65.

Baker, C. W., Carter, A. S., Cohen, L. R., & Brownell, K. D. (1999). Eating attitudes and behaviors in pregnancy and postpartum: Global stability versus specific transitions. *Annals of Behavioral Medicine*, 21, 143–8.

Barrett, A. E., & Robbins, C. (2008). The multiple sources of women's aging anxiety and their relationship with psychological distress. *Journal of Aging and Health*, 20, 32–65.

Bennett, K., & Stevens, R. (1996). Weight anxiety in older women. *European Eating Disorders Review*, 4, 32–9.

Bordo, S. (2003). *Unbearable weight: Feminism, western culture and the body*. Berkeley, CA: University of California Press.

Bromberger, J. T., & Lanza di Scalea, J. T. (2009). Longitudinal associations between depression and functioning in midlife women. *Maturitas*, 64, 145–59.

Cash, T. F. (2002). Cognitive-behavioral perspectives on body image. In T. F. Cash & T. Pruzinsky (eds.) *Body image: A handbook of theory, research and clinical practice*, pp. 38–46. New York: Guilford.

Cash, T. F. & Henry, P. E. (1995). Women's body images: The results of a national survey in the USA. *Sex Roles*, 33, 19–28.

Cash, T. F., Melnyk, S. E., & Hrabosky, J. I. (2004). The assessment of body image investment: An extensive revision of the Appearance Schemas Inventory. *International Journal of Eating Disorders*, 35, 305–16.

Cash, T. F., Winstead, B. A., & Janda, L. H. (1986). Body image survey report: The great American shape-up. *Psychology Today*, 19, 30–7.

Crawford, M., Lee, I-C., Portnoy, G., Gurung, A., Khati, D., Jha, P., *et al.* (2009). Objectified body consciousness in a developing country: A comparison of mothers and daughters in the US and Nepal. *Sex Roles*, 60, 174–85.

Deeks, A. A., & McCabe, M. P. (2001). Menopausal stage and age and perceptions of body image. *Psychology & Health*, 16, 367–79.

Demarest, J. & Allen, R. (2000). Body image: Gender, ethnic and age differences. *Journal of Social Psychology*, 140, 465–72.

Dillaway, H. E. (2005). (Un) Changing menopausal bodies: How women think and act in the face of a reproductive transition and gendered beauty ideals. *Sex Roles*, 53, 1–17.

Duncombe, D., Wertheim, E. H., Skouteris, H., Paxton, S. J., & Kelly, L. (2008). How well do women adapt to changes in their body size and shape across the course of pregnancy? *Journal of Health Psychology*, 13, 503–15.

Dunkel, T. M., Davidson, D., & Qurashi, S. (2010). Body satisfaction and pressure to be thin in younger and older Muslim and non-Muslim women: The role of Western and non-Western dress preferences. *Body Image*, 7, 56–65.

Dunkley, D. M., Masheb, R. M., & Grilo, C. M. (2010). Childhood maltreatment, depressive symptoms, and body dissatisfaction in patients with binge eating disorder: The mediating role of self-criticism. *International Journal of Eating Disorders*, 43, 274–81.

Festinger, L. (1954). A theory of social comparison processes. *Human Relations*, 7, 117–40.

Forbes, G. B., Adams-Curtis, L., Jobe, R. L., White, K. B., Revak, J., Zivcic-Becirevic, I., *et al.* (2005). Body dissatisfaction in college women and their mothers: Cohort effects, developmental effects, and the influences of body size, sexism, and the thin body ideal. *Sex Roles*, 53, 281–98.

Forman, M., & Davis, W. N. (2005). Characteristics of middle-aged women in inpatient treatment for eating disorders. *Eating Disorders*, 13, 231–43.

Garner, D. M. (1997). The 1997 body image survey results. *Psychology Today*, 30, 30–44; 75–80; 84.

Gravener, J. A., Haedt, A. A., Heatherton, T. F., & Keel, P. K. (2008). Gender and age differences in associations between peer dieting and drive for thinness. *International Journal of Eating Disorders*, 41, 57–63.

Green, SP., & Pritchard, M. E. (2003). Predictors of body image dissatisfaction in adult men and women. *Social Behavior and Personality*, 31, 215–22.

Grogan, S. (2008). *Body image: Understanding body dissatisfaction in men, women, and children*. New York: Routledge.

Gupta, M. A. & Schork, N. J. (1993). Aging-related concerns and body image: Possible future implications for eating disorders. *International Journal of Eating Disorders*, 14, 481–6.

Heatherton, T. F., Mahamedi, F., Striepe, M., Field, A. E., & Keel, P. (1997). A 10-year longitudinal study of body weight, dieting and eating disorder symptoms. *Journal of Abnormal Psychology*, 106, 117–25.

Heinberg, L. J. & Guarda, A. S. (2002). Body image issues in obstetrics and gynecology. In T. F. Cash & T. Pruzinsky (eds.) *Body image: A handbook of theory, research and clinical practice*, pp. 351–60. New York: Guilford.

Hrabosky, J. I., & Grilo, C. M. (2007). Body image and eating disordered behavior in a community sample of Black and Hispanic women. *Eating Behaviors*, 8, 106–14.

Huang, C. K., & Miller, T. A. (2007). The truth about over-the-counter topical anti-aging products: A comprehensive review. *Aesthetic Surgery Journal*, 27, 402–12.

Jenkin, W. & Tiggemann, M. (1997). Psychological effects of weight retained after pregnancy. *Women and Health*, 25, 89–98.

Keel, P. K., Gravener, J. A., Joiner T. E. Jr., & Haedt, A. A. (2010). Twenty-year follow-up of bulimia nervosa and related eating disorders not otherwise specified. *International Journal of Eating Disorders*, 43, 492–7.

Keery, H., van den Berg. P., & Thompson, K. (2004). An evaluation of the Tripartite Influence Model of body dissatisfaction and eating disturbance with adolescent girls. *Body Image*, 1, 237–51.

Koch, P. B., Mansfield, P. K., Thurau, D., & Carey, M. (2005). 'Feeling Frumpy': The relationships between body image and sexual response changes in midlife women. *Journal of Sex Research*, 42, 215–23.

Kozar, J. M., & Damhorst, M. L. (2009). Comparison of the ideal and real body as women age: Relationships to age identity, body satisfaction and importance, and attention to models in advertising. *Clothing & Textiles Research Journal*, 27, 197–210.

Lerner, R. M., & Jovanovic, J. (1990). The role of body image in psychosocial develop-
ment across the life span: A developmental contextual perspective. In T. F. Cash &
T. Pruzinsky (eds.) *Body images: Development, deviance and change*, pp. 110–27. New York:
Guilford.

Levine, M. P., & Murnen, S. K. (2009). 'Everybody knows that mass media are/are not [pick
one] a cause of eating disorders': A critical review of evidence for a causal link between
media, negative body image, and disordered eating in females. *Journal of Social and
Clinical Psychology*, 28, 9–42.

Lewis, D., & Cachelin, F. M. (2001). Body image, body dissatisfaction, and eating attitudes
in midlife and elderly women. *Eating Disorders: The Journal of Treatment & Prevention*, 9,
29–39.

Marcus, M. D., Bromberger, J. T., Wei, H-L., Brown, C., & Kravitz, H. M. (2007). Prevalence
and selected correlates of eating disorder symptoms among a multiethnic community
sample of midlife women. *Annals of Behavioral Medicine*, 33, 269–77.

Markey, C. N., Markey, P. M., & Birch, L. L. (2004). Understanding women's body
satisfaction: The role of husbands. *Sex Roles*, 51, 209–16.

Matz, P. E., Foster, G. D., Faith, M. S., & Wadden, T. A. (2002). Correlates of body image
dissatisfaction among overweight women seeking weight loss. *Journal of Consulting and
Clinical Psychology*, 70, 1040–4.

McCabe, M. P., & Ricciardelli, L. A. (2004). Weight and shape concerns of boys and men.
In JK. Thompson (ed.) *Handbook of eating disorders and obesity*, pp. 606–34. Hoboken,
NJ: John Wiley & Sons Inc.

McCabe, M. P., Ricciardelli, L. A., & James, T. (2007). A longitudinal study of body change
strategies of fitness center attendees. *Eating Behaviors*, 8, 492–6.

McKinley, N. M. (1999). Women and objectified body consciousness: Mothers' and daughters' body experience in cultural, developmental, and familial context. *Developmental
Psychology*, 35, 760–9.

McKinley, N. M. (2006a). The developmental and cultural contexts of objectified body
consciousness: A longitudinal analysis of two cohorts of women. *Developmental Psychology*,
42, 679–87.

McKinley, N. M. (2006b). Longitudinal gender differences in objectified body consciousness and weight-related attitudes and behaviors: Cultural and developmental contexts in
the transition from college. *Sex Roles*, 54, 159–73.

McKinley, N. M., & Lyon, L. A. (2008). Menopausal attitudes, objectified body consciousness, aging anxiety, and body esteem: European American women's body experiences in
midlife. *Body Image*, 5, 375–80.

McLaren, L., Hardy, R., & Kuh, D. (2003). Women's body satisfaction at midlife and lifetime body size: A prospective study. *Health Psychology*, 22, 370–7.

McLaren, L., Kuh, D., Hardy, R., & Gauvin, L. (2004). Positive and negative body-related
comments and their relationship with body dissatisfaction in middle-aged women.
Psychology & Health, 19, 261–72.

McLean, S. A., Paxton, S. J., & Wertheim, E. H. (2010). Factors associated with body
dissatisfaction and disordered eating in women in midlife. *International Journal of Eating
Disorders*, 43, 527–36.

Midlarsky, E., & Nitzburg, G. (2008). Eating disorders in middle-aged women. *Journal of
General Psychology*, 135, 393–407.

Paa, H. K., & Larson, L. M. (1998). Predicting level of restrained eating behavior in adult women. *International Journal of Eating Disorders*, 24, 91–4.

Patrick, J. H., & Stahl, S. T. (2009). Understanding disordered eating at midlife and late life. *Journal of General Psychology*, 136, 5–20.

Paxton, S. J., & Phythian, K. (1999). Body image, self-esteem, and health status in middle and later adulthood. *Australian Psychologist*, 34, 116–21.

Perez, M., Hernandez, A., Clarke, A., & Joiner, T. E. (2007). Analysis of bulimic symptomatology across age and geographic locations. *Eating Behaviors*, 8, 136–42.

Pliner, P., Chaiken, S., & Flett, G. (1990). Gender differences in concern with body weight and physical appearance over the life span. *Personality and Social Psychology Bulletin*, 16, 263–73.

Procopio, C. A., Holm-Denoma, J. M., Gordon, K. H., & Joiner, T. E. (2006). Two–three-year stability and interrelations of bulimotypic indicators and depressive and anxious symptoms in middle-aged women. *International Journal of Eating Disorders*, 39, 312–19.

Rallis, S., Skouteris, H., Wertheim, E. H., & Paxton, S. J. (2007). Predictors of body image during the first year postpartum: A prospective study. *Women & Health*, 45, 87–104.

Rodin, J., Silberstein, L., & Striegel-Moore, R. (1985). Women and weight: A normative discontent. In T. B. Sonderegger (ed.) *Psychology and gender*, pp. 267–307. Lincoln, NE: University of Nebraska Press.

Rozin, P. & Fallon, A. (1988). Body image, attitudes to weight, and misperceptions of figure preferences of the opposite sex: A comparison of men and women in two generations. *Journal of Abnormal Psychology*, 97, 342–5.

Sarwer, D. B., & Crerand, C. E. (2004). Body image and cosmetic medical treatments. *Body Image*, 1, 99–111.

Share, T. L., & Mintz, L. B. (2002). Differences between lesbians and heterosexual women in disordered eating and related attitudes. *Journal of Homosexuality*, 42, 89–106.

Slevec, J. H., & Tiggemann, M. (2010). Attitudes toward cosmetic surgery in middle-aged women: Body image, aging anxiety, and the media. *Psychology of Women Quarterly*, 34, 65–74.

Slevec, J. H., & Tiggemann, M. (2011). Media exposure, body dissatisfaction, and disordered eating in middle-aged women: A test of the sociocultural model of disordered eating. *Psychology of Women Quarterly*, 35, 617–27.

Stevens, C. & Tiggemann, M. (1998). Women's body figure preferences across the life span. *Journal of Genetic Psychology*, 159, 94–102.

Stice, E. (2002). Risk and maintenance factors for eating pathology: A meta-analytic review. *Psychological Bulletin*, 128, 825–48.

Stokes, R., & Frederick-Recascino, C. (2003). Women's perceived body image: Relations with personal happiness. *Journal of Women & Aging*, 15, 17–29.

Thompson, J. K., & Stice, E. (2001). Thin-ideal internalisation: Mounting evidence for a new risk factor for body-image disturbance and eating pathology. *Current Directions in Psychological Science*, 10, 181–3.

Thompson, J. K., Heinberg, L. J., Altabe, M., & Tantleff-Dunn, S. (1999). *Exacting beauty: Theory, assessment, and treatment of body image disturbance*. Washington, DC: American Psychological Association.

Thompson, S. C., Thomas, C., Rickabaugh, C. A., Tantamjarik, P., Otsuki, T., Pan, D., *et al.* (1998). Primary and secondary control over age-related changes in physical appearance. *Journal of Personality*, 66, 583–605.

Tiggemann, M. (1992). Body-size dissatisfaction: Individual differences in age and gender, and relationship with self-esteem. *Personality and Individual Differences, 13,* 39–43.

Tiggemann, M. (2004a). Body image across the adult life span: Stability and change. *Body Image,* 1, 29–41.

Tiggemann, M. (2004b). Dietary restraint and self-esteem as predictors of weight gain over an 8-year time period. *Eating Behaviors,* 5, 251–9.

Tiggemann, M., & Lacey, C. (2009). Shopping for clothes: Body satisfaction, appearance investment, and functions of clothing among female shoppers. *Body Image,* 6, 285–91.

Tiggemann, M., & Lynch, J. (2001). Body image across the lifespan in adult women: The role of self-objectification. *Developmental Psychology,* 37, 243–53.

Tiggemann, M., & McGill, B. (2004). The role of social comparison in the effect of magazine advertisements on women's mood and body dissatisfaction. *Journal of Social & Clinical Psychology,* 23, 23–44.

Tiggemann, M., & Stevens, C. (1999). Weight concern across the life-span: Relationship to self-esteem and feminist identity. *International Journal of Eating Disorders,* 26, 103–6.

Tiggemann, M., Martins, Y., & Kirkbride, A. (2007). Oh to be lean and muscular: Body image ideals in gay and heterosexual men. *Psychology of Men & Masculinity,* 8, 15–24.

Tiggemann, M., Martins, Y., & Churchett, L. (2008). Beyond muscles: Unexplored parts of men's body image. *Journal of Health Psychology,* 13, 1163–72.

Voda, A. M., Christy, N. S., & Morgan, J. M. (1991). Body composition changes in menopausal women. *Women and Therapy,* 11, 71–96.

Wardle, J., Waller, J., & Fox, E. (2002). Age of onset and body dissatisfaction in obesity. *Addictive Behaviors,* 27, 561–73.

Webster, J., & Tiggemann, M. (2003). The relationship between women's body satisfaction and self-image across the life span: The role of cognitive control. *Journal of Genetic Psychology,* 162, 241–52.

Wertheim, E. H., Paxton, S. J., & Blaney, S. (2004). Risk factors for the development of body image disturbances. In J. K. Thompson (ed.) *Handbook of eating disorders and obesity,* pp. 463–94. Hoboken, NJ: John Wiley & Sons Inc.

Wilcox, S. (1997). Age and gender in relation to body attitudes: Is there a double standard of aging? *Psychology of Women Quarterly,* 21, 549–65.

CHAPTER 14

APPEARANCE IN LATER LIFE

LUCIE BAKER

EYAL GRINGART

INTRODUCTION

THERE are two common contradictory perspectives on body image in older adulthood. One proposes that body image dissatisfaction increases with age as normative ageing changes people's bodies so that they are increasingly discrepant from Western society's cultural ideal of thinness, muscularity, and youthfulness (Bordo, 1993; Lamb et al., 1993; Lien et al., 2001). The second perspective holds that body image concerns wane in older adulthood, particularly among women, as social pressures emphasizing the importance of appearance become less pronounced (Feingold & Mazzella, 1998).

To date, only a few published studies on body image considered older adulthood and none seem to have been specifically devoted to this population. In this chapter we report on our 4-year research (2007–2010) in which we developed an integrative model of body image and a quantitative measure with which we investigated body image satisfaction in older adulthood. We argue that body image is a significant concern to older adults. Further, we propose that body image dissatisfaction in older adulthood is psychologically injurious.

An Integrative Model of Body Image Development

Pruzinsky and Cash (2002) acknowledged that a single problem perspective was a significant hindrance to the advancement of knowledge in body image research. Cash (1990) argued that the term 'body experience' could be more appropriate than the term 'body image' since image did not reflect the complexity of the construct. A series of focus groups we carried out with older men and women, aged 68–89 years, confirmed that several aspects contributed to older adults' body image development and day-to-day experience. This led us to propose an integrative model of body image development (see Fig. 14.1) taking into account issues that were found relevant to both younger and older populations.

According to the integrative model, outlined in Fig. 14.1, body image satisfaction is mediated by a perceived discrepancy between body ideal and body reality, the smaller the perceived discrepancy the greater the satisfaction. These domains are influenced by individuals' sociocultural environments; health and function; physical and personal characteristics. Addressing the perceived discrepancy, to enhance body image satisfaction, involves a range of strategies that facilitate body presentation, which is continually checked via self-evaluation and social feedback. Over time, the information obtained via self-evaluation and social feedback is

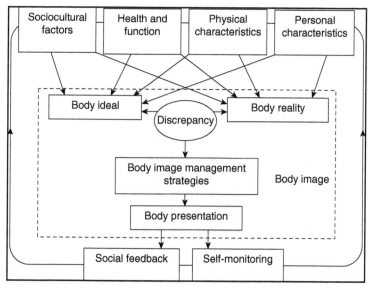

Figure 14.1. Integrative model of body image development.

reintegrated with the primary domains that influence body ideal and body reality development, thus allowing for continuous changes in body image.

Whilst the focus here is on older adults aged 65 and over, it is important to bear in mind that ageing is a lifelong process of change starting from birth if not conception. Ageing is accompanied by many bodily changes, yet, it is not solely about the body. Ageing occurs within a sociocultural context and thus includes the accumulation of experiences within these settings. Hence, sociocultural factors (see Fig. 14.1) refer to the influences that originate from individuals' immediate and wider environment throughout their life and that are internalized as sociocul- turally appropriate norms and expectancies. This includes familial, social, and cultural interactions.

Whilst sociocultural factors influence everyone, not just older adults, we found that to understand older adults' body image we needed to take into account the time, in a historical sense, at which participants grew up and the sociocultural environments they have lived within. Participants highlighted the importance of parental upbringing in communicating values pertaining to self-presentation, which remain with individuals throughout their life. For example: *'It's how we were brought up and back then we had clothes for school, clothes for home, clothes for church, you know, but we always had to be well presented, that was important and that's stayed with us all our life'* [female, 85 years].

Participants also noted a link between physical appearance, personal and social qualities as well as a need to conform to sociocultural standards. For example: *'Everyone that came in had a tie on and I felt... not good at all because I was the only fellow without a tie'* [male, 85 years].

Our findings supported previously held views that older adults' body image satisfaction is largely mediated by health and physical as well as functional abilities (Paxton & Phythian 1999). These encompass one's overall health status, movement, gross and fine motor skills, and sense of balance. Older adults' definition of body image reflected this notion. For example: *'Your image would depend to a large degree... on your physical condition'* [male, 85 years].

Participants highlighted physical limitations in terms of health and function both generally and in the context of their personal circumstances. For example: *'It's not that you don't want to do it but your body won't let you'* [female, 78 years] and *'Your body is a machine... we're living longer and the body, that machine, starts to break down and so the body doesn't last as long as you live'* [male, 85 years].

Given older adults' increased vulnerability to a range of health challenges and functional impairments (Janelli, 1993), some changes in the body's health and function may be inevitable. How individuals respond to such changes depends on whether they feel that they have control over their body's condition or whether they feel that they are victims of an unrepairable body. Feelings such as these are likely to determine the way in which older adults view their body as well as their related aspirations.

Whilst some participants indicated that, with age, one becomes less concerned with appearance and more concerned with health; this does not imply that physical appearance is no longer important. Physical characteristics (see Fig. 14.1) pertain to the physical features that affect appearance, such as body weight and shape, but also include factors related to ageing, such as wrinkles.

Despite societal attempts at imposing norms on what one should look like, certain personal characteristics, such as self-confidence, self-esteem, and self-acceptance, may act in a protective manner. As an 86-year-old female participant stated: 'It's your opinion of yourself, your self confidence in a way. I'm as good as anybody else, or poor old me, I'm not very good... if you've got good self-esteem... what you look like shouldn't really bother you. You just have to be yourself'.

In accord, personal characteristics (see Fig. 14.1) refer to personal traits and self-concept variables that may affect how individuals view their body as well as the extent to which they engage in body image management strategies and self monitoring. Whilst all older adults agreed that looking good was important, their realistic view was evidenced by comments such as: 'It's all in your mind. You've just got to do the best you can with what you've got' [female, 68 years] or, 'You have to be at peace with yourself, not be envious of others. It's really a state of mind more than anything' [female, 86 years].

Whilst acceptance may be key to countering feelings of shame or inadequacy, this notion was not shared across participants with some indicating a discrepancy between their sense of self (felt age) and their ageing bodies (chronological age), resulting in an uneasy feeling regarding their changing image. This was illustrated by comments such as: 'I would like my body to [...] have less wrinkles because when I look in the mirror it's just not me anymore' [female, 89 years] or, 'I've lost a great deal of weight and...it's hardly me' [female, 84 years].

Participants also related declining physical abilities to a feeling of shame because they had to be dependent upon others for small tasks, such as changing a light bulb or hooking up a curtain. So whilst one's personal characteristics, such as self-confidence, can act in a protective fashion, other feelings, such as shame or feelings of discrepancy between the mind and the body, as described earlier, can have an adverse effect.

Body ideal refers to the way an individual would like his/her body to be in terms of physical appearance, fitness, and/or functional ability and health. Body reality refers to the perception of the body as it is, looks, and feels, affected by the ageing process and previous lifestyle variables. The discrepancy between body reality and body ideal represents the extent of one's body image dissatisfaction.

It has been suggested that mature individuals reach a point of self-acceptance (Allport, 1961). It has further been argued that, during older adulthood, previously set high body ideal expectations are replaced by more realistic goals as older adults are more likely to compare themselves to realistic prototypes rather than to youthful ideals (Grogan, 2007). Whilst this could, theoretically, lead to increased harmony between body ideal and body reality, our participants made several comments pertaining to the discrepancy between their body reality and body ideal. For instance: *'I would like to have a bit taken off around my hips'* [female, 85 years] or, *'Gravity always wins in the end, you know, we'd all need breast lifts and face lifts'* [female, 68 years].

Nevertheless, the way in which individuals cope with unwelcomed changes of their body, due to ageing or as a result of their own actions, appears similar, namely, utilizing body image management strategies (see Fig. 14.1). These refer to all the strategies, such as the use of cosmetics and anti-ageing skin care products, as well as hairstyling, jewellery and clothing, dieting, and exercising, that a person may engage in order to enhance body image satisfaction. As stated by an 86-year-old female participant: *'You can't completely change your looks but you can make them so that you are happy with them'.*

It has been argued that the body is the material property of its owner, who in turn has a responsibility to control and monitor its performance and appearance (Goffman, 1963). Others, such as Sparkes (1997), pointed out the numerous opportunities individuals had in order to attain the culturally defined standards of body ideal. Taking the view that the fear of old age and bodily ageing has become an integral part of many people's life, Gilleard and Higgs (2000) described the wide range of body-care options available as 'age-resisting practices' (p. 59), thus adding a more contemporary dimension to that of responsibility (Goffman, 1963) and opportunity (Sparkes, 1997).

Whether by resistance to ageing, responsibility or opportunity, humans seem to have always engaged in management strategies in order to either achieve a body that they feel is more socially acceptable (Reischer & Koo, 2004) or that is a more accurate reflection of themself (Featherstone 1991). In accord, the wide variety of activities that older adults engage was raised by a number of participants. The more controllable aspects of body management, such as clothing, hair care, make up for women and shaving for men, were commonly cited as means to create a favourable body presentation. For example: *'Getting dressed and doing our hair and putting a bit of make up on. That makes us feel good'* [female, 74 years]. *'If I'm going out, doesn't matter where, I wouldn't dream of going out... anywhere without shaving [...] no one is going to see me, but I have to shave, it's important to me'* [male, 85 years].

As discussed previously, health and function are salient aspects of older adult's body image and all focus group participants reported trying to maintain their physical fitness, mainly by walking, which they also felt was socially beneficial. As an 85-year-old female participant said: *'It gets you out of the house and you meet people and chat to your neighbours along the way. That's important when you're by yourself. It gets you out of the house'.* Another 68-year-old female participant said *'it's great walking the dog, not only I exercise but I meet all sorts of people'.*

It is also important to point out that participants highlighted that engaging in activities such as walking was not something new to them, thus indicating the importance of lifestyle habits adopted earlier in life. As an 85-year-old male participant said: '*An exercise routine is something which is a lifetime lifestyle*'.

The promotion of healthy behaviours, communicating warnings against self-inflicted illnesses triggered by behaviours such as smoking, alcohol consumption, overeating, or lack of exercise are a constant reminder of individuals' responsibility for their body (Gilleard, 2002). As personal emphasis on health and function appear to increase as people age, older adults may be more receptive to messages related to such responsibility. Yet previous research indicated that factors, such as weight loss or maintenance, enhancement of body tone and overall physical attractiveness, have been consistently identified as reasons for exercising (Silverstein et al., 1988). Thus, whilst reporting being increasingly aware of their health and fitness, older adults' motivation to engage physical activity may be significantly related to their desire to control their body presentation (Marquez & McAuley, 2001).

Whether or not a satisfactory body presentation is achieved after appearance management strategies are applied is related to a number of factors. These include self-monitoring, which is facilitated by comparing oneself to others as well as to prototypes, and feedback from others. Social feedback communicates to the individual the approval or disapproval of their body presentation as displayed in the wider social context.

Participants pointed out several methods by which they evaluate their physical appearance and expressed their desire to be perceived as well presented. In accord with previous research (e.g. Douglas, 1970; Frost, 2001), participants also considered the processes by which people give meaning to appearance and the social consequences of these meanings, which are important aspects of social feedback. For example, one 82-year-old male participant explained: '*I have to make an effort to present an image of lively, fit… old man [because] my son and my daughter whenever they're with me they're looking for signs of ageing and senility*'.

This participant further explained that his children used his physical appearance, particularly his neatness and ability to properly dress, to monitor his ability of living independently. By contrast, other participants suggested that, with age, social feedback became less important and, therefore, other people's opinion had less impact on the way they felt about their body. For example, an 85-year-old male participant stated: '*I think that what I think about my body is more important than what my neighbour or anyone else thinks. At my age, I don't feel the need to parade around like a peacock and impress anyone*'. Similarly, an 81-year-old female participant said: '*I want to look a well presented person, and I do my hair and my make up everyday but it's for me really, not anyone else*'.

This same participant, however, later said that her family's opinion was important to her, suggesting that the opinion of significant others still mattered. Playing down the importance of others' opinion and emphasizing one's own could reflect a defence mechanism providing self empowerment for the use of various body care strategies.

Some participants viewed their ageing body as divorced from their self whilst others perceived the two as intertwined. Self acceptance (Ranzijn & Luszcz, 1999) may thus mediate the significance attached to social feedback, with those who have accepted ageing-related changes being less affected by such feedback than those who did not.

According to Weiss (1999), one of the most important features of body image is the body's ability to alter and adapt to internal as well as external changes. This ability is important in terms of adaptation to ageing-related changes. Over time, social feedback and self-monitoring inform the primary domains that influence body ideal and body reality development. The feedback loop in the integrative model of body image development emphasizes that the body is a dynamic construct and that its perception evolves and fluctuates over time.

Whilst Western society, in general, values agelessness (Gilleard & Higgs, 2000), ageing is universal and unavoidable. By taking into account factors such as declining health and functional ability, the integrative model is more encompassing than previous ones. It also acknowledges that the experience of aging can be positive, (Andrews 1999, 2009) and includes a focus on positive adjustments and adaptation to normative age-related bodily changes.

THE BODY IMAGE SCALE FOR OLDER ADULTS (BIS-OA)

Following the formulation of the integrative model of body image development we constructed and validated a measure of body image, specific to older adults (Baker & Gringart, submitted a). Based on domains of the integrative model of body image development and validated with a sample of 785 older adults, the BIS-OA provides a tool to further the knowledge in body image research among older adults.

The BIS-OA comprises 19 items within four subscales. The subscales are: Body–Self Relations, which corresponds to comparisons between a person's body reality and body ideal; Body Image Management, which relates to strategies to decrease discrepancies between body reality and body ideal; Lifestyle, which relates to body image management strategies in terms of lifestyle practices, (e.g. adequate physical activity and healthy diet); and Health Evaluation, which relates to ratings of physical health.

The BIS-OA uses a 6-point Likert type scale rating statements from 1 (strongly disagree) to 6 (strongly agree). The scores of the BIS-OA can be summed to provide a score of respondents' overall body image satisfaction and the subscales can provide further details. Subscale scores allow insight into the particular areas and their relative contribution to respondents' body image satisfaction. The BIS-OA includes items such as; 'My physical fitness is very good for my age'; and 'I have always been confident about my physical appearance'. The measure demonstrated good internal consistency (Cronbach's alpha reliability coefficients were 0.92 for the overall score and ranged between 0.81 to 0.90 for the subscales) (Baker & Gringart, submitted a, b) and test retest reliability ($r = 0.92$, $p <0.01$) (Baker & Gringart, submitted a).

In a study using the BIS-OA to explore body image in older adulthood among 240 older adults (115 males and 125 females aged 65–85 years), we found that women's overall scores were relatively similar across age groups as were their scores on the Body Image Management, Lifestyle and Health Evaluation subscales (Baker & Gringart, submitted b). Women's scores on the Body-Self Relations subscale, however, were higher among the oldest group (79–85 years). This suggests that, as they age, older women may become more accepting of their body reality. Alternatively, it may be an indication that they have been able to successfully address perceived discrepancies between their body reality and body ideal by means of body image management or lifestyle strategies.

Contrary to suggestions that women are more dissatisfied with their body image than are men (e.g. Davison & McCabe 2005), men of all age groups reported lower scores on all measures of body image with the exception of the 65–71 years group, who reported more favourable scores on the Body–Self Relations subscale than did their female counterparts. One gender difference was that males in the 65–71 and 72–78 years age groups reported significantly lower levels of involvement in body image management strategies than all other female groups. This is consistent with previous research (e.g. Baker & Gringart, 2009) suggesting that, in attempting to buffer ageing related effects on appearance, older women are more likely to engage in the more controllable aspects of personal grooming, than are men.

The two significant predictors of males' self-esteem were the BIS-OA's Health Evaluation subscale and the Body–Self Relations subscale. These results are in accord with previous research indicating the importance of health and functional abilities in older adults' perception of their bodies (Paxton & Phythian, 1999). The only significant predictor of females' self-esteem was the BIS-OA's Body–Self Relations subscale. This suggests that the ability to address discrepancies between body ideals and body reality to a level that is satisfactory is a significant predictor of self-esteem in older adulthood across gender.

The two significant predictors of males' satisfaction with life were the BIS-OA's Lifestyle and Body–Self Relations subscales. Similar to patterns for self-esteem, the only significant predictor of females' satisfaction with life was the BIS-OA's Body–Self Relations subscale. More favourable scores on the BIS-OA's Body–Self Relations subscale may reflect a person's ability to minimize the discrepancy between his or her body ideal and body reality. This perspective is in accord with previous research suggesting that perceived control is a significant predictor of life satisfaction in older adulthood (Sparks et al., 2004). Likewise, one's ability to make lifestyle choices could be related to perceived control but also to the social interactions that are associated with a healthy lifestyle.

Following our qualitative and quantitative investigations, we argue that body image is both important and relevant to older adults, and suggest that monitoring and facilitating body image satisfaction among older adults could contribute to well-being and the quality of lived experience among people in this age group.

CONTEXT AND FUTURE DIRECTIONS

Worldwide, the number of adults, aged over 60 years, tripled from 205 million in 1950 to 606 million in 2000. This number is expected to reach nearly 2 billion by 2050, as the first cohort of the baby boomers (those born from 1946 to 1965) reach the age of 65 by 2011 and contribute to this figure (United Nations, 2001). Whilst this unprecedented growth rate in the ageing population, relative to the rest of the population, has brought ageing related issues to the forefront of the thinking of governments and healthcare providers, ageing issues were relevant prior to this demographic trend and will continue to be significant beyond the baby boomers generation.

Furthermore, the current decade is recognized as 'a time of increased concerns with the body' (Grogan, 2007, p. 206). As noted earlier, in aiming to understand body image issues in older adults we need to consider the time, in a historical sense, during which people grew up, and the social and cultural environments they have lived within. While hair care or skin care products are now widely promoted to men, this has not always been the case. Thus, to the extent that lifestyle practices affect people's appearance, it is likely that future cohorts will have different concerns to the one examined in our research.

Likewise, technological and medical advancements have resulted in an extensive range of body image management strategies that are more accessible and socially acceptable than ever before (Hogle, 2005). Although people aged 65 and over currently make up only a small percentage of all cosmetic surgery consumers, there are indications of a steady increase in the number of older adults undertaking such procedures. As public acceptance of such procedure increases, future generations of older adults may adopt more positive views toward this intervention. Longitudinal studies should be undertaken to provide important information about processes that occur in response to societal changes in terms of body image satisfaction, the changes in strategies employed to reduce discrepancies between body reality and body ideal, and their psychological ramifications.

CONCLUSION

Whilst older adults' body image has been largely overlooked within psychological gerontology, the findings presented in this chapter demonstrate that contrary to popular beliefs, body image is important to older adults. Our findings indicate that older adults' ability to address the discrepancy between their body reality and body ideal can have significant implications. It is also necessary to understand the normal physiological changes associated with ageing and to consider how these changes within the body are experienced in different ways by older people. Mobility, for example may be particularly important to those who have been involved in physical activity throughout their lives but may be less important to those leading more sedentary lifestyles. Thus, aspects that are valued by the person throughout their adult life are likely to remain important in older adulthood and attempts to preserve efficacy in these domains as well as finding ways to compensate for their losses could be encouraged. Nonetheless, it is also imperative that practitioners, researchers, and policy-makers 'resist the temptation of agelessness' (Andrews, 1999, p. 316), and aim to promote well-being rather than reinforce the idea that aging without showing the physical signs of growing old is feasible, necessary, or desirable.

Given that relatively minor body image concerns can lead to unhealthy outcomes, further investigation into factors that protect against body image dissatisfaction as well as those that hinder or enhance such satisfaction is warranted. This work will inform professionals working with older adults and assist in the development of preventative as well as therapeutic interventions, which are likely to help older adults develop a positive body image that will contribute to psychosocial strengths and enhance their quality of life. Finally, older adults should be informed of the importance many of their counterparts place on body image to promote the idea that these concerns are both normal and appropriate. Further research and understanding of body image issues in later life could counter the idealization of agelessness and facilitate world views that would foster instead, a celebration of ageing.

REFERENCES

Allport, G. W. (1961). *Patterns and growth in personality*. New York: Holt, Rinehart & Winston.

Andrews, M. (1999). The seductiveness of agelessness. *Ageing and Society*, 19, 301–18.

Andrews, M. (2009). The narrative complexity of successful ageing. *International Journal of Sociology and Social Policy*, 29, 73–83.

Baker, L. & Gringart, E. (2009). Body image and self-esteem in older adulthood. *Ageing & Society*, 29, 977–95.

Baker, L. & Gringart, E. (submitted a). *Development and psychometric evaluation of the Body Image Scale for Older Adults (BIS-OA)*. Manuscript submitted for publication.

Baker, L. & Gringart, E. (submitted b). *Body image, self-esteem and satisfaction with life in older adulthood.* Manuscript submitted for publication.

Bordo, S. (1993). *Unbearable weight: Feminism, Western culture and the body.* Los Angeles, CA: University of California Press.

Cash, T. F. (1990). The psychology of physical appearance: Aesthetics, attributes and images, in T. F. Cash and T. Pruzinsky (eds.), *Body images: Development deviance and change,* pp. 51–79. New York: Guilford.

Davison, T. E. & McCabe, M. P. (2005). Relationships between men's and women's body image and their psychological, social, and sexual functioning. *Sex Roles,* 52, 463–75.

Douglas, M. (1970). *Natural symbols: Explorations in cosmology.* London: The Cresset Press.

Featherstone, M. (1991). *Consumer culture and postmodernism.* Sage: London.

Feingold, A. & Mazzella, R. (1998). Gender differences in body image are increasing. *Psychological Science,* 9, 190–95.

Frost, L. (2001). *Young Women and the Body: A Feminist Sociology.* Palgrave: New York.

Gilleard, C. (2002). Women, aging and body talk. In L. Anderson (ed.), *Cultural gerontology,* pp. 139–60. Westport, CN: Auburn House.

Gilleard, C. & Higgs, P. (2000). *Cultures of ageing: Self, citizen and the body.* London: Prentice Hall.

Goffman, E. (1963). *Stigma: Notes on the management of spoiled identity.* Englewood Cliffs, NJ: Prentice Hall.

Grogan, S. (2007). *Body image: Understanding body dissatisfaction in men, women, and children* (2nd edn.). London: Routledge.

Hogle, L. (2005). Enhancement technologies and the body. *Annual Review of Anthropology,* 34, 695–716.

Janelli, L. M. (1993). Are there body image differences between older men and women? *Western Journal of Nursing Research,* 15, 327–39.

Lamb, C. S., Jackson, L. A., Cassidy, P. B., & Priest, D.J. (1993). Body figure preferences of men and women: A comparison of two generations. *Sex Roles,* 28, 345–58.

Lien, A., Pope, H. G., & Gray, J.J. (2001). Cultural expectations of muscularity in men: The evolution of playgirl centerfolds. *International Journal of Eating Disorders,* 29, 90–3.

Marquez, D. X. & McAuley, E. (2001). Physique anxiety and self-efficacy influences on perceptions of physical evaluation. *Social Behavior and Personality,* 29, 649–60.

Paxton, S. J. & Phythian, K. (1999). Body image, self-esteem, and health status in middle and late adulthood. *Australian Psychologist,* 34, 116–21.

Pruzinsky, T. & Cash, T. F. (2002). Understanding body images: Historical and contemporary perspectives. In T. F. Cash & T. Pruzinsky (eds.) *Body image: A handbook of theory, research, and clinical practice,* pp. 3–12. New York: Guilford.

Ranzijn, R. & Luszcz, M. (1999). Acceptance: A key to well-being in older adults? *Australian Psychologist,* 34(2), 94–8.

Reischer, E. & Koo, K.S. (2004). The body beautiful: Symbolism and agency in the social world. *Annual Review of Anthropology,* 33, 297–317.

Silverstein, L. R., Striegel-Moore, R. H., Timko, C., & Rodin, J. (1988). Behavioral and psychological implications of body image dissatisfaction: Do men and women differ? *Sex Roles,* 19, 219–32.

Sparkes, A. C. (1997). Reflections on the socially constructed physical self. In K. R. Fox (ed.) *The physical self: From motivation to well-being,* pp. 83–110. Champaign, IL: Human Kinetics.

Sparks, M., Zehr, D., & Painter, B. (2004). Predictors of life satisfaction: Perceptions of older community-dwelling adults. *Journal of Gerontological Nursing, 30,* 47–53.

United Nations (2001). *World population ageing: 1950–2050.* Available at: http://www.un. org/esa/population/publications/worldageing19502050/ (accessed 28 April 2010).

Weiss, G. (1999). *Body images: Embodiment as intercorporeality.* New York: Routledge.

INDIVIDUAL DIFFERENCES IN ADJUSTMENT AND DISTRESS

CHAPTER 15

....

GENDER

....

HELEN J. FAWKNER

THIS chapter has three aims; to examine who is affected by appearance related concerns (i.e. rates of dissatisfaction as a function of gender), the ways in which men and women are affected (e.g. differences in the sources of, antecedents to, and adjustive strategies as a consequence of dissatisfaction), and why men and women may experience dissatisfaction relating to their appearance.

BODY IDEALS
....

It is well documented, in both academic and popular literature, that the female ideal is a slender, full-breasted, and well-toned body (Rodin et al., 1985; Grogan, 2008; Koff et al., 2010). This physique is typified by models, actors, and celebrities, and has been described as 'physically impossible' for most women to attain as it is the 'Barbie-doll stereotype' (Marchessault, 2000). Further, this ideal has become increasingly slender since the 1950s (Fallon & Rozin, 1985), despite secular trends demonstrating that among the general population, women are increasingly taller and heavier. In fact, 25% of UK women are a size 18 (US 16) or larger (Mintel, 2010).

Thinness alone however, will not suffice; muscle tone is also important (Bordo, 2003), but women must not be too muscular! (Choi, 2000a). Thus, it is not surprising the majority of (Western) women experience body dissatisfaction (Grogan, 2008). This dissatisfaction is so pervasive that more than 25 years ago it was labelled 'normative discontent' (Rodin et al., 1985). Further, body dissatisfaction appears to be consistent among women irrespective of age, relationship status, educational level, or occupational status (Stevens & Tiggemann, 1998).

The male ideal is mesomorphic; an athletic, slender, well-proportioned, v-shaped physique. There 'should' be good muscular development of the shoulders, chest, arms, and abdomen, with a slim waist and hips (Pope et al., 2000; Fawkner & McMurray, 2002; Olivardia et al., 2004,). Although some males idealize the hyper-mesomorphic physique, typified by body-builders (Tucker, 1984), this extreme is often perceived to be 'unnatural' and a sign of narcissism (Filiault & Drummond, 2010).

As for women, the men's ideal has become more extreme; increasingly muscular and lean over a similar time period, and is equally unattainable for the average male (Pope et al., 2000; Leit et al., 2001). Pope et al. claimed that the male ideal is difficult to obtain without the use of steroids.

RATES OF APPEARANCE DISSATISFACTION

It is difficult to assess the exact percentage of individuals who experience dissatisfaction as the rate is partly an artefact of how dissatisfaction is measured. One method involves participants being presented with an array of silhouettes (very thin to obese) and being asked to select the figures that best represent their current size and their ideal. Any discrepancy is considered indicative of dissatisfaction. In studies employing this methodology, the majority of women chose an ideal figure that was thinner than their perceived current figure (e.g. Cororve-Fingeret et al., 2004; Cachelin et al., 2006). This difference is typically greater for White women than women from other ethnic groups (Kronenfeld et al., 2010; Phillips & de Man, 2010).

In contrast, early studies employing this methodology with men led to the erroneous assumption that they experienced body satisfaction, as comparisons of the average ratings for the figures selected as current and ideal were almost identical (e.g. Fallon & Rozin, 1985; Rozin & Fallon, 1988; Tiggemann, 1991). Nevertheless, the current-ideal congruence reported was a statistical artefact as the direction of the discrepancy was not considered. When the direction of discrepancy was considered, current-ideal discrepancy was reported (Drewnowski & Yee, 1987; Frederick et al., 2007) by as many as 95% of men (Mishkind et al., 1986). There was, however, variation in the direction of this discrepancy; approximately equal numbers of men selected a smaller ideal as those who selected a larger ideal (Mishkind et al., 1986; Drewnowski & Yee, 1987) and the latter choice has been interpreted as a desire for a muscular physique. Studies that have employed silhouettes that depict changes in muscularity support this interpretation (Lynch & Zellner, 1999; Morrison et al., 2003; Olivardia et al., 2004; Tiggemann et al., 2007). Again, these findings contrast with results for women in that ethnicity does not seem to have an effect; the mesomorphic ideal is valued across cultures (e.g. Mellor et al., 2004, 2008, 2009).

Body Areas That are the Source of Dissatisfaction

Research with global measures paints a clearer picture of the similarities and differences in appearance dissatisfaction as a function of gender. Data collected via *Psychology Today* magazine suggests an increasing percentage of men and women have reported dissatisfaction with their weight, shape, and other aspects of their appearance (Berscheid et al., 1972; Cash et al., 1986; Garner & Kearney-Cooke, 1997).

In studies spanning three cohorts, across three decades, more women than men reported dissatisfaction with their overall appearance (1972: 23% of women vs. 15% of men, 1985: 38% of women vs. 34% of men, 1996: 56% of women vs. 43% of men). Similarly, more women than men reported dissatisfaction with their weight (1972: 48% of women vs. 35% of men, 1985: 55% of women vs. 45% of men, 1996: 66% of women vs. 53% of men). Furthermore, the 1996 study revealed that 89% of weight dissatisfied women wanted to lose weight, while men were split between those who wished to lose weight and those who wished to gain weight.

Dissatisfaction with every individual body part, with the exception of height, showed a steady increase, and the pattern of dissatisfaction remained the same; women were predominantly dissatisfied with their lower bodies; stomach (50% in 1972 vs. 71% in 1996), and hips and thighs (49% in 1972 vs. 61% in 1996). This pattern of dissatisfaction is echoed in other research (Grogan, 2008). Men reported the greatest dissatisfaction with their abdomens (36% in 1972 vs. 63% in 1996), muscle tone (25% in 1972 vs. 45% in 1996), and chests (18% in 1972 vs. 38% in 1996). In fact, more men then women expressed dissatisfaction with their chest/breasts in the 1996 survey (38% vs. 34% respectively).

Despite the caution that is required in interpreting these data due to recruiting, sampling, and scale measurement biases inherent in these studies (Cash, 2002b), these results illustrate a high prevalence of body dissatisfaction among men and women. Some researchers have argued these data suggest that the gender gap is narrowing, but this conclusion is challenged by a meta-analysis of 222 studies conducted over a 50-year period (Feingold & Mazzella, 1998). This study shows the effect sizes for gender increased significantly over time, with female respondents increasingly over-represented among those expressing body dissatisfaction, while body satisfaction among men has remained the same, or declined less steeply than the decline for women in the same period.

Antecedents to Dissatisfaction

Cash (1996, 2002a) proposed that four types of factors shape body image; physical attributes, personality attributes, cultural influences, and interpersonal experiences.

Further, he hypothesized a bidirectional relationship among body image attitudes and adjustive strategies.

This model is equally applicable to men and women, although gender directly influences satisfaction and is linked to differences in some antecedents to body image. Many of these antecedents are covered in detail elsewhere in this book, thus, only pertinent gender differences among these relationships will be considered. I will selectively examine the role of physical attributes, and how gender may intertwine with some psychological factors (i.e. self-esteem), interpersonal factors (i.e. relationship status), and cultural factors (e.g. media images, sexual orientation) as antecedents to body image. Further, pertinent gender differences in adjustive strategies (dieting, exercise, steroid use, cosmetic surgery) will be considered.

Physical factors: breast and penis size

The effects of size and weight have been written about extensively, so are not addressed in this chapter (see Grogan, 2008). Instead, physical characteristics that are markers of gender are examined. Just as muscles are equated with masculinity, so is penis size (Bordo, 1999; Fox and Fawkner, 2004; Fawkner, 2005). Little research examines the role of men's genitals in body satisfaction (Bordo, 1999), despite many men expressing dissatisfaction with the size of their penis (Edwards, 1998; Fox & Fawkner, 2004; Lever et al., 2006; Martins et al., 2008).

Actual penis size is normally distributed (Lever et al., 2006). Most men view their own as average (Lee, 1996; Son et al., 2003; Lever et al., 2006), but there is disagreement as to whether more men underestimate (Lee, 1996; Son et al., 2003) or overestimate (Lever et al., 2006) the relative size of their penis. Fewer men who rate their penis as 'modestly' sized are satisfied with their size (10%), compared with men who believe they are average sized (40%) or 'endowed' (70%) (Edwards, 1998). Similar findings were noted by Lever et al. (2006).

Men who were satisfied with their penises also experienced higher levels of global body satisfaction (Fox and Fawkner, 2004; Morrison et al., 2005; Lever et al., 2006; Tiggemann et al., 2008). Thus, as with the other physical marker of masculinity (musculature), penis size is a source of dissatisfaction for many men and also influences global body satisfaction.

The research examining men's preferences for women's breast size is equivocal. Some evidence indicates women with larger breasts are rated by men as more physically attractive (e.g. Gitter et al., 1983; Furnham et al., 1990). Experimental evidence suggests such women receive more male attention; they are more likely to offered a lift by male motorists (Morgan et al., 1975), or approached for a date in a public place (Gueguen, 2007). That said, some research shows men rate women with medium (Kleinke & Staneski, 1980) or small breasts (Furnham & Swami, 2007) as more attractive. Further, recent research has suggested that preferred breast size may be influenced by the ethnicity of the men who are 'judging' attractiveness and the ethnicity of the women being 'judged' (Swami et al., 2009). Whatever men's preferences, breasts clearly feature in judgments of attractiveness, thus, it is not surprising that many women are concerned with the appearance of their breasts (Thompson & Tantleff, 1992; Koff & Benavage, 1998; Goodman & Walsh-Childers, 2004; Frederick et al., 2008).

In the largest of these studies, Frederick et al. (2008) noted younger and thinner women expressed concern that they had small breasts, and older and heavier women were concerned with 'droopiness'. Breast dissatisfaction was associated with real-life behaviours; women who were dissatisfied reported they were less likely to undress in front of their partners, attempted to conceal their breasts during intimacy, and felt less comfortable in a swimsuit. These women were also more likely to report global body dissatisfaction.

Psychological factors: self-esteem

Body satisfaction and self-esteem are related but independent constructs. Research has revealed that body dissatisfaction is associated with low self-esteem for both genders (Silberstein et al., 1988; Paxton & Phythian, 1999) and cross-culturally (e.g. Davis & Katzman, 1998). Gender appears to influence the nature of this relationship. Specifically, the relationship between body dissatisfaction and self-esteem is stronger for women than for men (Furnham & Greaves, 1994; Davis, 1997), however, the effect of the relationship appears to differ as a function of gender. Silberstein et al. (1988) reported that self-esteem was moderately, negatively correlated with the absolute values of current-ideal discrepancies and moderately, positively correlated with the body esteem scores for males, but not females. Self-esteem for men with current-ideal congruence was higher than for men with current-ideal discrepancy, regardless of whether they desired to gain or lose weight. For women, there was no difference in self-esteem between those who desired to be thinner and those who did not. Silberstein et al. hypothesized that women who experience weight dissatisfaction resemble rather than deviate from their peers, and weight dissatisfaction may be less unique and distinctive for women. Thus, it is possible that dissatisfaction with weight in men sets them apart from their peers, and may have more serious psychological consequences.

Cultural factors: media images and sexual orientation

Two important cultural factors that influence body image are media images and sexual orientation. A detailed account is beyond the scope of this chapter, but it is worth noting that correlational and experimental research shows that both men and women are affected by exposure to idealized media images and the effects seem similar for men and women (see Chapter 18). In contrast, much research suggests an interaction between sexual orientation and gender; non-heterosexuality appears to be a protective factor for women but a risk factor for men (e.g. Siever, 1994). Yet, a recent meta-analysis suggests that gender may trump sexual orientation for women. Again, suggesting that irrespective of sexual orientation, body dissatisfaction is normative for women. See Chapter 16.

Interpersonal factors: relationship status

Both the presence and quality of interpersonal relationships have a strong influence on body image attitudes. A satisfying relationship (Fawkner, 2005) or feeling that one's partner finds one attractive is associated with body satisfaction (Garner & Kearney-Cooke, 1997; Tantleff-Dunn & Gokee, 2002). Of interest, recent work by Hearty (2010) suggests an interaction between age and gender. Specifically, the most dissatisfied participants in this study were young single women. It is of concern that in 2010, much of young women's satisfaction with their appearance still appears to be derived from reflected appraisal of their bodies.

GENDER AND THE CONSEQUENCES OF DISSATISFACTION

Dieting behaviour

Dieting is more frequent amongst women as compared with men. For example, Mintel estimated that 25% of UK men compared with 43% of women were dieting with the intention of losing or controlling their weight (Leith, 2006). This is possibly because dieting is viewed as more gender appropriate for women (Bordo, 2003, Gough, 2007). In contrast, men tend to exercise rather than diet for the purposes of weight control (Drewnowski & Yee, 1987; Grogan & Richards, 2002; Grogan et al., 2006a). Other weight control methods differ; women are more likely to use diet pills and laxatives (Braun et al., 1999; Johnson et al., 1999), men are more likely to use saunas and steam baths (Johnson et al., 1999).

The meaning ascribed to dieting also differs as a function of gender (Grogan, 2008). Women are more likely to explain their dieting as being motivated by a desire for slimness or increased confidence and self-esteem (Furnham & Greaves, 1994). In contrast, many men who 'diet' report behaviour more akin to healthy eating practices; eating more fruit and vegetables and reducing fat consumption (Grogan, 2008), or engaging in high-protein diets in an effort to bulk up (McCreary & Sasse, 2002; Leith, 2006).

Linked with dieting; eating disorder diagnoses generally exhibit a gender bias. Although the diagnosis of anorexia nervosa and bulimia nervosa are increasing amongst men (e.g. Strong et al., 2000), rates are still significantly higher amongst women (Croll et al., 2002) and only binge-eating disorder occurs equally among men and women (Spitzer et al., 1993). Of concern however, is the finding that outcomes for men with an eating disorder are often worse; only 20% of men compared with 50% of females had a good outcome (i.e. maintenance of body weight between 85% and 115% of the matched population mean weight, regular sexual activity, normal eating habits). More men (50%) compared with women (40%) had a poor outcome (i.e. body weight significantly outside the 85–115% of matched population mean weight with or without sexual activity), and the majority of men (70%) were still pre-occupied with their diets and physiques as compared with only 30% of the women (Oyebode et al., 1988).

Exercise

Although men, compared with women, are less likely to report that they exercise for appearance-related reasons, they do still exercise for weight control (Grogan et al., 2006a,b), particularly older men (Davis et al., 1995). Exercise has been shown to improve body image in both men (Tucker, 1983) and women (Choi, 2000b), but the relationship between exercise and body image is complicated, and the findings equivocal. A detailed exploration of this research is beyond the scope of this chapter (see instead Chapter 22), however a small number of studies show no differences in body image as a function of exercise status (e.g. Pasman & Thompson, 1988), and others have shown exercisers to be more dissatisfied with their bodies (e.g. Armstrong et al., 1992). The bulk of research suggests exercisers are more satisfied with their bodies, especially when participation is not at an elite level (Stoutjesdyk & Jevne, 1992), does not involve weight restrictions (Thiel et al., 1993), or place a premium on thinness or muscularity as an aesthetic demand of participation (Fawkner, 2005).

Steroid use

Steroid use is more common amongst men than women (Beel, 1996; Peters et al., 1997). Although men and women have similar motivations for use (i.e. increased muscularity) (Wright et al., 2000), increasingly, many male users are 'aesthetes'; not involved in competitive sport or jobs requiring strength or the appearance of strength (Peters et al., 1997; Pope et al., 2000; Fawkner, 2005). Concerns, or rather a lack of concerns regarding steroid use are also quite similar, except that women expressed some particular anxieties about the masculinizing effects of steroids (e.g. voice deepening, balding, being 'too big'), and effects on fertility, which may render them 'unfeminine' (e.g. Grogan et al., 2004; Grogan et al., 2006b). Interestingly, men did not appear to be concerned about the feminizing effects that steroids can have (see Grogan et al., 2004; Grogan et al., 2006b), such as decreasing the size of their testicles, or their fertility. Both men and women firmly believed that the harm is not in using steroids, but in 'misusing' steroids (Grogan et al., 2006b).

Cosmetic surgery

There has been a significant increase in the number of individuals undergoing cosmetic surgery in Western nations (Castle et al., 2002; Sarwer and Crerand, 2004; British Association of Aesthetic Plastic Surgeons (BAAPS), 2010). Among the reasons for the increase are that surgery has become more 'normal', attitudes toward surgery are more positive, and surgery less invasive, safer, has a faster recovery time, and procedures are marketed directly to the consumer (Sarwer and Crerand, 2004; Grogan, 2008).

Although more women still undergo these procedures, the rate of increase is greater among men than women; a 21% vs. 5% increase in 2009 (BAAPS, 2010). Further, there were striking similarities in the procedures undertaken as a function of gender (BAAPS, 2010). Amongst women, the three most popular procedures were breast augmentation, blepharoplasty (eyelid surgery), and breast reduction, and for men; rhinoplasty (nose reshaping), blepharoplasty, and breast reduction. There is much debate about the motivations and agency of individuals undergoing cosmetic surgery. Recent work with men who have sought breast reduction for gynaecomastia (Singleton et al., 2009, 2010) is in line with Davis' (1995, 2002) argument that the surgery gives an individual a sense of bodily control and normality. Nevertheless, attitudes towards men who undergo cosmetic surgery are still quite negative, they were more likely to be viewed as self-conscious, insecure or vain, rather than assertive or confident (Fawkner, 2005).

WHY MEN AND WOMEN MAY EXPERIENCE DISSATISFACTION

Objectification theory offers an explanation for why more women than men may experience dissatisfaction. It is suggested that all women are objectified, their bodies made available for the consumption and pleasure of others, therefore, their sense of worth is contingent upon how closely they match the cultural ideal (Fredrickson & Roberts, 1997). According to this theory, men, as compared with women, are less objectified and therefore experience less dissatisfaction.

That said, the literature reviewed in this chapter suggests that men are following in the footsteps of women and increasingly experiencing dissatisfaction. Mishkind et al. (1986) suggested three sociocultural changes might explain the increased body consciousness among men. First, a decline in purely masculine domains within society has resulted in increased muscularity being one of the few ways available for men to express their masculinity. Second, the leading causes of death are now preventable diseases (e.g. cardiovascular disease) (Sarafino, 2002), and increased importance is placed upon the self-management of one's health. Erroneously, being healthy has become equated with looking healthy. Finally, cultural attitudes towards the male body have changed, men's bodies are increasingly visible in popular culture, and actively targeted by the advertising industry, challenging traditional masculine icons and encouraging viewers of these images to become more aware of how they look (Mort, 1988).

Summary

The research to date suggests that more women than men experience body dissatisfaction, though a significant proportion of both genders are dissatisfied. Both men and women commonly report dissatisfaction with body aspects that correspond with their respective gender-based ideals. Interestingly however, both genders often misperceive what is attractive to the opposite sex (e.g. Fallon & Rozin, 1985; Jacobi & Cash, 1994; Frederick & Haselton, 2003; Olivardia et al., 2004).

There are similarities in antecedents to body dissatisfaction for men and women (e.g. dissatisfaction with sexual organs, media exposure, relationship satisfaction), as well as differences (e.g. self-esteem, ethnicity, sexual orientation). Further, there are gender differences in behavioural indicators of dissatisfaction (dieting, exercise, steroid use, cosmetic surgery), and again, these are tied to men's and women's body-ideals. Increasing sexual objectification of the body may be partially responsible for increasing levels of dissatisfaction amongst men and women, especially the recent increases amongst men.

References

Armstrong, J. E., Lange, E. & Mishra, S. (1992). Reported exercise practices and self-image of adult male and female recreational exercisers. *Family and Community Health*, 14, 20–8.

Beel, A. (1996). The profile, attitudes and behaviours of steroid users: How do they compare to the general population. 7th International Conference of Drug Related Harm. Hobart, Australia.

Berscheid, E., Walster, E. & Bohrnstedt, G. (1972). *A Psychology Today* questionnaire. Body image. *Psychology Today*, 6, 57–65.

Bordo, S. (1999). *The male body,* New York: Farrer, Strauss, and Giroux.

Bordo, S. (2003). *Unbearable weight: Feminism, western culture, and the body (10th anniversary ed.).* Berkeley, CA: University of California.

Braun, D. L., Sunday, S. R., Huang, A. & Halmi, K. (1999). More males seek treatment for eating disorders. *International Journal of Eating Disorders, 26,* 413–24.

British Association Of Aesthetic Plastic Surgeons (2010). Britons over the moob: Male breast reduction nearly doubles in 2009 available from: http://www.baaps.org.uk/about-us/audit/584-britons-over-the-moob-male-breast-reduction-nearly-doubles-in-2009 (accessed 5 March 2012).

Cachelin, F. M., Monreal, T. K. & Juarez, L. C. (2006). Body image and size perceptions of Mexican American women. *Body Image, 3,* 67–75.

Cash, T. F. (1996). The treatment of body image disturbances. In J. K. Thompson (ed.) *Body image, eating disorders, and obesity: An integrative guide for assessment and treatment,* pp. 83–107. Washington, DC: American Psychological Association.

Cash, T. F. (2002a). Cognitive-behavioral perspectives on body image. In T. F. Cash & T. Pruzinsky (eds.) *Body image. A handbook of theory, research, and clinical practice,* pp. 38–46. New York: The Guilford Press.

Cash, T. F. (2002b). A 'negative body image'. Evaluating epidemiological evidence. In T. F. Cash & T. Pruzinsky (eds.) *Body image. A handbook of theory, research, and clinical practice,* pp. 269–76. New York: The Guildford Press.

Cash, T. F., Winstead, B. A. & Janda, L. H. (1986). Body image survey report: The great American shape-up. *Psychology Today, 20,* 30–7.

Castle, D. J., Honigman, R. J. & Phillips, K. A. (2002). Does cosmetic surgery improve psychosocial wellbeing? *Medical Journal of Australia, 176,* 601–4.

Choi, P. Y. L. (2000a). *Femininity and the physically active woman,* London: Women's Press.

Choi, P. Y. L. (2000b). Looking good and feeling good: Why do fewer women than men exercise? In J. Ussher (ed.) *Women's health,* pp. 372–9. Leicester: BPS Books.

Cororve-Fingeret, M., Gleaves, D. H. & Pearson, C. A. (2004). On the methodology of body image assessment: The use of figural rating scales to evaluate body dissatisfaction and the ideal body standards of women. *Body Image, 1,* 207–212.

Croll, J., Neumark-Sztainer, D., Story, M. & Ireland, M. (2002). Prevalence and risk and protective factors related to disordered eating behaviors among adolescents: Relationship to gender and ethnicity. *Journal of Adolescent Health, 31,* 166–75.

Davis, C. (1997). Body image, exercise, and eating behaviors. In K. Fox (ed.) *The physical self. From motivation to well being,* pp. 143–74. Champaign, IL: Human Kinetics.

Davis, C., Fox, J., Brewer, H. & Ratusny, D. (1995). Motivations to exercise as a function of personality characteristics, age, and gender. *Personality & Individual Differences, 19,* 165–74.

Davis, C. & Katzman, M. A. (1998). Chinese men and women in the United States and Hong Kong. Body and self-esteem ratings as a prelude to dieting and exercise. *International Journal of Eating Disorders, 23,* 99–102.

Davis, K. (1995). *Reshaping the female body. The dilemma of cosmetic surgery.* London: Routledge.

Davis, K. (2002). A dubious equality: Men and women in cosmetic surgery. *Body and Society, 8,* 49–65.

Drewnowski, A. & Yee, D. K. (1987). Men and body image: Are males satisfied with their body weight? *Psychosomatic Medicine, 49,* 626–34.

Edwards, R. (1998). *The definitive penis size survey results* (6th ed.). http://www.sizesurvey.com

Fallon, A. E. & Rozin, P. (1985). Sex differences in perceptions of desirable body shape. *Journal of Abnormal Psychology,* 94, 102–5.

Fawkner, H. J. (2005). Body image attitudes in men: An examination of the antecedents and consequent adjustive strategies and behaviours. Unpublished PhD Thesis, University of Melbourne, Australia.

Fawkner, H. J. & Mcmurray, N. E. (2002). Body image in men: Self-reported thoughts, feelings, and behaviors in response to media images. *International Journal of Men's Health,* 1, 137–61.

Feingold, A. & Mazzella, R. (1998). Gender differences in body image are increasing. *Psychological Science,* 9, 190–5.

Filiault, S. M. & Drummond, M. J. N. (2010). "Muscular but not 'roided out": Gay male athletes and performance-enhancing substances. *International Journal of Men's Health,* 9, 62–81.

Fox, C. & Fawkner, H. J. (2004). Sizing up the Man. A qualitative exploration of the importance of penis size to men. ASSERT 2004, National Sexology Conference, Sydney, Australia. Sydney, Australia.

Frederick, D. A., Buchanan, G. M., Sadehgi-Azar, L., Peplau, L. A., Haselton, M. G., Berezovskaya, A. & Lipinski, R. E. (2007). Desiring the muscular ideal: Men's body satisfaction in the United States, Ukraine, and Ghana. *Psychology of Men & Masculinity,* 8, 103–17.

Frederick, D. A. & Haselton, M. G. (2003). Muscularity as a communicative signal. International Communications Association, San Diego. San Diego.

Frederick, D. A., Peplau, A. & Lever, J. (2008). The Barbie mystique: Satisfaction with breast size and shape across the lifespan. *International Journal of Sexual Health,* 20, 200–11.

Fredrickson, B. L. & Roberts, T.-A. (1997). Objectification theory. *Psychology of Women Quarterly,* 21, 173.

Furnham, A. & Greaves, N. (1994). Gender and locus of control. Correlates of body image dissatisfaction. *European Journal of Personality,* 8, 183–200.

Furnham, A. & Swami, V. (2007). Perception of female buttocks and breast size in profile. *Social Behaviour and Personality,* 35, 1–8.

Furnham, A., Hester, C. & Weir, C. (1990). Sex differences in the preferences for specfic female body shapes. *Sex Roles,* 22, 743–54.

Garner, D. M. & Kearney-Cooke, A. (1997). The 1997 body image survey results. *Psychology Today,* 30, 30–44.

Gitter, G. A., Lomranz, J., Saxe, L. & Bar-Tal, Y. (1983). Perceptions of female physique characteristics by American and Israeli students. *The Journal of Social Psychology,* 121,7–13.

Goodman, J. R. & Walsh-Childers, K. (2004). Sculpting the female breast: How college women negotiate the media's ideal breast image. *Journalism & Mass Communication Quarterly,* 81, 657–74.

Gough, B. (2007). 'Real men don't diet:' An analysis of contemporary newspaper representations of men, food, and health. *Social Science and Medicine,* 64, 326–37.

Grogan, S. (2008). *Body image. Understanding body dissatisfaction in men, women, and children* (2nd edn.). London: Routledge.

Grogan, S., Connor, M. & Smithson, H. (2006a). Sexuality and exercise motivations: Are gay men and heterosexual men most likely to be motivated by concern about weight and appearance? *Sex Roles,* 55, 567–72.

Grogan, S., Evans, R., Wright, S. & Hunter, G. (2004). Femininity and muscularity: Accounts of seven females bodybuilders. *Journal of Gender Studies*, 13, 49–61.

Grogan, S. & Richards, H. (2002). Body image; Focus groups with boys and men. *Men and Masculinities*, 4, 219–33.

Grogan, S., Shepherd, S., Evans, R., Wright, S. & Hunter, G. (2006b). Experiences of anabolic steroid use: Interviews with men and women steroid users. *Journal of Health Psychology*, 11, 849–60.

Gueguen, N. (2007). Women's bust size and men's courtship solicitation. *Body Image*, 4, 386–90.

Hearty, P. (2010). Body satisfaction and appearance investment: The influences of gender and relationship status. Unpublished BSc (Hons) Thesis, Leeds Metropolitan University, UK.

Jacobi, L. & Cash, T. F. (1994). In pursuit of the perfect appearance: Discrepancies among self-ideal percepts of multiple physical attributes. *Journal of Applied Social Psychology*, 24, 379–96.

Johnson, C., Powers, P. S. & Dick, R. (1999). Athletes and eating disorders: The National Collegiate Athletic Association study. *International Journal of Eating Disorders*, 26, 179–88.

Kleinke, C. L. & Staneski, R. A. (1980). First impressions of female bust size. *The Journal of Social Psychology*, 110, 123–34.

Koff, E. & Benavage, A. (1998). Breast size perception and satisfaction, body image, and psychological functioning in Caucasian and Asian American college women. *Sex Roles*, 38, 655–73.

Koff, E., Lucas, M., Migliorini, R. & Grossmith, S. (2010). Women and body dissatisfaction: Does sexual orientation make a difference? *Body Image.*, 7, 255–58.

Kronenfeld, L. W., Reba-Harrelson, L., Von Holle, A., Reyes, M. L. & Bulik, C. M. (2010). Ethnic and racial differences in body size perception and satisfaction. *Body Image*, 7, 131–6.

Lee, P. A. (1996). Survey report: Concept of penis size. *Journal of Sex and Marital Therapy*, 22, 131–5.

Leit, R. A., Pope, H. G., Jr. & Gray, J. J. (2001). Cultural expectations of muscularity in men: The evolution of Playgirl centerfolds. *International Journal of Eating Disorders*, 29, 90–3.

Leith, W. (2006). We used to settle for one like this; now we all want one like this. *Observer Women*, February.

Lever, J., Frederick, D. A. & Peplau, L. A. (2006). Does size matter? Men's and women's views on penis size across the lifespan. *Psychology of Men & Masculinity*, 7, 129–43.

Lynch, S. M. & Zellner, D. A. (1999). Figure preferences in two generations of men: The use of figure drawings illustrating differences in muscle mass. *Sex Roles*, 40, 833–43.

Marchessault, G. (2000). One mother and daughter approach to resisting weight preoccupations. In B. Miedema, J. M. Stoppard, & V. Anderson (eds.) *Women's bodies, women's lives*, pp. 203–26. Toronto: Sumach Press.

Martins, Y., Tiggemann, M. & Churchett, L. (2008). The shape of things to come: Gay men's satisfaction with specific body parts. *Psychology of Men & Masculinity*, 9, 248–56.

McCreary, D. R. & Sasse, D. K. (2002). Gender differences in high school students' dieting behaviour and their correlates. *International Journal of Men's Health*, 1, 195–213.

Mellor, D., McCabe, M., Ricciardelli, L. & Ball, K. (2004). Body image importance and body dissatisfaction among Indigenous Australian adolescents. *Body Image*, 1, 289–97.

Mellor, D., McCabe, M., Ricciardelli, L. & Merino, M. E. (2008). Body dissatisfaction and body change behaviors in Chile: The role of sociocultural factors. *Body Image*, 5, 205–15.

Mellor, D., McCabe, M., Ricciardelli, L., Yeow, J., Daliza, N. & Hapidzal, N. F. B. M. (2009). Sociocultural influences on body dissatisfaction and body change behaviors among Malaysian adolescents. *Body Image*, 6, 121–8.

Mintel (2010). Size matters. A quarter of UK women now size 18 or above. http://www. mintel.com/press-centre/press-releases/587/size-matters-a-quarter-of-uk-women-now-size-18-or-above (accessed August 18, 2010).

Mishkind, M. E., Rodin, J., Silberstein, L. R. & Striegel-Moore, R. H. (1986). The embodiment of masculinity: Cultural, psychological, and behavioral dimensions. *American Behavioral Scientist*, 29, 545–62.

Morgan, C., Lockard, J., Fahrenbuch, C. & Smith, J. (1975). Hitchhiking: Social signals at a distance. *Bulletins of the Psychonomic Society*, 5, 459–61.

Morrison, T. G., Bearden, A., Ellis, S. R. & Harriman, R. (2005). Correlates of genital perceptions among Canadian post-secondary students. *Electronic Journal of Human Sexuality*, 8. http://www.ejhs.org/volume8/GenitalPerceptions.htm

Morrison, T. G., Morrison, M. A. & Hopkins, C. (2003). Striving for bodily perfection? An exploration of the drive for muscularity in Canadian men. *Psychology of Men and Masculinity*, 4, 111–20.

Mort, F. (1988). Boys own? Masculinity, style and popular culture. In R. Chapman & J. Rutherfords (eds.) *Male order: Unwrapping masculinity*, pp. 193–224. London: Lawrence and Wishart.

Olivardia, R., Pope, H. G., J. R., Borowiecki, J. J. & Cohnae, G. H. (2004). Biceps and body image: The relationship between muscularity, and self esteem, depression, and eating disorder symptoms. *Psychology of Men & Masculinity*, 5, 112–20.

Oyebode, F., Boodhoo, J.-A. & Schapira, K. (1988). Anorexia nervosa in males: Clinical features and outcome. *International Journal of Eating Disorders*, 7, 121–4.

Pasman, L. & Thompson, J. K. (1988). Body image and eating disturbance in obligatory runners, obligatory weightlifters, and sedentary individuals. *International Journal of Eating Disorders*, 7, 759–69.

Paxton, S. J. & Phythian, K. (1999). Body image, self-esteem, and health status in middle and later adulthood. *Australian Psychologist*, 34, 116–21.

Peters, R., Copeland, J., Dillon, P. & Beel, A. (1997). *Patterns and correlates of anabolic-androgenic steroid use.* Sydney, New South Wales, Australia, National Drug and Alcohol Research Centre, University of New South Wales.

Phillips, N. & De Man, A. F. (2010). Weight status and body image satisfaction in adult men and women. *North American Journal of Psychology*, 12, 171–84.

Pope, H. G., JR., Phillips, K. A. & Olivardia, R. (2000). *The Adonis complex. The secret crisis of male body obsession*, New York: The Free Press.

Rodin, J., Silberstein, L. & Streigel-Moore, R. (1985). Women and weight: A normative discontent. In T. B. Sondregger (ed.) *Psychology and gender*, pp. 267–307. Lincoln, NE: University of Nebraska Press.

Rozin, P. & Fallon, A. (1988). Body image, attitudes to weight, and misperceptions of figure preferences of the opposite sex: A comparison of men and women in two generations. *Journal of Abnormal Psychology*, 97, 342–5.

Sarafino, E. P. (2002). *Health psychology: Biopsychosocial interactions.* New York: John Wiley & Sons, Inc.

Sarwer, D. B. & Crerand, C. E. (2004). Body image and cosmetic medical treatments. *Body Image,* 1, 99–111.

Siever, M. D. (1994). Sexual orientation and gender as factors in socioculturally acquired vulnerability to body dissatisfaction and eating disorders. *Journal of Consulting and Clinical Psychology,* 62, 252–60.

Silberstein, L. R., Striegel-Moore, R. H., Timko, C. & Rodin, J. (1988). Behavioral and psychological implications of body dissatisfaction: Do men and women differ? *Sex Roles,* 19, 219–32.

Singleton, P., Fawkner, H., Foster, S. & White, A. (2010). The road to surgery for gynecomastia: What can health professionals learn from men's experiences? Paper presented at Appearance Matters 4. Bristol University.

Singleton, P., Fawkner, H., White, A. & Foster, S. (2009). Men's experience of cosmetic surgery: A phenomenological approach to discussion board data. *Qualitative Methods in Psychology Newsletter,* 8, 17–23.

Son, H., Lee, H., Huh, J., Kim, S. W. & Paick, J. (2003). Studies on self-esteem of penile size in young Korean military men. *Asian Journal of Andrology,* 5, 185–9.

Spitzer, R. L., Yanovski, S. Z., Wadden, T., Wing, R., Marcus, M. D., Stunkard, A., *et al.* (1993). Binge eating disorder: Its further validation in a multisite study. *International Journal of Eating Disorders,* 13, 137–53.

Stevens, C. & Tiggemann, M. (1998). Women's body figure preferences across the lifespan. *Journal of Genetic Psychology,* 159, 94–102.

Stoutjesdyk, D. & Jevne, R. (1992). Eating disorders among high performance athletes. *Journal of Youth and Adolescence,* 22, 271–82.

Strong, S. M., Williamson, D. A., Netemeyer, R. G. & Geer, J. H. (2000). Eating disorder symptoms and concerns about body differ as a function of gender and sexual orientation. *Journal of Social and Clinical Psychology,* 19, 240–55.

Swami, V., Jones, J., Einon, D. & Furnham, A. (2009). Men's preferences for women's profile waist-to-hip ratio, breast size, and ethnic group in Britain and South Africa. *British Journal of Psychology,* 100, 313–25.

Tantleff-Dunn, S. & Gokee, J. L. (2002). Interpersonal influences on body image development. In T. F. Cash & T. Pruzinsky (eds.) *Body image. A handbook of theory, research, and clinical practice,* pp. 108–16. New York: The Guilford Press.

Thiel, A., Gottfried, H. & Hesse, F. W. (1993). Subclinical eating disorders in male athletes: A study of low weight category in rowers and wrestlers. *Acta Psychiatra Scandinavia,* 88, 259–65.

Thompson, J. K. & Tantleff, S. (1992). Female and male ratings of upper torso: Actual, ideal, and stereotypical conceptions. *Journal of Social Behavior & Personality,* 7, 345–54.

Tiggemann, M. (1991). Body-size dissatisfaction: Individual differences in age and gender, and relationship to self-esteem. *Personality and Individual Differences,* 13, 39–43.

Tiggemann, M., Martins, Y. & Churchett, L. (2008). Beyond muscles. *Journal of Health Psychology,* 13, 1163–72.

Tiggemann, M., Martins, Y. & Kirkbride, A. (2007). Oh to be lean and muscular: Body image ideals in gay and heterosexual men. *Psychology of Men & Masculinity,* 8, 15–24.

Tucker, L. A. (1983). Weight training: A tool for the improvement of self and body concepts of males. *Journal of Human Movement Studies*, 9, 31–37.

Tucker, L. A. (1984). Physical attractiveness, somatotype, and the male personality: A dynamic interactional perspective. *Journal of Clinical Psychology*, 40, 1226–34.

Wright, S., Grogan, S. & Hunter, G. (2000). Motivations for anabolic steroid use among body builders. *Journal of Health Psychology*, 5, 566–72.

....

CHAPTER 16

LESBIAN, GAY, AND BISEXUAL SEXUALITIES: APPEARANCE AND BODY IMAGE

....

CAROLINE HUXLEY
NIKKI HAYFIELD

INTRODUCTION

....

THIS chapter critically discusses lesbian, gay, and bisexual people's appearance and body image. First, LGB (lesbian, gay, and bisexual) appearance norms and their functions will be described. Second, we will discuss research comparing the body satisfaction of different groups, and possible protective or harmful influences. While we use the common umbrella term 'LGB', the bulk of the literature focuses on lesbians and/or gay men, but seldom includes bisexual people.

LGB Appearance

Although scholars writing of LGB history and identity have tended to *mention* appearance, it has rarely been brought to the fore. However, there is a small body of literature which has identified the existence and importance of appearance norms for lesbians and gay men. The most documented of these are gay men as effeminate and lesbian women as 'butch'. Less well documented are the reciprocal appearance norms of gay men as overtly masculine and lesbian women as overtly feminine or 'femme'.[1] There appear to be no equivalent appearance norms for bisexual people (e.g. Holliday, 1999; Clarke & Turner, 2007; Hayfield, 2011, submitted a,b; Huxley et al., submitted).

The masculine butch lesbian 'look' is produced through particular styles of short hair, comfortable shoes, and 'masculine' clothes and gestures (e.g. Esterberg, 1996; Winn & Nutt, 2001; Krakauer & Rose, 2002; Clarke & Turner, 2007; Johnson et al., 2007). Meanwhile, the effeminate gay man is feminized through his (tighter) clothing and his mannerisms (e.g. Cole, 2000; Clarke & Turner, 2007).[2] These appearance norms can serve a number of functions in the context of individuals' personal and social identities, such as coming out, being recognized, and belonging within LGB communities.

Coming Out

When LGB people first come out they often change their appearance in order to incorporate some of the appearance norms popular within contemporary LGB communities (e.g. Krakauer & Rose, 2002; Maltry & Tucker, 2002). In this sense, the newly-identified individual can look to other LGB people as role models (e.g. Cole, 2000; Krakauer & Rose, 2002), both to 'dress the part' and to resist the (gendered) dress codes of (an arguably heterosexual, hegemonic, and heteronormative) mainstream society can be an empowering expression of self identification,

---

[1] Butch looks and identities have been more widely written about than femme looks, although in more recent years there has been some discussion of 'femme' identities (e.g. Hemmings, 1999; Maltry & Tucker, 2002; Luzzatto & Gvion, 2004; Levitt & Hiestand, 2005). We note that some LGB looks are historically understood to be aligned with associated gender roles, and that appearance is about more than just adornment of the body. However, it is beyond the scope of this chapter to discuss in depth the notion of embodied identities (see for example Rothblum, 2002) and instead we stay at the level of the purely aesthetic in order to map the usefulness and limitations of appearance.

[2] These appearance norms mirror the early theorization of gay men and lesbians as 'inverts', the opposite sex 'trapped' in the wrong body. These conceptualizations have a deep rooted history going as far back as the sex researchers of the late 1800s and early 1900s, including Richard von Kraft-Ebbing and Henry Havelock Ellis (see, for example, Newton 1991; Terry, 1999; Oosterhius, 2000; Maltry & Tucker, 2002).

as well as an assertion of pride in that identity (e.g. Holliday, 1999; Ingebretsen, 1999; Entwistle, 2000; Schorb & Hammidi, 2000; Maltry & Tucker, 2002; Eves, 2004; Clarke & Turner, 2007). Critically, appearance can also serve to signify one's sexual identity, or 'come out' to others (Rothblum, 1994; Esterberg, 1996; Rudd, 1996; Lewis & Rolley, 1997; Clarke & Turner, 2007).

RECOGNITION

Because lesbians and gay men are often able to recognize others' sexuality through visual cues, appearance can also function as a form of communication (Rudd, 1996; Winn & Nutt, 2001; Krakauer & Rose, 2002) and *visual* identity becomes a key aspect of sexual identity. Those who are 'in the know' (Clarke & Turner, 2007: 267) may be able to recognize a diverse range of particular nuanced subcultural looks, both for gay men (e.g. Rudd, 1996, Cole, 2000) and lesbians (e.g. Rothblum 1994; Kaiser, 1998; Winn & Nutt, 2001; Clarke & Turner, 2007). This ability to recognize others' sexuality through appearance has even developed its own terminology and is colloquially referred to as 'gaydar' (e.g. Nicholas, 2004).

Recognition is useful as a form of sexual signalling to recognize and attract appropriate others (Rothblum, 1994; Winn & Nutt, 2001; Krakauer & Rose, 2002; Rothblum, 2002; Luzzatto & Gvion, 2004; Levitt & Hiestand, 2005) and can also serve to reify and acknowledge lesbian and gay identities (e.g. Esterberg, 1996; Schorb & Hammidi, 2000). Recognition also allows lesbians and gay men to signal their belonging within LGB culture in order to become a part of it (Rothblum, 1994; Rudd, 1996; Entwistle, 2000; Ciasullo, 2001; Krakauer & Rose, 2002; Rothblum, 2002; Huxley et al., submitted).

COMMUNITIES

Appearance norms also serve a wider function in helping LGB people connect with and fit into (what would once have been hidden) LGB communities. Appearance norms have aided in the creation and maintenance of cohesive communities, and therefore of a shared identity (e.g. Rudd, 1996; Cole, 2000; Luzzatto & Gvion, 2004). Accordingly it is often in shared social space that codes of appearance are most clearly situated (Rothblum, 1994; Luzzatto & Gvion, 2004).

To belong within communities can be important for many lesbians and gay men because they provide places of acceptance where group identities encompassing shared values can be formed (e.g. D'Augelli & Garnets, 1995). Critically, they are safe spaces away from the gaze of voyeuristic or homophobic individuals. Further, looking and being looked at have been acknowledged as an enjoyable part of subculture (e.g. Ainley, 1995; Levitt & Hiestand, 2005).

In order to protect the sanctity of community, lesbian and gay appearance norms often become a regime or a 'uniform' (Rothblum, 1994; Cole, 2000; Schorb & Hammidi, 2000; Hayfield, 2011; Huxley et al., submitted). Gay and lesbian appearance is necessarily policed, meaning that those who do not conform to lesbian and gay aesthetics may struggle to feel that they belong, or may even have their authenticity questioned (Holliday, 1999; Ciasullo, 2001; Eves, 2004; Levitt & Hiestand, 2005; Clarke & Turner, 2007; Hayfield, 2011). Therefore, looking the part is an important aspect to belonging within LGB social spaces.

THE RISKS OF RECOGNITION

So far the focus has been on the advantageous functions of LGB appearance norms, however, there may be disadvantages or risk to appearance communicating sexuality, particularly within wider heterosexual society. It has been suggested that some of the subtler appearance norms allow lesbians to identify each other 'without being identifiable by the dominant culture' (Rothblum, 1994, p. 92; see also Winn & Nutt, 2001; Krakauer & Rose, 2002; Clarke & Turner, 2007) in part because LGB appearance is not only about *what* is worn, but also about *how* it is worn (Kaiser, 1998). The functions of appearance norms are primarily situated within a lesbian and gay context, where it is safe to be out, rather than within mainstream heterosexual society (Smyth, 1998).

Little research has considered whether heterosexual audiences are able to assess sexuality through appearance.[3] However, it is likely that heterosexual individuals will understand enough from appearance to 'get the message'. Research (much of which is now somewhat dated) has concluded that 'inappropriate' displays of gender (understood to reveal lesbian and gay identification) led to dislike, negative evaluation (often as 'unattractive' and 'deviant'), and stigmatization (Laner & Laner, 1980; Unger et al., 1982; Rothblum, 1994; Rudd, 1996). As a result, visibility can incur societal disapproval, discrimination and hate crimes, such as homophobic violence (Eves, 2004; Krakauer & Rose, 2002; Huxley, submitted), particularly for gay men (e.g. Ingebretsen, 1999; Cole, 2000).

Therefore the revelation of sexuality can carry the risk of rejection or hostility, and can be a threat to the safety of the individual, both emotionally and physically. For this reason those gay men and lesbians who are able to 'pass' as heterosexual may find it advantageous to do so[4] (Rothblum, 1994). However, they may receive

---

[3] However this is an area which NH has researched as a part of her doctoral thesis. Heterosexual students were broadly able to recognize some broad lesbian and gay appearance norms, but were less able to engage with any nuanced or detailed descriptions of lesbian and gay (or bisexual) appearance (Hayfield, 2011; submitted a,b).

[4] Dressing 'the part' has often been understood as partly a class issue, with middle-class individuals less likely, and working class individuals more likely, to convey their sexuality through their appearance (e.g. Rothblum, 1994).

criticism from other lesbians and gay men (who do reveal their sexuality) for their adherence to heterosexual norms (e.g. Walker, 1993; Rothblum, 2002) or for being closeted (e.g. Winn & Nutt, 2001). To conclude, appearance norms serve a number of useful functions but also carry a number of risks for lesbians and gay men.

But What About Bisexuality?

What is notably lacking in the literature is any clear understanding of bisexual people's appearance. Where they have been included in research they have often been too few in number to be classed a separate group. Consequently bisexual people have often been merged within groups of lesbians and gay men. However, there are some qualitative studies which have considered bisexuality.

Bisexual people may use appearance in similar ways to lesbians and gay men. Taub (1999) conducted a qualitative study in the US, which specifically focused on bisexual women's appearance. She concluded that some women changed their appearance when they came out as bisexual; they adopted lesbian norms, and/or felt less pressure to conform to (heterosexual) cultural norms of appearance for women. Similarly, the one bisexual man who took part in Holliday's (1999) UK-based research identified that he wore bright colours and bent the rules of his employer's dress codes. He linked these behaviours with resistance to rigid heter-onormative dress codes. These findings indicate that bisexual people's appearance may indeed function in a similar way as it does for lesbians and gay men.

Taub (1999) also found that some of her participants changed their appearance according to the gender of their current partner, although others did not, making it difficult to draw even tentative conclusions other than to say that it is possible that bisexual people's appearance may change according to their relationships.

It is also possible that bisexual people have their own appearance norms, just as they have their own distinct community (see, Barker et al., 2008) although to date no research appears to have identified this. Alternatively, bisexual people may not have their own 'look', and may not be able to use their appearance to express or identify themselves or others (Clarke & Turner, 2007; Holliday, 1999). Clarke and Turner (2007) highlighted that further research could help in understanding the specificity of bisexual appearance.[5] While some research has now taken place with bisexual women (e.g. Taub, 1999; Huxley, 2010; Hayfield, 2011; submitted b) it would appear that none has explored bisexual men and their appearance practices. Overall, it remains uncertain whether bisexual people are able to draw on appearance in similar ways to lesbians and gay men.

---

[5] We acknowledge that previous researchers (Rothblum, 2002; Clarke & Turner, 2007) have high-lighted the lack of research in this area. We, and others, are striving to contribute to understandings of the topic.

Body Image

While it is clear that sexual identity is uniquely linked to physical appearance, less clearly defined is how sexuality is related to feelings about body size and shape. We will now review the research which explores lesbian and gay men's body satisfaction and possible influences that may affect it. Again, bisexual people (and those who identify in other ways, such as 'queer' or 'non-heterosexual') have generally been excluded from such research, and therefore very little is known about their body image concerns. Wherever possible we have described research that includes bisexual people, but this is an area that needs more attention.

Differences in Body Satisfaction

Quantitative evidence has generally found that gay men report higher levels of body dissatisfaction than heterosexual men (e.g. Kaminski et al., 2005; Yelland & Tiggemann, 2003; also see Morrison et al. (2004) for a meta-analysis of existing research). However, many body satisfaction scales were originally developed with women (e.g. The Physical Appearance State and Trait Anxiety Scale (PASTAS) (Reed et al., 1991)) and may not always be appropriate for use with men (Kaminski et al., 2005). Using a scale specifically designed to measure men's body satisfaction, Kaminski and colleagues (2005) found that gay men reported more body dissatisfaction, a greater drive for muscularity, more fear of fatness, and a stronger drive for thinness than heterosexual men.

Although such evidence suggests that gay men experience more anxiety in relation to their body size, it has been theorized that the prevalence of body dissatisfaction is actually similar for both gay and heterosexual men (Pope et al., 2000). Pope and colleagues theorized that differences have been found because gay men are more willing to admit to body-related concerns than are heterosexual men.

Similar research exploring differences between lesbian and heterosexual women has produced mixed findings. Some studies have concluded that lesbian women are significantly less dissatisfied with their body size and shape than heterosexual women (e.g. Polimeni et al., 2009), while other studies have found no significant differences (e.g. Legenbauer et al., 2009; Peplau et al., 2009; Huxley, 2010; Hayfield, 2011; submitted b). Morrison et al. (2004) conducted a meta-analysis of existing evidence, including 27 different papers on body satisfaction and sexuality. Their findings suggested no differences between the lesbian and heterosexual women in terms of body satisfaction, but the authors criticized the frequent discrepancies in both age and weight between groups of lesbian and heterosexual women (the lesbian participants were often older and heavier). In the analysis of the studies in which lesbian and heterosexual participants were demographically similar, results suggested that lesbian women were 'slightly' more satisfied with their bodies than the heterosexual women.

A very small number of studies have included bisexual women, finding no differences in their body satisfaction compared to lesbian and heterosexual women (LaTorre & Wendenburg, 1983; Polimeni et al., 2009).

We will now briefly explore the ways in which the social influences of LGB subculture and same-sex relationships may shape body image concerns.[6]

LGB Subculture

There are contrasting theories about the influence of LGB communities on lesbian women's body image. According to Brown (1987) such communities reject the traditional emphasis on women's appearance and weight, and are more accepting of diverse female bodies. Accordingly, lesbian women should be more content with their body size than heterosexual women (e.g. Polimeni et al., 2009). However, Dworkin (1988) argued that LGB subculture *cannot* protect lesbian women from experiencing body image concerns, as all women, regardless of sexuality, grow up and live in mainstream society. Consequently all are subjected to the same pressures to conform to body shape ideals and will experience equivalent body dissatisfaction (e.g. Peplau et al., 2009).

Empirical research supports both Brown's (1987) and Dworkin's (1988) theories. Heffernan (1996) found significant differences in the degree of weight concern between women who were involved in LGB 'activities' and those who were not. In contrast, Beren et al. (1996) found that lesbian women's affiliation to LGB communities was not significantly related to their body satisfaction. Cogan (1999) argued that although lesbian subculture may promote positive messages about women's bodies, and value 'healthy' or 'natural' body shapes, such messages cannot protect women from internalizing mainstream society's thin beauty ideals or experiencing body dissatisfaction.

Research with gay men has been more consistent. There is huge emphasis on appearance and particular body shapes and sizes within gay subculture (Tucker, 1998). Certain ideals, such as slim, toned, and muscular bodies are highly valued (Morrison et al., 2004), and gay and bisexual men often feel that they are being judged on whether they conform to these standards (Morgan & Arcelus, 2009). This emphasis on appearance is so strong that Blotcher (1998) described gay subculture as having 'given its approval to a culture of body fascism' (p. 359).

---

[6] We choose to focus on LGB subcultures and same-sex partner relationships but acknowledge that there are many potential sexuality-related influences on body image concerns (e.g. discrimination, political ideology, and so on) which are beyond the scope of this chapter to explore.

Empirical evidence has found that affiliation to LGB communities was a signifi-cant predictor of gay men's body dissatisfaction (e.g. Beren et al., 1996). Qualitative explorations of young gay men's body image reported that they felt that LGB social space (the 'scene') was highly competitive with regard to appearance (Morgan & Arcelus, 2009). This competition was particularly emphasized for single men, who felt pressure to look attractive in order to meet a partner.

ROMANTIC/SEXUAL RELATIONSHIPS

Relationships may also have an impact on gay men, lesbian women, and bisexual people's body satisfaction. Rothblum (1994) argued that physical appearance is seen as particularly important for heterosexual women in terms of their social and sexual attractiveness to men. As lesbian women are less likely to be concerned with male gaze, they may feel able to resist social pressures to conform to the thin ideal body shape that is depicted as being attractive to men (Atkins, 1998). In contrast, appearance and body size may be particularly important to gay men in terms of their attractiveness to other men (Brand et al., 1992), particularly in the context of a gay subculture that values appearance (Morgan & Arcelus, 2009).

Legenbauer and colleagues (2009: 230) compared lesbian and heterosexual women's and gay and heterosexual men's 'preference for thinness and attractive-ness in a partner'. Male participants (both heterosexual and gay) reported a higher preference for thinness and attractiveness in a partner than did either heterosexual or lesbian women. It is possible, then, that people who wish to be attractive to men (e.g. heterosexual women, gay men, and possibly bisexual people) may experience the most pressure to be thin and attractive (Brand et al., 1992). Similarly, a qualita-tive study with bisexual women suggested that they experience lessened pressure to conform to mainstream ideals when in same-sex relationships, compared to their experiences within different-sex relationships (Taub, 1999).

There are different ways in which same-sex relationships and partners may shape body image concerns. However, there is little research in this area, with particularly scant focus on men's relationships. Research with women indicates that same-sex attractions can have a positive influence on body satisfaction (Huxley, 2010; Huxley et al., 2011). Lesbian women have described applying different stan-dards of 'beauty' to themselves once they realized that they were attracted to women who do not conform to mainstream ideals (Beren et al., 1997; Huxley et al., 2011). Body-size comparisons between partners could also influence body satisfaction. Qualitative research with lesbian and bisexual women found that they generally described feeling more confident if they felt they were slimmer than their female partner, or more self-conscious if they felt they were bigger (Huxley et al., 2011).

LIMITATIONS AND CRITIQUES OF APPEARANCE AND BODY IMAGE LITERATURE

Studies that have explored appearance issues with people identifying as LGB have tended to be qualitative, and situated within constructionist and critical paradigms. Accordingly this has produced research with small samples, which have often relied upon data from interviews with mainly white, middle-class participants from the UK or US. While such research has enabled deep and rich meanings to be interpreted, quantitative research of the topic could also be useful. Larger samples and more transferable findings could contribute to results being disseminated more widely.

A major flaw in previous quantitative research on body image and sexuality is the way in which researchers have used subcategories. Sexuality can be regarded in terms of sexual orientation, behaviour, attractions, or self-identity, and previous research has often assumed that scales measuring sexual *behaviour* could be used to categorize participants into universally-acknowledged and understood sexual *identities* (Bohan, 1996). Much research into sexuality and body image has asked participants to indicate the nature of their current attractions and behaviours on Kinsey-type 7-point Likert scales (Kinsey, 1953) which tend to range from 'exclusively heterosexual' through to 'exclusively homosexual'. *Researchers* then label participants as 'heterosexual', 'gay', or 'lesbian' based on their responses (e.g. Brand et al., 1992; Beren et al., 1996). One major flaw of this technique is that researcher-imposed labels are not always congruent with participants' sexual identities (Morris & Rothblum, 1999).

Other problems with existing quantitative research include the different recruitment methods used for different participants (Morrison et al., 2004). Heterosexual people are often recruited from undergraduate populations, while LGB participants may be recruited from specifically LGB communities or social networks (e.g. Beren et al., 1996). This technique has been criticized for producing non-representative samples with very particular characteristics, because people who engage in such social networks are seen as relatively comfortable with their sexuality (Rothblum et al., 2002). These recruitment strategies also often result in under-representation of less educated, lower social classes and non-white populations (Platzer, 1998). It is also problematic that in many of the studies cited here there are notably more participants in the heterosexual groups than LGB groups. For example, in one study with a sample of over 55,000 participants, fewer than 800 identified as lesbian, and fewer than 1700 as gay men (Peplau et al., 2009).

CONCLUSION

There is now a body of literature and research (albeit small) on topics of appearance, body image, and sexual identity. We would argue that research on lived visual identities remains worthy of further exploration. Further, there is very little research that has investigated the specificity of bisexual appearance or how bisexual identities are connected to body image (for the exceptions to this see LaTorre & Wendenburg, 1983; Holliday, 1999; Taub, 1999; Clarke & Turner, 2007; Polimeni et al., 2009; Hayfield, 2011, submitted b; Huxley, 2010).

Future research would also do well to consider the ways in which appearance and body image might map onto the intersections of identity, rather than focusing on sexual identity alone. Further, many people may not identify with sexual identity labels such as 'gay', 'lesbian', 'bisexual'. Hence while inviting 'LGB' people to take part in research has provided the vital underpinnings of an understanding of visual identities and appearance ideals, a move beyond these categories is now necessary.

In sum, existing theory and research has explored appearance and body image in relation to sexual identity in a number of ways. However, future research would do well to expand upon this with a wider range of participants, who identify their sexual identity in different ways, and with a more varied and sensitive use of methods in order to glean a deeper understanding of the topic.

References

Ainley, R. (1995) *What is she like? Lesbian identities from the 1950s to the 1990s.* London: Cassell.

Atkins, D. (1998). Introduction: Looking Queer. In D. Atkins (ed.) *Looking Queer: Body Image and Identity in Lesbian, Bisexual, Gay and Transgender Communities*, pp. xxiv–li. New York: Harrington Park Press.

Barker, M., Bowes-Catton, H., Iantaffi, A., Cassidy, A., & Brewer, L. (2008). British bisexuality: A snapshot of bisexual representations and identities in the United Kingdom. *Journal of Bisexuality*, 8(1/2), 141–62.

Beren, S. E., Hayden, H. A., Wilfley, D. E., & Grilo, C. M. (1996). The influence of sexual orientation on body dissatisfaction in adult men and women. *International Journal of Eating Disorders*, 20(2), 135–41.

Beren, S. E., Hayden, H. A., Wilfley, D. E., & Striegel-Moore, R. H. (1997). Body dissatisfaction among lesbian college students: The conflict of straddling mainstream and lesbian cultures. *Psychology of Women Quarterly*, 21(3), 431–45.

Blotcher, J. (1998). Justify my love handles: how the queer community trims the fat. In D. Atkins (ed.) *Looking Queer: Body Image and Identity in Lesbian, Bisexual, Gay, and Transgender Communities*, pp. 359–66. London: Harrington Park Press.

Bohan, J.S. (1996). *Psychology and Sexual Orientation: Coming To Terms.* London: Routledge.

Brand, P. A., Rothblum, E.D., & Solomon, L.J. (1992). A comparison of lesbians, gay men, and heterosexuals on weight and restrained eating. *International Journal of Eating Disorders*, 11(3), 253–9.

Brown, L. S. (1987). Lesbians, Weight, and Eating: New Analyses and Perspectives. In Boston Lesbian Psychologies Collective (eds.) *Lesbian Psychologies: Explorations and Challenges*, pp. 294–59. Urbana-Champaign, IL: University of Illinois Press.

Ciasullo, A. (2001). Making her (in)visible: Cultural representations of lesbianism and the lesbian body in the 1990s. *Feminist Studies,* 27(3), 577–608.

Clarke, V. & Turner, K. (2007). Clothes maketh the queer? Dress, appearance and the construction of lesbian, gay and bisexual identities. *Feminism & Psychology,* 17(2), 267–76.

Cogan, J. C. (1999). Lesbians walk the tightrope of beauty: Thin is in but femme is out. *Journal of Lesbian Studies,* 3(4), 77–89.

Cole, S. (2000). *Don we now our gay apparel: Gay men's dress in the twentieth century.* Oxford: Berg.

D'Augelli, A. R., & Garnets, L. D. (1995). Lesbian, gay, and bisexual communities. In A. R. D'Augelli and C. J. Patterson (eds.) *Lesbian, gay, and bisexual identities over the lifespan: Psychological perspectives,* pp. 293–320. Oxford: Oxford University Press.

Dworkin, S. H. (1988). Not in man's image: Lesbians and the cultural oppression of body image. *Women & Therapy,* 8(1–2), 27–39.

Entwistle, J. (2000). *The fashioned body: Fashion, dress, and modern social theory.* Cambridge: Polity Press.

Esterberg, K. G. (1996). 'A certain swagger when I walk': Performing lesbian identity. In S. Seidman (ed.) *Queer Theory/Sociology,* pp. 259–79. Oxford: Blackwell Publishers Ltd.

Eves, A. (2004). Queer theory, butch/femme identities and lesbian space. *Sexualities,* 7(4), 480–96.

Hayfield, N. J. (2011). Bisexual women's visual identities: A feminist mixed-methods exploration. Unpublished doctoral dissertation. University of the West of England, Bristol.

Hayfield, N. (submitted a). 'Never judge a book by its cover?': Students' understandings of lesbian, gay, and bisexual appearance.

Hayfield, N. (submitted b). The (in)visibility of (bi)sexuality: An exploration of bisexual appearance and visual identities.

Heffernan, K. (1996). Eating disorders and weight concern among lesbians. *International Journal of Eating Disorders,* 19(2), 127–38.

Hemmings, C. (1999). Out of sight, out of mind? Theorizing femme narrative. *Sexualities,* 2(4), 451–64.

Holliday, R. (1999). The comfort of identity. *Sexualities,* 2(4), 475–91.

Huxley, C. J. (2010). *An exploration of the sociocultural influences affecting lesbian and bisexual women's body image.* Unpublished doctoral dissertation, University of the West of England, Bristol, UK.

Huxley, C. J. (submitted). Lesbian and bisexual women's experiences of sexuality–based discrimination and their appearance concerns.

Huxley, C. J., Clarke, V., & Halliwell, E. (2011). 'It's a comparison thing isn't it?': Lesbian and bisexual women's accounts of how partner relationships shape their feelings about their body and appearance. *Psychology of Women Quarterly,* 35(3), 415–27.

Huxley, C. J., Clarke, V., & Halliwell, E. (submitted). 'If you're girly you can't possibly be gay': lesbian and bisexual women discuss their appearance.

Ingebretsen, E. (1999). Gone shopping: The commercialization of same-sex desire. *Journal of Gay, Lesbian, and Bisexual Identity,* 4(2), 125–48.

Johnson, K. L., Gill, S., Reichman, V., & Tassinary, L.G. (2007). Swagger, sway, and sexuality: Judging sexual orientation from body motion and morphology. *Journal of Personality and Social Psychology,* 93(3), 321–34.

Kaiser, S. B. (1998). *The social psychology of clothing: symbolic appearances in context.* New York: Macmillan.

Kaminski, P. L., Chapman, B. P., Haynes, S. D., & Own, L. (2005). Body image, eating behaviours, and attitudes toward exercise among gay and straight men. *Eating Behaviors*, 6(3), 179–87.

Kinsey, A., Pomeroy, W., Martin, C., & Gebhard, P. (1953). *Sexual Behavior in the Human Female*. Philadelphia, PA: W.B. Saunders.

Krakauer, I. D., & Rose, S. M. (2002). The impact of group membership on lesbians' physical appearance. *Journal of Lesbian Studies*, 6(1), 31–43.

Laner, M. R., & Laner, R. H. (1980). Sexual preference or personal style. *Journal of Homosexuality*, 5(4), 339–56.

LaTorre, R. A. & Wendenburg, K. (1983). Psychological characteristics of bisexual, hetero-sexual and homosexual women. *Journal of Homosexuality*, 9(1), 87–97.

Legenbauer, T., Vocks, S., Schafer, C., Schutt-Stromel, S., Hiller, W., Wagner, C., & Vogele, C. (2009). Preference for attractiveness and thinness in a partner: influence of internalization of the thin ideal and shape/weight dissatisfaction in heterosexual women, heterosexual men, lesbians and gay men. *Body Image*, 6(3), 228–34.

Levitt, H. M., & Hiestand, K. R. (2005). Gender within lesbian sexuality: Butch and femme perspectives. *Journal of Constructivist Psychology*, 18(1), 39–51.

Lewis, R., & Rolley, K. (1997). (Ad)dressing the dyke: Lesbian looks and lesbians looking. In M. Nova, A. Blake, I. MacRury, & B. Richards (eds.) *Advertising and Consumption*, pp. 291–308. New York: Routledge.

Luzzatto, D., & Gvion, L. (2004). Feminine but not femme. *Journal of Homosexuality*, 48(1), 43–77.

Maltry, M., & Tucker, K. (2002). Female fem(me)ininities. *Journal of Lesbian Studies*, 6(2), 89–102.

Morgan, J. F., & Arcelus, J. (2009). Body image in gay and straight men: a qualitative study. *European Journal of Eating Disorders*, 17(6), 435–43.

Morris, J. F., & Rothblum, E. (1999). Who fills out a 'lesbian' questionnaire? The interrelation-ship of sexual orientation, years 'out', disclosure of sexual orientation, sexual experience with women, and participation in the lesbian community. *Psychology of Women Quarterly*, 23(3), 537–57.

Morrison, M. A., Morrison, T. G., & Sager, C. L. (2004). Does body satisfaction differ between gay men and lesbian women and heterosexual men and women? A meta-analytic review. *Body Image*, 1(2), 127–38.

Newton, E. (1991). The mythic mannish lesbian: Radclyffe Hall and the new woman. In M. B. Duberman, M. Vicinus, & G. Chauncey Jr. (eds.) *Hidden from history: Reclaiming the gay and lesbian past*, pp. 281–93. London: Penguin Group.

Nicholas, C. L. (2004). Gaydar: Eye-gaze as identity recognition among gay men and lesbians. *Sexuality and Culture*, 8(1), 60–86.

Oosterhuis, H. (2000). *Stepchildren of nature: Krafft-Ebing, psychiatry, and the making of sexual identity*. London: The University of Chicago Press.

Peplau, L. A., Frederick, D. A., Yee, C., Maisel, N., Lever, J., & Ghavami, N. (2009). Body image satisfaction in heterosexual, gay, and lesbian adults. *Archives of Sexual Behaviour*, 38(5), 713–25.

Platzer, H. (1998). The concerns of lesbians seeking counseling: a review of the literature. *Patient Education & Counseling*, 33 (3), 225–32.

Polimeni, A. -M., Austin, S. B., & Kavanagh, A. M. (2009). Sexual orientation and weight, body image and weight control practices among young Australian women. *Journal of Women's Health*, 18(3), 355–62.

Pope, H. A., Phillips, K. A., & Olivardia, R. (2000). *The Adonis Complex: The Secret Crisis of Male Body Obsession.* New York: The Free Press.

Reed, D. L., Thomson, J. K., Brannick, M. T., & Sacco, W. P. (1991). Development and validation of the physical appearance state and trait anxiety scale (PASTAS). *Journal of Anxiety Disorders,* 5, 323–32.

Rothblum, E. D. (1994). Lesbians and physical appearance: Which model applies? In B. Greene and G.M. Herek (eds.) *Lesbian and gay psychology: Theory, research, and clinical applications,* pp. 84–97. Thousand Oaks, CA: Sage Publications.

Rothblum, E. D. (2002). Gay and lesbian body images. In T.F. Cash & T. Pruzinsky (eds.) *A handbook of theory, research and clinical practice,* pp. 257–65. New York: The Guildford Press.

Rothblum, E. D., Factor, R., & Aaron, D. L. (2002). How did you hear about the study? Or, how to reach lesbian and bisexual women of diverse ages, ethnicity and educational attainment for research projects. *Journal of the Gay and Medical Association,* 6(3), 53–9.

Rudd, N. A. (1996). Appearance and self-presentation research in gay consumer cultures: Issues and impact. *Journal of Homosexuality,* 31(1/2), 109–34.

Schorb, J. R., & Hammidi, T. N. (2000). Sho-lo showdown: The do's and don'ts of lesbian chic. *Tulsa Studies in Women's Literature,* 19(2), 255–68.

Smyth, C. (1998). How do we look? Imaging butch/femme. In S. R. Munt (ed.) *Butch/femme: Inside lesbian gender,* pp. 82–9. London: Cassell.

Taub, J. (1999). Bisexual women and beauty norms: A qualitative examination. In J. C. Cogan and J. M. Erickson (eds.) *Lesbians, Levis and Lipstick: The Meaning of Beauty in Our Lives,* pp. 27–36. New York: The Haworth Press.

Terry, J. (1999). *An American obsession: Science, medicine, and homosexuality in modern society.* Chicago, IL: The University of Chicago Press.

Tucker, N. (1998). Contradictions of the spirit: theories and realities of lesbian body image. In D. Atkins (ed.) *Looking Queer: Body Image and Identity in Lesbian, Bisexual, Gay, and Transgender Communities,* pp. 37–46. London: Harrington Park Press.

Unger, R. K., Hilderbrand, M., & Madar, T. (1982). Physical attractiveness and assumptions about social deviance: some sex-by sex comparisons. *Personality and Social Psychology Bulletin,* 8(2), 293–301.

Walker, L. (1993). How to recognise a lesbian: the cultural politics of looking like what you are. *Signs: Journal of Women in Culture and Society,* 18(4), 866–90.

Winn, J., & Nutt, D. (2001). From closet to wardrobe? In A. Guy, E. Green, & M. Banim (eds.) *Through the wardrobe: Women's relationships with their clothes,* pp. 221–36. New York: Berg.

Yelland, C., & Tiggemann, M. (2003). Muscularity and the gay ideal: body dissatisfaction and disordered eating in homosexual men. *Eating Behaviors,* 4(2), 107–16.

CHAPTER 17

CULTURE AND ETHNICITY

HABIB NAQVI

KRYSIA SAUL

RESEARCHERS and practitioners need to recognize that however expert they may be in the psychology of appearance, as individuals, groups, and societies, we all view appearance through different lenses of culture and ethnicity. These lenses offer differential perceptions of what constitutes 'beauty', as well as providing distinct means by which individuals may adjust to an appearance-altering condition. The influence of culture and ethnicity in these domains is outlined and discussed in this chapter. This chapter also considers the importance of culturally sensitive research and patient-centred service provision in the field of appearance and disfigurement.

CONCEPTS OF RACE, ETHNICITY, AND CULTURE

Race, ethnicity, and culture are terms commonly used in health literature, often in confusing and contradictory ways. These concepts originated with the global expansion of European societies from the late 15th century onwards, a process that brought Europeans increasingly into contact with other societies. The contemporary usage of the term 'race' surfaced during the middle of the 19th century as part of the general emergence and expansion of scientific inquiry. As a result, novel ways of classifying the world emerged including ideas about racialized differences relating to natural, observable, and physical characteristics that separate and define groups of people (Dubow, 1995).

The science of 'race' characterized human diversity as a 'division between fixed and separate races rooted in biological difference and the product of divergent heritages' (Mason, 2000, p. 6). The still dominant, though intensely challenged, concept of 'race' is a biological one. Developed to extend the taxonomic classification below the level of species, 'race' from the biological sciences perspective refers to one of the divisions of humankind as differentiated by physical characteristics. The strategy for developing this classification was based upon the observation and measurement of physical features. Many features were studied, but emphasis was placed upon those that were externally visible, including skin colour, eye colour, hair type, and the shape of the head and features such as the nose and lips.

A related sociodemographic term commonly used in health literature is 'ethnicity'. The concept of 'ethnicity' is neither simple nor precise, but can be viewed as another way of thinking about human diversity and refers to the social group to which a person belongs to based upon shared language, religious belief, and culture. Values and traditions that are distinctive, maintained between generations, and lead to a sense of identity, kinship, and group belonging are also a key characteristic (Senior & Bhopal, 1994). The concept of 'ethnicity' is often used in such a way that makes it indistinguishable from 'race'. Such use also draws upon boundaries on the basis of physical appearance. However, this criterion would be of little use in countries in which almost everyone has the same skin colour. This is therefore a strong argument for physical appearance being a marker of race rather than ethnicity. A number of South Asian groups, for instance, those living in Kashmir (an area of the Himalayas), are light skinned, making it difficult for an outsider to label them as South Asian, even though Kashmiris may self-define themselves as such.

Health literature relating to ethnic differences in access to services, health outcomes, and the experience of having a health condition is large and ever growing. In contrast, the relationship of ethnicity and race with psychological variables and concepts is less well researched and documented. For example, within the discipline of health psychology, the psychological and social consequences of living with a visible difference as well as the individual's experience of being visibly different, are well documented amongst Caucasian populations (Lansdown et al., 1997; Rumsey & Harcourt, 2005). However, little research exists regarding the extent to which different cultural and ethnic groups view the socially constructed representations of such differences (see, for example, Hughes et al., 2009).

DEFINITIONS OF BEAUTY

Physical appearance, the public representation of one's personal self in society, accords us membership with a social or cultural group even though that attribution may be incorrect. We make unconscious and mistaken assumptions about an individual's appearance, based on cultural visual cues such as colour and facial features. Group membership and self-image, both constituents of self-identity, define us as individuals and are important for our sense of self. From our identity, we derive a feeling of belonging to and likeness with others, drawn from shared customs, practices, languages, and cultural values that are based on nationality and ancestry but also shared ethnicity, religion or other common interests.

Pressure to conform to socially defined norms that accord group membership or status can perpetuate meanings of beauty, good health and otherness, though such norms are often culturally specific. The Suruwaha tribe, an isolated Amazonian hunting tribe, bury or abandon children with physical disabilities to die in the jungle much like the ancient Greeks of Sparta. The custom arises from the belief that people with disabilities and others have 'bad souls' who will return to haunt the tribe unless their last breath is taken underground. The traditional practice of stretching the lips of Mursi women in Southwest Ethiopia to hold huge lip-plates, has been said to raise their social status as the size of the lip-plate at the time of marriage determines the dowry to be paid in cattle. However, Turton (2004) suggests that the wearing of lip plates appears to mark the boundary between the biological self and the social self, 'cultural identity and political autonomy', viewed by Mursi women as an 'expression of female social adulthood and reproductive potential'. More recently, the practice has become an economic asset as lip-plates are a popular tourist attraction. Notions of wealth, affluence, and social status are often accorded to those deemed healthy and beautiful though these values vary across cultures; for example, voluptuous (traditionally built, (McCall Smith, 2009)) women are valued in parts of Africa in contrast to Western societies where thinness is preferred. Similarly, attractive people are more likely to be selected for highly paid, prestigious jobs and considered to have better social skills in the West, although in countries like China where the culture is based on the Confucian value of internal goodness, less importance may be placed on external beauty (Chiu & Babcok, 2002).

Historically there is a strong association between physical features, good health, and personality traits and morals. The desire for light skin appears universal, although meanings of skin colour—'whiteness'—remain significant markers of social and cultural distinctions between and within ethnic groups. In Japan, light skin is associated with femininity, moral virtue, motherhood and identity; in Korea with nobility and superiority whilst in the Indian sub-continent a wheaten complexion is an indicator of status, privilege and respect (Lewin, 2005). Fair skin, hairlessness and flawless skin—traditional Chinese symbols of refinement—have now been replaced with the desire for white skin and large breasts as signifiers of health (Johansson, 1998. pp. 59–60). In Brazil, a 'folk taxonomy' of appearance groups people along a continuum of colour (Edmonds, 2007) even though skin colour alone—dark, fair, brown—cannot define any particular race, ethnicity, or culture or adequately describe the skin types and pigmentations that vary so greatly among

African Americans (Talakoub & Wesley, 2009). Not everyone wants a Westernized appearance and Brazilian surgeons, recognizing that patients from different ethnic groups have different and unique cosmetic aspirations, have altered their preopera-tive health checks to ensure that surgical techniques take account of the differences in skin pathophysiology, mechanisms of aging, and unique anatomic structure and their impact on, for example, dyschromia—discoloration of the skin.

Social desirability and the perceived value of presenting the self in a certain way have encouraged people within the Western world to alter their appearance. In the US, cultural, social and economic perceptions of appearance have led many to undergo cosmetic surgery to diminish or eradicate ethnic origins that mark them as different from the majority population: for Jews, noses; for South East Asians, eyes; for Africans, noses and lips (Gilman, 1999). Surgeons have claimed to help over-come problems associated with social exclusion as aesthetic surgery enabled indi-viduals to 'pass' as members of the preferred social group leading some to view the medicalization of appearance as a tool that has altered the ethnic composition of America (Kaw, 1991).

LAY REPRESENTATIONS OF CAUSATION

That individual spiritual identities and religious beliefs are central to day-to-day functioning, and often provide guidelines for living, is well acknowledged (Clark & Dawson, 1996), yet the role of these in relation to appearance-related adjustment has yet to be explored in depth. Amongst the wide variety of influences upon health decisions and treatment choice, religion and culture can also be included. The pos-itive psychological and physiological effects of religious and cultural practice include social support (Wilson, 2000), a source of inspiration (Walsh, 1998), relaxation (Benson et al., 1975), and lower rates of depression, stress, and anxiety (Holland et al., 1998). However, it can be argued that religious and cultural beliefs can also be linked to negative influences of guilt and punishment. Furthermore, researchers have suggested that certain religious beliefs may restrain healthcare utilization, with beliefs and practices of certain religions conflicting with medical recommendations (Gall et al., 2005).

South Asian populations, in particular, are reported to place a high value on religion (van der Veer, 2002) and tend to rely upon religious faith to deal with various circumstances including those relating specifically to health issues (see, for example, Bhopal, 2007). A prominent feature of South Asian religions is a belief in predestination or fate. Fatalism, the belief that an individual's health condition is predetermined by a higher power or being and not within the individual's control, is a construct recognized in health psychology (see, for example, Wallston et al., 1976; Peyrot & Rubin, 1994). An individual with fatalistic beliefs perceives health status as being beyond one's control and rather a result of fate, luck or the will of God.

Research has found that fatalism is linked to both educational level and knowledge of chronic conditions such as diabetes (Conrad et al., 1996), and the perceived seriousness of the particular condition (Lange & Piette, 2006). In Hughes at al.'s (2009) qualitative study exploring British South Asian community views about individual people whose appearance differed from 'the norm', participants offered a number of explanations to elucidate the origins of visible differences or disfigurements. The concept of individual culpability was raised by participants who thought that individuals' past or present actions may be the cause for their visible difference. Consequently, participants referred to 'karma' (the belief that one's actions have consequences requiring atonement (Dalal, 2002), a concept that is shared by many religions) as being responsible for facial scarring or disfigurement caused during an accident or a fight; or a mother's immoral or deviant actions from the past or present resulting in her bearing a visibly different child: *'People are so suspicious of how come all of a sudden this has happened to your child or what were they doing so bad that this has happened to their child'* (Hughes et al., 2009 p. 247). For the majority of participants in this study, however, explanations of causation had their foundations embedded within external religious factors and fatalism. There was a general acceptance that the occurrence of a visible difference in appearance is the will of the creator and sustainer of the world and that any such characteristic should be accepted: *'First we would have to accept it as God's will… I would accept it as my fate and destiny'*, was the response from an older Sikh man (p. 246).

A tendency towards a fatalistic view of life is also found embedded in Asian language and discourse. In the Hindi language, for example, catching a cold is expressed as: 'a cold has come to me'—that is, 'a cold has caught me'. This implies that the person with the cold has no control over their health status. Control is not thought to be possible, let alone desirable, within the Islamic faith. The term 'Inshallah' (God willing) is used by Muslims, not just from South Asia but from all over the world, when making a decision, intending to take an action or planning an event. Indeed, the literal translation of the word 'Islam' is 'submission'.

Often situated alongside religious explanations of appearance and visible differences are cultural myths. Respondents in Hughes et al.'s (2009) study, for example, reported an attribution for the origins of visible difference to a variety of myths including engagement in sexual activity during the state of pregnancy, becoming pregnant during a lunar eclipse and being insensitive to those that have a visible difference. The gradual shift from mythical explanations of visible difference towards more biomedical interpretations of such conditions occurred in the UK, and other European cultures, immediately after the Victorian era. In Hughes et al.'s (2009) study, South Asians living in the UK articulated medical and other causal explanations for a visible difference. A number of respondents acknowledged the role of genetics and inheritance in lay explanations of causation. It may not be unreasonable to suggest that the exposure to current Western thought regarding visible difference coupled with changes in social structure and education levels amongst first and subsequent immigrant generations is resulting in a gradual shift of emphasis from cultural mythological explanation to biomedical justification that is not divorced from religious connotations.

FACTORS INFLUENCING
ADJUSTMENT AND DISTRESS

Living with disfigurement may adversely affect a person's perceptual and subjective body image, quality of life, and self-esteem (Rumsey & Harcourt, 2005), their identity and social interaction (Thompson & Kent, 2001). The process of adjustment to disfigurement therefore involves a multifaceted, complex mix of physical, psychosocial, and cultural factors (Clarke & Cooper, 2001). Family dynamics, marriage, religion, acculturation, the media, and health beliefs all affect adjustment as they define behavioural norms, assumptions, rules, and relationships (Adamson & Doud Galli, 2009).

Superficially, many cultures may appear ambivalent towards disfigurement but it raises complex and contradictory emotions that may hinder individual adjustment. These emotions partly result from cross-cultural superstitions, religious, and folk beliefs, although no one religious or cultural community can be considered a homogenous group. For example, Asian American perspectives on cleft palate vary between immigrant Chinese—some of whom believe eating rabbit during pregnancy causes cleft palate in infants—and Vietnamese, Hmong communities and other Asian groups. Fear, anxiety, moral judgement, 'retribution for sinful acts' are also common responses to disfigurement: *'There are stories in our religion about these people. Therefore we are scared of these people'* (Hughes et al., 2009 p. 247). The Buddhist belief that, in this world, nothing happens to a person that he does not for some reason or other deserve, is not dissimilar to the Christian teaching 'For whatsoever a man soweth, that shall he also reap' (Galatians VI (King James Version)). Yet such views coexist with pity and compassion: *'If I see such a person I feel very sad. I want these people to be treated the same as others'* (Hughes et al., 2009 p. 248). Indeed, social stigma, pride, and ostracism, sit uneasily alongside the Islamic obligation to provide care for people of all physical and mental abilities within an accepting and inclusive community.

Families often provide the main source of physical, emotional and economic support for people with disabilities, thereby largely determining the quality of their lives (Landsdown at al., 1991). Within South Asian cultures, the family unit or 'biraderi' (as referred to in Hindi and Urdu languages) includes extended family members, whereas in most Western cultures the family is nuclear in its structure. As such, shared family values and obligations can provide vulnerable members with a sense of security and belonging within the wider community. In India, a country of diverse cultural and religious heritages, family, and religion are the two decisive factors in shaping rehabilitation practices in society (Dalal, 2002). Nevertheless, despite common language and customs, social systems supporting those living with visible difference vary because family values, traditions and religions are not specific to any particular culture. In Israel, for example, Arab parents are more likely than Jewish parents to seek supportive frameworks for children with disabilities beyond the extended family (Mikulincer et al., 1993). Some families may feel a sense of burden, stigma and shame and respond in ways that serve the interests of the family reputation rather than those of the person with a disfigurement. Mistaken fears of contagion from unsightly skin lesions associated with cuteanous leishmaniasis mean Afghanistani parents isolate children from school and wider society (Kassi et al., 2008). Intolerance and limited marriage expectations are not uncommon among the families of those living with visible difference. This has shown to be particularly prominent amongst South Asian populations. Hughes et al. (2009) reported feelings of responsibility amongst relatives to care for an individual with a disfigurement and these feelings reflect an additional sense of burden if the individual happened to be a female: '*The disfigured female in the family is terribly embarrassing*' was a response from a female elder of the Bangladeshi community living in the UK (Hughes et al., 2009, p. 247). Indeed, participants in Hughes et al.'s study showed more tolerance towards males with disfiguring conditions, especially if they are capable of earning a living. The views amongst younger participants clearly highlighted the notion that having a disfigurement had a negative impact on marriage prospects, especially for females: '*I think parents would be worried about their child's marriage if their child was disfigured*' was a statement from a young Pakistani woman (p. 247).

Disfigurement often poses a threat to core cultural values and is associated with mistaken assumptions; Iranians who have sustained a burn injury are assumed to be infertile, while Latin Americans believe cancer is a punishment for premarital sex. Cancer is a particularly socially stigmatizing experience for American Latina women. The diagnosis changes their status within family relationships partly because their role changes from carer to someone needing care, but also because male partners see the loss of reproductive organs such as the breast or the uterus as destroying a woman's identity and femininity (Ashing-Giwa et al., 2006).

Ethnic diversity often relates to multiple faiths, familial structures, obligations, and responsibilities which together with varied levels of superstition, knowledge, and education, inform health beliefs, behaviours, and outcomes. Studies among Israeli Arabs and Jews show how social values like levels of spirituality, education, conservatism, gender, and exposure to disability or disfigurement influence adjustment towards visible difference (Florian & Katz, 1983). Similarly, O'Malley et al. (1999) found significant association between acculturation and health behaviour among the American Hispanic community when measures included ethnicity as well as language, education and socioeconomic factors. Perhaps, as more cultures are exposed to diverse concepts of beauty, a broader education and more sensitively orientated health practices, younger members of ethnic minority groups may challenge traditional, cultural, and religious value systems and familial authority (Modood et al., 1994) that impact on perceptions of illness and disfigurement:

Some people believe that illness comes from Allah, this attitude is wrong. Allah has given the medicine same as the illness and science have developed treatment. Some people feel that one day Allah will give the disease and I will go to doctor, I do not need to do check-ups early; this attitude makes us suffer, it makes delay to get the disease caught. Religion should not be an issue in this situation (Szczepura et al., 2008).

RESEARCH AND THE ENGAGEMENT
OF COMMUNITIES

As ascertained from this chapter thus far, there is a paucity of research exploring the views of different cultural and ethnic groups relating to appearance and visible differences. Consequently, there is a need to extend our knowledge and understanding in this field, and (as the next section in this chapter will outline) to relate this knowledge and understanding to both policy and practice. A means of extending our knowledge base is through research. Given that issues of disfigurement, stigma and shame may be particularly bound to cultural and ethnic membership (Papadopoulos et al., 1999; Hughes et al., 2009), the necessity for applied research is a priority.

Research, in general, is merely an estimation of the 'real world' (Johnson, 2005). Consequently, to ensure the generalizability of research findings, it is important that all groups participate. Should the views and representations of a significant minority be omitted, then that bias becomes inherent within the research, and the conclusions blemished.

The ideal research study in multicultural and multiethnic societies would be inclusive of all ethnic groups. Such a study would produce data that would facilitate comparable across all ethnic groups and subgroups and be interpreted in ways that could be used to inform improvements in healthcare provision. The lack of research examining differential ethnic and cultural experiences and representations in the field of appearance and disfigurement may in part be due to the methodological challenges, including those relating to accessing relevant populations, sampling techniques, and appropriate outcome measures. Furthermore, the specific nature and how prevalence of many disfiguring and appearance-related conditions, often results in small sample sizes.

Ethnicity as a variable that distinguishes human populations, is extremely important to the structure and function of society, and is therefore a valued variable in research. However, many commentators state that ethnic minority groups are less willing to participate in research (Shavers et al., 2002; Wendler et al., 2006). In relation to ethnic research in the field of appearance and disfigurement, it is more the case that little research has been initiated rather than ethnic groups being reluctant to participate in it. For any study area that has attracted little attention, qualitative approaches may be more suitable than quantitative research methodology. Hughes et al.'s (2009) study exploring South Asian community views about individuals with visible differences employed a qualitative methodology of focus group interviews using a community engagement approach (Pearce et al., 2004; Johnson, 2005). The notion that there should be strong community involvement in the design, conduct, and reporting of research that is of community relevance is difficult to argue against (see also Chapter 48).

Community engagement is an ideal approach where it is important to understand the meaning and interpretation of social arrangements surrounding potentially sensitive topics, such as those stemming from disfigurement and appearance-related conditions. In an attempt to initiate discussion and depersonalize the potentially sensitive issues of appearance and disfigurement, researchers can utilize the approach of asking participants to report on the wider community's views. Indeed this approach has been successfully used when examining views relating to a range of sensitive health topics within ethnic minority communities (see, for example, Johnson, 2006). Furthermore, the community engagement approach can help to overcome barriers such as those of language, culture, and religious understanding.

Constructs most commonly cited as being central to adjustment to disfigurement and appearance include self-esteem, body image, and social anxiety (Rumsey & Harcourt, 2004). Quantitative research in this area has involved mainly white participants and has used a number of established tools and scales to assess the importance of these constructs. These constructs and the measures and scales used to assess them have, in the main, been developed and trialled upon white populations in the US, Western Europe, or Australia. Culturally-sensitive measures developed with involvement from people from a range of ethnic backgrounds would be a valuable resource for planning policy and care provision that meets the needs of all population groups.

CULTURALLY SENSITIVE APPLICATIONS AND INTERVENTIONS

The need to provide health interventions that address 'culturally discordant encounters among physicians, patients and their families' (Kagawa-Singer & Kassim-Lakha, 2003, p. 578) is increasingly recognized among researchers, health professionals, and policy-makers. Moves towards a culturally sensitive mind-set have perhaps highlighted the negative influence of racial markers on healthcare outcomes. Yet in general, we fail to acknowledge the distinction between cultural and ethnic characteristics, and the negative impact this might have on the provision of appearance-related healthcare (and other) services among ethnic minority groups. Classificatory systems continue to focus on easily measured, high level, simple groupings that disguise diverse cultural heritages; 'South Asian', for example, implies ancestry in the Indian subcontinent, but ignores the diverse religious beliefs, educational, and socioeconomic backgrounds and dialects of the several subgroups (Bhopal et al., 1991) to which many post-war UK immigrants belong.

Language and meaning are particularly important when exploring perceptions of 'disfigurement' which are informed by what each cultural group regards as beautiful. Ethnic minority attitudes to disfigurement draw on multiple meanings ranging 'from 'ugly' to any abnormality or unevenness in the colour, shape, or features of the face, including scarring and birthmarks' (Hughes, 2009, p. 246). As in Western cultures, disfigurement may be associated with disability, mental or physical illness causing stigma and shame. Policy-makers acknowledge that 'language and words are used and understood differently in different contexts' when discussing disability or ethnicity (Department of Health, 2008). The Department of Health's recommendation to use 'South Asian rather than Asian to refer to people of Bangladeshi, Indian or Pakistani heritage' reflects to some extent the recognition that ethnic minority communities have different healthcare needs and preferences (p. 39).

Understanding the values and beliefs of ethnic minority groups is important for the establishment of effective health strategies capable of providing relevant support to individuals living in communities that perceive disfigurement negatively for spiritual, cultural, or social reasons. Many body image concerns may be broadly shared, yet the detail may vary between ethnic groups (Altabe, 1998). For example, Greenhalgh (1998) found the similarities between Bangladeshi and non-Bangladeshi perceptions of body image, and the cause and nature of diabetes as striking as their differences. This 'complex value hierarchy' underpinning ethnic minority groups may however mean that education and awareness-raising alone may not be sufficient to address the 'moral conflicts between individual and collective goals' (Grace et al., 2008, p. 1006), or dispel long-held assumptions that buttress the shame and stigma currently associated with disfigurement.

Effective communication including the appropriate use of language and words, are essential for good healthcare outcomes within all healthcare encounters but particularly so for patients whose health beliefs and concerns may not reflect the needs of national or local populations (Johnson, 2005). It may be difficult to translate concepts and words used in research and healthcare accurately where there is no direct equivalent in the language and culture of particular minorities. Thus, reliance on the use of a professional interpreter who 'just translates what you say, doesn't seem to add any explanations for the patient, stays in the background and lets me and the patient carry on the conversation' (Hadziabdic et al., 2010, p. 264) will not necessarily lead to better health outcomes. To improve understanding of health and disease, and provide effective and culturally sensitive treatment, researchers and healthcare providers alike need to demonstrate a broader awareness of the role of religion and other cultural attributes in the healthcare beliefs and practices of ethnic minority groups. Johnson (2005) reminds us that health and social care services are more likely to be beneficial when they are relevant to people's needs and concerns. Thus working with minority communities is more likely to lead to recommendations arising from research that will be sensitive to these concerns.

Professional perceptions of other health beliefs are also variable, such as the mistaken belief that Bangladeshis associate obesity with health and fertility (Grace et al., 2008). There is a danger that patients' concerns about appearance may be trivialized and assumptions made about their emotional resources and coping strategies if underlying cultural concerns are not recognized. This has implications for the training of doctors and healthcare professionals who work at the interface between the lay perception of illness and disfigurement and their personal system of health beliefs (Montgomery & Schubart, 2010) which may often be in conflict with those of their patients. Health professionals could be encouraged to develop the skills they need to communicate and deliver care more sensitively and effectively to members of ethnic minority groups, using resources such as PROCEED (Professionals Responding to Cancer and Ethnic Diversity) developed in response to growing concern about inequalities in healthcare experienced by patients with different ethnic and cultural backgrounds (Medical News Today, 31 March 2006). The key message here is that while perhaps we can never fully appreciate the multiplicity of values within all ethnic groups that shape and perpetuate perceptions of disfigurement or any other health condition, those working to support them need, on a continuous basis, to reflect upon their own cultural and ethnic origins, values and beliefs, and develop an awareness of how others perceive their worlds.

A means of gaining a better understanding of the diversity encompassed within ethnic groups is through community engagement. The advantages of this are not merely restricted to the process of conducting ethnic research, as highlighted above; such benefits can also be extended to policy and practice within the healthcare system. In the UK, the NHS White Paper, *Equity and excellence: Liberating the NHS* (Department of Health, 2010), commits the government to promoting equality and the NHS to eliminating discrimination and reducing inequalities. The White Paper describes the aim of greater empowerment for patients and communities in decisions that impact upon their healthcare, together with appropriate balance between local accountability and technical expertise. Should this be achieved, it would be a significant step towards an environment in which effective policies and practices could be developed to meet the needs of people from different ethnic groupings who are distressed by their appearance.

REFERENCES

Adamson, P. & Doud Galli, S. (2009). Modern concepts of beauty. *Plastic Surgical Nursing,* 29, 5–9.

Altabe, M. (1998). Ethnicity and body image: Quantitative and qualitative analysis. *International Journal of Eating Disorders,* 23, 153–59.

Ashing-Giwa, K., Padilla, G., Bohorquez, D. E., Tejero, J. S., & Garcia, M. (2006). Understanding the breast cancer experience of Latina women. *Journal of Psychosocial Oncology,* 24, 19–52.

Benson, H., Greenwood, M., & Klemchuck, H. (1975). The relaxation response: psychophysiologic aspects and clinical applications. *International Journal of Psychiatry & Medicine,* 6, 87–98.

Bhopal, R. S., Phillimore, P., & Kohli, H. S. (1991). Inappropriate use of the term 'Asian': an obstacle to ethnicity and health research. *Journal of Public Health Medicine,* 13, 244–6.

Bhopal, R. (2007). *Ethnicity, Race, and Health in Multicultural Societies. Foundations for better epidemiology, public health and health care.* New York: Oxford University Press.

Cash, T. & Pruzinsky, T. (1990). *Body images: development, deviance and change.* New York: Guilford Publications.

Chiu, R. & Babcock, D. (2002). The Relative Importance of facial attractiveness and gender in Hong Kong selection decisions. *International Journal of Human Resource Management,* 13, 141–55.

Clarke, A. & Cooper, C. (2001). Psychological rehabilitation after disfiguring injury or disease: investigating the training needs of specialist nurses. *Journal of Advanced Nursing,* 34, 18–26.

Conrad, E., Brown, P., & Conrad, P. (1996). Fatalism and breast cancer in black women. *Annals of Internal Medicine,* 125, 941–42.

Clark, J. & Dawson, L. (1996). Personal religiousness and ethical judgements: An empirical analysis. *Journal of Business Ethics,* 15, 359–70.

Dalal, A. K. (2002). Disability rehabilitation in a traditional Indian society. *Asia Pacific Disability Rehabilitation Journal,* 13, 17–26.

Department of Health. (2008). *Equality impact assessment: summary tool and guidance for policy makers.* http://www.dh.gov.uk/prod_consum_dh/groups/dh_digitalassets/documents/digitalasset/dh_107580.pdf (accessed 03 September 2010).

Department of Health. (2010). *Equity and excellence: Liberating the NHS.* http://www.dh.gov.uk/prod_consum_dh/groups/dh_digitalassets/@dh/@en/@ps/documents/digitalasset/dh_117794.pdf (accessed 03 September 2010).

Dubow, S. (1995). *Scientific Racism in Modern South Africa.* New York: Cambridge University Press.

Edmonds, A. (2007). 'The poor have the right to be beautiful': cosmetic surgery in neoliberal Brazil. *Journal of the Royal Anthropological Institute,* 13, 363–81.

Florian, V. & Katz, S. (1983). The impact of cultural, ethnic and national variables on attitudes towards the disabled in Israel. *International Journal of Intercultural Relations,* 7, 167.

Gall, T., Charbonneau, C., Clark, N., *et al.* (2005). Understanding the nature and role of spirituality in relation to coping and health: A conceptual framework. *Canadian Psychology,* 46, 88–104.

Gilman, S. (1999). By a nose: on the construction of 'foreign bodies'. *Social Epistemology,* 13, 49–58.

Grace, C., Begum, R., Subhani, S., Kopelman, P., & Greenhalgh, T. (2008). Prevention of type 2 diabetes in British Bangladeshis: qualititative study of community, religious, and professional perspectives. *British Medical Journal*, 337, a1931.

Greenhalgh, T., Helman, C., & Chowdhury, A. M. (1998). Health beliefs and folk models of diabetes in British Bangladeshis: a qualitative study. *British Medical Journal*, 316, 978–83.

Hadziabdic, E., Albin, B., Heikkila, K., & Hjelm, K, (2010). Healthcare staff perceptions of using interpreters: a qualitative study. *Primary Health Care Research & Development*, 11, 260–70.

Holland, J., Kash, K., Passik, S., *et al.* (1998). A brief spiritual beliefs inventory for use in quality of life research in life threatening illness. *Psychooncology*, 7, 460–69.

Hughes, J., Naqvi, H., Saul, K., Williams, H., Johnson, M., Rumsey, N., & Charlton, R. (2009). South Asian community views about individuals with a disfigurement. *Diversity in Health and Care*, 6, 241–53.

Hunt, S. (2005). *Religion and Everyday Life*. New York: Routledge.

Johansson, P. (1998). White skin, large breasts: Chinese beauty product advertising as cultural discourse. *China Information*, 13, 59–84.

Johnson, M. (2005). Engaging communities and users: Health and social care research with ethnic minority communities. In J. Nazroo (ed.) *Research with Minority Groups: Issues and Solutions*, pp. 48–64. London: Taylor & Francis.

Johnson, M. (2006). Ethnicity. In A. Killoran, C. Swann, & M. Kelly (eds.) *Public Health Evidence: Changing the health of the public*. Oxford: Oxford University Press.

Kagawa-Singer M, and Kassim-Lakha, S. (2003). A strategy to reduce cross-cultural miscommunication and increase the likelihood of improving health outcomes. *Academic Medicine*, 78, 577–87.

Kaw, E. (1991). Medicalisation of racial features: Asian American women and cosmetic surgery. *Medical Anthropology Quarterly*, 7, 74–89.

Lange, L. & Piette, J. (2006). Personal models for diabetes in context and patients' health status. *Journal of Behavioural Medicine*, 29, 239–53.

Lansdown, R., Lloyd, J. & Hunter, J. (1991). Facial deformity in childhood: severity and psychological adjustment. *Child Care Health Development*, 17, 165–71.

Lansdown, R., Rumsey, N., Bradbury, E., Carr, T., & Partridge, J. (1997). *Visibly Different: Coping with Disfigurement*. London: Butterworth Heinemann.

Lewin, E. (2005). Perceptions about skin colour and heritage: The experience of Anglo-Indian women in Western Australia. *Social Identities*, 11, 621–51.

Mason, D. (2000). *Race and Ethnicity in Modern Britain*. Oxford: University Press.

Medical News Today, 2006. PROCEED: New ethnic diversity training launched for health professionals. *Medical News Today* 31 March. http://www.medicalnewstoday.com/medicalnews.php?newsid=40581 (accessed 4 November, 2010).

McCall Smith, A. (2009). *Tea Time for the Traditionally Built: A No. 1 Ladies' Detective Agency, Book 10*. London: Little Brown.

Mikulincer, M., Weller, A., & Florian, V. (1993). Sense of Closeness to Parents and Family Rules: A Study of Arab and Jewish Youth in Israel. *International Journal of Psychology*, 28, 323–35.

Modood, T., Beishon, S., & Virdee, S. (1994). *Changing Ethnic Identities*. London: Policy Studies Institute.

Montgomery, K.S. & Schubart, K.J. (2010). Heath Promotion in Cuturally Diverse and Vulnerable Populations. *Home Health Care Management & Practice*, 22, 131.

O'Malley, A., Kerner, J., Johnson, A., & Mandelblatt, J. (1999). Acculturation and breast cancer screening among hispanic women in New York City. *American Journal of Public Health*, 89, 219–27.

Papadopoulos, L., Bor, R., & Legg, C. (1999). Coping with the effects of vitiligo: A preliminary investigation into the effects of cognitive-behavioural therapy. *British Journal of Medical Psychology*, 72, 385–96.

Pearce, N., Foliaki, S., Sporle, A., *et al.* (2004). Genetics, race, ethnicity and health. *British Medical Journal*, 328, 1070–2.

Peyrot, M. & Rubin, R. (1994). Structure and correlates of diabetes-specific locus of control. *Diabetes Care*, 14, 605–9.

Rozario, S. (2007). Growing up and living with neurofibromatosis 1 (NF1): a British Bangladeshi case study. *Journal of Genetic Counselling*, 16, 551–9.

Rumsey, N. & Harcourt, D. (2004). Body image and disfigurement: issues and interventions. *Body Image*, 1, 83–97.

Rumsey, N. & Harcourt, D. (2005). *The Psychology of Appearance*. Maidenhead: Open University Press.

Senior, P. & Bhopal, R. (1994). Ethnicity as a variable in epidemiological research. *British Medical Journal*, 309, 327–9.

Shavers, V., Lynch, C., & Burmeister, L. (2002). Racial differences in factors that influence the willingness to participate in medical research studies. *Annals of Epidemiology*, 12, 248–56.

Szczepura, A., Price, C., & Gumber, A. (2008). Breast and bowel cancer screening uptake patterns over 15 years for UK south Asian ethnic minority populations, corrected for differences in socio-demographic characteristics. *BMC Public Health*, 8, 346 doi:10.1186/1471–2458-8-346.

Talakoub, L. & Wesley, N. (2009). Differences in perceptions of beauty and cosmetic procedures performed in ethnic patients. *Seminars in Cutaneous Medicine & Surgery*, 28, 115–29.

Thompson, A. & Kent, G. (2001). Adjusting to disfigurement: processes involved in dealing with being visibly different. *Clinical Psychology Review*, 21, 663–82.

Turton, D. (2004). Lip plates and the people who take photographs: uneasy encounters between Mursi and tourists in southern Ethiopia. *Athropology Today*, 20, 3–8.

Van Der Veer, P. (2002). Religion in South Asia. *Annual Review of Anthropology*, 31, 173–87.

Wallston, B., Wallston, K., Kaplan, G., & Maides, S. (1976). Development and validation of the Health Locus of Control (HLC) Scale. *Journal of Consulting Clinical Psychology*, 21, 3–20.

Walsh, F. (1998). *Strengthening family resilience*. New York: The Guilford Press.

Wendler, D., Kington, R., Madans, J., *et al.* (2006). Are racial and ethnic minorities less willing to participate in health research? *PLOS Medicine*, 3, 201–10.

Wilson, L. (2000). Implementation and evaluation of church-based health fairs. *Journal of Community Health Nursing*, 17, 39–48.

CHAPTER 18

···

INFLUENCE OF THE MEDIA

···

EMMA HALLIWELL

PHILLIPPA C. DIEDRICHS

THE mass media play a large role in defining and moulding cultural ideals and norms. In the context of appearance, the media helps to shape beauty ideals by showing certain body sizes and features more frequently, and by depicting them as more beautiful and desirable. Analyses of the dimensions and features of body types and appearances frequently displayed in the media, and the narratives surrounding these images, consistently show that the media endorses and reinforces current Western beauty ideals. These ideals emphasize the importance of a thin body shape for women, a lean and muscular body shape for men, facial symmetry, and a clear and youthful complexion. Compared to the appearance of people in the general population, women and men who embody these ideals are drastically over-represented in magazines, on television, and in films (Spitzer et al., 1999; Fouts & Vaughan, 2002). This means that only a minority of women and men in the general population have bodies that bear any resemblance to those idealized in the media.

Many studies have demonstrated that exposure to idealized, and often sexualized, media images can harm individual's psychological well-being, although some people appear to be more vulnerable to negative effects than others. There is now a growing body of research which suggests that media images that depict more realistic appearances may prevent these negative effects. This chapter presents an overview of the empirical evidence and the psychosocial theories that address the influence of the media on body image and appearance concerns.

THE CONTENT OF THE MEDIA

The bodily dimensions of the ideal woman and man represented in the media have changed over time. The ideal body weight for women, as depicted by magazine images of fashion and glamour models, has decreased over the last 50 years. Since the 1990s the average model has been more than 20% underweight (Wiseman et al., 1992). Further, the recent trend for 'size zero' fashion models and actresses represents the glorification of women with a BMI of less than 16, a point at which starvation is common and anorexia nervosa more prevalent (Dittmar, 2008). The ideal body for men has also become increasingly muscular and visible in magazines (Leit et al., 2001; Rohlinger, 2002). This shift in masculine beauty is also evident in children's action toys, which have become more muscular over time, to the extent that modern action figures have bodies at the very extremes, or even beyond the limits, of actual human attainment (Pope et al., 1999). Alongside analysis of the bodily dimensions of beauty displayed in the media, it is also important to consider the way in which these 'beautiful' bodies are framed.

The sexualization and objectification of bodies in the media has increased over the last 30 years, highlighting the media's tendency to emphasize the centrality of appearance to identity, attractiveness, and success (Reichert et al., 1999). In addition, there has been a recent shift in the way this sexualization is framed. Rather than women being displayed merely as objects of male desire, women are now portrayed as actively choosing to display themselves sexually, in order to demonstrate their independence and liberation (Gill, 2007, 2008). The sexualization of media imagery is also evident in the dress and pose of young female models in teenage magazines, whereby the content of these magazines encourages a focus on sexual attractiveness among readers who often have not reached puberty (Tankard Reist, 2010). Similar changes have occurred in representations of men's bodies in the media. The most frequent representation of masculinity in men's magazines in both 1987 and 1997 was of the erotic male (Rohlinger, 2002). However, in the later magazines other signs of objectification were also displayed; the male models were shown as distracted from the scene, with heads or face obscured, and without clothes. The sexualization and objectification of the body in media images symbolizes the prioritization of physicality over other aspects of identity, and presents the body as of supreme importance, as signifying the whole person (Rohlinger, 2002).

As Bordo (1993) has argued, contemporary Western ideals of beauty are also distinctly racialized, privileging 'white' features—such as blue eyes, blonde hair, a slimmer body shape, and glossy, moving hair—and presenting them as universal 'ideals'. For instance, an analysis of advertisements contained within three of the most popular women's fashion and lifestyle magazines in the US from 2001–2002 found that 91% of the models were white (Frith et al., 2005). The same study looked at women's magazines in Taiwan and Singapore, and found that despite these countries having predominantly Chinese populations, their magazines displayed white models more frequently than Chinese models. More recently, however, the influence of black beauty ideals can be seen in the shift towards a more voluptuous, but extremely toned, body ideal displayed by the likes of Beyonce, and the idealization of athletic bodies for both men and women (Bordo, 2009).

Although much less researched, congenital and acquired visible difference (disfigurement) is another aspect of appearance that is excluded from media images. Wardle and Boyce (2009) analysed the content of 1 year's primetime, and 1 month's daytime, television programming in the UK. They found that people with visible differences were rarely shown on television. Furthermore, when they were featured, characters with visible differences were presented in stereotypical and derogatory ways. For example, scarring was used to identify 'baddies', and individuals with burns depicted as withdrawn and reclusive. The reliance on myths surrounding visible differences in media representations can have a damaging impact on public attitudes towards, and the psychosocial adjustment of, individuals' living with visible differences. To address this, UK charities, such as Changing Faces (2010), have developed high profile, public awareness campaigns aimed at promoting media representations of visible differences that are inclusive and non-discriminatory.

THEORETICAL EXPLANATIONS FOR THE MEDIA'S IMPACT ON BODY IMAGE AND WELL-BEING

In this section we explore the impact that media representations of beauty ideals can have on people. We will begin by discussing theoretical accounts of the processes through which beauty ideals in the media impact on individual's body image concerns. Then we will review evidence to support this link.

Two prominent theories highlighting the role of media images with idealized appearances in the development of psychological health problems are sociocultural theory and self-objectification theory. Sociocultural theory states that individuals experience body dissatisfaction because they cannot match unrealistic appearance standards displayed in the media. This can lead to participation in a range of body shaping behaviours such as dieting and excessive exercise, and for some individuals the associated distress and behaviour reach clinical levels (Thompson et al., 2004). Stice and associates (e.g. Stice, 1994; Stice & Shaw, 2002) further specify mechanisms through which sociocultural pressures to adhere to beauty ideals portrayed can lead to disordered eating. This model posits that perceived pressure concerning appearance from the media, and from other sources such as family, peers and partners, leads to disordered eating through body dissatisfaction and the internalization of cultural beauty ideals as personal standards for success and appearance.

Self-objectification theory (Fredrickson & Roberts, 1997) was originally formulated to explain how women's socialization is related to psychological health problems. However, it has also been successfully applied to understanding the development of body image and eating problems among men (Moradi & Huang, 2008). The theory posits that exposure to idealized and sexualized images fosters the development of an observer's perspective on oneself, whereby individuals begin to feel like they are an object to be looked at and evaluated based on their appearance (Fredrickson & Roberts, 1997). Through this process of self-objectification, the appearance of the body becomes more highly valued than the competence and ability of the body. In turn, individuals engage in high levels of body monitoring and appearance surveillance, which leads to body shame, anxiety and decreased awareness of bodily sensations. Ultimately, this can lead to the development of eating disorders, depression, and sexual dysfunction.

Fredrickson and Roberts (1997) argue that repeated exposure to direct and indirect pressures to match cultural beauty ideals leads individuals to believe that their motivation to improve their appearance is freely chosen, or even natural. Internalization of appearance in sociocultural theory implies a similar internal attribution for appearance behaviours (Thompson & Stice, 2001). This is a key component of each theory because when the desire to be beautiful is constructed as a personal choice, rather than an externally imposed prescription, individuals are more willing to strive for an idealized appearance and become more vulnerable to feedback that they do not meet societal standards (Spitzack, 1990). There is a large body of research which supports the central tenets of sociocultural and self-objectification theory by demonstrating that exposure to unrealistic and idealized media images can have a negative impact on women's and men's health.

EMPIRICAL INVESTIGATIONS OF THE IMPACT OF MEDIA IMAGES

Parallels are frequently drawn between the decreasing size of the female body ideal in the media and both escalating levels of women's body dissatisfaction and increases in the incidence of eating disorders (e.g. Striegel-Moore et al., 1986; Jacobi & Cash, 1994). Similarly, as the muscularity and objectification of male bodies in the media has increased, there has been a corresponding increase in men's concerns with appearance and body dissatisfaction (e.g. Pope et al., 2000; Thompson et al., 2004). It is also clear, however, that not all individuals are equally affected by media imagery, and critics of this viewpoint often question how such a prevalent causal factor (i.e. idealized media images), could account for what is still a relatively limited effect (i.e. severe body image concerns, and fairly rare conditions such as eating disorders)? It is true that although body dissatisfaction amongst men and women is normative, only a small proportion develop eating disorders. Nonetheless, Levine and Murnen (2009) note that when you have a combination of risk factors (e.g. media exposure, genetic factors, history of dieting), it is perfectly plausible that common risk factors can account for the incidence of less prevalent problems. In addition, there is a substantial body of literature which demonstrates that exposure to idealized media imagery can negatively influence women's and men's body image.

Media impact on women's body image concerns

Numerous studies have examined associations between media representations of female beauty and women's body image concerns and self-esteem. Correlational studies consistently demonstrate that increased media exposure is associated with increased body dissatisfaction (e.g. Botta, 2003; Tiggemann, 2005b). These studies typically involve a questionnaire design, whereby researchers correlate scores on measures of self-reported exposure to the media, internalization and awareness of beauty ideals, and body image. Meta-analyses of correlational studies also report a positive association between exposure to body-focused magazines and TV and body dissatisfaction (e.g. Grabe et al., 2008). However, correlational studies fail to tell us the direction of the relationship between media consumption and body image. Do body dissatisfied women seek out idealized media images, or, do idealized media images cause negative body image? Experimental and prospective studies can help to unravel this relationship.

Experimental studies demonstrate that a specific incident of media exposure can lead to an immediate change in body image. This type of research typically involves showing individuals either magazine or television images that depict idealized bodies or no bodies (control images), and then measuring and comparing body image-related variables for the different images. Meta-analyses of these studies demonstrate that exposure to thin bodies idealized in the media has a small to moderate negative effect on body- and weight-dissatisfaction, negative affect, internalization of the thin ideal and eating behaviour amongst adolescents and young adult women across countries such as Australia, Canada, UK, and the US (Groesz et al., 2001, 2008; Want, 2009). Individual studies suggest that this negative exposure effect is also experienced by women in later adulthood, and by girls as young as 5 years (Dittmar & Howard, 2004b; Halliwell & Dittmar, 2004; Dittmar et al., 2006).

Whilst the majority of research in this area has examined the impact of media exposure on body and weight dissatisfaction, body esteem, or mood, a few studies have looked specifically at the impact of media images on self-objectification. Harper and Tiggemann (2008) found that viewing advertisements featuring thin models leads to increased self-objectification among women, compared to viewing control images without models. Halliwell et al. (2010) found that framing women as actively courting sexual attention was associated with greater state self-objectification than exposure to images framing women as passive sex objects. These findings suggest that the recent trend for framing women in media images as sexually agentic may be more damaging than earlier representations of women as passive objects and suggest that future research should examine the framing and context of media images as well as the dimensions of the bodies displayed.

A common criticism of the experimental media exposure literature is the short-term nature of the research, which means that it is often unclear whether the negative effects of thin ideal media imagery persist over time. Although there are some inconsistencies in regards to the impact of different mass media (i.e. television vs. magazines), there is now a growing body of prospective studies with findings that are largely consistent with the experimental and correlational literature. In large-scale, prospective cohort studies of North American pre-adolescent and adolescent girls, Field and colleagues found that trying to look like women in magazines, television, and films predicted the onset of purging, dieting and weight concern 1 year later (Field et al., 1999, 2001). Tiggemann (2006) studied Australian adolescent girls and found that reading fashion magazines and watching soap operas predicted increased internalization of the thin beauty ideal and drive for thinness 1 year later, although there was no effect for body dissatisfaction. In an innovative study, Stice et al. (2001) gave North American adolescent girls either a 15-month subscription to a fashion magazine or no subscription. Although there was no effect on girls' body image 15 months later, girls with a magazine subscription who also reported lower levels of social support at baseline were more likely to report increased pressure to be thin, body dissatisfaction, dieting, and bulimic symptomatology at follow-up. Overall, this research suggests that media exposure is a risk factor for the development of negative body image among girls and women, but that some girls and women may be more vulnerable than others.

Media impact on men's body image concerns

Compared to research with women, there has been considerably less research into the effects of exposure to idealized media images on men's body image. While some studies have found no effect on men's weight satisfaction (Hargreaves & Tiggemann, 2009), drive for muscularity (Johnson et al., 2007) or body self-consciousness (Kalodner, 1997), a recent meta-analysis of 25 correlational and experimental studies concluded that, on average, exposure to idealized, attractive muscular media images is associated with greater psychological dysfunction and lower body satisfaction and body esteem among men (Barlett et al., 2008). Moreover, the effect size of media exposure on men's body image is similar to that found for women. There are several issues that emerge as important from individual studies that are not reflected in the meta-analysis, possible due to the small number of studies in this area.

Two of the earliest experimental exposure studies found that exposure to male models had a negative impact on men's overall body satisfaction (Grogan et al., 1996; Ogden & Mundray, 1996). More recently, research has found that exposure to idealized male models leads to lower satisfaction specifically with muscularity compared to exposure to control, no model, advertisements (Lorenzen et al., 2004; Baird & Grieve, 2006; Hargreaves & Tiggemann, 2009).

Relatively few studies have compared the effects of exposure to male models who display different levels of muscularity. Arbour and Ginnis (2006) compared the impact of exposure to images of muscular and hyper-muscular models on young men's body satisfaction. Men's pre-existing dissatisfaction with their own level of muscularity moderated the effect of exposure to the media images; men who initially reported high muscularity dissatisfaction reported greater general body dissatisfaction after exposure to muscular models than after exposure to hyper-muscular models. However, a follow-up study demonstrated that the muscular models were viewed as more attractive than the hyper-muscular images. Therefore, it is impossible to determine if the differing muscularity of the models, or the difference in attractiveness, was responsible for these effects. This confound of size with the attractiveness of models was also evident in some of the early exposure research with women (Halliwell & Dittmar, 2004). A more recent study by Diedrichs and Lee (2010), however, compared the impact of advertisements featuring no models with advertisements depicting muscular or non-muscular male models, and controlled for model attractiveness. After controlling for attractiveness, there was no difference in the impact of viewing muscular models on young men's body image in comparison to viewing non-muscular models or no models. However, viewing media images depicting attractive, average-size male models was associated with more positive body image than viewing no models.

To date there has been almost no research that has examined the long-term influence of media images depicting idealized male bodies on men's body image. However, one study examined the long-term and cumulative impact of viewing sexualized media images on men's body image and objectification. Aubrey (2006) found that for college-aged women and men exposure to sexually objectifying television shows was associated with increase self-objectification a year later. Interestingly, exposure to objectifying television and magazines also increased body surveillance in men but not in women, suggesting that men are particularly vulnerable to media exposure in this respect. However, it may also be that any demonstrable impact of the media on surveillance amongst women was diluted by the impact of other pressures to body monitor from sources such as friends and family, that are not so strong for men.

The research surrounding the influence of idealized media images on adolescent boys' body image is less clear. Some studies using correlational designs have found that exposure to the media is associated with increased body dissatisfaction, the use of food supplements, and an increased desire to lose fat and gain muscle mass (Botta, 2003; McCabe & Ricciardelli, 2003; Ricciardelli & McCabe, 2003; Carlson Jones et al., 2004). However, most of these studies find small effects, and other experimental studies find no effect on body dissatisfaction (Hargreaves & Tiggemann, 2002a, 2003, 2004; Humphreys & Paxton, 2004). Similarly, prospective studies with pre-adolescent boys have produced conflicting results (e.g. Ricciardelli et al., 2006; Moriarty & Harrison, 2008). It has been suggested that the inconsistent findings for boys may be due to pubertal growth; during puberty, boys generally grow in the direction of the muscular ideal and therefore they may not feel affected by muscular media imagery (Humphreys & Paxton, 2004). However, while it appears that adolescent boys may not be adversely affected by media images of the muscular ideal to the extent that young girls are influenced by the thin ideal, the research with adult men indicates that when these adolescent boys progress into adulthood it is likely that exposure to such images will become detrimental to their body image. Of course, prospective and longitudinal research with adolescent boys and young men is needed to confirm this.

A more complex picture

The meta-analyses in this area are valuable because they demonstrate, overall, the role of media images in fuelling body dissatisfaction among women and men. However, the picture is somewhat more complex, as a number of studies suggest there is considerable variability in individual's responses to media exposure. Often the role of individual difference factors has been ignored or downplayed in the literature, but actually it is very important as it indicates the complex nature of the media's influence on body image and the need to understand the *psychological processes* through which media messages influence individuals' concerns (Tiggemann, 2005a; Halliwell et al., 2007; Dittmar, 2008).

Two meta-analyses have found that women who have pre-existing body image concerns and have internalized the thin beauty ideal are more strongly affected by media exposure (Groesz et al., 2001; Want, 2009). Individual studies have also identified various factors that moderate the effect of idealized media on women's body image. They suggest that higher levels of trait body dissatisfaction, self-monitoring, chronic appearance-related self-discrepancies, appearance schemas and disordered eating symptomatology are associated with stronger negative effects of the media on body image (e.g. Posavac et al., 1998; Hargreaves & Tiggemann, 2003; Bessenoff, 2006; Dittmar et al., 2009).

Turning to men, currently there is no consistent picture of what individual difference factors influence the impact of idealized media imagery on men's body image. Arbour & Ginnis (2006) found prior levels of muscularity dissatisfaction, but not generalized body dissatisfaction, influenced susceptibility to negative exposure effects. Hargreaves & Tiggemann (2009) concurred that general appearance dissatisfaction did not moderate the exposure effect, although men who were highly invested in their appearance were particularly vulnerable to negative effects after viewing television commercials featuring muscular men. On the other hand, Agliata and Tantleff-Dunn (2004) and Diedrichs and Lee (2010) found that internalization of current beauty ideals, the consistent moderator of media exposure amongst women (e.g. Dittmar & Howard, 2004b; Halliwell & Dittmar, 2004; Diedrichs & Lee, 2011), did not influence exposure effects among men.

It is evident that a clearer theoretical understanding of the factors determining *when* and *how* women and men are influenced by media images is needed to make sense of these findings. This will also help address the important question posed by Polivy and Herman (2004) who ask, given the strong evidence for the negative effects of idealized media on body image, why do women and men still choose to read fashion and lifestyle magazines? It is clear that women and men are not naïve, passive consumers of the media. In contrast, we know that women have a complex and critical understanding of the messages being portrayed through the use of idealized bodies in advertising (e.g. Malson et al., 2011). Similarly, focus groups with men suggest that they are often very critical of idealized, muscular media images and that they frequently dismiss them as being unrealistic and unappealing (e.g. De Visser et al., 2009; Diedrichs et al., 2011). Theories regarding how individuals process media images can help to answer these questions.

Theoretical Accounts of Media Processing: Moderators and Mediators

Cognitive-processing models

Self-discrepancy theory and self-schema theory are both cognitive-processing models which propose that the nature of an individual's self-representations determine the way in which they respond to media messages. They argue that individuals differ in the extent to which they hold appearance schemas or self-discrepancies, and that these differences account for an individuals' vulnerability to media exposure and the psychological processes through which media exposure leads to affective outcomes.

Self-schema theory argues that all individuals develop at least a basic appearance-related schema, that is a cognitive structure containing information about appearance (Altabe & Thompson, 1996). However, some individuals develop very elaborate and salient representations of their appearance. These individuals are referred to as 'appearance schematic' and it is thought that these schema increase an individual's awareness of, and attention to, appearance-related information in the environment.

Therefore, schematicity is conceptualized as an individual difference factor that can account for an individual's vulnerability to negative media exposure effects. Consistent with self-schema theory, research has demonstrated that appearance schematic women report stronger negative media exposure effects than aschematic women (e.g. Jung et al., 2001; Lavin & Cash, 2001; Hargreaves & Tiggemann, 2003). Furthermore, self-schema theory argues that media exposure activates an individual's pre-existing schemas or knowledge structures about one's appearance, and it is through this activation that individuals come to experience negative emotions in response to media exposure (Hargreaves & Tiggemann, 2002b). Again, there is empirical support for this claim (e.g. Hargreaves & Tiggemann, 2003; Brown & Dittmar, 2005).

Self-discrepancy theory (SDT) has been used to propose a similar but more specific account of psychological processing that links media exposure to affective outcomes (Dittmar et al., 2009). SDT proposes that discrepancies within an individual's self-concept cause negative affect and psychological dysfunction. For a detailed discussion of this theory in relation to body image see Halliwell & Dittmar (2006). Most importantly in relation to media effects, Higgins (1987) makes a distinction between chronic self-discrepancies linked to a chronic vulnerability to particular emotions and temporarily accessible self-discrepancies that are associated with transiently experienced emotions. Stable, or chronic, self-discrepancies predict body-related outcomes, such as body dissatisfaction or disordered eating (e.g. Strauman et al., 1991; Szymanski & Cash, 1995; Harrison, 2001). They also guide an individual's attention to and processing of environmental information. Consistent with theory, individuals with large chronic appearance-discrepancies are particularly vulnerable to the effects of exposure to body-ideals in the media (Bessenoff, 2006; Dittmar & Halliwell, 2008).

However, environmental input, such as media images of models, will also activate temporary self-discrepancies which, theoretically, will lead to body dissatisfaction and negative affect (Dittmar & Halliwell, 2008). It is also likely that the discrepancies activated by media exposure are domain specific and related to the specific nature of the media image. For example, exposure to male models is likely to give rise to temporary self-discrepancies in men that are specific to the domain muscularity and, as a consequence, negative affect about body build and muscularity should be stronger than negative affect about general appearance or other domains of the self. Indeed, Blond's (2008) meta-analysis revealed that stronger media exposure effects were found for measures that focus on specific body parts than for measures of overall body dissatisfaction.

Research has indicated that temporary appearance-related self-discrepancies mediate the impact of media exposure on body dissatisfaction amongst young men (Dittmar & Halliwell, 2008) and amongst young women (Dittmar et al., 2009). In each case media exposure activated discrepancies that specifically related to the body ideal, i.e. muscularity in men and thinness in women, and crucially, that it was these specific discrepancies that were related to increases in negative body-focused affect.

In summary, there is evidence that activation of appearance schema and temporary appearance-related discrepancies represent important psychological processes which determine the impact of media exposure. Whilst there is much similarity between these constructs, there is also an important difference; schema theory focuses on the activation of pre-existing information about appearance, whereas self-discrepancy activation focuses on the creation of temporary appearance-related discrepancies there and then which relate to specific aspects of the exposure images. Therefore, discrepancy activation theory proposes a more specific explanatory mechanism, as the specific nature of discrepancy activated by particular media images are important in determining the emotional and behavioural consequences of exposure. There is also evidence that the existence of both chronic appearance-related self-discrepancies and appearance schemas make individuals susceptible to media exposure effects. Both of these constructs are strongly related to internalization, and the extent to which women internalize the thin ideal may be a central vulnerability factor which underlies these and other moderators identified in the literature (Halliwell & Dittmar, 2008).

Social-comparison theory

The cognitive-processing models are clearly valuable in unpicking some of the inconsistencies in the media exposure literature. However, the most widely used theory, and the model that can best account of the inconsistencies in the literature, is social comparison theory (Festinger, 1954). Indeed, social comparison mechanisms have been shown to be more powerful in explaining exposure effects than schema activation (Birkeland et al., 2005; van den Berg & Thompson, 2007). Social comparison theory proposes that individuals continually evaluate themselves in order to assess their own standing on a wide range of characteristics. Festinger (1954) proposed that, in the absence of objective information about norms and standards, individuals will make subjective comparisons with other people around them. The aim of these comparisons is accurate self-evaluation. Generally, a social comparison with someone who is considered superior to oneself on the comparison dimensions is referred to as an upward comparison. In contrast, a comparison with someone who is considered inferior is referred to as downward comparison.

Women report that they make spontaneous comparisons with media models and television actors (Smith & Leach, 2004). Due to the unrealistic nature of these images these will be upward comparisons, evaluating oneself against these comparison targets can explain the negative effect of media exposure found in much of the research (Groesz et al., 2001). This is supported by evidence that appearance satisfaction is lower amongst women who view appearance-related commercials after being instructed to engage in appearance-related social comparisons, than amongst women instructed to focus on the product or given neutral instructions (Cattarin et al., 2000).

However, further developments in social comparison theory suggest individuals are motivated to engage in social comparisons not only for self-evaluation, but also for self-improvement and self-enhancement (Wood, 1989). This is consistent with evidence that restrained eaters self-enhance in response to viewing thin models. They report higher appearance self-esteem and rate their own and actual ideal body size as smaller than dieters who have viewed plus-size models, or no model control images (Mills et al., 2002). Further, they report higher social self-esteem and more positive self-image after exposure to thin models than to control images (Joshi et al., 2004). Mills et al. (2002) propose that dieters use media models as inspirational figures, because these models represent an ideal-self on an important dimension, and that they self-enhance in response to comparisons with thin models. Self-improvement motives can also explain why men who use the gym report less body-focused negative affect after viewing idealized male models than after control images, particularly because the extent of their self-enhancement was explained by individual motivation to increase muscularity through exercise (Halliwell et al., 2007). The similarity between the dieters and exercisers in these studies is that both are actively trying, and expecting, to change their body shape and, therefore, are likely to make appearance-related comparisons motivated by self-improvement.

Two studies have explicitly manipulated motivation for appearance comparisons with models. Both studies suggest that comparisons motivated by self-improvement or self-enhancement avoid negative media exposure effects (Martin & Gentry, 1997; Halliwell & Dittmar, 2005). However, in contrast to the studies with restrained eaters and exercisers, there was no evidence of a positive impact of media exposure.

The positive exposure effects amongst individuals expecting to change their body shape are consistent with the notion that some women temporarily 'buy into', and imagine themselves as, the idealized image portrayed (Myers & Biocca, 1992). Indeed, this affiliation with the idealized image is also posited to be central to self-enhancement and self-improvement effects. It is interesting that different methods of inducing self-improvement and self-enhancement seem to have a different impact on outcomes. The comparison instructions used by Martin and Gentry (1997) and Halliwell and Dittmar (2005) for self-improvement referred to 'becoming more like the person you would ideally like to be'. In contrast, Tiggemann et al. (2009) induced a fantasy viewing condition that required participants to imagine themselves in the place of the model and imagine how much fun her life would be. They demonstrated that this fantasy processing was associated with more positive mood after exposure to ideal media images.

It is reasonable to suppose that men and women will tend to use a variety of processing motives when viewing media, according to both individual differences and also the framing of the images. Advertising can be seen as actively promoting a self-improvement motivation for comparison through the suggestion that a particular product can make you a more ideal person (Dittmar, 2008). Products often promise greater attractiveness. Qualitative research suggests that self-evaluation and self-improvement motives are frequently used by young women when making comparisons with models in the media (Martin & Kennedy, 1993). Furthermore, Tiggemann et al. (2009) found that women often engage in more than one processing strategy, so they may engage in appearance-related comparisons and fantasy processing simultaneously. Clearly, the impact of exposure will depend on the type and combination of processing individuals engage in when viewing an image.

However, it is important to note here that any immediate positive exposure effects may still be problematic in the longer term (Myers & Biocca, 1992; Tiggemann et al., 2009). As beauty ideals for both men and women displayed in the media are unrealistic and in some cases biologically unachievable due to computer manipulation techniques such as airbrushing, attempts to match these ideals are unlikely to be successful in the long run, and the more permanent exposure effects are therefore likely to be negative. Furthermore, the targets for 'fantasy processing' or 'self-enhancement comparisons' are unhealthy for most men and women, and immediate increases in mood associated with viewing these images may simply increase the tendency to internalize these ideals and increase their risk of body image problems (Mills et al., 2002). However, self-improvement comparisons or fantasy processing does go some way to explaining why people choose to read magazines.

Alternative Images in Advertising

Despite the complexity of the research findings in this area, it is important to remember that the meta-analyses clearly demonstrate a negative impact of idealized bodies in the media for a large proportion of the population. Clearly then, there is a need to investigate ways in which these negative effects may be reduced or prevented. Considerable attention has been paid to interventions that aim to provide adolescent consumers with skills to deconstruct and critique unrealistic, idealized media images (see Chapters 32 and 37). However, a relatively small body of research has also examined the potential for developing alternative advertising images that avoid increasing body dissatisfaction and yet may still be effective in selling products.

Qualitative research indicates that women and men are keen to see a shift in the content of advertising. Diedrichs et al. (2011) examined young adult consumers' opinions on idealized media images and body image. As can be seen in the following quotes, both women and men expressed dissatisfaction with current media images and suggested that they would like to see advertising that features more diversity and 'everyday people'.

[I would like the media to] *just to see the beauty in everyday items, like everyday people. Like, a good old 17 year old boy running down the road with braces and bad skin and whatever. That's normal and there is some good in that. And, to not show that and not advertise that to people is not a good thing.* Lauren, 19 years.

[I would like to see] *more realistic women. I mean not like always, um, stick thin models. Just like an everyday person, who's probably not necessarily going to be the most good looking person, but, just to make it a bit more real.* Wesley, 19 years.

However, despite consumer demand for more realistic and representative depictions of beauty in the media, and extensive criticism of the use of ultra-thin models in advertising from politicians and advocacy groups (Liberal Democrats, 2009; Australian Government, 2010; Girlguiding UK, 2010), the advertising industry argues that 'thinness' sells, whereas 'fatness' does not. The London-based Premier agency, which represents the top models Naomi Campbell and Claudia Schiffer, was reported as saying that agencies, advertisers, and magazines were only responding to consumer demand:

Statistics have repeatedly shown that if you stick a beautiful skinny girl on the cover of a magazine you sell more copies… Agencies would say that we supply the women the advertisers, our clients, want. The clients would say that they are selling a product and responding to consumer demand. At the end of the day, it is a business and the fact is that these models sell the products (Gillian, 2000, p. 7).

Some fashion designers have also claimed that models with body sizes more representative of the general public are not appealing to consumers and may cause health problems such as obesity (Connolly, 2009; Rawi, 2010). The claim that 'thinness sells' acts to justify the almost exclusive use of thin models in idealized media images, regardless of possible detrimental impacts on girls and women. However, there is little research evidence to support this claim.

There is some evidence that attractiveness sells (Caballero & Solomon, 1984; Kahle & Homer, 1985). Research supports the notion that highly attractive models are more effective than normally attractive models at selling appearance relevant products (Bower & Landreth, 2001). However, a recent series of studies suggest that the body size of models is relatively unimportant in successful advertising. Data collected from undergraduate women and men, teachers, advertising professionals, and women with a history of eating-disorders shows that average-size female models (UK size 14–18) are rated as equally effective in advertisements as thin models traditionally seen in the media (UK size 8–12) (Dittmar & Howard, 2004a; Halliwell & Dittmar, 2004; Halliwell et al., 2005; Diedrichs & Lee, 2011). These studies examined advertisements for both appearance- and non-appearance-related products. Similarly, a study focusing on male models demonstrated that attractive, average-size male models are perceived by undergraduate men and women to be as effective in advertisements as muscular male models (Diedrichs & Lee, 2010). As previously noted, the attractiveness of a model influences the perceived effectiveness of advertising and theses effect hold as long as the average-size and thin or muscular models are equally attractive. However, the important finding is that more realistic body sizes do not compromise the effectiveness of the advertisement. Furthermore these, and other studies have also demonstrated that exposure to average-size female and male models is not associated with increased body dissatisfaction compared to viewing no-model control images and, in some studies, actually led to a relief effect and increased state body satisfaction amongst undergraduate women and men who internalized current beauty ideals, teachers, and women with a history of eating disorders (Dittmar & Howard, 2004b; Halliwell & Dittmar, 2005; Diedrichs & Lee, 2010, 2011).

The findings from the studies investigating the use of average-size models in advertisements are promising, as they suggest that providing a greater diversity in the bodies displayed in the media would not damage advertising effectiveness but may reduce levels of body anxiety. Although this evidence around body-size diversity does not address the media's idealization of other aspects of appearance (e.g. clear skin, a youthful appearance) or sexualization, the methodologies used in these studies offer a very applied route that researchers can take to strengthen arguments for change in the media.

CONCLUSIONS AND DIRECTIONS FOR FUTURE RESEARCH

Research in this area has focused on media effects amongst white, middle-class, young, and able-bodied people and on weight and shape dimensions of body image. There is a substantial body of work in this area and a number of conclusions can be drawn for these groups. However, there is a need for a broader research focus to incorporate other aspects of media images, other aspects of body image and self-evaluation, and more diverse populations. Clearly the media communicates very complex messages about cultural standards of beauty, femininity, and masculinity. The strength of experimental investigations of media effects is that they can isolate the impact of specific aspects of an image. It is valuable to combine evidence from such studies with qualitative investigations to gain a more detailed understanding of the influence of the media on body image concerns.

In this chapter we have discussed how research has begun to unpick some of the complexities in the media's influence on body image. The effect of media images is not straightforward and varies according to aspects of the advertising image, as demonstrated by examinations of comparison motives activated by particular advertising slogans or the degree of sexualization of an image, and by individual differences in the consumers of these images. Therefore, it is likely that the influence of media images on an individuals' body image will vary across time and situation.

However, the majority of the experimental and prospective research confirms that exposure to idealized media images does have a negative impact on many people. It is clear that the standards of attractiveness idealized in the media are unrealistic and unhealthy. The available evidence demonstrates that the contemporary images of ultra-thin, ultra-muscular, and highly sexualized bodies are damaging to individuals' well-being. Therefore, evidence suggesting that healthier body shapes can be effectively used in advertising is very promising and campaigns to promote diversity in the bodies idealized in the media are welcome.

REFERENCES

Agliata, D., & Tantleff-Dunn, S. (2004). The impact of media exposure on male's body image. *Journal of Social & Clinical Psychology, 23,* 7–22.

Altabe, M. N., & Thompson, J. K. (1996). Body image: A cognitive self-schema construct? *Cognitive Therapy and Research, 20,* 171–93.

Arbour, K. P., & Ginnis, K. A. (2006). Effects of exposure to muscular and hypermuscular media images on young men's muscularity dissatisfaction and body dissatisfaction. *Body Image, 3,* 153–61.

Aubrey, J. S. (2006). Effects of sexually objectifying media on self-objectification and body surveillance in undergraduates: Results of a 2-year panel study. *Journal of Communication, 56,* 366–86.

Australian Government. (2010). *Voluntary industry code of conduct on body image.* http://www.youth.gov.au/

Baird, A. L., & Grieve, F. G. (2006). Exposure to male models in advertisements leads to a decrease in men's body dissatisfaction. *North American Journal of Psychology, 8,* 115–22.

Barlett, C. P., Vowels, C. L., & Saucier, D. A. (2008). Meta-analyses of the effects of media images on men's body-image concerns. *Journal of Social & Clinical Psychology, 27,* 279–310.

Bessenoff, G. R. (2006). Can the media affect us? Social comparison, self-discrepancy, and the thin ideal. *Psychology of Women Quarterly, 30,* 239–51.

Birkeland, R., Thompson, J. K., Herbozo, S., Roehrig, M., Cafri, G., & van den Berg, P. (2005). Media exposure, mood, and body image dissatisfaction: An experimental test of person versus product priming. *Body Image, 2*(1), 53–61.

Blanton, H., & Stapel, D. A. (2008). Unconscious and spontaneous and. complex: The three selves model of social comparison assimilation and contrast. *Journal of Personality and Social Psychology, 24,* 1018–32.

Blond, A. (2008). Impacts of exposure to images of ideal bodies on male body dissatisfaction: A review. *Body Image, 5,* 244–50.

Bordo, S. (1993). *Unbearable weight: Feminism, western culture and the body.* Berkeley, CA: University of California Press.

Bordo, S. (2009). 'Not just `a white girl's thing': The changing face of `food and body image problems'. In H. Malson and M. Burns (eds.) *Critical Feminist Approaches to Eating Dis/Orders*, pp. 46–60. London: Routledge.

Botta, R. (2003). For your health? The relationship between magazine reading and adolescents' body image and eating disturbances. *Sex Roles, 48,* 389–99.

Bower, A. B., & Landreth, S. (2001). Is beauty best? Highly versus normally attractive models in advertising. *Journal of Advertising, 30,* 1–12.

Brown, A., & Dittmar, H. (2005). Think 'thin' and feel bad: The role of appearance schema activation, attention level, and thin-ideal internalization for young women's responses to ultra-thin media ideals. *Journal of Social & Clinical Psychology*, 24, 1088–113.

Caballero, M. J., & Solomon, P. J. (1984). Effects of model attractiveness on sales response. *Journal of Advertising*, 13, 17–23.

Carlson Jones, D., Vigfusdottir, T. H., & Lee, Y. (2004). Body image and the appearance culture among adolescent girls and boys: An examination of friend conversations, peer criticism, appearance magazines, and the internalisation of appearance ideals. *Journal of Adolescent Research*, 19, 323–39.

Cattarin, J. A., Thompson, J. K., Thomas, C., & Williams, R. J. (2000). Body image, mood, and televised images of attractiveness: The role of social comparison. *Journal of Social & Clinical Psychology*, 19, 220–39.

Changing Faces. (2010). *Face Equality*. http://www.changingfaces.org.uk/Face-Equality (accessed 16 November 2010).

Connolly, K. (2009). Karl Lagerfeld says only 'fat mummies' object to thin models. *The Guardian*, 12 October. http://www.guardian.co.uk/

De Visser, R. O., Smith, J. A., & McDonnell, E. J. (2009). 'That's not masculine': Masculine capital and health-related behaviour. *Journal of Health Psychology*, 14, 1047–58.

Diedrichs, P. C., & Lee, C. (2010). GI Joe or average Joe? The impact of average-size and muscular male fashion models on men's and women's body image and advertisement effectiveness. *Body Image*, 7, 218–26.

Diedrichs, P. C., & Lee, C. (2011). Waif goodbye! Average-size female models promote positive body image and appeal to consumers. *Psychology & Health*, 26, 1273–91.

Diedrichs, P. C., Lee, C., & Kelly, M. (2011). Seeing the beauty in everyday people: A qualitative study of young Australians' opinions on body image, the mass media and models. *Body Image*, 8, 259–66.

Dittmar, H. (ed.) (2008). *Consumer culture, identity and well-being: The search for the 'good life' and the 'body perfect'*. Hove: Psychology Press.

Dittmar, H., & Halliwell, E. (2008). Think 'ideal' and feel bad? Using self-discrepancies to understand negative media effects. In H. Dittmar (ed.). *Consumer culture, identity and well-being: The search for the 'good life' and the 'body perfect'* pp. 147–72. Hove: Psychology Press.

Dittmar, H., Halliwell, E., & Ive, S. (2006). Does Barbie make girls want to be thin? *Developmental Psychology*, 42, 283–92.

Dittmar, H., Halliwell, E., & Stirling, E. (2009). Understanding the impact of thin media models on women's body-focused affect: The roles of thin-ideal internalization and weight-related self-discrepancy activation in experimental exposure effects. *Journal of Social & Clinical Psychology*, 28, 43–72.

Dittmar, H., Halliwell, E., Tiggemann, M., & Levine, M. P. (2009). *The impact of media images on body image and behaviours: A summary of the scientific evidence*. http://www.libdems.org.uk/

Dittmar, H., & Howard, S. (2004a). Professional hazards? The impact of models' body size on advertising effectiveness and women's body-focused anxiety in professions that do and do not emphasises the cultural ideal of thinness. *British Journal of Social Psychology*, 43, 477–97.

Dittmar, H., & Howard, S. (2004b). Thin-ideal internalization and social comparison tendency as moderators of media models' impact on women's body-focused anxiety. *Journal of Social & Clinical Psychology*, 23(6), 768–91.

Festinger, L. (1954). A theory of social comparison processes. *Human Relations, 7,* 117–40.

Field, A. E., Camargo, C. A., Barr Taylor, C., Berkey, C. S., & Colditz, G. A. (1999). Relation of peer and media influences to the development of purging behaviors among preadolescent and adolescent girls. *Archives of Pediatric Adolescent Medicine, 153,* 1184–89.

Field, A. E., Camargo, C. A., Barr Taylor, C., Berkey, C. S., Roberts, S. B., & Colditz, G. A. (2001). Peer, parents, and media influences on the development of weight concerns and frequent dieting among preadolescent and adolescent girls and boys. *Pediatrics, 107,* 54–60.

Fouts, G., & Vaughan, K. (2002). Television situation comedies: Male weight, negative references, and audience reactions. *Sex Roles, 46,* 439–42.

Fredrickson, B. L., & Roberts, T. A. (1997). Objectification theory: Toward understanding women's lived experiences and mental health risks. *Psychology of Women Quarterly, 21,* 173–206.

Frith, K., Shaw, P., & Cheng, H. (2005). The construction of beauty: A cross-cultural analysis of women's magazine advertising. *Journal of Communication, 55,* 56–70.

Gill, R. (2007). *Gender and the media.* Cambridge: Polity Press.

Gill, R. (2008). Empowerment/sexism: Figuring female sexual agency in contemporary advertising. *Feminism and Psychology, 18,* 35–60.

Gillian, A. (2000). Skinny models 'send unhealthy message'. *The Guardian,* 31 May, 7.

Girlguiding UK. (2010). *Tell us the truth—Girls call for honesty over airbrushing.* http://www.girlguiding.org.uk/system_pages/small_navigation/latest_news/tell_us_the_truth.aspx (accessed 18 November, 2010).

Grabe, S., Ward, L. M., & Hyde, J. S. (2008). The role of the media in body image concerns among women: A meta-analysis of experimental and correlational studies. *Psychological Bulletin, 134,* 460–76.

Groesz, L. M., Levine, M. P., & Murnen, S. K. (2001). The effect of experimental presentation of thin media images on body satisfaction: A meta-analytic review. *International Journal of Eating Disorders, 31,* 1–16.

Grogan, S., Williams, Z., & Conner, M. (1996). The effects of viewing same-gender photographic models on body-esteem. *Psychology of Women Quarterly, 20,* 569–75.

Halliwell, E., & Dittmar, H. (2004). Does size matter? The impact of model's body size on women's body-focused anxiety and advertising effectiveness. *Journal of Social and Clinical Psychology, 23,* 104–22.

Halliwell, E., & Dittmar, H. (2005). The role of self-improvement and self-evaluation motives in social comparisons with idealised female bodies in the media. *Body Image, 2,* 249–61.

Halliwell, E., & Dittmar, H. (2006). Associations between appearance-related self-discrepancies and young women's and men's affect, body satisfaction, and emotional eating: A comparison of fixed-item and participant-generated self-discrepancies. *Personality and Social Psychology Bulletin, 32,* 447–58.

Halliwell, E., Dittmar, H., & Howe, J. (2005). Short research note: The impact of advertisements featuring ultra-thin or average-size models on women with a history of eating disorders. *Journal of Community & Applied Social Psychology, 15,* 405–413.

Halliwell, E., Dittmar, H., & Orsbom, A. (2007). The effects of exposure to muscular male models among men: Exploring the moderating role of gym use and exercise motivation. *Body Image, 4,* 278–87.

Halliwell, E., Malson, H., & Tischner, I. (2011). The effects of contemporary framings of women in advertising on weight-concern and self-objectification. *Psychology of Women Quarterly, 35,* 38–45.

Hargreaves, D. A., & Tiggemann, M. (2002a). The effect of television commercials on mood and body dissatisfaction: The role of appearance-schema activation. *Journal of Social & Clinical Psychology*, 21, 287–308.

Hargreaves, D. A., & Tiggemann, M. (2002b). The role of appearance schematicity in the development of adolescent body dissatisfaction. *Cognitive Therapy and Research*, 26, 691–700.

Hargreaves, D. A., & Tiggemann, M. (2003). The effect of 'thin ideal' television commercials on body dissatisfaction and schema activation during early adolescence. *Journal of Youth and Adolescence*, 32, 367–73.

Hargreaves, D. A., & Tiggemann, M. (2004). Idealised media images and adolescent body image: 'comparing boys and girls'. *Body Image*, 1, 351–61.

Hargreaves, D. A., & Tiggemann, M. (2009). Muscular ideal media images and men's body image: Social comparison processing and individual vulnerability. *Psychology of Men & Masculinity*, 10, 109–19.

Harper, B., & Tiggemann, M. (2008). The effect of thin ideal media images on women's self-objectification, mood, and body image. *Sex Roles*, 58, 649–57.

Harrison, K. (2001). Ourselves, our bodies: Thin-ideal media, self-discrepancies, and eating disorder symptomatology in adolescents. *Journal of Social & Clinical Psychology*, 20, 289–323.

Higgins, E. T. (1987). Self-discrepancy: A theory relating self and affect. *Psychological Review*, 94, 319–40.

Higgins, E. T. (1999). When do self-discrepancies have specific relations to emotions? The second-generation question of Tangney, Niedenthal, Covert, and Barlow (1999). *Journal of Personality and Social Psychology*, 77, 1313–17.

Humphreys, P., & Paxton, S. J. (2004). Impact of exposure to idealised male images on adolescent boys' body image. *Body Image*, 1, 253–66.

Jacobi, L., & Cash, T. F. (1994). In pursuit of the perfect appearance: Discrepancies among self- and ideal-percepts of multiple physical attributes. *Journal of Applied Social Pyschology*, 24, 379–96.

Johnson, P. J., McCreary, D. R., & Mills, J. S. (2007). Effects of exposure to objectified male and female images on men's psychological wellbeing. *Psychology of Men & Masculinity*, 8, 95–102.

Joshi, R., Herman, C. P., & Polivy, J. (2004). Self-enhancing effects of exposure to thin-body images. *International Journal of Eating Disorders*, 35, 333–41.

Jung, J., Lennon, S. J., & Rudd, N. A. (2001). Self-schema or self-discrepancy? Which best explains body image? *Clothing and Textiles Research Journal*, 19, 171–84.

Kahle, L. R., & Homer, P. M. (1985). Physical attractiveness of the endorser: A social adaptation perspective. *The Journal of Consumer Research*, 11, 954–61.

Kalodner, C. R. (1997). Media influences on male and female non-eating disordered college students: A significant issue. *Eating Disorders: The Journal of Treatment and Prevention*, 5, 47–57.

Lavin, M. A., & Cash, T. F. (2001). Effects of exposure to information about appearance stereotyping and discrimination on women's body images. *International Journal of Eating Disorders*, 29, 51–8.

Leit, R. A., Pope, H. G., & Gray, J. J. (2001). Cultural expectations of muscularity in men: The evolution of playgirl centrefolds. *International Journal of Eating Disorders*, 29, 90–3.

Levine, M. P., & Murnen, S. K. (2009). 'Everybody knows that mass media are/are not [pick one] a cause of eating disorders': A critical review of evidence for a causal link between media, negative body image, and disordered eating in females. *Journal of Social & Clinical Psychology*, 28, 9–42.

Liberal Democrats. (2009). Airbrushed ads damaging a generation of young women says Swinson [Press Release]. http://www.libdems.org.uk/

Lorenzen, L. A., Grieve, F. G., & Thomas, A. (2004). Exposure to muscular male models decreases men's body satisfaction. *Sex Roles*, 51, 743–8.

Malson, H., Halliwell, E., Tischner, I., & Rudolfsdotir, A. (2011). Post-feminist advertising laid bare: Young women's talk about the sexually agentic woman of 'midriff' advertising. *Feminism and Psychology*, 21, 174–99.

Martin, M. C., & Gentry, J. W. (1997). Stuck in the model trap: The effects of beautiful models in ads on female pre-adolescents and adolescents. *Journal of Advertising*, 26, 19–34.

Martin, M. C., & Kennedy, P. F. (1993). Advertising and social comparison: Consequences for female preadolescents and adolescents. *Psychology & Marketing*, 10, 513–30.

McCabe, M. P., & Ricciardelli, L. A. (2003). Sociocultural influences on body image and body changes among adolescent boys and girls. *The Journal of Social Psychology*, 143, 5–26.

Mills, J. S., Polivy, J., Herman, C. P., & Tiggemann, M. (2002). Effects of exposure to thin media images: Evidence of self-enhancement among restrained eaters. *Personality and Social Psychology Bulletin*, 28, 1687–99.

Moradi, B., & Huang, Y.-P. (2008). Objectification theory and psychology of women: A decade of advances and future directions. *Psychology of Women Quarterly*, 32, 377–98.

Moriarty, C. M., & Harrison, K. (2008). Television exposure and disordered eating among children: A longitudinal panel study. *Journal of Communication*, 58, 361–81.

Myers, P. N., & Biocca, F. A. (1992). The elastic body image: The effect of television advertising and programming on body image distortions in young women. *Journal of Communication*, 42, 108–33.

Ogden, J., & Mundray, K. (1996). The effect of the media on body satisfaction: the role of gender and size. *European Eating Disorders Review*, 4, 171–82.

Polivy, J., & Herman, C. (2004). Sociocultural idealization of thin female body shapes: An introduction to the special issue on body image and eating disorders. *Journal of Social and Clinical Psychology*, 23(1), 1–6.

Pope, H. G., Gruber, A. J., Mangweth, B., Bureau, B., deCol, C., Jouvent, R., *et al.* (2000). Body image perception among men in three countries. *American Journal of Psychiatry*, 157, 1297–301.

Pope, H. G., Olivardia, R., Gruber, A., & Borowiecki, J. (1999). Evolving ideals of male body image as seen through action toys. *International Journal of Eating Disorders*, 26, 65–72.

Posavac, H. D., Posavac, S. S., & Posavac, E. J. (1998). Exposure to media images of female attractiveness and concern with body weight among young women. *Sex Roles*, 38, 187–201.

Rawi, M. (2010). Designer Julien Macdonald attacks plus-size models, branding them 'a joke'. *The Daily Mail*, 17 June. http://www.dailymail.co.uk

Reichert, T., Lambiase, J., Morgan, S., Carstarphen, M., & Zavoina, S. (1999). Cheesecake and beefcake: No matter how you slice it, sexual explicitness in advertising continues to increase. *Journalism and Mass Communication Quarterly*, 76, 7–20.

Ricciardelli, L. A., & McCabe, M. P. (2003). Sociocultural and individual influences on muscle gain and weight loss strategies among adolescent boys and girls. *Psychology in the Schools*, 40, 209–23.

Ricciardelli, L. A., McCabe, M. P., Lillis, J., & Thomas, K. (2006). A longitudinal investigation of the development of weight and muscle concerns among preadolescent boys. *Journal of Youth and Adolescence*, 2, 177–87.

Rohlinger, D. A. (2002). Eroticizing men: Cultural influences on advertising and male objectification. *Sex Roles,* 46, 61–74.

Sirgy, M. J. (1985). Using self-congruity and ideal congruity to predict purchase motivation. *Journal of Business Research,* 13, 195–206.

Smith, H. J., & Leach, C. W. (2004). Group membership and everyday social comparison experiences. *European Journal of Social Psychology,* 34, 297–308.

Snyder, M., & DeBono, K. G. (1985). Appeals to image and claims about quality: Understanding the psychology of advertising. *Journal of Personality and Social Psychology,* 49, 586–97.

Spitzack, C. (1990). *Confession excess.* Albany, NY: State University of New York Press.

Spitzer, B. L., Henderson, K. A., & Zivian, M. T. (1999). Gender differences in population versus media body sizes: A comparison over four decades. *Adolescence,* 24, 677–87.

Stice, E. (1994). Review of the evidence for a sociocultural model of bulimia nervosa: An explanation of the mechanisms of action. *Clinical Psychology Review,* 14, 633–61.

Stice, E., & Shaw, H. E. (2002). Role of body dissatisfaction in the onsent and maintenance of eating pathology: A synthesis of research findings. *Journal of Psychosomatic Research,* 53, 985–93.

Stice, E., Spangler, D., & Agras, W. S. (2001). Exposure to media-portrayed thin-ideal images adversely affects vulnerable girls: A longitudinal experiment. *Journal of Social and Clinical Psychology,* 20, 270–88.

Strauman, T. J., Vookles, J., Berenstein, V., Chaiken, S., & Higgins, E. T. (1991). Self-discrepancies and vulnerability to body dissatisfaction and disordered eating. *Journal of Personality and Social Psychology,* 61, 946–56.

Striegel-Moore, R. H., Silberstein, L. R., & Rodin, J. (1986). Toward an understanding of risk factors for bulimia. *American Psychologist,* 41, 246–63.

Szymanski, M. L., & Cash, T. F. (1995). Body-image disturbances and self-discrepancy theory: Expansion of the Body-Image Ideals Questionnaire. *Journal of Social & Clinical Psychology,* 14, 134–46.

Tankard Reist, M. (ed.). (2010). *Getting real: Challenging the sexualisation of girls.* North Melbourne: Spinifex Press.

Thompson, J. K., & Stice, E. (2001). Thin-ideal internalization: Mounting evidence for a new risk factor for body-image disturbance and eating pathology. *Current Directions in Psychological Science,* 10, 181–83.

Thompson, J. K., Heinberg, L. J., Altabe, M. N., & Tantleff-Dunn, S. (2004). *Exacting beauty: Theory, assessment and treatment of body image disturbance.* Washington, DC: American Psychological Association.

Tiggemann, M. (2005a). The state of body image research in clinical and social psychology. *Journal of Social & Clinical Psychology,* 24, 1202–10.

Tiggemann, M. (2005b). Television and adolescent body image: The role of program content and viewing motivation. *Journal of Social & Clinical Psychology,* 24, 361–81.

Tiggemann, M. (2006). The role of media exposure in adolescent girls' body dissatisfaction and drive for thinness: Prospective results. *Journal of Social & Clinical Psychology,* 25, 523–41.

Tiggemann, M., Polivy, J., & Hargreaves, D. A. (2009). The processing of thin ideals in fashion magazines: A source of social comparison or fantasy? *Journal of Social & Clinical Psychology,* 28, 73–93.

Van den Berg, P., & Thompson, J. K. (2007). Self-schema and social comparison explanations of body dissatisfaction: A laboratory investigation. *Body Image,* 4, 29–38.

Want, S. C. (2009). Meta-analytic moderators of experimental exposure to media portrayals of women on female appearance satisfaction: Social comparisons as automatic processes. *Body Image*, 6, 257–69.

Wardle, C., & Boyce, T. (2009). *Media coverage and audience reception of disfigurement on television*. London: The Healing Foundation and Cardiff University.

Weilage, M., & Hope, D. A. (1999). Self-discrepancy in social phobia and dysthymia. *Cognitive Therapy and Research*, 23, 637–50.

Wiseman, C. V., Gray, J. J., Mosimann, J. E., & Ahrens, A. H. (1992). Cultural expectations of thinness in women: An update. *International Journal of Eating Disorders*, 11, 85–9.

Wood, J. V. (1989). Theory and research concerning social comparisons of personal attributes. *Psychological Bulletin*, 106, 231–48.

CHAPTER 19

··

THE ROLE OF
THE FAMILY

··

REBECCA BELLEW

WE are constantly surrounded by ideals of appearance and beauty: thin models, glamour celebrities, the latest fashion, and the opinions of friends and family. Our emotional and behavioural reactions to these encounters can be extremely varied. Some people embrace these ideals, altering their appearance and striving to meet them; others may reject them, choosing instead other ways of looking. Living in a society in which these ideals are forcibly expressed may leave some anxious that they do not, or cannot, measure up; others, however, may treat these ideals with indifference. But why do people have such varied responses? Our understanding of appearance evolves from our social and cultural experiences; these may include our interactions with our peers, the media, our cultural environment, and our family. This chapter will explore how the family uniquely contributes to individuals' experience of appearance and to their values, attitudes, and behaviours.

The first section explores two overarching ways in which the family contributes to our understanding of appearance: through the information that families offer, and their guidance in interpreting social and cultural information. The latter sections explore other more specific, familial factors that may affect appearance adjustment, including the family's influence when a member has a visible difference of appearance, the child's gender, and the family's relative importance compared to other sociocultural influences. It concludes with recommendations for future research. Interspersed throughout the chapter are quotes from interviews with children with a visible difference and their families, taken from my own research, with the intention of illustrating individual experiences in more detail.

THE FAMILY: A SOURCE OF INFORMATION

You know you've got to find a happy medium between ... controlling the way they look to suit what you think's appropriate and letting them be their own person as they're growing up, and fitting in [quote from a father].

From birth, children learn about the meaning and value of appearance through observation and interactions with their family (Davis, 1992; Ogle & Damhurst, 2003). Children learn from those around them how they *should* look and how to manage and modify their appearance appropriately (Birch, 1990; Ogle & Damhurst, 2003). Family members can communicate different messages to each other about appearance and can convey these in different ways.

Direct messages

Children are provided with information about appearance values, attitudes, and behaviours through explicit communication from their parents. For example, one study found that over a third of parents had directly encouraged their daughters to lose weight (Wertheim et al., 1999). If parents make comments about a child's weight and encourage them to diet, their children have been found to be consistently more likely to demonstrate moderate weight-loss attempts, weight concerns, and body dissatisfaction (e.g. Thelen & Cormier, 1995; Benedikt et al., 1998; Smolak et al., 1999; Ricciardelli et al., 2000; Vincent & McCabe, 2000; Ata et al., 2007; Haines et al., 2008). This association appears to be especially evident among daughters, with research suggesting that girls receive more messages about their appearance, more weight-related teasing, and more pressure to lose weight than sons do (e.g. Rodin et al., 1985; McCabe & Ricciardelli, 2003; Smolak et al., 2005; Ata et al., 2007). Maternal relationships have been associated with appearance dissatisfaction in children more often than fraternal relationships (e.g. Smolak et al., 1999; Kiang & Harter, 2006); however, comments about appearance seem to have the greatest impact when they are received from both parents (Smolak et al., 1999).

The majority of research has discussed direct messages from family members to their children that are concerned weight-related appearance. Far less research relating to other aspects of appearance (Gillen & Lefkowitz, 2009; Frisen & Holmqvist, 2010). Some studies have reported that families which promoted positive messages about appearance were associated with children who demonstrated a more positive body image and higher levels of body satisfaction (e.g. Swarr & Richards, 1996; Ricciardelli et al., 2000; Bearman et al., 2006). Other research has suggested that adolescents with a positive body image actually report few positive comments about their bodies from their families, with several reporting negative comments (e.g. Calogero et al., 2009). Both findings are not necessarily contradictory; their seemingly differing conclusions may stem from the methods and hypotheses driving them. Indeed, it may be equally possible that positive messages from parents are associated with more positive appearance outcomes, but that these positive messages are few in number compared to the negative messages received by those with negative outcomes. Furthermore, the influence of the content of these messages has also often been overlooked. There is also evidence that families of adolescents with positive body image impart messages about appearance that are concerned with external, malleable aspects of appearance, such as clothes and hairstyle, rather than about the young person's body shape or size (Frisen & Holmqvist, 2010). This suggests that a more positive view towards one's own appearance may stem from receiving more positive messages about appearance, or messages that are concerned with easily changeable aspects of appearance.

Research has suggested that whether or not messages are interpreted as a pressure to change appearance may be crucial (Vincent & McCabe, 2000). Much research considers only the surface value of the meaning of messages and their frequency, overlooking other elements relating to the delivery of these messages, which are likely to impact on their interpretation. This will be influenced by additional cues, such as tone of voice, context, and the perceived motives of the message givers. Other additional factors intrinsic to the child may also influence the interpretation, for example, those with more positive appearance beliefs may process information in a different way to those with a more negative body image (Frisen & Holmqvist, 2010). Thus, messages that may be interpreted by others (e.g. researchers) as positive or negative from surface-level information may not be interpreted in the same way by the recipient in the familial context (Frisen & Holmqvist, 2010).

Modelling

Appearance-related messages can also be absorbed by children indirectly though exposure to parents' and siblings' own appearance-related attitudes and behaviours (Bandura, 1977; Ogle & Damhorst, 2003). Research suggests that appearance-related values and behaviours modelled by parents, such as weight control and eating practices, may only be adopted by their children in particular instances, (e.g. Heel et al., 1997; Benedikt et al., 1998; Cromley et al., 2010). The impact of this kind of modelling has more consistently been demonstrated within mother and daughter relationships compared with other family relationships. For example, Benedikt et al. (1998) found that mothers' reports of their own body dissatisfaction and use of extreme weight-loss behaviours did predict their daughters' more extreme weight-loss behaviours, but not their daughters' moderate weight-loss attempts. Similarly, Wertheim et al. (1999) found that more extreme restrained eating by fathers was associated with similar behaviours by their daughters. Cromley et al. (2010) found that parental engagement in less severe forms of weight-control behaviour was associated with adolescents' engagement in unhealthy forms of weight-control behaviour. However, other research has not demonstrated the role of modelling behaviour from both mothers and fathers in the transmission of appearance-related information (e.g. Moreno & Thelan, 1993; Kanakis & Thelan, 1995; Byely et al., 2000; Fulkerson et al., 2002).

The inconsistency in these research findings may relate to differences in the methods and design between studies, or it may be indicative that modelling as a process is not the fundamental cause of differences in appearance adjustment. In the main, research has found that parental encouragement to change appearance more consistently predicts the appearance-related behaviour of their offspring (e.g. Pike & Rodin, 1991; Thelen & Cormier, 1995; Smolak et al., 1999; Wertheim et al., 1999). Furthermore, research has found that the influence of maternal modelling on daughters' eating attitudes and body image was only significant when daughters also experienced high levels of negative comments about their appearance and were actually encouraged to diet (Kichler & Crowther, 2001). Thus, modelling as a process would seem to be mediated by other factors, such as observations of parental dissatisfaction with their bodies (e.g. Benedikt et al., 1998) and negative appearance-related comments.

Teasing and criticism

Appearance-related teasing and criticism have been shown to reinforce ideals of appearance. Teasing about appearance within families seems to be most frequently associated with siblings, especially brothers, followed by mothers and fathers (e.g. Rieves & Cash, 1996; Keery et al., 2005; Neumark-Sztainer et al., 2002[1]). Both males and females seem to experience similar levels of appearance-related teasing (Phares et al., 2004). Facial characteristics and weight seem to be the most common focus of teasing (Rieves & Cash, 1996).

Familial teasing has been associated with a range of negative outcomes in children. Girls who experience appearance-related teasing and criticism by family members are more likely to engage in weight control behaviours, and have demonstrated higher levels of body dissatisfaction, negative social comparisons, internalization of sociocultural thinness, restrictive and bulimic eating behaviours, lower self-esteem, and depression, than girls who reported they were not teased (e.g. Levine et al., 1994; Keery et al., 2005; Neumark-Sztainer et al., 2010). Teasing from fathers and older brothers has been associated with higher levels of negative outcomes (Keery et al., 2005). In fact Field et al. (2001) found that when adolescents reported that weight was important to their fathers, they were more likely to diet. As fathers are traditionally viewed as messengers of society's views, their opinions, even if delivered in a jovial or

---

[1] This research differs in its conclusions concerning which parent is responsible for most teasing.

indirect way, may carry particular importance for family members (Kearney-Cooke, 2002; Keery et al., 2005). Nevertheless, females have reported pressure to lose weight from family and friends to be a more salient influence on negative body image and eating attitudes than levels of teasing (Ata et al., 2007). Thus, familial teasing may not be as instrumental in affecting body dissatisfaction as other familial values and opinions about appearance.

The Family: Guiding Our Understanding

I think we're quite a close and loving family. At least I hope we are. Sometimes they fall out. But most of the time they're there for each other [quote from a mother].

As well as providing us with information about appearance, our families shape our personalities, and our understandings of relationships outside of our family. Although these experiences are not primarily focused on physical looks, they will influence how we approach, interpret, and give value to, the social information around us.

Relationships and interactions in the family environment have been associated with body satisfaction, and a vulnerability or resilience to experience social pressures to change appearance. Research influenced by attachment theory[2] has found that higher body satisfaction was related to experiences of secure attachments (e.g. Cash et al., 2003), whereas insecure attachments have been associated with eating problems in clinical and non-clinical populations (e.g. Ward et al., 2000; Kiang & Harter, 2006). Social cues about appearance may be more salient to those who have high attachment anxiety (McKindley & Randa, 2005). In both general and student populations, low body satisfaction has been associated with pressure to lose weight in women who have more anxious attachments, however the same pattern is not evident in those with more avoidant attachments (e.g. Cash et al., 2003; McKindley & Randa, 2005). Thus, for those who are emotionally close to their families, and susceptible to feelings of rejection (high in attachment anxiety), cues about losing weight may be particularly salient, and may leave members more vulnerable to experiencing low body satisfaction. Furthermore, those who avoid closeness in relationships (high in avoidant attachment) are less likely to be cued to attend to their appearance, and are therefore less vulnerable to experiencing lower body

---

[2] Through relationships with significant others (attachments), individuals develop representations of themselves and others (see Bowlby, 1969/1982; Main et al., 1985). Individuals with secure attachments experience attachment figures as responsive and caring, and see themselves as worthy of care, experiencing low anxiety and avoidance in relationships. However, individuals with insecure attachment may either experience relationships that are high in anxiety (where relationships are continually monitored and individuals are sensitive to rejection or threats of security in a relationship), or, individuals may experience avoidant attachment relationships (in which they avoid closeness with their attachment figures (Fraley & Shaver, 2000)).

satisfaction (McKindley & Randa, 2005). Other research, however, has reported that both highly anxious and avoidant attachments predicted eating disorder symptomology in undergraduate students (Kiang & Harter, 2006). The authors do not hypothesize as to why both attachment styles may be important in predicting eating disorder symptomology. Further consideration is needed of the role of family attachments in the aetiology of eating disorders.

Family relationships which are warmer and more supportive have been associated with positive body image and body satisfaction in children (Swarr & Richards, 1996; Bearman et al., 2006). Furthermore, greater family cohesion, independence, and open expressiveness within the family have been shown to predict more positive psychosocial adjustment in adolescents with burns injures (Blakeney et al., 1990). Openness and willingness to discuss issues of appearance may help young people to negotiate their own feelings, and this may be especially valuable if they have a visible difference. In families who are overprotective and more guarded, children may not be encouraged to raise their appearance concerns or may feel unable to do so (Bradbury, 1997).

Family experiences in childhood also contribute to the development of personality characteristics which impact upon social experiences (Leary & Kowalski, 1995; Thompson & Kent, 2001). A proneness to experiencing shame, low self-esteem, and appearance consciousness are all suggested to originate from feelings of rejection and striving for acceptance (Thompson & Kent, 2001; Gilbert, 2002). For example, proneness to experiences of shame[3] is suggested to originate from two sources; temperament and socialization (Lewis, 1971). Gilbert (1997) suggests that during early socialization, experiences of inadequacy and a failure to be seen as a good and able child can result in a heightened vulnerability to experiencing shame and other self-conscious emotions. Such experiences have been associated with negative adjustment to appearance, in those with eating disorders and visible differences (see Gilbert & Miles, 2002).

DISFIGUREMENT

Yeah I think it's alright to be different, cos if everyone was exactly the same it would be quite boring [quote from an 11-year-old boy].

Having a disfigurement or visible difference can set an individual apart from others. Whilst some describe predominantly negative experiences associated with having a visible difference, others emphasize the minor role their disfigurement plays in their lives, and others describe a positive experience (Rumsey, 2002).

---

[3] Shame involves viewing the self as essentially inadequate, bad or worthless and a sense that exposure of the self as such would lead to rejection by others (Lewis, 1971).

Demographic variables and the physical nature of the visible difference have been repeatedly demonstrated as poor predictors of distress (Rumsey, 2002; Thompson & Kent, 2001). Disfigurements may be present at birth, so the role the family plays in the development of appearance values, attitudes, and behaviours can be continual. Or, if the visible difference is acquired after birth, the values, attitudes, and behaviours of family members may be challenged and redefined as a result. In all cases, parents' views about their child's disfigurement are likely to be influential in relation to the child's development (Rumsey & Harcourt, 2004).

There has been limited research investigating the role of the family in adjustment for young people with disfigurements, with most focusing on the role of peers and social support. Some research has suggested that disfigurements which are evident at birth may impact negatively on early infant–parent relationships (e.g. Chamlin, 2006), however, in the long term, rates of insecure attachment in children with a visible difference are no different from those in the general population (Bradbury & Hewison, 1994; Speltz et al., 1997).

Several researchers have suggested that family support is a critical element in positive psychosocial adjustment (e.g. Bradbury & Hewison, 1994; Sproul et al., 2009; Simons et al., 2010) and that it is associated with fewer psychological difficulties in children with disfigurements (e.g. Dennis et al., 2006). Key to promoting a supportive family environment may be the experience of less stress and fewer parental concerns associated with their child's appearance. These characteristics have also been associated with more family cohesion and adaptation (e.g. Miller et al., 1999; Dennis et al., 2006). An overprotective parenting style may promote an environment in which children do not feel comfortable discussing appearance for fear that it may cause distress to the family (Bradbury, 1997). Thus families who experience relationships as warm, close and agreeable, yet experience high levels of independence (i.e. cohesive families (Minuchin, 1974)) are likely to experience more positive psychosocial adjustment.

OTHER SOCIOCULTURAL INFLUENCES

Well it's impossible to know how big school is going to affect them isn't it. You know I sort of think well Sally's going in there fairly confidently but will she come out the person she's gone in? [quote from a mother].

Research presented here offers significant support for the key role played by the family in the development of a young person's appearance values, attitudes and behaviours, however, there are of course other social and cultural factors influencing experiences of appearance. Research is divided as to the relative importance of messages from family members compared to other sociocultural sources. Some research suggests the family plays a more important role in predicting adolescents' body satisfaction than other sociocultural influences (e.g. Stanford & McCabe, 2005). Conversely, other research has found that peers exert greater pressure on adolescents to conform to appearance ideals (e.g. Dunkley et al., 2001; Stice et al., 2002). With an adult sample, Gillen and Lefkowitz (2009) have reported that most negative messages about the body were received through the media, while more positive messages were received from family and peers.

Life stage may have a significant role in determining which sociocultural sources are most influential at one time (Tantleff-Dunn & Gokee, 2002). Early family interactions may act to influence children's early processing of appearance-related information, as well as providing information about societal standards of appearance. Harter (1999) has reported that adolescents who felt their appearance was important in determining their general self-worth, experienced lower self-esteem and greater depression, than those who believed their self-worth determined how they felt about their appearance. Family interactions may guide the development of this outlook; with more positive family relationships acting as a buffer to other more negative sociocultural influences (Bearman et al., 2006; Ata et al., 2007), especially those encountered later in adolescence, when peers and the media become a more significant part of social life. Further research is needed to explore if it is this positive family experience that leads to the development of more positive appearance values, attitudes or behaviours, or an underlying personality trait or positive disposition that leads to a more positive family experience.

FUTURE RESEARCH

Research exploring the influences on adjustment to appearance and the development of appearance values, attitudes, and behaviours has focused largely on other sociocultural influences, such as peers and the media, rather than the role of the family. Within the research that has been conducted, and consequently this chapter, there has been a focus on the impact of parents on the offspring's weight-related appearance and body image. Much more research is needed to expand knowledge in this area: to inform interventions for parents and for those negatively affected by appearance concerns or related issues. Broader investigations of the effects of the whole family environment on appearance values, attitudes, and behaviours will advance understanding of how other sociocultural and psychological factors intertwine with family influences. For example, until recently, research relating to people with a visible difference has focused mainly on the role of peers. More research exploring the contribution of the family to appearance satisfaction would be valuable in informing care provision and designing effective interventions.

The design of research to date has been largely associative and cross-sectional, thus casual connections between the family environment and appearance adjustment have not clearly been demonstrated. Longitudinal research would help to distinguish the protective factors which contribute to high levels of satisfaction with appearance, and would guide a conceptualization of how different sociocultural sources, including the family, may be more or less influential at different stages of the life span. The vast majority of research has also been driven by a negative, pathologizing view about the nature of adjustment to appearance, especially amongst people with a visible difference. A more complete picture of familial influence would benefit from research, such as that by Frisen and Holmqvist (2010) and my own research, focusing on the correlates and predictors of more positive outcomes, such as family support.

Future research must also be designed to consider the influence of the subtleties associated with different types of appearance-related messages. For example, little research has considered the meaning of messages from the point of view of the message giver. For example, mothers may be unaware of the impact of the appearance-related messages they are conveying to their daughters, and of their consequences (Ogle & Damhorst, 2003). It is not simply the presence of negative or positive messages that promotes negative or positive appearance-related thoughts, but how these messages are interpreted (Frisen & Holmqvist, 2010). It is clear further research investigating the influence of direct messages must also consider the role of the non-verbal cues associated with the message and the young person's interpretation of both the content and delivery of the message. Research must also consider the impact of behaviours and values, even when not specifically directed at the family member. The use of more qualitative research in this area may provide richer and more detailed insights into the subtleties of appearance-related messages within the family about appearance and their interpretation.

To date, the majority of research with the family has been focused on mother–daughter relationships. Much more research is needed to explore other interactions, for example, those with the father, especially in light of the increased influence of men in both home and child rearing roles. Furthermore, as individuals do not experience their family as a single entity, research focusing on the whole family environment as well as interactions within them, may provide useful insights.

Research in this area has been limited by unrepresentative samples, having been carried out in predominantly American or Australian, white, middle-class environments. Gillen and Lefkowitz (2009) report few differences between ethnic groups in relation to the perceptions concerning appearance-related messages; however, more research with families from ethnically diverse groups should be explored. Sample sizes, especially in clinical populations, have also been relatively small, thereby preventing complex interactions between variables from being fully examined. This may be part of the reason why research thus far has not been able to produce a multifaceted model of the role of the family in appearance adjustment and distress. Research within the visible difference literature has largely neglected the role of the family. In addition, researchers have more often recruited participants receiving treatment in the health-care system or who are in contact with self-help and support groups. Within my own research I have endeavoured to recruit through primary care settings in order to achieve a more representative sample. However, this approach has resulted in a low response rate. Investigation has suggested this may be the result of parental fear: that by involving their child in the research they would be highlighting to their child that appearance is worthy of consideration, when they had previously down-played its importance. It is difficult to know how this obstacle can be overcome. Perhaps offering more substantial, obvious, or personal benefits to children, such as educational information promoting positive appearance self-esteem, would provide parents more comfort.

There are a number of issues of measurement, in relation to research investigating the family environment and appearance. Studies have used a wide range of tools to assess appearance and body image, including some condition-specific measures. This makes comparisons between studies problematic. Given that research indicates that the type, extent, and severity of visible difference consistently fail to adequately predict adjustment (see Rumsey, 2002), research using measures of appearance-related adjustment, such as the Derriford Appearance Scale (DAS) (Carr et al., 2005) may be appropriate. Furthermore, quantitative measurement of more appearance-related satisfaction in children and young people is extremely challenging. Measures currently under development aim to facilitate the measurement of appearance satisfaction in adolescents and younger children in the near future.

Additionally, existing quantitative measurements of the family environment are problematic. Most research in the UK has employed the Family Environment Scale (Moos, 1996), the Family Adaptability and Cohesion Scale IV (Olson et al., 2007), or the McMaster family assessment device (Epstein et al., 1983) which were all developed in the US. The Family Perception Scale (Tiffin, 2006) is a new scale which is shorter, and which has been developed from the accounts of adolescents in England.

CONCLUSIONS

Appearance-related values, attitudes, and behaviours develop throughout childhood, yet the exact role of the family in the development and maintenance of body dissatisfaction is still unclear. However, a likely model seems to be emerging in which the family contribute to appearance adjustment most strongly in childhood, and appearance-related values, attitudes, and behaviours are then developed and modified later in adolescence and adulthood through experience with friends and romantic partners in the context of other social and cultural influences.

References

Ata, R. N., Ludden, A. B., & Lally, M. M. (2007). The effects of gender and family, friend, and media influences on eating behaviors and body image during adolescence. *Journal of Youth and Adolescence*, 36, 1024–37.

Bandura, A. (1977). *Social learning theory*. Englewood Cliffs, NJ: Prentice Hall.

Bearman S. K., Presnell K., & Stice, M. E. (2006). The skinny on body dissatisfaction: A longitudinal study of adolescent girls and boys. *Journal of Youth and Adolescence*, 35(2), 229–41.

Benedikt, R.,Wertheim, E. H., & Love, A. (1998). Eating attitudes and weight-loss attempts in female adolescents and their mothers. *Journal of Youth and Adolescence*, 27(1), 43–57.

Birch, L. L. (1990). Development of food acceptance patterns. *Developmental Psychology*, 26, 515–19.

Blakeney, P., Portman, S., & Rutan, R. (1990). Familial values as factors influencing long-term psychological adjustment of children after severe burn injury. *Journal of Burn Care Rehabilitation*, 11, 472–75.

Bowlby, J. (1969/1982). *Attachment and loss: Vol. 1, Attachment*. New York: Basic Books.

Bradbury, E. (1997). Understanding the problems. In R. Lansdown, N. Rumsey, E. Bradbury, A. Carr, & J. Partridge (eds.) *Visibly different: Coping with disfigurement*, pp. 180–93. Oxford: Butterworth-Heinemann.

Bradbury, E. T. & Hewison, J. (1994). Early parental adjustment to visible congenital disfigurement. *Child: Care, Health and Development*, 20, 251–66.

Byely, L., Archibald, A. B., Graber, J., & Brooks-Gunn, J. (2000). A prospective study of familial and social influences on girls' body image and dieting. *International Journal of Eating Disorders*, 28, 155–64.

Calogero, R. M., Herbozo, S., & Thompson, J. K. (2009). Complimentary weightism: The potential costs of appearance-related commentary for women's self-objectification. *Psychology of Women Quarterly*, 33, 120–32.

Carr, T., Moss, T., & Harris, D. (2005). The DAS24: A short form of the Derriford Appearance Scale (DAS59) to measure individual responses to living with problems of appearance. *British Journal of Health Psychology*, 10(2), 285–98.

Cash, T. F., Theriault, J., & Annis, N. W. (2003). Body image in an interpersonal context: Adult attachment, fear of intimacy, and social anxiety. *Journal of Social and Clinical Psychology*, 23, 89–103.

Chamlin, S. L. (2006). The psychosocial burden of childhood atopic dermatitis. *Dermatologic Therapy*, 19(2), 104–7.

Cromley, T., Neumark-Sztainer, D., Story, M., & Boutelle, K. (2010). Parent and family associations with weight-related behaviors and cognitions among overweight adolescents. *Journal of Adolescent Health*, 47(3), 263–9.

Davis, F. (1992). *Fashion, culture, and identity*. Chicago, IL: University of Chicago Press.

Dennis, H., Rostill, H., Reed, J., & Gill, S. (2006). Factors promoting psychological adjustment to childhood atopic eczema. *Journal of Child Health Care*, 10(2), 126–39.

Dunkley, T. L., Wertheim, E. H., & Paxton, S. J. (2001). Examination of a model of multiple sociocultural influences on adolescent girls' body dissatisfaction and dietary restraint. *Adolescence*, 36(142), 265–79.

Epstein, N. B., Baldwin, L. M., & Bishop, D. S. (1983). The McMaster family assessment device. *Journal of Marital and Family Therapy*, 9, 171–80.

Field, A. E., Camargo, C. A. Jr., Taylor, C. B., Berkey, C. S., Roberts, S. B., & Colditz, G. A. (2001). Peer, parent, and media influences on the development of weight concerns and frequent dieting among preadolescent and adolescent girls and boys. *Pediatrics*, 107, 54–60.

Fraley, R. C. & Shaver, P. R. (2000). Adult romantic attachment: Theoretical developments, emerging controversies, and unanswered questions. *Review of General Psychology*, 4(2), 132–54.

Frisen, A. & Holmqvist, K. (2010). What characterizes early adolescents with a positive body image? A qualitative investigation of Swedish girls and boys. *Body Image*, 7, 205–212.

Fulkerson, J. A., McGuire, M. T., Neumark-Sztainer, D., French, S. A., & Perry, C. L. (2002). Weight-related attitudes and behaviors of adolescent boys and girls who are encouraged to diet by their mothers. *International Journal of Obesity*, 26, 1579–87.

Gilbert, P. (1997). The evolution of social attractiveness and its role in shame, humiliation and therapy. *British Journal of Medical Psychology*, 70, 113–47.

Gilbert, P. (2002). Body shame: A biopsychosocial conceptualisation and overview with treatment implications. In P. Gilbert and J. Miles (eds.) *Body shame: Conceptualisation, research and treatment*, pp. 3–54. London: Routledge.

Gilbert, P. & Miles, J. (2002). *Body shame: Conceptualisation, research and treatment.* London: Routledge.

Gillen M. M. & Lefkowitz, E., (2009). Emerging adults' perceptions of messages about physical appearance. *Body Image*, 6, 178–85.

Haines, J., Neumark-Sztainer, D., Hannan, P., & Robinson-O'Brien, R. (2008). Child versus parent report of parental influences on children's weight-related attitudes and behaviors. *Journal of Pediatric Psychology*, 33(7), 783–8.

Harter, S. (1999). *The construction of the self: A developmental perspective.* New York: Guilford.

Heel, P. K, Heatherton, T. F., Harnden, J. L., & Hornig, C. D. (1997). Mothers, fathers and daughters: dieting and disordered eating. *Eating Disorders: The Journal of Treatment and Prevention*, 5, 216–28.

Kanakis, D. & Thelen, M. (1995). Parental variables associated with bulimia nervosa. *Addictive Behaviors*, 20, 491–500.

Kearney-Cooke, A. (2002). Familial influences on body image development. In T. F. Cash and T. Pruzinsky (eds.) *Body image: A handbook of theory, and clinical practices*, pp. 99–107. New York: Guilford.

Keery, H., Boutelle, K., van den Berg, P., & Thompson, J.K. (2005). The impact of appearance-related teasing by family members. *Journal of Adolescent Health*, 37, 120–27.

Kiang, L. & Harter, S. (2006). Sociocultural values of appearance and attachment processes: An integrated model of eating disorder symptomatology. *Eating Behaviors*, 7, 134–51.

Kichler, J. C. & Crowther, J. H. (2001). The effects of maternal modelling and negative familial communication on women's eating attitudes and body image. *Behaviour Therapy*, 32, 443–57.

Leary, M. & Kowalski, R. (1995). *Social Anxiety.* London: Guildford Press.

Levine, M. P., Smolak, L., & Hayden, H. (1994). The relation of sociocultural factors to eating attitudes and behaviours among middle school girls. *Journal of Early Adolescence*, 14(4), 471–90.

Lewis, H. B. (1971). *Shame and guilt in neurosis.* New York: International Universities Press.

Main, M., Kaplan, N., & Cassidy, J. (1985). Security in infancy, childhood, and adulthood: A move to the level of representation. In I. Bretherton and E. Waters (eds.) *Growing* points in attachment theory and research. *Monographs of the Society for Research in Child Development*, 50, 66–106.

McCabe, M. & Ricciardelli, L. (2003). Sociocultural influence's on body image and body changes among adolescent boys and girls. *Journal of social psychology*, 143(1), 5–26.

McKinley, N. M. & Randa, L. A. (2005). Adult attachment and body satisfaction. An exploration of general and specific relationship differences. *Body Image*, 2, 209–18.

Miller, A. C. Pit-ten Cate, I. M., Watson, H. S., & Geronemus, R. G. (1999). Stress and family satisfaction in parents of children with facial port-wine stains. *Pediatric Dermatology*, 16(3), 190–97.

Minuchin, S. (1974). *Families and Family Therapy*. Harvard University Press.

Moos, R. H. (1996). *Community Oriented Programs Environment Scale manual* (3rd edn.). Palo Alto, CA: Mind Garden.

Moreno, A. & Thelen, H. (1993). Parental factors related to bulimia nervosa. *Addictive Behaviors*, 18, 681–9.

Neumark-Sztainer, D., Bauer, K.W., Friend, S., Hannan, P.J., Story, M., & Berge, J.M. (2010). Family weight talk and dieting: How much do they matter for body dissatisfaction and disordered eating behaviors in adolescent girls? *Journal of Adolescent Health*, 47(3), 270–6.

Neumark-Sztainer, D., Falkner, N., Story, M., Perry, C., Hannan, P. J., & Mulert, S. (2002). Weight-teasing among adolescents: correlations with weight status and disordered eating behaviors. *International Journal of Obesity*, 26(1), 123–31.

Ogle, J. P. & Damhorst, M. L. (2003). Mothers and daughters: Interpersonal approaches to body and dieting. *Journal of Family Issues*, 24, 448–87.

Olson, D. H., Gorall, D. M., & Tiesel, J. W. (2007). *FACES IV Manual*. Minneapolis, MN: Life Innovations.

Phares, V., Steinberg, A. R., & Thompson, J. K. (2004). Gender differences in peer and parental influences: Body image disturbance, self-worth, and psychological functioning in preadolescent children. *Journal of Youth and Adolescences*, 33(5), 421–9.

Pike, K. M. & Rodin J. (1991). Mothers, daughters, and disordered eating. *Journal of Abnormal Psychology*, 100, 198–204.

Ricciardelli, L. A., McCabe, M. P., & Banfield, S. (2000). Body image and body change methods in adolescent boys: Role of parents, friends, and the media. *Journal of Psychosomatic Research*, 49(3), 189–97.

Rieves, L. & Cash, T. F. (1996). Social developmental factors and women's body-image attitudes. *Journal of Social Behaviour and Personality*, 11(1), 63–78.

Rodin, J., Silberstein, L. R., & Striegel-Moore, R. H. (1985). Women and weight: A normative discontent. In T. B. Sonderegger (ed.), *Nebraska symposium on motivation*, pp. 267–308. Lincoln, NE: University Press of Nebraska.

Rumsey, N. (2002). Body image & congenital conditions with visible differences. In T. F. Cash and T. Pruzinsky (eds.) *Body image: A handbook of theory, research, and clinical practice*, pp. 226–33. New York: Guilford.

Rumsey, N., & Harcourt, D. (2004). Body image and disfigurement: Issues and interventions. *Body Image*, 1, 83–97.

Simons, M. A., Ziviani, J. & Copley, J. (2010). Predicting Functional Outcome for Children on Admission After Burn Injury: Do Parents Hold the Key? *Journal of Burn Care & Research*, 31(5), 750–65.

Smolak, L., Levine, M. P., & Schermer, F. (1999). Parental input and weight concerns among elementary school children. *International Journal of Eating Disorders*, 25, 263–71.

Smolak, L., Murnen, S. K., & Thompson, J. K. (2005). Sociocultural influences and muscle building in adolescent boys. *Psychology of Men and Masculinity*, 6(4), 227–39.

Speltz, M. L., Endriga, M. C., Fisher, P. A., and Mason, C. A. (1997). Early predictors of attachment in infants with cleft lip and/or palate. *Child Development*, 68(1), 12–25.

Sproul, J. L., Malloy, S., & Abriam-Yago, K. (2009). Perceived Sources of Support of Adult Burn Survivors. *Journal of Burn Care & Research*, 30(6), 975–82.

Stanford, J. N. & McCabe, M. P. (2005). Sociocultural influences on adolescent boys' body image and body change strategies. *Body Image*, 2, 105–13.

Stice, E., Presnell, K., & Spangler, D. (2002). Risk factors for binge eating onset in adolescent girls: A 2-year prospective investigation. *Health Psychology*, 21(2), 131–8.

Swarr, A. E. & Richards, M. H. (1996). Longitudinal effects of adolescent girls' pubertal development, perceptions of pubertal timing, and parental relations on eating problems. *Developmental Psychiatry*, 32, 636–46.

Tantleff-Dunn, S., & Gokee, J. L. (2002). Interpersonal influences on body image development. In T. F. Cash, & T. Pruzinksy (Eds.), *Body image: A handbook of theory, research, and clinical Practice*, pp. 108–116. New York: Guilford Press.

Thelen, M. H., & Cormier, J. F. (1995). Desire to be thinner and weight control among children and their parents. *Behavior Therapy*, 26(1), 85–99.

Thompson, A. & Kent, G. (2001). Adjustment to disfigurement: Processes involved in dealing with being visibly different. *Clinical Psychology Review*, 21(5), 663–82.

Tiffin, P. A. (2006). Family Perception Scale Manual. Unpublished.

Vincent, M. & McCabe, M. (2000). Gender differences among adolescents in family and peer influences on body dissatisfaction, weight loss, and binge eating behaviors. *Journal of Youth and Adolescence*, 29, 205–21.

Ward, A., Ramsay, R., & Treasure, J. (2000). Attachment research and eating disorders. *British Journal of Medical Psychology*, 73, 35–51.

Wertheim, E.H., Mee, V., & Paxton, S.J. (1999). Relationships among adolescent girls' eating behaviours and their parents' weight related attitudes and behaviors. *Sex Roles*, 41, 169–87.

CHAPTER 20

INFLUENCE OF PEERS

LINA A. RICCIARDELLI

DAVID MELLOR

PEERS play an important role in influencing children's and adolescents' body image and appearance concerns, and they exert their influence in a range of ways. As early as 1967, Elkind argued that adolescents are preoccupied with the way they appear to other people and assume that others, 'their imaginary audience', are highly involved in evaluating their appearance. A large number of 'their others' are peers and friends.

In the chapter we begin by examining how peers exert their direct influence via negative comments such as teasing, encouragement, modelling, discussions, peer networks, and social comparisons. We then examine the associations between peer relationships and appearance/body image concerns. Peers provide an important socializing role (Dunn, 2005) and positive peer relationships and acceptance by peers are important indicators of children's and adolescents' mental health (Ladd & Asher, 1985). There is extensive evidence showing that children and adolescents who have poor relationships with their peers are at an increased risk of psychopathology, which can be manifested in a variety of ways including depression, social difficulties, severe loneliness, social anxiety, school adjustment difficulties, juvenile delinquency, and suicide (Hodges et al., 1999; Nolan et al., 2003). The role of friends will be specifically examined. Friends can provide social support and intimacy; they may help children and adolescents to cope with insecurities, and serve as a buffer against emotional difficulties. Moreover, friends may assist children to develop an image of themselves as competent and worthy via self-evaluations and social comparisons (Dunn, 2005). In addition, we will consider how the influence of peers and friends may vary according to gender, age, and cultural group. For example, girls and boys differ in the structure of their peer interactions; girls spend more time in quieter, smaller group activities whereas boys spend more time in competitive and active games (Rose & Rudoph, 2006). Further, girls' friendships are likely to be more intense and intimate than those of boys whereas boys are likely to have less emotional support from their friends but engage in more structured activities such as team sports (Rose & Rudoph, 2006). Finally, we cannot assume that the influences of peers are invariant across different cultural groups, as some cultures place greater importance on the family and other sociocultural influences than peers.

PEER PRESSURE

Peer pressure has been described as the primary mechanism for transmitting group norms (Lieberman et al., 2001). Moreover, it has been suggested that peers exert their influence by offering desirable rewards to those who conform to group norms and/or undesirable consequences to those who resist them. Conceptualizations of peer pressure in relation to body image include direct reports of teasing, encouragement, and modelling of body change strategies, discussions about body image and appearance concerns, as well as adolescents' perceptions of their peers/friends' interest in this domain.

Several studies have shown that peer pressure is a correlate of body image concerns among adolescent girls and boys. For example, Lieberman et al. (2001) found that an overall assessment of peer pressure and more specific measures that examined teasing and attributions about the importance of weight and shape for popularity and dating were associated with lower body esteem among 14-year-old girls. Similarly, Peterson et al. (2007) found that higher perceived pressures from peers, parents and the media were related to higher levels of body dissatisfaction among both 16-year-old girls and boys. In another study, peer pressure and the relative attractiveness of peers were found to be significant predictors of social physique anxiety among 15-year-old girls and boys (Mack et al., 2007).

Other studies suggest that peer pressure may be more important for boys than girls. For example, Muris et al. (2005) found that a combined measure which assessed parent and peer pressure to decrease weight, self-esteem, and the importance placed on body image was associated with greater body dissatisfaction among 13-year-old boys, but only body mass index and self-esteem were associated with body dissatisfaction among the same aged girls. However, it is important to further examine the interplay among some of the studied variables when evaluated in multivariate models. Presnell et al. (2004) found that for 17-year-old girls and boys perceived pressure to be thin from peers predicted increases in body dissatisfaction over the 9-month period in their univariate analyses. Peer pressure was not significant in the multivariate model, when negative affect was also examined. Presnell and colleagues suggested that peer pressure is likely to overlap with other variables such as negative affect and self-esteem, so it is not easy to fully evaluate its effects using survey methods.

In another study, Rayner et al. (2010) found that a comprehensive assessment of peer pressure did not predict body dissatisfaction but body dissatisfaction was found to prospectively predict 12-year-old girls' perception of peer influences after 1 and 2 years. This finding is important as it is usually assumed that peers influence body image and appearance concerns rather than vice versa. However, the relationship is likely to be a bidirectional one. Adolescents who see themselves more negatively may seek out peers and an environment which reinforces their negative self-perceptions, feelings, and attitudes.

Several studies have also examined the influence of peer pressure among preadolescents. Ricciardelli et al. (2003) did not separate perceived peer pressure from that attributed to parents or the media, as the pressure for each of these sources was found to be highly interrelated among their sample of 9-year-old girls and boys. Overall pressure to lose weight and pressure to increase muscle was associated with body dissatisfaction among girls; pressure to lose weight was associated with body dissatisfaction and the importance placed on weight among boys; and pressures to increase muscle was associated with the importance placed on muscles among both girls and boys (Ricciardelli et al., 2003). In addition, a follow-up study showed that pressure to increase muscles predicted the importance placed on weight and muscles among boys when tested 8 and 16 months later (Ricciardelli et al., 2006). However, these relationships were not found among girls, thus again suggesting that other factors such as body mass index and self-esteem may be more important for girls.

Other studies have separated pressures from peers from other sources. However, these studies have only included girls. In one study, Sinton and Birch (2006) demonstrated a positive relationship between appearance-related interactions with other girls (these include social comparisons and weight talk) and appearance schemas among 11-year-old girls. In another study, Clark and Tiggemann (2006) found that peer appearance conversations were associated with the internalization of appearance ideals, and with lower body esteem among 10-year-old girls (Clark & Tiggemann, 2007). However, as with adolescent girls, the peer appearance conversations were not found to predict body image concerns 1 year later (Clark & Tiggemann, 2008).

Other research has focused on younger girls aged between 5–8 years. As found among older girls, the perceived peer desire for thinness was significantly correlated with girls' own desire for thinness, and girls who engaged in more peer discussions with their friends and imitated others more often had lower appearance satisfaction (Dohnt & Tiggemann, 2006a). Moreover, in this study, perception of peers' desire for thinness also predicted the girls' desire for thinness, appearance satisfaction and self-esteem 1 year later (Dohnt & Tiggemann, 2006b). It is important to note that the girls in this study were specifically asked to consider what they thought their best friend and other girls in class looked like, and what they thought their best friend would like to look like. The specific focus on their best friend as opposed to peers more generally is likely to have had a different impact. The role of friends is considered more fully, later in this chapter.

In addition to cross-sectional and longitudinal studies, several researchers have conducted experimental studies to more fully understand the nature and impact of peer pressure. All these studies have included young adult women. Consistently, laboratory studies have shown that an exposure to social pressure to be thin leads to increased body dissatisfaction. In one study, Stice et al. (2003) randomly assigned women to a control condition or one in which an ultra-thin confederate voiced complaints about how fat she felt and her intentions to lose weight. The women who were exposed to the peer pressure to be thin showed significant increases in body dissatisfaction whereas the control group did not. In addition, the negative effects on body dissatisfaction and other body image concerns have been found to be higher among women who are more prone to social comparisons and/or who place more importance on their body image (e.g. Shomaker & Furman, 2007).

Experimental manipulations can also be used to challenge norms by convincing women that their peers do not endorse the sociocultural norms of thinness. Strahan et al. (2007) found that adult women who were exposed to thin images, but were also told that their peers criticized the images, did not restrain their eating to the same extent as participants who were only exposed to the thin images. Further studies are now needed to also test this model among adolescent girls and males.

PEER TEASING

Although appearance-related teasing by peers is often conceptualized as part of peer pressure, there are many studies that have specifically examined teasing. As has been argued and summarized by Jones, Newman and Bautista (2005), teasing by peers is a common yet challenging aspect of the adolescent experience at school; it is primarily verbal and increases dramatically during early adolescence. Moreover, given the concern with acceptance and social changes within friendship and peer groups that occur during adolescence, teasing within peer interactions is especially salient and an essential part of adolescent culture. Hayden-Wade et al. (2005) defined teasing as a form of personal communication, directed by an agent toward a target, which combines elements of aggression, humour, and ambiguity.

A large number of studies have shown that female adolescents who are teased about their weight, body shape, and appearance tend to exhibit poorer body image and are more likely to diet (Liberman et al., 2001). This has been highlighted in retrospective accounts of college women where three-quarters of participants reported that they were teased repeatedly and/or criticized about their appearance by their peers and friends; they found this upsetting, and many thought it had a negative impact on their body image (Rieves & Cash, 1996). In another study, recalled childhood teasing about appearance (height, weight, hair colour) was related to fear of negative evaluations, depressive symptoms, and loneliness in adulthood (Faith et al., 2008).

Male adolescents also perceive appearance-related teasing at levels that are similar or higher than females (Jones & Crawford, 2005), and appearance-related criticism by peers has also been found to be positively correlated with body dissatisfaction among males (Jones et al., 2004; cf. Smolak & Stein, 2006). Moreover, this relationship is already well established among preadolescent girls and boys (e.g. Gardner et al., 1997). Often it is overweight children who are more likely to be frequent targets of peers' appearance-related teasing, however, it is also children who were concerned about being overweight in the case of girls or 'too skinny' in the case of boys. For example, Frisén et al. (2009) found that 10-year-old girls and boys who expressed beliefs about being 'too fat' reported greater frequencies of peer victimization. The girls also reported being subject to appearance teasing, threats, and overt physical aggression whereas boys with beliefs about being 'too skinny' generally reported more frequent experiences of victimization and threats by peers.

In another study, Hayden-Wade et al. (2005) found that 78% of overweight children (10–14-year-olds) versus 37.2% of non-overweight children reported having been teased or criticized about some aspect of their appearance. The overweight children were teased significantly more for weight-related (89.1% vs. 31.3%) than for non-weight-related aspects of appearance. The overweight children also reported that teasing occurred more frequently and lasted for more years, and that they found the teasing to be more upsetting. Peers, in general, were the most common source of teasing for the overweight children while specific peers were more commonly identified by the non-overweight. The correlates of weight-related teasing were wide-ranging and very negative. The degree of weight-related teasing was correlated with weight concerns, negative self-perceptions, loneliness, and the liking of sedentary/isolative activities.

Longitudinal studies have also often supported the relationship between appearance/weight-related teasing and body image concerns (cf. Jones, 2004). For example, Eisenberg et al. (2006) found that between one-third and just under half of the females in their study reported weight-related teasing at the start of the study, and this was associated with lower self-esteem and body dissatisfaction and higher depression among both girls and boys from both middle and high schools 5 years later. On the other hand, Paxton et al. (2006) found that weight teasing predicted body dissatisfaction after 5 years but only among 12-year-old boys. This result was not found among 15-year-old boys or among the girls. The authors argued that different influences may affect girls and boys, and the changes in the peer environment over middle to late adolescence may contribute to the weakening of peer influences on increases in body dissatisfaction. However, studies that examine the nature of these differences are now needed.

Positive Communication versus Negative Communication

Less is known about the impact of positive communication (i.e. perceived frequency of positive comments about appearance), as this dimension has been studied less frequently. In one study Kichler and Crowther (2009) found that 10-year-old girls perceived more positive communication than negative communication about shape and weight from their family members and peers. However, positive communication was not related to body dissatisfaction; this relationship held only for negative communication (Kichler & Crowther, 2009). Ricciardelli et al. (2000) also found that boys from grade 7 (12–13 years) and grade 9 (14–15 years) reported primarily positive messages about their bodies from both female friends and their mothers. These were in the form of praise or compliments (e.g. 'You've got a good body'; 'You've got pretty big muscles'; 'You're tall and got pretty good legs'). These positive messages were significantly related to the boys' satisfaction with body shape and their satisfaction with muscles.

In another study, Frisén and Holmqvist (2010) specifically interviewed 15 boys and 15 girls aged between 10–15 years, who were highly positive about their bodies. These adolescents reported that their friends and family liked their looks; they reported very few negative comments and the adolescents did not place much importance on these, nor were they bothered by any of these remarks. More studies that focus on adolescents who have a positive image will help to reveal more about the protective sociocultural factors that influence and determine satisfaction with body image and appearance. Far too much emphasis in the field has been on factors implicated in the development of a negative body image at the expense of identifying those contributing to the development of a positive body image.

Weight and Appearance Talk and the Peer Culture

Extensive work has highlighted the role of 'fat talk' or more broadly, discussions about weight, in the case of girls. Several studies have found that discussions about weight among 13-year-old girls were associated with body dissatisfaction (e.g. Levine et al., 1994; Vincent & McCabe, 2000). In addition, other studies have more fully investigated 'peer interactions' and the nature of the peer group (e.g. Paxton et al., 1999; Hutchinson & Rapee, 2007).

In one of the first comprehensive studies, Paxton et al. (1999) found that adolescent friendship cliques among 15-year-old girls shared similar levels of body image concerns, dietary restraint, and the use of extreme weight-loss behaviours. Furthermore, perceived peer group attitudes and behaviours toward weight-related concerns predicted individual member behaviours. Another interesting finding to emerge was that girls within friendship groups were very similar to one another with respect to body mass index, depression, and self-esteem, thus suggesting that 'friendship-group similarities go deeper than shared behaviors to similar beliefs of self-worth and mood' (Paxton et al., 1999, p. 263).

In another study, Dunkley et al. (2001) found that adolescent girls who showed the most body dissatisfaction and dietary restraint lived in a subculture supporting a thin ideal and encouraging dieting. Perceived pressure from peers, parents, and media were all significant correlates but peers were perceived to add the strongest pressure to be thin when girls' actual size was accounted for. This pressure was communicated via fat talk, teasing, and social comparisons. Social comparisons are discussed in later sections.

Peer groups often engage in discussions about physical attractiveness, clothing, and other aspects of appearance, which is a behaviour that Jones (2004) refers to as 'appearance training'. This training sets the norms and expectation for the group members and sets the parameters for what is idealized, acceptable, and unacceptable; and some peer groups are more focused on appearance concerns than others. In a longitudinal study that spanned 1 year, Jones (2004) found that peer appearance conversations predicted social comparisons change which in turn predicted body dissatisfaction change in 12-year-old girls. Among 12-year-old boys, those who initially endorsed the ideal images of appearance were more likely to express greater body dissatisfaction. None of the peer appearance context measures prospectively predicted social comparisons or internalized appearance ideals. Jones argued that the importance of appearance issues may develop later for boys because they start and exit puberty after girls do, and move into the cultural glorification of muscularity associated with manhood during the high school and college years. However, the adoption of ideal images as their appearance goal may be an important first step in boys' participation in the appearance culture. In contrast, girls are embedded in the appearance culture from an early age, so appearance goals appear to be well established at an earlier stage.

The nature of peer groups, with a focus on peer crowds, has been examined by Mackey and La Greca (2008). Peer crowds are reputation-based peer groups, or more specifically, large social networks of similarly stereotyped individuals who may or may not spend time together. However, membership of peer crowds reflects adolescents' peer status and reputation, as well as the primary attitudes and behaviours by which they are known to their peers. Peer crowd affiliation also provides adolescents with a sense of identity and belonging, and opportunities for social interactions. Mackey and La Greca (2008) classified six types of crowds among

15-year-old girls: 'Populars' who are involved in activities concerned about image; 'Brains' who do well in school and enjoy academic activities; 'Jocks' who are athletic and on school sport teams; 'Burnouts' who skip school and get into trouble; 'Alternatives' who rebel against the norm in clothing or ideas, do not conform to social ideals; and 'Average' who do not identify with any particular peer crowd.

Mackey and La Greca (2008) found that girls affiliating with the Jocks appeared to be at lower risk for engaging in weight control behaviours, as they reported less concern about their own weight and fewer perceived peer norms about thinness. In contrast, girls identifying with the Alternatives reported more concern with their weight and appearance than others girls and also were more likely to engage in weight control behaviours. Girls identifying as Average, or not belonging to any particular peer crowd, reported more weight control behaviours than other girls, independent of their own or perceived peer weight norms. However, none of the examined variables described the girls who identified highly with the Brains or Popular peer crowds. Clearly additional examinations of the nature and impact that peer crowds have on adolescents is needed, and further studies also need to include boys. Studies that incorporate a wider arrange of individual measures that target peer pressures within the context of peer crowds may also enhance current understanding.

SOCIAL COMPARISONS

Another potential way that peers may exert their influence is indirectly via social comparisons. Peers or similar others are often the target chosen for social comparisons and these comparisons are often used to explain how individuals evaluate their own attributes, behaviours, and other characteristics (see Buunk & Gibbons, 2007). The main purpose of social comparisons is to evaluate or to enhance some aspects of the self (Suls et al., 2002). In particular, individuals utilize social comparisons when they need to both reduce uncertainty about their abilities, performance, and other socially-defined attributes, and when they need to rely on external standards against which to judge themselves (White et al., 2006). They are especially salient in the domain of appearance and body image, as there are no objective criteria for determining attractiveness.

There has been extensive research in the field which has shown a strong association between appearance-related social comparisons and body image concerns among both adolescent and adult women (e.g. Dittmar & Howard, 2004; Jones, 2004; Halliwell & Harvey, 2006). This has included a large number of cross-sectional studies and an increasing number of experiments, but very little longitudinal research. The targets of social comparisons have included both peers and celebrities. Moreover, most researchers have assumed that women are engaging in upward social comparisons (comparisons with women who are super-slender, and therefore have the idealized body shape), as the effects of appearance-related social compari-sons have been found to be consistently negative. Very little work has examined the possibility that women may also engage in downward social comparisons, and how appearance-related social comparisons are related to social comparisons in other domains (cf. Strahan et al., 2006).

Several studies have also examined appearance-related social comparisons and body image concerns among males (Ricciardelli & McCabe, 2007). However, associa-tions between those variables have not been found in all these studies (e.g. Ricciardelli et al., 2000; Humphreys & Paxton, 2004; Jones, 2004; cf Smolak et al., 2005). Interestingly, the findings from earlier studies have been more equivocal than those of recent studies. This partly reflects a general trend in the literature which clearly shows either that many of the relationships demonstrated in work with women are not supported in work with men, or that the findings are still inconclusive (Ricciardelli & McCabe, 2004). However, the state of the field also reflects the problem that many researchers have utilized measures with males which have been primarily developed and validated with women. In addition, two studies with adolescent males (Jones, 2004; Ricciardelli et al., 2000) and one with adult males (Strahan et al., 2006) have shown that males engage in fewer appearance-related social comparisons than women. More specifically, in our work with adolescent boys, we found that almost half of the boys interviewed did not make social comparisons (Ricciardelli et al., 2000). Moreover, most of the boys who made social comparisons reported feeling more positive or neutral about their body. Therefore, the nature of boys' social com-parisons is more likely to be downward than upward.

Consistent with this suggestion, Strahan et al. (2006) found that when describing their appearance, adult men made more downward than upward social compari-sons, and these were associated with a positive body image. In contrast, adult women made more upward than downward comparisons, and these were associ-ated with a more negative body image. Interestingly, the men and women did not differ in the number of upward and downward comparisons made when describing their social skills; however, upward social comparisons in this domain were associ-ated with more negative self-views. Women were also more likely to compare their appearance to more unobtainable targets such as models and celebrities. Men, on the other hand, were more likely to focus on sporting persons and on functional attributes such as health and fitness. In addition, two of the most frequent targets college men have been found to use in their social comparisons are friends and other males at school (Karazsia & Crowther, 2009).

Social comparisons are likely to be even more important during preadolescence, as this is the time when social comparisons first appear and they have been shown to play a role in other developmental domains such as in overall self-evaluation and academic performance (Holt, 2005). Three studies were located which have exam-ined the relationship between social comparisons and body image concerns among preadolescents. Holt and Ricciardelli (2002) found that 10-year-old boys engaged in more social comparisons with adults while the same aged girls engaged in more social comparisons with their peers. However, social comparisons were not associated with body dissatisfaction for either girls or boys. It may perhaps be that the figure rating scale used by Holt and Ricciardelli (2002) was not sufficiently sensitive to accurately detect the degree of body image concerns among children. In another study, Blowers et al. (2003) found that social comparisons (the target was not specified) were associated with body dissatisfaction among 11-year-old girls. Similarly, Fraser et al. (2010) found that social comparisons with peers were associated with more body image concerns among 10-year-old girls. Blowers et al. (2003) used the Body Dissatisfaction subscale from the Eating Disorder Inventory while Fraser et al. (2010) used the Body Esteem scale for children. Both of these measures appear to be more sensitive than figure rating scales in detecting individual differences in children's body image concerns (Ricciardelli & McCabe, 2001).

Peer Relationships

Same-gender and other-gender relationships play an important function during adolescence, as this is the time when adolescents' bodies are changing; they compare themselves to others; and they develop an interest in dating and sex (Simmons & Blyth, 1987; Levine et al., 1994). In one study, McCabe et al. (2002) found that 13-year-old boys with poor same-gender peer relations reported greater body dissatisfaction while boys with poor opposite-gender peer relations placed greater importance on their bodies. On the other hand, 13-year-old girls with negative same-gender peer relations reported greater body dissatisfaction and also placed more importance on their bodies. Girls' opposite-gender relationships were not correlated with either body image dimension (McCabe et al., 2002). Additional studies are needed, as often researchers do not separate the influence of same-gender versus opposite-gender relationships.

Additional differences between girls' and boys' relationships were more fully illustrated by Palmqvist and Santavirta (2006), who found that 14-year-old girls engaged in more discussion with their peers concerning both intimate and general matters than did boys of the same age. In addition, Palmqvist and Santavirta (2006) found that closer peer relationships were associated with more dissatisfaction with physical appearance and weight, but only among the girls. The researchers argued that it is possible that boys feel they are not expected to be as talkative or as sociable in peer relationships as girls, hence their relationships may not be as influential.

An individual's physical appearance can also have an impact on how others perceive and interact with him or her, with unattractive individuals receiving negative evaluations from their peers and reduced social contact. In one study with 13-year-olds, Davison and McCabe (2006) found that positive self-rated physical attractiveness, a low tendency to conceal their bodies, and low social physique anxiety were associated with positive same-gender peer relations among girls whereas none of the examined variables were associated with positive same-gender peer relations among boys. On the other hand, positive self-rated physical attractiveness, satisfaction with their bodies and low social physique anxiety were associated with positive opposite-gender peer relations among both girls and boys. These findings suggest that appearance-related concerns are central to the ways girls interact and relate with other girls but they are less important for boys' interactions with other boys. However, appearance concerns are important for both genders when interacting with the opposite gender. Longitudinal studies are needed to more fully examine the direction of these associations. As summarized by Davison and McCabe (2006): 'although a negative body image may contribute to problematic psychosocial function, poor interpersonal skills and social anxiety may contribute to negative evaluations of appearance' and 'such relationships may well be bidirectional' (p. 27).

Another dimension of peer influence that has been outlined is 'appearance-based rejection sensitivity' (Appearance-RS (Park et al., 2009)). Appearance-RS is defined as 'the degree to which individuals anxiously expect to be rejected based on their physical appearance' (Park et al., 2009, p. 108; e.g. 'How concerned or anxious would you be that your date might be less attracted to you because of the way you looked?'). Park et al. (2009, p. 108) have argued that:

Appearance concerns are rooted not just in intrapsychic concerns about how one looks, but in how one appears to others in concerns of being rejected by others based on one's appearance. ... Appearance-RS affects how social information about appearance is perceived, processed, and applied to oneself and to others. Specifically, the more sensitive individuals are to appearance rejection, the more lonely and rejected they feel when asked to list dissatisfying aspects of their appearance and the more negative they feel following an ambiguous experience of appearance rejection. Following a direct instance of appearance-based rejection, these individuals become socially avoidant and seek to withdraw from close others and from social interactions more generally.

In their study, Park et al. (2009) found adult women showed greater sensitivity to appearance rejection than men. In addition, it was only among women that perceptions of peer conditional acceptance based on appearance (e.g. 'If I had a better body, I think I would be more popular among my friends and peers') were found to be associated with Appearance-RS. On the other hand, greater perceived media pressures were associated with Appearance-RS among both women and men. These findings are consistent with the view that appearance concerns are more central for women but they also suggest that women place more importance on peers' conditional acceptance of their appearance. Further research that includes both longitudinal and experimental studies is now required to determine cause and effect relations among the peer influences and Appearance-RS.

FRIENDS

Although much of the focus of research has been on the influence of peers, other research has more specifically examined the influence of friends. This has included studies that focus on sociocultural messages and other pressures explicitly transmitted by friends; and the provision of social support by friends.

Friend pressure

The evidence for the influence of pressure exerted by friends on body image concerns is still not conclusive. Weight-related attitudes and behaviour of best girl friend (e.g. 'I think my best friend tries to lose weight') have been found to be related to body dissatisfaction in 9–12-year-old girls (Sands & Wardle, 2003). Jones et al. (2004) also found that girls and boys (12- and 14-year-olds) who reported more frequent conversations with their friends about appearance reported greater internalized appearance ideals and body dissatisfaction (Jones et al., 2004). Similarly, Paxton et al. (2006) found that body dissatisfaction after 5 years was predicted by friend dieting among 12-year-old girls. However this relationship was not found among 12-year-old boys or among the 15-year-olds, thus highlighting the need to more closely examine differences according to gender and age. In another study, Shroff and Thompson (2006) found that a range of measures that assessed 'friend pressure' (i.e. perceived friend preoccupation with weight and dieting and appearance conversations with friends) were associated with body dissatisfaction among 14-year-old girls.

In contrast to these studies, Van den Berg et al. (2007) found that among adolescent girls, dieting by friends predicted media body comparisons but not body dissatisfaction. Body dissatisfaction was predicted by self-esteem, magazine exposure, weight teasing, and media body comparisons. Among adolescent boys, body dissatisfaction was only predicted by the media variables. Likewise, Woelders et al. (2010) found that initial friendship group levels of body dissatisfaction did not predict body image and dieting 1 year later among 13-year-old adolescent girls. More research is needed which more fully separates the effects of friends from peers but these effects need to be assessed by methods that can more clearly separate their influences (i.e. not self-reports or survey methods). Moreover, it may be that the quality of the friendships and other individual factors, such as negative affect and self-esteem moderate these effects.

Friend support

One of the important roles of friends is to provide emotional security and protect against the impact of stresses and life-strains (Schultz & Paxton, 2007).

Several studies have shown that lower levels of peer support are associated with higher body image concerns among adolescent girls (e.g. Stice & Whitenton, 2003; Alta et al., 2007).

In one study, Gerner and Wilson (2005) examined the relationship between four dimensions of friendship and body image concerns among 15-year-old adolescent girls. The dimensions included acceptance by friends, perceived social support, friendship intimacy, and the perceived impact of thinness on male and female friendships. All dimensions were found to be associated with girls' body image concerns, with the largest unique predictor being perceived impact of thinness on males. In addition, poor acceptance by friends predicted the perceived impact of thinness on male and female friendships. A main limitation of the study, as with much of the work in this field, is that the conclusions are based on concurrent correlational data and that all assessments relied on self-reports.

In another study Schultz and Paxton (2007) specifically examined the positive aspects of friendships (i.e. quality of friend communication, friend trust, and peer acceptance), and negative aspects of friendships (i.e. friend conflict, friend alienation, and social anxiety and insecurity) in relation to body image and eating concerns among 15-year-old girls. There was no relationship between the positive aspects of friendships and body image concerns. On the other hand, girls with greater body image and eating concerns reported more negative aspects of friendships including conflict and alienation, and greater social anxiety and insecurity. Interestingly, these relationships generally disappeared when analyses controlled for depressive symptoms. The findings are consistent with research suggesting that depressive symptoms contribute to a negative view of the quality of social relationships and social functioning (Schultz & Paxton, 2007). Another possibility argued by Schultz and Paxton (2007) is that conflicted friendships and poorer social functioning precede body concerns and disturbed eating. Difficulties relating to peers may lead girls to engage in restrictive eating practices in an effort to bring increased social approval, acceptance and belonging. Moreover, existing image concerns and eating disturbances may also interfere with a girl's capacity to sustain healthy relationships with peers. Longitudinal studies are now needed to more fully understand the nature and development of these associations, and additional studies are also needed to understand whether the role of friendships differs for boys.

CULTURAL DIFFERENCES

To date, there have been only a small number of studies that have examined the pressure from peers and/or friends from countries outside Australia, the US, or the UK. Two studies have shown that peers are at least as important as the family and the media. In one study, Xu et al. (2010) found that peer pressure to increase muscles was the most important influence associated with body dissatisfaction among

12–16-year-old boys in China. On the other hand, body dissatisfaction in girls was predicted by pressure to lose weight from peers, adult relatives, and the media. In another recent study, Mousa et al. (2010) only examined sociocultural pressures among 12-year-old schoolgirls in Jordan. However, as found among Chinese girls, pressures from the peers, family, and the media were all associated with Jordanian girls' body image concerns.

The influence of peers may not be as important or the same in all cultures. For example, Ricciardelli et al. (2004) found that 14-year-old Indigenous Australian adolescents reported perceived messages to lose weight from their friends with lower frequency than did the non-Indigenous participants. Moreover, these messages (and other sociocultural messages from other sources—parents and the media) were not associated with Indigenous girls' body dissatisfaction or the importance they placed on their body image. A possible explanation for these findings is that Indigenous girls may have a very positive self-image and high self-esteem, which is more similar to non-Indigenous boys (Ricciardelli et al., 2000; Ricciardelli & McCabe, 2001a). This positive self-image may protect Indigenous girls from the sociocultural messages that could increase their levels of body dissatisfaction and body image importance. In contrast, perceived pressure from male friends (and other sources) was associated with body image concerns among Indigenous boys. These findings are consistent with gender differences on self-esteem that have been found among minority groups. In contrast to white girls, who tend to report lower levels of self-esteem in comparison to white boys, minority girls demonstrate higher levels of self-esteem than minority boys (Twenge & Crocker, 2002).

In another study, Mellor et al. (2008) found that the influence of peers was less important in Chile than in other countries such as Australia. The main predictor of body dissatisfaction for both adolescent girls and boys (12–18-year-olds) was perceived pressure from adults, not peers, to lose weight. The family may be more influential for Chilean adolescents because their family structures are more cohesive or authoritarian than in some other cultural groups. However, more research is needed to further understand these differences.

Moreover, different cultural groups living in the same country may experience peer pressures differently. For example, Mellor et al. (2009) found that perceived pressure from peers to lose weight was associated with body dissatisfaction among 12–18-year-old Malay girls. However, this relationship was not found among the boys or among the Chinese and Indians in Malaysia. Interestingly, the Malay adolescents reported greater perceived pressures to lose weight from peers than Chinese adolescents. On the other hand, the Chinese girls were more influenced by the media than either their peers or families but there was no clear pattern for the Indian adolescents. One of the main limitations of the study was that the Indian sample may have been too small to detect any significant relationships. However, further studies are needed to more fully understand how girls and boys from different cultures are influenced by the various sociocultural pressures.

Conclusions

Our review has highlighted the centrality of peers and friends in understanding children's and adolescents' body image and appearance concerns. These relationships are also likely to be important for adults; however, the majority of the reviewed studies have not included adults. The focus in the majority of studies was on the negative aspects of peer pressure and peer relationships, however, increasing research is now also examining the positive dimensions of peers and friends. More work is needed to more fully understand how age, gender, culture, body mass index, negative affect, self-esteem, and the importance placed on appearance may moderate the influence of peers on body image and appearance concerns. In addition, the majority of the researchers have employed self-reports and correlational designs, which means that it is often not easy to separate peer influences from other sociocultural influences and/or separate causes from effects. Qualitative, longitudinal and/or experimental studies are needed to verify and more fully delve into many of the findings. In addition, the majority of studies have only examined adolescents' perceived messages based on self-reports, so these now need to be studied in relation to actual messages from peers and friends. Future studies also need to obtain independent data from peers and friends, and to compare this to adolescents' perceptions and self-reports, and examine the factors that may explain any discrepancies.

References

Alta, R. N., Ludden, A. B., & Lally, M. M. (2007). The effects of gender and family, friend, and media influences on eating behaviours and body image during adolescence. *Journal of Youth and Adolescence*, 36, 1024–37.

Blowers, L. C., Loxton, N. J., Grady-Flesser, M., Occhipinti, S., & Dawe, S. (2003). The relationship between sociocultural pressure to be thin and body dissatisfaction in preadolescent girls. *Eating Behaviors*, 4, 229–44.

Buunk. A. P., & Gibbons, F. X. (2007). Social comparison: The end of a theory and emergence of a field. *Organizational Behavior and Human Decision Processes*, 102, 3–21.

Clark, L., & Tiggemann, M. (2006). Appearance culture in nine- to 12- year- old girls: media and peer influences on body dissatisfaction. *Social Development*, 15, 628–43.

Clark, L., & Tiggemann, M. (2007). Sociocultural influences and body image in 9- to 12- year old girls: The role of appearance schemas. *Journal of Clinical Child and Adolescent Psychology*, 36, 76–86.

Clark, L., & Tiggemann, M. (2008). Sociocultural and individual psychological predictors of body image in young girls: A prospective study. *Developmental Psychology*, 44, 1124–34.

Davison, T. E., & McCabe, M. P. (2006). Adolescent body image and psychosocial functioning. *The Journal of Social Psychology*, 146, 15–30.

Dittmar, H., & Howard, S. (2004). Ideal-body internalization and social comparison tendency as moderators of thin media models' impact on women's body-focused anxiety. *Journal of Social and Clinical Psychology*, 23, 747–70.

Dunn, J. (2005). *Children's friendships: The beginning of intimacy.* Blackwell publishing: Melbourne

Dunkley, T. L., Wertheim, E. H., & Paxton, S. J. (2001). Examination of a model of multiple sociocultural influences on adolescent girls' body dissatisfaction and dietary restraint. *Adolescence,* 36, 265–79.

Dohnt, H. K., & Tiggemann, M. (2006a). Body image concerns in young girls: The role of peers and media prior to adolescence. *Journal of Youth and Adolescence,* 35, 141–51.

Dohnt, H. K., & Tiggemann, M. (2006b). The contribution of peer and media influences to the development of body satisfaction and self-esteem in young girls: A prospective study. *Developmental Psychology,* 42, 929–36.

Eisenberg, M. E., Neumark-Sztainer, D., Haines, J., & Wall, M. (2006). Weight-teasing and emotional well-being in adolescents: Longitudinal findings from project EAT. *Journal of Adolescent Health,* 38, 675–83.

Elkind, D. (1967). Egocentrism in adolescence. *Child Development,* 38, 1025–34.

Faith, M. A., Storch, E. A., Roberti, J. W., & Ledley, D. R. (2008). Recalled childhood teasing among non-clinical, non- college adults. *Journal of Psychopathology and Behavioral Assessment,* 30, 171–9.

Fraser, J.K., Sproal, A.W., & Ricciardelli, L.A. (2010). Social comparisons and perceived media pressure in relation to body image concerns among 8 to 11 year old girls. Unpublished manuscript. Deakin University, Melbourne, Australia.

Frisén, A., & Holmqvist, K. (2010). What characterizes early adolescents with a positive body image? A qualitative investigation of Swedish girls and boys. *Body Image,* 7, 205–12.

Frisén, A., Lunde, C., & Hwang, P. (2009). Peer victimization and its relationship with perceptions of body composition. *Educational Studies,* 35, 337–48.

Gardner, R.M., Sorter, R.G., & Friedman, B.N. (1997). Developmental changes in children's body images. *Journal of Social Behavior and Personality,* 12, 1019–36.

Gerner, B., & Wilson, P. H. (2005). The relationship between friendship factors and adolescent girls' body image concern, body dissatisfaction, and restrained eating. *International Journal of Eating Disorders,* 37(4), 313–20.

Halliwell, E., & Harvey, M. (2006). Examination of a sociocultural model of disordered eating among male and female adolescents. *British Journal of Health Psychology,* 11, 235–48.

Hayden-Wade, H. A., Stein, R. I., Ghaderi, A., Saelens, B. E., Zabinski, M. F., & Wilfley, D. E. (2005). Prevalence, characteristics, and correlates of teasing experiences among overweight children vs. non-overweight peers. *Obesity Research,* 13, 1381–92.

Hodges, E. V. E., Boivin, M., Vitaro, F., Bukowski, W. M. (1999). The power of friendship: Protection against an escalating cycle of peer victimization. *Developmental Psychology,* 35, 94–101.

Holt, K. E. (2005). Preventing weight and muscle concerns among preadolescents. Unpublished doctoral thesis. Deakin University, Melbourne, Australia.

Holt, K. E., & Ricciardelli, L. A. (2002). Social comparisons and negative affect as indicators of problem eating and muscle preoccupation among children. *Applied Developmental Psychology,* 23, 285–304.

Hutchinson, D. M., & Rapee, R. M. (2007). Do friends share similar body image and eating problems? The role of social networks and peer influences in early adolescence. *Behaviour Research and Therapy,* 45, 1557–77.

Humphreys, P., & Paxton, S. J. (2004). Impact of exposure to idealised male images on adolescent boys' body image. *Body Image,* 1, 253–66.

Jones, D. C. (2004). Body image among adolescent girls and boys: A longitudinal study. *Developmental Psychology,* 40, 823–35.

Jones, D. C., & Crawford, J. (2005). Adolescent boys and body image: Weight and muscularity concerns as dual pathways to body dissatisfaction. *Journal of Youth and Adolescence,* 34, 629–36.

Jones, D. C., Vigfusdottir, T., & Lee, Y. (2004). Body image and the appearance culture among adolescent girls and boys: An examination of friend conversations, peer criticism, appearance magazines, and the internalization of appearance ideals. *Journal of Adolescent Research,* 19, 323–9.

Jones, D. C., Newman, J. B., & Bautista, S. (2005). A three-factor model of teasing: The influence of friendship, gender, and topic on expected emotional reactions to teasing during early adolescence. *Social Development,* 14, 421–39.

Karazsia, B. T., & Crowther, J. H. (2009). Social body comparison and internalization: Mediators of social influences on men's muscularity-orientated body dissatisfaction. *Body Image,* 6, 105–12.

Kichler, J. C., & Crowther, J. H. (2009). Young girls' eating attitudes and body image dissatisfaction. *Journal of Early Adolescence,* 29, 212–32.

Ladd, G.W., & Asher, S.R. (1985). Social skills training children's peer relations: Current issues in research and practice. In L. L'Abate & M. A. Milan (eds.) *Handbook of social skills training and research,* pp. 219–44. New York: Wiley.

Lieberman, M., Gauvin, L., Bukowski, W. M., & White, D. R. (2001). Interpersonal influence and disordered eating behaviors in adolescent girls the role of peer modeling, social reinforcement, and body-related teasing. *Eating Behaviors,* 2, 215–36.

Levine, M. P., Smolak, L., Moodey, A. F., Shuman, M. D., & Hessen, L. D. (1994). Normative developmental challenges and dieting and eating disturbances in middle school girls. *International Journal of Eating Disorders,* 15, 11–20.

Mack, D. E., Strong, H. A., Kowalski, K. C., & Crocker, P. E. (2007). Does friendship matter? An examination of social physique anxiety in adolescence. *Journal of Applied Social Psychology,* 37, 1248–64.

Mackey, E. R., & La Greca, A. M. (2008). Does this make me look fat? Peer crowd and peer contributions to adolescent girls' weight control behaviours. *Journal of Youth and Adolescence,* 37, 1097–110.

McCabe, M. P., Ricciardelli, L. A., & Finemore, J. (2002). The role of puberty, media and popularity with peers on strategies to increase weight, decrease weight and increase muscle tone among adolescent boys and girls. *Journal of Psychosomatic Research,* 52, 145–53.

Mellor, D., McCabe, M., Ricciardelli, L., & Merino, M. E. (2008). Body dissatisfaction and body change behaviours in Chile: The role of sociocultural factors. *Body Image,* 5, 205–15.

Mellor, D., McCabe, M., Ricciardelli, L., Yeow, J., Daliza, N., & Hapidzal, N. F. M. (2009). Sociocultural influences on body dissatisfaction and body change behaviors among Malaysian adolescents. *Body Image,* 6, 121–8.

Mousa, T. Y., Mashal, R. H., Al-Domi, H. A., & Jibril, M. A. (2010). Body image dissatisfaction among adolescent schoolgirls in Jordan. *Body Image,* 7, 46–50.

Muris, P., Meesters, C., van de Blom, W., & Mayer, B. (2005). Biological, psychological, and sociocultural correlates of body change strategies and eating problems in adolescent boys and girls. *Eating Behaviors,* 6, 11–22.

Nolan, S. A. Flynn, C., & Garber, J. (2003). Prospective study between rejection and depression in young adolescents. *Journal of Personality and Social Psychology*, 85, 745–55.

Park, L. E., DiRaddo, A. M., & Calogero, R. M. (2009). Sociocultural influence and appearance-based rejection sensitivity among college students. *Psychology of Women Quarterly*, 33, 108–19.

Palmqvist, R., & Santavirta, N. (2006). What friends are for: The relationship between body image, substance use, and peer influence among Finnish adolescents. *Journal of Youth and Adolescence*, 35, 203–17.

Paxton, S. J., Eisenberg, M. E., & Neumark-Sztainer, D. (2006). Prospective predictors of body dissatisfaction in adolescent girls and boys: A five-year longitudinal study. *Developmental Psychology*, 42, 888–99.

Paxton, S. J., Schutz, H. K., Wertheim, E. H., & Muir, S. L. (1999). Friendship clique and peer influences on body image concerns, dietary restraint, extreme weight loss behaviors, and binge eating in adolescent girls. *Journal of Abnormal Psychology*, 108, 255–66.

Peterson, K. A., Paulson, S. E., & Williams, K. K. (2007). Relations of eating disorder symptomology with perceptions of pressures from mother, peers, and media in adolescent girls and boys. *Sex Roles*, 57, 629–39.

Presnell, K., Bearman., S. K., & Stice, E. (2004). Risk factors for body dissatisfaction in adolescent boys and girls: A prospective study. *International Journal of Eating Disorders*, 36, 389–401.

Rayner, K. E., Schniering, C. A., Rapee, R. M., & Hutchinson, D. M. (2010). A longitudinal investigation of perceived peer influence in the development of body dissatisfaction and disordered eating in early adolescent girls. Unpublished manuscript. Macquarie University, Sydney, Australia.

Ricciardelli, L. A., & McCabe, M. P. (2001). Self-esteem and negative affect as moderators of sociocultural influences on body dissatisfaction, strategies to decrease weight, and strategies to increase muscles among adolescent boys and girls. *Sex Roles*, 44, 189–207.

Ricciardelli, L.A., & McCabe, M.P. (2004). A biopsychosocial model of disordered eating and the pursuit of muscularity in adolescent boys. *Psychological Bulletin*, 130, 179–205.

Ricciardelli, L. A., & McCabe, M. P. (2007). The pursuit of muscularity among adolescent boys. In J.K. Thompson and Cafri, G. (eds.) *The muscular ideal; psychological, social and medical perspectives*, pp. 199–216. Washington DC: APA.

Ricciardelli, L. A., McCabe, M. P., & Banfield, S. (2000). Body image and body change methods in adolescent boys: Role of parents, friends, and the media. *Journal of Psychosomatic Research*, 49, 189–97.

Ricciardelli, L. A., McCabe, M. P., Holt, K. E., & Finemore, J. (2003). A biosocial model for understanding body image and body change strategies among children. *Applied Developmental Psychology*, 24, 475–95.

Ricciardelli, L. A., McCabe, M. P., Ball, K., & Mellor, D. (2004). Sociocultural influences on body image concerns and body change strategies among Indigenous and non-Indigenous Australian adolescent girls and boys. *Sex Roles*, 51, 731–41.

Ricciardelli, L. A., McCabe, M. P., Lillis, J., & Thomas, K. (2006). A longitudinal investigation of the development of weight and muscle concerns among preadolescent boys. *Journal of Youth and Adolescence*, 35, 168–78.

Rieves, L., & Cash, T. F. (1996). Social developmental factors and women's body image attitudes. *Journal of Social Behavior and Personality*, 11, 63–78.

Rose, A. J., & Rudoph, K. D. (2006). A review of sex differences in peer relationship processes: Potential trade-offs for the emotional and behavioral development of girls and boys. *Psychological Bulletin, 132*, 98–131.

Sands, E. R., & Wardle, J. (2003). Internalization of ideal body shapes in 9-12-year-old girls. *International Journal of Eating Disorders, 33*, 193–204.

Schultz, H. K., & Paxton, S. J. (2007). Friendship quality, body dissatisfaction, dieting and disordered eating in adolescent girls. *British Journal of Clinical Psychology, 46*, 67–83.

Shomaker, L. B., & Furman, W. (2007). Same-sex peers' influence on young women's body image: An experimental manipulation. *Journal of Social and Clinical Psychology, 26*, 871–95.

Shroff, H., & Thompson, J. K. (2006). Peer influences, body-image dissatisfaction, eating dysfunction and self-esteem in adolescent girls. *Journal of Health Psychology, 11*, 533–51.

Simmons, R.G., & Blyth, D.A. (1987). *Moving into adolescence: The impact of pubertal change and school context.* Hawthorne, NJ: Aldine.

Sinton, M. M., & Birch, L. L. (2006). Individual and sociocultural influences on pre-adolescent girls' appearance schemas and body dissatisfaction. *Journal of Youth and Adolescence, 35*, 165–75.

Smolak, S., Murnen, S. K., and Thompson, J. K. (2005). Sociocultural influences and muscle building in adolescent boys. *Journal of Men and Masculinity, 6*, 227–39.

Smolak, L., & Stein, J. A. (2006). The relationship of drive for muscularity to sociocultural factors, self-esteem, physical attributes gender role, and social comparison in middle school boys. *Body Image, 3*, 121–9.

Stice, E. & Whitenton, K. (2003). Risk factors for body dissatisfaction in adolescent girls: A longitudinal investigation. *Developmental Psychology, 38*, 669–78.

Stice, E., Maxfield, J., & Wells, T. (2003). Adverse effects of social pressure to be this on young women: An experimental investigation of the effects of 'fat talk'. *International Journal of Eating Disorders, 34*, 108–17.

Strahan, E. J., Spencer, S. J., & Zanna, M. P. (2007). Don't take another bite; How sociocultural norms for appearance affect women eating behavior. *Body Image, 4*, 331–42.

Strahan, E. J., Wilson, A. E., Cressman, K. E., & Buote, V. M. (2006). Comparing to perfection: How cultural norms for appearance affect social comparisons and self-image. *Body Image, 3*, 211–27.

Suls, J., Martin, R., & Wheeler, L. (2002). Social comparison: Why, with whom, and with what effect? *Current Directions in Psychological Science, 11*, 159–63.

Twenge, J. M., & Crocker, J. (2002). Race and self-esteem: Meta-analyses comparing Whites, Blacks, Hispanics, Asians, and American Indians, and comment on Gray-Little and Hafdahl (2000). *Psychological Bulletin, 128*, 371–408.

Van den Berg, P., Paxton, S. J., Keery, H., Wall, M., Guo, J., & Neuwmark-Sztainer, D. (2007). Body dissatisfaction and body comparison with media images in males and females. *Body Image, 4*, 257–68.

Vernberg, E. M. (1990). Psychological adjustment and experiences with peers during early adolescence: Reciprocal, incidental or unidirectional relationships? *Abnormal Child Psychology, 18*, 197–98.

Vincent, M. A., & McCabe, M. P. (2000). Gender differences among adolescents in family, and peer influences on body dissatisfaction, weight loss, and binge eating behaviors. *Journal of Youth and Adolescence, 29*, 205–21.

White, J. B., Langer, E. J., Yariv, L., & Welch, J. C. (2006). Frequent social comparisons and destructive emotions and behaviors: The dark side of social comparisons. *Journal of Adult Development*, 13, 36–44.

Woelders, L. C., Larsen, J. K., Scholte, R., Cillessen, A. H., & Engels, R. C. (2010). Friendship group influences on body dissatisfaction and dieting among adolescent girls: A prospective study. *Journal of Adolescent Health*, 47, 456–62.

Xu, X., Mellor, D., Kiehne, M., Ricciardelli, L. A., McCabe, M. P., Xu, Y. (2010). Body dissatisfaction, engagement in body change behaviours and sociocultural influences on body image among Chinese adolescents. *Body Image*, 7, 156–64.

CHAPTER 21

ADULT PSYCHOSOCIAL ADJUSTMENT TO VISIBLE DIFFERENCES: PHYSICAL AND PSYCHOLOGICAL PREDICTORS OF VARIATION

TIMOTHY P. MOSS

BEN ROSSER

WE all respond differently to our own appearance—otherwise, the psychological research and practice in this field would be limited to understanding and changing the external, social meanings of appearance to reduce discrimination and stigma. However, it is clear that within similar social and cultural environments, there is a great deal of variation in the well-being of both clinical and non-clinical populations in relation to appearance (Harris & Carr, 2001). The purpose of this chapter is to explore some of the main contending explanations for this variation, as well as to propose some areas of less well-developed theory that could bear the subject of further work. Initially, we will consider the most intuitive explanations—physical severity, and the location of the difference. We will go on to explore how coping processes play a role in adjustment, highlighting the focus in this area on negative outcomes rather than positive adjustment. The second part of this chapter will focus on some key cognitive underpinnings to adjustment, in relation to the self, attention, interpretation of ambiguity, and memory. There are areas of explicit omission in this chapter. We have not, for example, considered the role of social comparison or exposure to the media, as these are discussed elsewhere in this volume (see Chapter 18).

SEVERITY

The range and diversity of appearance-altering conditions is vast. Similarly, within any one diagnostic category, there are large variations in the extent to which any one condition will have a noticeable impact upon appearance, based upon such factors as size, symmetry, colour contrast with surrounding tissue, and texture. Other physical issues—for example, the extent to which appearance issues are cyclical over time (e.g. eczema), or stable (e.g. amputation)—also vary within and across conditions. When searching for predictors of psychosocial adjustment to different or altered appearances, these external characteristics are the most salient variables. Among the lay population, and those with a more normative appearance, the objective severity of an appearance difference is often suggested as the most likely cause of distress. The line of thinking—conscious or non-conscious—is perhaps like this: 'I know what it is like to have a minor difference of appearance, and I don't like it; if this was to be greater, I would feel much worse'. There is perhaps also a degree of self-serving downward comparison involved; 'I have days when I don't like the way I look, and I feel self-conscious. At least I don't have anything that marks me out too much, though; if it was more severe, it would be harder to cope'. A subjective severity—adjustment relationship is implicit within social-cognitive theorizing (Moss & Carr, 2004) and clinical practice (Kleve et al., 2002). The relationship between the self-rated severity of appearance, and associated distress, seems to bear this out. The strength of this relationship is evident in a number of studies—for example, with skin scarring (Brown et al., 2010), facial lipoatrophy (characterized by a 'sunken' facial appearance associated with some medical conditions), and general plastic surgery (Rumsey et al., under review).

The scientific literature was, for some time, not clear on the importance of objective severity in explaining adjustment. Some studies seemed to suggest a major role for objective appearance severity, consistent with intuitive explanations. More recently, an absence of meaningful relationships between severity and adjustment has been demonstrated in studies in a number of conditions. Andrews et al. (2010) prospectively investigated 70 burned adults. Congruent with earlier findings, they found no relationship between the severity of the burn and depressive symptoms. Finzi et al. (2007) have demonstrated that the extent of psoriasis amongst over 1500 Italian adults with the condition was unrelated to their general mental health (as assessed by the General Health Questionnaire and the Brief Symptom Inventory), consistent with earlier findings of, for example, Fortune et al. (2002). We can observe similar negative findings in head and neck cancer (Baker, 1992), vitiligo (Thompson et al., 2002), or craniofacial disfigurement (Sarwer et al., 2001). For characteristics that can be very accurately objectively measured, such as scar size, or the degree of facial lipoatrophy, studies have reported no correlations between objective measures and psychological distress (Brown et al., 2010). A small number of studies—e.g. Leary et al. (1998), investigating psoriasis—have claimed an association. However, these results tend not to stand up well under close scrutiny. For example, the Leary et al. paper used self-reported severity, introducing an element of subjectivity into the measure. More importantly, they did not differentiate between the extent of severity associated by having a visible difference, and the extent of severity accounted for by increased physical symptomatology.

Does this plethora of negative findings mean that there is no relationship between objective severity and distress? Crucially, almost all the work investigating objective severity and distress has been posited on the assumption of a linear relationship— that is, that greater severity would be associated with greater distress. Moss (2005) investigated 400 plastic surgery patients who completed a measure of psychological distress and behavioural dysfunction related to self-consciousness of appearance. Severity in half of the sample was objectively rated by plastic surgeons, whilst severity amongst the remainder was subjectively rated by the patients themselves. Unsurprisingly, the subjective severity of appearance difference was directly and strongly related to psychological symptomatology. However, there was a significant, though smaller effect, for objective severity. This was not linear, however, but followed an inverted U pattern. A portion of the variability in adjustment was accounted for by objective severity such that those with the least and most severe difference of appearance were less distressed than those with moderate levels of severity. Possible interpretations of this finding, discussed by Moss (2005), include the suggestion that the minor and severe extremes of the severity spectrum will elicit a more predictable, and thus more manageable, social response.

Physical location is similarly used as a lay predictor of distress, most notably in relation to visibility. Two large datasets cast doubt on the expected role of visibility. Moss (1997), with 535 general plastic surgery patients, demonstrated that the greatest level of distress was associated not with body sites normally visible, (the head/face, and hands), but rather, with the torso. This finding was replicated in recent research by Rumsey et al. (under review), in which for women, though not men, the body site most associated with poor adjustment was the torso. The explanation for this is likely to be twofold. Firstly, the obvious sexual significance of the breasts and abdomen amongst women increases the psychological stake when these body sites are felt to be flawed or damaged; the subjective sense of oneself as a sexually desirable is threatened. Secondly, less normally visible body sites require a different kind of interpersonal management to normally visible sites. With appearance issues related to a normally hidden body site, one is faced with the practical dilemma of how to reveal this, and to whom, and in what circumstances, as well as the psychological burden of carrying a secret (cf. Pachankis, 2007).

In relation to understanding adjustment to visible differences, then, it is clear that the obvious physical characteristics of severity and location are less useful than may be first thought. It is for this reason that it is necessary to turn to more psychologically-based explanations of individual differences, in coping, personality, and in cognitive processing.

Coping

The field of coping has been widely explored in psychology (e.g. Lazarus, 1993). The cognitive-motivational coping theory presents coping as an ongoing, cyclical transaction between the individual and the environment. Coping may be emotion focused (changing the meaning of the stressor), problem focused (changing the 'real' world), or avoidant. On the basis of what we know about the difficulties associated with visible differences, we would expect that socially avoidant coping would be more often associated with distress. Avoidant coping is rarely adaptive, as it prevents the disproof of maladaptive cognitions, and limits experience which can provide meaning and resilience. Training and support (e.g. Clarke & Castle, 2007) has focused primarily on essentially emotion focused responses (for example, the unhelpful thought 'They are staring at me because I am a freak and will never speak to me' might be replaced by the more adaptive 'They are staring at me because they have a natural inclination to notice the unusual. Although I am unusual looking, that doesn't mean they won't like me'). This is often combined with problem focused, approach-oriented skills training, aimed at eliciting positive social responses as well as changing the meaning of situations. However, problem focused coping alone—doing something to change the source of the stressor—is less helpful in situations which cannot be controlled. For example, if one is subject to stares, comments, and double takes on the basis of physical appearance, other than camouflage make-up, there is little in the way of practical steps that can be done to stop this.

Some studies have included coping measures as outcome variables within their designs. Within the general population, it is evident that avoidant coping mediates general (non-clinical) appearance bullying and well-being. This is largely congruent with the findings of groups with visible differences. For example, Desmond et al. (2007) showed in a sample of participants with traumatic upper limb amputations that avoidance predicted anxiety and depression.

In understanding adjustment to psoriasis, Finzi et al. (2007) have investigated the extent and efficacy of coping attempts. Behavioural disengagement (an avoidant coping strategy) and emotional venting (expressing negative feelings to others) were independent predictors of minor and major psychological distress.

Scharloo et al. (2000) also investigated coping with psoriasis. Social support seeking, distraction, and active coping were all related to positive outcomes (less anxiety and depression) at 1 year from initial assessment. Contradicting Finzi at al. (2007), they reported that emotional expression was associated with better outcomes. However, it must be noted that the measure of coping used was more idiosyncratic, and perhaps less focused on expression of *negative* emotions. Other strategies which have been reported associated with improved quality of life in psoriasis include confrontation, and optimism (Wahl et al., 2006).

Perhaps the best work on coping in relation to visible differences has been in the burns community. For example, Andrews et al. (2010) and Kildal et al. (2005) showed avoidant coping was associated with the worst outcomes on burn-specific outcome measures of psychosocial outcomes, and use of emotional support associated with the best outcomes. Similarly, Fauerbach et al. (2002) in a study of adults with burns found that emotion focused coping was associated with increased body image dissatisfaction. Specifically, emotional venting and mental disengagement predicted poor body image satisfaction, and when used together, predicted a worse outcome than either used alone.

A significant body of work, familiar to those following the burns outcome literature, has been produced by Fauerbach and colleagues, which has been associated with more sophisticated theorizing about coping than many others writing in the field. Fauerbach et al.'s (2009) study with burned adults, showed that both approach and avoidant coping were assessed in relation to psychological distress in a sample at risk of post-traumatic stress disorder (PTSD). Approach-based coping was conceptualized as coping which involved actively processing information about their burn or the incident causing their burn. Avoidant coping was seen as actively attempting to suppress burn-related thoughts. They found that approach/avoidance conflict (that is, trying to manage competing coping tendencies) was associated with a poorer outcome than just approach or avoidance alone.

Beyond Coping

It is important to recognize an implicit drawback in the underlying assumption of much of the coping literature, generally in psychology and more specifically in the area of visible differences. Coping is conceived of as managing the negative impact of unpleasant events. An alternative view is that traumatic events and conditions can be the catalyst for a more fundamental process of personal psychological development. Until recently, how people drew on strengths and resilience to adjust positively was rarely considered. The idea that having a different appearance could be a route to finding meaning in life and developing stronger relationships was little recognized in the literature. In part, this may be through the expectations researchers have brought with them from a history in the health sector, which despite the rhetoric of treating the 'whole person', has remained essentially illness-centred with a focus on pathology. Current work involves using ideas taken directly from the positive psychology movement, directed at human growth and 'nurturing what is best' (Seligman & Csikszentmihalyi, 2000) rather than pathology. Until recently, observations which were consistent with this perspective (e.g. Cochrane & Slade, 1999, noting some of their research participants with cleft lips perceived positive gains arising from their cleft; Liber et al. (2008) identifying more emotional stability and agreeableness in burned adolescents than non-burned equivalents) were undertheorized. We are now in a position to begin to consider the mechanisms by which this might take place. One means is through the process of adapting to visible difference, as this necessitates a confrontation with strongly held personal values. Personal values are multifaceted, with a degree of cultural specificity, and include distinctions between, for example, transcendental and materialistic values. It is conceivable that individuals who *become* visibly different may find that their ability to accommodate this change within the framework of their personal values may impact on their ability to cope. At present, this set of ideas remains a working hypothesis and invites empirical evaluation.

A chapter on individual differences could address many other potential variables which differentiate people, and relate these to adjustment to appearance. For example, there is good work on personality—e.g. Andrews et al. (2010), who in a prospective study of adult burns survivors showed that neuroticism significantly predicted depressive symptoms at 3-month follow-up. However, interesting as this may be from an academic perspective, given the essential stability of personality, deep exploration of this set of variables does not necessarily lend itself to intervention.

A great deal more work has been carried out investigating cognitive processes in relation to visible differences, including work on the self-concept, attentional processing, interpretation of ambiguity, and memory. It is to these areas that we now turn.

SELF-CONCEPT

Appearance and self

Appearance plays a crucial role in our experience and expression of self. It is a pathway allowing us to be recognized as an individual and to interact with the external world around us. It is a means by which we express our internal state, are perceived and interpreted (Zebrowitz & Montepare, 2008); it is a means by which we are capable of perceiving, interpreting, and recognizing others. Although each individual's identity is a unique combination of defining attributes, personal experience, and self-evaluation, it is argued that appearance features ubiquitously as a component of self. The impact of appearance on self-conception and evaluation, however, is notably variable across individuals irrespective of the presence or absence of a visible difference (Harris & Carr, 2001; Rumsey & Harcourt, 2004). Consequently, to understand individual differences in appearance adjustment it is necessary to consider individual differences in the way we conceive appearance within our understanding of self.

The self-concept can be conceived of as a cognitive structure comprising all information constituting one's understanding of self. This information is peculiar to the individual and their personal history and may take many forms, such as physical attributes, beliefs and values, experiences, and interpersonal roles. The grouping and organization of this content represents the importance and interrelationships between the different domains of self. The most central, accessible and affective self-domains are termed self-schemas (cf. Markus, 1977). They represent amalgamates of information relevant to specific domains upon which expectation is based and information processing is directed. Schema theory considers the self-concept to be a collection of self-schemas, the unifying nature of which has been proposed to be useful in understanding appearance adjustment (Thompson & Kent, 2001).

The following sections will consider the individual attributes of self-concept content and organization. Comprehensive understanding of the role of self-conception in appearance adjustment, however, requires consideration of how these attributes interrelate.

Self-concept content

Appearance concerns are characterized, in part, by negative self-evaluations of appearance. Individuals with high levels of concern are likely to experience a more negative perception of their appearance (Lavin & Cash, 2001), which may be accompanied by negative affective and decreased mood (Altabe & Thompson, 1996). Meta-analysis of research into the impact of media presentation of idealized models has demonstrated a relationship between presentation and subsequent negative self-evaluation and body dissatisfaction (Want, 2009). The effect appears to be moderated by pre-existing concern. There is indication, therefore, that appearance adjustment is related to the valence and evaluative quality of information about appearance stored within the self-concept. Furthermore, the emotional and self-appraising outcomes of considering this information are more negative in individuals with higher levels of concern.

Previous experience and social evaluation are important sources of information informing our understanding of self. Social comparison processes (cf. Festinger, 1954) have frequently been suggested as a source of understanding and evaluating appearance. Internalization of unrealistic idealized models of appearance and attractiveness has been associated with persistent downward social comparison and increased appearance concern (Groesz et al., 2002). In addition, discrepancy between the perceived ideal and actual self based on appearance demonstrates a robust relationship with body dissatisfaction (Cash & Deagle, 1997). Increased ideal-actual self-discrepancy has also been associated with an increased affective evaluation and response, both in relation to appearance and global self-concept (Halliwell & Dittmar, 2006). Thus, adjustment appears at least partially related to an individual's internalization of ideals within the self-concept, and negative evaluation of appearance and self based on those ideals.

A negative conception of appearance alone, however, does not necessarily determine the high levels of psychological distress characterizing appearance concern. It is possible to have negative beliefs without those beliefs impacting negatively on behaviour. It has even been argued that negative content integrated within the self-concept may facilitate maintenance of a healthy and balanced self-conception (McMahon et al., 2003). Furthermore, the relation between objective accuracy of the information stored and adjustment is not unidirectional. Inaccurate information may be employed as a protective bias toward positive self-evaluation (Tester & Gleaves, 2005), and conversely, accurate information does not necessarily preclude the occurrence of body dissatisfaction (Grave et al., 2008).

Appearance adjustment is frequently understood through subjective evaluation by the individual. Research into psychosocial variables in people living with a cleft lip and palate has emphasized subjective over objective measure of visible difference in predicting depressive symptoms (Feragen et al., 2010). The research also demonstrated the buffering influence that positive social interactions and support may have. Social context presents as a powerful influence informing our understanding of appearance and self. Social interaction, comparisons, and pressures may all contribute to self-conceptions of appearance; however, subjective evaluation of the impact on self-worth varies greatly across individuals. Overall, self-perception of appearance rather than objective evaluation appears critical in mediating the relationship between appearance, experience, and adjustment outcome.

Self-concept organization

The information content about appearance stored within the self-concept represents the descriptive and evaluative conception of this domain. Social interactions and comparisons assist the evaluation of appearance. Internalization and self-discrepancy present as vulnerability factors in the development and maintenance of negative descriptions and evaluations of self associated with appearance concern. Evaluation of appearance, however, does not predict impact. Individual differences in adjustment may be understood not only in terms of one's conceptualization of appearance but also by how this information relates to and is integrated with other self-concept domains.

Cash (2005) asserts the importance of investment, alongside evaluation, in understanding body image disturbances and appearance adjustment. The salience of appearance as a self-defining domain moderates the impact of negative content. Furthermore, greater investment in appearance demonstrates association with increased internalization and self-discrepancy, and ultimately more body dissatisfaction and impact on psychosocial functioning (Cash et al., 2004).

Personal evaluation of self-worth may become contingent on perceived success or failure in central domains. Appearance-contingent self-worth has been specifically emphasized as potentially maladaptive due to its reliance on external comparison and validation. Consequently, elevation of the salience of appearance within the self-concept may increase vulnerability and negative consequences on self-esteem. VanDellen et al. (2009) reported that individuals with more appearance-contingent self-worth not only rated appearance as more central to their definition of self but also perceived that social evaluation and acceptance/rejection from others was most likely to be dependent on this domain. This indicates that individuals with high levels of appearance concern may judge themselves negatively based on this domain and may believe others do the same. Perceived social rejection can have significant implications for sense of worth and belonging. The social relevance of appearance may explain why poor adjustment can be so affective and isolating, and why social skills training and positive interactions may be useful in diminishing this negative experience (Corry et al., 2009).

The presence of appearance-contingent evaluations of self-worth may relate to the clarity and stability of the conception of 'self'. Individuals with an unstable and ill-defined sense of self are more likely to internalize perceived social standards and consider their appearance as a means of self-definition and evaluation (Vartanian, 2009). Unstable conceptions of self and employment of attributes requiring external validation for self-worth may mean the individual is more vulnerable to threat against the appearance domain of self. Conversely, flexibility in self-definition can be protective when a domain is challenged. Functional and adaptive structuring of the self-concept can take many forms and relates to the complex interplay between the multiple domains of self and the valence of information (Showers, 2002). The flexibility or rigidity of the self-concept, therefore, may potentially facilitate either positive or negative adjustment. To understand adjustment outcome the overall complexity of self-concept and the relative importance and integration of appearance content must also be incorporated into our view of the structure of the self-concept.

Hitherto the self-domain of appearance has been considered in isolation. However, in determining its impact, it is necessary to consider appearance relative to other self-domains. The relative salience of appearance in comparison with other domains is useful as it provides a scale for evaluation of importance—a numerical value can only be considered low or high in reference to other figures. Attributes considered central to self-definition are conceived to have greater impact on self-esteem, hold more affective content, and are chronically accessible (Sedikides, 1995). Consequently, the more central 'appearance' is to self-definition, the greater the influence this content has, the more emotionally charged this description and evaluation is, and the more likely this information is to be brought to mind and appear relevant. Increased accessibility of self-domains is also associated with information processing biases.

The association between adjustment and relative salience of appearance emphasizes the context of the self-concept. Self-complexity refers to the elaboration of self-domains and associated information that constitute this content. Self-complexity has been proposed as a moderator of threat posed by negative events (Linville, 1987). A more elaborate system of self-information was deemed to buffer the impact of negative information through reliance on positive information stored within the self-concept. A study of self-complexity in individuals with a range of visible differences by Moss and Carr (2004), however, suggested the converse may be true. In this study, individuals reporting a larger number of self-domains and information reported poorer adjustment than those with less complex self-concepts. The evidence indicates that any buffering affect self-complexity may have is dependent on the accessibility of positive information. Self-concepts dominated by large quantities of negative information may not have such a resource. The elaboration and connectedness of appearance and negative information may reflect the importance of the appearance domain and the repeated activation of this domain in perception and evaluation of the world.

Additionally, related research has illustrated that disordered eating may be related to the complexity of appearance within the self-concept rather than the complexity of the global self-concept. Stein and Corte (2007) reported that compared to controls, individuals with eating disorders reported more appearance information within the self-concept. Furthermore, this information was more interrelated with other self-domains and negative content. The indication may be that information relating to the appearance domain also features in other self-domains. Consequently, activation of any one of multiple self-domains may lead to the activation of the appearance domain as well. This relation was not, however, replicated in subsequent study where negativity was found to be related to disordered eating and interrelatedness was not (Stein & Corte, 2008). The inconsistency in results may reflect the proposition that compartmentalization and integration of appearance information within the self-concept can play both adaptive and maladaptive roles. Both separating information about appearance from other self-domains and integrating that information can have positive or negative outcomes. The valence of the content is emphasized as pivotal in determining the outcome. For example, positive adjustment may be related to both highly compartmentalized positive conception of appearance; or it may take the form of an evaluative integrative conception of self, balancing positive information against negative threats. Conversely, poor adjustment may relate to compartmentalization of negative appearance information without positive information to buffer its influence; or an integrative conception of self which inter-relates negative information. Flexibility in organizational strategy dependent on situation may prove most adaptive and relate to positive adjustment. These findings may aid an explanation of the variable outcomes related to self-concept stability and instability discussed previously.

Summary of the self-concept and appearance adjustment

Individual differences in appearance adjustment are not related to a specific type of self-concept. Instead, adjustment is associated with complex inter-relationships between variables relating to both self-concept content and organization. The valence of appearance-related information stored relates to the type of impact this information will have. In addition, internalization of unrealistic ideals and related self-discrepancies may compound negative evaluation. The context in which this information exists, however, is considered critical in understanding the magnitude of its impact. Self-concept complexity, relative importance, contingent self-worth, and the integration or compartmentalization of appearance information all contribute to our understanding of adjustment outcome. Although there is not a prototypical good or poor self-concept for appearance adjustment, arguably the current evidence suggests that a more adaptive experience of appearance relates to a highly positive conception of the appearance domain, a diminution of its importance, or flexible reliance on more positively conceived self-domains and information. Conversely, poor adjustment appears associated with negative content considered highly important and self-defining, with a lack of accessible positive information to provide a protective buffer.

INFORMATION PROCESSING AND APPEARANCE ADJUSTMENT

Cognitive psychology conceives each individual as an active, albeit often automatic and unconscious, contributor to their own perception and experience. Our view and understanding of the world is considered to be largely influenced by subjective expectation (top-down processing), rather than solely being the product of direct perception (bottom-up processing). In short, we are not simply passive perceivers of our environment; we contribute to its construction. Our past experiences may not only enable us to predict outcomes of events and interactions, they may actually direct perception and interpretation to be consistent with expectation. The most established expectations and associated processing biases are considered to be unconscious and automatic in activation, often contributing to perception without the individual's awareness (Markus, 1977). In terms of appearance adjustment, there exists the potential for appearance concerns to lead and inform information processing, thus dominating perception in a manner that reinforces and exacerbates concern. Research into adjustment and cognitive processing has suggested appearance concern may be related to biases at all stages of processing from attention and discrimination to interpretation and recall. The following discussion will expand upon cognitive biases in processing appearance information and their implications.

Attention

Evidence relating information processing biases and psychological distress is relatively robust within the field of anxiety (Bar-Haim et al., 2007). High levels of anxiety have been associated with biased attention toward threatening stimuli and biased interpretation of ambiguous stimuli as threatening. The resultant self-reinforcing perceptual cycle is termed hyper-vigilance (Mathews, 1990). Similar, although less robust effects have been found between depression and the perception of negative stimuli. A potential difference between these two cycles is the stage at which they are activated (Mogg & Bradley, 2005). The experience of appearance concern can be partially characterized in terms of anxiety and depression (Carr et al., 2000). Consequently, a comparable appearance-focused cycle of concern may exist in individuals with high levels of appearance concern.

Investigation into appearance-related attentional biases has demonstrated that individuals with high levels of concern may preferentially attend to appearance-related information (Labarge et al., 1998; Rosser et al., 2010). Shafran et al. (2007) measured Visual Dot-Probe task response latencies to photographs relating to eating, shape, and weight in a sample of individuals with eating disorders. Compared to the control group, the clinical sample demonstrated quicker responses to negative appearance stimuli and slower responses to positive appearance stimuli. In other groups of non-clinical appearance-concern relating to 'drive for thinness', the direction of preferential attention in those with higher levels of concern has been related not only to appearance-related information but specific body regions (Hewig et al., 2008). Areas such as waist, hips, legs, and arms received more attention than the face. This particular preference may be a product of the type of appearance concern present (i.e. drive for thinness), or it may demonstrate evidence that appearance-related attentional bias are tailored to the individual's specific concern.

The research discussed suggests that individuals with high levels of appearance concern preferentially attend to information that reinforces that concern. The specificity of the information may demonstrate individual differences in attention to bodily region, upward social comparison, and negative affect associated with this information. It is suggested that such attention may rapidly generate negative evaluations and body dissatisfaction (Brown & Dittmar, 2005). Conversely, positive adjustment may be associated with protective attentional biases directing attention toward positive aspects of one's own appearance and negative aspects of others (Jansen et al., 2005). The direction of causality between appearance-directed attention and level of concern was not explored within the research discussed. Smith and Rieger (2006), however, experimentally manipulated attention to weight/shape stimuli in a sample of the general population. Greater attention to appearance stimuli was related to increased body dissatisfaction. The authors suggest that rather than such attention biases causing appearance concern; attention and appearance concern may be interactively related to one another. This proposition supports the cognitive cycle of exacerbation outlined previously.

Interpretation

Critical to the perceptual cycle of attention is an accompanying interpretative bias. Interpretation of information provides the basis for evaluation of environment and interactions; correspondingly, psychological disorders such as anxiety and depression have been associated with increased interpretation of information as condition congruent (Mathews & Macleod, 2005). Similarly, preferential interpretation of stimuli as appearance-related has been theorized as a contributing factor to the experience and maintenance of appearance concern in a variety of groups, including eating disorders (Vitousek & Hollon, 1990), visible differences (Moss & Carr, 2004), and general concern (Markus et al., 1987). Employing a 'Situation Interpretation Test', Cooper (1997) found that individuals with eating disorders more frequently employed appearance-based explanations in interpretation of ambiguous scenarios. Utilizing the same methodology, comparable results have been found in obese children with appearance concerns (Jansen et al., 2007). The interpretational bias took two forms; firstly, increased endorsement of appearance as responsible for negative events involving the self; secondly, increased endorsement of appearance responsible for positive events involving others. Once again there is indication that appearance concerns relate to the individual's perception and evaluation of the world, not only in judgements about the self but also in comparative appraisals of others.

Investigation into self-concept organization of appearance-related information in individuals with visible differences by Moss and Carr (2004) reported larger numbers of adjectives being identified as self-descriptive and appearance-related.

This evidence may potentially be the product of a more elaborated conception of the appearance domain of self, and/or an increased perceived relevance of appearance-based explanation. Related research found that, in female university students, higher levels of body dissatisfaction were associated with an increased likelihood of interpreting appearance-related comments as negative (Altabe et al., 2004). This interpretation bias was exaggerated further if the alleged source of the comment was male. These results reiterate the social role of appearance and the importance of information valence.

Throughout the research discussed, negative valence has typically featured alongside appearance interpretation biases. Relevant to this observation, recent investigation of appearance concerns in the general population found that an interpretation bias toward appearance information was only evident when accounting for valence interpretation (Rosser et al., 2010). After controlling for current level of affect, high levels of appearance concern were associated with increased propensity to interpret ambiguous words as appearance-related and negative simultaneously; no bias was present when considering the two attributes in isolation. The associated emotional content of information on perception and evaluation further illustrates the need to consider the integration of information about appearance in order to understand adjustment to it.

Memory

Frequent perception and employment of appearance-related information in interpretation is proposed to increase information accessibility, not only in subsequent perception but also biasing retrospective evaluation and recall toward the incorporation of appearance-related content (Williamson et al., 2004). Study within the general population has demonstrated a general preferential recall of weight versus muscle in women and men respectively (Unterhalter et al., 2007). More specifically, Altabe and Thompson (1996) found experimental appearance priming enhanced recall of appearance-related information, but only when the information was self-referent. In combination this evidence provides support of Markus et al.'s (1987) claim that self-conceptions of appearance are universal in their presence but peculiar in their content and salience. The evidence also illustrates that one can gain an understanding of individual concern through the type of cognitive biases exhibited.

Investigation of information accuracy and quantity of recall of appearance-related information has demonstrated some evidence of enhanced recall of body and food related stimuli in individuals with eating disorders (Williamson et al., 2004); although others have found the converse (Legenbauer, 2010). The research outlined, however, did not employ ideographic categorization of information, nor was the level of self-reference of information evaluated, which may have contributed to the inconsistency. The results are at present inconclusive and there is a need for further investigation.

The inconsistent results may reflect a lack of consideration of content-specificity of the appearance domain within the self-concept and associated memory biases. Furthermore, accessibility of information, arguably, relates more closely to speed and likelihood of access rather than quantity of content available or accuracy of information recalled. Consequently, the ease of appearance-information access and likelihood of false recognition may demonstrate a more consistent association with level of adjustment than elaboration or accuracy of that recall.

The presence of appearance-biased memory in individuals with appearance concerns entails that recollection is manipulated to conform to negative expectation and evaluation based on appearance. Consequently, regardless of the objective relevance of 'appearance' to the recalled event it still features as a means of interpretation.

Implications

The implications of the appearance processing biases in attention, interpretation, and memory discussed have been alluded to throughout. Firstly, the evidence of a relationship between these biases and appearance adjustment suggests that although they cannot necessarily be considered a determining factor in the process of an individual developing appearance concerns, they may well serve to maintain and exacerbate those concerns. Secondly, the emotional impact of readily accessing negative, self-referent appearance information is demonstrated in frequent reports of decreased mood and negative body evaluations. Finally, appearance-directed perception has been observed in some form at all levels of processing, from current attention and interpretation to retrospective recall and evaluation, suggesting that individuals with high levels of appearance concern may conceive the world as a place dominated by information that reinforces those concerns.

CONCLUSIONS

The aim of this chapter was to give an overview of some of the candidate theories put forward to explain individual differences in adjustment to appearance problems. While an exhaustive review would be a book in itself, we have endeavoured to cover some of the more common explanations (physical characteristics, coping), some of the more sophisticated and stronger explanations (self-concept-based models, cognitive theories), as well as suggesting areas likely to be worth pursuing in the future (positive psychology and post-traumatic growth). The task for those working in this area in the future has moved on now from challenging widely held beliefs to one of theoretical integration of findings, and practical application. We would argue strongly that it is crucial that these two facets of appearance psychology move in tandem. Good theory will produce sophisticated, testable interventions with known parameters, and facilitate communication and direction amongst researchers and practitioners. Well-crafted interventions will inform theory development by directing researchers to challenging, anomalistic, or limited outcomes, testing theory in the glare of the 'real world'. The synchrony between these spheres of work is becoming a characteristic and strength of this field. We anticipate a flourishing collaboration to the ultimate benefit of those living with different appearances.

REFERENCES

Altabe M. & Thompson, J. K. (1996). Body image: A cognitive self-schema construct? *Cognitive Therapy and Research*, 20(2), 171–93.

Altabe, M., Wood, K., Herbozo, S. & Thompson, J. K. (2004). The Physical Appearance Ambiguous Feedback Scale (PAAFS): A measure for indexing body image related cognitive bias. *Body Image*, 1, 299–304.

Andrews, R. M., Browne, A. L., Drummond, P. D., & Wood, F. M. (2010). The impact of personality and coping on the development of depressive symptoms in adult burns survivors. *Burns*, 36(1), 29–37.

Baker, C. A., (1992), Factors associated with rehabilitation in head and neck cancer. *Cancer Nursing*, 15(6), 395–400.

Bar-Haim, Y., Lamy, D., Pergamin, L., Bakermans-Kranenburg, M. J., & van IJzendoorn, M. H. (2007). Threat-related attentional bias in anxious and nonanxious individuals: A meta-analytic study. *Psychological Bulletin*, 133, 1–24.

Brown, A. & Dittmar, H. (2005). Think "thin" and feel bad: The role of appearance schema activation, attention level, and thin-ideal internalization for young women's responses to ultra-thin media ideals. *Journal of Social and Clinical Psychology*, 24(8), 1088–113.

Brown, B. C., Moss, T.P., McGrouther, D. A., & Bayat, A. (2010). Skin scar preconceptions must be challenged: Importance of self-perception in skin scarring. *Journal of Plastic Reconstructive and Aesthetic Surgery*, 63(6), 1022–9.

Carr, T., Harris, D., & James, C. (2000). The Derriford Appearance Scale (DAS-59): A new scale to measure individual responses to living with problems of appearance. *British Journal of Health Psychology*, 5, 201–15.

Cash, T. F. (2005). The influence of sociocultural factors on body image: Searching for constructs. *Clinical Psychology: Science and Practice*, 12, 438–42.

Cash, T. F. & Deagle, E.A. (1997). The nature and extent of body-image disturbances in anorexia nervosa and bulimia nervosa: A meta-analysis. *International Journal of Eating Disorders*, 22, 107–25.

Cash, T. F., Melnyk, S. E., & Hrabosky, J.I. (2004). The assessment of body image investment: An extensive revision of the appearance schemas inventory. *International Journal of Eating Disorders*, 35, 305–16.

Clarke, A. & Castle, B. (2007) *Handling Other People's Reactions: Communicating with Confidence When You Have a Disfigurement*. London: Changing Faces.

Cochrane, V. M. & Slade, P. (1999). Appraisal and coping in adults with cleft lip: Associations with well-being and social anxiety. *British Journal of Medical Psychology*, 72, 485–503.

Cooper, M. (1997). Bias in interpretation of ambiguous scenarios in eating disorders. *Behaviour Research and Therapy*, 35, 619–26.

Corry, N., Pruzinsky, T. & Rumsey, N. (2009). Quality of life and psychosocial adjustment to burn injury: Social functioning, body image, and health policy perspectives. *International Review of Psychiatry*, 21(6), 539–48.

Crocker, J. & Knight, K. M. (2005). Contingencies of self-worth. *Current Directions in Psychological Science*, 14(4), 200–3.

Desmond, D. M. (2007). Coping, affective distress, and psychosocial adjustment among people with traumatic upper limb amputations. *Journal of Psychosomatic Research*, 62(1), 15–21.

Fauerbach, J. A., Heinberg, L. J., Lawrence, J. W., Bryant, A. G., Richter, L., & Spence, R. J. (2002). Coping with body image changes following a disfiguring burn injury. *Health Psychology*, 21(2), 115–21.

Fauerbach, J. A., Lawrence, J. W., Fogel, J., Richter, L., Magyar-Russell, G., McKibben, J. B. A., et al. (2009). Approach-avoidance coping conflict in a sample of burn patients at risk for posttraumatic stress disorder. *Depression and Anxiety*, 26(9), 838–50.

Feragen, K. B., Kvalem, I. L., Rumsey, N., & Borge, A. I. H. (2010). Adolescents with and without a facial difference: The role of friendships and social acceptance in perceptions of appearance and emotional resilience. *Body Image*, 7(4), 271–9.

Festinger, L. (1954). A theory of social comparison processes. *Human Relations*, 7, 117–40.

Finzi, A., Colombo, D., Caputo, A., Andreassi, L., Chimenti, S., Vena, G., et al. (2007). Psychological distress and coping strategies in patients with psoriasis: The PSYCHAE study. *Journal of the European Academy of Dermatology and Venereology*, 21, 1161–9.

Fortune, D. G., Richards, H. L., Griffiths, C. E. M., & Main, C. J. (2002). Psychological stress, distress and disability in patients with psoriasis: Consensus and variation in the contribution of illness perceptions, coping and alexithymia. *British Journal of Clinical Psychology*, 41, 157–74.

Grave, R. D., Calugi, S., & Marchesini, G. (2008). Underweight eating disorder without over-evaluation of shape and weight: Atypical anorexia nervosa? *International Journal of Eating Disorders*, 41, 705–12.

Groesz, L. M., Levine, M. P., & Murnen, S. K. (2002). The effect of experimental presentation of thin media images on body satisfaction: A meta-analytic review. *International Journal of Eating Disorders*, 31, 1–16.

Halliwell, E. & Dittmar, H. (2006). Associations between appearance-related self-discrepancies and young women's and men's affect, body satisfaction, and emotional eating: A comparison of fixed-item and participant-generated self-discrepancies. *Personality and Social Psychology Bulletin*, 32, 447–58.

Harris, D. L. & Carr, A. T. (2001). Prevalence of concern about physical appearance in the general population. *British Journal of Plastic Surgery*, 54, 223–6.

Hewig, J., Cooper, S., Trippe, R. H., Hecht, H., Diplin-Ing, Straube, T. & Miltner, W. H. R. (2008). Drive for thinness and attention toward specific body parts in a nonclinical sample. *Psychosomatic Medicine*, 70, 729–36.

Jansen, A., Nederkoorn, C. & Mulkens, S. (2005). Selective visual attention for ugly and beautiful body parts in eating disorders. *Behaviour Research and Therapy*, 43, 183–96.

Jansen, A., Smeets, T., Boon, B., Nederkoorn, C., Roefs, A. & Mulkens, S. (2007). Vulnerability to interpretation bias in overweight children. *Psychology and Health*, 22, 561–74.

Kildal, M., Willebrand, M., Andersson, G., Gerdin, B., & Ekselius, L. (2005). Coping strategies, injury characteristics and long-term outcome after burn injury. *Injury-International Journal of the Care of the Injured*, 36(4), 511–18.

Kleve, L., Rumsey, N., Wyn-Williams, M. & White, P. (2002). The effectiveness of cognitive-behavioural interventions provided at Outlook: A disfigurement support unit. *Journal of Evaluation in Clinical Practice*, 8(4), 387–95.

Labarge, A. S., Cash, T. F., & Brown, T. A. (1998). Use of a modified Stroop task to examine appearance-schematic information processing in college women. *Cognitive Therapy and Research*, 22, 179–90.

Lavin, M. A. & Cash, T. F. (2001). Effects of exposure to information about appearance stereotyping and discrimination on women's body images. *International Journal of Eating Disorders*, 29, 51–8.

Lazarus, R. S., (1993). Coping theory and research: Past, present and future. *Psychosomatic Medicine*, 55, 234–47.

Leary, M. R., Rapp, S. R., Herbst, K. C., Exum, M. L., & Feldman, S. R. (1998). Interpersonal concerns and psychological difficulties of psoriasis patients: Effects of disease severity and fear of negative evaluation. *Health Psychology*, 17(6), 530–6.

Legenbauer, T., Maul, B., Rühl, I., Kleinstäuber, M. & Hiller, W. (2010). Memory bias for schema-related stimuli in individuals with bulimia nervosa. *Journal of Clinical Psychology*, 66(3), 302–16.

Liber, J. M., Faber, A. W., Treffers, P. D. A., & Van Loey, N. E. E. (2008). Coping style, personality, and adolescent adjustment 10 years post-burn. *Burns*, 34(6), 775–82.

Linville, P. W. (1987). Self-complexity as a cognitive buffer against stress-related illness and depression. *Journal of Personality and Social Psychology*, 52, 663–76.

Markus, H. (1977). Self-schemas and information processing about the self. *Journal of Personality and Social Psychology*, 35, 63–78.

Markus, H., Hamill, R., & Sentis, K.P. (1987). Thinking fat: Self-schemas for body weight and the processing of weight relevant information. *Journal of Applied Social Psychology*, 17(1), 50–71.

Mathews, A. & MacLeod, C. (2005). Cognitive vulnerability to emotional disorders. *Annual Review of Clinical Psychology*, 1, 167–95.

Mathews, A. (1990). Why worry? The cognitive function of anxiety. *Behaviour Research and Therapy*, 28, 455–68.

McMahon, P. D., Showers, C. J., Rieder, S. L., Abramson, L. Y., & Hogan, M. E. (2003). Integrative thinking and flexibility in the organization of self-knowledge. *Cognitive Therapy and Research*, 27(2), 167–84.

Mogg, K. & Bradley, B. P. (2005). Attentional bias in generalized anxiety disorder versus depressive disorder. *Cognitive Therapy and Research*, 29, 29–45.

Moss, T. P. & Carr, T. (2004). Understanding adjustment to disfigurement: The role of the self-concept. *Psychology & Health*, 19(6), 737–48.

Moss, T. P. (1997). Individual Differences in Psychological Adjustment to Perceived Abnormalities of Appearance. PhD thesis, University of Plymouth, UK.

Moss, T. P. (2005). The relationships between objective and subjective ratings of disfigurement severity, and psychological adjustment. *Body Image*, 2, 151–9.

Pachankis, J. E. (2007). The psychological implications of concealing a stigma: A cognitive-affective-behavioral model. *Psychological Bulletin, 133,* 328–45.

Rosser, B., Moss, T. & Rumsey, N. (2010). Attentional and interpretative biases in appearance concern: An investigation of biases in appearance-related information processing. *Body Image, 7,* 251–4.

Rumsey, N. & Harcourt, D. (2004). Body image and disfigurement: Issues and interventions. *Body Image, 1,* 83–97.

Rumsey, N., Charlton, R., Clarke, A., Harcourt, D., James, H., Jenkinson, E., *et al.* (under review). Factors associated with distress and positive adjustment in people with disfigurement: evidence from large multi-centered study.

Sarwer, D., Whitaker, L. & Bartlett, S. (2001). Psychological functioning of adolescents born with craniofacial anomalies. *Craniofacial Surgery, 9,* 224–6.

Scharloo, M., Kaptein, A. A., Weinman, J., Bergman, W., Vermeer, B. J., & Rooijmans, H. G. M. (2000). Patients' illness perceptions and coping as predictors of functional status in psoriasis: A 1-year follow-up. *British Journal of Dermatology, 142*(5), 899–907.

Sedikides, C. (1995). Central and peripheral self-conceptions are differentially influenced by mood: Tests of the differential sensitivity hypothesis. *Journal of Personality and Social Psychology, 69*(4), 759–77.

Seligman, M. E. P., & Csikszentmihalyi, M. (*2000*). Positive psychology: An introduction. *American Psychologist, 55,* 5–14

Shafran, R., Lee, M., Cooper, Z., Palmer, R.L. & Fairburn, C.G. (2007). Attentional bias in eating disorders. *International Journal of Eating Disorders, 40,* 369–80.

Showers, C.J. (2002). Integration and compartmentalization: A model of self-structure and self-change. In D. Cervone & W. Mischel (eds.) *Advances in personality science,* pp. 271–91. New York: Guilford.

Smith, E. & Rieger, E. (2006). The effect of attentional bias toward shape- and weight-related information on body dissatisfaction. *International Journal of Eating Disorders, 39,* 509–15.

Stein, K. F. & Corte, C. (2007). Identity impairment and the eating disorders: Content and organization of the self-concept in women with anorexia nervosa and bulimia nervosa. *European Eating Disorders Review, 15,* 58–69.

Stein, K. F. & Corte, C. (2008). The identity impairment model: A longitudinal study of self-schemas as predictors of disordered eating behaviors. *Nursing Research, 57*(3), 182–90.

Tester, M. L. & Gleaves, D. H. (2005). Self-deceptive enhancement and family environment: Possible protective factors against internalization of the thin ideal. *Eating Disorders, 13,* 187–99.

Thompson, A. & Kent, G. (2001). Adjusting to disfigurement: Processes involved in dealing with being visibly different. *Clinical Psychology Review, 21*(5), 663–82.

Thompson, A. R., Kent, G., & Smith, J. A. (2002). Living with vitiligo: Dealing with difference. *British Journal of Health Psychology, 7,* 213–25.

Unterhalter, G., Farrell, S., & Mohr, C. (2007). Selective memory biases for words reflecting sex-specific body image concerns. *Eating Behaviors, 8,* 382–9.

vanDellen, M. R., Hoy, M. B. & Hoyle, R. H. (2009). Contingent self-worth and social information processing: Cognitive associations between domain performance and social relations. *Social Cognition, 27*(6), 847–66.

Vartanian, L. R. (2009). When the body defines the self: Self-concept clarity, internalization, and body image. *Journal of Social and Clinical Psychology, 28*(1), 94–126.

Vitousek, K. B. & Hollon, S. D. (1990). The investigation of schematic content and processing in eating disorders. *Cognitive Therapy and Research,* 14, 191–214.

Wahl, A. K., Mork, C., Hanestad, B. R., & Helland, S. (2006). Coping with exacerbation in psoriasis and eczema prior to admission in a dermatological ward. *European Journal of Dermatology,* 16(3), 271–5.

Want, S.C. (2009). Meta-analytic moderators of experimental exposure to media portrayals of women on female appearance satisfaction: Social comparisons as automatic processes. *Body Image,* 6, 257–69.

Williamson, D. A., White, M. A., York-Crowe, E., & Stewart, T.M. (2004). Cognitive-behavioral theories of eating disorders. *Behavior Modification,* 28, 711–38.

Zebrowitz, L. A. & Montepare, J. M. (2008). Social psychological face perception: Why appearance matters. *Social and Personality Psychology Compass,* 2(3), 1497–517.

SECTION 2.3

CONSEQUENCES
OF APPEARANCE
CONCERNS

....

CHAPTER 22

APPEARANCE AND EXERCISE

....

JAMES BYRON-DANIEL

THIS chapter examines the relationship between body image and exercise, as an example of the consequences that appearance concerns can have on lifestyle and health behaviours. Research into the effects of physical activity on psychological states has almost universally found improvements in anxiety, depression, and negative affect (Biddle & Mutrie, 2008), and given its beneficial impact on physical health, motivating people to increase their levels of physical activity is a major focus within public health. How a person feels about his or her appearance may be an important determinant of physical activity (Hausenblaus et al., 2004) and as body image dissatisfaction is so widespread and low levels of physical activity are so common (Oja, 1995), it is appropriate to examine the links between these phenomena. Firstly, this chapter considers briefly the relationship between exercise and body dissatisfaction. It then explores how appearance can act as a motivator or a barrier to exercise, before considering the use of physical activity as an intervention to boost body satisfaction. The relevance of the environment in which exercise takes place is then considered, and areas for further research are highlighted.

THE RELATIONSHIP BETWEEN EXERCISE AND BODY DISSATISFACTION

....

There is considerable ambiguity about the relationship between exercise and body image and disparity in research findings is common in this field of investigation.

Gillison et al. (2006) found that adolescents perceiving themselves to be overweight and who felt pressurized to lose weight were more motivated to exercise, and some correlational findings suggest that the levels of concern that people have about their physique are negatively associated with the amount of exercise they undertake (Lantz et al., 1997). In contrast, Cumming et al. (2009) found no association in 13–15-year-olds between body image and physical activity. In adults, negative associations have been shown between body image, social physique anxiety (SPA), and physical activity participation (Hausenblas & Fallon, 2002; Sebire et al., 2009). The most widely accepted interpretation of this research is that poor body satisfaction and high levels of fear of negative appearance-related evaluations by others may deter people from exercising, whereas individuals who are happy with the way they look and/or are disinterested in what others think may not be negatively affected in terms of physical activity participation.

There is some suggestion that age might moderate this relationship. Treasure et al. (1998) found that SPA affected adherence to a 12-week walking programme and that this anxiety was moderated by age, with younger participants adhering less if they had greater SPA. The opposite was found in university students (Lantz et al., 1997). There are also mixed findings in terms of the intensity and frequency of exercise required to have positive effects on body image (Randsell et al., 1998).

Is Appearance A Motivator for Exercise, or A Barrier?

Research findings are somewhat contradictory as to whether or not appearance is a motivator for exercise, suggesting self-presentational and body image concerns can lead to both increasing and decreasing levels of physical activity (Furnham et al., 2004; Hausenblas & Fallon, 2006). A substantial number of studies have investigated this relationship, employing a variety of methodologies and outcome measures. For the sake of brevity this chapter does not review all of this research, rather it offers a summary of the key findings and highlights questions that remain unanswered.

Common motivations for exercising include improving fitness and health, increasing social engagement and deriving psychological benefit. Many people are also motivated to exercise for appearance related reasons, be that to become thinner, lose weight, or to become more muscular or toned (Marquez & McAuley, 2001; Williams & Cash, 2001). Weight loss has been the most frequently cited motivator for physical activity amongst women in both quantitative and qualitative work (Bulley et al., 2009). DiBartolo et al. (2007) argue that weight-related reasons for exercise can be linked to eating disorders and low self-esteem. These motivations are not particularly surprising considering the current cultural ideals to which men, women, and young people are exposed. A key question is whether exercising in an attempt to achieve these 'ideals' has a different effect on participation in physical activity compared to exercising for other reasons.

Self-determination theory (SDT) hypothesizes that motives to exercise are either intrinsic or extrinsic (Deci & Ryan, 1985). Intrinsic motivation is demonstrated when people exercise for 'internal' reasons, for example, because they believe that exercise is a route to improving their own health and fitness. Motives such as enhancing physical appearance and weight control in order to match up to societal ideals are characteristic of people who are extrinsically motivated. People who are externally motivated do not usually participate in exercise in the longer term (Culos-Reed et al., 2002; Markland & Ingledew, 2007) and those with higher social physique anxiety are more likely to exercise for extrinsic reasons (Gillison et al., 2006; Niven et al., 2009). Tiggemann and Williamson (2000) suggest that these motives are associated with lower body satisfaction, whilst health and fitness (i.e. internal) motivations have the opposite association. In one of the few prospective studies in this area Gillison et al. (2011) found that pressure to lose weight (extrinsic motivation) predicted drop-out from exercise regimes and was negatively associated with activity uptake.

A number of studies have reported that appearance and self-presentational concerns act as a barrier to physical activity (Zabinski et al., 2003; Defourche et al., 2006). Qualitative interviews with women suggested that perceived negative social consequences of exercise, in particular self-presentational concerns, were associated with a lack of exercise participation (Buman et al., 2009). Tiggemann and Williamson (2000) investigated motivations to exercise, psychological well-being (including body satisfaction), self-esteem, and amounts of physical activity, in a cross-sectional study. A significant negative relationship was found between amount of exercise and body satisfaction. Women reported exercising more for reasons of weight control, toning, and mood enhancement than did men. Across the whole sample, a desire for weight control and toning was associated with lower body satisfaction while motivations focused on health and fitness reasons were associated with enhanced self-esteem. However, other research has found the opposite (i.e. being unhappy with appearance is a major motivator for physical activity (Chen et al., 2010)), whilst some studies have found no relationship at all (Pelegrini & Petroski, 2009).

Blouin and Goldfield (2006) explored appearance-related motivations in different groups of exercisers, measuring body image, drive for muscularity and other related concepts in bodybuilders compared with runners and martial artists. They found that the bodybuilders had significantly higher body dissatisfaction and were more likely to use steroids and be at risk of body image disturbance compared to the other exercisers. Drive for muscularity may also be associated with more problematic behaviours associated with exercise, such as dependence and drug abuse (Zelli et al., 2010).

Bulley et al. (2009) reported that exercise is often associated with a feeling of obligation or duty, and that many barriers have to be overcome in order to achieve the level of physical activity that participants feel they 'should' do. Greenleaf et al. (2006) found that a thin, lean, and toned ideal had been internalized by all but one of the participants in their study. Many of the participants believed they could achieve their ideal body through exercise, yet reported uncertainty about doing so (i.e. concern over 'having to exercise all the time'). The study highlights the notion that an 'ideal body' was attainable and deserved, but only through extreme effort.

Research is needed to explain and tease out the mediating and moderating variables if we are to fully understand the role of body dissatisfaction as a motivator or inhibitor of physical activity. In addition, more qualitative work is needed to build upon these accounts relating to the perceived pressure of exercising, with a focus on identifying barriers and pressures associated with specific appearance goals and motivations.

Researchers should also broaden the focus of their attention to include midlife and older adults, as the links between appearance concerns and physical activity are likely to vary across the lifespan. Studies of older people (52–87 years of age) suggest that factors other than body image and appearance are important for physical activity participation. Hardy and Grogan (2009) suggest that health, enjoyment, and social motivations were most prominent for this age group. Men have reported becoming less involved in physical activities as they get older, with a progressive decline in investment in muscularity, physical fitness, and traditional masculine traits (power, dominance, and sexual virility). This may reflect their frustration at becoming further removed from the male ideal (Baker & Gringart, 2009). Exactly how motivations related to physical activity (including those that are appearance-related) evolve over a lifespan is unclear, since no longitudinal investigations have been conducted.

The research literature suggests a trend that, for some people at least, extrinsic appearance motivations are negatively related to exercise participation. It has been suggested that a more effective way to increase physical activity would be to focus on the health benefits of exercise, and to emphasize the necessity for long-term behaviour change to achieve a change in one's physique. Despite the challenges of achieving and maintaining changes to appearance through exercise (James, 2000), many see physical activity as a way to potentially improve their levels of satisfaction with their looks and body image. A number of research studies have investigated this possibility and these are briefly considered in the following sections, and also in Chapter 40.

CAN EXERCISE INTERVENTIONS IMPROVE BODY SATISFACTION?

Unlike the seemingly contradictory findings of research examining the relationships between appearance-related motivations and uptake of exercise, the results of studies examining the impact of exercise interventions on participants' perceptions of their appearance are more consistent, with the majority reporting positive effects on body image (Campbell & Hausenblaus, 2009). Anderson et al. (2006) investigated 8 weeks of brisk walking in sedentary women and found that walking groups improved body image. Forty-minute circuit training sessions held over 6 weeks have been found to improve body esteem (alongside reductions in BMI) in adults, suggesting that a combination of resistance training and cardiovascular activities can have positive effects (Duncan et al., 2009). A longer intervention of twice weekly 45-minute exercise sessions held over 6 months, found significant improvements in social physique anxiety and physical self-perceptions in adults (Lindwell & Lindgren, 2005).

Positive effects of exercise interventions have also been found in children and adolescents. Daley and colleagues (2006) conducted a randomized controlled trial of exercise in overweight young people. They demonstrated that an 8-week intervention significantly increased physical self-worth, and that this was not necessarily associated with physiological changes. Duncan et al. (2009) examined the impact of circuit training in 10–11-year-old boys and girls and found that children in the exercise group had significant improvements in body-esteem compared to the control group.

However, although the majority of studies have reported benefits from exercise interventions, others have shown no effect on perceptions of appearance dissatisfaction. Arbour and Ginis (2008), for example, found that women who used pedometers to give feedback on the amount of walking they were doing, reported a significant improvement in satisfaction with physical functioning, but no significant effect was found for satisfaction with physical appearance. Zabinski et al. (2001) found no difference in body image after a 15-week physical activity programme.

It may be that the nature of the exercise that people engage in moderates the effect on body image and appearance concerns. There is currently a lack of data relating to the impact of acute exercise sessions. In the limited research that has been done, one study suggests that a single session of acute activity can be effective at improving body satisfaction (McInman & Berger, 1993; Vocks et al., 2009) although this positive effect has not been found in other work (Stock & Byron-Daniel, in preparation). There is some suggestion that higher levels of drive for thinness, body dissatisfaction, and weight concern at baseline are associated with greater change in body satisfaction after an acute exercise session, although this requires further investigation. For some people, the physical changes achieved only through more sustained exercise interventions, such as increases in muscle mass and tone, may be necessary to achieve improvements in body satisfaction, however this may not be the case for all (Williams & Cash, 2001).

Campbell and Hausenblas (2009) conducted a meta-analysis of the effects of 57 exercise interventions on body image. Overall, they found small significant effect sizes, suggesting that exercise interventions do improve body image, although much of the variance in this relationship remains unexplained. Larger effects were found for females compared to males, possibly due to the dearth of research focusing on men. Men are clearly concerned about different aspects of their appearance, with nearly half reporting that they wanted to actually gain weight, and specifically to become more muscular (Pope et al., 2000). There was also a suggestion that effects were larger for older participants and for those with higher BMI. Campbell and Hausenblas concluded that actual fitness levels and body composition did not moderate the effects of interventions, suggesting that an improvement in fitness levels is not a requirement for improvements in body image. Also, no moderating effects were found in relation to the duration and intensity of the exercise, thus the dose–response relationship remains unclear. Frequency of exercise was, however, found to have an effect suggesting that greater exercise frequency in a specified period led to greater gains in body image.

Exercise interventions have tended to target appearance-related beliefs and aspirations of individuals in order to motivate them to exercise (Jones et al., 2004). Yet this focus may feed the desire to exercise predominantly for weight loss and other aesthetic reasons, and this may ultimately be detrimental to long term participation in exercise. Future work should focus on helping people overcome their internal barriers to physical activity, such as emphasizing the health and enjoyment benefits that exercise can provide.

In summary, exercise interventions have shown promise in improving body image, but there are still a number of gaps in our understanding and several caveats that require consideration. It seems that actual changes in body composition and weight are not always required for benefits in body image to accrue, suggesting that changes to self-perceptions relating to appearance may occur through psychological rather than physical mechanisms. Whether exercise fosters good body image and feelings about appearance in perpetuity remains unknown, as long-term follow-up of participants in exercise interventions is rare.

THE RELEVANCE OF THE EXERCISE ENVIRONMENT

Exercise takes place in a multitude of environments, including private spaces such as in the home, or more public arena such as gyms and parks. Decisions about whether and where to exercise may, in part, be related to appearance. For example, women high in social physique anxiety may be more likely to avoid exercising in public (Belling, 1992).

In many public exercise spaces, such as gyms, mirrors are a prominent feature. Mirrored environments have been linked to an increased awareness of physique (Katula et al., 1998) and increased feelings of vulnerability to others' evaluation of one's physical appearance. Ginis et al. (2003) found that regardless of how they felt about their bodies at baseline, women felt worse when exercising in front of a mirror compared to a wall. Exercising in front of mirrors or other people may actually 'knock out' the psychological advantages of exercise (Chmelo et al., 2009). This might be particularly important for those who start with high levels of social physique anxiety and body image dissatisfaction (Katula et al., 1998). The initiation of physical activity for people with high body image concerns may be more likely in environments with less of an emphasis on appearance.

Tight, figure-hugging clothing is 'the uniform' in some exercise environments. Women who prefer exercise environments which de-emphasize revealing clothing have been found to be higher in social physique anxiety (Crawford & Eklund, 1994). It appears that some people can protect themselves from the potential negative effects of mirrors and tight clothing, for example by exercising away from mirrored areas, wearing clothing that drapes and hides body contours, and by avoiding exercise environments that engender social physique anxiety (Brewer et al., 2002).

The research in this field supports the need to develop a body friendly environment, where people of all shapes and sizes can feel comfortable taking part in physical activity and exercise. This should be taken into consideration when planning and implementing physical activity interventions. Furthermore, the role of social support and peer networks in increasing acceptance of body shapes and engagement in exercise needs to be investigated since these are aspects that have been largely overlooked in previous research.

Conclusions: Ways Ahead and Unanswered Questions

This chapter has outlined some of the research into associations between exercise/physical activity and perceptions of appearance and body satisfaction, with a particular focus on motivations to exercise, exercise interventions, and the exercise environment. It appears that exercise interventions can have a positive effect on body image, but that initial motivations are crucial in determining how people feel about their own appearance after physical activity. In particular, research suggests that appearance concerns may act as a barrier to some people engaging in physical activity. The exercise environment itself may also be crucial in encouraging, or discouraging, people with appearance motivations and concerns to become active. It is evident that appearance is extremely important in relation to exercise participation yet much about this relationship remains unclear, particularly as the methodology and measures used in research to date have been so variable.

A host of key questions remain to be answered. For example, what factors mediate and moderate the relationship between body (dis)satisfaction and exercise? How stable are appearance-related motivations to exercise, and how important are appearance motivations throughout a person's exercising life? What would be the ideal mode, duration, and frequency if one were to use exercise as an intervention for body image improvement? Future research needs to look prospectively and longitudinally at these questions. In addition, the experience of the 'average' exerciser should be captured in order to assess the generalizability of the research to date (much of which has been carried out with habitual exercisers) to the population as a whole. There is also a surprising lack of qualitative research in this area, although current investigations may well provide much needed detailed accounts of exercisers experience of physical activity in relation to appearance motivations (Townsend et al., in preparation).

As the benefits of exercise for psychological well-being and physical health are clear, a better understanding of the links between appearance concerns and engagement in physical activity across the lifespan should be a priority for researchers, practitioners, and policy-makers in psychology and public health. Early indicators suggest that existing exercise interventions targeted at encouraging people to increase physical activity for weight loss and body image reasons may actually have the opposite effect, and may, for some, actually feed negative emotions associated with exercise and render them less likely to start or maintain an exercise regime. Overcoming these associations may begin to help break down barriers to participation in exercise and physical activities and should be a focus of research and public health strategy in the future.

References

Anderson, A. E. (1995). Eating disorders in males. In K. D. Brownell & C. G. Fairburn (eds.) *Eating Disorders and Obesity*, pp. 177–87. New York: Guilford Press.

Arbour, K. P. & Martin Ginis, K. A. (2008). Improving body image one step at a time: Greater pedometer step counts produce greater body image improvements. *Body Image*, 5(4), 331–6.

Baker, L. & Gringart, E. (2009). Body image and self-esteem in older adulthood. *Ageing & Society*, 29(6), 977–95.

Biddle, S. & Dovey, T. (2009). Obesity: Is physical activity the key? *The Psychologist*, 22 (1), 32–5.

Biddle, S. & Mutrie, N. (2008). *Psychology of physical activity: Determinants, well-being and interventions*. London: Routledge.

Brewer, B. W., Diehl, N. S., Cornelius, A. E., Joshua, M. D., Van Raalte, J. L., Shaw, D., et al. (2002). Exercising caution: Social physique anxiety and protective self-presentational behavior. *Journal of Science and Medicine in Sport*, 7, 47–55.

Blouin, A. G. & Goldfield, G. S. (1995). Body image and steroid use in male bodybuilders. *International Journal of Eating Disorders*, 18(2), 159–65.

Bulley, C., Donaghy, M., Payne, A., & Mutrie, N. (2009). Personal meanings, values and feelings relating to physical activity and exercise participation in female undergraduates: A qualitative exploration. *Journal of Health Psychology*, 14, 751–60.

Buman, M., Giacobbi, L., Yasova, D., & McCrae, C. (2009). Using the constructive narrative perspective to understand physical activity reasoning schema in sedentary adults. *Journal of Health Psychology*, 14, 1174–8.

Campbell, A. & Hausenblas, H. A. (2009). Effects of exercise interventions on body image: A meta-analysis. *Journal of Health Psychology*, 14, 6, 780–93.

Chen, L., Fox, K. R., & Haase, A. M. (2010). Body image and physical activity among overweight and obese girls in taiwan. *Women's Studies International Forum*, 33(3), 234–43.

Chmelo, E. A., Hall, E. E., Miller, P. C., & Sanders, K. N. (2009). Mirrors and resistance exercise, do they influence affective responses? *Journal of Health Psychology*, 14(8), 1067–74.

Crawford, S. & Eklund, R. C. (1994). Social physique anxiety, reasons for exercise, and attitudes toward exercise settings. *Journal of Sport & Exercise Psychology*, 16, 70–82.

Culos-Reed, S. N., Brawley, L. R., Martin, K. A., & Leary, M. R. (2002). Self- presentation concerns and health behaviors among cosmetic surgery patients. *Journal of Applied Social Psychology*, 32, 560–9.

Cumming, S. P., Standage, M., Gillison, F. B., Dompier, T. P. & Malina, R. M. (2009). Biological maturity status, body size, and exercise behaviour in British youth: A pilot study. *Journal of Sports Science*, 27(7), 677–87.

Daley, A., Copeland, R., & Wright N. (2006). Exercise therapy as a treatment for psychopathology in obese and morbidly obese adolescents: Randomised controlled trial. *Pediatrics*, 118, 2126–34.

Davis, C. (1990). Body image and weight preoccupation: A comparison between exercising and non-exercising women. *Appetite*, 15(1), 13–21.

Deci, E. & Ryan, R. (1985). *Intrinsic motivation and self-determination in human behaviour.* New York: Plenum Press.

Deforche, B. I., De Bourdeaudhuij, I. M., & Tanghe, A. P. (2006). Attitude toward physical activity in normal-weight, overweight and obese adolescents. *Journal of Adolescent Health*, 38(5), 560–8.

DiBartolo, P. M., Lin, L., Montoya, S., Neal, H., & Shaffer, C. (2007). Are there 'healthy' and 'unhealthy' reasons for exercise? examining individual differences in exercise motivations using the function of exercise scale. *Journal of Clinical Sport Psychology*, 1(2), 93–120.

Duncan, M. J., Al-Nakeeb, Y., & Nevill, A. M. (2009). Effects of a 6-week circuit training intervention on body esteem and body mass index in British primary school children. *Body Image*, 6(3), 216–20.

Furnham, A. & Greaves, N. (1994). Gender and locus of control correlates of body image dissatisfaction. *European Journal of Personality*, 8(3), 183–200.

Furnham, A., Titman, P., & Greaves, N. (1994). Gender and locus of control correlates of body image dissatisfaction. *Psychological Medicine*, 13, 829–37.

Gillison, F. B., Standage, M., & Skevington, S. M. (2006). Relationships among adolescents' weight perceptions, exercise goals, exercise motivation, quality of life and leisure-time exercise behaviour: A self-determination theory approach. *Health Education Research*, 21(6), 836–47.

Gillison, F. B., Standage, M., & Skevington, S. M. (2011). Motivation and body-related factors as discriminators of change in adolescents' exercise behaviour profiles. *Journal of Adolescent Health*, 48, 44–51.

Ginis, K., Prapavessis, H., & Haase, A. (2008). The effects of physique-salient and physique non-salient exercise videos on women's body image, self-presentational concerns, and exercise motivation. *Body Image*, 5, 164–72.

Ginis, K., Jung, M., & Gauvin, L. (2003). To see or not to see: Effects of exercising in mirrored environments on sedentary women's feeling states and self-efficacy. *Health Psychology*, 22, 4, 354–61.

Greenleaf, C., McGreer, R., & Parham, H. (2006). Physique attitudes and self-presentational concerns: Exploratory interviews with female group aerobic exercisers and instructors. *Sex Roles*, 54(3–4), 189–99.

Hardy, S. & Grogan, S. (2009). Investigating older adults' influences and motivations to engage in physical activity. *Journal of Health Psychology*, 14, 7, 1036–46.

Hausenblas, H., Brewer, B., & Van Raalte, J. (2004). Self-presentation and exercise. *Journal of Applied Sport Psychology*, 16, 3–18.

Hausenblas, H. A. & Martin, K. A. (2000). Bodies on display: Predictors of social physique anxiety in female aerobic instructors. *Women in Sport and Physical Activity Journal*, 9, 1–14.

Hausenblas, H. A. & Fallon, E. A. (2002). Relationship between body image, exercise behavior, and exercise dependence symptoms. *International Journal of Eating Disorders*, 32, 179–85.

Heywood, S. & McCabe, M. P. (2006). Negative affect as a mediator between body dissatisfaction and extreme weight loss and muscle gain behaviors. *Journal of Health Psychology*, 11(6), 833–44.

Jones, L. W., Sinclair, R. C., Rhodes, R. E., & Courneya, K. S. (2004). Promoting exercise behaviour: An integration of persuasion theories and the theory of planned behaviour. *British Journal of Health Psychology*, 9(4), 505–21.

Katula, J. A., McAuley, E., Mihalko, S. L., & Bane, S. M. (1998). Mirror, mirror on the wall . . . Exercise environment influences on self-efficacy. *Journal of Social Behavior and Personality*, 13, 319–32.

Kiernan, M., Rodin, J., Brownell, K. D., Wilmore, J. H., & Crandall, C. (1992). Relation of level of exercise, age, and weight-cycling history to weight and eating concerns in male and female runners. *Health Psychology*, 11(6), 418–21.

Lantz, C. D., Hardy, C. J., & Ainsworth, B. E. (1997). Social physique anxiety and perceived exercise behavior. *Journal of Sport Behavior*, 20, 83–93.

Lindwall, M. & Lindgren, E. (2005). The effects of a 6-month exercise intervention programme on physical self-perceptions and social physique anxiety in non- physically active adolescent Swedish girls. *Psychology of Sport and Exercise*, 6(6), 643–558.

Markland, D. & Ingledew, D. K. (2007). Exercise participation motives: A self-determination theory perspective. In M. S. Hagger & N. L. D. Chatzisarantis (eds.) *Intrinsic motivation and self-determination in exercise and sport*, pp. 23–34. Champaign, IL: Human Kinetics.

Marquez, D. X. & McAuley, E. (2001). Physique anxiety and self-efficacy influences on perceptions of physical evaluation. *Social Behavior and Personality*, 29, 649–60.

McInman, A. D. & Berger, B. G. (1993). Self-concept and mood changes associated with aerobic dance. *Australian Journal of Psychology*, 45(3), 134–40.

Niven, A., Fawkner, S., Knowles, A. M., Henretty, J., & Stephenson, C. (2009). Social physique anxiety and physical activity in early adolescent girls: The influence of maturation and physical activity motives. *Journal of Sports Sciences*, 27(3), 299–305

Neumark-Sztainer, D. (2009). Preventing obesity and eating disorders in adolescents: What can health care providers do? *Journal of Adolescent Health*, 44(3), 206–13.

Oja, P. (1995). Descriptive epistemology of health-related physical activity and fitness. *Research Quarterly for Exercise and Sport*, 66, 303–12.

Pelegrini, A. & Petroski, E. (2009). Physical inactivity and its association with nutritional status, body image dissatisfaction and sedentary behaviour in adolescents of public schools. *Revisita Paulista de Pediatria*, 27, 4.

Pope, H., Phillips, K., & Olivardia, R. (2000). *The Adonis Complex*. London: Free Press.

Ransdell, L. B., Wells, C. L., Manore, M. M., Swan, P. D., & Corbin, C. B. (1998). Social physique anxiety in postmenopausal women. *Journal of Women & Aging*, 10, 19–39.

Sebire, S. J., Standage, M., & Vansteenkiste, M. (2009). Examining intrinsic versus extrinsic exercise goals: Cognitive, affective, and behavioral outcomes. *Journal of Sport and Exercise Psychology*, 31(2), 189–210.

Smolak, L. & Stein, J. (2006). The relationship of drive for muscularity to sociocultural factors, self-esteem, physical attributes gender role, and social comparison in middle school boys. *Body Image*, 3(2), 121–9.

Stock, N. and Byron-Daniel, J. (in preparation). The effect of acute exercise on body image satisfaction and affect in women.

Strahan, E. J., Wilson, A. E., Cressman, K., & Buote, V. (2006). Comparing to perfection: How cultural norms for appearance affect social comparisons and self-image. *Body Image*, 3, 211–27.

Teixeira, P. J., Going, S. B., Houtkooper, L. B., Cussler, E. C., Metcalfe, L. L., Blew, R. M., *et al.* (2006). Exercise motivation, eating, and body image variables as predictors of weight control. *Medicine & Science in Sports & Exercise*, 38(1), 179–88.

Tiggemann, M., & Williamson, S. (2000). The effect of exercise on body satisfaction and self-esteem as a function of gender and age. *Sex Roles*, 43(1/2), 119–27.

Townsend, D., Byron-Daniel, J., Halliwell, E. & Harcourt, D (submitted). 'I feel happier because I have hope that I can do whatever I want with my body': Exploring the body image of new exercisers.

Treasure, D. C., Lox, C. L., & Lawton, B. R. (1998). Determinants of physical activity in a sedentary obese female population. *Journal of Sport & Exercise Psychology*, 20, 218–24.

Vocks, S., Hechler, T., Rohrig, S., & Legenbauer, T. (2009). Effects of a physical exercise session on state body image: The influence of pre-experimental body dissatisfaction and concerns about weight and shape. *Psychology & Health*, 24(6), 713–28.

Williams, P. A. & Cash, T. F. (2001). Effect of a circuit training program on the body images of students. *International Journal of Eating Disorders*, 30, 75–82.

Zabinski, M. F. Calfas, J. K., Gehrman, C. A., Wilfley, D. E., & Sallis, J. F. (2001). Effects of a physical activity intervention on body image in university seniors: Project GRAD. *Annals of Behavioural Medicine*, 23(4), 247–52.

Zelli, A., Lucidi, F., & Mallia, L. (2010). The relationships among adolescents' drive for muscularity, drive for thinness, doping attitudes, and doping intentions. *Journal of Clinical Sport Psychology*, 4(1), 39–52.

....

CHAPTER 23

UNDERSTANDING THE 'TOO FAT' BODY AND THE 'TOO THIN' BODY: A CRITICAL PSYCHOLOGICAL PERSPECTIVE

....

IRMGARD TISCHNER

HELEN MALSON

INTRODUCTION

....

IN Quentin Blake's children's story, *Patrick*, a young man, Patrick, and two children, Kath and Mick, meet a tinker and his wife.

'Look at our procession' shouted Kath. 'Isn't it fun!' 'How can he enjoy it?' asked the tinker's wife. 'He's very thin and I don't know what to do for him. …. Let me play my violin and see what happens,' said Patrick. So he played a tune, and you see what happened. The tinker

Figure 23.1 *Patrick.* © A. P. Watt on behalf of Quentin Blake.

started to get fatter. He lost his cough, and his cold, and his stomach-ache, and his headache; until he was well and smiling and happy again (Blake, 1970, p. 29).

Under the text is a series of five pictures of an initially slim man, dramatically increasing in girth until in the final picture the now dancing, happy man is positively rotund and might easily be described as obese (Fig. 23.1). This is clearly not a recent publication. How, it might be asked today, could anyone—whether male or female—be happy about such a transformation in body weight and shape? Sure, he was initially perhaps a little thin (for a man) but even at the third picture he's looking 'flabby'. And surely at that final size he's 'grossly corpulent' and heading for, if not already succumbed to, serious ill health?

In *Patrick*, the tinker's weight-gain is both felicitous and magical. In contemporary everyday life such a transformation from slimness to obesity would, rather obviously, not only be experienced and perceived very differently, most likely as an unmitigated disaster rather than a cause for celebration; but it would also in most academic and clinical as well as popular contexts be attributed to 'poor lifestyle choices': to eating (far) too much 'bad food' and 'failing' to exercise. From a critical psychological perspective this scene from *Patrick* is interesting, first, because it highlights a dramatic shift in cultural values and beliefs surrounding fat and thin bodies and, second, because, by relating a story of weight-gain caused only by magic, it further highlights the force of culturally dominant explanations of how people become 'too fat' or indeed 'too thin'. In this chapter our aim is to map out some of this cultural shift. Drawing on a range of interviews and focus groups conducted with 'too fat' and 'too thin' women and men we begin by exploring some key continuities and discontinuities in the cultural values and beliefs accruing around 'too fat' and 'too thin' bodies before then drawing out the ways in which these cultural perceptions shape the regulation and self-regulation of eating in 'too fat' and 'too thin' people.

The political gendered aesthetics of body weight

Since the 1960s, a slim or thin body has been a key signifier of 'femininity' in Western cultures (e.g. Smith, 1990; Bordo, 1993; Malson, 1998; Orbach, 2006).

Slenderness was never the only criterion of feminine attractiveness—being young, white, able-bodied, blond, and blue-eyed have also featured strongly (Bordo, 1993)—but in late 20th- and early 21st-century Western/Westernized contexts, slimness has been an 'essential' and arguably the most vociferously promoted measure of women's (heterosexualized) beauty (Wolf, 1991). The achievement and/or maintenance of this idealized slim/thin body, has therefore, until quite recently, been framed almost exclusively as an issue of gendered aesthetics; and 'dieting', as the primary means of achieving this 'ideal', an issue for women's magazines, its prescriptions on a par with (though arguably rather more important than) 'how to' tips on applying make-up. And, while 'dieting' in pursuit of an attractive slim body—along with other practices of feminine beautification—has frequently been presented as a trivial issue of vanity (Orbach, 1993), it is nevertheless loaded with considerable personal and cultural significance. Numerous feminist scholars have argued that a range of gendered body 'ideals' and practices of body-modification— foot-binding, wearing corsets, stilettos, or make-up, dieting, cosmetic surgery, and so forth—represent ways of subjugating and objectifying women (Coward, 1984; Ussher, 1991; Wolf, 1991; Orbach, 2008). Thus, the idealization and pursuit of thinness has been interpreted as reflecting a cultural repudiation and fear of female flesh (Bordo, 1993) and of girls' and women's needs and desires (Orbach, 1993); as reflecting an infantilization of women and a social requirement that women should both literally and metaphorically take up less space than men (Chernin, 1983); and as a response to the lack of control women in patriarchal cultures have over their lives (Lawrence, 1987). From this perspective thinness and dieting can be seen to be not only about (female) beauty but also about a range of culturally prescribed characteristics of 'proper' heteronormative femininity while, conversely, fatness becomes construed not only as unattractive but as 'failed femininity' (Malson, 1998).

In short, for over half a century slenderness has been imbued with considerable cultural currency as a key index of girls' and women's beauty *and* of feminine subjectivity. Its promotion through the media, the dieting and fashion industries, and everyday discourse, has for a long time been associated with near ubiquitous body dissatisfaction and restrictive dieting amongst women (Polivy & Herman, 1985; Orbach, 1993) and with eating disorders such as anorexia and bulimia (Bordo, 1993; Orbach, 1993, Grogan, 1999; Halliwell et al., 2005; Bordo, 2009). And, as we will discuss further later, whilst body dissatisfaction and dieting have been described as descriptively and prescriptively normative for women (Polivy & Herman, 1985; Wolf, 1991), disordered eating has been viewed primarily as an individual psychopathology somehow caused by (at least in part) and yet distinct from this normative discontent (see Bordo, 1993; Malson & Burns, 2009; Eckermann, 2009). Thus, the thin female body, whilst idealized, is at the same time, if it is deemed 'too thin', also pathologized (cf. Malson & Ussher, 1996; Malson & Swann, 1999; LeBesco, 2009) such that women at both ends of the weight spectrum are marginalized (Swami et al., 2010).

Moralizing 'healthy' and 'unhealthy' body weight

The cultural equations of slimness/thinness with feminized beauty and of fatness with unattractiveness clearly still hold. And, as numerous studies have illustrated, thinness and fatness have and still do accrue numerous meanings—for example, self-denial/gluttony, self-control/self-indulgence, discipline/laziness, self-destruction/self-comforting—in addition to beauty and femininity (e.g. Bordo, 1993; Malson & Burns, 2009). Now, however, with national and global concerns about the alleged health consequences of an 'obesity epidemic', the message that beautiful bodies are slim is further overwritten by a framing of body fat as a health issue.

Research investigating the relationship(s) of body weight to health has produced conflicting findings and numerous authors (Cogan & Ernsberger, 1999; Gard, 2005; Miller, 2005; Campos et al., 2006; LeBesco, 2009) maintain that evidence used to support the notion that a high body weight is a risk factor per se is sparse and based on flawed research. Nevertheless, the mainstream perspective that obesity constitutes a severe health risk is generally accepted as commonsensical truth (Cogan & Ernsberger, 1999; Campos, 2004; Gard, 2005). Hence, health is equated with 'normal' body weight, defined as a body mass index (BMI) of 18–25. And, while non-normative body weights above *or* below that range are thus presented as causing many adverse health conditions (e.g. Saguy & Riley, 2005), the overwhelming emphasis in both government-sponsored and popular health-promotion discourse is on the dangers of overweight not underweight bodies (Campos, 2004; Gard, 2009). As such fat bodies (and weight-gain) are almost invariably presented as (always) unhealthy and thin/slim bodies (and weight-loss) as (always) healthy (Aphramor & Gingras, 2008; LeBesco, 2009; Rice, 2009).

In this context then, while the longer-standing gendered aesthetics and gender power-relations remain in place, the issue of body weight and its management also take on new meanings—of health, responsibility, and good (neo-liberal) citizenship—which apply to everyone regardless of gender, body weight, or any other indices of identity (Malson, 2008, 2009; Markula et al., 2008). Moreover, despite numerous explanations for the causes of overweight and obesity including genetics and environmental factors, in the early 21st century body weight is considered primarily a consequence of an individual's lifestyle choices in respect of dietary intake and exercise and is thus seen as a matter of individual responsibility (e.g. Saguy & Riley, 2005). Based on a simple energy-balance approach, the dictate is most often to 'just eat less and move more' to solve the 'obesity problem'. While lifestyle clearly is important for health, the evidence that 'excess' fat is a simple consequence of poor diet and overeating are highly contested (e.g. Aphramor & Gingras, 2008; Gard, 2009). Thus it has been asserted that the 'war on obesity' is based on the faulty assumptions that

- 'overweight' and 'obesity' are major contributors to morbidity and mortality;
- to be healthy and happy, people have to be thin;

- people can change their weight at will, with long-term sustained weight loss being achievable for everybody;
- dieting works and improves health;
- 'overweight' and 'obese' individuals have no willpower, eat too much, and do not exercise enough. (cf. Cogan & Ernsberger, 1999)

Despite considerable evidence contradicting these assumptions (Campos, 2004; Gard, 2009; Aphramor 2008), weight loss 'dieting' is promoted to entire populations as an efficient way of improving health (Aphramor & Gingras, 2008; LeBesco, 2009). A glance across the magazine shelves of any larger newsagent highlights this cultural prominence. Numerous titles specializing in body transformation are on offer, ranging from slimming magazines such as *Slim at Home* and the official magazines of commercial slimming clubs, which are aimed near-exclusively at women, to those such as *Fitness, Men's Health,* and *Diet and Health* targeting men as well as women, that couch weight loss dieting in broader discourses of health and fitness. As might be expected, slimming magazines tend to feature headlines like 'Lose Fat Fast' and 'Drop a Stone', offering 'real life' accounts of women losing large amounts of weight as a 'guarantee' of 'looking fab' and 'feeling great'. Aimed at women audiences these magazines clearly illustrate the intertwining of the newer healthist framing of weight loss with the longer-standing dictum that 'slim is feminine and beautiful and fat is ugly and repulsive' (Germov & Williams, 1999; LeBesco & Braziel, 2001). Those magazines targeting a mixed or male audience tend, as noted earlier, to emphasize health maximization over appearance enhancement in promoting weight loss diets. At the same time, however, pressures on men to achieve a particular look are increasing with the 'ideal' masculine body being presented as tall, strong, muscular, and lean (see, e.g. Frith & Gleeson, 2004; Bell & McNaughton, 2007; Monaghan, 2007; Gill 2008a, b; Monaghan, 2008). Being a 'fat bastard' is no longer a culturally accepted option on aesthetic as well as health-related grounds (cf. Monaghan, 2008) so that body dissatisfaction amongst boys and men is increasing and men as well as women are now engaged in 'body projects' that are perhaps as much about gendered aesthetics and the regulation of normative gender identity as they are about health (Gill et al., 2005; Tiggemann et al., 2008).

The promotion of slenderness and dieting implies that achieving or maintaining a medically sanctioned body size (and thereby health) is a matter of individual responsibility. This neo-liberal framing of health/weight (as amenable to modification and as an individual's responsibility) interfaces with the cultural idea of the body as malleable and as a project to be worked on in pursuit of a 'better look' rather than as a natural object (Malson, 2008). As such, bodies become constituted and experienced as always flawed but always perfectible—in terms of maximizing both health and aesthetics—and indeed the pursuit of this 'perfection' has become a normative '*duty*' of good citizenship *and* 'correct' embodiment of gender (Featherstone, 1991; Lupton, 1996).

In this context 'correct' body-weight management becomes a highly charged moral imperative articulated in the collective knowingness that 'the fat subject is lazy, not willing to commit to change or to the dictates of healthy living' (Murray, 2005, p. 155). The 'fat' body has thus come to signify amongst other things, a failed body project, a lack of self-discipline, laziness, and irresponsibility (Lupton, 1996; cf. Murray, 2005; Throsby, 2007) and a failing of gender (Gill et al., 2005; Gill, 2008a; Monaghan, 2008) whilst the thin/slim body signifies the obverse of all this. That these moral values are read off 'fat' and 'thin' bodies is not only evident in discourses of health and health promotion, but also reflected by research findings documenting the considerable and widespread discrimination to which 'fat' individuals are subjected (e.g. Puhl & Brownell, 2003; Schwartz et al., 2003; Blaine & Williams, 2004; Swami et al., 2010).

POLICING THE 'TOO FAT' AND THE 'TOO THIN'

The investment many people have in the notion that being slim is inherently good was borne out in a recent web-blog following an article by Lucy Aphramor, promoting the 'Health at Every Size' (HAES) paradigm (Aphramor, 2009). Numerous readers felt provoked to defend the slim equals good dictum, and probably their own efforts to stay slim, with statements such as:

I can see how they're judged, but why is that such a bad thing? Being judgemental is only wrong, if you make bad judgements. Equating obesity with physical laziness and greed is an accurate judgement for the overwhelming majority of obese people. What is wrong with telling the truth and saying that obesity is unattractive and for many an indicator of undesirable personality traits? HAES is a ridiculous concept pandering to the inability of a minority to take some responsibility for themselves. (Danot, in web-blog following Aphramor, 2009).

As the following interview quotes illustrate, this culturally prevalent judgement of fat people as morally and aesthetically repellent clearly shapes the lived experiences of those deemed 'too fat':

Emily: If, if *I* didn't feel other people looking at me and thinking 'yuk' (.) then I would go [swimming] / I: hmm / yes, it is that simple actually, isn't it?

Alli: I've come home from places before (.) I've gone to parties, and I am talking about 10 years ago now but I've gone to parties and I remember I went to the loo and I caught a glimpse of myself in the mirror and uh thought oh God you're just a ugly monstrosity and you know just burst into tears and went home.

Negative judgements based on body weight, however, are not reserved for 'fat' people: they are directed at individuals at both ends of the body weight spectrum. As noted earlier, while slim/thin bodies, particularly for girls and women, are ubiquitously idealized, the 'too thin' body is pathologized and denigrated. Thus whilst the 'anorexic' body is often envied (Hsu, 1989), derogatory stereotypes of 'anorexia' as self-inflicted and of 'anorexic' girls as spoilt, vain, self-obsessed fashion-victims also circulate (Malson, 2008; Katzman & Lee, 1997). In the interview extracts which follow, Nicky talks about doctors viewing her through this derogatory lens while Denise distances herself from her diagnosis for this same reason:

Nicky: They [doctors] think it's to do with vanity and the media /H: right/ but it's so much more deeper than that /H: right (inaud.)/ Like it's called the slimmer's disease which is a load of rubbish anyway.

Denise: I would definitely not call myself anorexic [...] So when people say to me: Oh you're anorexic, or, you're in the anorexic unit, /H: right/ it just makes my back prickle. I hate it. /H: mm right / I really do. I think it's uhh (.) in a way it's because even in *my mind*, even though *I've* been with people who who are, who would call themselves anorexics, /H: mm/ still in my mind is the old stereotype of (.) what *the media* portray as (.) as anorexic, / H: right/ sort of um self-inflicted, spoilt brat, /H: right/ selfish, um (.) unnecessary. You know: Well why can't you just eat, / H: right mm/ things like that. Um (.) and other people sort of see it as pathetic and that.

Both 'too fat' and 'too thin' bodies, then, are highly scrutinized and judged negatively. Whilst the 'fat' body is always denigrated, however, the scrutiny of the 'too thin' body swings between idealization and pathologization. Celebrity magazines praise female celebrities for their slenderness and weight loss but at the same time often berate them for being 'anorexic'; media coverage of Victoria Beckham being a prime example of this vacillation.

Regulating the eating of 'too fat' and 'too thin' people

There is, then, a complex web of value-laden meanings, produced by dominant cultural discourses of food, health, gender, and appearance, which converge on 'too fat' and 'too thin' individuals. The consequences of this for judging those deemed 'too fat' or 'too thin' are reflected in the following extracts:

Lynn: I thought people must look at me and think I'm, that person's mental uh like, you know. Like sort of walk round town and you'll see someone who's schizophrenic, you know, with all the homeless people and everything. And I'd think they'd look at me and they'd think I'm like that /Jane: mm/ so I stopped going out /H: mm/ so that people wouldn't see me.

Scrumpz: I suppose (.) just sit there and eat all day (.) that's what people think /I: hmm/ so, which isn't true /I: Hmm/ (.) which then gives you a complex when you go out, if you *do* go out to eat, it sort of, well me personally I sit there and I'm looking around, 'who's looking at me, who's looking at me' /I: hmmm/ uhm, I sort of avoid eating in front of people.

Blade: It's like if you're uhm, I could take you shopping now and if we went up to uhm a a queue with all slim people in, and I come up with my trolley, they would actually see what I was buying / I: hmm / to prove to theirselves 'that's why she's fat' /I: mhm/ and you know that that do, you know, nobody up to now said anything /I: mhm/ uhm but you can tell that they're doing that look.

The consequences of cultural 'knowing' about body weight are clearly apparent in Lynn's reflection on her pathologized thinness and in Scrumpz's and Blade's comments about their denigrated fatness. Lynn felt she was judged as 'mental' for being 'too thin' and thus stops going out whilst Scrumpz and Blade talk about being subjected to stares and monitoring. Scrumpz represents the experience of going out for a meal as affecting her as other people's opinion of 'fat' individuals 'give you a complex' which she sees as stopping her from eating out whilst Blade talks about being monitored and judged by 'slim people' while shopping for food. However, whilst Blade constitutes 'slim people' as the policing agents, many 'fat' participants included themselves in this social monitoring:

Jenny: I think that a fat person walking down the road eating a doughnut (.) gets more attention than a thin person walking down the road eating a doughnut /I: mm/ um, and (.) and and and would get more attention from *me* as well and that's where I feel so conflicted because I, I feel fat and happy or whatever (.) but I would (.) I guess I wouldn't ever want to be smaller than a size 16, I can't see /I: mm/ I can't really see see that (.) but I'd I'd quite like to be maybe maybe I just want to be a size 18.

Much as Denise, quoted earlier, talks about subscribing to derogatory stereotypes of 'anorexics', Jenny, as a 'fat' woman, positions herself alongside others as actively critical of other people's fatness. Although she also expresses a conflict between her experience of herself as 'fat and happy' and her judgemental gaze, she nevertheless seems unable to extricate herself from dominant discourses that construct 'fat' individuals as unhealthy, uncontrolled overeaters—a construction which is again apparent in the following quotes:

Rich: I'm, I'm quite self-conscious about eating in public / I: mhm / (. .) uhm (.) ech, not so bad with restaurants and things like that but if, but nearer the classic thing is when there's something like a buffet or something like that / I: mhm / I always take great care not to, not to take too much /I: mhm/ because I feel self-conscious (.) you know, that I'm fulfilling a stereotype /I: mhm/ you know, that if I, if I *if, you know I would really love a plate full of stuff* but, yeah, will, uh, a a a mound of of things, but on the other hand it would just fulfil the stereotype.

Don: Yeah, now that you mentioned that uh, that does affect me uhm, I often have something to eat before I go to a buffet here /I: mhm/ so I don't appear greedy /I: mhm/ uh, because I would like to have lots of food and I like eating nice food, I would like to have lots of food, but (.) uhm like, like you said, I, I (.) beware putting ideas into people's heads that uh, you know, he's having a lot and, look, he's quite big, or (obese), so I'd often have something to eat before I went to buffet so I didn't kind of uh appear as greedy as I was, *so to speak.*

In the preceding excerpts from a focus group with 'large' men (Tischner, 2009, 2010) participants construe their eating as self-regulated in response to others' judgemental gazes. To avoid 'fulfil[ling] the stereotype' of fat people as gluttonous they either avoid eating in public altogether or consciously restrict the amount of food they eat in public. In the following quote this construction and regulation of fat people is extended to manifest itself as a cultural prohibition against fat people eating in public view.

Jacqueline: I don't know it's probably a stroke of paranoia and also *maybe* it is happening, but I always feel that when I go in a restaurant, my partner who is also big that we get put nearer the back so we are not seen near the front of the restaurant to be eating food as two big people /I: hmm/ and that seems to have happened quite a lot you know.

Jacqueline's being seated out of sight at the back of restaurants can be understood as an act designed to avoid a public view not only of fat people but also of (their assumed) uncontrolled eating. The cultural horror of 'uncontrolled eating' is undoubtedly associated now most strongly with those deemed 'too fat'. But it also has a considerably longer genealogy. A moral requirement to control bodily desires can be traced through from Christian practices of, for example, fasting and self-flagellation to the Cartesian dualist view of personhood that divides mind, will, or spirit from body and that continues to inform a plethora of Western cultural ideas and practices (Bordo, 1993; Malson, 1998). Within this framework the body becomes constituted and experienced as alien, eruptive, and disruptive: it requires the mind's control. Eating thus appears as a bodily and therefore dangerous, alien desire, as the mind's failure to properly control the body. This cultural image of eating as uncontrolled bodily desire which underpins Jacqueline being seated at the back of restaurants can also be seen to mobilize 'eating disordered' practices such as self-starvation and binge/purging:

Nicky: I know that you have to eat to live but um (.) when at the time it seemed like an awful thing to do /H: mm/ and re' like a disgusting thing to do.

Zoe: I would just run into the like kitchen and like four o'clock in the morning, like have a bowl of cereal, like *two* muffins and like toast, like and would eat so much and then I couldn't like, I felt like I had eaten half of it before I'd even realised what I was doing. You know /H: mm/ and I was like, you know, this is so weird [...] my body was just eating it before my mind could /H: could think about it/ was awake enough to stop it from doing it.

Michelle: A cream cake can be really threatening and frightening [...] I know that food's got a lot of power over *me* because it I start (.) if I start eating and sort of (.) if I don't have that control then I could quite easily (.) blow it.

Jane: I just wanted to rid of all this weight an' /H: right/ (.) it made me feel I was better cos there was less fat /H: mm/ as if there was less/H: mm/ less bad [...] I just wanted to get down to like a stone or something.

The moralistic construction of bodies as eruptive and requiring control, and of eating as therefore a disgusting bodily urge and as a failure of the mind's control can, we would argue, be viewed as a culturally embedded understanding which contributes to the production of *both* anti-fat discrimination and 'eating disordered' practices. It is part of the cultural palimpsest behind Rick's and Don's avoidance of eating in public, Jacqueline's being seated at the back of restaurants, and the cultural sanction against 'a fat person walking down the road eating a doughnut'. But it is also behind Nicky's and Michelle's self-starvation and Zoe's experience of binge/purging. In popular, academic, and clinical discourses, uncontrolled eating is clearly associated with fat bodies, not thin bodies, but the abject cultural imagining of uncontrolled eating is implicated in the experiences and practices of those deemed 'too thin' as well as those deemed 'too fat'.

CONCLUSION

To summarize, body weight represents one of the most culturally significant aspects of appearance. While 'too fat' bodies are clearly denigrated and 'too thin' bodies idealized as well as pathologized, both are imbued with a plethora of cultural meanings relating to aesthetics, gender identities, moral worth, health, good citizenship, and so forth. As we have sought to illustrate, this 'collective knowingness' (Murray, 2005) about body weight significantly shapes the lived experiences and practices of those deemed 'too fat' or 'too thin'. And, in the context of the early 21st century where appearance is so vociferously prioritized, where body weight is so prominently represented as *the* index of health and health is presented as a matter of individual responsibility, this matrix of meanings accruing to body weight undoubtedly also shape, though less dramatically, the experiences and practices of most individuals regardless of their BMI. Messages that urge us all to maintain or strive for medically sanctioned body weights and watch what we eat are now near-ubiquitous but are, we have argued, also potentially harmful. They reproduce the commonsensical 'truth' that thinness and weight loss are inherently good and thus occlude their potential detrimental effects not only of fat-phobic discrimination but also of, for example, malnutrition, reduced bone density (Aphramor, 2008), deterioration in mental health (Kiefer et al., 2000), and disordered eating practices (Bordo, 1993; Wooley & Garner, 1994; Austin, 1999; Burns & Gavey, 2004; Rich & Evans, 2005). As Burns and Gavey (2008) assert, the discourses that construct any weight gain as potentially dangerous and weight loss as always healthy also produce a rationale that allows for problematic dietary practices like purging to be constructed as healthy. As such, the discourses intended to promote healthy lifestyles may also mobilize practices that can be (mentally and physically) harmful to individuals of any size.

This argument that diets and weight loss can in fact be harmful has led to an alternative approach to health promotion: HAES (Miller, 2005; Miller & Jacob, 2001; Liebman, 2005; Aphramor & Gingras, 2008) which maintains that health is possible for people of any size and calls for a focus on increasing health by promoting healthy eating (not to be confused with weight loss diets) and exercise, regardless of body weight. Thus, rather than focusing on promoting weight loss for the 'overweight' and 'obese', HAES seeks to promote healthier lifestyles (rather than weight loss) for all. The approach thus avoids the automatic construction of 'fat' people as health villains and at the same time recognizes the possibility of unhealthy lifestyles amongst thin/slim people. Thus, in contrast with weight-focused health promotion, HAES also avoids sanctioning problematic weight-loss practices as beneficial since it rejects the notion that 'slim is always good and fat always bad'. It thereby also disrupts our 'cultural knowingness' about body weight where gendered, aesthetic, moralistic, and health-related values all converge to produce the fat body as abject and which are arguably re-articulated and endorsed in contemporary mainstream health promotion (Gard, 2005; Markula et al., 2008; LeBesco, 2009). The HAES approach may provide a solution to the seeming dilemmas of untangling the conflicting and complex evidence regarding the relationship(s) between health and weight (see Gard, 2009) and of promoting health without creating the iatrogenic effects of fat-phobic discrimination, 'disordered eating', and widespread body dissatisfaction and distress outlined earlier. The HAES representation of health as independent of body weight and its emphasis on 'healthy lifestyles' (for people of any size) rather than body weight will no doubt have little effect on aesthetic imperatives to be slim or on many other cultural values accruing to body weight, but it may at least mitigate some of the pernicious ways in which 'cultural knowing' about body weight shapes people's lives.

REFERENCES

Aphramor, L. (2008). Weight and health: Changing attitudes and behaviours. *Health Psychology Update*, 17(1), 42–5.

Aphramor, L. (2009). All shapes and Sizes. *The Guardian*, 9 May. http://www.guardian.co.uk/commentisfree/2009/may/09/obesity-weight-health

Aphramor, L. & Gingras, J. (2008). Sustaining imbalance – evidence of neglect in the pursuit of nutritional health. In S. Riley, M. Burns, H. Frith, S. Wiggins, & P. Markula (eds.) *Critical Bodies—Representations, Identities and Practices of Weight and Body Management*, pp. 155–74. Basingstoke: Palgrave Macmillan.

Austin, S. B. (1999). Fat, loathing and public health: The complicity of science in a culture of disordered eating. *Culture, Medicine and Psychiatry*, 23(2), 245–68.

Bell, K. & McNaughton, D. (2007). Feminism and the invisible fat man. *Body & Society*, 13(1), 107–31.

Blaine, B. & Williams, Z. (2004). Belief in the controllability of weight and attributions to prejudice among heavyweight women. *Sex Roles*, 51(1–2), 79–84.

Blake, Q. (1970). *Patrick*. Harmondsworth: Puffin.

Bordo, S. (1993). *Unbearable Weight, Feminism, Western Culture, and the Body*. Berkeley, CA: University of California Press.

Bordo, S. (2009). Not just 'a white girl's thing': The changing face of food and body image problems. In H. Malson & M. Burns (eds.) *Critical Feminist Approaches to Eating Dis/Orders*, pp. 46–60. London: Routledge.

Burns, M. & Gavey, N. (2008). Dis/orders of weight control: bulimic and/or 'healthy weight' practices. In S. Riley, M. Burns, H. Frith, S. Wiggins, & P. Markula (eds.) *Critical Bodies—Representations, Identities and Practices of Weight and Body Management*, pp. 139–54. Basingstoke: Palgrave Macmillan.

Burns, M. & Gavey, N. (2004). 'Healthy weight' at what cost? 'Bulimia' and a discourse of weight control. *Journal of Health Psychology*, 9(4), 549–65.

Campos, P. (2004). *The Obesity Myth*. Camberwell: Viking (Penguin Group).

Campos, P., Saguy, A., Ernsberger, P., Oliver, E., & Gaesser, G. (2006). The epidemiology of overweight and obesity: public health crisis or moral panic? *International journal of epidemiology*, 35(1), 55–60.

Chernin, K. (1983). *Womansize: the tyranny of slenderness*. London: Women's Press.

Cogan, J. C. & Ernsberger, P. (1999). Dieting, weight, and health: Reconceptualizing research and policy. *Journal of Social Issues*, 55(2), 187–205.

Coward, R. (1984). *Female desire*. London: Paladin.

Eckermann, L. (2009). Theorising self-starvation: Beyond risk, governmentality and the normalizing gaze. In H. Malson & M. Burns (eds.) *Critical Feminist Approaches to Eating Dis/Orders*, pp. 9–21. London: Routledge.

Featherstone, M. (1991). The body in consumer culture. In M. Featherstone, M. Hepworth, & B. S. Turner (eds.) *The Body: social process and cultural theory*, pp. 170–96. London: Sage.

Frith, H. & Gleeson, K. (2004). Clothing and embodiment: Men managing body image and appearance. *Psychology of Men & Masculinity*, 5(1), 40–8.

Gard, M. (2009). Understanding obesity by understanding desire. In H. Malson & M. Burns (eds.) *Critical Feminist Approaches to Eating Dis/Orders*, pp. 35–45. London: Routledge.

Gard, M. (2005). *The obesity epidemic: science, morality and ideology*. London: Routledge.

Germov, J. & Williams, L. (1999). Dieting women. In J. Sobal and D. Maurer (eds.) *Weighty Issues*, p. 117. New York: Walter de Gruyter, Inc.

Gill, R. (2008a). Body talk: Negotiating body image and masculinity. In S. Riley, M. Burns, H. Frith, S. Wiggins, & P. Markula (eds.) *Critical Bodies—Representations, Identities and Practices of Weight and Body Management*, pp. 101–16. Basingstoke: Palgrave Macmillan.

Gill, R. (2008b). Empowerment/sexism: Figuring female sexual agency in contemporary advertising. *Feminism & Psychology*, 18(1), 35–60.

Gill, R., Henwood, K., & McLean, C. (2005). Body projects and the regulation of normative masculinity. *Body & Society*, 11(1), 37–62.

Grogan, S. (1999). *Body image: understanding body dissatisfaction in men, women and children*. London: Routledge.

Halliwell, E., Dittmar, H., & Howe, J. (2005). The impact of advertisements featuring ultra-thin or average-size models on women with a history of eating disorders. *Journal of Community & Applied Social Psychology*, 15(5), 406–13.

Hsu, L. K. G. (1989). The gender gap in eating disorders: why are the eating disorders more common among women? *Clinical Psychology Review*, 9, 393–407.

Katzman, M. A. & Lee, S. (1997). Beyond body image: the integration of feminist and transcultural theories in the understanding of self starvation. *International Journal of Eating Disorders*, 22(4), 385–94.

Kiefer, I., Leitner, B., Bauer, R., & Rieder, A. (2000). Body weight: the male and female perception. *Sozial- und Praventivmedizin*, 45(6), 274–8.

Lawrence, M. (ed.) (1987). *Fed up and hungry: women, oppression and food.* London: Women's Press.

LeBesco, K. (2009). Weight management, good health and the will to normality. In H. Malson and M. Burns (eds.) *Critical Feminist Approaches to Eating Dis/orders*, pp. 146–55. Hove: Routledge.

LeBesco, K. & Braziel, J. E. (2001). Editors' Introduction. In J. E. Braziel and K. LeBesco (eds.) *Bodies out of bounds: fatness and transgression*, pp. 1–15. Berkeley, CA: University of California Press.

Liebman, M. (2005). Promoting healthy weight: lessons learned from WIN the Rockies and other key studies. *Journal of Nutrition Education & Behavior*, 37(Suppl 2), S95–100.

Lupton, D. (1996). *Food, the body and the self.* London: Sage.

Malson, H. (2009). Appearing to disappear - postmodern femininities and self-starved subjectivities. In H. Malson & M. Burns (eds.) *Critical Feminist Approaches to Eating Dis/Orders*, pp. 135–45. London: Routledge.

Malson, H. (2008). Deconstructing un/healthy body-weight and weight management. In S. Riley, M. Burns, H. Frith, S. Wiggins & P. Markula (eds.) *Critical Bodies—Representations, Identities and Practices of Weight and Body Management*, pp. 27–42. Basingstoke: Palgrave Macmillan.

Malson, H. (1998). *The thin woman: feminism, post-structuralism and the social psychology of anorexia nervosa.* New York: Routledge.

Malson, H. & Burns, M. (2009). Re-theorising the slash of dis/order: An introduction to critical feminist approaches to eating dis/orders. In H. Malson and M. Burns (eds.) *Critical Feminist Approaches to Eating Dis/Orders*, pp. 1–16. London: Routledge, London.

Malson, H. & Swann, C. (1999). Prepared for consumption: (dis)orders of eating and embodiment. *Journal of Community & Applied Social Psychology*, 9(6), 397–405.

Malson, H. & Ussher, J. (1996). Body poly-texts: discourses of the anorexic body. *Journal of Community & Applied Social Psychology*, 6(4), 267–80.

Markula, P., Burns, M., & Riley, S. (2008). Introducing critical bodies: Representations, identities and practices of weight and body management. In S. Riley, M. Burns, H. Frith, S. Wiggins, & P. Markula (eds.) *Critical Bodies*, pp. 1–22. Basingstoke: Palgrave Macmillan.

Miller, W. C. (2005). The weight-loss-at-any-cost environment: how to thrive with a health-centered focus. *Journal of Nutrition Education and Behavior*, 37(Suppl. 2), S89–93.

Miller, W. C. & Jacob, A. V. (2001). The health at any size paradigm for obesity treatment: the scientific evidence. *Obesity Reviews*, 2(1), 37–45.

Monaghan, L. F. (2008). *Men and the War on Obesity.* London: Routledge.

Monaghan, L. F. (2007). Body mass index, masculinities and moral worth: men's critical under-standings of appropriate weight-for-height. *Sociology of health & illness*, 29(4), 584–609.

Murray, S. (2005). (Un/Be)Coming out? Rethinking fat politics. *Social Semiotics*, 15(2), 154.

Orbach, S. (1993). *Hunger strike: the anorectic's struggle as a metaphor for our age* (New edn.). London: Penguin.

Orbach, S. (2006). *Fat is a feminist issue: the anti-diet guide; Fat is a feminist issue II: conquering compulsive eating* (New edn.) London: Arrow.

Orbach, S. (2008). *Bodies.* London: Profile.

Polivy, H. & Herman, C. P. (1985). Dieting and binging. *American Psychologist*, 40(2), 193–201.

Puhl, R. M. & Brownell, K. D. (2003). Psychosocial origins of obesity stigma: toward changing a powerful and pervasive bias. *Obesity Reviews*, 4(4), 213–27.

Rice, C. (2009). How big girls become fat girls: The cultural production of problem eating and physical inactivity. In H. Malson & M. Burns (eds.) *Critical Feminist Approaches to Eating Dis/Orders*, pp. 97–109. London: Routledge.

Rich, E. & Evans, J. (2005). 'Fat ethics'—The obesity discourse and body politics. *Social Theory & Health*, 3(4), 341–58.

Saguy, A. C. & Riley, K. W. (2005). Weighing both sides: morality, mortality, and framing contests over Obesity. *Journal of Health Politics& Policy & Law*, 30(5), 869–921.

Schwartz, M. B., Chambliss, H. O., Brownell, K. D., Blair, S. N., & Billington, C. (2003). Weight bias among health professionals specializing in obesity. *Obesity Research*, 11(9), 1033–9.

Smith, D. E. (1990). *Texts, facts, and femininity: exploring the relations of ruling*. London: Routledge.

Swami, V., Pietschnig, J., Stieger, S., Tovée, M. J., & Voracek, M. (2010). An investigation of weight bias against women and its associations with individual difference factors. *Body Image*, 7(3), 194–9.

Throsby, K. (2007). "How could you let yourself get like that?": Stories of the origins of obesity in accounts of weight loss surgery. *Social Science & Medicine*, 65, 1561–71.

Tiggemann, M., Martins, Y., & Churchett, L. (2008). Beyond muscles: Unexplored parts of men's body image. *Journal of Health Psychology*, 13(8), 1163–72.

Tischner, I. (2010). Dissertation abstracts and summaries: The experience of 'being large': A critical psychological exploration of 'fat' embodiment. *Body Image*, 7(4). http://about.elsevier.com/bodyimage/Vol7Iss4/BI-7–4–0001/index.html.

Tischner, I. (2009). The Experience of 'Being Large: A Critical Psychological Exploration of 'Fat' Embodiment. PhD (unpublished thesis), University of the West of England, Bristol.

Ussher, J. (1991). *Women's madness: Misogyny or mental illness?* Hemel Hempstead: Harvester Wheatsheaf.

Wolf, N. (1991). *The beauty myth*. London: Vintage.

Wooley, C. S. & Garner, D. M. (1994). Controversies in management: Dietary treatments for obesity are ineffective. *British Medical Journal*, 309, 655.

CHAPTER 24

APPEARANCE CONCERNS, DIETARY RESTRICTION, AND DISORDERED EATING

VICTORIA LAWSON

THE evidence for appearance concerns as one of the variables that can mediate the development of eating disorders is compelling and there is now an established body of literature which explores this (e.g. Gowers & Shore, 2001; Stice & Shaw, 2002; Grogan, 2008). Eating disorders are relatively rare, with prevalence estimates at approximately 2.7% of the UK population for anorexia nervosa and bulimia nervosa (National Institute for Health and Clinical Excellence, 2004). However, disordered eating behaviours and concerns about appearance in relation to weight are not limited to diagnosed patients and there is evidence that some degree of disordered eating is widespread in the general population. This is perhaps not surprising given the entrenched cultural idealization of thinness in Western society as a marker of attractiveness, success, and health and commonly accepted myths about the malleability of our bodies, which are strongly supported by the media and a multi-million pound diet industry. These disordered eating behaviours and concerns about appearance in relation to weight can have consequences for both physical and psychological health that in some cases are recognized as severe. Those working in the field have highlighted the devastating effects of weight-related appearance concerns, eloquently critiquing the social constructions that control women through their body size (Orbach, 1983) and have challenged beliefs that body size should in any way determine self-worth.

To further complicate this picture, since the 1990s there has been a dramatic increase in the number of people in the developed world who are overweight/obese (Zimmerman, 2011) alongside a very significant change in the environment, particularly in relation to the variety and availability of food and more sedentary lifestyles. There is mounting scientific evidence of the links between obesity, physical ill health, and increased mortality, including physiological evidence relating to how central adipose (fat) cells may function in hormone secretion and inflammatory regulation—hence their link to type 2 diabetes, heart disease, and cancer (Cross-Government Obesity Unit, 2009). In addition to risks associated with physical health, the pervasive nature of weight stigma in Western society towards those who are overweight presents psychological and social risks to individuals (Puhl & Heuer, 2009). Given that the majority of the adult population in England have been classified by their body mass index (BMI) as either overweight (38.3%) or obese (23%), the increased physical and psychological health risks cannot be ignored (NHS Information Centre, 2009).

There is an inherent tension between how to raise awareness of the potential health risks of overweight and obesity whilst avoiding the reinforcement of appearance stereotypes and the associated potential for psychological distress. This is particularly difficult given the responsibility, indeed blame, placed on people who are overweight or obese, with weight gain widely viewed as a wholly individual problem, rather than one situated in a complex and often stigmatizing social context. The interactions between individual and societal factors can be illustrated by the (albeit somewhat contradictory) evidence surrounding certain eating behaviours, particularly dietary restriction, occurring as a response to weight-related appearance concerns and the dilemma of how those interested in the promotion of health should encourage realistic *and* healthy responses to being overweight. In considering the role that appearance plays in this debate this chapter will consider:

- Appearance concerns and perceptions of body size in people without a diagnosed eating disorder.
- The challenges to both psychological and physical health posed by the environment.
- The links between weight-related appearance concerns and disordered eating.
- How to raise awareness of the potential physical health risks of overweight/obesity without fuelling appearance concerns and/or using stigmatizing appearance-related messages.

This chapter discusses research that often defines weight in terms of healthy, overweight and obese according to BMI. This measurement needs to be treated with a degree of caution as it was originally developed as an epidemiological measurement tool of population based data, not as a measure of individual overweight. For further discussion of this issue see Tischner and Malson (Chapter 23, this volume), and the National Obesity Observatory (2009).

APPEARANCE CONCERNS AND PERCEPTIONS
OF BODY SIZE IN PEOPLE WITHOUT
A DIAGNOSED EATING DISORDER

Weight-related appearance concerns can affect anyone, regardless of actual body size: people who are underweight can have 'fear of fat' (Russell, 1979), if in a healthy weight range they can still feel overweight and be keen to lose weight, and if over-weight they can be harshly self-judgemental. At a clinical level, appearance concerns, also known as body dysmorphia, are defined in the Diagnostic and Statistical Manual of Mental Disorders (DSM) IV as a 'preoccupation with an imagined or slight defect in appearance that causes significant distress such as clinical depression, anxiety or suicidal thoughts' (Frances et al., 2000, p. 468). This can be related to any aspect of body dissatisfaction (not only weight) and such self views are rooted in both psychological and social constructions. In relation to weight-related appearance concerns, this usually involves a distorted evaluation of body size, a negative evaluation of one's own size and a discrepancy between current and ideal body size (Grogan, 2008), and can disrupt perceptions, thoughts and behaviours, as is often the case for people with anorexia and bulimia nervosa. Both the preoccupation with appearance and attempts to achieve the 'ideal' body size can result in anxiety, low self-esteem, feelings of failure and eating disorders. However, these processes and symptoms can also exist in the non-clinical population and there is a need to safeguard the physical and psychological health of people who are underweight, healthy weight, or overweight but who are restricting their dietary intake in an unhealthy way, as well as the health of people who are overweight, yet unaware that they may need to modify their lifestyle to reduce potential health risks.

Much of the research on eating disorders has focused on those identified as having a clinical condition, the majority of whom are girls and young women, either in a healthy weight range or underweight. These findings do not necessarily apply to a more general population, many of whom are at least moderately overweight. Levels of weight concern in the general adult population have been measured using population-based cross-sectional studies. These have highlighted the prevalence of a significant misperception between perceived and actual body size. This misperception is bidirectional with healthy weight/underweight participants identifying themselves as overweight but also overweight/obese participants identifying themselves as being a healthy weight.

In a study of 16,720 adults, 34% of women and 25% of men who were a healthy weight identified themselves as overweight (Yaemsiri et al., 2011). Not surprisingly, many participants who overestimated their body size also wanted to weigh less, but more surprisingly, 66% of all the women in the study who were a healthy weight wanted to weigh less, regardless of whether they had identified themselves as overweight (compared to 12% of the men). This suggests a level of concern that bears much more relation to appearance than health. Similar studies have found a smaller but still significant trend for healthy weight participants, particularly women, to perceive themselves as overweight (Johnson et al., 2008; Raheman & Berenson, 2010).

In addition to the psychological consequences of these perceptions, these findings have potentially serious physical health implications since people who are currently a healthy weight and who overestimate their body size are significantly more likely to report using unhealthy weight control behaviours such as diet pills and excessive restraint, as well smoking more cigarettes to suppress their appetite (Rahman & Berenson, 2010). From these and other studies, there appears to be a social patterning to weight concern and subsequent behaviours, predominantly characterized by gender, ethnicity, age, and socioeconomic status (SES). In particular, higher levels of weight concern associated with varying degrees of disordered eating such as dietary restriction are seen amongst adolescent girls and women from higher SES groups (see Wardle et al., 2004; Gavin et al., 2010).

Conversely, underestimation of weight is common amongst some participants who are overweight. In the Yaemsiri et al. study, 23% women and 48% of men who were overweight or obese incorrectly identified themselves as a healthy weight. This misperception is supported by Rahman and Berenson (2010) in whose study of a sample of 2,224 women aged 18–25, 23% of those who were overweight or obese incorrectly classified themselves as being a healthy weight. Similarly in a UK longitudinal study of 1,836 adults in the general population, 25% of people who were overweight or obese categorized themselves as being a healthy weight (Johnson et al., 2008). These are somewhat surprising findings, given the high profile public health campaigns about the impact of weight and the media fascination with body size. This underestimation of weight also appears to be increasing, with a small but significant increase in the prevalence of this misperception. Johnson et al. noted an increase of 6% from the previous data collection point 8 years earlier, despite an actual increase in overweight and obesity in the UK of approximately 10% (NHS Information Centre, 2009). The authors suggest that this increase in misperception might in part be due to social comparison processes; as overweight and obesity become more common, individuals may no longer perceive themselves as overweight compared with the rest of the population.

On one level, this misperception could be taken as an encouraging reduction in levels of weight-related appearance concern for approximately a quarter of people who are overweight or obese, and perhaps might even suggest a low incidence of weight stigma experiences within this group. However, this underestimation of overweight and obesity is potentially problematical from a physical health point of view, as people may be less likely to view weight-related health messages as personally relevant and less motivated to make changes in eating and activity behaviours (Kuk et al., 2009).

The Challenges to Both Psychological and Physical Health Posed by the Environment

In recent years there have been dramatic changes to the food and activity environment in the West. A huge variety of highly palatable, energy dense foods have become available at a lower cost, alongside increasingly sedentary work and leisure activities, resulting in a so called obesogenic environment (Swinburn et al., 1999). As a consequence, the environment has become much more challenging for people with weight-related appearance concerns and associated unhealthy eating behaviours as it provides a higher likelihood of weight gain with less opportunity for control. If this situation is internalized as an individual (rather than an environmental) problem, both psychological and physical consequences are likely to result. Similarly, people who are overweight or obese now have more opportunity to gain rather than to lose weight. There is mixed to poor evidence for psychological causes being the main driver for overeating in the general population. Instead, passive overconsumption can be seen, at least in part, as a response to substantial changes in the environment including aggressive marketing by the food industry (Zimmerman, 2011), and this behaviour that has become normalized over time. Overeating can be viewed as a direct response to a deregulated food industry and ubiquitous advertising messages that encourage us to eat to reward ourselves or others, to celebrate, to treat ourselves when happy, when sad or when bored. In such an environment it could be argued that some form of personal dietary restriction might be a necessary and indeed healthy response to a culture that is increasingly orientated around food (Tillatson, 2003) and there is a need for people whose health is potentially at risk due to their weight to be aware of this.

The Links between Weight-Related Appearance Concerns and Disordered Eating

Within a weight-related appearance concerns framework, dietary restriction or changes to other eating behaviours represent attempts to bring the current body size closer to the ideal and are a response to weight-related appearance concerns. As previously discussed, for healthy weight women, particularly young women, appearance-related weight concerns can be associated with binge eating, extreme dietary restriction, and even starvation. Dietary restriction has attracted particular controversy over recent years because of concerns about its negative consequences on psychological and physical health and its role in the development and maintenance of eating disorders.

Disordered eating behaviours which are adopted to deliberately change body weight can be understood on a continuum from diagnosed eating disorders to more general disordered eating. Roy and Gauvin (2010) have classified the disordered eating that might be found in the general population as either 'unhealthy' or 'extremely unhealthy'. Unhealthy behaviours would include skipping meals, fasting, very low calorie diets/using food substitutes, excessive exercising, and smoking for weight loss/maintenance. It could also include excluding particular food groups and adopting nutritionally inadequate 'fad' diets. Extremely unhealthy behaviours would include purging/vomiting and the use of laxatives, diuretics, and/or steroids. Most of these behaviours are a form of dietary restriction, i.e. consciously limiting food intake as a method of weight loss or weight maintenance (Herman & Polivy, 1975). From a clinical perspective, food intake would be at a level where an individual was consuming less than was needed for a healthy weight (BMI 18.5–24.9) or the person was losing weight too rapidly.

Dietary restriction has also been identified as a possible causal factor in the increase in overweight and obesity due to both psychological and physiological mechanisms (Ogden, 2003). At a non-clinical level, additional aspects of restricting food intake can include a preoccupation with food and overeating/binges in response to episodes of restraint, the 'What the hell effect' (Herman and Polivy, 1984) and, as a consequence, cycles of weight gain and loss. Food restriction has been implicated in low mood, promoting unrealistic expectations about body shape malleability, vulnerability to emotional eating, and impaired cognitive functioning. Paradoxically, it has also been suggested that dietary restriction may play a contributory part in the development of obesity by triggering overeating in those who perceive a discrepancy between their current and ideal body weight or size but who might actually be a healthy weight or only moderately overweight. For some people who are overweight/obese, excessive or continued dietary restriction can exacerbate the problem it is supposed to solve and lead to a familiar cycle of being 'on' or 'off' a diet.

However, the relationship between restraint and under- or overeating is complex. It may be that people who exhibit restrained behaviours do so because they are prone to overeating, or alternatively the restraint behaviour may trigger the overeating. Also, not everyone who diets regains weight and many people who have lost weight or wish to maintain their current weight practice some form of dietary restriction, either consciously or automatically through habit (Wing & Phelan, 2005).

The nature of restraint can also vary. Dietary restriction might relate to all food, therefore leading to physical hunger, or it might relate to certain foods the desire for which is driven by physiological as well as psychological mechanisms; although most foods are judged to be more palatable when hungry, more desirable foods are eaten by humans and animals to the point of overconsumption, even in the absence of hunger (Lowe & Levine, 2005). This, together with arguments derived from evolutionary perspectives that overconsumption of highly palatable, energy-dense foods is adaptive and driven by a biological imperative, indicates how difficult it is for many people to self-regulate food intake in the current environment without some level of self imposed dietary restriction. Indeed, it has been argued that the frequency of weight regain following weight loss is 'evidence of the potency of the food environment' (Lowe & Levine, 2005, p. 208). Susceptibility to the food environment can also inform the current understanding of how the fat mass and obesity associated 'obesity genes' (FTO or fat mass and obesity-associated gene) may be expressed. This gene is not thought to directly cause weight gain but rather to influence eating behaviours in relation to satiety, sensitivity to food cues and the palatability of food (Frayling et al., 2007).

The desirability or otherwise of dietary restriction then, can be viewed differently according to the triggers and consequences which accompany it: 'Asking whether dietary restraint is desirable is akin to asking if taking drugs is desirable, when "drug taking" could range from prescribed medications for illness to ... heroin' (Lowe, 2003, p. 46S). For example, healthy dietary restraint might include restricting portion sizes, avoiding snacking/unplanned eating, and limiting certain high fat/high sugar foods.

How Should Awareness of the Potential Physical Health Risks of Overweight/ Obesity be Raised without Fuelling Appearance Concerns and Using Stigmatizing Appearance-Related Messages?

It is clear then that there are a range of complex interactions between appearance concerns and disordered eating behaviours in people across the spectrum of weight. The competing imperatives and consequences of appearance ideals and physical health risks give health promoters and policy-makers a significant dilemma. One attempt to at least partially reconcile these two positions is the non-dieting treatment approach. The goals of this can vary, but broadly speaking it includes a focus on improving self-esteem and body image, education about the difficulty of weight loss from a biological perspective, and encouraging the use of internal cues such as hunger rather than external cues (including appearance ideals) to achieve a personally optimal or natural weight. This approach shows some promise, however, a review of the evidence from a number of non-dieting studies indicates that although these have had beneficial effects on self-esteem, they have not been effective in changing body weight (Foster & McGuckin, 2002). A more recent approach is the development of third-generation cognitive approaches using techniques such as mindfulness which aim to reduce automaticity of unhealthy eating behaviours and increase self-acceptance (Lillis et al., 2009). Although promising, this research is at a relatively early stage in development and much more evidence is required. In practice, it is often the responsibility of individual healthcare practitioners to be aware of, and negotiate, these issues.

In conclusion, the challenge remains as to how to frame health messages that promote both psychological and physical well-being in an environment which is increasingly oriented towards appearance ideals, yet is at the same time, obesogenic. Public health messages need to be framed in such a way that they do not directly or indirectly reinforce appearance ideals that may contribute to psychological distress, yet discouraging any sort of dietary restriction for people who are prone to weight gain or currently obese would seem to be irresponsible. There is a need to challenge unrealistic and unhealthy expectations that individuals can or should attain a culturally sanctioned body, and health should be emphasized as both the reason for, and the outcome of behaviour change. In addition, the language and images used to communicate these messages should challenge, rather than covertly support, the cultural idealization of thinness as a marker of health.

REFERENCES

Cross-Government Obesity Unit (2009). *Healthy Weight, Healthy Lives: One Year On.* London: Department of Health.

Foster, G. D. & McGuckin, B. G. (2002). Nondieting approaches: principles, practices, and evidence. In T. A. Wadden & A. J. Stunkard (eds.) *Handbook of Obesity Treatment,* pp. 494–512. New York: Guilford Press.

Frances, A. and American Psychiatric Association Task Force on DSM-IV (2000). *Diagnostic and statistical manual of mental disorders: DSM-IV-TR: text revision.* Washington, DC: American Psychiatric Association.

Frayling, T. M., Timpson, N. J., Weedon, M. N., Zeggini, E., Freathy, R. M., Lindgren, C. M., et al. (2007). A common variant in the FTO gene is associated with body mass index and predisposes to childhood and adult obesity. *Science, 316,* 889–94.

Gavin, A. R., Simon, G. E., & Ludman, E. J. (2010). The association between obesity, depression, and educational attainment in women: the mediating role of body image dissatisfaction. *Journal of Psychosomatic Research, 69*(6), 573–81.

Gowers, S. & Shore, A. (2001) Development of weight and shape concerns in the aetiology of eating disorders. *British Journal of Psychiatry, 179,* 236–42.

Grogan, S. (2008) *Body image: Understanding body dissatisfaction in men, women and children* (2nd edn.). New York: Routledge/Taylor & Francis Group.

Herman, C. P. & Polivy, J. (1984). A boundary model for the regulation of eating. *Research Publications—Association for Research in Nervous & Mental Disease*, 62, 141–56.

Herman, C. P. & Polivy, J. (1975). Anxiety, restraint, and eating behavior. *Journal of Abnormal Psychology*, 84(6), 666–72.

Johnson, F., Cooke, L., Croker, H., & Wardle, J. (2008). Changing perceptions of weight in Great Britain: comparison of two population surveys. *British Medical Journal*, 337, a494.

Kuk, J. L., Ardern, C. I., Church, T. S., Hebert, J. R., Sui, X., & Blair, S. N. (2009). Ideal weight and weight satisfaction: association with health practices. *American Journal of Epidemiology*, 170(4), 456–63.

Lillis, J., Hayes. S. C., Bunting, K., & Masuda, A. (2009). Teaching acceptance and mindfulness to improve the lives of the obese: a preliminary test of a theoretical model. *Annals of Behavioral Medicine*, 37(1), 58–69.

Lowe, M. R. (2003). Self-regulation of energy intake in the prevention and treatment of obesity: is it feasible? *Obesity Research*, 11(Suppl), 44S–59S.

Lowe, M. R. & Levine, A. S. (2005). Eating motives and the controversy over dieting: eating less than needed versus less than wanted. *Obesity Research*, 13(5), 797–806.

National Institute for Health and Clinical Excellence (2004). *Eating disorders: Core interventions in the treatment and management of anorexia nervosa, bulimia nervosa and related eating disorders [CG9]*. London: National Institute for Health and Clinical Excellence.

National Obesity Observatory (2009). *Body Mass Index as a measure of obesity*. http://www.noo.org.uk/publications/719/Body_Mass_Index_as_a_measure_of_obesity.

NHS Information Centre (2009). *Health survey for England 2008: physical activity and fitness: summary of key findings*. London: Information Centre.

Ogden, J. (2003). *The psychology of eating: from healthy to disordered behavior*. Oxford: Blackwell.

Orbach, S. (1983). Food, fatness and femininity. *Practitioner*, 227(1379), 860.

Puhl, R. M. & Heuer, C. A. (2009). The stigma of obesity: a review and update. *Obesity*, 17(5), 941–64.

Rahman, M. & Berenson, A. B. (2010). Self-perception of weight and its association with weight-related behaviors in young, reproductive-aged women. *Obstetrics & Gynecology (New York)*, 116(6), 1274–80.

Roy, M. & Gauvin, L. (2010). Having a personal weight goal that mismatches healthy weight recommendations increases the likelihood of using unhealthy behaviors among a representative population-based sample of adolescents. *Eating Behaviors*, 11(4), 281–87.

Russell, G. (1979). Bulimia nervosa: an ominous variant of anorexia nervosa. *Psychological Medicine*, 9(3), 429–48.

Stice, E. & Shaw, H. (2004). Eating disorder prevention programs: a meta-analytic review. *Psychological Bulletin*, 130(2), 206–27.

Stice, E. & Shaw, H. E. (2002). Role of body dissatisfaction in the onset and maintenance of eating pathology: A synthesis of research findings. *Journal of Psychosomatic Research*, 53(5), 985–93.

Swinburn, B., Egger, G., & Raza, F. (1999). Dissecting obesogenic environments: the development and application of a framework for identifying and prioritizing environmental interventions for obesity. *Preventive Medicine*, 29(6), 563–70.

Tillotson, J. E. (2003). Pandemic obesity: agriculture's cheap food policy is a bad bargain. *Nutrition Today*, 38(5), 186–90.

Wardle (2000). Intentional weight control and food choice habits in a national representa-tive sample of adults in the UK. *International Journal of Obesity*, 24(5), 534–40.

Wardle, J., Robb, K. A., Johnson, F., Griffith, J., Brunner, E., Power, C., & Tovee, M. (2004). Socioeconomic variation in attitudes to eating and weight in female adolescents. *Health Psychology*, 23(3), 275–82.

Wing, R. R. & Phelan, S. (2005). Long-term weight loss maintenance. *American Journal of Clinical Nutrition*, 82, 222S–5S.

Yaemsiri, S., Slining, M. M., & Agarwal, S. K. (2011). Perceived weight status, overweight diagnosis, and weight control among US adults: the NHANES 2003–2008 Study. *International Journal of Obesity*, 35, 1063–70.

Zimmerman, F. J. (2011). Using marketing muscle to sell fat: the rise of obesity in the modern economy. *Annual Review of Public Health*, 32, 285–306.

....

CHAPTER 25

COSMETIC PROCEDURES

....

CANICE E. CRERAND

LEANNE MAGEE

DAVID B. SARWER

INTRODUCTION

....

ACCORDING to the American Society of Plastic Surgeons (ASPS), approximately 12.5 million cosmetic surgical and minimally invasive cosmetic treatments were performed in the US in 2009. The British Association of Aesthetic Plastic Surgeons (BAAPS) reported that in 2010 the number of private cosmetic procedures had tripled since 2003 (2011). The majority consisted of minimally invasive, non-surgical procedures such as botulinum toxin (Botox®) injections and soft tissue fillers (ASPS, 2010). The estimated cost of the cosmetic treatments undertaken in the US was $10 billion in 2009. Between 2008 and 2010 the UK market for cosmetic surgery is estimated to have grown by 17% to reach an estimated worth of £2.3 billion (Mintel, 2010). These numbers are often shocking to both medical professionals and lay persons alike. Perhaps even more staggering, these statistics are likely to be a conservative underestimate, as they do not reflect the procedures that are performed by all medical specialists.

The popularity of cosmetic surgery is likely to result from an interaction of a number of factors (Sarwer & Magee, 2006). Improvements in safety as well as the now widespread use of direct-to-consumer marketing have probably contributed to the growth of cosmetic procedures. The mass media and entertainment industries have long endorsed cosmetic surgery. This has been particularly evident over the past decade with the emergence of reality-based television programmes which feature individuals before and after cosmetic surgery. The bombardment of mass media ideals of beauty, coupled with the dissatisfaction that many people, especially women, experience with regard to their physical appearance, are likely to have contributed as well (Sarwer & Magee, 2006). Finally, society's acceptance of the use of medicine to enhance appearance, perhaps paired with a greater awareness of the importance of physical appearance in daily life, has potentially fuelled the increases in cosmetic surgery.

As the popularity of cosmetic medical treatments has grown, so has interest in the psychological aspects of these procedures. There is now a relatively large body of research which has examined the psychological aspects of cosmetic surgery, dating back to the pioneering work of Edgerton and colleagues in the US in the 1960s. Interest in the psychological aspects of these procedures seems intuitive. In some of the earliest work in this area, cosmetic procedures were described as being analogous to psychiatric treatment (Sarwer et al., 1998c). Understanding the psychological characteristics of patients who desire and undergo cosmetic procedures is important for practical reasons as well. Plastic surgeons have long been interested in identifying and 'screening out' patients with certain personality characteristics or psychiatric disorders which may contribute to poor outcomes.

This chapter will review psychological studies of cosmetic surgery patients. Because there is growing interest in understanding the psychological characteristics of patients who undergo specific procedures (e.g. rhinoplasty), this chapter will review the psychological studies that have been conducted in specific patient populations, including persons undergoing facial and body procedures. The chapter concludes with a discussion of the psychiatric disorders which may be most relevant to this population, namely body dysmorphic disorder (BDD) and eating disorders.

Facial Cosmetic Procedures

Rhinoplasty

Historically, rhinoplasty (reshaping of the nose) has been one of the most popular cosmetic surgical procedures, with over 250,000 performed in the US in 2009 (ASPS, 2010) and over 4,000 in the UK (BAAPS, 2011). The psychological characteristics of rhinoplasty have long been of interest to surgeons and mental health professionals, as the first reports in the literature date back to the 1940s and 1950s.

The first studies of rhinoplasty patients relied primarily upon clinical interviews of patients and revealed significant levels of psychopathology (Linn et al., 1949; Hill et al., 1950). This is probably due to the fact that most of these early investigators worked from a psychodynamic theoretical orientation to conceptualize the desire for rhinoplasty. Accordingly, the nose was thought to be symbolic of the penis, and pursuit of rhinoplasty was interpreted as a representation of the patient's unconscious displacement of sexual conflicts onto the nose (Book, 1971).While these conceptualizations seem almost comical today, they endured and influenced the field for decades.

A second generation of cosmetic surgery research took place during the 1970s and 1980s, and researchers used psychometrically validated measures to evaluate patients' personality characteristics and changes in functioning postoperatively (Sarwer et al., 1998c; Sarwer & Crerand, 2004). Studies from this era reported less preoperative psychopathology among rhinoplasty patients (Hay, 1970; Wright &Wright, 1975; Micheli-Pellegrini & Manfrida, 1979; Robin et al., 1988). Other studies reported psychosocial improvements postoperatively (Hay, 1973; Wright &Wright, 1975; Micheli-Pellegrini & Manfrida, 1979; Marcus, 1984). Nonetheless, many of these studies used small sample sizes or failed to include appropriate control groups, which calls into question the validity of the findings.

In the past two decades, studies have continued to use improved methodologies, including use of reliable and valid self-report measures; clinical interviews with established diagnostic criteria; pre-and postoperative assessments; and suitable control groups (e.g. Goin & Rees, 1991; Sarwer et al., 1997; Borges-Dinis et al., 1998; Rankin et al., 1998; Ercolani et al., 1999b; Hern et al., 2002; de Arruda Alves et al., 2005; Litner et al., 2008; Moss & Harris, 2009). In contrast to earlier investigations, the majority of these studies suggest that most rhinoplasty patients do not have significant psychopathology. Such findings are supportive of surgeons' clinical experiences with rhinoplasty patients, namely that the majority of patients are psychologically healthy individuals who are dissatisfied with the size and shape of their noses. Improvements in quality of life, symptoms of anxiety, depression, and self-esteem, increased satisfaction with facial appearance, and decreased self-consciousness have been documented postoperatively (deArruda Alves et al., 2005; Litner et al, 2008; Moss & Harris, 2009).

However, recent studies also suggest that some patients suffer from significant psychopathology. Several studies have reported increased symptoms of obsessiveness and BDD in this population (Veale et al., 2003; Zojaji et al., 2007; Pecorari et al., 2010). An investigation of predictors of interest in rhinoplasty found that lower levels of education and appearance satisfaction; greater investment in appearance; BDD symptoms; and history of being teased about appearance were predictive of interest in this procedure (Javo & Sorlie, 2010). Such reports of psychopathology, specifically BDD, highlight the importance of preoperative psychological screening for patients who desire rhinoplasty (Crerand et al., 2007).

Anti-aging procedures

Rhytidectomy and blepharoplasty

The two most popular surgical procedures used to combat the aging face are rhytidectomy (facelift) and blepharoplasty (eye lift). In 2009, 103,625 facelifts and 203,309 blepharoplasty procedures were performed in the US (ASPS, 2010), with 4,756 facelifts and 5,779 eyelifts reported in 2010 in the UK (BAAPS, 2011).

Similar to early studies of rhinoplasty patients, the first studies of facelift patients found evidence for high levels of psychopathology. Patients were typically described as dependent and depressed. One study reported that nearly 70% of patients met criteria for a psychiatric diagnosis preoperatively (Webb et al., 1965). Interestingly, most patients in this sample reported postoperative psychosocial improvements and did not experience symptom exacerbations after surgery (Webb et al., 1965). Studies using standardized measures reported similar improvements in psychological symptoms postoperatively (Rankin et al., 1998; Goin et al., 1980).

More contemporary studies have examined the body image concerns of these patients. For example, in one of the first empirical studies, patients reported higher levels of dissatisfaction with their aging facial appearance, but they were satisfied with their overall body image (Sarwer et al., 1997). Compared to rhinoplasty patients, rhytidectomy and/or blepharoplasty patients have reported greater investment in their appearance as well as greater satisfaction with their overall body image (Sarwer et al., 1997). Postoperatively, patients reported decreases in body image dissatisfaction for the feature that was treated, but no changes in overall body image (Sarwer et al., 2002). In a study that compared women who sought cosmetic surgery (primarily facelifts) to a control group, greater appearance investment was reported among the cosmetic surgery patients, but no differences in self-esteem or psychopathology symptoms were found (Muhlan et al., 2007). Interestingly, a study using the Derriford Appearance Scale found that facelift patients reported increased satisfaction with both facial and bodily appearance postoperatively (Litner et al., 2008), suggesting that surgery did have an impact on overall body image. Improvements in quality of life and self esteem have also been reported postoperatively (de Arruda Alves et al., 2005). Taken together, these findings suggest that individuals who pursue anti-aging surgical procedures are typically psychologically healthy, but do experience more dissatisfaction with facial appearance and a greater investment in appearance. They also appear to experience improvements in body image postoperatively.

Minimally invasive procedures

In 2009, nearly 11 million minimally invasive cosmetic procedures were performed in the US (ASPS, 2010). For the past several years, these procedures have surpassed the popularity of the more traditional anti-aging surgical procedures such as facelifts. For example, nearly 4.8 million botulinum toxin (Botox®) injections were performed in 2009, making it the most popular of all cosmetic treatments (ASPS, 2010). Botox® is typically injected into the face in order to reduce the appearance of wrinkling. Other popular minimally invasive procedures include soft tissue fillers (e.g. fat or collagen injections), which can be used to add fullness to the lips. The Independent Healthcare Advisory Services (IHAS) estimate that over 200,000 injectable cosmetic treatments are carried out each year in the UK (IHAS, 2011). Chemical peels and microdermabrasion are commonly used to improve skin discolorations and texture, and can diminish the appearance of acne-related scarring. In 2009, 1,142,949 chemical peels and 910,168 microdermabrasion procedures were performed in the US (ASPS, 2010).

Despite their increasing popularity, few studies have examined the psychological characteristics of patients who seek these procedures. In a study of 30 patients who received Botox® injections for facial wrinkles, over 50% of those studied reported improvements in their appearance and almost 50% reported greater confidence in their appearance (Sommer et al., 2003). A study that evaluated the psychosocial benefits associated with alpha hydroxy acid, a topical treatment that is often used to reduce roughness and fine wrinkling, found that patients reported significant improvements in appearance and relationship satisfaction after treatment (Fried & Cash, 1998). While these studies suggest that minimally invasive procedures can have psychosocial benefits, more research is needed to further evaluate the psychosocial impact of these procedures.

COSMETIC PROCEDURES OF THE BODY

Cosmetic breast augmentation

Breast augmentation has been the most popular cosmetic surgical procedure in recent years. Over 289,000 cosmetic breast augmentation procedures were performed in the US 2009 (ASPS, 2010) and 9,430 in the UK in 2010 (BAAPS, 2011). This 787% increase in the US since 1992 is striking given the Food and Drug Administration (FDA) ban on silicone gel-filled breast implants between 1992 and 2006 due to concerns about their association with a number of significant health issues (see also Chapter 8). Following a decade of research which repeatedly found no association between silicone gel-filled breast implants and specific diseases (e.g. cancer and connective tissue disease; Sanchez-Guerrero et al., 1995; Silverman et al., 1996; Bondurant et al., 2000; Jensen et al., 2002; Holmich et al., 2003), the FDA re-approved the use of silicone breast implants for women age 22 and older (http://www.fda.gov). Despite this recent controversy, half of all breast augmentations in 2009 were performed with silicone implants (ASPS, 2010). Probably as a result of both the popularity and controversy, there is a large literature on the psychological aspects of breast augmentation (Sarwer, 2007).

Descriptive characteristics

Women from a wide range of age, racial, and socioeconomic groups seek cosmetic breast augmentation. Despite this heterogeneity, women who receive breast implants differ from their peers in several ways. Compared to other women, they are more likely to have had more sexual partners, report a greater use of oral contraceptives, be younger at their first pregnancy, have a history of terminated pregnancies, have a higher divorce rate, and use alcohol and tobacco more frequently (Beale et al., 1980; Schlebusch & Levin, 1983; Cook et al., 1997; Brinton et al., 2000; Fryzek et al., 2000; Kjoller et al., 2003). Many have been reported to have a below average body weight leading to concern that some may have eating disorders (Cook et al., 1997; Brinton et al., 2000; Fryzek et al., 2000; Didie & Sarwer, 2003; Kjoller et al., 2003; Sarwer et al., 2003).

Studies of preoperative psychological status

Numerous studies have investigated the preoperative psychological status of women interested in breast augmentation. Early studies characterized patients as having increased symptoms of depression, anxiety, guilt, and low self-esteem (Sihm et al., 1978; Beale et al., 1980; Schlebusch & Levin 1983; Sarwer et al., 2000). More recent investigations using valid and reliable psychometric measures have found significantly less preoperative psychopathology (Young et al., 1994; Didie & Sarwer, 2003; Kjoller et al., 2003; Sarwer et al., 2003).

The most profound psychological effects of breast augmentation may occur in the realm of body image (Sarwer et al., 1998c; Sarwer & Crerand, 2004; Sarwer, 2007). Women seeking breast augmentation have unique body image concerns, including greater dissatisfaction with their breasts, greater investment in their overall appearance, greater concern with their appearance in social situations, and more frequent appearance-related teasing compared to other women with similar breast size who are not seeking augmentation (Sarwer et al., 1998a; Didie & Sarwer, 2003; Sarwer et al., 2003; Banbury et al., 2004; Van Soest et al., 2009). Augmentation candidates also rated their ideal breast size, as well as the breast size preferred by women, as significantly larger than did controls (Sarwer et al., 2003).

Psychosocial outcomes and postoperative complications

Far fewer studies have examined postoperative psychosocial changes among breast augmentation patients, but early clinical interview-based studies generally reported improvements, or at least no change, in self-esteem and depressive symptoms after surgery (Edgerton et al., 1961; Ohlsen et al., 1978; Sihm et al., 1978). More recent psychometric investigations are equivocal, with one study reporting a decrease in depressive symptoms after surgery (Schlebusch & Marht, 1993) and another reporting increased symptoms in 30% of patients in the immediate postoperative period (Meyer & Ringberg, 1987). A recent study of 155 women undergoing cosmetic surgery (primarily breast augmentation or reduction) found that lower levels of preoperative psychological problems assessed by the Hopkins Symptom Checklist were associated with greater levels of body image satisfaction and self-esteem post-operatively (von Soest et al., 2009).

Studies have suggested that women experience improvements in body image following cosmetic surgery (e.g. Sihm et al., 1978; Young et al., 1994; Cash et al., 2002; Sarwer et al., 2002), with up to 90% of breast augmentation patients reporting improved body image 2 years postoperatively (Cash et al., 2002). Clinical reports and empirical studies suggest that the vast majority of women are satisfied with the outcome of breast augmentation (Schlebusch & Marht, 1993; Young et al., 1994; Gabriel et al., 1997; Cunningham et al., 2000; Cash et al., 2002), but psychosocial outcomes may be tempered by the occurrence of postoperative complications, which are negatively related to postoperative satisfaction (Handel et al., 1993; Cash et al., 2002; Jacobsen et al., 2004). Up to 25% of women experience a surgical or implant-related complication, such as implant rupture/deflation, capsular contracture, pain, breast asymmetry, scarring, loss of nipple sensation, and breastfeeding difficulties (Fiala et al., 1993; Sanchez-Guerrero et al., 1995; Silverman et al., 1996; Bondurant et al., 2000; Brinton et al., 2001; Fryzek et al., 2001a, b; Jensen et al., 2002; Kjoller et al., 2002; Holmich et al., 2003). Approximately 10% of augmentation patients experience a complication within five years of implantation, and 23.8% experience complications severe enough to require additional surgery (Fryzek et al., 2001a, b; Kjoller et al., 2002). In a large prospective study, Cash and colleagues (2002) found that women who experienced postoperative complications reported less favourable improvements in self-image than women who did not. Women with socially detectable complications, such as capsular contracture, reported lower satisfaction and poorer body image than women who had non-detectable or no complications. The groups did not differ in rates of satisfaction at 24 months after surgery, but those with socially detectable complications viewed the risk-benefit ratio of surgery less favourably.

Breast implants and suicide

Within the past decade, epidemiological studies have suggested that breast implant patients have a two to three times greater risk of suicide compared to population estimates (Brinton et al., 2001; Koot et al., 2003; Pukkala et al., 2003; Jacobsen et al., 2004; Brinton et al., 2006; Villeneuve et al., 2006; Lipworth et al., 2007). Rates of suicide are highest among women who undergo augmentation at age 40 or later and who have had implants for a longer duration of time (Brinton et al., 2006; Villeneuve et al., 2006). The exact nature of the relationship between breast implants and suicide is unclear. Rather than there being a cause and effect relationship between breast augmentation and suicide, it is likely that some women seeking breast augmentation present for surgery with certain personality characteristics or life experiences that are in and of themselves risk factors for suicide such as more frequent substance use or increased divorce rate (Sarwer et al., 2007).

Much of the research regarding the relationship between breast augmentation and suicide has intuitively focused on the presence of pre-existing psychopathology (McLaughlin et al., 2003; Sarwer, 2003; Sarwer et al., 2007). Women with breast implants have a higher rate of outpatient psychotherapy or psychopharmacological treatment compared to other women (Sarwer, 2007), which may be indicative of psychological and psychiatric distress that contribute to increased risk for suicide. In addition, when compared to women who underwent other cosmetic procedures or breast reduction, women with breast implants have a higher rate of previous psychiatric hospitalization (Jacobsen et al., 2004), which is a strong predictor of suicide among women in the general population (Sarwer et al., 2007).

Given these findings, additional prospective epidemiological and empirical studies of the relationship between breast implants and suicide are needed, as are studies that examine the postoperative psychosocial impact of breast augmentation. Despite the methodological limitations of both clinical interview-based and psychometric investigations, it is likely that breast augmentation candidates present for surgery with a variety of psychological symptoms. Whether some of these symptoms serve as contraindications for surgery has yet to be established. Given the limited number of studies that have specifically investigated the postoperative psychosocial benefits of breast augmentation, it is premature to definitively conclude that the procedure confers more general psychological benefits (Sarwer & Crerand, 2004; Sarwer, 2007).

Liposuction and abdominoplasty

Approximately two-thirds of American adults are considered to be overweight or obese, as defined by a body mass index (BMI) greater than $25kg/m^2$ (Flegal et al., 2010). Obesity is associated with increased body image dissatisfaction (Sarwer et al., 2005a) and, more significantly, medical comorbidities such as type 2 diabetes. Although designed for body contouring purposes, many individuals erroneously believe that liposuction and abdominoplasty are permanent solutions to obesity.

Liposuction

Over 198,000 men and women in the US underwent liposuction in 2009, with a figure of 3,369 for 2010 in the UK, making it the most fourth most popular surgical procedure in the US (ASPS, 2010) and the sixth in the UK (BAAPS, 2010). Few, if any, studies have investigated the pre- and postoperative psychological status of liposuction patients. Many patients often mistakenly believe that liposuction leads to significant weight loss. The typical weight loss associated with liposuction has not been well-documented. One study of 14 overweight women reported a mean weight loss of 5.1kg by 6 weeks postoperatively, with an additional 1.3kg weight loss by 4 months (Giese et al., 2001). Studies investigating changes in lipids and insulin sensitivity following liposuction have been equivocal (Samdal et al., 1995; Baxter, 1997; Klein et al., 2004).

Many patients erroneously believe that liposuction will result in 'washboard abs', smooth thighs, and permanent removal of fat deposits in treated areas. Though liposuction reduces the number of fat cells in a local area of the body, the remaining fat cells may still expand if weight increases, and if fat cells are not removed in a consistent fashion, residual pockets of fat may remain. Most patients, however, report satisfaction with their results and maintain a more proportional shape, even if they do gain some weight postoperatively (Dillerud & Haheim, 1993; Rohrich et al., 2004). Nearly 50% of patients reported weight gain after surgery, and up to 29% claimed that their fat returned to the site of the surgery (Dillerud & Haheim, 1993; Rohrich et al., 2004).

People with excessive weight or shape concerns require particular attention prior to surgery. Women and men with formal eating disorders, as discussed in detail later in this chapter, may seek liposuction as an inappropriate means to control their weight. A recent, large study of Norwegian women found that the presence of eating disorder symptoms was a significant predictor of interest in liposuction (Javo & Sorlie, 2010). Case reports suggest that liposuction can exacerbate eating disorder symptoms (Willard et al., 1996).

Abdominoplasty

Over 115,000 'tummy tuck' procedures were performed in the US in 2009, representing an 84% increase since 2000 (ASPS, 2010). The figure for the UK in 2010 is 3,147, which interestingly represented a decrease of 7.5% compared with previous years (BAAPS, 2011). This increase may be partly attributed to the rising number of individuals with extreme obesity who undergo bariatric surgery for weight loss. Bariatric procedures typically result in a weight loss of approximately one-third of operative body weight and significant improvements in obesity-related comorbidities and psychosocial status (Sarwer et al., 2005b). Unfortunately, many patients are left with excess folds of skin and fat which may contribute to increased body image dissatisfaction (Sarwer et al., 2008). This may motivate some patients to seek abdominoplasty and related body contouring procedures. In 2009, approximately 8,200 lower body lifts were performed in the US, and following massive weight loss, an additional 16,000 breast lifts, 5,600 thigh lifts, and 6,200 upper arm lifts were performed to remove loose and sagging skin (ASPS, 2010). Case reports suggest that these individuals experience psychosocial improvements and a decrease in the physical discomfort associated with the excess skin (Rhomberg et al., 2003). Improvements in body image have also been reported (Pecori et al., 2007).

In one study documenting psychosocial changes associated with abdominoplasty, women endorsed significant improvements in overall body image dissatisfaction and abdominal dissatisfaction 8 weeks after surgery, but they did not report significant improvements in self-concept or general life satisfaction (Bolton et al., 2003). These results are consistent with other postoperative studies suggesting that the impact of cosmetic surgery procedures may be limited to specific improvements of body image discontent, but not necessarily general psychosocial functioning (Sarwer et al., 2002).

Other body enhancement procedures

An unknown number of men and women who are dissatisfied with the appearance of their genitalia pursue enhancement or beautification procedures. Men may undergo procedures to lengthen or widen their genitals. Women may seek surgery to reduce the size of the labia minora. Although some individuals may seek these procedures because of functional deficits (e.g. urination problems), there can be a significant aesthetic component to the pursuit of cosmetic genital surgery (Miklos & Moore, 2008). Patients are often motivated for surgery out of embarrassment, either when undressed or wearing tight clothing (Choi & Kim, 2000; Perovic et al., 2003), or by beliefs that their genitalia are abnormal or deformed (Goodman, 2009). However, little else is known abut the psychological characteristics of these patients. Considering the nature of these procedures, it is possible that a significant percentage of these patients are suffering from BDD or other psychiatric disorders. There are several case reports of individuals who have performed self-surgeries, such as injecting their genitals with various substances (e.g. Cohen et al., 2001).

There is also a growing trend towards postpartum plastic surgery, also known as 'Mommy Makeovers,' designed to help women restore or improve their post-pregnancy bodies. Such makeovers often involve multiple surgical procedures to treat stretched skin and increased or changed breast and abdominal tissue. Exact figures for this type of surgery are difficult to estimate, as 'Mommy Makeover' is a marketing rather than surgical term and can represent various combinations of surgical procedures.

PSYCHIATRIC DISORDERS IN COSMETIC POPULATIONS

Given the number of persons who seek cosmetic procedures, it is likely that all psychiatric diagnoses are represented within this population. However, disorders with a body image component, such as BDD and eating disorders, may be more common among persons who pursue cosmetic surgery.

Body dysmorphic disorder

BDD is a psychiatric disorder characterized by a preoccupation with an imagined or slight defect in appearance that causes emotional distress and/or significant impairment in daily functioning (APA, 2000). BDD is relatively new to the psychiatric nomenclature in the US, as it was only recognized as a formal psychiatric disorder in 1987 (APA, 1987). However, decades earlier, case reports and descriptions of persons with BDD symptoms were published in the plastic surgery literature, including descriptions of 'insatiable' and 'minimal deformity' patients (Edgerton et al., 1960; Knorr et al., 1967).

BDD is thought to affect 1–2% of the general population (APA, 2000). However, the prevalence of BDD in cosmetic surgery populations is notably higher. Among US cosmetic surgery patients, rates of BDD range from 7–8% (Sarwer et al., 1998b; Crerand et al., 2004). Among rhinoplasty patients, 20.7% reported symptoms of BDD (Veale et al., 2003). Studies of BDD in international samples have reported comparable rates (e.g. Aouizerate et al., 2003; Vulink et al., 2006). Persons with BDD also seek appearance-altering procedures from other specialists (e.g. dermatologists, dentists) (Crerand et al., 2005).

Non-psychiatric treatments

Persons with BDD often pursue cosmetic treatments as a means of decreasing their appearance preoccupations. In a study of 250 persons with BDD who underwent cosmetic procedures, 76% sought and 66% received treatment, with dermatological procedures and cosmetic surgery being the most popular (Phillips et al., 2001). Similarly, in a sample of 200 persons with BDD, non-psychiatric treatment was sought by 71% and received by 64% (Crerand et al., 2005). The most commonly received treatments were topical acne agents, rhinoplasty, collagen injections, electrolysis, and tooth whitening (Crerand et al., 2005).

The outcomes of cosmetic procedures in persons with BDD are typically poor (Crerand et al., 2005; Crerand et al., 2010), with patients frequently reporting dissatisfaction with the results of their procedures (Veale et al., 2000). Cosmetic procedures rarely impact BDD severity in the long-term, with the majority of non-psychiatric treatments received by patients with BDD resulting in either no change or a worsening in symptoms (Phillips et al., 2001; Crerand et al., 2005). Even in cases where persons report improvement in the appearance of their 'defects,' the results are often temporary, and preoccupation may shift to another body part (Tignol et al., 2007; Crerand et al., 2010). Of greater concern, there is evidence that patients with BDD may become violent towards their providers or pursue legal action against them (Crerand et al., 2008). Suicidality is also common among persons with BDD (Phillips & Menard, 2006), and dissatisfaction with postoperative outcomes could trigger suicidal ideation or attempts. Some patients have even been known to take matters into their own hands and have attempted their own cosmetic procedures or revisions (Veale, 2000). These concerns, coupled with the evidence for poor treatment outcomes, suggest that BDD should be considered a contraindication for cosmetic surgery (Crerand et al., 2008; Crerand & Sarwer, 2010). Psychiatric and psychological treatments are more appropriate and effective interventions avenues to effectively address their needs (Phillips, 2010; Veale, 2010).

Eating disorders

Eating disorders such as anorexia and bulimia nervosa are characterized by extreme body image dissatisfaction, specifically with weight and shape (APA, 2000). Given the excessive emphasis that individuals with eating disorders place on their appearance, these disorders may occur with increased frequency among those who seek cosmetic surgery. Persons with eating disorders may mistakenly believe that cosmetic surgery will improve their extreme dissatisfaction with their bodies and low self-esteem.

Surprisingly, no studies to date have examined the prevalence of eating disorders in patients seeking cosmetic surgery; however, a recent study reported that the presence of eating pathology in women was a significant predictor of interest in liposuction (Javo & Sorlie, 2010). Some case studies have noted exacerbations of eating disorder symptoms following breast augmentation, lipoplasty, rhinoplasty, and chin augmentation (Yates et al., 1988; McIntosh et al., 1994; Willard et al., 1996). A case report of five breast reduction patients with bulimia found that four of the women experienced an improvement in their eating disorder symptoms and reductions in emotional distress postoperatively (Losee et al., 1997). The improvements in eating disorder symptoms were maintained 10 years postoperatively, although other factors in addition to surgery may have been responsible for symptom improvement (Losee et al., 2004). Future studies are needed to further evaluate the prevalence of eating disorders in cosmetic populations before and after cosmetic procedures.

CONCLUSION

Studies suggest that people who seek cosmetic procedures experience a wide variety of psychological symptoms. While early investigations conceptualized the desire for cosmetic treatments as pathological, recent studies with improved methodologies indicate that the majority of cosmetic surgery patients are psychologically healthy. Most people who pursue cosmetic treatments appear to be motivated by a desire to improve their body image as opposed to psychopathology. However, for a minority of patients, psychiatric disorders may underlie their pursuit of appearance-altering procedures.

Future studies are needed to address the motivations of patients who seek cosmetic procedures (particularly minimally invasive and body contouring procedures) and the relationships between treatment outcomes, body image, and psychopathology. While more men now seek cosmetic procedures, empirical studies of gender differences in body image and other psychological characteristics among those who seek cosmetic procedures are lacking. Future studies should utilize appropriate control groups and standardized pre- and postoperative assessments (including structured clinical interviews and psychometrically sound self-report measures). While there is evidence that patients experience psychosocial improvements postoperatively, more research is needed to determine the long-term impact of these procedures.

The literature reviewed in this chapter has implications for clinical practice. Some degree of preoperative body image dissatisfaction and psychosocial distress may be normative in cosmetic populations. However, a subgroup of patients present with pathological levels of body image dissatisfaction, characteristic of psychiatric disorders such as BDD and eating disorders. Because of these concerns, preoperative psychological screenings should be conducted for persons who desire cosmetic procedures. Since persons with BDD and eating disorders may be more likely to present for surgical rather than psychiatric treatment, cosmetic treatment providers are well-positioned to identify such patients and to provide appropriate referrals to mental health professionals.

Acknowledgement

This chapter was supported, in part, by funding from National Institute of Dental and Craniofacial Research (Grant # K23 DE020854–01) to Dr Crerand.

REFERENCES

American Psychiatric Association. (1987). *Diagnostic and statistical manual of mental disorders* (3rd edn. rev.). Washington, DC: APA Press.

American Psychiatric Association. (2000). *Diagnostic and statistical manual of mental disorders* (4th edn., text rev.). Washington, DC: APA Press.

American Society of Plastic Surgeons. (2010). *National clearinghouse of plastic surgery statistics.* Arlington Heights, IL: ASPS.

Aouizerate, B., Pujol, H., Grabot, D., Faytout, M., Suire, K., Braud, C., *et al.* (2003). Body dysmorphic disorder in a sample of cosmetic surgery applicants. *European Psychiatry*, 18, 365–8.

Banbury, J., Yetman, R., Lucas, A., Papay, F., Graves K., & Zins, J. E. (2004). Prospective analysis of the outcome of subpectoral breast augmentation: sensory changes, muscle function, and body image. *Plastic and Reconstructive Surgery*, 113, 701–7.

Baxter, R. A. (1997). Serum lipid changes following large-volume suction lipetomy. *Aesthetic Surgery Journal*, 17, 213–15.

Beale, S., Lisper, H., & Palm, B. (1980). A psychological study of patients seeking augmentation mammaplasty, *British Journal of Psychiatry*, 136, 133–8.

Bolton, M. A., Pruzinsky, T., Cash, T. F., & Persing, J. A. (2003). Measuring outcomes in plastic surgery: Body image and quality of life in abdominoplasty patients. *Plastic and Reconstructive Surgery*, 112, 619–25.

Bondurant, S., Ernester, V. R., & Herdman, R. (2000). *Committee on the Safety of Silicone Breast Implants, Division of Health Promotion and Disease Prevention. Safety of Silicone Breast Implants.* Washington, DC: National Academy Press.

Book, H. E. (1971). Sexual implications of the nose. *Comprehensive Psychiatry*, 12(5), 450–5.

Borges-Dinis, P., Dinis, M., & Gomes, A. (1998). Psychosocial consequences of nasal aesthetic and functional surgery: A controlled prospective study in an ENT setting. *Rhinology*, 36, 32–6.

Brinton, L. A., Brown, S. L., Colton, T., Burich, M. C., & Lubin, J. (2000). Characteristics of a population of women with breast implants compared with women seeking other types of plastic surgery. *Plastic and Reconstructive Surgery*, 5, 919–27.

Brinton, L. A., Lubin, J. H., Burich, M. C., Colton, T., Hoover, R. N. (2001). Mortality among augmentation mammoplasty patients. *Epidemiology*, 12, 321–6.

Brinton, L. A., Lubin, J. H., Murray, M. C., Colton, T., & Hoover, R. N. (2006). Mortality rates among augmentation mammoplasty patients: an update. *Epidemiology*, 17, 162–69.

The British Association of Aesthetic Plastic Surgeons (BAAPS) (2010). *Annual Audit.* http://www.baaps.org.uk/about-us/audit/584-britons-over-the-moob-male-breast-reduction-nearly-doubles-in-2009

The British Association of Aesthetic Plastic Surgeons (BAAPS) (2011). *Annual Audit.* http://www.baaps.org.uk/about-us/audit/854-moobs-and-boobs-double-ddigit-rise

Cash, T. F., Duel, L. A., & Perkins, L. L. (2002). Women's psychosocial outcomes of breast augmentation with silicone gel-filled implants: a 2-year prospective study. *Plastic and Reconstructive Surgery*, 109, 2112–21.

Choi, H. Y., & Kim, K. T. (2000). A new method for aesthetic reduction of labia minora (the Deepithelialized Reduction Labioplasty). *Plastic and Reconstructive Surgery*, 105, 419–22.

Cohen, J. L., Kreoleian, C. M., & Krull, E. A. (2001). Penile paraffinoma: Self-injection with mineral oil. *Journal of American Academic Dermatology*, 45, S222–4.

Cook, L. S., Daling, J. R., Voigt, L. F., deHart M. P., Malone K. E., Stanford, J. L., *et al.* (1997). Characteristics of women with and without breast augmentation, *Journal of the American Medical Association*, 277, 1612–17.

Crerand, C. E., & Sarwer, D. B. (2010). Cosmetic treatments and body dysmorphic disorder. *Psychiatric Annals*, 40, 344–8.

Crerand, C. E., Sarwer, D. B., Magee, L., Gibbons, L. M., Lowe, M. R., Bartlett, S. P., *et al.* (2004). Rate of body dysmorphic disorder among patients seeking facial plastic surgery. *Psychiatric Annals*, 34(12), 958–65.

Crerand, C. E., Phillips, K. A., Menard, W., & Fay, C. (2005). Non-psychiatric medical treatment of body dysmorphic disorder. *Psychosomatics*, 46, 549–55.

Crerand, C. E., Gibbons, L. M., & Sarwer, D. B. (2007). Psychological characteristics of revision rhinoplasty patients. In D. G. Becker & S. S. Park (ed.) *Revision Rhinoplasty*, pp. 32–41. New York: Thieme Medical Publishers.

Crerand, C. E., Franklin, M. E., & Sarwer, D. B. (2008). Patient safety: Body dysmorphic disorder and cosmetic surgery. *Plastic & Reconstructive Surgery* 122(4S), 1–15.

Crerand, C. E., Menard, W., & Phillips, K. A. (2010). Surgical and minimally invasive cosmetic procedures among persons with body dysmorphic disorder. *Annals of Plastic Surgery*, 65, 11–16.

Cunningham, B. L., Lokeh, A., & Gutowski, K. A. (2000) Saline-filled breast implant safety and efficacy: a multicenter retrospective review. *Plastic and Reconstructive Surgery*, 105, 2143–9.

De Arruda Alves, M. C., Abla, L. E. F., Santos, R. A. S., & Ferreira, L. M. (2005). Quality of life and self-esteem following rhytidoplasty. *Annals of Plastic Surgery*, 54, 511–14.

Didie, E. R., & Sarwer, D. B. (2003). Factors that influence the decision to undergo cosmetic breast augmentation surgery. *Journal of Women's Health*, 12, 241–53.

Dillerud, E., & Haheim, L. L. (1993). Long term results of blunt suction lipectomy assessed by a patient questionnaire survey. *Plastic and Reconstructive Surgery*, 92, 35–42.

Edgerton, M. T., Jacobson, W. E., & Meyer, E. (1960). Surgical-psychiatric study of patients seeking plastic (cosmetic) surgery: Ninety-eight consecutive patients with minimal deformity. *British Journal of Plastic Surgery*, 13, 136–45.

Edgerton, M. T., Meyer, E., & Jacobson, W. E. (1961). Augmentation mammaplasty II: Further surgical and psychiatric evaluation. *Plastic and Reconstructive Surgery*, 27, 279–302.

Ercolani, M., Baldaro, B., Rossi, N., & Trombini, G. (1999). Five year follow-up of cosmetic rhinoplasty. *Journal of Psychosomatic Research*, 47, 283–6.

Fiala, T. G., Lee, W. P. A., & May, J. W. (1993) Augmentation mammoplasty: Results of a patient survey. *Annals of Plastic Surgery*, 30, 503–9.

Flegal, K. M., Carroll, M. D., Ogden, C. L., & Curtin, L. R. (2010). Prevalence and trends in obesity among US adults, 1999–2008. *Journal of the American Medical Association*, 303, 235–41.

Fried, R. G., & Cash, T. F. (1998). Cutaneous and psychosocial benefits of alpha hydroxyl acid use. *Perceptual and Motor Skills*, 86, 137–8.

Fryzek, J. P., Weiderpass, E., Signorello, L. B., Hakelius, L., Lipworth, L., Blot, W. J., et al. (2000). Characteristics of women with cosmetic breast augmentation surgery compared with breast reduction surgery patients and women in the general population of Sweden. *Annals of Plastic Surgery*, 45, 349–56.

Fryzek, J. P., Signorello, L. B., Hakelius, L., Feltelius, N., Ringberg, A., Blot, W. J., et al. (2001a). Self-reported symptoms among cosmetic breast implant and breast reduction surgery. *Plastic and Reconstructive Surgery*, 107, 206–13.

Fryzek, J. P., Signorello, L. B., Hakelius, L., Lipworth, L., McLaughlin, J. K., Blot, W. J., et al. (2001b). Local complications and subsequent symptom reporting among women with cosmetic breast implants. *Plastic and Reconstructive Surgery*, 107, 214–21.

Gabriel, S. E., Woods, J. E., O'Fallon, W. M., Beard, C. M., Kurland, L. T., Melton, L. J., 3rd. (1997). Complications leading to surgery after breast implantation. *New England Journal of Medicine*, 336, 677–82.

Giese, S. Y., Bulan, E. J., Commons, G. W., Spear, S. L., Yanovski, J. A. (2001). Improvements in cardiovascular risk profile with large-volume liposuction: A pilot study. *Plastic and Reconstructive Surgery*, 108, 510–19.

Goin, M. K., & Rees, T. D. (1991). A prospective study of patients' psychological reactions to rhinoplasty. *Annals of Plastic Surgery*, 27, 210–15.

Goin, M. K., Burgoyne, R. W., Goin, J. M., & Staples, F. R. (1980). A prospective psycho-logical study of 50 female face-lift patients. *Plastic and Reconstructive Surgery*, 65, 436–42.

Goodman, M. P. (2009). Female cosmetic genital surgery. *Obstetrics and Gynecology*, 113, 154–9.

Handel, N., Wellisch, D., Silverstein, M. J., Jensen, J. A., & Waisman, E. (1993). Knowledge, concern and satisfaction among augmentation mammaplasty patients. *Annals of Plastic Surgery*, 30, 13–22.

Hay, G. G. (1970). Psychiatric aspects of cosmetic nasal operations. *British Journal of Psychiatry*, 116, 85–97.

Hay, G. G., & Heather, B. B. (1973). Changes in psychometric test results following cosmetic nasal operations. *British Journal of Psychiatry*, 122, 89–90.

Hern, J., Hamann, J., Tostevin, P., Rowe-Jones, J., & Hinton, A. (2002). Assessing psycho-logical morbidity in patients with nasal deformity using the CORE questionnaire. *Clinical Otolaryngology*, 27, 359–64.

Hill, G., & Silver, A. G. (1950). Psychodynamic and esthetic motivations for plastic surgery. *Psychosomatic Medicine*, 12, 345–52.

Holmich, L. R., Kjoller, K., Fryzek, J. P., Høier-Madsen, M., Vejborg, I., Conrad, C., et al. (2003). Self-reported diseases and symptoms by rupture status among unselected Danish women with cosmetic silicone breast implants. *Plastic and Reconstructive Surgery*, 111, 723–32.

Independent Healthcare Advisory Services (IHAS) (2010). *Safeguards to be introduced for provision of Injectable Cosmetic Treatments as Quality Mark announced.* http://www.inde-pendenthealthcare.org.uk/index.php?/safeguards-to-be-introduced-for-provision-of-injectable-cosmetic-treatments-as-quality-mark-announced.html

Jacobsen, P. H., Holmich, L. R., McLaughlin, J. K., Johansen, C., Olsen, J. H., Kjøller, K., et al. (2004). Mortality and suicide among Danish women with cosmetic breast implants. *Archives of Internal Medicine*, 164, 2450–5.

Javo, I. M., & Sorlie, T. (2010). Psychosocial characteristics of young Norwegian women interested in liposuction, breast augmentation, rhinoplasty, and abdominoplasty: A pop-ulation-based study. *Plastic and Reconstructive Surgery*, 125, 1536–43.

Jensen, B., Wittrup, I. H., Friss, S., Kjøller, K., McLaughlin, J. K., Bliddal, H., et al. (2002). Self-reported symptoms among Danish women following cosmetic breast implant sur-gery. *Clinical Rheumatology*, 2002, 21, 35–42.

Kjoller, K., Holmich, L. R., Jacobsen, Friis, S., Fryzek, J., McLaughlin, J. K., et al. (2002). Epidemiological investigation of local complications after cosmetic breast implant sur-gery in Denmark. *Annals of Plastic Surgery*, 48, 229–37.

Kjoller, K., Holmich, L. R., Fryzek, J. P., Jacobsen, Friis, S., McLaughlin, J. K., et al. (2003). Characteristics of women with cosmetic breast implants compared with women with other types of cosmetic surgery and population-based controls in Denmark. *Annals of Plastic Surgery*, 50, 6–12.

Klein, S., Fontana, L., Young, V. L., Coggan, A. R., Kilo, C., Patterson, B. W., et al. (2004). Absence of an effect of liposuction on insulin action and risk factors for coronary heart disease. *New England Journal of Medicine*, 350, 2549–57.

Koot, V. C., Peeters, P. H., Granath, F., Grobbee, D. E., & Nyren, O. (2003). Total and cause specific mortality among Swedish women with cosmetic breast implants: A prospective study. *British Medical Journal*, 326, 527–8.

Knorr, N. J., Edgerton, M. T., & Hoopes, J. E. (1967). The 'insatiable' cosmetic surgery patient. *Plastic and Reconstructive Surgery,* 40, 285–89.

Linn, L., & Goldman, I. B. (1949). Psychiatric observations concerning rhinoplasty. *Psychosomatic Medicine,* 11, 307–315.

Lipworth, L., Nyren, O., Weimin, Y., Fryzek, J.P., Tarone, R. E., & McLaughlin, J. K. (2007).Excess mortality from suicide and other external causes of death among women with cosmetic breast implants. *Annals of Plastic Surgery,* 59, 119–23.

Litner J. A., Rotenberg B. W., Dennis, M., Adamson, P. A. (2008). Impact of cosmetic facial surgery on satisfaction with appearance and quality of life. *Archives of Facial Plastic Surgery,* 10, 79–83.

Losee, J. E., Serletti, J. M., Kreipe, R. E., & Caldwell, E. H. (1997). Reduction mammaplasty in patients with bulimia nervosa. *Annals of Plastic Surgery,* 39, 443–46.

Losee, J. E., Jiang, S., Long, D. E., Kreipe, R. E., Caldwell, E. H., & Serletti, J. M. (2004). Macromastia as an etiologic factor in bulimia nervosa: 10-year follow-up after treatment with reduction mammoplasty. *Annals of Plastic Surgery,* 52, 452–7.

Marcus P. (1984). Psychological aspects of cosmetic rhinoplasty. *British Journal of Plastic Surgery,* 37, 313–18.

McIntosh, V. V., Britt, E., & Bulik, C. M. (1994). Cosmetic breast augmentation and eating disorders. *New Zealand Medical Journal,* 107, 151–2.

McLaughlin J. K., Lipworth, L., & Tarone, R. E. (2003). Suicide among women with cosmetic breast implants: a review of the epidemiologic evidence. *Journal of Long Term Effects of Medical Implants,* 13, 445–50.

Meyer, L., & Ringberg, A. (1987). Augmentation mammaplasty-psychiatric and psychosocial characteristics and outcome in a group Swedish women. *Scandanavian Journal of Plastic and Reconstructive Surgery,* 21, 199–208.

Micheli-Pellegrini, V., & Manfrida, G. M. (1979). Rhinoplasty and its psychological implications: Applied psychology observations in aesthetic surgery. *Aesthetic Plastic Surgery,* 3, 299–319.

Miklos, J. R., Moore, R. D. (2008). Labiaplasty of the labia minora: Patients' indications for pursuing surgery. *Journal of Sexual Medicine,* 5, 1492–5.

Mintel Oxygen (Mintel International Group Ltd.) (2010). *Cosmetic Surgery – UK – June 2010.* http://oxygen.mintel.com/index.html

Moss, T. P., Harris, D. L. (2009). Psychological change after aesthetic plastic surgery: A prospective controlled outcome study. *Psychology, Health, & Medicine,* 14, 567–72.

Muhlan, H., Eisenmann-Klein, M., Schmidt, S. (2007). Psychological features in a German sample of female cosmetic surgery candidates. *Aesthetic Plastic Surgery,* 31, 746–51.

Ohlsen, L., Ponten, B., & Hambert, G. (1978). Augmentation mammaplasty: A surgical and psychiatric evaluation of the results. *Annals of Plastic Surgery,* 2, 42–52.

Pecorari, G., Gramaglia, C., Garzaro, M., Abbate-Daga, G., Cavallo, G. P., Giordano, C., *et al.* (2010). Self-esteem and personality in subjects with and without body dysmorphic disorder traits undergoing cosmetic rhinoplasty: preliminary data. *Journal of Plastic, Reconstructive, and Aesthetic Surgery,* 63, 493–8.

Pecori, L., Cervetti, G. G. S., Marinari, G. M., Migliori, F., Adami, G. F. (2007). Attitudes of morbidly obese patients to weight loss and body image following bariatric surgery and body contouring. *Obesity Surgery,* 17, 68–73.

Perovic, S. V., Radojicic, Z. I., Djordjevic, M. L., & Vukadinovic W. (2003). Enlargement and sculpturing of a small and deformed glans. *Journal of Urology,* 170, 1686–90.

Phillips, K. A. (2010). Pharmacotherapy for body dysmorphic disorder. *Psychiatric Annals*, 40, 325–32.

Phillips, K. A., Menard, W. (2006). Suicidality in body dysmorphic disorder: a prospective study. *American Journal of Psychiatry*,163, 1280–2.

Phillips, K. A., Grant, J. E., Siniscalchi, J., & Albertini, R. S. (2001). Surgical and non-psychiatric medical treatment of patients with body dysmorphic disorder. *Psychosomatics*, 42, 504–10.

Pukkala, E., Kulmala, I., Hovi, S. L., Hemminki, E., Keskimäki, I., Pakkanen, M., *et al.* (2003). Causes of death among Finnish women with cosmetic breast implants, 1971–2001. *Annals of Plastic Surgery*, 51, 339–42.

Rankin, M., Borah, G. L., Perry, A. W., & Wey, P. D. (1998). Quality-of-life outcomes after cosmetic surgery. *Plastic and Reconstructive Surgery*, 102, 2139–45.

Rhomberg, M., Pulzi, P., & Piza-Katzer, H. (2003). Single-stage abdominoplasty and mastopexy after weight loss following gastric banding. *Obesity Surgery*, 13, 418–23.

Robin, A. A., Copas, J. B., Jack, A. B., Kaeser, A. C., & Thomas, P. J. (1988). Reshaping the psyche: The concurrent improvement in appearance and mental state after rhinoplasty. *British Journal of Psychiatry*, 152, 539–43.

Rohrich, R. J., Broughton, G., Horton, B., Lipschitz, A., Kenkel, J. M., & Brown, S. A. (2004). The key to long-term success in liposuction: A guide for plastic surgeons and patients. *Plastic and Reconstructive Surgery*, 114, 1945–52.

Samdal, F., Birkeland, K. I., Ose, L., & Amland, P. F. (1995). Effect of large-volume liposuction on sex hormones and glucose- and lipid metabolism in females. *Aesthetic Plastic Surgery*, 19, 131–5.

Sanchez-Guerrero, J., Colditz, G. A., Karlson, E. W., Hunter, D. J., Speizer, F. E., & Liang, M. H. (1995). Silicone breast implants and the risk of connective-tissue diseases and symptoms. *New England Journal of Medicine*, 332, 1666–70.

Sarwer, D. B. (2003). Discussion of causes of death among Finnish women with cosmetic breast implants, 1971–2001. *Annals of Plastic Surgery*, 51, 343–44.

Sarwer, D. B. (2007).The psychological aspects of cosmetic breast augmentation. *Plastic and Reconstructive Surgery*, 120(7 Suppl 1), 110S–7S.

Sarwer, D. B., & Crerand, C. E. (2004). Body image and cosmetic medical treatments. *Body Image: An International Journal of Research*, 1, 99–111.

Sarwer, D. B., & Magee, L. (2006). Physical appearance and society. In D. B. Sarwer, T. Pruzinsky, T. F. Cash, R. M. Goldwyn, L. A. Persing, & L. A. Whitaker (eds.) *Psychological Aspects of Reconstructive and Cosmetic Surgery: Empirical, Clinical, and Ethical Issues*, pp. 23–26. Philadelphia, PA: Lippincott, Williams, and Wilkins.

Sarwer, D. B., Whitaker, L. A., Wadden, T. A., & Pertschuk, M. J. (1997). Body image dissatisfaction in women seeking rhytidectomy or blepharoplasty. *Aesthetic Surgery Journal*, 17, 230–4.

Sarwer, D. B., Bartlett, S. P., Bucky, L. P., LaRossa, D., Low, D. W., Pertschuk, M. J., *et al.* (1998a). Bigger is not always better: body image dissatisfaction in breast reduction and breast augmentation patients. *Plastic and Reconstructive Surgery*, 101, 1956–61.

Sarwer, D. B., Wadden, T. A., Pertschuk, M. J., & Whitaker, L. A. (1998b). Body image dissatisfaction and body dysmorphic disorder in 100 cosmetic surgery patients. *Plastic and Reconstructive Surgery*, 101, 1644–9.

Sarwer, D. B., Wadden, T. A., Pertschuk, M. J., & Whitaker, L. A. (1998c). The psychology of cosmetic surgery: A review and reconceptualization. *Clinical Psychology Review*, 18, 1–22.

Sarwer, D. B., Nordmann, J. E., & Herbert, J. D. (2000). Cosmetic breast augmentation surgery: A critical overview. *Journal of Women's Health*, 9, 843–56.

Sarwer, D. B., Wadden, T. A., & Whitaker, L. A. (2002). An investigation of changes in body image following cosmetic surgery. *Plastic and Reconstructive Surgery*, 109, 363–9.

Sarwer, D. B., LaRossa, D., Bartlett, S. P., Low, D. W., Bucky, L. P., & Whitaker, L. A. (2003). Body image concerns of breast augmentation patients. *Plastic and Reconstructive Surgery*, 112, 83–90.

Sarwer, D. B., Thompson, J. K., & Cash, T. F. (2005a). Obesity and body image in adulthood. *Psychiatric Clinics of North America*, 28, 69–87.

Sarwer, D. B., Wadden, T. A., & Fabricatore, A. N. (2005b). Psychosocial and behavioral aspects of bariatric surgery. *Obesity Research*, 13, 639–48.

Sarwer, D. B., Brown, G. K., & Evans, D. L. (2007). Cosmetic breast augmentation and suicide. *American Journal of Psychiatry*, 164, 1006–113.

Sarwer, D. B., Thompson, J. K., Mitchell, J. E., Rubin, J.P. (2008). Psychological considerations of the bariatric surgery patient undergoing body contouring surgery. *Plastic and Reconstructive Surgery*, 121, 423e–34e.

Schlebusch, L., & Levin, A. (1983). A psychological profile of women selected for augmentation mammaplasty. *South African Medical Journal*, 64, 481.

Schlebusch, L. & Marht, I. (1993). Long-term psychological sequelae of augmentation mammaplasty. *South African Medical Journal*, 83, 267–71.

Sihm, F., Jagd, M., & Pers, M. (1978). Psychological assessment before and after augmentation mammaplasty. *Scandanavian Journal of Plastic Surgery*, 12, 295–8.

Silverman, B. G., Brown, S. L., Bright, R. A., Kaczmarek, R. G., Arrowsmith-Lowe, J. B., Kessler, D. A. (1996). Reported complications of silicone gel breast implants: An epidemiologic review. *Annals of Internal Medicine*, 124, 744–56.

Sommer, B., Zschocke, I., Bergfeld, D., Sattler, G., & Augustin, M. (2003). Satisfaction of patients after treatment with botulinum toxin for dynamic facial lines. *Dermatologic Surgery*, 29, 456–60.

Tignol, J., Biraben-Gotzamanis, L., Martin-Guehl, C., Grabot, D., Aouizerate, B. (2007). Body dysmorphic disorder and cosmetic surgery: Evolution of 24 subjects with a minimal defect in appearance 5 years after their request for cosmetic surgery. *European Psychiatry*, 22, 520–4.

Veale, D. (2000). Outcome of cosmetic surgery and 'DIY' surgery in patients with body dysmorphic disorder. *Psychiatric Bulletin*, 24, 218–20.

Veale, D. (2010). Cognitive behavioral therapy for body dysmorphic disorder. *Psychiatric Annals*, 40, 333–40.

Veale, D., De Haro, L., Lambrou, C. (2003). Cosmetic rhinoplasty in body dysmorphic disorder. *British Journal of Plastic Surgery*, 56, 546–51.

Villeneuve, P. J., Holowaty, E. J., Brisson, J., Xie, L., Xie, L., Ugnat, A. M., Latulippe, L., *et al.* (2006). Mortality among Canadian women with cosmetic breast implants. *American Journal of Epidemiology*, 164, 334–41.

von Soest, T., Kvalem, I. L., Roald, H. E., Skolleborg, K. C. (2009). The effects of cosmetic surgery on body image, self-esteem, and psychological problems. *Journal of Plastic, Reconstructive, and Aesthetic Surgery*, 62, 1238–44.

Vulink, N. C., Sigurdsson, V., Kon, M., Bruijnzeel-Koomen, C. A., Westenberg, H. G., Denys, D. (2006). Body dysmorphic disorder in 3–8% of patients in outpatient dermatology and plastic surgery clinics. *Ned Tijdschr Geneeskd*, 150, 97–100.

Webb, W. L., Slaughter, R., Meyer, E., Edgerton, M. (1965). Mechanisms of psychosocial adjustment in patients seeking 'face-lift' operation. *Psychosomatic Medicine, 27,* 183–92.

Willard, S. G., McDermott, B. E., & Woodhouse, L. (1996). Lipoplasty in the bulimic patient. *Plastic and Reconstructive Surgery, 98,* 276–8.

Wright, M. R., & Wright, W. K. (1975). A psychological study of patients undergoing cosmetic surgery. *Archives of Otolaryngology, 101,* 145–51.

Yates, A., Shisslak, C. M., Allender, J. R., & Wolman, W. (1988). Plastic surgery and the bulimic patient. *International Journal of Eating Disorders, 7,* 557–60.

Young, V. L., Nemecek, J. R., & Nemecek, D. A. (1994). The efficacy of breast augmentation: Breast size increase, patient satisfaction, and psychological effects. *Plastic and Reconstructive Surgery, 94,* 958–69.

Zojajii, R., Javanbakht, M., Ghanadan, A., Hosien, H., & Sadeghi, H. (2007). High prevalence of personality abnormalities in patients seeking rhinoplasty. *Otolaryngology-Head and Neck Surgery, 137,* 83–7.

SECTION 2.4

EXPERIENCES OF PEOPLE WHO HAVE A VISIBLE DIFFERENCE

CHAPTER 26

CONGENITAL CONDITIONS

KRISTIN BILLAUD FERAGEN

INTRODUCTION

PEOPLE's perception is automatically drawn to aspects of appearance that differ from what is expected. Consequently, individuals with a congenital condition resulting in a difference of the face or body have to cope with a social visibility that most people do not experience on a daily basis. The consequences of this visibility may impact upon the affected person's feelings, thoughts, and behaviours, and in addition, may influence the responses of other people. It is the complex interplay of these individual and social factors that determines the psychological and psychosocial consequences of living with a visible difference.

Many of the existing studies in this area of research have been based on two assumptions (Rumsey & Harcourt, 2005). The first is that concerns about appearance, and the processes involved in such concerns, differ between individuals with and without a visible difference. The second assumption is that negative experiences will result from the difference in appearance, and that the nature and intensity of these experiences will be directly related to the degree of visible difference. Assumptions of risk are based on the close associations between self-perceptions and appearance (Harter, 1999), in addition to stereotypes, sociocultural norms, and an increasing use of cosmetic surgery, that may conspire to render individuals with congenital anomalies more unusual and therefore noticeable, and hence more socially vulnerable (Bull & Rumsey, 1988; Pruzinsky et al., 2006). These suppositions have, in the past, contributed to a problem-focused approach to research when exploring the question of adjustment to a congenital condition. More recent research, however, demonstrates that the range of emotions, cognitions, and behaviours of individuals with congenital conditions is comparable to that found in people who are generally dissatisfied with their 'normal' appearance (Rumsey, 2002). Further, review studies state that most individuals with a congenital condition cope well (Endriga & Kapp-Simon 1999; Hunt et al., 2005). Such findings challenge the assumption of the inevitability of psychological problems and indicate processes of strength and resilience in some individuals with a visible difference.

Congenital Conditions Affecting Appearance

A congenital condition is defined as having existed pre-memory (Harris, 1997), meaning that the affected individual has no experience of what life is like without the condition. Several congenital conditions can potentially affect an individual's appearance. These conditions involve various body sites, and differ with respect to severity and degree of visibility. Congenital conditions will also vary as to whether or not they are paired with impairments in cognitive function or other medical problems, factors that may alter the psychological impact of a condition on an individual or a child's parents. Further, while some congenital conditions are present at birth but their visibility reduces over time due to treatment, other conditions, such as neurofibromatosis, develop over time, resulting in more apparent visible differences with age. The psychological challenges and experiences of people living with different congenital conditions might, therefore, differ, depending on the specific characteristics of their condition.

Congenital conditions can be classified according to the type or affected body site (Harris, 1997), and may involve the head and neck (craniofacial conditions), other parts of the body, or the vascular or nervous systems.

Congenital conditions involving the head and neck

The most common condition involving the head and neck is a cleft of the lip and/or palate, affecting approximately 1–2 per 1,000 newborns (Sivertsen et al., 2008). The embryologic development of the face and the palate takes place between the 5th and 11th week of gestation (Watson, 2002). Interference with the processes of cell fusion during facial development may result in a cleft. Dependent on the timing of the disturbance, the degree of cleft varies; it may involve, separately or in combination, the lip, the alveolus, and/or the palate. In addition, the cleft may be unilateral (left- or right-sided), or bilateral. The causes of this failure of neural crest cells to migrate properly and fuse are still not completely understood, but involve interactions of both genetic and environmental factors (Jugessur & Murray, 2005).

A large number of other conditions exist involving the head, face, or neck, most of which are rare. They may result from a failure by a part of the face or head to develop (hemifacial microsomias). Other conditions include complex facial clefts, the absence of an ear or an eye, or an underdevelopment of some facial structures, e.g. the cheek and jaw bones (Treacher Collins syndrome). Other conditions are characterized by a premature fusion of the suture lines of the skull, resulting in craniosynostoses (Crouzon and Apert syndrome).

Congenital conditions involving the nervous system

Neurofibromatosis type 1 is a genetically-inherited neurocutaneous disorder, affecting the growth and formation of nerve cells. The prevalence of this disorder is approximately 1 per 3,000 people (Ferner et al., 2007). The disorder causes neural crest cells to proliferate excessively throughout the body, forming tumours on body nerves. The disease is characterized by visible 'café au lait' patches, peripheral neurofibromas, and deformed bones. Changes start at birth (Mouridsen & Sorensen 1995), and symptomatology, intensity, and progression are extremely variable in this congenital condition.

Congenital conditions involving vascular development

Vascular anomalies are congenital errors in vascular development and can be divided into haemangiomas (vascular tumours) and vascular malformations (Buckmiller et al., 2010). Haemangiomas affect 1% of children, while vascular malformations, such as port-wine stains are ten times less common (Sandler et al., 2009). Vascular malformations are present at birth and they do not regress. Haemangiomas, on the other hand, proliferate between the ages of 6–10 months and usually disappear completely before the child is 10 years old (Hoornweg et al., 2009). The majority of these lesions occur in a visible location on the head or neck (Buckmiller et al., 2010).

Congenital conditions involving other body parts

These include the failure of part of a limb to develop—resulting for example in a missing breast, hand, or foot, or in a shape anomaly. The prevalence of such congenital conditions is the same as those involving the head and neck (Harris, 1997). Failure of the fingers or toes to separate (syndactyly) and growth of extra digits (polydactyly) are congenital anomalies which also occur relatively frequently.

PSYCHOLOGICAL ADJUSTMENT: RESEARCH FINDINGS

Research provides an inconsistent picture of the psychological adjustment of people living with a congenital condition (Rumsey & Harcourt 2004), indicating the involvement of multifaceted and complex processes. In order to understand the psychological consequences of conditions affecting appearance, one needs to take into account the immense variation in affected body sites, the severity of a condition, and the specific challenges associated with the different conditions. In addition, there are a number of individual, situational, and societal factors that affect psychological functioning. However, in spite of the complexity of variables involved and the differences in findings, research points to a consensus regarding some of the reported challenges and difficulties, for both the affected persons and their families (Rumsey, 2002). Specifically, living with such a condition can have a potential impact upon self-perceptions, interpersonal experiences, emotional adjustment, and cognitive functioning (see, e.g. Benjamin et al., 1993; Lansdown et al., 1997). These are considered in the following sections, and illustrated with quotes from published research and clinical settings with children or adults with a congenital visible difference.

Self-perceptions and satisfaction with appearance

My appearance always gets in the way. So I try to show other people who I really am, by using my personality [girl, aged 14].

I do not ask for surgery in order to be beautiful. I just want to feel normal [female, aged 22].

Studies have demonstrated an association between the severity of a congenital condition and 'objective' evaluations of appearance (Okkerse et al., 2001). A visible difference may also have a negative impact on the individual's self-perceptions of appearance (Thomas et al., 1997; Millard & Richman, 2001), supporting the theoretical assumption that internalizations of cultural appearance ideals may affect self-perceptions negatively (Harter, 1999). Such findings do not, however, indicate an association between severity of a condition and psychological adjustment, as is often presumed by many health professionals and people in general. The associations between objective and subjective evaluations of appearance, and their relations to psychological adjustment, are much more complex and multifaceted. The fact that degree of visible difference does not predict level of psychological distress is one of the most consistent findings in the present field of research (Benjamin et al., 1993; Rumsey & Harcourt, 2004; Ong et al., 2007). It is the individual's subjective appearance satisfaction, and the extent to which he or she believes the congenital condition is visible to others, that appear to be the best predictors of psychological adjustment (Wolkenstein et al., 2001; Rumsey & Harcourt, 2004; Moss, 2005).

Self-evaluations of appearance and social experiences are strongly intertwined (Cash, 2002). Appearance-related comments from peers about weight or shape (Smolak, 2002), or about a child's differing appearance (Thompson & Kent, 2001) might affect the child's self-perceptions. Accordingly, a child with a facial difference might internalize other people's reactions to the congenital condition as his or her own views (Thompson & Kent, 2001), and interpret ambiguous social experiences in light of these 'self-views' (Tantleff-Dunn & Gokee, 2002). Although both theory and empirical findings point to a heightened risk of negative self-perceptions when there is a difference in appearance (Turner et al., 1997; Harter, 1999; Levine & Smolak, 2002; Bilboul et al., 2006), there are also findings which contradict this view, pointing to average or above average scores on self-perception measures (Kapp-Simon et al., 1992; Barton & North, 2007; Feragen et al., 2010). The variation in findings may partly be due to methodological issues. Other explanations for the conflicting results might be differences in the level of importance the person attaches to his or her appearance (Moss & Carr, 2004), and whether the individual interprets ambiguous social experiences as negative, neutral, or positive responses to the visible difference (Feragen et al., 2009).

Psychosocial experiences and interactions

Of course people are curious! I would be curious too [boy, aged 10].

When unknown people stare at me, I feel like the Elephant-man, and I want to disappear. This feeling is in strong contrast to the inner strength I feel at work or with my friends [male, aged 34].

The disadvantages I suffer as a result of having lost my right eye are insignificant in comparison with those problems raised by my actually looking different (Marc Crank, cited in Lansdown et al., 1997, p. 27).

Several decades ago, Macgregor (1953) identified particular aspects of social experiences that were affected in people with an unusual appearance, such as the inability to feel anonymous as a result of continuous unwanted attention. Such attention includes verbal or non-verbal reactions from others, comments and questions, staring, surprise, aversion, or social discomfort. In spite of individual differences, many similarities are reported in the experiences of people affected by a visible difference, and across a wide range of conditions (Mouridsen & Sorensen, 1995; Lansdown et al., 1997; Rumsey et al., 2003; Weinstein & Chamlin 2005). Clinical experience suggests that the lack of control over other people's responses to the visible difference enhances a sense of social vulnerability, a vulnerability that may turn into anxieties associated with forming relationships and meeting new people. Studies have consequently searched for an association between visible conditions and behavioural inhibition, but have yet to paint a clear picture (for a review, see Endriga & Kapp-Simon, 1999). Nevertheless, for some individuals, the burden of negative social experiences associated with a visible difference is profound, and surpasses the impact of medical problems related to a specific condition.

An association between appearance concerns, emotional distress, and negative social experiences—such as comments, criticism, staring, or teasing—has been demonstrated in adolescents without a visible difference (Adams & Bukowski, 2008), and in people with a visible skin disorder (Magin et al., 2008). Some studies have reported a high frequency of teasing and appearance-related bullying in children with visible differences (Benjamin et al., 1993; Hunt et al., 2006; Turner et al., 1997), and more than 60% of parents of children with birthmarks reported concerns about their child being teased at school (Sandler et al., 2009). Further, children who looked at a video showing unfamiliar peers with a facial port-wine stain believed that the facial difference would attract teasing and staring from others. The participants' willingness to become friends with the affected child, was not, however, affected by this belief (Demellweek et al., 1997). One study (Feragen & Borge, 2010) found an interaction between cleft visibility and gender, indicating that a visible difference had a more negative impact on girls than on boys. However, this association was fully mediated by experiences of peer harassment, highlighting the importance of interpersonal experiences for subjective perceptions of appearance. Negative experiences, or expectations of them, clearly contribute to negative self-appraisals and social comparisons, as well as to social isolation and emotional distress.

While the negative social consequences of a visible difference have been investigated from many different perspectives, few studies have explored the effects of positive social experiences—such as close friendships, romantic relationships and social acceptance—on people with congenital conditions. It is well known from general psychology that friendships and social acceptance may act as a buffer against emotional difficulties (Pedersen et al., 2007; McElhaney et al., 2008), a perspective that remains generally under-represented in research on conditions affecting peoples' physical appearance (La Greca & Bearman, 2000). Some studies have investigated the role of friendships, supporting the view that social relationships may be important protective factors for persons with a facial difference (Meyerson, 2001; Feragen et al., 2010).

Until recently, social difficulties encountered by people with a visible difference have been interpreted, primarily, as a consequence of an unusual appearance. More recently, researchers have also investigated, and have found, neurodevelopmental markers of interpersonal difficulties in children and adults with congenital conditions (Barton & North, 2004; Nopoulos et al., 2005; Boes et al., 2007). One study compared different congenital conditions (Snyder & Pope, 2010), and reported that children with haemangiomas, in contrast to the group with craniofacial conditions, did not show deficits related to social function. Since both groups had visible conditions, the result could indicate possible differences in neurodevelopmental function. Consequently, a neurocognitive perspective on congenital conditions may inform our understanding of how biological components interact with the psychological risks related to visible difference (Nopoulos et al., 2002).

Emotional functioning and health

I think about my appearance each day. Often I feel that I do not fit in. However, when I am with my friends, those who do not care, I feel good [girl, aged 15].

People stared at me. Children stood and stared. Every time I went out I had to shut down all my emotions beforehand and try to block everything out (Linda, aged 21, in Lytsy, 2006, p. 79).

Negative self-perceptions of appearance carry a risk of emotional distress within adolescent samples generally (Dekker et al., 2007), as well as for people with weight-related appearance concerns (Eisenberg et al., 2006) and adults with a visible difference (Ramstad et al., 1995). The findings regarding emotional health are equivocal, however. Some studies have indeed found a higher incidence of depressive symptoms in individuals with congenital conditions (Wolkenstein et al., 2001; Hunt et al., 2006), and a Danish study reported a higher incidence of suicide in adults with a cleft than in comparison samples (Christensen et al., 2004). Yet another study found that fewer depressive symptoms were reported by adolescents with a cleft than by adolescents in a reference group without congenital conditions (Feragen et al., 2010). This disparity in findings illustrates the complexity of psychological adjustment: while many individuals with a congenital and visible condition demonstrate good emotional health, others may be at risk for developing significant emotional distress.

An association between generalized anxiety and the presence of a wide range of visible medical conditions has also been indicated (Benjamin et al., 1993; Berk et al., 2001; Rumsey et al., 2003). This association suggests that anticipated and actual negative social experiences impact on emotional health. Negative experiences (e.g. staring or personal questions) may lead the affected person to behave in a less socially skilled manner, such as initiating fewer conversations or making less eye contact (Kapp-Simon and McGuire 1997; Richman 1997; Adachi et al., 2003; Frederickson et al., 2006; Slifer et al., 2006). Social skills have been shown to mediate other people's perceptions of a disfigurement (Rumsey et al., 1986), so that a problematic interaction style linked to social anxiety might reinforce a negative perception of the person with a facial difference, leading to a spiralling cycle of problems (Robinson et al., 1996).

Quality of life

I've never connected my self-confidence to my appearance. I can't change my appearance or the way people see me. All I can do is decide what I choose to feel and respond to. And I can have an effect on people by being how I am as a person (Sandra, aged 22, in Lytsy, 2006, p. 21).

Measuring quality of life has become a way of assessing the impact of a medical condition on the affected individual. Again, however, findings do not provide a consistent picture. Some studies have demonstrated good quality of life, or no negative effects of a congenital condition on perceived life quality (Hoornweg et al., 2009; Kramer et al., 2009; Sagheri et al., 2009; Mani et al., 2010). Reduced quality of life has been associated with patient dissatisfaction regarding appearance in adults with a cleft lip and palate (Marcusson et al., 2002) highlighting, once again, the importance of subjective appearance evaluations in psychological health. Another study compared quality of life in adolescents with conditions affecting facial appearance, adolescents with physical disabilities, and adolescents with attention deficit hyperactive disorder (ADHD) (Topolski et al., 2005). This study found that quality of life was reduced in all three study groups compared to the comparison group, indicating that risk was dependent on the presence of any medical condition, more than on the visibility of a condition.

Whilst parents of children with neurofibromatosis reported a profound impact of the disease on their child's quality of life (Graf et al., 2006), the affected children themselves reported significantly lower levels of distress (Krab et al., 2009). This inconsistency could be an effect of a well-known discrepancy between parent and child reports within psychology (Eiser & Morse, 2001). Alternatively, it may reflect the parents' higher level of anxiety and stress regarding their child's condition, while the child may be too young to fully understand the range of potential consequences.

Cognitive and neuropsychological function

Studies of children with craniofacial conditions and neurofibromatosis indicate that a higher than expected proportion of these children are at risk for associated developmental and cognitive problems (Milerad et al., 1997; Swanenburg et al., 2003; Hyman et al., 2005; Conrad et al., 2009). Such findings indicate that pathological developmental processes occur in association with some congenital conditions and affect cerebral development. Consequently, underlying cognitive difficulties may be a mediating or confounding variable in the design of some studies. The underlying mechanisms related to cognitive functioning should therefore be determined and understood in order to clarify the processes that are involved in the emotional health and psychosocial experiences of people with congenital conditions (Pride et al., 2010). As an example of this need to clarify findings, the reduced social skills of children with neurofibromatosis that were reported in one study were primarily associated with the concurrent presence of ADHD, an association that has been demonstrated by Barton and North (2004).

ADJUSTMENT IN A DEVELOPMENTAL PERSPECTIVE

When she was born, I took her in my arms so that she would not feel how ugly I thought she was. And because I did not want all the others around to think that I was a bad mother [mother of newborn child].

Of course I would like to look more like everybody else. But all other girls around me would like that too! [girl, aged 15].

During the child's first years of life, many families experience stress when having to cope with the pre- or postnatal diagnosis of a congenital condition. Challenges include understanding the consequences of a condition, learning to cope with its uncertain course, and coping with the stresses of surgery and treatment (Endriga & Kapp-Simon, 1999; Weinstein & Chamlin, 2005; Baker et al., 2009). Mother–child attachments have been investigated in craniofacial conditions affecting appearance, indicating few differences between children with clefts and controls (Maris et al., 2000). One study found more secure attachments in mother–child dyads when the child had a craniofacial condition. The results were interpreted as stemming from the increased protectiveness of the child's mother, probably related to the child's congenital condition (Coy et al., 2002).

Later in development, both the transitions from childhood to adolescence, and from adolescence to adulthood, are marked by distinct developmental tasks. These transitional periods include changes in appearance, changes in social interactions and friendship dimensions, and changes related to emotional development. Friendship patterns also change during the transition from childhood to adolescence. During childhood, friendships are more often based on common activities than during adolescence, and less often on characteristics such as self-disclosure and commitment (Newcomb & Bagwell, 1995). Adolescence is also characterized by a new dimension of friendship, this being the development of romantic experiences and relationships. Consequently, social difficulties in individuals with congenital conditions may have a different psychological impact depending on whether they are measured during childhood, adolescence, or adulthood.

One qualitative study explored the concerns of children with orofacial conditions with a particular focus on the transition from primary to secondary school

(Marshman et al., 2009), and found that the children described concerns about aspects of themselves that they developed during this time. The most visible and appearance-related developmental changes occur, however, during puberty, and call for a reorganization of body image and self-perceptions. Girls' satisfaction with body image declines significantly over the adolescent years, as revealed by longitudinal studies (Levine & Smolak, 2002). This decline in positive self-perceptions of appearance seems correlated with an increase in emotional problems such as depressive symptoms (Dekker et al., 2007). When investigating adjustment to a congenital condition, it is crucial to keep this broader developmental perspective in mind so that normal psychological mechanisms are not interpreted as being specific to people living with a visible condition.

PROTECTIVE FACTORS AND RESILIENCE

Sometimes I am glad I was born different. I have learned to look beyond appearances, and do not try to be like everybody else (girl, aged 14)

When I was 14, my mother told me: You can choose to feel sorry about yourself, or you can choose to stand up and do something about it. I chose the second option, and it worked! (girl, aged 16)

The positive aspects of being born without a lower jaw have definitely outweighed the negative aspects. Having to handle social situations differently from how other people do. I've also had to test my limits a bit more than other people to see what I can manage (Sandra, aged 22, in Lytsy, 2006, p. 24).

In order to study processes of resilience in a given population, risk factors have to be presented and their impact discussed. Risk can be a single event but is more often a sequence of stressful experiences, as for children with a congenital condition. In this population, risk factors may be associated with the complications and consequences related to the medical condition, with treatment and surgery, and/or with the presence of associated developmental or cognitive difficulties. In addition, risk may be associated with negative psychosocial experiences, or with negative self-perceptions resulting from a visible difference. Hence, findings of positive adjustment in individuals with a visible condition could indicate the presence of protective factors that provide resilience against the difficulties associated with the condition.

The question of resilience in craniofacial health was first raised by Clifford (1983), but was then left unexplored until two decades later (Mouradian, 2001; Strauss, 2001). There are still few studies explicitly focusing on those who cope well, even if they usually represent the largest proportion of a sample (Eiserman, 2001). Qualitative studies have illustrated how a focus on coping may reveal unique and positive outcomes related to the experiences of living with a facial difference (Eiserman, 2001;

Meyerson, 2001; Edwards et al., 2005). This group's levels of emotional health and social experiences, as well as satisfaction with appearance, have also been reported to be above what is found in the general population (Berger & Dalton, 2009; Hoornweg et al., 2009; Feragen et al., 2010). Furthermore, young adults with a cleft and parents of children with this condition have reported a range of positive outcomes resulting from living with a cleft, such as better self-understanding, greater personal strength, more effective ability to regulate emotions, and a greater sense of belonging (Baker et al., 2009).

INTERVENTIONS AND CLINICAL PRACTICE

In order to tailor preventive work and effective clinical interventions, an initial understanding of the challenges associated with living with a visible condition is essential. Interventions should subsequently aim to minimize those aspects of risk that have been identified by empirical research. However, the variation and complexity involved in psychological adjustment to a visible condition points to the need for an individual approach in clinical practice.

The strong link between social experiences and subjective appearance evaluations (Cash, 2002) suggests there is value in strengthening aspects of social experience when seeking to prevent and treat appearance-concerns (Kapp-Simon, 1995). This can be done by broadening the person's repertoire of social skills, thereby strengthening social competence. Positive social skills encourage favourable reactions from others, which further strengthen a person's self-perceptions (Rumsey, 2002). Indeed, such interventions have been demonstrated to be useful in the treatment of appearance concerns (Robinson et al., 1996; Kapp-Simon et al., 2005). Equally important are interventions aimed at reducing teasing behaviours and strengthening protective factors, such as friendships and social support.

The individual's subjective perceptions of his or her social experiences are strongly associated with their emotional impact. People are selective in their interpretation of social experiences, and tend to focus on information supporting their internalized view of themselves. In a similar way, an individual's satisfaction with appearance is based on cognitions and subjective evaluations, providing tools for intervention. Knowledge of these tendencies provides an opportunity to focus on these perceptions when planning psychological interventions (Clarke, 1999). Accordingly, a cognitive-behavioural approach has been demonstrated to improve social confidence and perceptions of social support in individuals with a visible difference (Kleve et al., 2002; Maddern et al., 2006). Interestingly, Kleve et al. (2002) showed that participants perceived their disfigurement as less noticeable after the intervention. From a clinical perspective, this finding illustrates the notion of malleable self-perceptions of appearance.

Psychosocial care provided at an individual level should coexist with interventions provided through healthcare systems. Further, professionals working in the field of visible differences have a responsibility to inform the community at a broader level, and to challenge stereotypes and sociocultural values affecting the lives of people living with a visible condition. The presence of stereotypes and prejudices also support the importance of public education, and the need to work on the social, political, and economic forces that support and sustain appearance ideals (Rumsey & Harcourt, 2005). At the individual level, the child and the parents of children with a congenital condition should be given information about how they can increase the positive coping repertoire of their child, and turn the challenges of living with a medical condition into a strengthening experience. (Interventions to support people living with a visible difference are discussed in depth in Chapter 38.)

METHODOLOGICAL ISSUES AND
FUTURE RESEARCH

Knowledge concerning the psychological impact of a visible and congenital condition is still largely dominated by research on craniofacial conditions, and within this, mainly on people with cleft lip/palate. Samples including other congenital conditions remain sparse in comparison, restricting our knowledge concerning specific psychological challenges that might be associated with conditions such as neurofibromatosis or vascular anomalies.

Many studies on the impact of visible differences are still limited by methodological problems, in spite of an increase in the quality of methodology over the last decades (Pope & Speltz, 1997). First, most studies are limited by small sample sizes (Hunt et al., 2005; Hyman et al., 2005). In order to address this problem, studies often include people with different conditions in the same study, without a careful account of the potential differences between them that might influence the results (Speltz & Richman, 1997). There is also a lack of knowledge concerning gender differences in terms of adjustment to a visible difference—again due to small sample sizes—which impede comparisons across gender. Furthermore, a large number of studies are based on samples of widely differing ages, thereby increasing the risk of confounding the results on the basis of development variability. In addition, the research field struggles with a lack of representative samples with regards to the population under study, variation in the use of concepts, measures and instruments, a lack of longitudinal studies, and difficulties in finding appropriate comparison or control groups (Rumsey & Harcourt, 2004; Hyman et al., 2005). Consequently, the validity of results as well as the ability to generalize them can sometimes be questionable.

Future research should aim at counteracting the methodological problems described earlier. Research should also be based on different methods and methodologies in order to broaden our understanding of living with a visible difference. A better understanding is needed of what supports positive outcomes and coping, in order to capitalize on this knowledge in clinical interventions. Other areas of research which are under-represented concern people from a wider range of ethnic and subcultural groups, in addition to older adults with congenital conditions. Moreover, while clinical experience suggests that changes of school, starting a new job, or a relationship break-up may be particularly hard for people with a visible difference, there is still a lack of research on the impact of periods of transition on children and adults.

Future research should take particular care to investigate the psychological consequences of a congenital condition in light of general psychological knowledge and theories. This will enable us to differentiate between normal psychological and developmental processes, and those that are specific to people with a visible difference.

CONCLUSION

Complex factors are involved in adjustment to a congenital condition, some of them more briefly presented than others in the present chapter. These include interpersonal experiences, self-perceptions, emotional responses, cognitive processes, and developmental issues. These multifaceted processes—which may occur at an individual, social, and/or sociocultural level—are often difficult to capture and measure in empirical studies. In addition, methodological issues make interpretation and generalization across studies difficult. Despite the enormous range of congenital conditions, however, there seem to be more similarities than differences with regards to the experiences of those affected. In summary, individuals living with congenital and visible conditions appear to be at greater risk of experiencing negative self-perceptions and interpersonal difficulties. Yet it is also clear that many cope effectively with the social and emotional challenges they encounter by restricting the impact of these challenges on their self-perceptions. Some people even have the capacity to transform the challenge of living with a visible difference into a positive experience. A balanced understanding of the experience of living with differences resulting from congenital conditions considers the whole breadth of people's experience, and includes mechanisms of resilience and successful coping as well as specific challenges and difficulties.

REFERENCES

Adachi, T., Kochi, S., & Yamaguchi, T. (2003). Characteristics of nonverbal behavior in patients with cleft lip and palate during interpersonal communication. *Cleft Palate–Craniofacial Journal*, 40, 310–16.

Adams, R. E. & Bukowski, W. M. (2008). Peer victimization as a predictor of depression and body mass index in obese and non-obese adolescents. *Journal of Child Psychology and Psychiatry*, 49, 858–66.

Baker, S. R., Owens, J., Stern, M., & Willmot, D. (2009). Coping strategies and social support in the family impact of cleft lip and palate and parents' adjustment and psychological distress. *Cleft Palate–Craniofacial Journal*, 46, 229–36.

Barton, B. & North, K. (2004). Social skills of children with neurofibromatosis type 1. *Developmental Medicine and Child Neurology*, 46, 553–63.

Barton, B. & North, K. (2007). The self-concept of children and adolescents with neurofibromatosis type 1. *Child: Care, Health, and Development*, 33, 401–8.

Benjamin, C. M., Colley, A., Donnai, D., Kingston, H., Harris, R., & Kerzin-Storrar, L. (1993). Neurofibromatosis type 1 (NF1): knowledge, experience, and reproductive decisions of affected patients and families. *Journal of Medical Genetics*, 30, 567–74.

Berger, Z. E. & Dalton, L. J. (2009). Coping with a cleft: psychosocial adjustment of adolescents with a cleft lip and palate and their parents. *Cleft Palate–Craniofacial Journal*, 46, 435–43.

Berk, N. W., Cooper, M. E., Liu, Y. E., & Marazita, M. L. (2001). Social anxiety in Chinese adults with oral-facial clefts. *Cleft Palate–Craniofacial Journal*, 38, 126–33.

Bilboul, M. J., Pope, A. W., & Snyder, H. T. (2006). Adolescents with craniofacial anomalies: psychosocial adjustment as a function of self-concept. *Cleft Palate–Craniofacial Journal*, 43, 392–400.

Boes, A. D., Murko, V., Wood, J. L., *et al.* (2007). Social function in boys with cleft lip and palate: relationship to ventral frontal cortex morphology. *Behavioural Brain Research*, 181, 224–31.

Buckmiller, L. M., Richter, G. T., & Suen, J. Y. (2010). Diagnosis and management of hemangiomas and vascular malformations of the head and neck. *Oral Diseases*, 16, 405–18.

Bull, R. & Rumsey, N. (1988). *The Social psychology of facial appearance*. London: Springer-Verlag.

Cash, T. F. (2002), Cognitive-behavioral perspectives on body-image. In T. F. Cash and T. Pruzinsky (eds.) *Body image. A handbook of theory, research, and clinical practice*, pp. 38–46. New York: Guilford Press.

Christensen, K., Juel, K., Herskind, A. M., & Murray, J. C. (2004). Long term follow up study of survival associated with cleft lip and palate at birth. *British Medical Journal*, 328, 1405.

Clarke, A. (1999). Psychosocial aspects of facial disfigurement: Problems, management and the role of a lay-led organization. *Psychology, Health and Medicine*, 4, 127–42.

Clifford, E. (1983). Why are they so normal? *Cleft Palate Journal*, 20, 83–4.

Conrad, A. L., Richman, L., Nopoulos, P., Dailey, S. (2009). Neuropsychological functioning in children with non-syndromic cleft of the lip and/or palate. *Child Neuropsychology*, 15, 471–84.

Coy, K., Speltz, M. L., & Jones, K. (2002). Facial appearance and attachment in infants with orofacial clefts: a replication. *Cleft Palate–Craniofacial Journal*, 39, 66–72.

Dekker, M. C., Ferdinand, R. F., van Lang, N. D., Bongers, I. L., van der Ende, J., & Verhulst, F. C. (2007). Developmental trajectories of depressive symptoms from early childhood to late adolescence: gender differences and adult outcome. *Journal of Child Psychology and Psychiatry*, 48, 657–66.

Demellweek, C., Humphris, G. M., Hare, M., & Brown, J. (1997). Children's perception of, and attitude towards, unfamiliar peers with facial port-wine stains. *Journal of Pediatric Psychology*, 22, 471–85.

Edwards, T. C., Patrick, D. L., Topolski, T. D., Aspinall, C. L., Mouradian, W. E., & Speltz, M. L. (2005). Approaches to craniofacial-specific quality of life assessment in adolescents. *Cleft Palate–Craniofacial Journal*, 42, 19–24.

Eisenberg, M. E., Neumark-Sztainer, D., Haines, J., & Wall, M. (2006). Weight-teasing and emotional well-being in adolescents: longitudinal findings from Project EAT. *Journal of Adolescent Health*, 38, 675–83.

Eiser, C. & Morse, R. (2001). Can parents rate their child's health-related quality of life? Results of a systematic review. *Quality of Life Research*, 10, 347–57.

Eiserman, W. (2001). Unique outcomes and positive contributions associated with facial difference: expanding research and practice. *Cleft Palate–Craniofacial Journal*, 38, 236–44.

Endriga, M. C. & Kapp-Simon, K. A. (1999). Psychological issues in craniofacial care: state of the art. *Cleft Palate–Craniofacial Journal*, 36, 3–11.

Feragen, K. B. & Borge, A. I. (2010). Peer harassment and satisfaction with appearance in children with and without a facial difference. *Body Image—an International Journal of Research*, 7, 97–105.

Feragen, K. B., Borge, A. I., & Rumsey, N. (2009). Social experience in 10-year-old children born with a cleft: exploring psychosocial resilience. *Cleft Palate–Craniofacial Journal*, 46, 65–74.

Feragen, K. B., Kvalem, I. L., Rumsey, N., & Borge, A. I. H. (2010). Adolescents with and without a facial difference: The role of friendships and social acceptance in perceptions of appearance and emotional resilience. *Body Image—an International Journal of Research*, 7, 271–9.

Ferner, R. E., Huson, S. M., Thomas, N., *et al.* (2007). Guidelines for the diagnosis and management of individuals with neurofibromatosis 1. *Journal of Medical Genetics*, 44, 81–8.

Frederickson, M. S., Chapman, K. L., & Hardin-Jones, M. (2006). Conversational skills of children with cleft lip and palate: a replication and extension. *Cleft Palate–Craniofacial Journal*, 43, 179–8.

Graf, A., Landolt, M. A., Mori, A. C., & Boltshauser, E. (2006). Quality of life and psychological adjustment in children and adolescents with neurofibromatosis type 1. *Journal of Pediatrics*, 149, 348–53.

Harris, D. (1997) Types, causes and physical treatment of visible differences, In R. Lansdown, N. Rumsey, E. Bradbury, T. Carr, and J Partridge (eds.) *Visibly different. Coping with disfigurement*, pp. 79–90. Oxford: Butterworth-Heinemann.

Harter, S. (1999). *The construction of the self. A developmental perspective*. New York: The Guilford Press.

Hoornweg, M. J., Grootenhuis, M. A., & van der Horst, C. M. (2009). Health-related quality of life and impact of haemangiomas on children and their parents. *Journal of Plastic, Reconstructive and Aesthetic Surgery*, 62, 1265–71.

Hunt, O., Burden, D., Hepper, P., & Johnston, C. (2005). The psychosocial effects of cleft lip and palate: a systematic review. *European Journal of Orthodontics*, 27, 274–85.

Hunt, O., Burden, D., Hepper, P., Stevenson, M., & Johnston, C. (2006). Self-reports of psychosocial functioning among children and young adults with cleft lip and palate. *Cleft Palate–Craniofacial Journal*, 43, 598–605.

Hyman, S.L., Shores, A., & North, K. N. (2005). The nature and frequency of cognitive deficits in children with neurofibromatosis type 1. *Neurology*, 65, 1037–44.

Jugessur, A. & Murray, J.C. (2005). Orofacial clefting: recent insights into a complex trait. *Current Opinion in Genetics and Development*, 15, 270–8.

Kapp-Simon, K. A. (1995). Psychological interventions for the adolescent with cleft lip and palate. *Cleft Palate–Craniofacial Journal*, 32, 104–8.

Kapp-Simon, K. A., Simon, D. J., & Kristovich, S. (1992). Self-perception, social skills, adjustment, and inhibition in young adolescents with craniofacial anomalies. *Cleft Palate–Craniofacial Journal*, 29, 352–6.

Kapp-Simon, K. A. & McGuire, D. E. (1997). Observed social interaction patterns in adolescents with and without craniofacial conditions. *Cleft Palate–Craniofacial Journal*, 34, 380–4.

Kapp-Simon, K. A., McGuire, D. E., Long, B. C., & Simon, D. J. (2005). Addressing quality of life issues in adolescents: social skills interventions. *Cleft Palate–Craniofacial Journal*, 42, 45–50.

Kleve, L., Rumsey, N., Wyn-Williams, M., & White, P. (2002). The effectiveness of cognitive-behavioural interventions provided at Outlook: a disfigurement support unit. *Journal of Evaluation in Clinical Practice*, 8, 387–95.

Krab, L. C., Oostenbrink, R., de Goede-Bolder, A., Aarsen, F. K., Elgersma, Y., & Moll, H. A. (2009). Health-related quality of life in children with neurofibromatosis type 1: contribution of demographic factors, disease-related factors, and behavior. *Journal of Pediatrics*, 154, 420–5.

Kramer, F. J., Gruber, R., Fialka, F., Sinikovic, B., Hahn, W., & Schliephake, H. (2009). Quality of life in school-age children with orofacial clefts and their families. *Journal of Craniofacial Surgery*, 20, 2061–6.

La Greca, A. M. & Bearman, K. J. (2000). Children with pediatric conditions: can peers' impressions be managed? And what about their friends? *Journal of Pediatric Psychology*, 25, 147–9.

Lansdown, R., Rumsey, N., Bradbury, E., Carr, T., & Partridge, J. (1997). *Visibly different. Coping with disfigurement*. Oxford: Butterworth-Heinemann.

Levine, M. P. & Smolak, L. (2002), Body image development in adolescence. In T. F. Cash and T. Pruzinsky (eds.) *Body image. A handbook of theory, research, and clinical practice*, pp. 74–82. New York: Guilford Press.

Lytsy, A. (2006). *Another face*. Stockholm: Bulls Graphics.

MacGregor, F. C. (1953). Some psychological hazards of plastic surgery of the face. *Plastic and Reconstructive Surgery*, 12, 123–30.

Maddern, L. H., Cadogan, J. C., & Emerson, M. P. (2006). 'Outlook': A psychological service for children with a different appearance. *Clinical Child Psychology and Psychiatry*, 11, 431–43.

Magin, P., Adams, J., Heading, G., Pond, D., & Smith, W. (2008). Experiences of appearance-related teasing and bullying in skin diseases and their psychological sequelae: results of a qualitative study. *Scandinavian Journal of Caring Sciences*, 22, 430–6.

Mani, M., Carlsson, M., & Marcusson, A. (2010). Quality of Life Varies with Gender and Age among Adults Treated for Unilateral Cleft Lip and Palate. *Cleft Palate–Craniofacial Journal*, 47, 491–8.

Marcusson, A., Paulin, G., & Ostrup, L. (2002). Facial appearance in adults who had cleft lip and palate treated in childhood. *Scandinavian Journal of Plastic and Reconstructive Surgery and Hand Surgery*, 36, 16–23.

Maris, C. L., Endriga, M. C., Speltz, M. L., Jones, K., – DeKlyen, M. (2000). Are infants with orofacial clefts at risk for insecure mother-child attachments? *Cleft Palate–Craniofacial Journal*, 37, 257–65.

Marshman, Z., Baker, S. R., Bradbury, J., Hall, M. J., & Rodd, H. D. (2009). The psychosocial impact of oral conditions during transition to secondary education. *European Journal of Paediatric Dentistry*, 10, 176–80.

McElhaney, K. B., Antonishak, J., & Allen, J.P. (2008). 'They like me, they like me not': popularity and adolescents' perceptions of acceptance predicting social functioning over time. *Child Development*, 79, 720–31.

Meyerson, M. D. (2001). Resiliency and success in adults with Moebius syndrome. *Cleft Palate–Craniofacial Journal*, 38, 231–5.

Milerad, J., Larson, O., Hagberg, C., & Ideberg, M. (1997). Associated malformations in infants with cleft lip and palate: a prospective, population-based study. *Pediatrics*, 100, 180–6.

Millard, T. & Richman, L. C. (2001). Different cleft conditions, facial appearance, and speech: relationship to psychological variables. *Cleft Palate–Craniofacial Journal*, 38, 68–75.

Moss, T. P. (2005). The relationships between objective and subjective ratings of disfigurement severity, and psychological adjustment. *Body Image—an International Journal of Research*, 2, 151–9.

Moss, T. & Carr, T. (2004). Understanding adjustment to disfigurement: the role of the self-concept. *Psychology and Health*, 19, 737–48.

Mouradian, W. E. (2001). Deficits versus strengths: ethics and implications for clinical practice and research. *Cleft Palate–Craniofacial Journal*, 38, 255–9.

Mouridsen, S. E. & Sorensen, S. A. (1995). Psychological aspects of von Recklinghausen neurofibromatosis (NF1). *Journal of Medical Genetics*, 32, 921–4.

Newcomb, A. F. & Bagwell, C. L. (1995). Children's friendship relations: A meta-analytic review. *Psychological Bulletin*, 117, 306–47.

Nopoulos, P., Choe, I., Berg, S., Van, D. D., Canady, J., & Richman, L. (2005). Ventral frontal cortex morphology in adult males with isolated orofacial clefts: relationship to abnormalities in social function. *Cleft Palate–Craniofacial Journal*, 42, 138–44.

Nopoulos, P., Richman, L., Murray, J., & Canady, J. (2002). Cleft palate and craniofacial conditions. *Cleft Palate–Craniofacial Journal*, 39, 123–4.

Okkerse, J. M., Beemer, F. A., Cordia-de, H. M., Heineman-de Boer, J. A., Mellenbergh, G. J., & Wolters, W. H. (2001). Facial attractiveness and facial impairment ratings in children with craniofacial malformations. *Cleft Palate–Craniofacial Journal*, 38, 386–92.

Ong, J., Clarke, A., White, P., Johnson, M., Withey, S., & Butler, P. E. (2007). Does severity predict distress? The relationship between subjective and objective measures of appearance and psychological adjustment, during treatment for facial lipoatrophy. *Body Image—an International Journal of Research*, 4, 239–48.

Pedersen, S., Vitaro, F., Barker, E. D., & Borge, A. I. H. (2007). The timing of middle-childhood peer rejection and friendship: linking early behavior to early-adolescent adjustment. *Child Development*, 78, 1037–51.

Pope, A. W. & Speltz, M. L. (1997). Research of psychosocial issues of children with craniofacial anomalies: progress and challenges. *Cleft Palate–Craniofacial Journal*, 34, 371–3.

Pride, N., Payne, J. M., Webster, R., Shores, E. A., Rae, C., & North, K. N. (2010). Corpus callosum morphology and its relationship to cognitive function in neurofibromatosis type 1. *Journal of Child Neurology*, 25, 834–41.

Pruzinsky, T., Sarwer, D. B., Cash, T. F., Goldwyn, R. M., Persing, J. A., & Whitaker, L. (2006), Multiple perspectives on the psychology of plastic surgery, In D. B. Sarwer, S. P. Bartlett, L. P. Bucky, et al. (eds.) *Psychological aspects of reconstructive and cosmetic plastic surgery. Clinical, empirical, and ethical perspectives*, pp. 3–11. Philadelphia, PA: Lippincott Williams and Wilkins.

Ramstad, T., Ottem, E., & Shaw, W. C. (1995). Psychosocial adjustment in Norwegian adults who had undergone standardised treatment of complete cleft lip and palate. II. Self-reported problems and concerns with appearance. *Scandinavian Journal of Plastic and Reconstructive Surgery and Hand Surgery*, 29, 329–36.

Richman, L. C. (1997). Facial and speech relationships to behavior of children with clefts across three age levels. *Cleft Palate–Craniofacial Journal*, 34, 390–5.

Robinson, E., Rumsey, N., & Partridge, J. (1996). An evaluation of the impact of social interaction skills training for facially disfigured people. *British Journal of Plastic Surgery*, 49, 281–9.

Rumsey, N. (2002). Body image and congenital conditions with visible differences, In T.F. Cash and T. Pruzinsky (eds.) Body image. A handbook of theory, research, and clinical practice, pp. 226–33. New York: The Guilford Press.

Rumsey, N., Bull, R., & Gahagan, D. (1986). A developmental study of children's stereotyping of facially deformed adults. *British Journal of Psychology*, 77, 269–74.

Rumsey, N., Clarke, A., & White, P. (2003). Exploring the psychosocial concerns of outpatients with disfiguring conditions. *Journal of Wound Care*, 12, 247–52.

Rumsey, N. & Harcourt, D. (2004). Body image and disfigurement: issues and interventions. *Body Image—an International Journal of Research*, 1, 83–97.

Rumsey, N. & Harcourt, D. (2005). *The psychology of appearance*. Maidenhead: Open University Press.

Sagheri, D., Ravens-Sieberer, U., Braumann, B., & von Mackensen, S. (2009). An Evaluation of Health-Related Quality of Life (HRQoL) in a group of 4–7 year-old children with cleft lip and palate. *Journal of Orofacial Orthopedics*, 70, 274–84.

Sandler, G., Adams, S., & Taylor, C. (2009). Paediatric vascular birthmarks—the psychological impact and the role of the GP. *Australian Family Physician*, 38, 169–71.

Sivertsen, A., Wilcox, A., Johnson, G. E., Abyholm, F., Vindenes, H. A., & Lie, R. T. (2008). Prevalence of major anatomic variations in oral clefts. *Plastic and Reconstructive Surgery*, 121, 587–95.

Slifer, K. J., Pulbrook, V., Amari, A., et al. (2006). Social acceptance and facial behavior in children with oral clefts. *Cleft Palate–Craniofacial Journal*, 43, 226–36.

Smolak, L. (2002), Body image development in children, In T.F. Cash & T. Pruzinsky (eds.) *Body image. A handbook of theory, research, and clinical practice*, pp. 65–73. New York: Guilford Press.

Snyder, H. & Pope, A. W. (2010). Psychosocial adjustment in children and adolescents with a craniofacial anomaly: diagnosis-specific patterns. *Cleft Palate–Craniofacial Journal*, 47, 264–72.

Speltz, M. L. & Richman, L. (1997). Progress and limitations in the psychological study of craniofacial anomalies. *Journal of Pediatric Psychology*, 22, 433–8.

Strauss, R. P. (2001). 'Only skin deep': health, resilience, and craniofacial care. *Cleft Palate–Craniofacial Journal*, 38, 226–30.

Swanenburg, D. V, Beemer, F. A., Mellenbergh, G. J., Wolters, W. H., & Heineman-de Boer, J. A. (2003). An investigation of the relationship between associated congenital malformations and the mental and psychomotor development of children with clefts. *Cleft Palate–Craniofacial Journal*, 40, 297–303.

Tantleff-Dunn, S. & Gokee, J. L. (2002), Interpersonal influences on body image development, In T.F. Cash and T. Pruzinsky (eds.), *Body image. A handbook of theory, research, and clinical practice*, pp. 108–116. New York: Guilford Press.

Thomas, P. T., Turner, S. R., Rumsey, N., Dowell, T., & Sandy, J. R. (1997). Satisfaction with facial appearance among subjects affected by a cleft. *Cleft Palate–Craniofacial Journal*, 34, 226–31.

Thompson, A. & Kent, G. (2001). Adjusting to disfigurement: processes involved in dealing with being visibly different. *Clinical Psychology Review*, 21, 663–82.

Topolski, T. D., Edwards, T. C., & Patrick, D. L. (2005). Quality of life: how do adolescents with facial differences compare with other adolescents? *Cleft Palate–Craniofacial Journal*, 42, 25–32.

Turner, S. R., Thomas, P. W., Dowell, T., Rumsey, N., & Sandy, J. R. (1997). Psychological outcomes amongst cleft patients and their families. *British Journal of Plastic Surgery*, 50, 1–9.

Watson, A. C. H. (2002), Embryology, aetiology and incidence, In A. C. H. Watson, D. A. Sell, and P. Grunwell (eds.) *Management of cleft lip and palate*, pp. 3–15. London: Whurr Publishers.

Weinstein, J. M. & Chamlin, S. L. (2005). Quality of life in vascular anomalies. *Lymphatic Research and Biology*, 3, 256–9.

Wolkenstein, P., Zeller, J., Revuz, J., Ecosse, E., & Leplege, A. (2001). Quality-of-life impairment in neurofibromatosis type 1: a cross-sectional study of 128 cases. *Archives of Dermatology*, 137, 1421–5.

CHAPTER 27

TRAUMA—WITH SPECIAL REFERENCE TO BURN INJURY

JULIE WISELY

SARAH GASKELL

INTRODUCTION

THIS chapter focuses on the experience of those whose appearance is changed as the result of a traumatic event. Traumatic events typically include road traffic accidents, industrial accidents, violent attacks, and burns sustained through fires or other means. When injuries occur, individuals are often confronted with a traumatic, life-threatening situation that is of sudden onset, with little or no warning. Even more minor injuries can cause considerable pain, discomfort, hospitalization, scarring, and physical limitations. The physical and psychological challenges initiated by this are further exacerbated by medical treatments which are often themselves traumatic, lengthy, and fraught with potential setbacks and uncertain outcomes. The pain, loss of function, changes in skin sensation and disfigurement caused by a traumatic injury often provoke a range of adverse emotional reactions and undoubtedly impact on an individual's body image. There appears also to be something particularly stigmatizing about scars resulting from these kind of injuries. There is nothing like such a scar to tell a film audience that a character is a bad apple; think of Al Pacino in *Scarface* (1983) and 'Freddy' from *A Nightmare on Elm Street* (1984) and 'Two-face' and 'The Joker' in '*Batman: The Dark Night*' (2008). Even children's films feature examples of malevolent characters with damaged skin. The Disney film *The Lion King* (1994) stars Jeremy Irons as the voice of the merciless villain who is named after his 'scar' (seen across his eye).

Much has been documented about how the experience of a traumatic injury which results in a visible difference can impact on the individual—from personal accounts, qualitative investigations, and from larger, quantitative studies. Most of the research in this area tends to focus on the negative impact of traumatic and disfiguring injuries. Two themes emerge here—the impact on the self (feelings, behaviour, self-esteem, and body image) and the impact on relationships with others (from strangers through to intimate partners). These themes are not entirely independent—for example, feelings (such as depression or anxiety) can undoubtedly affect the way we face social situations and interact with others. However, these two strands provide a useful way to structure our exploration of people's experiences in this field. As we shall see, there is much interest in identifying characteristics that may place individuals at risk of poor adjustment post injury. However, more recently the literature has focused on those who seem to cope well. Whilst this literature is relatively small, it yields some interesting findings—some of which we shall show has been put to good effect in therapeutic interventions and support initiatives for patients and their families.

To illustrate these points, this chapter will focus specifically on the area of visible difference acquired through a traumatic burn injury. At its most extreme, a burn can be described as 'the most extensive and frightening [injury] a person can receive' (Van Loey & Van Son, 2003). There has been a significant amount of research conducted around the experience of burn injury and many of the findings apply equally to visible differences acquired through other traumatic injuries.

SETTING THE CONTEXT

The majority of burns are the result of scalds or flames—accounting for more than 75% of all cases (Vyrostek et al., 2001). Contact, flash, electrical, and chemical injuries also occur. Most injuries are accidents sustained either at home or at work. However, acts of deliberate self-harm or self-immolation (attempted suicide by burning) and injuries resulting from assault, abuse, or neglect are also all too frequently reported. Burn injuries are experienced by approximately 250,000 people in the British Isles each year. They can range from a trivial wound requiring self-treatment, through to a severe injury, requiring the highest levels of intensive care and extensive surgery. Convincing data however from both the UK and the US would suggest that most burn injuries are small, covering less than 10% of the body and that only around 5% require inpatient treatment (National Burn Care Review

(NBCR), 2001; Latenser, 2007). Significantly, there is a gender imbalance in this form of trauma. Reliable long-term data suggests that across almost all age groups, 70% of patients are male (Rajipura, 2002), possibly because males are more likely to engage in high-risk forms of lifestyle and employment compared to females. Significant geographical variations exist in the prevalence of burns, thought to be attributed to socio/demographic factors (NBCR, 2001).

It would also seem that burn injuries are more common in people who are psychologically vulnerable in the first place. There is a large body of evidence to indicate that psychiatric and psychological disorders are over-represented in burn-injured populations compared to the normal population (see Klinge et al., (2009) for a review). For example, a significant subset of children who sustain severe burn injuries present with specific symptomatology (e.g. attention deficit hyperactivity disorder, conduct disorder) that are accompanied by supervision and monitoring challenges and may mean children are more likely to engage in impulsive risk-taking behaviours (Tarnowski et al., 1991). Risk factors reported amongst adult populations include alcoholism, deliberate self-harm, psychosis, impulsive risk-taking, substance abuse, depression, anxiety, and personality disorders (see Patterson et al., 1993 for a review). Thus practitioners and researchers in this field need to be acutely aware not only of the psychological harm that the trauma of a burn injury can cause, but also the possibility that psychological vulnerabilities contribute to causing the injury in the first place, as well as influencing the subsequent impact it may have.

THE JOURNEY TO RECOVERY

Improvements in the treatment of burns and other forms of traumatic injury mean that increasing numbers of people across all age groups are surviving more extensive injuries (Feller et al., 1980). Consequently, many survivors are now confronted with greater psychological challenges, in a much longer journey to recovery. In the case of burns, the aims of treatments are to minimize pain and the risk of infection, achieve wound healing in a timely fashion, preserve physical function, minimize cosmetic deformity, and support prompt physical and psychological rehabilitation (Hartford & Kealey, 2007). The UK National Burn Care Review refers to this as the recovery of form, function and feeling (NBCR, 2001). Depending on the severity of the injury, the individual may spend time in the Intensive Care Unit (ICU). This can be a very distressing time—not only because of the struggle for survival but also because of confusion, disorientation, pain, and uncertainty about outcome. Intubation (to provide a means of mechanical ventilation) that limits speech and therefore direct communication can add to the experience of stress.

Once the patient is stabilized, effort is devoted to the care of the burn wound. This phase of treatment is typically the most painful as the patient is subjected to a variety of aversive procedures (e.g. intravenous placements, dressing changes, wound cleansing, skin grafting). A critical concern during this period is that of serious infection of the wounds. Physio- and occupational therapy are introduced early in the process of recovery with the aim of gently increasing mobility and preventing the development of skin contractures. Psychological support for the patient and their family also ideally begins early in this hospitalization phase. Initially wounds look unpleasant and raw and patients have to accept that they will improve. It is not uncommon for patients to want to avoid looking at wounds, or facing their reflection for the first time; supporting the burns patient to take this first step towards adjustment to their new appearance is an important role for family members and the burns care team.

Rehabilitation continues into the longer term after leaving hospital when patients and their families must face the stresses associated with an extensive rehabilitation programme. Individuals must negotiate the difficult transition from social isolation during their hospital stay to reconnection with their former life. Transition home is often when appearance concerns come to the fore. One burns survivor, Amy Acton, describes the 'secure cocoon' of the burns centre, and then feeling 'surprised, shocked and sometimes completely overwhelmed' as she had to contend with the curious stares of others once discharged to her community (Acton, 2004). Up until this point, as many burns survivors will explain, the focus is on physical healing and the goal of being 'well' enough to leave hospital; the reality of how living with a burn injury can go on to impact on life over the longer term is also often not at the forefront of people's minds. Coping with the stigmatization of scarring during this resocialization period can also be overwhelming for families (Knudson-Cooper & Thomas, 1988).

In the initial stages post-discharge, patients usually attend regular outpatient clinics where their wounds are managed. At this stage it is likely that they will still be wearing cumbersome dressings and splints. Once wounds have healed, individuals then progress to the 'scar management' phase of rehabilitation. Procedures are introduced to prevent hypertrophic scarring (scars which become raised), such as the application of skin emollients, massage, and compression dressings—custom-made pressure garments. This stage of treatment may last for many years, as burn scars can take around 2 years to mature and become stable. Over time, colour fades and scars become less rigid and obvious. Phillips (2005) highlights that during this maturation period, anxiety and uncertainly about the eventual outcome is common. During this process of change many feel optimistic that eventually everything will 'be OK', but if not carefully managed expectations may become unrealistic, leading to disappointment, delaying the process of adaptation to the new, changed appearance.

After the relief of losing the bulky dressings, patients may then be required to wear specially tailored, tight-fitting pressure garments. As well as being uncomfortable to wear, they can also be a source of curiosity for the general public. A commonly reported complaint by burns patients in these early stages is having to answer endless questions about what happened, as well as enduring staring, name calling, and teasing. Acton (2004) again captures the feelings of many at this stage, expressing how she 'was not prepared for this and had no idea how to cope with people's reactions'. She says it took her more than 2 years to feel comfortable in social situations and learn how to appreciate her body again, learning that the way she responded could have a huge impact on how others behaved towards her.

James Partridge, a burns survivor and founder of the charity Changing Faces (http://www.changingfaces.org.uk), has proposed that recovering from a burn involves moving through several stages (Partridge, 2005). He suggests that in the first months after the burn injury, the focus is on survival and physical aspects of recovery and rehabilitation. Key psychological issues at this time include coping with pain, grief, acute stress reactions, and early anxiety about appearance. He argues that as recovery progresses into the post-hospital discharge stage, the level of professional and social support starts to decrease and socialization becomes a central challenge. During this post-discharge stage patients may shift between a pre-burn or temporarily scarred vision of the self and an identity as a person with a permanent disfigurement. A range of emotions including anger, shame, grief, and low mood are likely to be common. Partridge proposes that this stage may last from several months to several years post-burn. He also suggests a third stage, which he terms 'advocacy'. At this stage some survivors are somehow able to transform their sense of self by adopting attitudes which are incompatible with society's ideal about attractiveness and beauty in order to rebuild a sense of self-esteem (Partridge, 2005).

In summary, the physical effects of thermal injury, particularly when they involve large areas of the body surface, are profound, and the process of recovery is physically arduous and psychologically challenging.

The Psychological and Social Impact of Burn Injury

A visible difference can have a profound impact on the affected person. People who acquire visible disfigurements through trauma face the dual challenge of managing and adjusting to their own emotional responses, as well as dealing with the behaviour of others.

Impact on emotions and behaviour

Given the unpleasant experience of burn injury itself, it is no surprise that individuals who have been burned experience higher than average levels of psychological distress. Many studies have focused on levels of distress during the phase of hospitalization post injury and a number of psychological and psychiatric symptoms have been documented in both adults and children. These include delirium, anxiety, acute stress reactions, depression, anger, survivor guilt, grief, psychosis, behavioural regression, and aggressiveness (Molinaro, 1978; Kolman, 1983; Patterson et al., 1993; Tedstone et al., 1998). Distressed emotional responding can also occur in members of the patient's family—particularly guilt, helplessness, anger, and fear (Wright & Fulwiler, 1974; Phillips & Rumsey, 2008).

Key emotional and behavioural issues are as follows.

Pain

The pain associated with the treatment of burn injuries is recognized to be particularly aversive and can be difficult to manage adequately. It is often made worse by anticipatory anxiety and feelings of helplessness (Maron & Bush, 1991). Problems associated with undermanaged burn treatment pain in children include distress resulting in uncooperativeness during treatments and dressing changes, and negative interactions between children and nurses. Staff members can also have a difficult time adjusting not only to the child's aversive responses to them, but also to the conflict between the roles of caregiver and paingiver (Miller et al., 1988). It has been observed that children whose pain is better managed recover more quickly, cope better with post-hospital adjustment, and comply better with prescribed exercises and wearing pressure garments (Maron, 1991). Further, a link has been established between longer-term emotional symptoms, including the development and maintenance of suicidal ideation, and acute pain following burn injury in adults, (Edwards et al., 2007). It is clear that well-managed pain leads to better physical, psychological, and (through higher levels of adherence to the wearing of pressure garments) aesthetic outcomes, underscoring the importance of time spent by the multidisciplinary burns team assessing and treating pain. As well as traditional pharmacological approaches to pain management, psychological interventions which teach adaptive coping skills have important benefits in terms of reducing pain and increasing patient satisfaction (Frenay et al., 2001). For example, teaching how to use distraction during dressing changes, or learning how to manage the anxiety that acts to exacerbate their experience of pain.

Post-traumatic stress disorder (PTSD)

Several studies have highlighted the prevalence of symptoms of acute and post-traumatic stress symptoms following burn injury and other traumatic disfiguring injuries in both adults and children (Saigh, 1989; Powers et al., 1994; Fauerbach et al., 1997; Yu & Dimsdale, 1999; Rusch et al., 2000; Thombs et al., 2005; Dyster-Aas et al., 2008). The experience of ICU has been associated with the development of such symptoms, likely to be related to the confusion and distressing memories that patients often have about their ICU stay (Jones et al., 2001). However, in the weeks following any traumatic event, acute stress symptoms will be common and to some extent normal. The experience of burn injury has been described as an example of 'continuous traumatic stress' because of the prolonged impact on the individual of the burn accident itself, the ongoing painful aspects of treatment and the difficulties then presented by reintegrating back to society with a more conspicuous appearance (Gilboa et al., 1994). For some patients, dressing changes can be as psychologically traumatic as their initial injury (Blalock et al., 1994).

Depression and anxiety

Published research on the prevalence of depression and anxiety suggests raised rates ranging from 25–65% over the first year post-injury. Numerous studies have reported that the experience of anxiety is common in burn populations over the longer term. Excluding those with pre-existing psychiatric diagnoses, 26.6% of adult burn patients have been shown to experience clinically significant levels of anxiety 2 years after hospital discharge (West & Spinks, 1988). Even patients with small injuries (less than 1% total body surface area) have been reported to experience clinically significant levels of psychological distress post-burn (Shakespeare, 1998; Tedstone & Tarrier, 1998). This less than straightforward relationship between injury severity and resulting psychological distress is mirrored in the literature reporting on traumatic injuries in general (O'Donnell et al., 2003).

In one of the only UK-based studies examining the long-term impact of burn injury, Phillips (2005) reported on a group of burn-injured adults and found that time is not necessarily a healer. Within this sample, levels of general anxiety, social anxiety, and depression dipped around discharge from hospital, but by 6–2 months had started to re-establish themselves. A number of reasons for this have been postulated. Realizing the permanency of scarring, awareness of functional limitations, concerns regarding the resumption of previous social and occupational roles, and the re-traumatization associated with legal or compensation cases may all help to explain the pattern of psychological adjustment post-burn (Tedstone et al., 1998; Phillips, 2006). As such, it should not be assumed that psychosocial needs diminish over time; instead, it is important to recognize that the process of psychological adaptation can continue for months or even years post-burn and that there will be a wide variation in individual reactions.

The trouble associated with a literature focused solely on identifying psychopathology is that it can leave the reader with the impression that long-term symptoms of distress are an inevitable consequence of a significant burn injury. However, the majority of adult burn survivors appear to adjust quite well to their injuries and certainly for some people, these symptoms are transient and will pass with time (Patterson et al., 1993). Similarly in a review of the paediatric literature, it has been concluded that only a minority of children with burns are at risk of longer-term psychosocial difficulties (Tarnowski et al., 1991). However, just as there is a risk of over-psychopathologizing people with burns, an over-reliance on standardized measures (e.g. of depression) as a barometer of psychological state may hide genuine problems. While a person who has substantial facial burns may be bitterly unhappy, angry, and distressed about their appearance, they may not score as clinically depressed on a recognized measure. Thus, the role of the burn care team is to skilfully identify those whose adjustment is causing them substantial distress so that appropriate intervention can be offered if and when necessary. Given the wide range of responses, and the fluctuations in levels of adjustment over time (Phillips, 2006), there is certainly evidence that levels of anxiety, depression, and social anxiety should be routinely screened for at least 2 years post-burn and preferably beyond.

IMPACT ON BODY IMAGE AND SELF-ESTEEM

There is agreement in the literature that people with visible differences report negative self perceptions and unfavourable levels of self-esteem in response to their own feelings and the reactions of others to their appearance. The loss of a body part or acquisition of a disfigurement following many sorts of trauma, including burn injury, can cause changes not only in appearance, but also in function. This, along with the abrupt and particularly stigmatizing nature of changes in appearance, has been postulated as one of the main challenges in adjusting to burn injury (Patterson et al., 1993). The inability to recognize the self, or an enforced change to the appearance one is accustomed to, represents a profound disruption to the self concept. Psychoanalytical approaches to the skin emphasize its importance to people as a container or frontier for themselves (Gilboa, 2001). If someone suffers a sudden skin injury (such as a burn) the body boundaries are threatened, and so the psychological self is also threatened. Other clinicians describe this as a process of grieving akin to a bereavement response, including elements of denial, anger, distress, anxiety and depression, followed by a gradual process of adaptation (Bradbury, 1997).

In considering the impact on body image, the age at which the injury is sustained is an important factor. It has been observed that children burned before the age of 2 require minimal body-image adaptation because the injury becomes a part of their 'normal' body image (Stoddard, 1982). This is consistent with the developmental literature on body image which documents that it is at approximately the end of the second year that children develop a sense of body image (Fisher, 1986). However, this is no guarantee that there will not be an emotional response to body damage later in life. The school-age child has a much clearer conception of body image and is aware of cultural standards of appearance. Children at this age will also have at least some memory of the pre-injury appearance, and therefore are likely to have to mourn the losses sustained. The literature on 'normal' body image development in adolescence does not document any critical developmental issues, though there is a general acceptance of a 'heightening of concern about the security of the body' during this period (Fisher, 1986). Within the burn literature, adolescence appears to be an especially challenging time with respect to body image adjustment, and some young people may evidence problems at this stage of development even if they have not done so earlier in life (Sawyer et al., 1983). Like adolescents, it is thought that younger adults may derive more of their sense of self esteem from their appearance and believe that others may evaluate them largely on the basis of their looks (Orr et al., 1989). In support of this, some researchers have found more psychological problems in adolescents and individuals in their 20s following burn injury (Long & Devault, 1990; Wallace, 1993).

Only limited research has been conducted on the older adult age group (over 65s), exploring appearance concerns. Harris and Carr (2001) reported that the importance attached to outward appearance appears to decrease with age. However, further research has suggested the picture may be more complicated than this (Spicer, 2002). Standard psychometrics administered in an outpatient clinic for individuals with dermatology problems showed lower levels of social anxiety and social avoidance in older adults than younger and middle aged adults. There was however, marked variation within the sample of older adults with one-third reporting high levels of appearance concern, embarrassment and avoidance of social activities. In fact, most of the older adults surveyed felt appearances were still important—but they suggested that their concern had shifted from one of a desire to look attractive to one of propriety—to appear clean, tidy and smart. Many felt their appearance concerns were not fully appreciated by clinicians.

IMPACT ON SOCIAL INTERACTIONS AND RELATIONSHIPS

Whatever the cause of disfigurement, whether acquired or congenital, the difficulties most frequently reported relate to encounters with strangers, meeting new people, and making new friends (Robinson, 1997). Over and above the adjustment to a new self image ('How happy am I with my appearance?'), there are therefore considerable implications for the trauma survivor's social world ('How comfortable am I in social situations—are others accepting me, or stigmatizing me?').

There are numerous examples documented about the very real changes in behaviour of others towards individuals with a visible difference (from ignoring through to staring and bullying), as well as explanations as to why other people behave as they do (see Bull & Rumsey (1988) for a detailed review). Visible differences, like burn scarring, can seriously impact on social interactions. Feelings of self-consciousness can take over and people can become preoccupied with their appearance and the effects this may be having on others. Such preoccupations can escalate; the person begins actively to search for signs that others have noticed the disfigurement or are feeling uncomfortable. Ultimately, a self-fulfilling prophecy can occur where the person anticipates negative reactions in every encounter and thus behaves defensively, or in a shy or aggressive manner, which in itself invites negativity from others. Of particular note in the case of a traumatic injury such as a burn is the fact that social encounters may also be affected by physical limitations of non-verbal expression. Burns to the face can lead to restricted facial movements which can make it difficult for others to read facial expressions. This can lead to hesitancy and awkwardness in social interactions which can result in a downward spiral of aversive emotional responses, maladaptive thought processes ('Everyone is looking at me', 'I look terrible', 'This conversation is not going well'). Partridge first described the concept of the SCARED syndrome, which was further developed by the charity Changing Faces (Partridge, 1990; Clarke & Castle, 2007). The SCARED syndrome is a model that describes how communication can sometimes go wrong between a person with a disfigurement and someone meeting this person (see Table 27.1). The model highlights the fact that sometimes neither party knows what to do to communicate effectively, so both may want to get away quickly. When these situations occur the result may be for both parties to want to avoid similar encounters in the future. Avoidance will not only result in unfavourable self-perceptions (further lowering self-esteem), but will also decrease the likelihood of further opportunities to practise social skills and have a potentially positive encounter.

Table 27.1 The SCARED syndrome

Someone with a facial disfigurement may feel or behave 'scared':

Feeling		Behaviour
self-conscious	S	shy
conspicuous	C	cowardly
angry, anxious	A	aggressive
rejected	R	retreating
embarrassed	E	evasive
'different'	D	defensive

Other people can feel and behave 'scared':

Feeling		Behaviour
sorry, shocked	S	staring, speechless
curious, confused	C	clumsy
anxious	A	asking, awkward
repelled	R	recoiling, rude
embarrassed	E	evasive
distressed	D	distracted

Reproduced from Clarke, A and Castle, B, *Handling Other People's Reactions: Communicating with confidence when you have a disfigurement.* © 2007, Changing Faces.

Research, specific to the burns population, highlights a tendency towards increased social withdrawal. For example, post-burn individuals tend to report an increase in family interactions and a decrease in relationships with non-family members (Andreasen et al., 1972; Browne et al., 1985). There are also reports of less involvement in social roles such as work (Browne et al., 1985), time spent with friends, and decreased involvement in activities that emphasize physical appearance such as dancing and swimming (Andreasen et al., 1972; Bergamasco et al., 2002).

Although it appears that post-burn the family unit becomes a 'safer' place to spend time, the whole family will experience the impact of the burn injury and resulting disfigurement. Partridge (1990) highlights the varied reactions of friends and relatives—some showing total commitment to helping and supporting, yet others avoiding and even completely rejecting the person who has been disfigured. Parents may suffer from feelings of guilt, anger, or depression and siblings who may have witnessed the accident can feel frightened and need support in their own right. Disciplinary problems may emerge as a child takes advantage of the changes in normal family patterns. There is some evidence that signs of dysfunction within the family may increase over the longer term, with 2 years' post-burn being a particularly vulnerable time, (Phillips, in Psychosocial Working Party Report for the National Burn Care Group, 2006).

Over and above changes in the dynamics of family relationships, parents, siblings, partners, and children of burned parents will have concerns about how best to support their loved ones. When asked what, in her view, were the hardest things to deal with following burn injury, a young child of a father who had sustained an injury stated:

Going places because my Dad doesn't like being in crowds or going out to eat ... Another thing is trying to explain to people in school what is wrong because they don't really understand and they make a fuss (Phillips, 2006).

The importance of addressing the psychosocial needs of family members therefore, should also be paramount.

A related area that is often overlooked is that of intimacy and sexual functioning (Whitehead, 1993). Several studies have reported significantly decreased sexual satisfaction post burn injury and again it seems that this is not necessarily related to burn size or site (e.g. Andreasen et al., 1972; Tudahl et al., 1987). The key difference found was between men and women. Whereas men reported an 82.5 % level of sexual satisfaction as compared to an ideal of 100%, women reported much lower satisfaction (52%). For women, level of sexual satisfaction was strongly related to body image and degree of physical dysfunction rather than burn size or location.

It is hard to consider the impact of burn injury without considering not just scarring and appearance change, but also the impact on physical function. As individuals survive bigger burn injuries, resulting long-term physical impairment is a reality. A significant social consequence is how this affects a person's ability to return to work. Several studies have examined levels of employment status post burn as an indicator of physical and overall health (Dyster-Aas et al., 2007). One major study reported on a group of 363 burn injured adults who were employed at the time of injury. By 2 years, 90% had returned to work, but of these only 37% had returned to the same job, with the same employer without accommodations (Brych et al., 2001). Difficulties returning to work have been particularly highlighted following hand injuries sustained in the work place, including post-trauma symptoms and anxiety about returning to work, as well as significant appearance concerns (Grunert et al., 1992). Thus significant job disruption after a traumatic injury can be a further social consequence.

INFLUENCES ON POST-BURN RECOVERY AND OUTCOME

Traditionally, research studies, by virtue of trying to highlight the impact of burns and other injuries on the individual, do tend to be biased towards presenting negative findings to the neglect of the positive. For example, in one study a number of patients reported positive comments relating to personal matters, for example taking better care of themselves, or worshipping life (Bergamasco et al., 2002). Although it may seem paradoxical to say that sustaining a burn injury can have a positive impact, there are undoubtedly people who cope well and return to normal functioning, as there are others who manage to improve their life in many ways post-burn.

Putting all this together, post burn outcomes can be considered in the form of a quadrant[1]:

1. Those with good pre-burn quality of life and function, for whom the burn represents a temporary, albeit painful, disruption from life's routine; one after which they will eventually resume their normal pre-injury functioning (Patterson et al., 1993). They may even have some visible scars, but manage and cope with these day to day. For example, a patient with facial burns who holds quite negative views about his own body image and appearance, but does not place so much value on this that it prevents him from having a positive sense of self-esteem. He jokes when asked about how he feels about his appearance, 'Well, I will never make the front cover of *Vogue*, but I was never going to anyway'. He had a happy and fulfilled life prior to the burn injury, with good social support around him, and despite experiencing a burn injury to the face, under traumatic circumstances, continues to lead a happy and fulfilled life.

---

[1] The clinical case examples described are for illustrative purposes and whilst they represent 'typical' presentations, the real identity of patients has been withheld for confidentiality purposes.

2. Those who have a good quality of life and high levels of confidence pre-burn and the impact of the burn is negative, leaving them with significantly lower post-burn functioning. For example, an inability to return to previous employment and difficulties with PTSD.
3. Those who have many pre-burn vulnerabilities, and find that the burn injury leaves them further disadvantaged. For example, these individuals start off on a lower footing (maybe as a result of drug and alcohol problems, social deprivation, vulnerable mental health, poor physical health). These risks factors act as obstacles to recovery and they struggle to engage in rehabilitation. Consider for example the man who drinks heavily and accidentally sets fire to himself whilst sitting in his armchair. He survives a major burn injury, but has lost all his belongings and his house (which was not insured). He leaves hospital with some level of physical disability and scarring, to live in a hostel, and then promptly returns to drinking. Or the woman with premorbid mental health problems, who is isolated and suffers from depression; she sets fire to herself in an attempt to take her life. She survives a significant injury, months of hospitalization, is physically disabled, significantly scarred, and despite making sure that mental health services are in place on discharge, she otherwise returns to her home facing the same difficulties, further exacerbated by the consequences of a major burn injury.
4. Those who pre-burn have many of the highlighted risk factors, but by virtue of the burn injury improve their quality of life and functioning post burn. For example, the alcoholic who has the opportunity to 'detox' whilst on the burns unit. Newly 'dry' he takes the opportunity to accept help and leaves hospital with support and financial benefits in place, feeling that he has a second chance to change his life; or the teenager heading down an 'antisocial behaviour' path, hanging out with the wrong crowd, who suffers a major traumatic burn injury whilst engaging in crime. She leaves hospital with visible scarring, physical disabilities, and PTSD. She, too, however, is eventually able to reflect on the route down which she was heading in life and feels thankful for her second chance. Although she initially struggles, she comes through the other side, eventually using her experiences to help and inspire others. She can reflect and see that she would not be the person she was today if it were not for the life changing burn injury she had sustained.

Although there is little research to verify what proportion of people may fall into each category, clinical experience would suggest that these outcomes clearly exist. Some people seem to be more resilient than others to adversity and even, in some cases adversity can result in a degree of positive growth. Tedeschi and Calhoun (1995) coined the term 'post-traumatic growth' (PTG) to describe positive life changes after exposure to traumatic events. Being faced with one's mortality may provoke a redefinition of personal goals and life priorities. One recently published study examined the possibility of posttraumatic growth following burn injury, and concluded that, similar to other populations who have experienced trauma and adversity, burns survivors also report PTG (Rosenbach & Renneberg, 2008). Their results were the first to show that whilst severe burn injury can have a major negative impact, such an aversive experience can also lead to positive change.

So, what determines which of the four quadrants a burns patient is likely to end up in? As highlighted earlier, it has been demonstrated time and time again that no correlation exists between the size or degree of disfigurement and the resulting psychological distress (Robinson, 1997; Kleve & Robinson, 1999; Patterson et al., 2000; Wallis et al., 2006). Other variables that may influence adjustment following burn injury have however been less thoroughly researched. And once again, it seems that much of the literature focuses on the prevalence of psychological maladjustment rather than on identifying variables that positively influence psychological adjustment.

Characteristics of the injury

Not all burns scars are visible in everyday life, by virtue of being on the head or hands. The majority of burn scars are hidden most of the time under clothing. There is a lively debate in the literature about whether it is more difficult to adjust to visible or hidden scars (Lawrence et al., 2004). It is well established that scars to the face can have a great impact on adjustment as our primary means of communication is face to face (MacGregor, 1970; Bull & Rumsey, 1988). Counterintuitively, some research has found that the impact of having a clearly visible difference is in some ways easier to predict and thus becomes easier to handle than one that is apparent only in particular situations. It is hard to hide a burns scar to the face, so the survivor is regularly forced into situations whereby he or she will have to deal with questions and unwanted staring, or adjust to a different reflection in the mirror. Cahners (1992) suggests that those with visible burns are forced to confront their anxieties and develop more efficient coping strategies. However, where scars are hidden it can be relatively easy to cover-up, avoid activities that reveal the scar and thus potentially delay the ability of the individual to adjust and adapt to that body part. This can have quite an impact on the individual, especially when situations such as new or intimate relationships are actively avoided. While the extent, type, and severity of a disfigurement fail to predict adjustment, a person's subjective perception of the noticeability his/her difference does appear to be a better predictor than ratings by a dispassionate observer or clinician (Harris 1997; Rumsey & Harcourt, 2004). Thus, whether scars are hidden or revealed, it is important for the burn care team to help patients reflect on how well their scarring is integrated into their self-image and relationships with others and to routinely include sexual health assessments (and interventions when required). It is particularly important not to assume that a hidden scar is less of a problem than one visible in everyday life.

Sociocultural factors

Little research has examined broad demographic variables that might impact on post-burn adjustment, let alone the nuances of cultural and social differences in response to changed appearances. It is generally assumed that darker skin tends to form more problem scars, and that this in turn may lead to greater psychological distress (McGrouther, 1997; Robert et al., 1999; Bayat et al., 2005). When it comes to gender, results so far have been contradictory (Newell, 2000). While burn injuries are more likely to happen to young adult men (Essleman et al., 2006), women are thought to be more likely to experience psychosocial issues regarding body image post burn (Fauerbach et al., 1999; Kleve & Robinson, 1999; Newell, 2000; Van Loey & VanSon, 2003). Some research however has contradicted this finding (Lawrence et al., 2004). The disparity in the literature highlights the complexity and heterogeneity of burn patients and the difficulty in predicting what factors influence adjustment (Klinge, 2009).

We do know that burn patients often come from lower socioeconomic backgrounds and while factors such as unemployment, homelessness, poverty, and substance misuse may increase the likelihood of sustaining a burn injury, it seems they also increase the risk of poorer psychological adjustment post-burn (Blakeney et al., 2008, Kramer et al., 2008). Those who do manage to return to work fare better in terms of psychological outcomes, it seems. It is likely that returning to the work place has positive effects such as greater social contact and support, thus offering the opportunity to improve social skills and learning to manage the reactions of others. Those individuals who return to work are also less likely to seek further reconstructive surgery, regardless of indexes of burn severity or injury location (Heinberg et al., 1997). This highlights the huge importance of incorporating interventions that target return to work within the care offered post-injury.

Pre-existing psychopathology

As reported earlier in this chapter, it is well recognized that burns patients have a higher incidence of pre-existing psychopathology than the general population and in turn premorbid mental health difficulties increase the risk of poor psychological adjustment post-burn injury (Noronha & Faust, 2006). A subset within this group are those who burn themselves intentionally, either in an act of deliberate self-harm, or a suicide attempt. There are few cases that challenge the clinical team more than the individual who has unsuccessfully committed suicide through self-immolation. The challenge to motivate and engage an individual who was feeling hopeless and depressed prior to the burn injury, who now more than likely faces a poorer quality of life, is huge. Likewise it can be hard for clinical teams to understand and empathize with the individual who has purposefully wounded and scarred themselves in an act of deliberate self harm. Burn wounds initiated or maintained by self harm can take on complex meanings for individuals, possibly distracting from emotional pain, self-punishment, or serving to keep others at arm's length. This is certainly an area that warrants further research in terms of both understanding why, but also how best to promote psychological recovery in these patient groups.

Psychological distress post-injury

In the absence of known premorbid psychopathology, it seems that psychological problems that develop due to the injury, such as PTSD, are generally associated with poorer functional outcomes and adjustment post-injury (Fauerbach et al., 1999; Corry et al., 2010). Patients often report that scars act as triggers or reminders of their traumatic accident; it seems understandable therefore that reaching a stage of acceptance might take longer in these circumstances. This highlights the importance of addressing issues around grief and trauma in psychological interventions post-injury and further research that could demonstrate improved outcomes if PTSD was successfully addressed (Bessell & Moss, 2007).

Coping styles and social interaction skills

Coping styles have been examined as factors that might aid in the quest to understand who adjusts well post-injury. Some have shown that avoidant coping styles such as avoiding social events, using alcohol or drugs, or distraction techniques are not so helpful as they can exacerbate fear of the particular situation and delay the development of more effective strategies. Others have tried to identify 'more helpful' coping strategies such as proposed 'self-talk' ('I know I look different, but at least I have other strengths') or proactive behavioural strategies such as initiating conversations. However, more recently it has been argued that it is not the actual strategies that people use, but rather the repertoire of strategies at their disposal that appears to be significant (Lansdown et al., 1997). If individuals have the ability and flexibility to use a range of different strategies then they are more able to respond to the varied and unpredictable demands of social situations (Robinson, 1997).

James Partridge puts forward a compelling case for the importance of developing good social interaction skills when one looks different. He comments, 'you will be scrutinised and automatic assumptions will be made in the public's mind, about your looks and your character. These connections are rarely flattering and will persist unless you challenge them' (Partridge, 1990). Several research studies have demonstrated the potential positive effects of social skills training. For example, Changing Faces have developed workshops incorporating social interaction skills training that have been found to be effective, albeit with a self-referred population who have been highly motivated to attend (Robinson et al., 1996). In a more representative hospital population, the NHS based Outlook service (a specialist hospital-based disfigurement support unit based at a district general hospital) has reported extremely positive results. Outlook offers individual interventions based on cognitive behavioural approaches including social interactional skills training (Trower et al., 1978).

While these studies are beginning to build an evidence base for the effectiveness of psychological interventions that develop helpful coping skills in the care and rehabilitation of individuals with disfiguring conditions, they are not without their shortcomings. None of the studies mentioned here contained control groups, sample sizes were small, and the participants were varied in relation to the cause, location, and severity of their disfigurement. A recent review of psychosocial interventions for individuals with visible differences concluded that much work still needs to be done (see Chapter 38). In highlighting the shortcomings of this work to date, future research in the form of randomized controlled trials and more accessible service provision, including Internet based-interventions were called for (see Besssel & Moss, 2007). The possibility that social skills can be developed or acquired continues to be a promising avenue for intervention and further research.

Family and social support

The 'buffering hypothesis' argues that social support is the most powerful factor in ameliorating stressful events (Cobb, 1976). It seems that the positive effects of stable social relationships correlate with better adjustment after burn injury (Patterson et al., 2000, Kildal, 2003, Wallis et al., 2006). It has been hypothesized that good relationships generate positive experiences for a burn survivor, and by increasing self esteem, the confidence then comes to approach social situations with strangers (Kildal, 2003, Noronha & Faust, 2006). Research suggests that the perceived sense of support is more important than actual support, and that probably having a supportive family is more important than friends (Bowden et al., 1980; Davidson et al., 1981; Browne et al., 1985; Orr et al., 1989). However, when parents (or spouses) experience their own difficulties in coming to terms with the trauma, this can hamper a child's/partner's adjustment. In addition, if social support is over solicitous, a person may cultivate feelings of worthlessness through over-reliance on help from others; social support in this sense can be unintentionally de-motivating and may lead to learned helplessness. This area has been particularly researched in considering influences on adjustment post-amputation, but is equally relevant to the visible differences acquired through other traumatic means.

Within the adolescent/young adult group, peer support acquires a particular importance, and the therapeutic gains offered by peer support are recognized to be extremely important for this group (Orr et al., 1989; Charkins, 1996). Peer support appears to offer something over and above the support received from family. It has been suggested that it may decrease isolation, increase knowledge about the condition, as well as provide coping strategies and a sense of hope (Macvean et al., 2008). Certainly one only has to enter 'burns support groups' into an Internet search engine to establish the extent of activity in this area. Support groups are particularly active in the US where they play an important part in post-burn rehabilitation (Munster, 1993). Although less prevalent in the UK, most of the larger burns facilities in the UK host a burns support group of some form.

Although burns survivors have argued the case for the importance of peer support (Acton, 2004; Acton et al., 2007) not all health professionals are convinced of its value. This may be because there are few studies demonstrating the benefits amongst survivors of trauma, but also, the support group format is not for everyone. Some survivors may not want to identify with a group that they see as stigmatized in some way (Rumsey & Harcourt, 2004). A retrospective report on setting up and running an adult support group for burns survivors recognized that discussing more sensitive issues was not always regarded as comfortable within the group setting but concluded that facilitator-led information-based groups had a place as part of the package of overall patient care along with individual sessions to supplement group discussions (Cooper & Burnside, 1996).

More recently a small qualitative study examining burns survivors' perceptions of the value of peer support also revealed positive views regarding the benefits. For example, a 39-year-old woman recently burned stated that 'seeing others wearing their burns proudly empowered me' (Badger & Royse, 2010, p. 305).

Burns Camps are a significant wing of the peer support spectrum, which in the UK have largely focused on children who have survived burn injuries. The concept stemmed from the recognition that children with burn injuries face many challenges, both physical and psychological, and therefore need long-term support away from the acute care setting (Verst, 1996). Camps are usually staffed by a group of burn care specialists, including nurses, doctors, therapists, psychologists, and play specialists, along with fire fighters, adult burns survivors and volunteers. Each camp programme is designed to offer children the opportunity to challenge themselves and exceed their physical expectations with the support of peers and their leaders. Whilst it has often been difficult to capture the benefit of camps quantitatively, qualitative evaluations have captured the sense of increased confidence, improved self-esteem, and the benefits of having had the opportunity to have shared the experience of having a burn with their peers that arise from these programmes (Biggs et al., 1997; Rimmer et al., 2007; Gaskell, 2007; Gaskell et al., 2010). Residential programmes for adult burns survivors are less common. However, one UK camp designed specifically to meet the needs of young people (16–25 years) who had sustained a burn injury either as a child or young adult, reported both positive quantitative outcomes and qualitative feedback (Gaskell et al., 2009). For example, as one young person who attended this programme reported:

I felt like I could be me instead of somebody else ... the barriers came down ... barriers go up with people who maybe don't understand ... it's almost like a protection ... whereas with the group we went away with, you don't need it (quote in conference presentation, Gaskell et al., 2009)

A final but important strand in the role that peer support can play are programmes that seek to train burn survivors to become mentors or role models for more recently injured patients. Survivors Offering Assistance in Recovery (SOAR) is a formalized hospital-based peer support programme organized in partnership with the Phoenix Society which currently runs in over 30 burns centre throughout the US. A recent study provided support for the high value burns survivors placed on the SOAR programme (Badger & Royse, 2010). Similarly, a number of burn camp programmes have developed leadership training programmes for burn survivors who have graduated from the burn camps. Again, the benefits of these initiatives have been documented (Gaskell, 2003) and illustrate the third stage of the recovery journey outlined by Partridge, 'advocacy'.

Therefore it seems that peer support-based psychosocial interventions offer something helpful to the experience of an individual trying to come to terms with an acquired disfigurement. The challenge, however, in the increasingly financially-strained economic climate will be to continue to show evidence for their efficacy. Although it is the case that support groups and residential camps will not suit everyone, it seems that they are most useful as part of a comprehensive package of support.

Concluding Thoughts

The challenges facing individuals who have acquired disfigurement following a traumatic injury are multifaceted. There are significant adjustments to be made in terms of overcoming a traumatic injury and enduring a gruelling treatment regimen, as well as coping with a changed appearance and potentially, physical disability. The far reaching effects of a traumatic injury which results in a changed appearance, whether major or minor, are seen at the level of the individual, the family, and the wider social world with which the survivor interacts. Although this chapter has focused largely on the area of burns, the range of possible social and psychological outcomes post-injury are great, whether the scars or other forms of visible difference such as amputation have resulted from burns or other forms of trauma. Responses can range from profound distress and despair, to renewed interest in life. Understanding better the factors important in influencing this journey to recovery, to acceptance and even advocacy remains an important avenue for investigation.

However, with what we have learned from the experiences of our patients and the post-burn adjustment literature to date, it should be possible to put this to good effect in the care and support provided for trauma survivors, both in the immediate aftermath of the injury and long into the recovery journey. Health and social care professionals are well placed to help individuals who have sustained a disfiguring injury tackle the challenges they face. Given the physical damage caused by such injuries, the majority of care and rehabilitation occurs in a medical setting. Historically this has placed an emphasis on interventions that will improve appearance and, theoretically, adjustment. Whilst surgical skill and technology have advanced considerably over recent years, there is a limit to what can be achieved. Also, as noted throughout this chapter, the severity of scarring or disfigurement does not reliably indicate the level of distress it causes, and coping successfully with the challenges of an unusual appearance will be determined by psychological rather than biomedical factors (Robinson, 1997; Rumsey, 1997). Thus while surgery may well be able to offer improvements in appearance in some cases, this will not invariably impact on distress. Psychological interventions in trauma rehabilitation are therefore key, despite the fact that national reviews have concluded that psychosocial care is currently lacking, (e.g. National Burn Care Review, 2001; Persson et al., 2009).

Appropriately trained and experienced psychosocial professionals are always likely to be a limited resource, and so a tiered approach to psychological care in burns has been advocated in the UK (Persson et al., 2009). Such models have also been advocated in other physical health areas in which the recognition of the importance of psychological factors has been highlighted (e.g. oncology) In this model, psychological care and promoting good adjustment after burn injury is the responsibility of the whole burn care team working at different levels of psychological skill. Frontline professionals, such as doctors, nurses, physio- and occupational therapists all have a role in communicating effectively, identifying, and dealing with distress, and recognizing when this reaches a level that would warrant more specialist help. Trained mental health professionals can then focus on providing specialist interventions for the more vulnerable patients, as well as providing training and supervision to the wider burn care team.

It is a challenge for every burn care team to develop an ethos in which appearance concerns can be discussed at every stage of the patient's care without that patient feeling stigmatized or as though they are not coping. However, when this is achieved, effective support and innovative interventions can be provided. Particularly important are thorough and holistic assessments of patients, instigated as soon as they enter the burn care setting; routinely implementing multifaceted approaches to pain management, incorporating both pharmacological and psychological components; preparing and supporting patients and their families in seeing their injuries for the first time; developing coping strategies for dealing with the reactions of others when leaving the hospital for the first time; support in returning to school or work, or having to make difficult decisions about future treatment. In all of this, burn care teams need to work together with patients, families, and their social contexts (e.g. schools, workplaces) to provide support and interventions in a variety of forms—individual, family, group, peer—to meet the range of different needs evident throughout the patient's recovery journey.

There are still many questions that remain: for example, understanding better the impact of psychological interventions on patient outcomes—can psychological outcomes that reduce distress/trauma, impact on functional outcomes? And conversely how does improved pain management impact on longer-term psychological adjustment? But we know enough from the experiences of our patients to date to significantly improve the services currently provided to trauma survivors, with the ultimate aim of smoothing the journey to recovery and enhancing outcomes for all.

REFERENCES

Acton, A. (2004). When we leave the hospital: A patient's perspective of burn injury. *British Medical Injury*, 329, 504–6.

Acton, A., Mounsey, E., & Gilyard, C. (2007). The burn survivor perspective. *Journal of Burn Care and Research*, 28, 615–20.

Andreasen, N. & Norris, A. (1972). Long-term adjustment and adaptation mechanisms in severely burned adults. *Journal of Nervous and Mental Disease*, 154, 352–62.

Badger, K. & Royse, D. (2010). Adult burn survivors' views of peer support: a qualitative study. *Social Work in Health Care*, 49, 299–313.

Bayat, A., Waller, J. M., Bock, O., Mrowietze, U., Ollier, W. E., & Ferguson, M. W. (2005). Genetic susceptibility to keloid disease: mutation screening of the TGFbeta3 gene. *Britsh Journal of Plastic Surgery*, 58(7), 914–21.

Bergamasco, E. C., Rossi, L. A., Amancio, A. da. C. G., & Carvalho, E. C. de. (2002). Body image of patients with burns sequellae: evaluation through the critical incident technique. *Burns*, 28, 47–52.

Bessell, A., & Moss, T. P. (2007). Evaluating the effectiveness of psychosocial interventions for individuals with visible differences: A systematic review of the empirical literature. *Body Image*, 4, 227–38.

Biggs, K. S., Heinrich, J. J., Jekel, J. F., & Cuono, C. B. (1997). The burn camp experience: variables that influence the enhancement of self-esteem. *Journal of Burn Care Rehabilitation*, 18, 93–8.

Blakeney, P., Thomas, C., Holzer, C. 3rd, Rose, M., Berniger, F., Meyer, W. J. 3rd. (2005). Efficacy of short-term, intensive social skills program for burned adolescents. *Journal of Burn Care and Rehabilitation*, 26, 546–55.

Blakeney, P., Rosenberg, L., Rosenberg, M., & Faber, A., (2008). Psychosocial care of persons with severe burns. *Burns*, 34, 433–40.

Blalock, S. J., Bunker, & B. J., DeVillis, R. (1994). Measuring health status among survivors of burn injury: Revisions of the burn Specific Health Scale. *Journal of Trauma*, 36, 508–15.

Bowden, M., Fdeller, I., Thorlen, D., Davidson, T., & James, M. (1980). Self-esteem of severely burned patients. *Archives of Physical and Medical Rehabilitation*, 61, 449–52.

Bradbury, E. (1997). Understanding the problems. In R. Lansdown, N. Rumsey, E. Bradbury, A. Carr, & J. Partridge (eds.) *Visibly different: Coping with disfigurement*, pp. 180–93. Oxford: Butterworth-Heinemann.

Browne, G., Byrne, C., & Brown, B. (1985). Psychosocial adjustment of burn survivors. *Burns*, 12, 28–35.

Brych, S. B., Engrav, L. H., Rivara, F. P., Ptacek, J. T., Lezotte, D. C., Esselman, P. C., *et al.* (2001). Time off work and return to work rates after burns: systematic review of the literature and a large two-centre series. *Journal of Burn Care and Rehabilitation*, 22, 401–5.

Bull, R. & Rumsey, N. (1988). *The social psychology of facial appearance.* New York: Springer-Verlag.

Cahners, S. (1992). Young women with breast burns. A self-help group by mail. *Journal of Burn Care and Rehabilitation*, 13, 44–7.

Cash, T. F. & Strachan, M. D. (2002). Cognitive–behavioural approaches to changing body image. In T. F. Cash & T. Pruzinsky (eds.) *Body Image: A handbook of theory, research and clinical practice*, pp. 478–86. New York: Guildford Press.

Charkins, H. (1996). *Children with facial difference: A parents' guide.* Bethesda: Woodbine House.

Clarke, A. & Castle, B. (2007). *Handling other people's reactions: Communicating with confidence when you have a disfigurement.* London: Changing Faces.

Cobb, S. (1976). Social support as a moderator of life stress. *Psychosomatic Medicine*, 38, 300–14.

Cooper, R., & Burnside, I. (1996). Three years of an adult burns support group: An analysis. *Burns*, 22, 65–8.

Corry, N. H., Klick, B. & Fauerbach, J. A. (2010). Posttraumatic stress disorder and pain impact functioning and disability after major burn injury. *Journal of Burn Care and Research*, 31(1), 13–25.

Davidson, T. I., Bowden, M. L., Tholen, D., James, M. H., & Feller, I. (1981). Social support and post-burn adjustment. *Archives of Physical Medicine and Rehabilitation*, 62, 274–8.

Dyster-Aas, J., Kildal, M., & Willebrand, M. (2007). Return to work and health-related quality of life after burn injury. *Journal of Rehabilitation Medicine*, 39(1), 49–55.

Dyster-Aas, J., Willerbrand, M., Wikehult, B., Gerdin, B., & Ekselius, L. (2008). Major depression and posttraumatic stress disorder symptoms following severe burn injury in relation to lifetime psychiatric morbidity. *Journal of Trauma Injury Infection and Critical Care*, 64, 1349–56.

Edwards, R., Smith, M., Klick, B., Magyar-Russell, G., Haythornthwaite, J., Holavanahalli, R., *et al.* (2007). Symptoms of depression and anxiety as unique predictors of pain-related outcomes following burn injury. *Annals of Behavioural Medicine*, 34, 313–22.

Fauerbach, J. A., Haythornthwaite, J., Lawrence, J. W., Richter, D., McGuire, M., Schmidt, C., & Munster, A. M. (1997). Psychiatric history affects post trauma morbidity in a burn injured adult sample. *Psychosomatics*, 38, 374–85.

Fauerbach, J. A., Lawrence, J. W., Munster, A. M., Palombo, D. A., & Richter, D. (1999). Prolonged adjustment difficulties among those with acute posttrauma distress following burn injury. *Journal of Behavioral Medicine*, 22(4), 359–78.

Fauerbach, J. A., Lawrence, J. W., Munster, A. M., Palombo, D. A., & Ritcher, D. (1999). Prolonged adjustment difficulties among those with acute posttrauma distress following burn injury. *Journal of Behavioural Medicine*, 22, 359–78.

Feller, I., Tholen, D., & Cornell, R. G. (1980). Improvement in burn care, 1965–1979. *Journal of the American Medical Association*, 244, 2074–8.

Fisher, S. (1986). *Development and structure of the body image*. Hillsdale, NJ: Lawrence Erlbaum.

Frenay M., Faymonville, M., Devlieger, A. A., & Vanderkelen, (2001). Psychological approaches during dressing changes of burned patients: a prospective randomised study comparing hypnosis against stress reducing strategy. *Burns*, 27(8), 793–9.

Gaskell, S. L. (2003). Evaluation of a young leader training programme for a paediatric burns camp. Oral presentation at the British Burns Association 36th Annual Meeting, Edinburgh.

Gaskell, S. L. (2007). The challenge of evaluating rehabilitative activity holidays for burn-injured children: qualitative and quantitative outcome data from a Burns Camp over a five-year period. *Journal of Developmental Neurorehabilitation*, 10(2), 149–60.

Gaskell, S. L., Wisely, J. A., Denley, S., Shah, M., & Dunn, K., (2009). The development of a burns camp for young adults. *Burns*, 35(Suppl 1), S42.

Gaskell, S. L., Cooke, S., Lunke, M., O'Shaughnessy, J., Kazbekov, M., & Zajicek, R. (2010). A pan-European evaluation of residential burns camps for children and young people. *Burns*, 36, 511–21.

Gilboa, D., Friedman, M., & Tsur, H. (1994). The burn as a continuous traumatic stress: implications for emotional treatment during hospitalization. *Journal of Burn Care and Rehabilitation*, 15(1), 86–91.

Gilboa, D. (2001). Long-term psychosocial adjustment after burn injury. *Journal of Burns* 27, 335–41.

Grunert, B. K., Devine, C. A., Matloub, H. S., Sanger, J. R., Yousif, N. J., Anderson, R. C., *et al.* (1992). Psychological adjustment following work-related hand injury: 18 month follow-up. *Annuals of Plastic Surgery*, 29, 537–42.

Harris, D. (1997). Types, causes and physical treatments of visible differences. In R. Landsdown, N. Rumsey, E. Bradbury, T. Carr, & J. Partridge (eds.) *Visabiliy different. Coping with disfigurment*, pp. 79–90. Oxford: Butterworth-Heinenmann.

Harris, D. L. & Carr, A. T. (2001). Prevalence of concern about physical appearance in the general population. *British Journal of Plastic Surgery*, 54, 223–26.

Hartford, C. E. & Kealey, G. P. (2007). *Care of outpatient burns*. In D. N. Herndon & J. H. Jones (eds.) Total Burn Care, pp. 67–80. Philadelphia, PA: WB Saunders.

Heinberg L. J., Fauerbach J. A., Spence, R. J., & Hackerman, F. (1997). Psychological factors involved in the decision to undergo reconstructive surgery after burn injury. *Journal of Burn Care & Rehabilitation*, 18 (4), 375–80.

Jones, C., Griffiths, R. D., Humphris, G. M., & Skirrow, P. M. (2001). Memory, delusions and the development of acute PTSD-related symptoms after intensive care. *Critical Care Medicine*, 29, 573–80.

Kildal, M. (2003). Perceived physical and psychological outcome after severe burn injury. *Comprehensive summaries of Uppsala Dissertations from the Faculty of Medicine*, 1247, 59.

Kleve, L. & Robinson, E. (1999). A survey of psychological need amongst adult burn-injured patients. *Burns*, 25, 575–9.

Klinge, K., Chamberlain, D. J., Redden, M., & King, L. (2009). Psychological adjustments made by postburn injury patients: an integrative literature review. *Journal of Advanced Nursing*, 65, 2274–92.

Knudson-Cooper, M. & Thomas, C. M. (1988). Psychosocial care of the severely burned child. In H. F. Carvajal, and D. Parks (eds.) *Burns in children: paediatric burn management*, pp. 345–62. Chicago, IL: Year Book Medical Publishers.

Kolman, P. B. (1983). The incidence of psychopathology in burned adult patients: a critical review. *Journal of Burn Care and Rehabilitation*, 4, 430–6.

Kramer, C., Gibran, N., Heimbach, D., Rivara, F., & Klein, M. (2008). Assault and substance abuse characterize burn injuries in homeless patients. *Journal of Burn Care & Research*, 29, 461–7.

Lansdowne, R., Rumsey, N., Bradbury, E., Carr, A. & Patridge, J. (1997). *Visibly different: Coping with disfigurement*. Oxford: Butterworth Heinemann.

Latenser, B. A., Miller, S. F., Bessey, P. Q., Browning, S. M., Caruso, D. M., Gomez, M., *et al.* (2007). National Burn Repository 2006: a ten-year review. *Journal of Burn Care and Research*, 28(5), 635–58.

Lawrence, J. W., Fauerbach, J. A., Heinberg, L., & Doctor, M. (2004). Visible vs hidden scars and their relation to body esteem. *Journal of Burn Care & Rehabilitation*, 25, 25–32.

Long D. & Devault, S. (1990). Disfigurement and adolescent development: exacerbating factors in personal injury. *American Journal of Forensic Psychology*, 8, 3–14.

MacGregor, F.C. (1970). Social and psychological implications of dentofacial disfigurement. *Angle Orthodontics*, 40, 231–3.

Maron, M. T. & Bush, J. P. (1991). Burn injury and treatment. In J. P. Bush & S. W. Harkins (eds.) *Children in pain: Clinical and research issues from a developmental perspective*, pp. 275–95. Berlin: Springer-Verlag.

Maron, M. T. (1991). Psychological adjustment of children and adolescents following burn injuries (Doctorate dissertation, Virgina Commonwealth University, 1991). *Dissertation Abstracts International*, 52, 1728B.

Macvean, M. L., White, V. M., & Sanson-Fischer, R. (2008). One to one volunteer support programs for people with cancer: A review of the literature. *Patient Education and Counselling*, 70, 10–24.

McGrouther, D.A. (1997). Facial disfigurement. *British Medical Journal*, 314, 991.

Molinaro, J. R. (1978). The social fate of children disfigured by burns. *American Journal of Psychiatry*, 135, 979–80.

Miller, M. D., Elliott, C. H., Funk, M., & Pruitt, S. D. (1988). Implications of children's burn injuries. In D. K. Routh (ed.) *Handbook of Pediatric Psychology*, pp. 426–47. New York: Guildford Press.

Munster, A. M. (1993). *Severe Burns: A Family Guide to Medical and Emotional Recovery (A Johns Hopkins Press Health Book)*. Baltimore, MD: The Johns Hopkins University Press.

National Burn Care Review Committee Report. (2001). *Standards and Strategy for Burn Care: A review of burn care in the British Isles*. British Burn Association.

Newell, R. (2000) *Body Image and Disfigurement Care: Routledge Essentials for Nurses*. London: Routledge.

Noronha, D. O. & Faust, J. (2006). Identifying the variables impacting post-burn psychological adjustments: a meta-analysis. *Journal of Pediatric Psychology*, 32, 380–91.

O'Donnell, M. L., Breamer, M., Bryant, R. A., Schnyder, U., & Shalev, A. (2003). Post-traumatic disorders following injury; an empirical and methodological review. *Clinical Psychology Review*, 23(4), 587–603.

Orr, D., Reznikoff, M., & Smith, G. (1989). Body image, self-esteem and depression in burn-injured adolescents and young adults. *Journal of Burn Care Rehabilitation*, 10, 454–61.

Patterson, D. R., Everett, J. J., Bombardier, C. H., Questad, K. A., Lee, V. K., & Marvin, J. A. (1993). Psychological effects of severe burn injuries. *Psychological Bulletin*, 113, 362–78.

Partridge, J. (1990). *Changing Faces: the challenge of facial disfigurement*. London: A Changing Faces Publication.

Partridge, J. (2005). Survival, socialization and advocacy. *Journal of Burn Care Rehabilitation*, 26, S32.

Patterson, D. R., Ptacek, J. T., Cromes, F., Fauerbach, J. A., & Engrav, L. (2000). The 2000 Clinical Research Award: describing and predicting stress and satisfaction with life for burn survivors. *Journal of Burn Care and Rehabilitation*, 21, 490–8.

Persson, M., Rumsey, N., Spalding, H., & Partridge, J. (2009). *Bridging the Gap.* Report for the National Burn Care Review Group. http://www.specialisedservices.nhs.uk

Phillips, C. (2005). CAR Burns Study: A Summary of the Quantitative Results and Recommendations for Care (in preparation; held at CAR office, UWE; 2005) referenced in National Burn Care Group, *Psychosocial Rehabilitation After Burn Injury, from the Psychosocial Working Party, NBCG March 2006.*

Phillips, C. & Rumsey, N. (2008). Considerations for the provision of psychosocial services for families following paediatric burn injury—A quantitative study. *Burns*, 34(1), 56–62.

Powers, P. S., Cruse, C. W., Daneils, S., & Stevens, B. (1994). Post-traumatic stress disorder in patients with burns. *Journal of Burn Care & Rehabilitation*, 15, 147–53.

Rajipura, A. (2002). The National Burn Repository Report 2002. American Burn Association. http://www.ameriburn.org

Rimmer, R, B., Fornaciari, G, M., Foster, K. N., Bay, C. R., Wadsworth, M. M., & Wood, M., et al. (2007). Impact of a pediatric residential burn camp experience on burn survivors perceptions of self and attitudes regarding the camp community. *Journal of Burn Care Research*, 28, 334–41.

Robert, R., Meyer, W., Bishop, S., Rosenberg, L., Murphy, L., & Blakeney, P. (1999). Disfiguring burns scars in adolescent self- esteem. *Burns*, 25(7), 581–5.

Robinson, E. (1997). Psychological research on visible differences in adults. In R. Lansdown, N. Rumsey, E. Bradbury, A. Carr, & J. Partridge (eds.) *Visibly different: Coping with disfigurement*, pp. 102–11. Oxford: Butterworth-Heinemann.

Rosenbach, C. & Renneberg, B. (2008). Positive change after severe burn injuries. *Journal of Burn Care & Research*, 29, 638–43.

Robinson, E., Clarke, A., & Cooper, C. (1996). *The psychology of facial disfigurement.* Facing the future, a guide for health professionals. London: Changing Faces.

Rumsey, N. & Harcourt, D. (2004). Body image and disfigurement: issues and inventions. *Body Image*, 1, 83–97.

Rumsey, N. J. (1997). Historical and anthropological perspectives on appearance. In R. Landsdown, N. Rumsey, E. Bradbury, A. Carr, & J. Partridge (eds.) *Visibly different: Coping with disfigurement*, pp. 91–101. London: Butterworth Heinemann.

Rusch, M. D., Grunert, B. K., Sanger J. R., Dzwierzynski, W. W., & Matloub, H. S. (2000). Psychological adjustment in children after traumatic disfiguring injuries: a 12-month follow-up. *Plastic and Reconstructive Surgery*, 107 (7), 1451–8.

Saigh, P. A. (1989). The validity of the DSM-III posttraumatic stress disorder classification as applied to children. *Journal of Abnormal Psychology*, 98, 189–92.

Stoddard, F. (1982). Coping with pain: A developmental approach to treatment of burned children. *American Journal of Psychiatry*, 139, 736–40.

Sawyer, M. G., Minde, K., & Zucker, R. (1982). The burned child, scared for life. *Burns Including Thermal Injuries*, 9, 205–13.

Sawyer, M. G., Minde, K., & Zuker, R. (1983). The burned child—scarred for life?: A study of the psychosocial impact of a burn injury at different developmental stages. *Burns*, 9, 205–13.

Shakespeare, V. (1998). Effect of small burn injury on physical, social and psychological health at 3–4 months after discharge. *Burns*, 24(8), 7394–4.

Spicer, J. (2002). Appearance-related concern in older adults with skin disorder: An exploratory study. Unpublished Doctoral Thesis, Exeter University.

Tarnowski, K. J., Rasnake, L. K., Gavaghan-Jones, M. P., & Smith, L. (1991). Psychosocial sequelae of paediatric burn injuries: A review. *Clinical Psychology Review*, 11, 371–98.

Tedstone, J. E., Tarrier, N., & Faragher, E. B. (1998). An investigation of the factors associated with an increased risk of psychological morbidity in burn injured patients. *Burns*, 24, 407–15.

Thombs, B. D., Fauerbach, J. A., & McCann U. D. (2005). Stress disorders following traumatic injury: assessment and treatment considerations. *Primary Psychiatry*, 12(5) 51–5.

Tudahl, L. A., Blades, B. C., & Munster, A. M. (1987). Sexual satisfaction in burn patients. *Journal of Burn Care and Rehabilitation*, 8, 292–93.

Tedeschi, R. G. & Calhoun, L. G. (1995). *Trauma and Transformation: growing in the aftermath of suffering*. Thousand Oaks, CA: Sage Publications, Inc

Trower, P., Bryant, B., Argyle, M., & Marziller, J. (1978). *Social Skills & Mental Health*. London: Methuen & Co Ltd.

Van Loey, N. E., & VanSon, M. J. (2003). Psychopathology and psychological problems in patients with burn scars: epidemiology and management. *American Journal of Clinical Dermatology*, 4, 245–72.

Verst, A. (1996). Burn camp: an unforgettable summer experience for children and teenagers. *Plastic Surgical Nursing*, 16, 240–2.

Vyrostek, S. B., Annest, J. L., & Ryan, J. L. (2001). *Surveillance for fatal and non-fatal injuries – United States, 2001*. Atlanta, GA: Office of statistics and programming. National Centre for Injury Prevention and Control.

West, J. & Spinks, P. (1988). *Clinical Psychology in action: a collection of case studies*. London: Wright.

Wright, L. & Fulwiler, R. (1974). Long range emotional sequelae of burns: Effects on children and their mothers. *Pediatric Research*, 8, 931–4.

Wallace, E. (1993). Nursing a teenager with burns. *British Journal of Nursing*, 2, 278–81.

Whitehead, T. L. (1993). Sexual health promotion of the patient with burns. *Journal of Burn Care & Rehabilitation*, 14, 221–6.

Wallis, H., Renneberg, B., Ripper, S., Germann, G., Wind, G., & Jester, A. (2006). Emotional distress and psychosocial resources in patients recovering from severe burn injury. *Journal of Burn Care & Research*, 27, 734–41.

Yu, B. & Dimsdale, J. (1999). Posttraumatic stress disorder in patients with burn injuries. *Journal of Burn Care & Rehabilitation*, 20, 426–33.

CHAPTER 28

VISIBLE DIFFERENCE ASSOCIATED WITH DISEASE: SKIN CONDITIONS

CHRISTINE BUNDY

WESTERN society attaches a great deal of importance to the complexion, and beauty is typically defined as an even skin tone that is free from blemishes, independent of skin colour. Advertisements link even skin tones with youth and general health, and beauty products promise a 'healthy glow' in exchange for, sometimes considerable, financial outlay.

In addition to its visual importance, the skin is our largest sensory organ which performs an important defence function against heat, cold, and external chemicals as well as helping to regulate body temperature. Synthesis of the pigment melanin, produced in the upper layer of skin (the epidermis), efficiently protects from ultra-violet (UV) rays in daylight and allows vitamin D, essential for growth and calcifica-tion of the bones, to be synthesized from sunlight. Any disruption to these functions because of trauma or disease can have a physical, social, and psychological impact on the person affected. Furthermore, skin is particularly susceptible to the effects of stress, which generates a physiological response (which may include increased sweating and blushing) . . . which in turn establishes a cognitive, emotional, and behavioural loop which can be distressing and difficult to interrupt.

54% of the population are affected by skin disease each year, and 15–25% of primary care consultations are due to skin disease (Schofield et al., 2009). Whilst many conditions can affect the appearance of the skin in different ways, this chapter focuses on acne, atopic eczema, vitiligo, psoriasis, and skin cancer as exemplars to highlight the psychosocial impact of an altered appearance due to disease and to consider the provision of psychosocial interventions for those affected.

Acne

Acne vulgaris presents as scaly, red areas and pus-filled spots accompanied by blackheads and whiteheads, most commonly on the body, face, upper chest, and back. Although it can affect any age group, acne is more common in adolescence and is thought to be stimulated by the increase in testosterone and other sex hormones released during puberty. Acne affects twice as many boys as girls and can occur in up to 85% of all young people during adolescence (Balkrishnan et al., 2006). The condition usually improves or disappears completely by the age of 20 but for a small proportion of people it persists into their adult life and can cause permanent skin damage.

Rarer, more severe forms of acne can include the formation of cysts and tends to affect deeper tissue, this can result in permanent scarring. Cysts can appear anywhere but are more usually found in the groin or axilla where sweat collects in perspiration ducts. This may be especially distressing for younger people, since appearance becomes crucial to psychosocial functioning during adolescence and social anxiety, depression, low self-esteem, poor self-image, excessive self-consciousness, and embarrassment are common amongst this group (Magin et al., 2006). In a large study of young people in New Zealand, Purvis and colleagues (2006) found symptoms of clinically relevant depression were reported by 1,294 (14.1%) students, whilst 432 (4.8%) reported symptoms of anxiety. A finding that is common across most skin conditions, including acne, is that the degree of psychological distress is not necessarily related to the severity of the condition but, surprisingly, Purvis et al.'s study found the presence of depressive symptoms did correlate with increasing acne severity. More than 2,000 students (23.6%) in their study reported having suicidal thoughts and 730 (7.8%) reported a suicide attempt in the previous 12 months.

The prevalence of body dysmorphic disorder (BDD) amongst people with acne has been found to range between 14.1% (according to assessment by a neutral observer) and 21.1% when self-reported (Bowe et al., 2007). Bowe et al. reported that the risk of BDD was increased two-fold in patients requiring systemic therapy for more severe acne.

A recent systematic review study by Dunn and colleagues (2011) confirmed previous findings that acne can negatively affect quality of life, self-esteem, and mood in adolescents. Furthermore, they supported the association between acne and increased incidence of anxiety, depression, and suicidal ideation. However, clinicians are generally not able to detect distress amongst their patients very accurately (Richards et al., 2004) and it is not possible to guess who is more susceptible to lower levels of well-being. Dunn and colleagues conclude that validated methods of assessment and the routine consideration of psychosocial aspects of acne during the consultation are essential, in order to identify those patients who are at particular risk for adverse psychosocial effects.

Topical and systemic treatments are often effective for acne and can result in improved psychological and social functioning in the short-term, but little is known about any longer-term effects and there are few reports of integrated medical and psychological approaches to managing people affected by it. Despite the established evidence that acne can result in disrupted psychological and social functioning, a search for studies focussing on beliefs about acne and links with adherence to treatment or health advice (or indeed any well-designed psychological interventions with people with acne), did not show any significant work. Given that there is still some confusion about the cause and effect relationship between acne and psychological distress (particularly depression and suicidal ideation), this area would benefit from longitudinal research to establish the longer-term effects of living with the condition and the impact of an integrated approach to clinical management.

A gap in our knowledge of the management of skin disease within primary care has been recognized (see Smith & Barker, 2006). We know that primary care clinicians do not always recognize or manage the psychological and social problems associated with many long-term medical conditions, but most of the management of acne and other skin conditions occurs in primary care, with only the most severely affected being seen in specialist services. The lack of knowledge and/or confidence about how to manage the psychosocial sequelae provides an opportunity for psychologists to develop training programmes to help primary care staff to provide better holistic care for patients with skin conditions.

Atopic Eczema

Eczema is a condition that affects 8–17% of adults under 60 years of age (Montnemery et al., 2003). Amongst adults, the highest prevalence is in those aged 16–24 years, and it tends to affect women more than men (around 16% of women in the UK are affected). The reason for this differential effect is unknown. Around 60% of women present when they become pregnant, but in around a quarter of those with pre-existing eczema, pregnancy improves their skin condition. Atopic eczema differs from other skin conditions with an external cause in that eczema is an inherited hypersensitivity to allergens such as pollen, foods, and animals. Those who are considered 'atopic' can also experience asthma and allergic rhinitis or hay fever.

Milder cases of eczema usually affect the folds of skin around the elbow flexures and the back of the knees where unsightly, dry, cracked, reddened areas of skin become itchy and weepy. This creates the itch–scratch cycle where scratching the areas stimulates cytokine release which subsequently intensifies the itch. Scratching also allows the transfer of bacteria from the nails which, in turn, can lead to infections. Severe eczema can be mistaken for psoriasis and vice versa, with the resultant inappropriate management.

Eczema usually first appears in childhood and 90% of cases appear before the age of 5 (Weston & Lane, 1991). Many children who present with eczema in infancy are clear of the condition by the age of 16 but some continue to suffer exacerbation and remission in adulthood. The impact on the family can be significant and includes stress, sleep deprivation, extra time taken to care for the child, and interruption to employment with its attendant indirect financial costs (Su et al., 1997). Reports of children being teased at school, especially during exercise classes or swimming activities, are common. Furthermore, disrupted sleep due to itching can leave the child sleepy and irritable which can affect learning. Family-based interventions to help parents manage a child who scratches and is irritable due to sleep disruption can help them to develop better ways of coping and managing any family tension. However, access to psychological services in the UK is limited and, where it is available, long waiting times can prevent timely treatment. There are few centres that offer specialist knowledge about skin conditions and integrated dermatology and psychology services are not yet established, other than in a few centres of excellence.

In later childhood and early adulthood, when physical appearance and attractiveness become increasingly important, the chronically inflamed, cracked, dry skin associated with eczema is often seen as unattractive and associated with distress. Other people often mistakenly believe it to be contagious and hesitate from touching people with eczema, which can further increase their distress and lead to social withdrawal. Sleeplessness from scratching can affect up to 60% of adults and young people (Lewis-Jones, 2006) and leads to daytime fatigue, which can also increase psychological distress.

Treatments for eczema include topical medicines (including emollients or moisturizers) that restore the skin's barrier function, and steroid-based creams that aim to modify the local inflammatory response. Regular moisturizing is essential to relieve the itching and prevent subsequent flare-ups. Light treatment, including UVB, may be used and, if the eczema is resistant to these first-line interventions, systemic and biological treatments similar to those used in psoriasis can be used, but bring with them the same unwanted side effects associated with psoriasis treatments (see later psoriasis section).

There are very few well-designed psychological interventions for people with eczema, which is surprising given the recognized role of stress in the inflammatory process in general and the psychosocial difficulties experienced by people with skin disease, specifically. Much of what is described as psychological is in fact an educational-based approach to inform people about their or their child's condition and to help them self-administer topical treatments. Ersser and colleagues' systematic review (2007) concluded that the studies in this area are, on the whole, of poor quality but those based on educational approaches are informative and those offering relaxation training do help people to control habitual scratching, resulting in fewer symptoms. They concluded there is a need for well-conducted randomized controlled studies in this area.

Vitiligo

Vitiligo affects about 1% of the total population and is characterized by the progressive development of scattered white patches of skin due to the loss of pigment cells. It often presents as symmetrical patches on exposed body parts such as the face or hands. Some studies have shown that vitiligo has a profound impact on psychological functioning including anxiety, depression and suicidal ideation (Sharma et al., 2001) and, as in other skin conditions, this is not necessarily related to the disease severity or the extent of area involved (Mattoo et al., 2001). Embarrassment, worry, and concern are common (Porter et al., 1986) as are disruptions to relationship development and sexual activity (Porter et al., 1990). People also report experiencing discrimination and the subsequent impact on their quality of life (Kent & Al'Abadie, 1996).However, some people cope well with the challenges presented by the condition and many develop great skill in using camouflage techniques to disguise it. This variability in adjustment has led some authors to propose that pre-existing vulnerabilities account for differences in reported distress within the vitiligo population, rather than it being a consequence for everyone who has the condition. Earlier studies claimed that stress could trigger vitiligo (Papadopoulos et al., 1998) but better controlled and more recent studies have not shown such a clear finding (Picadi et al., 2003).

Some research has shown psychological interventions to be beneficial for people with vitiligo. For example, Papadopoulos and colleagues (1999) reported improvements in self-esteem, body image, and quality of life after using a cognitive behaviour therapy (CBT) approach, but there are few studies to compare this with. As with many other skin conditions, there is a relative lack of well-controlled studies in this area and the evidence base comparing the relative efficacy of different interventions tends to be rather weak, making it difficult to draw firm conclusions on which to develop psychological services. Despite this, some patients clearly benefit from psychological support and the approach of identifying the most vulnerable people by using recognized measures and offering appropriate interventions (which do have an evidence base) would seem to be a reasonable strategy on which to build service development. Patients have reported, anecdotally, that they want integrated services rather than being referred to standard mental health services where practitioners are not familiar with their condition. This approach to service development is consistent with the evidence that supports the greater efficacy of condition-tailored, rather than generic, CBT approaches.

Psoriasis

Psoriasis is a chronic, inflammatory, immune-mediated condition, characterized by excessive growth and shedding of the upper layers of the skin. Whereas non-psoriatic skin takes around 28 days to replace the epidermis, psoriatic skin takes just 4 days. This excess skin-cell production and shedding or flaking is visible and can be very distressing, and presents as recurring periods of remission and exacerbation, or flare-ups. Reports of the prevalence of psoriasis vary but it is thought to affect between 1–3% of the population worldwide (Kimball et al., 2010), whilst a further 0.4–2.3% may have the condition but have not been formally diagnosed (Kurd et al., 2009). Although psoriasis can occur at any time in a person's life, the majority of those affected first report it appearing around early adulthood. There are two forms of psoriasis—around two-thirds of people diagnosed with the condition have type 1, which typically presents before the age of 30. It is thought to be hereditary, has more severe and extensive cutaneous involvement, and greater psychosocial impact (Ferrándiz et al., 2002). Type 2 occurs after the age of 30. Men and women are equally affected but there is a large variation between ethnic groups—it is most common in white skin and very rare amongst Japanese people, aboriginal Australians, Indians from the South Pacific, and Native American Indians (Menter, 2004; Langley et al., 2005).

The five main forms of psoriasis are labelled according to how they present. The most common, plaque psoriasis, is characterized by raised, thickened, red, scaly areas of skin called psoriatic plaques (Smith & Barker, 2006). These areas can be painful and extremely itchy and may appear in relatively small discrete areas of the body such as upper arms or lower limbs, or may involve most or all of the surface area of the skin including the scalp and eyes. Psoriasis can also affect the nails by causing discoloration, pitting, and loosening of the nail from its bed (onycholysis) and abnormal growth of the nail bed (hyperkeratosis).

The severity of psoriasis varies greatly and is graded clinically as mild, moderate, or severe according to the extent of body area affected: mild psoriasis affects less than 3% of the body, moderate affects 3–10%, and the severe form affects 10% or more.

Calculating the severity score includes the areas affected (head and neck, upper limbs, trunk, and lower limbs) plus three aspects of the lesions: redness, thickness, and scaliness. Valid and reliable measures of severity are widely used—the current gold standard being the Psoriasis Area and Severity Index (PASI) (Fredriksson & Pettersson, 1978) and the self-assessment version (SAPASI) which has a good level of agreement with the clinician-rated version (Sampogna et al., 2003).

However, psoriasis is not just a skin condition but rather a complex, long-term condition associated with immune system dysfunction (Christophers, 2001) that requires substantial patient understanding and cooperation if it is to be managed effectively. This systemic disease sometimes occurs alongside other conditions such as psoriatic arthritis (PsA) (Griffiths & Barker, 2007); Crohn's disease (Najarian & Gottlieb, 2003); diabetes mellitus and cardiovascular disease (CVD) (Henseler & Christophers, 1995). When these latter conditions occur simultaneously and are also associated with hyperlipidaemia (raised serum cholesterol levels), they are known collectively as the metabolic syndrome.

Around 6–11% of people with psoriasis develop associated inflammatory PsA (Gelfand et al., 2005). This can result in acute or chronic inflammation of the joints which can lead to stiffness, swelling, extreme pain, and sometimes permanent destruction of the joint structure leading to deformity. It commonly occurs in the spine and distal body regions, especially the fingertips, and can be disabling. So, in addition to managing the appearance of their skin, patients may also have disfigured joints, especially fingers and toes.

People with PsA are likely to experience additional stress which may impact on quality of life as their resources to meet demands are impaired by lowered physical, social and psychological functioning (Salaffi et al., 2009). A body of research has explored the relationship between stress and psoriasis. Stress affects immunity *indirectly* (via behaviours, for example, it may lead to people eating a poor diet, smoking and drinking) and also skin functioning *directly*, via dysregulation of the hypothalamic–pituitary–adrenal axis. The emergence of the field of psychoneuroimmunology (PNI) has re-established the central link between psychological and physical functioning. Evidence from recent PNI studies on chronically stressed people and controls have confirmed the link between changes in the immune system and altered healing processes. These studies show experimentally-induced wounds healed significantly slower in people who reported high levels of stress and had reduced levels of pro-inflammatory markers present (Kiecolt-Glaser et al., 1995; Marucha et al., 1998).

However, the relationship between stress and immune functioning is not simple or straightforward. Indeed, some inflammatory conditions have been shown to improve with periods of stress (Nisipeanu & Korczyn, 1993; Potter & Zautra, 1997), but the more usual observation is that stress exacerbates inflammatory conditions such as psoriasis.

Many people with psoriasis identify stress as either a trigger or a factor that exacerbates a recurrence or flare-up (Polenghi et al., 1994). Early studies looked to establish a link between stressful life events and psoriasis. For example, Fava et al. (1980) reported that 89% of participants recalled experiencing stressful life events 1 month before the onset of psoriasis compared with only 50% of patients with a fungal infection. Whilst other studies have also shown this link between stress and psoriasis (Invernizzi et al., 1988; Al'Abadie et al., 1994; Naldi et al., 2001), others have not (e.g. Payne et al., 1985). A study of 5,600 patients in the US showed around one-third of respondents claimed new patches of psoriasis had appeared at times of worry, while one-third did not claim this link and the remaining third were unclear about whether they had or not (Farber & Nall, 1974). One conclusion that can be drawn from these mixed findings is that some people are more susceptible to the effects of stress than others. Indeed, a more recent study of over 5,000 patients found differences between those who reported that stress played a major part in the exacerbation of their psoriasis and those that did not (Zachariae et al., 2004). The authors identified that those considered psychologically high stress reactors were more likely to be women, to have a family history of psoriasis, to report more severe psoriasis and poorer disease-related quality of life, and more frequent use of tobacco, antidepressants and tranquilizers. However, whether these people are more *physiologically* high stress reactors was not investigated in this study. The complete picture of the role of stress and immune functioning in people with psoriasis has yet to emerge.

Psoriasis is well recognized as a disfiguring and stigmatizing skin disease which can be associated with profound impairments to quality of life (Kimball et al., 2010). Patients with facial psoriasis often experience increased distress (Kent & Koehane, 2001; Richards et al., 2004), feelings of self-consciousness, shame, and embarrassment (Magin et al., 2009), increased stigma and psychological burden (Kimball et al., 2010), and, in some cases, an increased suicide risk (Kurd et al., 2010). This psychological burden can lead to the use of avoidant coping strategies (Magin et al., 2009) and may be the reason for excessive alcohol use, which in turn can exacerbate a psoriasis flare.

Recent work has focused on the degree of severity of the condition and distress, and patients' beliefs about psoriasis as predictors of distress. People living with psoriasis commonly report feeling distressed by other people's reactions to their appearance—strangers often stare and children comment on their appearance. Some people believe, erroneously, that it may be infectious (Magin et al., 2009). A recent review of the psychosocial impact of living with psoriasis argues that the stigma associated with visible skin lesions can create a strong psychological and social burden that is cumulative over time and affects the life course of people with psoriasis (Kimball et al., 2010). Kimball and colleagues report that people with psoriasis experience altered or impaired life potential as a direct effect of psoriasis and its treatment. The factors that make people more susceptible to this life-course impairment include greater perceived stigma, associated physical conditions (e.g. CVD, PsA) plus increased psychological comorbidity. This cumulative burden overwhelms people's ability to cope effectively and they may resort to maladaptive coping strategies, feelings of hopelessness and helplessness and a reduced sense of control over their life and the psoriasis. There is little longitudinal research in this area and although studies to date have not been able to determine cause and effect, single case studies support the view that having psoriasis is the driver for the associated life impairment (Kimball et al., 2010).

A recent, worldwide, online survey of the impact on individuals of living with psoriasis identified widespread effects across people and cultures. This work supports the cumulative life course impairment assertion (see Abbott laboratories: http://www.psoriasisuncovered.co.uk). This survey of 1,700 people from 17 countries asked participants to report the impact that psoriasis had had in four aspects of their lives: work, education, personal, and social. The majority of respondents were female (63%), had lived with their condition for 26 years or longer, and reported their psoriasis was moderately or very active. Sixty-seven per cent of those with active psoriasis believed it had impacted on their work life by limiting job opportunities and the salary they could command and needing time off work to manage their condition. Around a third felt they had been discriminated against in the workplace because of psoriasis. Over 60% felt that their ability to perform in educational settings had been adversely affected and this reinforced beliefs about reduced occupational choices due to psoriasis. Well over two-thirds of the sample claimed that their mental health, mood, and enthusiasm for life were reduced as a result of the condition. Linked to this, over two-thirds claimed they had difficulty forming intimate relationships and over 80% felt having psoriasis had reduced their self-esteem. Around 70% reported that they regularly cancelled social activities due to the condition.

It has been established for some time that the level of distress encountered by people with psoriasis is not directly proportional to the clinical severity of the condition (Fortune et al., 2004) and this is consistent with the findings from other skin conditions and long-term health conditions such as diabetes and CVD. Research suggests that people with psoriasis have a higher incidence of depression and anxiety (de Korte et al., 2004), suicide ideation (Gupta et al., 1993), and psychological distress, including worry (Fortune et al., 2002). Psoriasis is also linked with unhealthy behaviours including excess alcohol use (Kirby et al., 2008), smoking (Fortes et al., 2005), sedentary lifestyle (Magin et al., 2009), and increased body mass index (BMI) (Naldi et al., 2005).

As well as the effects of the condition itself, some of the treatments offered for psoriasis can be unpleasant to administer, odorous, and time-consuming. Biological medicines, in particular, can be associated with serious and, in some cases, life-threatening side effects.

Treatments for psoriasis follow a stepped care model. Specifically, topical treatments (often steroid based) and moisturizing ointments are used first, sometimes in conjunction with phototherapies (UVA and UVB) in controlled doses. If non-systemic treatments are unsuccessful, systemic medicines or immunosuppressant drugs and those that prevent excessive cell division may be introduced. The final, forth-line treatments, termed biologics, block the action of the immune system cells that play a role in psoriasis; these are used for severe forms of psoriasis. It is these systemic and biologic medicines that have the most serious side effects although phototherapy can result in greater risk of skin cancer.

In addition to these biomedical treatments, a range of psychological interventions including hypnotherapy, relaxation techniques, mindfulness-based stress reduction, and CBT have been used to help patients manage the psychosocial impact of psoriasis, but the strongest evidence supports CBT-based approaches (Roth & Fongay, 2005). Moreover, patients treated with tailored CBT for symptom management have shown improvements in *both* distress and psoriasis severity (Fortune et al., 2002). Delivery of CBT has traditionally been on a one-to-one or group basis, and both are effective (Fortune et al., 2002). However, access to psychological therapies in general, and specifically for people with psoriasis, has been, and continues to be, problematic with many eligible patients waiting for long periods to access suitably trained CBT therapists. Furthermore, dedicated service provision for patients with psoriasis only exists in highly specialized settings. For this reason alternative methods of CBT delivery have been developed for other long-term conditions and a review of computerized CBT programmes conducted by Tumur and colleagues (2007) concluded that this mode of delivery is effective, in particular for anxiety-based disorders. Baer and colleagues' editorial (2007) showed completion rates are increased if the participants are screened prior to accessing computerized support programme, if access is restricted via a password and if the programme is supported by phone, email, or face- to-face contact. The development of computer-based interventions for people living with a visible difference is considered in more detail in Chapter 39.

The relative lack of access to suitable psychological treatments particularly tailored to psoriasis has led to recent development of an online, CBT-based tailored programme for patients with mild to moderate psoriasis. This self-management programme (the Electronic-Targeted Intervention for Psoriasis (eTIPs) programme) has recently been shown to improve psychological distress and improve quality of life scores (Bundy et al., in press). A meta-analysis and review of CBT therapy by Butler and colleagues (2006) concluded that as 'Internet based CBT programmes have the advantage of being largely self administered, this type of treatment may be an excellent first step in stepped care approaches to managing distress and psychological morbidity in behavioral medicine populations', this may be especially so in psychological approaches to managing psoriasis.

SKIN CANCER

Skin cancers are the most prevalent cancers in the UK. They comprise non-melanoma skin cancers (both squamous cell carcinomas (SCCs) and basal cell carcinomas (BCCs)), and malignant melanomas. There is a high burden of disease from skin cancer, due to its high prevalence and the mortality attributable to it. The cause of skin cancers in the vast majority of individuals is excessive exposure to the UV radiation in sunlight. Malignant melanoma is generally related to intermittent acute exposure, SCC to chronic overexposure, and BCC to both forms of exposure. A study from the US has shown that people who have had non-melanoma skin cancer are also at greater risk of developing other forms of cancer and this suggests there may be a genetic predisposition to skin and other cancer risk (Chen et al., 2008).

The incidence of both malignant and non-malignant skin cancers has increased in the last 50 years. In particular there has been a three-fold increase of malignant melanoma rates in the 15–35-year age group over the past 35 years (Cancer Research UK 2012; http://www.cancerresearchuk.org). This is thought to be largely due to the numbers of people taking more holidays abroad and experiencing increased UV exposure as a result, plus the increased use of tanning beds particularly in the under 35 age group. Malignant melanoma is the second most common cancer in the under 18 age group and it is life-threatening—a quarter of the 8,000 cases diagnosed in the UK each year will die from it (Cancer Research UK 2012; http://www.cancerresearchuk.org). The concentration of tanning-bed salons is greatest in more economically deprived areas and malignant melanoma tends to be linked with lower socioeconomic status. Repeated sun burning before the age of 18 is thought to be a major risk factor for skin cancer, especially in those with fair skin types, those who do not tan easily, those with large numbers of freckles, and people prone to moles.

The main treatment for non-melanoma skin cancer is photodynamic or light therapy. However, it is not suitable for those that are deeper or malignant and, in these instances, surgical excision is the preferred option, although the scars can be extensive and may result in functional impairment, pain, and itching in addition to potential disfigurement, even if the melanoma is skilfully removed. This can be distressing and some people with scars from excision seek psychological support. It is important to note that the location, severity, or size of scarring is not always correlated with level of psychosocial sequelae (Partridge & Rumsey, 2003) which can include disruption to daily activities, sleep disturbance, anxiety, depression, loss of self-esteem, stigmatization, and post-traumatic stress reactions (Brown et al., 2010).

The diagnosis of cancer itself can create anxiety and lead to a host of psychosocial issues being raised, yet, despite the rise in numbers of skin cancers there is surprisingly little research on the psychosocial impact of skin cancer and its treatment, especially when compared with other types of cancer or the treatment associated with other visible differences, such as burns corrections or port-wine stain removal. This is an area that warrants more attention from psychologists both in public heath prevention strategies and, as the numbers of people living with the psychosocial burden of skin cancer increases, in treatment programmes to manage distress and secondary prevention.

At the very least, healthcare personnel should be able to assess and manage the minor distress that some patients experience, whilst identifying and referring on to specialist services those with greater levels of distress. They may require training to do this effectively. Access to specialist psychological services that understand patients' specific needs should be developed in order to meet the increasing demands from this group.

In conclusion, this chapter has given an overview of the psychosocial sequelae of five skin conditions which, although different in cause, severity, seriousness, and presentation, are very similar in terms of the psychological issues they present. Distress is common and many people report heightened levels of social anxiety and depressive symptoms. Sadly, there are too many reports of attempted suicide amongst people with skin conditions. The effect on patients' wider family and significant others is beyond the scope of this chapter and warrants investigation, as do beliefs about skin conditions and the associated degree of adherence to pre-scribed medicines or lifestyle changes,

Finally, the provision of psychological support for people affected by skin conditions needs to be addressed. It seems that CBT, whether face-to-face or online and within a stepped model of care is a potential way forward. Healthcare professionals working in dermatology may benefit from training to deliver the first steps of a tiered model of psychosocial care which should form part of their overall management plans. Expert psychological support should be integrated with, not separate from, medical management. In addition to increased medical and nursing training in psychological aspects of skin conditions, psychologists could benefit from some postgraduate train-ing that focuses on understanding key aspects of biology and medical management of skin disease. With lifestyle forming a significant part of the problems associated with many skin conditions, academic health and clinical psychologists should be focusing more research in this area and funding bodies would do well to consider an integrated biopsychosocial approach to funding research in dermatological conditions.

REFERENCES

Al'Abadie, M. S., Kent, G. G., & Gawkrodger, D. J. (1994). The relationship between stress and the onset and exacerbation of psoriasis and other skin conditions. *British Journal of Dermatology*, 130, 199–203.

Baer, L., Greist, J., & Marks, I. M. (2007). Computer-aided cognitive behaviour therapy. *Psychotherapy and Psychosomatics*, 76(4), 193–5.

Balkrishnan, R., Kulkarni, A. S., Cayce, K., & Feldman, S. R. (2006). Predictors of healthcare outcomes and costs related to medication use in patients with acne in the United States. *Cutis*, 77(4), 251–5.

Bowe, W. P., Leyden J. J., Crerand C. E., Sarwer, D. B., & Margolis, D. J. (2007). Body dysmorphic disorder symptoms among patients with acne vulgaris. *Journal of the American Academy of Dermatology*, 57(2), 222–30.

Brown, B. C., Moss, T. P., McGrouther, D. A., & Bayat, A. (2010). Skin scar preconceptions must be challenged: importance of self-perception in skin scarring. *Journal of Plastic, Reconstructive & Aesthetic Surgery*, 63(6), 1022–9.

Bundy, C., Pinder, B., Bucci, S., Griffiths, C. E. M., & Tarrier, N. (submitted). A Novel, Web-Based, Psychological Intervention for People with Psoriasis: The Electronic Targeted Intervention for Psoriasis (eTIPs) Study.

Butler, A. C., Chapman, J. E., Forman, E. M., & Beck, A. T. (2006). The empirical status of cognitive-behavioral therapy: a review of meta-analyses. *Clinical Psychology Review*, 26(1), 17–31.

Cancer Research UK. (2012). *Skin cancer statistics–key facts*. Available at http://info.cancerresearchuk.org/cancerstats/keyfacts/skin-cancer/ (accessed 27 April 2012).

Chen, J., Ruczinski, I., Jorgensen, T. J., Yenokyan, G., Yao, Y., & Alani, R., (2008). Non melanoma skin cancer and risk for subsequent malignancy. *National Cancer Institute*, 100(17), 1215–22.

Christophers, E. (2001). Psoriasis—epidemiology and clinical spectrum. *Clinical and Experimental Dermatology*, 26(4), 314–20.

de Korte, J., Sprangers, M. A., Mombers, F. M., & Bos, J. D. (2004). Quality of life in patients with psoriasis: a systematic literature review. *Journal of Investigative Dermatology Symposium Proceedings*, 9(2), 140–7.

Dunn, L. K., O'Neill, J. L., & Feldman, S. R. (2011). Acne in adolescents: Quality of life, self-esteem, mood, and psychological disorders. *Dermatology Online Journal*, 17(1), 1.

Ersser, S. J., Latter, S., Sibley, A., Satherley, P. A., & Welbourne, S. (2007). Psychological and educational interventions for atopic eczema in children (Cochrane review). *Cochrane Database of Systematic Reviews*, 3, CD004054.

Farber, E. M. & Nall, M. L. (1974). The natural history of psoriasis in 5600 patients. *Dermatologica*, 148, 1–14.

Fava, G. A., Perini, G. I., Santonastaso, P., & Fornasa, C. V. (1980). Life events and psychological distress in dermatological disorders: psoriasis, chronic urticaria and fungal infections. *British Journal of Medical Psychology*, 53, 277–83.

Ferrándiz, C., Pujol, R. M., García-Patos, V., Bordas, X., & Smandía, J. A. (2007). Psoriasis of early and late onset: A clinical and epidemiologic study from Spain. *Journal of the American Academy of Dermatology*, 46(6), 867–73.

Fortes, C., Mastroeni, S., Leffondré, K., Sampogna, F., Melchi, F., Mazzotti, E., *et al.* (2005). For the IDI Multipurpose Psoriasis Research on Vital Experiences (IMPROVE) Study Group. Relationship between smoking and the clinical severity of psoriasis. *Archives of Dermatology*, 141, 1580–4.

Fortune, D. G., Richards, H. L., Main, C. J., Kirby, B., Bowcock, S., & Griffiths, C. E. M. (2002). A Cognitive behavioural symptom management programme as an adjunct in psoriasis therapy. *British Journal of Dermatology*, 146, 458–65.

Fortune, D. G., Richards, H. L., Kirby, B., McElhone, K., Main, C. J., & Griffiths, C. E. (2004). Successful treatment of psoriasis improves psoriasis-specific but not more general aspects of patients' well-being. *British Journal of Dermatology*, 151(6), 1219–26.

Fredriksson, T. & Pettersson, U. (1978). Severe psoriasis—oral therapy with a new retinoid. *Dermatologica*, 157, 238–44.

Gelfand, J. M., Gladman, D. D., Mease, P. J., Smith, N., Margolis, D. J., Nijsten, T., *et al.* (2005). Epidemiology of psoriatic arthritis in the population of the United States. *Journal of the American Academy of Dermatology*, 53, 573.

Griffiths, C. E. M. & Barker, J. N. W. N. (2007). Psoriasis: pathogenesis and clinical features of psoriasis. *Lancet*, 370, 263–71.

Gupta, M. A., Schork, N., Gupta, A. K., Kirkby, S., & Ellis, C. N. (1993). Suicidal ideation in psoriasis. *International Journal of Dermatology*, 32, 188–90.

Henseler, T. & Christophers, E. (1995). Disease concomitance in psoriasis. *Journal of the American Academy of Dermatology*, 32, 982–6.

Invernizzi, G., Gala, C., Bovio, L., Conte, G., Manca, G., Polenghi, M., *et al.* (1988). Onset of psoriasis: the role of life events. *Medical Sciences Research*, 16, 143–4.

Kent, G. & Al'Abadie, M. (1996). Factors affecting responses on dermatology life quality index items among vitiligo sufferers. *Clinical and Experimental Dermatology*, 21, 330–3.

Kent, G. & Keohane, S. (2001). Social anxiety and disfigurement: the moderating effects of fear of negative evaluation and past experience. *British Journal of Clinical Psychology*, 40(Pt 1), 23–34.

Kiecolt-Glaser, J. K., Marucha, P. T., Malarkey, W. B., Mercardo, W. B., & Glaser, R. (1995). Slowing of wound healing by psychological stress. *Lancet*, 346, 1194–6.

Kimball, A. B., Gieler, U., Linder, D., Sampogna, F., Warren, R. B., & Augustin, M. (2010). Psoriasis: is the impairment to the patient's life cumulative? *Journal of the European Academy of Dermatology and Venereology*, 24, 989–1004.

Kirby, B., Richards, H. L., Mason, D. L., Fortune, D. G., Main, C. J., & Griffiths, C. E. M. (2008). Alcohol consumption and psychological distress in patients with psoriasis. *British Journal of Dermatology*, 158(1), 138–40.

Kurd, S. K. & Gelfand, J. M. (2009). The prevalence of previously diagnosed and undiagnosed psoriasis in US adults: results from NHANES 2003–2004. *Journal of the American Academy of Dermatology*, 60(2), 218–24.

Kurd, S. K., Troxel, B., Crits-Christoph, P., & Gelfand, J. M. (2010). The risk of depression, anxiety, and suicidality in patients with psoriasis. A population-based cohort study. *Archives of Dermatology*, 146(8), 891–5.

Langley, R. G. B., Krueger, G.G., & Grifiths, C. E. M. (2005). Psoriasis, epidemiology, clinical features, and quality of life. *Annals of the Rheumatic Diseases*, 64(Suppl 2), ii.18–ii.23.

Lewis-Jones, S. (2006). Quality of life and childhood atopic dermatitis: the misery of living with childhood eczema. *International Journal of Clinical Practice*, 60(8), 984–92.

Magin P., Adams J., Heading G., Pond, D., & Smith, W. (2006). Psychological sequelae of acne vulgaris: results of a qualitative study. *Canadian Family Physician*, 52, 978–9.

Magin, P., Adams, J., Heading, G., Pond, D., & Smith, W. (2009). The psychological sequelae of psoriasis: results of a qualitative study. *Psychology, Health & Medicine*, 14(2), 150–61.

Marucha, P. T., Kiecolt-Glaser, J. K., & Favagehi, M. (1998). Mucosa wound healing is impaired by examination stress. *Psychosomatic Medicine*, 60, 362–5.

Mattoo, S. K., Handa, S., Kaur, I., Gupta, N., & Malhotra, R. (2001). Psychiatric morbidity in vitiligo and psoriasis: a comparative study from India. *Journal of Dermatology*, 28, 424–32.

Menter, A. (2004). The effect of psoriasis on patients' quality of life and improvements associated with alefacept therapy. *Journal of Cutaneous Medicine and Surgery*, 8(Suppl 2), 20–5.

Montnemery, P., Nihlen, U., Goran Lofdahl, C., Nyberg, P., & Svensson, A. (2003). Prevalence of self-reported eczema in relation to living environment, socio-economic status and respiratory symptoms assessed in a questionnaire study. *BMC Dermatology*, 3, 4.

Najarian, D. J. & Gottlieb, A. B. (2003). Connections between psoriasis and Crohn's disease. *Journal of the American Academy of Dermatology*, 48, 805–21.

Naldi, L., Peli, I., Parazzini, F., & Carell, C. F. (2001). Family history of psoriasis, stressful life events, and recent infectious diseases are risk factors for a first episode of acute guttate psoriasis: results of a case controlled study. *Journal of the American Academy of Dermatology*, 44, 433–8.

Naldi L., Chatenoud L., Linder D., Belloni Fortina, A., Peserico, A., Virgili, A. R., *et al.* (2005). Cigarette smoking, body mass index, and stressful life events as risk factors for psoriasis: results from an Italian case control study. *Journal of Investigative Dermatology*, 125, 61–7.

Nisipeanu, P. & Korczyn, A. D. (1993). Psychological stress as a risk factor for exacerbations in multiple sclerosis. *Neurology*, 43, 1311–22.

Papadopoulos, L., Bor, L., Legg, C., & Hawk, J. L. M. (1998). Impact of life events on the onset of vitiligo in adults: a preliminary evidence for a psychological dimension in aetiology. *Clinical and Experimental Dermatology*, 23, 243–8.

Papadopoulos, L., Bor, R., & Legg, C. (1999). Coping with the disfiguring effects of vitiligo: a preliminary investigation into the effects of cognitive-behaviour therapy. *British Journal of Medical Psychology*, 72, 385–96.

Partridge, J. & Rumsey, N. (2003). Skin scarring: new insights may make adjustment easier. *British Journal of Medicine*, 326, 765.

Payne, R. A., Rowland Payne, C. M., & Marks, R. (1985). Stress does not worsen psoriasis? A controlled study of 32 patients. *Clinical and Experimental Dermatology*, 10, 239–45.

Picardi, A., Pasquini, P., Cattaruzza, M. S., Gaetano, P., Melchi, C. F., Baliva, G., *et al.* (2003). Stressful life events, social support, attachment security and alexithymia in vitiligo. A case-control study. *Psychotherapy and Psychosomatics*, 72, 150–8.

Polenghi, M. M., Molinari, E., Gala, C., Guzzi, R., & Finzi, A. F. (1994). Experience with psoriasis in a psychosomatic dermatology clinic. *Acta Dermato Venerologica (Suppl)*, 186, 65–6.

Porter, J. R., Beuf, A. H., Lerner, A. B., & Nordlund, J. J. (1986). Psychosocial effect of vitiligo: a comparison of vitiligo patients with normal subjects, with psoriasis patients, and with patients with other pigmentary disorders. *Journal of the American Academy of Dermatology*, 15, 220–4.

Porter, J. R., Beuf, A. H., Lerner, A. B., & Nordlund, J. J. (1990). The effect of vitiligo on sexual relationships. *Journal of the American Academy of Dermatology*, 22, 221–2.

Potter, P. & Zautra, A. J. (1997). Stressful life events' effects on rheumatoid arthritis activity. *Journal of Consulting and Clinical Psychology*, 65, 319–23.

Purvis, D., Robinson, E., Merry, S., & Watson, P. (2006). Acne, anxiety, depression and suicide in teenagers: a cross-sectional survey of New Zealand secondary school students. *Journal of Paediatrics and Child Health*, 42(12), 793–6.

Richards, H. L., Fortune, D. G., Weidmann, A., Sweeney, S. K., & Griffiths, C. E. (2004). Detection of psychological distress in patients with psoriasis: low consensus between dermatologist and patient. *British Journal of Dermatology*, 151(6), 1227–33.

Roth, A. & Fonagy, P. (2005). *What Works for Whom?: A Critical Review of Psychotherapy Research* (2nd edn.). London: The Guilford Press.

Salaffi, F., Carotti, M., Gasparini, S., Intorcia, M., & Grassi, W. (2009). The health-related quality of life in rheumatoid arthritis, ankylosing spondylitis, and psoriatic arthritis: a comparison with a selected sample of healthy people. *Health and Quality of Life Outcomes*, 18(7), 25.

Sampogna, F., Sera, F., Mazzotti, E., Pasquini, P., Picardi, A., Abeni, D. & The IDI Multipurpose Psoriasis Research On Vital Experiences (IMPROVE). (2003). Study group performance of the self-administered psoriasis area and severity index in evaluating clinical and sociodemographic subgroups of patients with psoriasis. *Archives of Dermatology*, 139, 353–8.

Schofield, J. K., Grindlay, D., William, H. C. (2009). *Skin conditions in the UK: a health needs assessment*. www.nottingham.ac.uk/scs/documents/documentsdivisions/documentsdermatology/hcnaskinconditionsuk2009.pdf (accessed 24 January 2011)

Sharma, N., Koranne, R. V., & Singh, R. K. (2001). Psychiatric morbidity in psoriasis and vitiligo: a comparative study. *Journal of Dermatology*, 28, 419–23.

Smith, C.H., Barker, J. N. W. N. (2006). Psoriasis and its management. *British Journal of Medicine*, 333, 380–4.

Su, J. C., Kemp, A. S., Varigos, G. A., & Nolan, T.M. (1997). Atopic eczema: its impact on the family and financial cost. *Archives of Disease in Childhood*, 76, 159–62.

Tumur, I., Kaltenthaler, E., Ferriter, M., Beverley, C., & Parry, G. (2007). Computerised cognitive behaviour therapy for obsessive–compulsive disorder: a systematic review. *Psychotherapy and Psychosomatics*, 76(4), 196–202.

Weston, W. L. & Lane, A. T. (1991). *Color textbook of pediatric dermatology*. St Louis, MO: Mosby-Yearbook.

Zachariae, R., Zachariae, H., Blomqvist, K., Davidsson, S., Molin, L., Mark, C., *et al.* (2004). Self-reported stress reactivity and psoriasis related stress of Nordic psoriasis sufferers. *Journal of the European Academy of Dermatology and Venereology*, 18, 27–36.

CHAPTER 29

WHEN TREATMENT AFFECTS APPEARANCE

HEIDI WILLIAMSON
MELISSA WALLACE

MANY surgical and medical treatments have the potential to alter appearance. However, whereas some seek to improve appearance, for example, cosmetic surgery or hormonal therapy for acne, those that aim to treat cancer and other conditions can result in temporary or permanent undesirable appearance changes. Here we focus on the latter and use a variety of familiar surgical and medical treatments, recognized as adversely changing appearance, to illustrate the common psychological and social appearance-related challenges experienced by patients. In addition, we investigate why some individuals appear to cope with an altered appearance better than others, touch upon the evidence base for interventions in this area, and provide opinion on the direction of future research. In addition to the treatments presented here, we acknowledge there are others that have a significant impact on appearance. This chapter is therefore not exhaustive, but will instead provide a more in depth focus on particular selected treatments.

Surgical Treatments

Surgical treatments can result in varying degrees of scarring or disfigurement with the potential to result in loss of function, lymphoedema, amputation, stoma formation, and reliance on prosthetics or external surgical devices. Differences in adjustment to an altered appearance make it difficult to predict the psychosocial impact of surgery on the individual. For some a scar may be viewed as a negative symbol, a reminder of the causative event, a source of stigma and pre-occupation, and therefore a major influence on psychosocial well-being:

I keep re-adjusting my clothes because I'm worried everyone else can see the same thing as me ... and I constantly worry about what I wear – what it looks like, does it cover my belly. If I lift my arms will it show? I can't relax and enjoy the moment ... I'm constantly fidgeting – checking round to see who's looking (young woman with an abdominal scar, Brown et al., 2008, p. 1055).

For others it may be viewed with pride, a positive symbol of one's experience on the journey to recovery: *'Yeah ... I'm quite proud of my scar'* (young female cancer survivor, Wallace et al., 2007, p. 1022).

Despite this caveat, some surgical treatments, either because of the extent of the appearance change they cause or the significance of the site involved, result in common psychosocial challenges and patterns of response. This section will focus on the experiences of those following surgical amputation, head and neck surgery, breast cancer surgery, and stoma formation—four specialist fields that can dramatically alter appearance, function and body image.

Amputation

Often as a last resort, after other medical and surgical interventions have failed, conditions such as cancer, vascular disease, and meningitis can result in the amputation of a limb(s). Relief from pain and illness can lead some to view amputation in a positive way, particularly those who regard the procedure as life saving (Jones et al., 1993), but nonetheless, such a rapid and highly visible change in appearance typically presents extraordinary psychological and social challenges.

Immediately post-amputation patients can experience feelings of shock, loss, and mutilation and many engage in behaviours to avoid looking at their stump (Sjodahl et al., 2004) and to conceal or disguise it with covers or clothes (Norris et al., 1998). Meeting friends and family for the first time following surgery can be particularly difficult, especially if other treatments, for example, chemotherapy, have altered appearance further and patients have to manage reactions of alarm or distress, staring, curiosity, and questioning (Sjodahl et al., 2004). Patients describe an initial response of hypervigilance to these reactions that typically subsides with the passage of time as they adjust to their altered body image. Support and acceptance of their appearance by friends and family can help with this process (Norris et al., 1998; Saradjian et al., 2007).

Horgan and MacLachlan's (2004) review of experimental and self-report studies provides considerable evidence of the social stigma associated with lower limb amputation; not only in relation to visible difference but also to physical disability as many have a temporary or permanent reliance on a wheelchair or walking aids (see also Chapter 3). Anxiety about saying the wrong thing and feeling uncomfortable in the presence of the individual with an amputation can lead others to ignore them, appear embarrassed, over-sympathetic, or patronizing (Gething, 1991; Gallagher and MacLachlan, 2001). Individuals can also feel that the role of the amputation in their life is over-emphasized and resent negative assumptions about their personality and functioning (Furst & Humphrey, 1983; Rybarczyk et al., 2000). For example, that the amputation is central to rather than merely one facet of their life or that they are highly misfortunate, when often they rate themselves as only marginally less fortunate after the amputation compared with before.

Positive adjustment to an amputation is more likely for those with an optimistic disposition and active coping skills (see Horgan & MacLachlan, 2004, for a review of the evidence), and for those who bolster their self-esteem by finding meaning in their loss or by drawing favourable comparisons between themselves and others deemed less fortunate: 'there were many who were worse off ... it's hard to feel sorry for yourself in that situation' (Sjodahl et al., 2004, p. 858).

Men with an upper limb amputation (ULA) have also reported some successful strategies to manage negative reactions by other people (Saradjian et al., 2007). These included managing people's curiosity and questions by honest open responses, using humour, attributing negative or demeaning reactions as the responsibility of the perpetrator, ('I'm not bothered by them, they're narrow-minded', p. 876), and by using a prosthesis to conceal the amputation. Prostheses can provide a sense of 'wholeness', normality, and much needed respite from unwanted attention and can also allow others to get to know the affected person before negative evaluations compromise social interactions.

There is evidence within the ULA literature that when compared with women, men are more concerned about the functionality of their prosthesis rather than its aesthetics (e.g. Murray & Fox, 2002). This is not always the case. Men also describe using a prosthetic limb to improve their appearance and to meet perceived social demands, especially in formal settings if they anticipate negative evaluation. For example, one participant in Saradjian et al.'s study recalled opting to wear his prosthesis to a wedding because: 'people don't want me on their wedding photographs *with [my] jacket sleeve tucked in [my] pocket'* (p. 879). Prosthetics that look more realistic are highly valued and have been found to increase adaptation to amputation and willingness to participate in normal activities (Donovan-Hall et al., 2002).

Despite these benefits, dependence on prosthetics for cosmetic cover can indicate an inability to deal with limb loss and feelings of shame (see Gallagher, 2004). While some individuals are able to find a balance between comfort and appearance—in that they are willing to remove their prosthesis in front of close friends or family, when swimming, or when straps rub painfully on sweaty skin—others become socially dependent and are never seen without it. One male described how: *'It can be boiling hot in the summer, I still put it on and it's very uncomfortable'* (Saradjian et al., 2007, p. 878). A similar behavioural response has been identified among other groups with visible differences, including those with a dependence on camouflage make-up or wigs. Reliance on only one coping strategy is believed to inhibit the development of alternatives, and ultimately increase anxiety for the individual who fears the prospect of accidentally or unavoidably revealing 'the real me' (Coughlan & Clarke, 2002).

Although many overcome the challenges of an amputation, for some the impact of an altered appearance results in negative changes in lifestyle and quality of life which do not improve with time (Sjodahl et al., 2004). Persisting hypervigilance to the reactions of others and heightened feelings of being judged and stigmatized are believed to contribute to feelings of body shame and self-consciousness, which can lead to anxiety, depression, isolation, and reduced social functioning (Rybarczyk et al., 1992, 1995; Saradjian et al., 2007). When comparing individuals with various degrees of disfigurement following amputation, self-consciousness can be a stronger predictor of distress than the *severity* of limb disfigurement (Williamson, 1995).

Research in the field of appearance psychology is currently exploring the role of information processing biases, such as hypervigilance, in reinforcing and exacerbating appearance concerns (see Rosser et al., 2010). This research is in its infancy, but the role of predisposing cognitive processing biases might offer some explanation for why certain individuals with an amputation experience greater feelings of being judged and stigmatized than others: an interesting area for further investigation.

Surgical treatment for head and neck cancer

Facial surgery, particularly for head and neck cancer (HNC), can have a profound psychosocial impact. HNC can occur in the mouth, throat, nose, ear, or eye region and treatment can result in scarring, changes in facial shape, paralysis, drooling, and difficulty with eating and speaking. Some may have prostheses or a highly visible temporary or permanent breathing stoma (hole in the neck). Developments in surgical techniques have revolutionized reconstruction capabilities, but nonetheless all patients will experience some degree of permanent appearance change, and treatments for advanced disease remain radical and dramatically alter appearance. Anxiety and depression is experienced by approximately 30–40% of patients (Semple et al., 2004) and anxiety can continue to escalate long after treatment has concluded (see Dropkin, 2001).

Findings are equivocal among the few studies that have attempted to disentangle the impact of disfigurement as a cause of this distress from other variables, including being diagnosed with a life threatening illness, physical dysfunction, and fear of cancer re-occurrence. This is possibly a consequence of using diverse methods to measure disfigurement and quality of life that often do not consider patient priorities or the importance they assign to their various concerns. Nonetheless, appearance concern is strongly implicated as a major contributor to the distress experienced by HNC patients.

Anticipation of disfigurement is associated with high levels of anxiety presurgery (Dropkin, 2001) and postoperatively patients often grieve for the loss of their previous appearance (see Piff, 1998). Many experience a negative impact on self-image (Gamba et al., 1992) and fears about re-entering society with an altered facial appearance can be as extreme and prominent as fears about recurring disease (Herzon & Bioshier, 1979). A further indication of the impact of living with an altered appearance is the repeated finding that patients tend to cope better with the ramifications of dysfunction than with those associated with disfigurement (Dropkin & Scott, 1983; Mast, 1999).

High levels of appearance-related distress are attributed to the importance individuals place on the head and neck area as the most individual and personal part of their body. The face provides expressions of emotion, intellect, and communication and is critical to identity, social interaction, and the development of close relationships. Social interactions can therefore be a major challenge, especially when surgery results in functional deficits that make it difficult or impossible to use facial expressions or to speak, and when highly visible scarring or disfigurement attracts curiosity and unwanted attention such as staring or negative remarks. Some individuals report feeling stigmatized, avoided, discounted, or misjudged, and provide accounts of people assuming their appearance points to intellectual impairment, criminal inclinations (or some other form of undesirable trait), difficulties making friends and in obtaining jobs (see Strauss, 1989; Kent, 2000).

As a result of these negative experiences patients can become socially isolated. Not only because others might avoid them, but also because feelings of self-consciousness and fear of negative evaluations can result in social anxiety and lead to self-imposed isolation from family, friends, and recreational activities (Dhooper, 1985; Rumsey et al., 2004; Hagedoorn & Molleman, 2006). Inevitably, the sum of these experiences lead to long-term problems with lowered self-esteem and loss of confidence (Robinson, 1997).

However, not all HNC patients struggle in this way (see Katz et al., 2003). Evidence of the extrinsic and dispositional factors that might be protecting these individuals is again inconclusive, indicating a complex multifactorial relationship between these factors and adjustment that is not yet fully understood. But nonetheless, severity of facial disfigurement, gender, social support, and personal assets such as social self-efficacy, are thought to play a role.

Appearance psychologists accept that as a result of individual differences in responses to disfigurement, one cannot predict the degree of psychological distress from the cause, type, and severity of a visible difference (Harris, 1997). Objective measures of the severity of facial disfigurement following surgery are therefore not necessarily related to measures of psychological adjustment (e.g. see Baker, 1992). Very often it is the individual's subjective assessment of how visible the facial difference is to others that determines psychological well-being. As a result surgeons can be surprised by the degree of distress caused by what they regard as only a minimal change in appearance, or by surgery they view as having a successful aesthetic outcome.

However, if large areas of the face are affected (particularly the central part of the face) and the disfigurement is extreme, immediately obvious and interferes with the social/communication process, then this degree of severity is likely to present a considerable and overwhelming psychosocial challenge (Clarke, 1999). Compared to those with minor disfigurement, patients experiencing severe disfigurement following HNC (measured by clinical assessment) tend to be more depressed, experience more appearance-related anxiety and social isolation, and experience a greater change to self-image and problems with romantic relationships. In some cases patients report that these disadvantages can outweigh the advantages of treatment (e.g. Gamba et al., 1992; Katz et al., 2003).

The impact of gender appears to be a less ambiguous factor in adjustment. In numerous studies women report more appearance concern and dissatisfaction with appearance post-surgery compared with men (e.g. see Khafif et al., 2007; Liu, 2008), and experience greater intensity of depressive symptoms and lower life happiness (Katz et al., 2003). The impact of disfigurement among females is also thought to contribute to comparative increases in length of postoperative hospital stay (Dropkin, 1997). Although the relationship between social support and adjustment is well established amongst all HNC patients (see Baker, 1992), women are particularly sensitive to its buffering effect and therefore at greater risk of poor adjustment if social support is poor (Katz et al., 2003).

Many researchers postulate that women are more vulnerable to the impact of disfigurement because most cultures value facial attractiveness in women more highly than in men. This phenomenon might account for Lockhart's (2000) finding that female nurses rated female patients as *more* disfigured than male patients even though the women had received identical procedures to the men. The effect of this perceptual bias was not evaluated in terms of interactions between nurse and patient, but nonetheless Lockhart warns nurses to be aware of the potential effect of gender-specific perceptions on their interactions.

The process of body image re-integration is believed to be another feature of positive adjustment (Dropkin, 1999, 2001). Self-care and re-socialization, employed during the postoperative period, have been identified as coping behaviours that contribute to this process and that can be facilitated by simple nursing interventions (Bowers, 2008). For HNC patients, mundane tasks associated with self-care (grooming and hygiene) become exceptionally demanding, with many wanting to avoid looking in the mirror and touching their scars (Gamba et al., 1992). Patients therefore benefit from practical and emotional support and encouragement to engage in self-care, by confronting their appearance in the mirror (which is usually alarming), touching their face, and managing changes in facial or neck contours that can make shaving, cleaning or the application of make-up challenging.

Re-socialization involves developing practical skills to re-establish sociality (listening, writing, and gesturing skills), and controlled exposure of their disfigurement to staff, family, and friends. Social exposure is not a comfortable process, but allows patients to confront the reactions of others to their appearance and provides validation of the severity of the disfigurement. The confrontation inherent in both self-care and re-socialization can lessen anxiety by increasing feelings of control and self-confidence and by reducing ambiguity about the extent and nature of their disfigurement. This affords an opportunity for reappraisal and can contribute towards acceptance of their new face (Dropkin, 1999, 2001).

Notwithstanding the potential benefits of controlled exposure in the early postoperative period, unfavourable reactions of shock or repulsion by visiting friends or family are a risk. They can be distressing to both parties and can have a lasting impact on the patient that can impair adjustment (McCormick, 1995). If relatives or friends are to be part of the adjustment process, Bower (2008) suggests that they too need to be prepared, coached, and supported, and made aware that appearance changes will be exacerbated by postoperative swelling and bruising.

The benefits of social skills in helping individuals with a variety of visible differences to manage the challenges and anxiety experienced during social interactions, is becoming increasingly recognized. More specific to the experiences of HNC patients is the finding by Hagedoorn and Molleman (2006) that those with severe facial disfigurement experience greater distress and social isolation, compared to those with less disfigurement, when they believe they are *not* capable of exercising control over the reactions and openness of others: that is to say when their social self-efficacy is low. Social self-efficacy appears to be an important asset that may moderate the relationship between the severity of facial disfigurement and distress.

The design and evaluation of interventions that attempt to improve social self-efficacy, via social skills training, offer promising results. For example, Fiegenbaum (1981) developed a social skills training programme for HNC patients that reduced social anxiety and improved self-confidence. Robinson et al. (1996) incorporated social skills training into a workshop for individuals with congenital and surgically acquired facial disfigurements that reduced social avoidance and distress. Clarke's (2001) social rehabilitation programme for HNC patients, delivered by specialist nurses trained in managing psychosocial issues, also proved successful in reducing social embarrassment and facilitating social functioning. These were small studies, the latter limited by lack of a control group, but having good social skills appears to be an effective coping strategy contributing towards adaptation to the psychosocial consequences of facial difference. Interventions described here may also be helpful to those struggling to adapt to the social consequences of other highly visible differences, such as amputation.

The success of any intervention to improve adjustment will also depend on the quality of the nurse–patient relationship, particularly the nurse's motivation and ability to initiate talk about appearance and to allow patients the time and context to express and identify their concerns. In theory, nurses can often discern the features of a helpful interaction and of good quality care, but in practice, barriers have been identified that prevent them from meeting these ideals (Konradsen et al., 2009).

Barriers identified by Konradsen et al. include not enough time to talk, a perceived lack of expertise or the assumption that there is little they can do to help, and fears they may make psychosocial problems worse. Opportunities to identify and discuss appearance concerns can also be missed by staff that are desensitized to disfigurement, judge others to be far worse, or assume the patient would instigate talk if their altered appearance was a problem. Patients are often given the impression that appearance concerns are secondary to survival and the immediate business of physical care, and therefore a 'luxury problem' that takes up valuable nursing time. These barriers and misperceptions can lead to a 'silencing process' between nurses and their patients that unintentionally inhibits appearance talk.

Nurses, and other members of the multidisciplinary team responsible for patient care, can support patients to adjust to their disfigurement by addressing these barriers. They can do this by validating and de-stigmatizing appearance concerns, talking openly about appearance, and examining any preconceived assumptions they hold that might be preventing an accurate assessment of appearance related needs. The use of routine measures to assess appearance or body image concerns can also be helpful to instigate appearance talk and identify individual concerns (see Millsopp et al., 2006).

Surgical treatment for breast cancer

Breast cancer is one of the most prevalent cancers in women. Survival rates have been improving for more than 20 years and women can now reduce the risk of a genetic predisposition by opting for prophylactic mastectomy. The number of women with an altered appearance resulting from the surgical removal of a section (lumpectomy) or the whole breast (mastectomy) will continue to grow as our population ages and as advances in cancer detection and treatment improve.

Breasts have always had social connotations of femininity, motherhood, and sexuality (Khan et al., 2000). Pressure via the media and interactions with others, further promotes the unrealistic dictate that for women to feel feminine, attractive, and sexy they must not only be beautiful and thin but have large and perfect breasts. Many women succumb to these pressures and premorbid appearance concerns in this area are likely to be exacerbated by breast loss and disfigurement.

Women can describe mastectomy (and even lumpectomy) as a psychologically painful experience which threatens their body image and sense of feminine, social and sexual identity (see Alfano & Rowland, 2006). Viewing the physical space caused by mastectomy and comparing their changed body to their former healthy self can trigger feelings of emptiness and grief. Some fear the stigma of looking 'monstrous' and shocking (Piot-Ziegler et al., 2010). To avoid distressing others and attracting negative attention, women are often motivated to conceal evidence of their mastectomy using clothing and by limiting their freedom of movement and social activity, for example, avoiding physical activities which expose evidence of mastectomy, such as swimming. The distress caused by visual and physical asymmetry and postural imbalance has led some women to consider bilateral mastectomy (Piot-Ziegler et al., 2010).

The perception of an inability to fulfil roles of motherhood (e.g. breastfeeding), and a physical discrepancy between what is socially expected in terms of idealized feminine images and their own reality, can also result in women feeling that their social identity has changed. Worries about intimacy and being sexually undesirable can also impact on current or potential romantic relationships. Revealing an altered appearance can be difficult, and some women go to great lengths to conceal their breast shape and scars from partners, for example, undressing in the dark and wearing clothing or bras to bed. Self-doubt about the sincerity of their partner's displays of affection and attempts to protect each other from further distress can lead to a physical and emotional distancing that overshadows relationships and creates communication problems (Piot-Ziegler et al., 2010).

Developments in treatments to conserve breast tissue (e.g. lumpectomy plus radiotherapy rather than mastectomy) and in reconstructive and plastic surgery following mastectomy, reflect greater recognition by healthcare providers of the negative impact of breast loss. Increasing uptake of reconstruction surgery also reflects the motivation of patients to restore their pretreatment appearance (Harcourt et al., 2003). With more surgical options available, many are confronted with the task of making a decision about treatment soon after diagnosis. This is an emotionally charged time when communication and decision-making can be difficult and complicated by numerous choices about the type and timing of breast and nipple reconstruction and surgery on the contralateral breast. Decision-aids aiming to empower patients in the decision-making process and reduce decisional errors are therefore proving helpful (e.g. see Whelan et al., 2004).

Many of the factors influencing decisions relate to appearance and body image. Among younger women in particular, concerns about anticipated disfigurement and expected loss of femininity play a role in choosing lumpectomy over mastectomy and reconstruction over mastectomy-only (Leinster et al., 1989). The motivation for reconstruction also includes the desire to restore feelings of wholeness, improve self-confidence, and avoid the need for breast prostheses (Margolis et al., 1989; Reaby, 1998). Reconstruction can also represent an opportunity to address previous dissatisfaction with breast size or shape, or can be chosen as a result of actual or perceived pressure from a significant other (Piot-Ziegler et al., 2010).

But not all women choose reconstruction. In some cases it is not an option because cancer treatment is a priority, and in others, women want to avoid the distress or complications of further surgery or fear that it will be viewed as an act of self-indulgent vanity (Schain et al., 1985). In these cases many women opt to wear a breast prosthesis which, although useful to create a breast shape, can also be experienced as inconvenient, potentially embarrassing, and a distressing reminder of cancer (Schain et al., 1985).

The impact of different surgical and reconstruction options upon psychosocial outcome has been researched at length. A substantial body of literature reports that women who undergo breast-conserving surgery or have immediate reconstructive surgery, are more likely to report a better body image and fewer appearance concerns than those with mastectomy or delayed reconstruction (e.g. Al-Ghazal et al., 2000; Nano et al., 2005). This evidence has given rise to the assumption that more extensive surgery and breast disfigurement and longer delays between mastectomy and reconstruction, will result in a poorer psychological outcome.

Again, sometimes, contradictory reports tell us that many women who undergo mastectomy (with or without reconstruction) can report high levels of body image satisfaction (see Berry et al., 1998). Furthermore, breast-conserving or reconstruction surgery provides no guarantee that women will avoid body image and appearance concerns. Depending on the size and location of the lump, a lumpectomy can still result in scarring, altered skin sensation, and breast disfigurement (Sneeuw et al., 1992). Equally, depending on the procedure used and its success, reconstruction procedures can leave extensive scarring around the breast, back, and abdomen and loss of skin sensation, all of which can lead to body image disruption and deterioration (Cederna et al., 1995; Harcourt et al., 2003). Women in Piot-Ziegler et al.'s (2010, p. 499) study also felt that a reconstructive breast 'would never re-establish their physical integrity or replace their lost femininity'.

For many it is not the *type* of intervention per se that determines outcome, rather it is satisfaction with the cosmetic result, particularly in relation to presurgery expectations of scarring and disfigurement (Constant et al., 2004). This finding is consistent with the experiences of other patient groups, including those treated with orthopaedic external fixation devices and those treated for skin and head and neck cancer (Meredith, 1979; Cassileth et al., 1983; Dropkin, 1999). Managing expectations and providing information about the anticipated impact of surgery on appearance is therefore good practice. However, as the information needs of patients varies between individuals and over time, Harcourt and Rumsey (2006) suggest that practitioners should tailor the amount, type, and form of information according to the patient's needs and include an evaluation of expectations of postoperative disfigurement and associated appearance concerns.

Rather than focusing purely on which procedure results in the best psychological outcome, efforts should therefore encompass the role of individual differences which may protect or predispose women to appearance-related and body image distress post-surgery. For example, research from within the field of appearance psychology has identified individual differences in adaptation to an altered appearance that are proposed to be a response to the degree of investment in physical appearance (i.e. the extent to which self-esteem depends on appearance) and the value patients place on specific body parts (White, 2000; Moss & Rosser, 2008). This theory is supported by a small body of research involving breast cancer patients. Irrespective of whether they undergo mastectomy or lumpectomy, women that place high importance on physical appearance or highly value their breasts, are more likely to experience appearance-related distress pre-surgery and greater difficulty adapting to an altered body image post-surgery. This is compared to those who place little importance on physical appearance and those with less apprehension about the appearance of their future breast shape and size (Carver et al., 1998; Kraus, 1999; Figueirdo et al., 2004). In Kraus's study those women who reported decreased bodily concerns also demonstrated stronger self-concepts and identities than those who placed high value on physical appearance.

Age might also predict appearance and body image distress. Regardless of which surgical option they choose, younger women tend to have a poorer body image post-surgery than older women. They can experience lowered overall quality of life which has been linked to less adaptive coping styles and concerns about partner relationships and sexual functioning (King et al., 2000; Nissen et al., 2001; Avis et al., 2005). This finding may again relate to increased appearance salience and premorbid appearance concerns, which are particularly prominent during early adulthood, a stage when women are expecting to develop permanent or new sexual relationships. This evidence has also led to speculation that women pursuing breast reconstruction for prophylactic or cancer-related mastectomy may be at high risk of body image problems because they tend to be younger and place a higher value on their breasts (see Frost et al., 2000; Nissen et al., 2001).

Formation of an abdominal stoma

An abdominal stoma is a permanent or temporary artificial opening in the abdomen to collect faecal or urinary waste into an appliance on the outside of the body. Underlying conditions that result in the need for stoma formation include bowel and urinary cancer, bladder dysfunction, or inflammatory bowel disease. The presence of the stoma, associated scarring, and the stoma appliance can change the appearance and function of the abdomen considerably. Appliances can usually be hidden under clothes, but even one that is performing well requires closer contact with faecal or urinary waste than is required with normal bowel or urinary functioning (Smith et al., 2007). Patients can experience smells and noises as faecal waste passes through the stoma. Leaks occur if appliances are poorly secured or the bag overfills.

If the stoma results in an increased sense of control over bodily functions (for those with inflammatory bowel disease or urinary incontinence) or disease progression (for those with cancer), then quality of life and self-esteem can increase for some patients (Jenkes et al., 1997; Rauch et al., 2004). However, despite advances in appliance technology and improved access to specialist nurses, the prevalence and extent of psychosocial morbidity generally remains high for those with an intestinal stoma. Individuals report distressing changes in body image and sexuality, and fears of public embarrassment and social rejection that often trigger anxiety and widespread changes in social functioning (Brown & Randle, 2005) similar to those described among individuals following amputation and head and neck surgery.

Nordstrom and Nyman (1991) suggest that body-image related factors are more likely to cause concern for women than men. However, both men and women can experience a strong sense of being sexually unattractive and self-conscious, which motivates many to keep the stoma secret and to avoid being seen naked. Decreased sexual activity and problems with intimate relationships are therefore a common consequence (Brown & Randle, 2005).

Novel research into the role of disgust as an impediment to adjustment and as a source of stigma may contribute to the understanding of individual differences in adaptation. A particular difficulty for those with an intestinal stoma is the link with defecation and sensory and cultural aversions to faeces (Manderson, 2005). Feeling 'disgust' is therefore a common response to the close proximity and appearance of faecal waste and to the appearance of the stoma itself. Investigation into the relationship between levels of the trait 'disgust sensitivity' and feelings of stigmatization among colostomy patients, suggests that more easily disgusted patients report higher levels of concern about being stigmatized, and poor adjustment. *Non-patients* with higher sensitivity to 'disgusting' stimuli were also less comfortable with the idea of close contact with a stoma patient (Smith et al., 2007). With only limited and cross sectional data available, Smith et al. are in debate as to whether it is a pre-existing high sensitivity to 'disgust' that increases poor adjustment, or whether people who adjust successfully become desensitized to bowel-disgust stimuli. Nonetheless, suggestions that as part of the process of adjustment patients need to manage their own and others feelings of 'disgust', are indicative of the need for further research.

MEDICAL TREATMENTS

Chemotherapy

The frequently debilitating toxic effects of chemotherapy, such as nausea and fatigue, can often be compounded by the personal impact of changes in appearance, including hair loss, weight gain, and skin changes. Even though they expect it to be temporary and irrespective of whether the degree of loss is partial or complete, women typically cite hair loss as one of the most common, feared, and ultimately distressing side effects of chemotherapy (Batchelor, 2001).

Hair reflects identity and sense of self and communicates messages associated with health, beauty, youthfulness, sexuality, and personality (Rosman, 2004), and the stigma attached to baldness is described by women as one of the most challenging aspects of chemotherapy. Among early stage breast cancer patients, for example, hair loss is often described as worse than the loss of a breast; whereas mastectomy can be concealed, hair loss is highly visible, serves as a constant reminder of the seriousness of their illness, and publicly marks the individual as having cancer (Tierney et al., 1992; De Frank et al., 2007; Lemieux et al., 2008).

Hair loss can have a significant and negative impact on body image and self-concept. Problems usually resolve as hair regrows (although patients may still have to adjust to an altered appearance if hair grows back with a different texture or colour) but sometimes psychosocial recovery is incomplete and body image changes do not return to normal despite hair re-growth (Baxley et al., 1984; Anderson & Johnson, 1994). In rare cases fear at the prospect of hair loss (and weight gain) can be so profound that patients contemplate or actually refused chemotherapy (Fawzy, et al., 1995, Williamson et al., 2010).

However, some patients view hair loss positively, either as a sign of the efficacy of chemotherapy (Rosman, 2004), of pride and courage (Boehmke & Dickerson, 2005), or as an 'explanation' for their behaviour, mood, or physical limitations—a benefit of other people guessing their cancer status merely by looking at them (Harcourt & Frith, 2008).

Much of the research investigating the impact of chemotherapy-induced hair loss has been with women, with very little focusing on that of men. It is often assumed that men cope more effectively with chemotherapy-induced hair loss than women because male baldness is more socially acceptable (see Vandegrift, 1994). This assumption may be based on a misconception. Evidence suggests that within Western societies the rate of appearance dissatisfaction amongst boys and men is on the rise (Humphreys & Paxton, 2004) with increasing numbers experiencing the negative social and emotional consequences of male pattern balding (see Cash, 2002). Indications that young men in particular may be experiencing negative and often similar feelings about chemotherapy-induced hair loss as women (Hilton et al., 2008), suggest that the appearance-related needs of boys and men also require attention.

Adolescents are particularly sensitive to the consequences of looking 'different' as a result of chemotherapy, or other surgical and medical treatments affecting appearance. Adolescence is a developmental stage when the usual processes of physical, social, and sexual development often result in individuals becoming acutely aware of their bodies (Holmbeck, 2002) and when physical appearance contributes more than any other factor to levels of overall self-esteem (Coleman & Hendry, 1999). Many are therefore disproportionately concerned about how they appear to others: 'I'm ugly, really fat, I've got a round face and I'm bald, I look like an old man!' (female adolescent receiving chemotherapy, Williamson, et al., 2010, p, 170).

Differences in response to hair loss are thought to be influenced by many factors. Among adolescents appearance issues tend to become more salient when the immediate effect of cancer and its treatment decline, as contact with other patients and hospital staff reduces, and as they start to compare themselves with healthy peers as opposed to other patients with cancer (Pendley et al., 1997). Individual variation in the degree of self-worth invested in appearance is also likely to play a role. For example, Wagner and Bye (1979) only identified body image distress in those women who had reported that their hair was particularly important to them.

The flexible use of a broad repertoire of coping strategies, including humour, banalization, social support, and attempts to prepare for, gather resources, and take control of hair loss can be helpful (Lansdown et al., 1997). Individuals take control of hair loss by cutting their hair short or shaving their head, using camouflage such as wigs, hats, line-drawn eye-brows, and false eyelashes, and by highlighting other features to distract themselves and others from hair loss using clothes, colour, make-up, and jewellery (Rosman, 2004; Williamson et al., 2010).

Social support is especially beneficial to adolescents. For example, the features of a 'peer-shield'—friends who adopt a strong caring attitude to shield the adolescent from appearance-related criticism and comments—can protect the adolescent against teasing, bullying, and unwanted attention (Larouche & Chin-Peuckert, 2006). Adolescents also find it helpful to be informative and dispel myths about the cause of appearance changes, and to manage potential negative reactions of shock and distress by warning family and peers of their altered appearance before they meet using text and photographic updates (Williamson et al., 2010).

As with those with an amputation who opt to wear their prosthetic limb to protect the sensibilities of others (see earlier), women report wearing a wig to protect their family from the distress associated with seeing them bald (Harcourt & Frith, 2008). Adolescents also describe choosing to conceal appearance changes to protect themselves during social events which they perceive to be threatening, or on 'bad days' when they feel emotionally vulnerable (Williamson et al., 2010). Although a highly valued strategy for concealing hair loss, wigs can be viewed as inconvenient and uncomfortable, and can emphasize feelings of abnormality (Harcourt & Frith, 2008).

Adolescents also describe them as another source of stigma, which motivates many to conceal their use: *'You've got to hide the fact that it's a wig or they (teasers) can be just as bad'* (Williamson et al., 2010, p. 171).

Highly-active antiretroviral therapy (HAART)

HAART refers to treatments which suppress viral replication in those who are HIV infected. While not curative, the rapid, discernible, and lasting changes in health and appearance as a result of HAART therapy are such that this condition has been reinterpreted as chronic rather than terminal. However, while HAART addresses appearance side effects associated with HIV-related illness, the treatment itself results in distinctive appearance changes.

The most common of these is lipodystrophy—changes in fat distribution across the body. This includes lipoatrophy (peripheral fat loss) in the legs, face, and buttocks, or lipoaccumulation (fat gain) in the abdomen, breasts, and what has become known as the characteristic 'buffalo hump' at the back of the neck. Facial lipoatrophy has distinctive features, including concavities in the temple and cheek areas, protruding facial bones and visible musculature. Other appearance changes include skin rashes, hyperpigmentation of the skin and nails, jaundice, scleral icterus (yellowing of the white of the eye), and hair loss (Hawkins, 2006).

The psychosocial impact of appearance-related side effects can by far-reaching:

With HIV I am not normal, I become deformed in all ways. My face, body, everything. Obviously, when your face and body deform, your mind starts to deform because it starts to affect you. Many patients have lost their desire to live due to the rejection. That rejection is due to external appearance. I think nothing is being done with respect to that (male, Varas-Diaz et al., 2005, p. 135).

Amongst 150 adult HIV patients, Martinez et al. (2005) found that the presence of illness or treatment side effects was strongly correlated with a perceived deterioration in body image. Lipodystrophy can be particularly difficult to manage and can result in low self-esteem, loss of control, depression (Collins et al., 2000), poor body image (Burgoyne et al., 2005), and can result in self-consciousness and social withdrawal: *'Very distressed about lipodystrophy ... did not go out for months and months ... stopped going to the gym ... huge psychological problems ... lost confidence socially* (male, Power et al., 2003, p. 138).

Power et al. (2003) also report that a sense of loss regarding aspects of their past appearance and feelings of denial were also experienced by some participants who no longer recognized their own appearance and struggled to accept appearance changes: *'You know you are just in front of the mirror and you say this is not me. It's someone else'* (female, 33 years, p. 138).

Many of these psychosocial outcomes are similar to those already described in this chapter, however, what is unique to HIV is that not only are the resultant appearance changes stigmatizing—but the disease is also (Sontag, 1989; Fife et al., 2000). Research on stigma identifies several conditions under which stigma is likely to develop and HIV appears to fulfil all of these conditions. For example, Goffman (1963) has categorized three types of stigma: abominations of the body (physical changes or deviations from the social norm); character imperfections; and tribal stigmas (stigma associated with a particular race, ethnicity, or sexual preference). HIV results in visible differences, is associated with character imperfections—because others perceive that infection has resulted from a lack of control or moderation in behaviour—and is associated with groups or 'tribes' that are typically marginalized or stigmatized within society, including homosexual men, intravenous drug users, sex workers, and those living in poverty. In addition, Lerner and Miller (1978), argue that where stigma is associated with death, the social impact of the stigma will be particularly severe; in part as a result of a fear of death and avoidance of any reminder of mortality and vulnerability by others. Similarly, social rejection in relation to illness is also related to perceived severity of the illness as determined by outcome and level of contagion. While HIV is no longer considered terminal, in many cases it is associated with death and remains incurable and infectious (Chapman, 2000).

An HIV positive test result immediately redefines someone who may not be experiencing any symptoms or manifestations of illness, as sick (Chapman, 2004). In the same way, where treatment for HIV is initiated prior to serious illness, this treatment may create appearance changes and markers of illness where previously there were none. Where the illness is stigmatized, the impact of this evidence of illness is particularly severe. Chapman et al. (1998) conducted a study using a body image measure designed specifically for patients with HIV. Participants with HIV (in contrast to the control group) perceived themselves as contaminated, and the authors linked this to perceptions of HIV/AIDS presented in the media and literature.

Disclosure of HIV status remains a complex issue for those who are HIV positive. The advent of HAART and its resultant visible side effects can force involuntary disclosure of HIV status, and compel those with HIV to deal with their own and others' perceptions of being recognizable as HIV-positive. Lipodystrophy in particular can 'out' patients. Patients are more likely to feel recognizable as HIV positive (Oette et al., 2002) and can feel deprived of their privacy and right to choose whether or not to disclose their HIV status (Ong et al., 2007; Innes et al., 2009): '*I am aware of my status since this happened ... more so than just taking the drugs. Because of lipodystrophy I look like a combination therapy user*' (male, 36 years, Power et al., 2003, p. 138).

Appearance change has also been found to play a significant role in the decision to decline HAART and in non-adherence to treatment regimens. Fear of appearance-related side effects, particularly lipodystrophy, is a common reason for declining HAART (Gellaitry et al., 2005; Rogowska-Szadkowska, 2009). Alfonso et al. (2005)

found that patients who declined were particularly fearful of the consequences of being stigmatized: *'I live in (a small town) and if I start to look sick, that stigma ... would bother me, it would make me feel I was not as good as them ... My self-esteem would definitely go down and my confidence would be badly hurt. Not taking meds is one way of taking care of myself to prevent that from happening.'* (p. 852). For those who commence treatment, appearance-related side effects can lead to poor treatment adherence or changes in drug regime (Munk, 1998), with many patients willing to increase their chance of death by 1% in order to avoid lipodystrophy (Lenert et al., 2002). In a way similar to those receiving other appearance-altering treatments, evidence suggests that the severity of disfigurement as a result of HAART side effects is not a useful predictor of appearance-related distress. Subjective rather than objective assessment of appearance has previously predicted psychological outcomes (Ong et al., 2007; Plankey et al., 2009).

Interventions to address the psychosocial impact of lipoatrophy have often focused on cosmetic procedures using a variety of injectable fillers. Patients can experience improvements in depression and anxiety scores as well as satisfaction with appearance (Kavouni et al., 2008). However, treatments can be temporary and there is a risk of undesirable appearance side effects (Moyle et al., 2006). Non-surgical interventions are rare, with the exception of a randomized controlled study conducted in Rwanda with 100 male and female participants with lipodystrophy. Participants who completed a 6-month, supervised exercise training programme reported positive changes to appearance and body image and displayed less fear of HIV status disclosure and fewer problems with shame, embarrassment, and concerns regarding dressing and style. The study measured objective changes in body fat distribution and found a significant decline in body fat percentage, waist circumference, and total body fat redistribution score (Mutimura et al., 2008). This intervention may have worked by impacting objective appearance in order to address psychosocial well-being, and although further evidence is required, offers a promising avenue for future interventions.

No interventions have been identified that train health professionals to address appearance-related issues resulting from HIV therapy. However, patient experiences and perceptions imply that training is needed, particularly to target those that question the need to manage appearance issues when physical health is so improved by drug regimes: *'I know someone whose doctor was virtually dismissive, you know this isn't an issue that we need to deal with, you've been through a lot of illness, you're lucky to be here really, you're on this combination therapy—you can't expect everything to be all right, you're just going to have to put up with it'* (male, 59 years, Power et al., 2003, p. 140). Such training may provide a valuable opportunity to improve care, promote adjustment to appearance changes and maintain adherence to treatment regimes.

CONCLUSION

This chapter represents only a selection of appearance-altering treatments and their psychosocial impact. We are aware that other treatments, such as radiotherapy, the use of life-saving cardiac and other external devices, bone marrow transplant, and treatment for prostate cancer can alter appearance, but there is very little research in these areas. Exploratory qualitative enquiry would be a good starting point to identify the impact of these treatments on appearance.

The psychosocial responses to the treatments presented here have demonstrated considerable overlap across different conditions. It may be useful to apply or adapt successful interventions for one condition to that of another; particularly those that identify and address appearance concerns before, as well as after treatment, those that focus on social skills and those that engage the support of significant others. Evidence also indicates that social stigma and negative assumptions about abilities and personality, and the condition itself, play a significant role that may hinder adaptation to a visible difference, and suggests that a wider societal approach to intervention design would be valuable too.

It is also apparent that for many individuals it is not simply the cause, nature or severity of appearance change that determines appearance-related distress but also pre-existing individual differences. These may include biases in appearance-orientated information processing, in the degree of investment placed in physical appearance, and the value placed on those parts of the body altered by treatment. Further research to understand individual differences in responses to appearance altering treatments, and to identify those at risk of poor adjustment, would therefore benefit from drawing on recent advances within the psychology of appearance research.

Health professionals are central to the success of any attempt to help patients manage their treatment-related appearance concerns. They need to be aware of the potential psychosocial impact of change and, as a matter of routine, provide opportunities for patients to raise appearance concerns and discuss them openly. However, as health professionals are often unsure how to address these concerns or where to refer their patients for further help, researchers need to identify and address their support and training needs (e.g. see Hood, 2010) and collaborate with clinical leaders to clarify and systemize appearance-related care pathways.

REFERENCES

Alfano C. M. & Rowland J. H. (2006). Recovery issues in cancer survivorship: A new challenge for supportive care. *Cancer Journal*, 12(5), 432–43.

Alfonso, V., Bermbach, N., Geller, J., & Montaner, J. (2005). Individual variability in barriers affecting people's decision to take HAART: a qualitative study identifying barriers to being on HAART. *AIDS Patient Care and STDs*, 20(12), 848–57.

Al-Ghazal, S. K., Fallowfield, L., & Blamey, R. W. (2000). Comparison of psychological aspects and patient satisfaction following breast conserving surgery, simple mastectomy and breast reconstruction. *European Journal of Cancer.* 36(15), 1938–43.

Anderson, M. S. & Johnson, J. (1994). Restoration of body image and self-esteem for women after cancer treatment: A rehabilitative strategy. *Cancer Practice,* 2, 345–9.

Avis, N. E., Crawford, S., & Manuel, J. (2005). Quality of life among younger women with breast cancer. *Journal of Clinical Oncology,* 23(16), 3322–30.

Baker, C. A. (1992). Factors associated with rehabilitation in head and neck cancer. *Cancer Nursing,* 15, 395–400.

Batchelor, D. (2001). Hair and cancer chemotherapy: consequences and nursing care—a literature study. *European Journal of Cancer Care,* 10, 147–63.

Baxley, K. O., Erdman, L. K., Henry, E. B., & Roof, B. J. (1984). Alopecia: Effect on cancer patients' body image. *Cancer Nursing,* 7, 499–503.

Berry, M. G., Al-Mufti, R. A., Jenkinson, A. D., Denton S., Sullivan, M., Vaus A., et al. (1998). An audit of outcome including patient satisfaction with immediate breast reconstruction performed by breast surgeons. *Annals of the Royal College of Surgeons of England,* 80, 173–7.

Boehmke, M. M. & Dickerson, S. S. (2005). Symptom, symptom experiences, and symptom distress encountered by women with breast cancer undergoing current treatment modalities. *Cancer Nursing,* 28(5), 382–9.

Bowers, B. (2008). Providing effective support for patients facing disfiguring surgery. *British Journal of Nursing,* 17(2), 94–8.

Brown, B. B., Mc Kenna, S. P. Siddhi, K., McGrouther, D. A., & Bayat, A. (2008). The hidden cost of skin scars: quality of life after skin scarring. *Journal of Plastic, Reconstructive and Aesthetic Surgery,* 62, 1049–58.

Brown, H. & Randle, J. (2005). Living with a stoma: A review of the literature. *Journal of Clinical Nursing,* 14, 74–81.

Burgoyne, R., Collins, E., Wagner, C., Abbey, S., Halman, M., Nur, M., et al. (2005). The relationship between lipodystrophy-associated body changes and measure of quality of life and mental health for HIV-positive adults. *Quality of Life Research,* 14, 981–90.

Carver, C. S., Pozo-Kaderman, C., Price, A. A., Noriega, V., Harris, S. D., & Derhagopian, R. P. (1998). Concerns about aspects of body image and adjustment in early stage cancer. *Psychosomatic Medicine,* 60, 168–74.

Cash, T. F. (2002). The psychological effects of androgenic alopecia in men. *Journal of the American Academy of Dermatology,* 26, 926–31.

Cassileth, B. R., Lusk, E. J., & Tenaglia, A. N. (1983). Patient's perceptions of the cosmetic impact of melanoma resection. *Plastic Reconstruction Surgery,* 71(1), 73–5.

Cederna, P. S., Yates, W. R., Chang, P., Cram, A. E., & Ricciardelli, E. J. (1995). Post-mastectomy reconstruction: comparative analysis of the psychosocial, functional, and cosmetic effects of transverse rectus abdominas musculacutaneous flap versus breast implant reconstruction. *Annals of Plastic Surgery.* 35(5), 458–68.

Chapman, E. (2004). Body image issues among individuals with HIV and AIDS. In T. F. Cash & T. Pruzinsky (eds.) *Body Image: a handbook of theory, research and clinical practice,* pp. 395–402. New York: Guilford.

Chapman, E. (2000). Conceptualisation of the body for people living with HIV: issues of touch and contamination. *Sociology of Health and Illness,* 22(6), 840–57.

Chapman, L. (1998). Body image and HIV: implications for support and care. *AIDS Care,* 10(2), S179–89.

Clarke, A. (1999). Psychosocial aspects of facial disfigurements: problems, management and the role of a lay-led organisation. *Psychology, Health and Medicine*, 4, 127–42.

Clarke, A. (2001). *Resourcing and training head and neck cancer nurse specialists to deliver a social rehabilitation programme to patients.* Unpublished doctoral thesis. City University, London, UK.

Collins, E., Wagner, C., & Walmsley, S. (2000). Psychosocial impact of the lipodystrophy syndrome in HIV infection. *AIDS Read*, 10, 546–50.

Constant, C. M. E., van Wersch, A. M. E., Menke-Pluymers, M. B. E., Tjong Joe Wai, R., Eggermont, A. M. M., & van Geel, A. N. (2004). Satisfaction and prothesis related complaints in women with immediate breast reconstruction following prophylactic and oncological mastectomy. *Psychology, Health & Medicine*, 9(1), 71–85.

Coleman, J. & C, Hendry, L. B. (1999). *The Nature of Adolescence.* London: Routledge.

Coughlan, G. & Clarke, A. (2002). Shame and burns. In P. Gilbert & B. Andrews (eds.) *Body shame*, pp. 155–70. Hove: Brunner-Routledge.

DeFrank, J. T., Mehta, C. B., Stein, K. D., & Baker, F. (2007). Body image dissatisfaction in cancer survivors. *Oncology Nursing Forum*, 34(3), E34–41.

Dhooper, S. S. (1985). Social work with laryngectomees. *Health Social Work*, 10, 217–27.

Donovan-Hall, M. K., Yardley, L., & Watts, R. J. (2002). Engagement in activities revealing the body and psychosocial adjustment in adults with a transtibial prosthesis. *Prosthetics and Orthotics International*, 26(1), 15–22.

Dropkin, M. J. (1997). Coping with disfigurement/dysfunction and length of hospital stay after head and neck cancer surgery. *ORL-Head and Neck Nursing*, 15, 22–6.

Dropkin, M. J. (1999). Body image and quality of life after head and neck cancer surgery. *Cancer Practice*, 7(6), 309–13.

Dropkin, M. J. (2001). Anxiety, coping strategies, and coping behaviors in patients undergoing head and neck cancer surgery. *Cancer Nursing*, 24(2), 143–8.

Dropkin, M. J. & Scott, D. W. (1983). Body image reintegration and coping effectiveness after head and neck surgery. *The Journal: Official publication of the society of Otolarngology and Head-Neck Nurses*, 2, 7–16.

Fawzy N. W., Secher L., Evans S., & Giuliano A. E. (1995). The Positive Appearance Centre: An innovative concept in comprehensive psychosocial cancer care. *Cancer Practice*, 3, 233–8.

Fiegenbaum, W. (1981). Social training program for clients with facial disfigurements: a contribution to the rehabilitation of cancer patients. *International Journal of Rehabilitation Research*, 4(4), 501–9.

Fife, B. L. & Wright, E. R. (2000). The dimension of stigma: a comparison of its impact on the self of persons with HIV/AIDS and Cancer. *Journal of Health and Social Behavior*, 41, 50–67.

Figueiredo, M. L., Cullen, J., Hwag, Y., Rowland, J. H., & Mandelblatt, J. S. (2004). Breast cancer treatment in older women: Does getting what you want improve your long-term body image and mental health? *Journal of Clinical Oncology*, 22(10), 4002–9.

Frost, M. H., Schaid D. J., Sellers, T. A., Slezak, J. M., Arnold P. G., *et al.* (2000). Long-term satisfaction and psychological and social function following bilateral prophylactic mastectomy. *Journal of the American Medical Association*, 284(2), 319–24.

Furst L. & Humphrey, M. (1983). Coping with the loss of a leg. *Prosthetics and Orthotics International*, 7, 152–6.

Gallagher, P. (2004). Introduction to the special issue on psychosocial perspectives on amputation and prosthesis. *Disability and Rehabilitation*, 26(14/15), 827–30.

Gallagher, P. & MacLachlan, M. (2001). Adjustment to an artificial limb: a qualitative study. *Journal of Health Psychology*, 6, 85–100.

Gamba, A., Romano, M., Grosso, T., & Tamburini, M. (1992). Psychosocial adjustment of patients surgically treated for head and neck cancer. *Surgery and Psychosocial Adjustment*, 14(3), 398–407.

Gellaitry, G., Cooper, V., Davis, C., Fisher, M., Leake Date, H., & Horne, R. (2005). Patients' perception of information about HAART: impact on treatment decision. *AIDS Care*, 17(3), 367–76.

Gething, L. (1991). Generality versus specificity of attitudes towards people with disabilities. *British Journal of Medical Psychology*, 65, 55–64.

Goffman, E. (1963). *Stigma: notes on the management of a spoiled identity*. New York: Simon and Schuster.

Hagedoorn, M. & Molleman, E. (2006). Facial disfigurement in patients with head and neck cancer: the role of social self-efficacy. *Health Psychology*, 25(5), 643–7.

Harcourt, D. & Frith, H. (2008). Women's experiences of an altered appearance during chemotherapy: an indication of cancer status. *Journal of Health Psychology*, 13(5), 597–606.

Harcourt, D. & Rumsey, N (2006). Altered body image. In N. Kearney & A. Richardson (eds.) *Nursing patients with cancer: principals and practice*, pp. 701–15. Edinburgh: Churchill Livingstone.

Harcourt, D., Rumsey, N., Ambler, N., Cawthorn, S. J., Reid, C., Maddox P., *et al.* (2003). The psychological effect of mastectomy with or without immediate breast reconstruction: a prospective, multi-centre study. *Plastic & Reconstructive Surgery*, 111(3), 1060–8.

Harris, D. (1997). Types, causes and physical treatment of visible differences. In R. Lansdown, N. Rumsey, E. Bradbury, T. Carr, & J. Partridge (eds.) *Visibly different: Coping with disfigurement*, pp. 79–90. Oxford: Butterworth-Heineman.

Hawkins, T. (2006). Appearance-related side effects of HIV-1 treatment. *AIDS Patient Care and STDs*, 20(1), 6–18.

Herzon, F. & Boshier. M. (1979). Head and neck cancer- emotional management. *Head and Neck Surgery*, 2, 112–18.

Hilton, S., Hunt, K., Emslie, C., Salinas, M., & Ziebland, S. (2008). Have many been over-looked? A comparison of young men and women's experiences of chemotherapy—induced alopecia. *Psycho-oncology*, 17, 577–83.

Holmbeck, G. N. (2002). A developmental perspective on adolescent health and illness. *Journal of Pediatric Psychology*. 27(5), 409–16.

Hood, C. (2010). Project to improve care for people coping with changes in body image. *Cancer Nursing Practice*, 9(2), 26–32.

Horgan, O. & MacLachlan M. (2004). Psychosocial adjustment to lower-limb amputation: a review. *Disability and Rehabilitation*, 26(14/15), 837–50.

Humphreys, P. & Paxton S. J. (2004). Impact of exposure to idealised male images on adolescent boys' body image. *Body Image*, 1(3), 253–66.

Innes, S., Levin, L., & Cotton, M. (2009). Lipodystrophy syndrome in HIV-infected children on HAART. *The Southern African Journal of HIV Medicine*, 10(4), 76–80.

Jenks, J. M., Morin, K. H., & Tomaselli, N. (1997). The influence of ostomy surgery on body image in patients with cancer. *Applied Nursing Research*, 10, 174–80.

Jones, L., Hall, M., & Schuld, W. (1993). Ability or disability? A study of the functional outcome of 65 consecutive lower limb amputees treated at the Royal South Sydney Hospital in 1988—1989. *Disability and Rehabilitation*, 15(4), 184–8.

Katz, M. R., Irish, J. C., Devins, G. M. Rodin, G. M., & Gullane, P. J. (2003). Psychosocial adjustment in head and neck cancer: impact of disfigurement, gender and social support. *Head and Neck*, 22, 103–15.

Kavouni, A., Catalan, J., Brown, S., Mandalia, S., & Barton, S. E. (2008). The face of HIV and AIDS: can we erase the stigma. *AIDS Care*, 20(4), 485–7.

Kent, G. (2000). Understanding the experiences of people with disfigurements: An integration of four models of social and psychological functioning. *Psychology, Health & Medicine*, 5(2), 11–129.

Khafif, A., Posen, J., Yagil, Y., Besier, M., Gil, Z., Ben-Yosef, R., *et al.* (2007). Quality of life in patients older than 75 years following major head and neck surgery. *Head and Neck*, 29(10), 932–9.

Khan, M. A., Sehgal, A., Mitra, B., Agarwal, P. N., Lal, P., & Malik, V. K. (2000). Psychobehavioural impact of mastectomy. *Journal of the Indian Academy of Applied Psychology*, 26(1–2), 65–71.

King, M. T., Kenny, P., Shiell, A., Hall, J., & Boyages J. (2000). Quality of life three months and one year after first treatment for early stage breast cancer: influence of treatment and patient characteristics. *Quality of life Research*, 9, 789–800.

Konradsen, H., Kirkevold, M. & Zoffman V. (2009). Surgical facial cancer treatment: the silencing of disfigurement in nurse patient interactions. *Journal of Advanced Nursing*, 65(11), 2409–18.

Kraus, P. L. (1999). Body image, decision making, and breast cancer treatment. *Cancer Nursing*, 22(6), 421–7.

Lansdown, R., Rumsey, N., Bradbury, E., Carr T., & Partridge J. (eds.) (1997). *Visibly different: coping with disfigurement*. London: Butterworth-Heinemann.

Larouche, S. S. & Chin-Peuckert, L. (2006). Changes in body image experienced by adolescents with cancer. *Journal of Pediatric Oncology Nursing*, 23(4), 200–9.

Leinster, S. J., Ashcroft, J. L., Slade, P. D., & Dewey, M. E. (1989). Mastectomy versus conservative surgery: Psychosocial effects of the patient's choice of treatment. *Journal of Psychosocial Oncology*, 7(1/2), 179–92.

Lenert, L. A., Feddersen, M., Sturley, A., & Lee, D. (2002). Adverse effects of medication and trade-offs between length of life and quality of life in human immunodeficiency virus infection. *American Journal of Medicine*, 113, 229–32.

Lemieux, J., Maunsell, E., & Provencher, L. (2008). Chemotherapy-induced alopecia and effects on quality of life among women with breast cancer: a literature review. *Psycho-oncology*, 17, 317–28.

Lerner, M. J. & Miller, D. T. (1978). Just world research and the attribution process: looking back and ahead. *Psychological Bulletin*, 85, 1030–51.

Liu, H. -E. (2008). Changes in satisfaction with appearance and working status for head and neck tumour patients. *Journal of Clinical Nursing*, 17, 1930–8.

Lockhart, J. S. (2000). Nurses' perceptions of head and neck oncology patients after surgery: severity of facial disfigurement and patient gender. *Plastic Surgical Nursing*, 20, 68–80.

Manderson, L. (2005). Boundary breaches: the body, sex, and sexuality after stoma surgery. *Social Science and Medicine*, 61, 405–15.

Margolis, G. J., Goodman, R. L., Rubin, A., & Pajac, T. M. (1989). Psychological factors in the choice of treatment for breast cancer. *Psychosomatics*, 30(2), 192–8.

Martinez, S. M., Kemper, C. A., Diamond, C., Wagner, G., & the California Collaborative Treatment Group. (2005). Body image in patients with HIV/AIDS: assessment of a new psychometric measure and its medical correlates. *AIDS Patient Care and STDs*, 1(3), 150–6.

Mast, B. A. (1999). Functional outcomes of microsurgical reconstruction of delayed complications following head and neck cancer ablation. *Annals of Plastic surgery*, 42, 40–5.

McCormick, M. (1995). Facing disfigurement. *Nursing New Zealand*, 1(2), 13–15.

Meredith, S. (1979). Formidible: that's the only word for the external fixation device—and for the care it demands. *RN Journal*, 42(12), 18–24.

Millsopp, L., Brandom, L., Humphris, G., Lowe D., Stat, C., & Rogers S. (2006). Facial appearance after operations for oral and oropharyngeal cancer: A comparison of case-notes and patient-completed questionnaire. *British Journal of Oral and Maxillofacial Surgery*, 44, 358–63.

Moore, I., M., Challinor, J., Pasvogel, A., Matthay, K., Hetter, J., & Kaemingk, K. (2003). Behavioural adjustment of children and adolescents with cancer: Teacher, parent and self-report. *Oncology Nursing Forum*, 30, E24–91.

Moss T. & Rosser B. (2008). Psychosocial adjustment to visible difference. *The Psychologist*, 21(6), 492–5.

Moyle, G. J., Brown, S., Lysakove, L., & Barton, S. E. (2006). Long-term safety and efficacy of poly-L-lactic acid in the treatment of HIV-related facial lipoatrophy. *HIV Medicine*, 7, 181–5.

Munk, B. (1998). Preparing for side effects. *POZ*, 8 (Special Treatment Supplement), 12.

Munstedt, K., Manthey, N., Sachsse, S., & Vahrson, H. (1997). Changes in self-concept and body image during alopecia induced chemotherapy. *Supportive Care in Cancer*, 5, 139–43.

Murray, C. D. & Fox J. (2002). Body image and prosthesis satisfaction in the lower limb amputee. *Disability Rehabilitation*, 24, 925–31.

Mutimura, E., Stewart, A., Crowther, N. J., Yarasheski, K. E., & Todd Cade, W. (2008). The effects of exercise training on quality of life in HAART-treated HIV-positive Rwandan subjects with body fat redistribution. *Quality of Life Research*, 17, 377–85.

Nano M. T., Gill P. G., Kollias J., Bochner, M. A., Malycha, P., & Winefield, H. R. (2005). Psychological impact and cosmetic outcome of surgical breast cancer strategies. *ANZ Journal of Surgery*, 75(11), 940–7.

Nissen, M. J., Swenson, K. K. Ritz, L. J., Farrell, J. B., Sladek, M. L., & Lally, R. M. (2001). Quality of life after breast carcinoma surgery: a comparison of three surgical procedures. *Cancer*, 91(7), 1238–46.

Nordstrom, G. M. & Nyman, C. R. (1991). Living with a urostomy. A follow up with special regard to the peristomal-skin complications, psychological and sexual life. *Scandinavian Journal of Urology and Nephrology*, 138(Suppl), 247–51.

Norris J., Kunnes-Connell, M., & Stockhard, S. S. (1998). A grounded theory of re-imaging. *Advances in Nursing Science*, 20, 1–12.

Oette, M., Juretzko, P., Kroidl, A., Sagir, A., Wettstein, M., Siegrist, J., *et al.* (2002). Lipodystrophy syndrome and self-assessment of wellbeing and physical appearance in HIV-positive patients. *AIDS Patient Care and STDs*, 16(9), 413–17.

Ong, J., Clarke, A., White, P., Johnson, M., Withey, S., & Butler, P. E. M. (2007). Does severity predict distress? The relationship between subjective and objective measures of appearance and psychological adjustment, during treatment for facial lipoatrophy. *Body Image*, 4, 239–48.

Pendley, J. S., Dahlquist, L. M., & Dreyer, Z. (1997). Body image and psychosocial adjustment in adolesent cancer survivors. *Journal of Pediatric Psychology*, 22(1), 29–43.

Piff, C. (1998). Body image: a patient's perspective. *British Journal of Theatre Nursing*, 8(1), 13–14.

Piot-Ziegler, C., Sassi, M.-L., Raffoul, W., & Delaloye J.-F. (2010). Mastectomy, body deconstruction, and impact on identity: A qualitative study. *British Journal of Health Psychology*, 15, 479–510.

Plankey, M., Bacchetti, P., Chengshi, J., Grimes, B., Hyman, C., Cohen, M., *et al.* (2009). Self-perception of body fat changes and HAART adherence in the women's interagency HIV study. *AIDS and Behaviour*, 13, 53–9.

Power, R., Tate, H. L., McGill, S. M., & Taylor, C. (2003). A qualitative study of the psychosocial implications of lipodystropy syndrome on HIV positive individuals. *Sexually Transmitted Infections*, 79, 137–41.

Rauch, P., Miny, J., Conroy, T., Neyton L., & Guillemin F. (2004). Life among disease-free survivors of rectal cancer. *Journal of Clinical Oncology*, 22, 354–60.

Reaby, L. L. (1998). Reasons why women who have mastectomy decided to have or not to have breast reconstruction. *Plastic and Reconstructive Surgery*, 101, 1810–18.

Robinson, E. (1997). Psychological research on visible differences in adults. In R. Lansdown N. Rumsey, E. Bradbury, A. Carr, & J. Partridge (eds.) *Visibly different: coping with disfigurement*, pp. 112–20. Oxford: Butterworth-Heinemann.

Robinson, E., Rumsey, N., & Partridge, J. (1996). An evaluation of the impact of social interaction skills training for facially disfigured people. *British Journal of Plastic Surgery*, 49, 281–9.

Rogowski-Szadkowska, D., Chlabicz, S., Oltarzewska, M. A., & Sawicka-Powierza, J. (2009). Which factors hinder the decision of Polish HIV-positive patients to take up antiretroviral therapy? *AIDS Care*, 21(3), 280–3.

Rosman S. (2004). Cancer and stigma: experience of patients with chemotherapy-induced alopecia. *Patient Education and Counselling*, 52, 333–9.

Rosser, B. A., Moss T., & Rumsey, N. (2010). Attentional and interpretative biases in appearance concern: An investigation of biases in appearance-related information processing. *Body Image*, 7, 251–4.

Rumsey, N., Clarke, A., White, P., Wyn-Williams M., & Garlick, W. (2004). Altered body image: appearance-related concerns of people with visible disfigurement. *Journal of Advanced Nursing*, 48(5), 443–53.

Rybarczyk, B., Nyenhuis D. L., Nicholas J. J, Schulz, R., Alioto, R. J., & Blair C. (1992). Social discomfort and depression in a sample of adults with leg amputations. *Archives of Physical and Medical Rehabilitation*, 73, 1169–73.

Rybarczyk, B., Nyenhuis D. L., Nicholas J. J., Cash, S., M., & Kaiser J. (1995). Body image, perceived social stigma, and the prediction of psychosocial adjustment to leg amputation. *Rehabilitation Psychology*, 49, 95–110.

Rybarczyk, B., Syzmanski, L. & Nicholas, J. J. (2000). Limb amputation. In R. G. Fink & T. R. Elliott (eds.) *Handbook of Rehabilitation Psychology*, pp. 29–47. Washington, DC: American Psychological Association.

Saradjian, A., Thompson, A. R., & Datta, D. (2007). The experience of men using an upper limb prosthesis following amputation: positive coping and minimizing feeling different. *Disability and Rehabilitation*, 30 (11), 871–83.

Schain, W. S., Wellisch, D., K., Pasnau, R. O., & Landsverk, J. (1985). The sooner the better: a study of psychological factors in women undergoing immediate versus delayed breast reconstruction. *American Journal of Psychiatry*, 142, 40–6.

Semple, C. J., Kate Sullivan, K., Dunwoody, L., & Kernohan G. (2004). Psychosocial interventions for patients with head and neck cancer. *Cancer Nursing*, 27(6), 434–44.

Sjodahl, G., Gard G., Jarnlo & G.-B. (2004). Coping after trans-femoral amputation due to trauma or tumour—a phenomenological approach. *Disability and Rehabilitation*, 26(14/15), 851–61.

Smith, D. M., Loewenstein, G., Rozin, P., Sheriff, R. L., & Ubel, P. A. (2007). Sensitivity to disgust, stigma and adjustment to life with a colostomy. *Journal of Research in Personality*, 41, 787–803.

Sneeuw K. C., Aaronson N. K., & Yarold J. R. (1992). Cosmetic and functional outcomes of breast conserving treatment for early stage breast cancer. 2. Relationship with psychosocial functioning. *Radiotherapy Oncology*, 25(3), 160–6.

Sontag, S. (1989). *AIDS and its metaphors.* New York: Farrar, Strauss and Giroux

Strauss, R. P. (1989). Psychosocial responses to oral and maxillofacial surgery for head and neck cancer. *Journal of Oral Maxillofacial Surgery*, 47, 343–8.

Tierney A. J., Taylor J., & Closs S. J. (1992). Knowledge, expectations and experiences of patients receiving chemotherapy for breast cancer. *Scandinavian Journal of Caring Science*, 6(2), 75–80.

Vandegrift, K., V. (1994). The development of an oncology alopecia wig program. *Journal of Intravenous nursing*, 17(2), 78–82.

Varas-Diaz, N., Toro-Alfonso, J., & Serrano-Garcia, I. (2005). My body, my stigma: body interpretations in a sample of people living with HIV/AIDS in Puerto Rico. *Qualitative Report*, 10(1), 122–42.

Wagner, L. & Bye, M. (1979). Body image and patients experiencing alopecia as a result of cancer chemotherapy. *Cancer Nursing*, 5, 365–9.

Wallace M. L., Harcourt D., Rumsey N., & Foot A. (2007). Managing appearance changes resulting from cancer treatment: resilience in adolescent females. *Psycho-oncology*, 16(11), 1019–27.

Whelan, T., Levine, M., Willan, A., Gafni, A., Sanders, K., Mirsky, D., *et al.* (2004). Effect of a decision aid on knowledge and treatment decision making for breast cancer surgery. *Journal of American Medical Association*, 292, 435–41.

White C. A. (2000). Body image dimensions and cancer: a heuristic cognitive behavioural model. *Psycho-oncology*, 9, 183–92.

Williamson, G. M. (1995). Restriction of normal activities among older adult amputees: the role of public self-consciousness. *Journal of Clinical Geropschology*, 1, 229–42.

Williamson, H., Harcourt, D., Halliwell, E., Frith, H., & Wallace M., (2010). Adolescents' and parents' experiences of managing the psychosocial consequences of an altered appearance during treatment for cancer. *Journal of Pediatric Oncology Nursing*, 27(3), 168–75.

CHAPTER 30

WHO IS AFFECTED BY APPEARANCE CONCERNS, IN WHAT WAY, AND WHY?: SUMMARY AND SYNTHESIS

NICHOLA RUMSEY

DIANA HARCOURT

THIS section has examined the nature of appearance concerns across the lifespan, explored a variety of factors that influence adjustment and levels of distress, and considered some of the consequences of appearance-related concerns, including the particular challenges facing people living with an appearance that is in any way different to the norm. These chapters raise many issues, including the importance of appearance for both males and females of all ages, the role of individual differences, psychological processes, and the influence of physical, social, and cultural environments.

The first group of chapters highlights how pressures for males and females to conform to appearance ideals at all ages are increasing and make clear that the foundations for appearance concerns are laid at an early age. But how early is not yet apparent, as research with young children is challenging. So far, most researchers and commentators have focused on girls and young women, yet the need to understand the extent and impact of appearance concerns amongst boys and young men is growing and calls for more research in this area have become more strident. For us, the importance of appearance to young children was brought into sharp relief when, whilst working on this book, we were visited by a 3-year-old boy. His clothes of choice were a selection of superhero costumes—complete with built-in muscles. Tears flowed when, because of the warm weather, the jumper worn under the costume was removed, reducing the bulk and appearance of his 'muscles'. When reluctantly removing the costume at bath time, he was at pains to demonstrate that he too had arm and chest 'muscles'—just like Batman and Superman.

Until now, attention has been focused primarily on young people and young adults, and the volume of appearance-related research declines as the age of participants increases. Is this because researchers themselves are buying in to the myth that appearance has less importance for older people? Or do researchers believe that prevention efforts should be focused on the early years? Preliminary work already suggests that the effects of appearance concerns and ageing anxiety on self-perceptions and disordered eating amongst midlife and older adults are considerable and are certainly not the preserve of younger people. Diedrichs et al.'s (in preparation) survey of 77,000 adults reported, for example, that over 50% of male and female respondents over the age of 40 felt ashamed of how they look. While the detail of the nature and consequences of appearance concerns might change over time, and although functional aspects of the body might change with age, there seems to be some consistency regarding the factors that contribute to appearance concerns across the lifespan, namely biological factors (e.g. weight, shape, and physical changes due to ageing, including puberty and menopause), social comparisons (although the targets for these may differ), the influence of others (including peers and family), and psychological processes involved in adjustment.

The possibility that the era in which people grew up is pivotal in determining levels of appearance concerns doesn't bode well for the current generations of young people and young adults who are living in a society that seems increasingly appearance-focused. Changes to appearance over time are less likely to be shrugged off as part of the ageing process and current levels of preoccupation across all ages may be a ticking time bomb. Media portrayals of bodies after normal appearance-altering events such as pregnancy (regularly depicted in the media by so-called 'yummy mummies') and the menopause (portrayed by images of thin and youthful middle aged celebrities), set new and unrealistic ideals for mid-life physiques. Researchers and commentators focus on the challenges associated with the rapid physical changes which take place during adolescence, yet menopause can bring extensive and, in some cases, unanticipated changes to physical appearance too. Mid-life women may be particularly sensitive to comments from families, especially partners. A shift in societal attitudes is needed, so that we celebrate ageing and the associated changes to appearance, rather than idealizing the impossibility of agelessness and the pursuit of supposedly age-defying interventions such as cosmetic surgery. There is still much to be learnt about appearance and ageing—and with pressures to increase the pension age of the current cohort of researchers, we wait to see whether interest in appearance research at this end of the lifespan increases!

The relatively small body of published work into appearance concerns in boys, young men, and adult males may reflect a view that this is a harder (or less pressing) issue to research amongst males than females. Whereas body ideals for women are clearly articulated and widely shared, they are more variable for men, with some seeking to achieve a muscular v-shape with broad shoulders and narrow waist whilst others aspire to thin and waif-like ideals more commensurate with those sought by females. Hair loss is an example of how appearance changes may be stereotypically seen as a natural consequence of ageing for a particular sex, yet responses to it still differ greatly, with some men embracing it whilst others find this more distressing and embark on a seemingly relentless quest to disguise the loss, or preserve or replace their locks.

Authors in this section have highlighted how measures developed with and for younger women are widely used in research with males because of the limited availability of measures specifically tailored to assess boys' and men's appearance issues. It is commonly believed that males are less comfortable discussing appearance issues than females and may disguise their efforts to achieve ideals and talk instead about aspirations of achieving prowess in physical activity. However, this is a burgeoning area and a relatively small number of studies (and recent reports in the media) suggest that men are willing and able to engage in appearance-related research if studies are presented and designed appropriately. Our experience has been that men are interested in taking part, but often prefer doing so through questionnaires with little, if any, face-to-face contact with the (often female) researchers. Online research (see Section 4) may be a fruitful means of engaging males in appearance research.

Across the lifespan, it is clear that some people are detrimentally affected by appearance concerns whilst others are content with their looks; some place no importance on appearance whilst others are very focused on it. But where is the boundary at which healthy interest and enjoyment in appearance becomes dysfunctional and/or unhealthy? The chapters in Section 2.2 have focused on the social and psychological factors which play a part in these individual differences in adjustment and distress, and the mechanisms through which psychological, interpersonal, and cultural factors intertwine to influence body (dis)satisfaction in men and women and the similarities and differences between them.

The range of sociocultural influences on appearance concerns is extensive. Habib Naqvi and Krysia Saul illustrate how views about appearance remain entrenched in some cultural groups, whilst elsewhere the emphasis on culturally-specific aspects reduces in favour of more globally shared ideals. Tensions between generations may be evident, with some younger people more attuned to Westernized ideals, and some older generations putting more emphasis on religious and cultural beliefs to guide their practices. Their chapter, together with Hannah Falvey's contribution in Section 1, highlights the need to engage more people from different ethnic groupings and generations in research and the development of policies and practices to ensure their needs are met effectively. This will require the use of culturally sensitive and appropriate methods.

Relationships, in terms of families, partners, and friendships, are clearly potent influences on the nature and extent of appearance concerns, not just in childhood, but yet again across the lifespan. We urgently need to better understand the ways in which families and friends can promote resilience (e.g. through influencing self-concept and self-esteem, and providing peer support and opportunities to develop and practice social skills) as well as maintain or exacerbate concerns (e.g. through censorious behaviours such as teasing). How does their role and influence change over a person's lifetime? The evaluative gaze does not cease even though, for some, the importance attached to various friends and family members will wax and wane over time. The perception of parents and their children will impact in both directions and again shift as both parties age and offspring become parents themselves. The issues relevant to people living with an inherited or genetic condition that has altered appearance (e.g. neurofibromatosis, Klinefelter's syndrome) warrant further research, and raise questions including to what extent does this altered appearance act as a familial tie? Are there benefits in terms of support from other family members who have the same condition? What is the impact on any family members who do not have the condition, and may therefore look very different to the rest of their family? Are there concerns about passing the condition on to subsequent generations? If so, how do these influence reproductive decision-making? What support is provided by health professionals such as genetic counsellors? Do they feel able to help patients with appearance-related concerns, in addition to the other issues that their condition may present?

Fathers' roles in the development of appearance concerns in their progeny have been largely neglected, as has the role of changing and more complex family groupings including step-families and the resulting introduction of additional siblings and parental figures. Yet again, most research has focused on the influence of family and friends on weight-related issues, with limited attention being paid to other aspects of appearance, such as clothing choices. Once more, the majority of research to date has concerned white middle-class families and friendship groups in the UK, US, and Australia, and more attention should be paid to the influence of other ethnic groupings.

Appearance also acts as a form of social communication across the lifespan, and Caroline Huxley and Nikki Hayfield's chapter demonstrates how choices about clothing can project an image in order to communicate or ascertain membership of a (sub) group, recognize and attract others, and signal belonging. Once again, although the image we present to the world can be the focus of overt attention and comment amongst young people, it remains a currency throughout adulthood and later in life and is a daily consideration for everyone to a greater or lesser extent (and for some a source of considerable preoccupation and expenditure). Impression management was popular within social psychology in the 1970s and 1980s, and although it currently receives less attention, it could contribute to our understanding of distress caused by discrepancies between our ideal and perceived selves. This has been discussed in detail by Timothy Moss and Ben Rosser, along with the range of strategies that have been shown to contribute to successful coping with appearance issues, in particular visible difference. Some situations are controllable through a person's own efforts, whereas others are not (e.g. someone staring or making unsolicited comments, or the content of the media), and the person can only choose how to respond in these circumstances. Being able to pick and choose from a range of different strategies can be beneficial, but might be unhelpful if they are conflicting (e.g. an approach-focused technique conflicting with an avoidant strategy).

Over time, different aspects of psychology come in and out of fashion—whilst positive psychology is in the ascendant at the moment, what about the role of personality, which has gone out of favour? Dispositional optimism has recently been highlighted as key in adjustment for people with visible differences (see Egan et al., 2011; Rumsey et al., under review). Within cleft lip and palate research, the emerging field of neurodevelopment/functioning is raising questions about whether psychosocial deficits are part of congenital syndromes, and beginning to shed new light on the interaction of biological components with psychological risks. We will follow developments in this field, and their impact on research in other areas, with great interest.

Emma Halliwell and Phillippa Diedrichs's careful examination of the media's influence illustrates that we are not just passive recipients of media messages, but that we actively engage with the magazines, TV, and celebrity culture which can feed appearance-related insecurities. There are 'nay sayers' who decry the influence of the media, but whether minor and transitory, or insidious and more major, its effects are now clearly evident. Some are affected more than others, and internalization has been highlighted as key in self-discrepancy and schema theories.

Whilst most research into the influence of the media has focused on weight and shape, other aspects (including the effects of beautiful faces, the impact of airbrushed images, and the portrayal of visible differences) are now creeping onto researchers' radars. The dominant images in the media are still of white Western people, even in other cultures. Likewise, people who have a visible difference are rarely shown in anything other than stereotypical ways and are usually portrayed as villains or withdrawn and reclusive. Recently, television programmes in the UK such as *Beauty and the Beast* (Channel 4, 2011) and *Katie Piper: My Beautiful Friends* (Channel 4, 2011) have presented people with a visible difference in a less derogatory and more positive light, with the potential to promote diversity of appearance. Yet, to what extent these programmes influence attitudes towards appearance, and in what way, is still unknown.

Chapters 22 to 25 focus on ways in which, as a consequence of appearance concerns, many people try to consciously change their appearance, for example, through diet, exercise, and cosmetic surgery. Contributors to this section have offered very different perspectives about diet and exercise, but it is clear that the physical and social environment has an influence to play in each. For example, James Byron-Daniel flags up how mirrors and clothing commonly associated with gyms may be intimidating to many, and thereby influence levels of appearance concerns, decisions about whether to exercise, and, if so, the type of physical activity engaged in, and where this takes place. Whilst appearance concerns might galvanize some people to increase their levels of physical activity, some will choose to do so in relative privacy (e.g. following an aerobics DVD in their own home), whilst others will choose a more public setting such as a gym—are these people who are already confident with their body to the extent that they feel comfortable revealing it in this way? In the UK, research by the YMCA (presented at the launch of the Campaign for Body Confidence, May 2011) reported that 42% of respondents would go into a gym if they could see that other people with their body shape were using the facilities. This led them to champion a campaign to encourage people of all shapes and sizes to engage in exercise, and to take steps to make their gyms more appealing and less intimidating (e.g. using people of various sizes in their advertising campaigns). Researchers need to establish the effectiveness of campaigns such as this, and to remember that many people who engage in regular physical activity do so away from gym settings and structured classes or environments. Interventions may be needed to encourage body conscious people to exercise in the company of others, for example, participating in team sports, or in very 'body revealing' environments such as swimming pools.

Diagnosable eating disorders such as anorexia and bulimia are merely the tip of the iceberg when it comes to people's use of diet as a means of trying to control their size and shape, with far greater numbers engaged in fasting, food restriction, skipping meals, and fad and yo-yo diets. Victoria Lawson highlights the role of social comparisons in self-judgements of weight (i.e. a person judging whether, in comparison with others, they are overweight, obese, normal, or underweight). She notes the pervasive influence of social constructions concerning weight, particularly in relation to images in the media, and the impact of obesogenic environments in which high calorific foods are omnipresent, readily available, and cheaper and easier to choose than healthier options. She argues that it is irresponsible not to encourage people to lose weight, but that interventions should focus more on health gains than on improvements to appearance. The links between this and James Byron-Daniel's consideration of the success of internal versus external motivations to exercise are clear. The message for those with an interest in promoting health is that interventions should avoid reinforcing appearance stereotypes and the use of stigmatizing messages about appearance, such as the view that thinness is desirable at any cost. Irmgard Tischner and Helen Malson's critical perspective towards the cultural currency of slimness and its consequences for physical health and well-being challenges prevailing societal definitions of obesity and associated health risks, particularly the implication that obesity on its own constitutes severe health risks. They advocate approaches which promote healthy eating and exercise for all, regardless of size.

The media, ubiquitous throughout this book, again plays a key role in formulating the environment in which appearance concerns are created and experienced, and in which 'solutions' for this supposed problem are promoted. The sharp rise in numbers of people undergoing cosmetic procedures is a shocking example of the actions some people will take in response to concerns about their looks (it is worth bearing in mind that the available statistics are probably an underestimate of the number of people pursuing cosmetic procedures of some kind or another, as the majority take place in the largely unregulated private sector. The implications of the regulation of the cosmetic surgery industry are considered by Alex Clarke in Chapter 36). The broader acceptance of cosmetic procedures as normative, the perceived malleability of appearance and the imperative to change it, and the endorsement of biomedicine as a legitimate way to tackle the increasing levels of body dissatisfaction, all provide evidence of the impact of the changing societal context. The publication of *My Beautiful Mommy* (Salzhauer, 2008) a picture book aimed at children of parents undergoing cosmetic surgery is indicative of how these procedures have become an accepted part of everyday life within some families. Canice Crerand and colleagues note that the risks of cosmetic procedures are rarely publicized in the media and, when published, may not be dwelt upon by providers. They highlight the need for screening tools and for the provision of appropriate psychological support and interventions as a routine part of the care pathway.

The complexities of the factors contributing to body image and appearance are becoming increasingly apparent. The number of constructs and variables (and their associated measures) is proliferating and the field is often bewildering for new researchers and practitioners drawn to the field. Psychologists talk of social comparison processes, internalization, cognitive biases, discrepancy theory, and schemas as discreet constructs and processes, and parcel them up separately in order to understand them fully. Yet the reality is more a combination of processes that work in parallel and are not mutually exclusive, rather than a neat series of boxes and arrows. Instead of increasing the fragmentation of research further, researchers could instead strive for greater coherence in the field. This could be achieved by establishing a broad consensus about an overarching framework of adjustment in relation to appearance, and within this framework, agreement about the main processes and key constructs within which the individual efforts of researchers could be located and understood. These issues are discussed in more detail in the final section (Section 5).

Whilst we are keen to encourage researchers and practitioners alike to consider appearance in terms of a spectrum according to levels of satisfaction as opposed to segregating people according to whether or not they have a visible difference, it remains important to consider the particular consequences of living with an altered appearance or visible difference. The issues raised in previous chapters are also pertinent to those living with a visible difference, and there are many similarities between the factors highlighted in the four chapters in Section 2.4 and those implicated in appearance-related distress and adjustment in the mainstream population (e.g. the multifactorial nature of adjustment, the importance of subjective interpretation of events, attention and information processing and the key role of the internalization of media and societal messages about appearance). Despite the enormous range of conditions resulting in disfigurement, there is surprising consistency in the problems and challenges they present. A recent study involving more than 1,200 people living with a range of visible differences (Rumsey et al, under review) has highlighted that people with disfigurements often report distress related to other aspects of their appearance, despite the attention paid to their visible difference by healthcare professionals. This study and these chapters remind us of the importance of acknowledging what are normal developmental processes rather than attributing all things negative to their unusual appearance, and of avoiding assumptions about the personal impact of any particular individual's experiences.

Overall, the chapters in Section 2 demonstrate the considerable volume of research that has taken place in recent years and identify gaps in our knowledge that still need to be addressed. The authors of these chapters have (as asked) focused on their own specialist area yet whether or not an individual reports appearance-related concerns will be determined by the simultaneous influence of many of these areas. The contributors to this section allude to the need for more research amongst men and older adults and across different ethnicities, with a particular emphasis on identifying protective factors contributing to resilience to appearance concerns and the development of appropriate interventions. Other areas in need of investigation include the role of appearance concerns and of visible difference in intimacy and sexual functioning, both for the affected person and potential or existing partners. Time is not necessarily a great healer when it comes to living with the challenge of a visible difference, but the cross-sectional designs employed in most studies mask this and more longitudinal research is needed. We also need to learn more about positive adjustment and post-traumatic growth after changes to appearance.

The issues raised in these chapters are of relevance to parents, teachers, clinicians, and policy-makers, in addition to researchers and practitioners who already have an interest in appearance issues. This section raises questions about what can be done to improve matters at individual, family, and societal levels, and how can supportive interventions best be provided? It is to these issues that we now turn in the next section.

References

Diedrichs, P. C., Rumsey, N., Halliwell, E. & Paraskeva, N. (in preparation). Body image in Britain: The prevalence of appearance concerns among 77630 adults.

Egan, K. Harcourt, D., Rumsey, N. & The Appearance Research Collaboration. (2011). A qualitative study of the experiences of people who identify themselves as having adjusted positively to a visible difference. *The Journal of Health Psychology.* 16, 739–49.

Rumsey, N., Charlton, R., Clarke, A., Harcourt, D., James, H., Jenkinson, E., et al (under review). Factors associated with distress and positive adjustment in people with disfigurement: evidence from a large multi-centred study.

Salzhauer, M. (2008). *My Beautiful Mommy.* Savannah, GA: Big Tent Books.

SECTION 3

WHAT NEEDS TO CHANGE AND HOW CAN CHANGE BE ACHIEVED?

CHAPTER 31

....

WHAT NEEDS TO CHANGE AND HOW CAN CHANGE BE ACHIEVED?: OVERVIEW

....

NICHOLA RUMSEY

DIANA HARCOURT

In Section 3 we move our attention beyond current understanding about the factors contributing to adjustment and distress in relation to appearance, to consider what needs to change, and how this change might be achieved. The first five chapters, in Section 3.1, examine interventions at a societal or professional level. Barrie Gunter's chapter focuses on the need to review media representations of appearance and the enormous challenges inherent in influencing this kind of change. He discusses a variety of approaches, including media literacy, ways in which the media and those working in this field might act to promote diversity (rather than narrow ideals) in appearance, and how the media might act as an agent of change.

Through the powerful personal perspective of someone who has survived extensive, disfiguring burns sustained in a car accident at the age of 18, James Partridge considers other ways of persuading the public to be more accepting of those with an unusual appearance. In his youth, James' good looks were central to his self-esteem and he freely admits to having 'used' looks to good advantage in social situations. He had joined his peers in buying in to societal stereotypes and as a result, in the early aftermath of his extensive burn injuries, interpreted his disfigurement as a personal disaster. Now, not only positively adjusted to his unique, post-burn looks, but also the CEO of the charity Changing Faces, which works to champion the cause of people with disfigurements, James knows well that prejudice and negative responses to an unusual appearance are frequently encountered in daily life. Even for those who adjust positively to disfigurement, it can take only one unwelcome comment to 'rock the boat'. In his chapter, James highlights the immense challenges inherent in changing social and societal attitudes, but is optimistic that this change can be achieved. He highlights the role lay-led organizations can play in this process by outlining his charity's recent campaign to promote 'Face Equality', and describing a series of posters of people with visible differences which have been displayed in many cities in England and which were designed to raise awareness, educate, and challenge viewers.

In the first of three chapters considering areas of the health services in need of change (all written by clinicians with a commitment to research), Julia Cadogan highlights the need to raise awareness in healthcare professionals about how to optimize psychosocial outcomes in people living with disfigurement. Julia describes her experience of the advantages of multidisciplinary care both for patients in hospital and for those attending outpatient clinics, and in raising the awareness of team members about psychosocial issues. To underline this point, she includes extracts of an interview with Katie Piper and highlights Katie's conviction, in the aftermath of treatment for burns caused by an acid attack, of the need for comprehensive rehabilitation including psychological support. Julia alludes to the challenges of convincing health service managers of the wisdom of including psychological care in core services and discusses the role care providers (including psychologists) can and should have in positioning psychological services and in commissioning care.

Susan Brown, who works as part of a team caring for patients and families affected by a cleft, raises the need for appropriate, authoritative, timely information for healthcare professionals who encounter unusual conditions, and also for the families of those who are affected. Without this information, families are likely to resort to unregulated, and often inappropriate, information gleaned from the Internet. Using her experience of coordinating the development of a series of DVDs, Susan outlines how this medium can be used to provide authoritative information for healthcare professionals and families, with input from people who have lived through a particular experience themselves. Susan's account also highlights a very positive use of service user involvement in the content, design, and filming of the DVDs.

Alex Clarke discusses the 'perfect storm' in the cosmetic surgery market created by a combination of public expectation driven by media hype and professional zeal, and the current lack of a regulatory framework for cosmetic procedures in UK.

Despite widespread acknowledgement of the need for regulation, there is a stand-off resulting from the reluctance of governments to legislate for robust regulation of cosmetic providers, presenting it instead as the responsibility of the various professional groups. This lacuna is potentially damaging for patients, many of whom fail to check the credentials of the providers of cosmetic services and some of whom may be incapable of making an informed choice about whether or not to undergo a procedure. The lack of regulation also reduces the credibility of the professionals providing these services. In contrast to France, where there has been a total ban on publicity and advertising of cosmetic surgery since 2009, advertising in the UK is also unregulated. Certainly when viewing the images and messages implicit in advertisements by many private providers, it is hard to maintain that the answer to questions of whether these are 'legal, honest and decent'—the standards applied by the Advertising Standards Authority to other forms of advertising—is 'yes'. In addition to the lack of appropriate protection for people seeking cosmetic procedures in the UK, Alex discusses the rise in cosmetic tourism and cost to NHS of increasing numbers of botched and failed procedures.

In Section 3.2, in the first of a series of four chapters considering how interventions to reduce appearance dissatisfaction might be provided at an individual or group level, Phillippa Diedrichs and Emma Halliwell discuss why educational settings provide a valuable opportunity and an appropriate setting in which to engage large groups of young people in interactions to address appearance-related concerns and to promote greater acceptance of diversity in appearance. They outline exciting progress in the ongoing search for the most effective techniques, theoretical orientation, and context in which to deliver these interventions and the challenges inherent in changing all aspects of attitudes, including beliefs, intentions, and behaviour. Phillippa and Emma's chapter also raises the need to take account of the undesired by-products of well-meaning interventions, for example, inadvertently focusing more attention on those with unusual, or different appearance, and thus increasing stigma rather than reducing it.

Elizabeth Jenkinson highlights the lack of current evidence for the effectiveness of psychological therapeutic interventions for adults, young people and children with visible differences, and the imperative of moving towards a more comprehensive evidence base. Elizabeth commends to readers the benefits of clinicians and researchers combining their expertise in the development and evaluation of interventions. She introduces a framework within which to consider interventions, based on the intensity of need of recipients. This framework is the product of collaboration between researchers and clinicians, and is discussed further in the summary and synthesis of this section.

Alyson Bessell offers readers a summary of different models of computer-based interventions and outlines the advantages and limitations of this mode of delivery. From the vantage point of having developed and evaluated Face IT, a computer-based intervention for people living with disfigurement, Alyson discusses the key issues and challenges in the design and evaluation of this type of intervention, highlighting the careful work necessary to develop and evaluate these programmes. She, like other authors in this volume, accentuates the importance of user involvement in the development of interventions in order to ensure they are relevant to the intended audience.

Finally, Sarah Grogan and Daniel Masterton use evidence from the fields of psychology, gender studies, sociology, and sport and exercise science, to explore the question of whether appearance concerns should be targeted in efforts to promote health through reductions in smoking, healthier eating, and avoidance of tanning. In doing so, they examine evidence for the direct impacts of appearance concerns on health behaviours, and also consider the potential 'side effects' of health promotion messages which target appearance concerns, including the possible reinforcement of existing stereotypes and the escalation of current appearance related anxieties mentioned by other authors in Section 2 (see Chapters 23 and 24).

The summary and synthesis at the end of this section centres around the challenges of categorizing and evaluating interventions, the role of the media, and the involvement of stakeholders.

SECTION 3.1

SOCIETAL INTERVENTIONS

....

CHAPTER 32

THE ROLE OF
THE MEDIA

....

BARRIE GUNTER

It has long been acknowledged that standards of human beauty are rooted in socio-cultural norms that evolve over generations and can be firmly conditioned in the prevailing social psyche (Grogan, 2008). These norms are rehearsed by individuals in a society and also through cultural artefacts or commodities that it produces. The latter include the mass media.

Concerns about physical appearance can occur among any age group but are especially prevalent among adolescent girls and young women when they experience puberty and find their identity in early adulthood (Crisp, 1992; see Chapter 13). In addition, individuals with visible differences may experience appearance-related insecurities and suffer social stigmatization (Barnes & Mercer, 2003). This chapter focuses on both of these appearance-related phenomena in relation to the role that the mass media play in shaping 'self' and 'other' perceptions and behaviours. Much of the research to date has examined the influence of television and magazines and has centred on the harmful effects of media representations on self-perceptions and dysfunctional behaviour, as well as on the shaping or reinforcement of distorted cultural norms concerning appearance (Wykes & Gunter, 2005). In this context, questions have been raised about the way appearance is represented and utilized by media producers (Wardle & Boyce, 2009).

A brief overview of the key theories that have been proposed to explain how the media might influence appearance concerns among consumers is followed by a consideration of the quality of the evidence relating to the extent and consequences of this influence. Finally, this chapter considers how positive change might be achieved in the media's representation of, and role in shaping, appearance and beauty ideals.

MEDIA INFLUENCES: THEORIES AND EXPLANATIONS

A number of psychological theories have been suggested to explain how media representations of appearance might influence viewers. These theories are reviewed in more detail by Halliwell and Diedrichs in Chapter 18, however, a brief overview is included here to offer readers a context for the present chapter.

According to social comparison theory (Festinger, 1954) in the context of appearance, people's confidence and satisfaction with the way they look can be influenced by the comparisons they make between their own appearance and the appearance of other people in real life and in the media. Women who exhibit a stronger tendency to make appearance-related social comparisons also tend to display greater body dissatisfaction than those who make fewer appearance-related comparisons (Cattarin et al., 2000).

According to objectification theory, the worth of a woman is defined in media imagery principally by her appearance and her sexual attractiveness. Such ideas can become internalized by both women and men (Frederickson & Roberts, 1997). Viewing images of sexualized and idealized female bodies in advertising, movies, music videos, and television programmes is associated with increased self-objectification in some women (Calogero & Thompson, 2009). With increasingly sexualized images of men in the media, self-objectification may also occur among men who feel pressurized by media role models to seek muscular physiques and to define themselves predominantly in terms of physical appearance.

In relation to the potential influence of media portrayals of people with unusual appearance on viewers, the medical model explains physical differences in relation to medical conditions that exist within the individual (Barnes & Mercer, 2003; Thoreau, 2006). Social models of disability move the debate away from the focus on medical conditions and argue instead that physical differences in appearance and function are a social issue, whereby individuals who do not conform to prevailing norms are also classified as if they are non-normative in other ways (Barnes & Mercer, 2003). The World Health Organization has argued that both models have their own strengths and weaknesses, and that some middle ground might be found in terms of a biopsychosocial model that incorporates elements of both of them (see Thoreau, 2006; Wardle & Boyce, 2009). Using this perspective, solutions to disfigurement can be both social (through a shift of public understanding and attitude) and medical (via plastic surgery).

Having briefly outlined some key theories devised to explain how appearance-related attitudes, beliefs, and behaviours are formed and might be influenced by the media, the next section turns to what is known about media representations of human appearance.

MEDIA REPRESENTATIONS OF HUMAN APPEARANCE

Research that has tracked media representations of beauty over time has noted a growing prevalence of thin female icons since the start of the 1960s. This was evidenced in the declining average measurements of *Playboy* centrefolds and models appearing in leading international fashion magazines (Garner et al., 1980; Silverstein et al., 1986; Sypeck et al., 2004; Luff & Gray, 2009; and see also Chapter 18).

Television programmes also over-represent below-average-weight women and muscular men (Fouts & Vaughan, 2002; Herbozo et al., 2004). Television provides vicarious reinforcement for people who conform to thin and muscular ideals, and vicarious punishment for those who do not. Researchers have analysed the verbal comments made about the weight and shape of characters depicted in North American prime time television comedies (for example, *Friends*, *Frasier*). Below average-weight female characters and muscular males received significantly more positive appearance-related comments and fewer negative comments than their average-weight or above-average-weight counterparts (Fouts & Vaughan, 2002). Further, negative comments about the average- and above-average-weight characters were followed by significantly more canned audience laughter than negative comments about the below-average-weight females or muscular males. This may suggest that not only is it undesirable to deviate from the thin and muscular ideals, but also that it is socially acceptable to ridicule those who do not conform.

Little attention has as yet been paid to the impact of 'new media', including those hosted by the Internet, including social networking, celebrity gossip sites, and pro-eating disorder sites. The impact of these, and the digitally enhanced self-depictions which populate social networking sites, have yet to be established.

Media aimed at children also promote thin and muscular beauty ideals. Herbozo et al. (2004) looked at appearance-related messages in popular children's videos and books. Female and male characters who were portrayed as attractive were more likely to have thin and muscular bodies, respectively. Overweight characters were more likely to be depicted as evil, unfriendly, and disliked by other characters, in comparison to characters conforming to appearance ideals. Klein and Shiffman (2005) analysed children's cartoons from the 1930s to 1990s and found a trend for overweight cartoon characters to appear less frequently over time, and for them to be depicted as less attractive, intelligent, pro-social, and lovable than their normal weight or underweight counterparts.

In examining media representations of disfigurement and physical disability, some historical investigations have identified shifts in their nature over the 1930s, 1970s, and 1990s. Initially, characters with physical disabilities or aesthetic differences were used in an exploitative fashion and were portrayed as physically and mentally abnormal, horrific, or as figures of fun. Next, a radical shift occurred in which such characters were shown as more heroic, and striving to overcome adversity. Finally, in the 1990s, there were signs that the character portrayals were becoming more rounded, with people with visible differences being depicted as having aspirations and concerns similar to those without physical and visible differences (Norden, 1994).

Not all studies have such comforting conclusions. A number of studies have examined the depiction of physical and aesthetic differences in cinema, highlighting the discrepancies in demographics, aspects of personality, dramatic prominence, and status of characters with a visible difference compared with depictions of characters without (Farnall & Smith, 1999; Wilde, 2005; Black & Pretes, 2007). In addition, an analysis of over 7,600 hours of UK television revealed a number of distinct representations of people with disfigurements (Wardle & Boyce, 2009). Items in factual programmes (e.g. news and documentaries) focussed largely on rare congenital conditions that result in extensive disfiguration, and mostly affect children. More common disfiguring conditions, such as those affecting the skin, were found most often in drama serials and in a minority of documentaries. Finally, there were portrayals that offered stereotypic views of disfigurement, such as 'bad guys' with scars, or people living as recluses on account of their extensive disfigurements. Again these representations were generally found in fictional programmes.

Media depictions such as those found by Wardle and Boyce (2009) may contribute to inaccurate and unhealthy stereotypes about people who are visibly different. Fortunately, the same study explored public opinion about the way television depicted physical disfigurement. They found that this depended to some extent on individuals' personal experiences. However, viewers with and without disfigurement shared a general sense of outrage at many of the portrayals of people with visible differences on television, particularly when these were considered to reinforce unhelpful stereotypes (including tropes associated with evil, bitterness, and reclusiveness), or to present disfigurement as a 'problem' which needed to be 'fixed'.

MEDIA INFLUENCES—BODY IMAGE PERCEPTIONS

Research that has tracked people's satisfaction with their appearance over time has found that both women and men have displayed declining satisfaction with their appearance. This has been attributed, at least in part, to exposure to increasingly unrealistic appearance ideals in the media (Levine & Murnen, 2009). This conclusion has been reinforced by evidence of the impact of media exposure on body image in questionnaire-based surveys and experimental studies (see Chapter 18).

Studies that have derived data from questionnaire responses, however, have a number of limitations. Measures of media exposure are often grounded in respondents' self-reports of the extent of their consumption of magazines or television. Such measures can yield inaccurate measurements of media consumption. Further, although sometimes content genres (e.g. editorial, advertising, news, gossip, and entertainment) are differentiated, there are often unsubstantiated assumptions made about exposure to relevant body shape role models within these different types of media outputs (Harrison, 1997, 2000). Even when specific television characters have been isolated for consideration, no allowances are made for the fact that they appear in programmes where they are surrounded by other actors with varying body shapes.

Experimental studies have been designed in an attempt to measure direct cause–effect relationships between short-term exposure to idealized images and viewers' self-perceptions of their appearance. The majority of the studies have concluded that participants exposed to magazine depictions of idealized models with thin and muscular body shapes often report negative body image and place a higher value on having a slender body shape.

Experimental research has also examined the effects of televised representations of idealized appearances and cosmetic surgery transformations on viewers. Televised representations of societal ideals of physical beauty and attractiveness have been found to trigger appearance and weight dissatisfaction, especially among individuals who already experience body dissatisfaction (see Chapter 2 for a review of this research). The viewing of television programmes about cosmetic surgery has also been linked to holding favourable attitudes towards cosmetic surgery, feeling pressure to have surgery, an increased likelihood of undertaking surgery in the future, reduced fear of surgery, lower body satisfaction, and a greater likelihood of engaging in disordered eating patterns among North American college women (Sperry et al., 2009).

In another study, women experienced a significant decline in self-esteem after watching a reality show about cosmetic surgery (Mazzeo et al., 2007). This effect persisted 2 weeks after viewing. Furthermore, white women who watched the cosmetic surgery programmes also reported that they felt that the media exert pressures on them to acquire a thin body shape and to control their physical appearance. Further research has also found that viewing a television sequence about cosmetic surgery encourages some women to want to change their appearance (Markey & Markey, 2010).

Although experimental research is only able to demonstrate the short-term effects of media exposure on body image, prospective research with adolescents suggests that media exposure can have a detrimental impact on body image over longer periods of time (e.g. Tiggemann, 2006). Furthermore, there is a general consensus of findings in the questionnaire, experimental, and prospective research which suggests that exposure to idealized media images has a negative effect on viewers' body esteem.

CLINICAL PROBLEMS ASSOCIATED
WITH MEDIA EXPOSURE

Perhaps the ultimate concern about the influences of mass media images of appearance rests not simply with changes in body self-perceptions, but also in behaviour that could be harmful to the individual. Body dissatisfaction and distorted perceptions of being too big have been associated with the onset of eating disorders such as anorexia nervosa and bulimia. If media representations of a slender ideal as the standard of beauty can trigger unfavourable self-evaluations about a person's own body shape and size, there are concerns that this could be the first stage in the development of a syndrome of potentially far more damaging behaviours (Arnett, 1995).

So far, there is limited empirical evidence on whether women with clinically diagnosed problems such as anorexia or bulimia have been influenced by media depictions. Some evidence has emerged, however, to show that women with these eating disorders displayed significant increases in their levels of body dissatisfaction after exposure to photographs of attractive models from fashion magazines (Hamilton & Waller, 1993). Such exposure also resulted in more exaggerated estimates of a participant's own body size (Waller et al., 1992).

Research with young and middle-aged women who were receiving outpatient treatment for eating disorders found that they did make comparisons between themselves and models depicted in fashion magazines. Some reported cutting out photographs from such magazines and pinning them to their bedroom walls. These magazines also provided dietary, health, and fitness advice which was eagerly consumed in their drive to be thin (Thomsen et al., 2001). In a review of the research examining the link between media exposure and eating disorders, Levine and Murnen (2009) concluded that current evidence suggests that media consumption is a variable, rather than causal, risk factor in the development of eating disorders.

There is a growing political and public concern that various forms of mass media play an important part in helping to shape this pattern of behaviour as influential cultural intermediaries (Grogan, 2008; Woolf, 2010). The question that naturally arises from this concern is what can we do about it?

WHAT NEEDS TO CHANGE AND
HOW CAN CHANGE BE ACHIEVED?

Mass media are influential agents of socialization in many societies, and for many, rival the role played by families and schools in the transmission of norms, values, and attitudes (Bryant & Oliver, 2009). Television, magazines, newspapers, radio, books, cinema, billboards, and other forms of advertising and the 'new media' (Internet and social networking sites) occupy much of our leisure time, and in relation to appearance ideals, present a skewed distortion of what is normal and acceptable. The evidence discussed earlier in this chapter indicates that these appearance-related messages are not benign.

Is media literacy the answer?

To date, most prevention efforts have focused on efforts to teach individual consumers how to resist unhealthy media imagery, rather than focusing on strategies to change the sociocultural environment. 'Media literacy' has been proposed as a solution to the damaging effects resulting from the consumption of idealized, perfected media images. Media literacy interventions encompass teaching individuals skills to critically analyse media and advertising messages and images, and the promotion of active behaviours and attitudes to foster resistance to media messages. The results of both brief and more intensive media literacy interventions have demonstrated some short-term gains, particularly when inter-session interactive activities and tasks are involved, but the results relating to more enduring effects are inconclusive. Existing studies have focused largely on young girls, rather than on young males or adult populations (Levine & Piran, 2004; Lopez-Guimera et al., 2011) and on psychological responses to media imagery. Little is yet known about the impacts of interventions on behavioural outcomes. In addition, most of these studies have reported on the impact of media literacy skills in response to consumption of television and magazines, rather than to responses to social networking and other new media.

Changes to media content:

As media literacy is clearly not the whole answer, it has become increasingly evident that a shift in the content of media is needed. In particular, it is clear from the research already reviewed that there needs to be a move towards greater diversity in the appearances of people depicted in the media, and a reduction in the reliance of appearance stereotypes in its messaging.

From the perspective of social comparison theory, the process of assimilation may explain how media imagery could be used to promote positive body image among consumers. Assimilation occurs when a person makes an upward comparison to a superior target and feels similar to the target in some way. Assimilation is proposed to result in improved affect and more positive self-evaluation because the discrepancy between the self and the superior target of comparison is minimized, and the individual is able to feel part of the superior group (Collins, 1996). If media images were more representative of the general population, it is possible that appearance comparisons could contribute to, or affirm appearance satisfaction, rather than promote dissatisfaction.

Based upon their extensive review of past media coverage of people with visible differences, Wardle and Boyce (2009) have made specific recommendations about the representations of people with disfigurements in the media. They maintain that the current focus on rare and more extreme forms of disfigurement should be reduced and replaced with regular depiction of people with more common, every-day differences. In relation to television and film, people with these more 'ordinary' disfigurements should be given a voice through appearances in a variety of roles, as reporters, presenters, and newscasters (see Chapters 18 and 33), and as characters with a variety of story lines in fictional pieces. Interestingly, Wardle and Boyce also recommended that people with disfigurements should have key roles behind the camera too, as producers, directors and media researchers.

Governments, politicians (Liberal Democrats, 2009; Quebec Government, 2009; Australian Government, 2010) and researchers (Halliwell & Dittmar, 2004; Diedrichs & Lee, 2010) in Australia, Europe, and the US have also called for greater body size diversity in media imagery to reduce body dissatisfaction and to prevent disordered eating. However, the fashion and advertising industries have argued that average-size models do not appeal to consumers and that their power to sell products will be significantly weaker. Until recently there has been little method-ologically sound research to inform government recommendations and to counter industry concerns. Recently however, a stream of research has examined viewers' responses to average-size fashion models, and has found that viewing average-size female and male models in advertisements is associated with positive consumer reactions and more healthy body image among women and men who internalized current beauty ideals, in comparison with viewing images of thin and muscular models, or no models.

Diedrichs et al. (2011) reported dislike and active rejection of current appearance ideals depicted in media imagery and an unease that advertisers rely on body dissatisfaction to sell products among a sample of young Australian women and men. There was also a prevailing belief amongst focus group participants that 'the mass media is dominated by narrow appearance ideals' and that 'women in the media are objectified', together with positive reactions to, and support for, increased body size diversity in media imagery. In additional studies, Diedrichs and Lee (2010) and Halliwell and Dittmar (2004) have found that average-size models are perceived by men and women to be as effective in selling products as advertise-ments using thin females or muscular males, or no models. Although this research focuses on intentions to buy rather than actual purchasing behaviour, the results suggest strongly that, in contrast to industry concerns, average-size models might provide an effective and healthy alternative to current approaches.

The images used in the advertising of cosmetic surgery—with the implicit message that an appearance which is altered to be closer to appearance ideals will result in the recipient attracting a good looking partner and acquiring a celebrity lifestyle—have also been a focus of concern amongst politicians and researchers. There have been calls in several countries for tighter regulation of this advertising, or an outright ban of advertising for cosmetic surgery. In response to the extremely high demand for cosmetic surgery in young Spanish girls, for example, the Spanish government passed a law banning the advertisement of beauty products and treatments that are marketed as ways of achieving appearance ideals. However, the impact of this ban is unknown (Paxton, 2011).

The educative potential of media

Commentators and researchers have suggested that the media can also be used as a force for good, by challenging appearance stereotypes and promoting diversity. For example, there is great potential for documentaries to educate viewers about types and causes of appearance differences, to promote less reliance on surgery and other biomedical solutions as the path to happiness and success, and to educate viewers about how to reduce appearance-related prejudice.

However, even if changes to the content and style of programming are achieved, it is very unlikely that one approach will fit all. An understanding of individual responses to the same programme content is still in its infancy, however, it is already clear that messages are received in very different ways, and one approach may be effective in changing beliefs, values and attitudes in only a segment of viewers. Sancho (2003), for example, revealed distinct groups in relation to the reception and interpretation of images about disabled people. Further research is needed, but it is likely that multiple approaches will be necessary.

Changes to media and advertising imagery will require shifts in the attitudes and practices of media professionals, and in those who drive the content and regulate the various media, advertising, and cosmetic industries. Although some media professionals regard television as having an educational remit and potential to act as a force for good, for example, in relation to the depiction of people with visible differences, this opinion is not universally held. Some media professionals regard television primarily as an entertainment medium with limited capacity to shift public understanding and opinion in a socially positive direction (Wardle & Boyce, 2009). There is no doubt that fear of losing audiences and hence, advertising revenue, will make significant change a difficult task.

The Internet is the mass communication channel of the future. Its power to influence appearance ideals in ways which may be harmful to vulnerable consumers is concerning. Yet, online health promoting interventions also show promise, and researchers must explore the potential of websites, chatrooms, blogs, and other burgeoning mobile technologies, as agents of change, (see Chapters 39, 46, and 47).

CONCLUSION

As things stand, predominant trends in media representations of human appearance place individuals of both sexes under increasing pressure to control their appearance and to project a 'look' that is deemed by commercial interests to be the gold standard. Those who do not conform to a cultural 'ideal' feel pressure to do so, even if that means putting themselves at risk. For those who feel powerless to conform, lowered self-confidence, anxiety, and depression can be spin-off side effects. Regardless of whether the empirical research to date has presented compelling evidence, the growing prominence of these trends is sufficiently serious to warrant continued efforts to understand them and their impact. In addition, effort should be invested in exploring the ways in which this impact can be reduced and how the media can be used as a force for change.

We have a very long way to go before, both through the media and more broadly in society, we are able—in the words of one of Diedrichs's participants—'to see beauty in everyday people' (Diedrichs et al., 2011). However, progress is being made. Activism and advocacy for change is spreading amongst commentators, policy-makers, and politicians. The Australian Government has recently announced a national strategy for addressing body image, including a voluntary industry code of conduct, which encourages media, fashion, and advertising industries to promote greater diversity in the appearance of people displayed. Politicians and researchers in the UK have been petitioning parliament and the Advertising Standards Authority (the national regulator of advertising in the UK) for a reduction in, or notification of, the use of airbrushing, and an increase in body shape diversity in media imagery (Liberal Democrats, 2009). Governments in Italy, Spain, Brazil, Argentina, Canada, and France have developed voluntary charters which attempt to promote body size diversity in media imagery and fashion shows (Boyer et al., 2009; Quebec Government, 2009). It remains to be seen whether these initiatives will be influential in producing change within the media.

REFERENCES

Altabe, M. N., & Thompson, J. K. (1996). Body image: A cognitive self-schema construct? *Cognitive Therapy and Research,* 20, 171–93.

Arnett, J. J. (1995). Adolescents' use of media for self-socialisation. *Journal of Youth and Adolescence,* 24(5), 511–18.

Australian Government. (2010). *Voluntary industry code of conduct on body image.* http://www.youth.gov.au

Barnes, C., & Mercer, G. (2003). *Disability*. Oxford: Blackwell.

Black, R. S., & Pretes, L. (2007). Victims and victors: representation of physical disability on the silver screen. *Research and Practice for Persons with Severe Disabilities (RPSD)*, 32(1), 66–83.

Boyer, V., Ameline, N., Beaudouin, P., Bignon, J., Blum, R., Bouchet, J.-C., *et al.* (2009). Private bill relating to the photographs of improved body images. http://www.assembleenationale.fr/13/propositions/pion1908.asp

Bryant, J., & Oliver, M. B. (eds.) (2009). *Media Effects: Advances in Theory and Research* (3rd edn.). New York and London: Routledge.

Calogero, R. M., & Thompson, J. K. (2009). Potential implications of the objectification of women's bodies for women's sexual satisfaction. *Body Image*, 6(2), 145–8.

Cattarin, J., Thompson, J. K., Thomas, C. M., & Williams, R. (2000). Body image, mood and televised images of attractiveness: The role of social comparison. *Journal of Social and Clinical Psychology*, 19(2), 220–39.

Collins, R. L. (1996). For better or worse: The impact of upward comparisons on self-evaluations. *Psychological Bulletin*, 119, 51–69.

Crisp, A. (1992). *Anorexia Nervosa: Let Me Be.* Hove: Lawrence Erlbaum Associates

Diedrichs, P. C., & Lee, C. (2010). GI Joe or average Joe? The impact of average-size and muscular male fashion models on men's and women's body image and advertisement effectiveness. *Body Image*, 7, 218–26.

Diedrichs, P. C., Lee, C., & Kelly, M. (2011). Seeing the beauty in everyday people: A qualitative study of young Australians' opinions on body image, the mass media and models. *Body Image*, 8, 259–66.

Durkin, K. (1985). *Television, Sex Roles and Children.* Milton Keynes: Open University Press.

Farnall, O., & Smith, K. A. (1999). Reactions to people with disabilities: personal contact versus viewing of specific media portrayals. *Journalism and Mass Communication Quarterly*, 76(4), 659–72.

Festinger, L. (1954). A theory of social comparison processes. *Human Relations*, 7, 117–40.

Fouts, G., & Vaughan, K. (2002). Television situation comedies: Male weight, negative references, and audience reactions. *Sex Roles*, 46, 439–42.

Frederickson, B. L., & Roberts, T. -A. (1997). Objectification theory: Toward understanding women's lived experiences and mental health risks. *Psychology of Women Quarterly*, 21, 173–206.

Garner, D. M., Garfinkel, P. E., Schwartz, D., & Thompson, M. (1980). Cultural expectations of thinness in women. *Psychological Rreports*, 47, 483–91.

Gitter, A., Lomeranz, J., & Saxe, L. (1982). Factors affecting perceived attractiveness of male physiques by American and Israeli students. *Journal of Social Psychology*, 118, 167–75.

Grogan, S. (2008). *Body Image: Understanding Body Dissatisfaction in Men, Women and Children* (2nd edn.). London: Routledge.

Halliwell, E., & Dittmar, H. (2004). Does size matter? The impact of model's body size on women's body-focused anxiety and advertising effectiveness. *Journal of Social and Clinical Psychology*, 23, 104–22.

Hamilton, K., & Waller, G. (1993). Media influences on body size estimation in anorexia and bulimia: An experimental study. *British Journal of Psychiatry*, 162, 837–40.

Harrison, K. (1997). Does interpersonal attraction to thin media personalities promote eating disorders? *Journal of Broadcasting and Electronic Media*, 41, 478–500.

Harrison, K. (2000). Television viewing, fat stereotyping, body shape standards, and eating disorder symptomatology in grade school children. *Communication Research,* 27(5), 617–40.

Herbozo, S., Tantleff-Dunn, S., Gokee-Larose, J., & Thompson, J. K. (2004). Beauty and thinness messages in children's media: A content analysis. *Eating Disorders,* 12, 21–34.

Klein, H., & Shiffman, K. S. (2005). Thin is 'in' and stout is 'out': What animated cartoons tell viewers about body weight. *Eating and Weight Disorders,* 10, 107–16.

Levine, M. P., & Murnen, S. K. (2009). 'Everybody knows that mass media are/are not [pick one] a cause of eating disorders': A critical review of evidence for a causal link between media, negative body image, and disordered eating in females. *Journal of Social & Clinical Psychology,* 28, 9–42.

Levine, M. P., & Piran, N. (2004). The role of body image in the prevention of eating disorders. *Body Image,* 1, 57–70.

Liberal Democrats. (2009). Airbrushed ads damaging a generation of young women says Swinson [Press Release]. http://www.libdems.org.uk/

Lopez-Guimear, G., Sanchez-Carracedo, D., Fauquet, J., Portell, M., & Raich, R. M. (2011). Impact of a school-based disordered eating prevention program in adolescent girls: General and specific effects depending on adherence to interactive activities. *Spanish Journal of Psychology,* 14, 293–303.

Luff, G. M., & Gray, J. J. (2009). Complex messages regarding a thin ideal appearing in teen-age girls' magazines from 1956 to 2005. *Body Image,* 6(2), 133–6.

Markey, C. N., & Markey, P. M. (2010). A correlational and experimental examination of reality television viewing and interest in cosmetic surgery. *Body Image,* 7(2), 165–71.

Mazzeo, S. E. Trace, S. E., Mitchell, K. S. & Gow, K. W. (2007). Effects of a reality TV cosmetic surgery makeover program on eating disordered attitudes and behaviours. *Eating Behaviour,* 8(3), 390–7.

Norden, M. (1994). *The Cinema of Isolation: A History of Disability in the Movies.* New Brunswick, NJ: Rutgers University Press.

Paxton, S. J. (2011). Public policy and prevention. In T. Cash & L. Smolak (eds.) *Body Image: A Handbook of Science, Practice and Prevention* (2nd edn.), pp. 460–8. New York: Guilford Press.

Quebec Government. (2009). *The Quebec charter for healthy and diverse body image.* http://www.ijoinonline.com/en/charter.php (accessed 14 July, 2010).

Sancho, J. (2003). *Disabling Prejudice: Attitudes towards disability and its portrayal on television.* London: British Broadcasting Corporation, Broadcasting Standards Commission, and Independent Television Commission.

Silverstein, B., Perdue, L., Peterson, B., & Kelly, E. (1986). The role of mass media in promoting a thin standard of bodily attractiveness for women. *Sex Roles,* 14(9/10), 519–32.

Sperry, S., Thompson, J. K., Sarwer, D. B., & Cash, T. F. (2009). Cosmetic surgery reality TV viewership: relations with cosmetic surgery attitudes, body image and disordered eating. *Annals of Plastic Surgery,* 62(1), 7–11.

Sypeck, M. F., Gray, J. J., & Ahrens, A. H. (2004). No longer just a pretty face: Fashion magazines' depictions of ideal female beauty from 1959 to 1999. *International Journal of Eating Disorders,* 36(3), 342–47.

Thomsen, S. R., McCoy, J. K., & Williams, M. (2001). Internalizing the impossible: Anorexic outpatients' experiences with women's beauty and fashion magazines. *Eating Disorders,* 9, 49–64.

Thoreau, E. (2006). Ouch! An examination of the self-representation of disabled people on the Internet. *Journal of Computer-Mediated Communication*, 11, 442–68.

Tiggemann, M. (2006). The role of media exposure in adolescent girls' body dissatisfaction and drive for thinness: Prospective results. *Journal of Social & Clinical Psychology*, 25, 523–41.

Waller, G., Hamilton, K., & Shaw, J. (1992). Media influences on body size estimation in eating disordered and comparison subjects. *British Review of Bulimia and Anorexia Nervosa*, 6, 81–7.

Wardle, C., & Boyce, T. (2009). *Media Coverage and Audience Reception of Disfigurement on Television*. Cardiff: The Healing Foundation and Wales office of Research & Development.

Wilde, A. (2005). Performing disability: Impairment, disability and soap opera viewing. In M. King and K. Watson (eds.) *Representing Health: Discourses of Health and Illness in the Media*. Basingstoke: Palgrave Macmillan.

Wiseman, C. V., Gunning, F. M., & Gray, J. J. (1993). Increasing pressure to be thin: Nineteen years of diet products in television commercials. *Eating Disorders: The Journal of Treatment and Prevention*, 1, 52–61.

Woolf, M. (2010). Minister demands airbrush health warning. *The Sunday Times*, 25 July, p. 7.

Wykes, M., & Gunter, B. (2005). *The Media and Body Image: If Looks Could Kill*. London: Sage.

....

CHAPTER 33

PERSUADING THE PUBLIC: NEW FACE VALUES FOR THE 21ST CENTURY

JAMES PARTRIDGE

TIME FOR CHANGE

....

'I'M not just a pretty face, you know'—it's a throwaway remark I sometimes make and it has the desired effect of challenging people's face values. Robert Redford apparently used to use the phrase too—and people probably thought 'Oh yeah'. Of course, he'd be worried that people thought he was all looks and no substance, dumb blond as it were. I'm the reverse: not much to look at—and maybe no substance too?

But when I say I'm not just a pretty face, I can see minds going into a spin because I clearly have a facial disfigurement (caused by burns) and I suspect people are quite relieved by the pro-active way I deal with it. But it—my face—is quite clearly not a pretty face. So I use the remark sardonically because, like Redford, I don't like the face value judgements that prevail—albeit without much acknowledgement that they do.

I was severely burned in 1970 at the age of 18 and have carried the visual effects of my wounds and subsequent brilliant reconstructive surgery ever since. I have what is called 'a disfigurement'—my face is a patchwork quilt of scars and skin grafts with a lovely smooth chin (skin from my back) that makes me look forever young!

But, contrary to what I am meant to think—assumed to think—according to today's culture's norms of appearance (perhaps even 'articles of faith'), I like my face very much, scars, asymmetry and all. I am very attached to it. And I am not alone in my view either. I think my family likes my face—and I know lots of other people with disfigurements who like their faces and have families who do too.

But when I make my 'pretty face' comment, I can often feel people wince because, I think, they can appreciate the irony and maybe see the implication: in a different culture, my face might be judged 'pretty'—or, as in African tribes, of high status—but in this one, I have to live with the stigma and disadvantage of not having a like-able face.

That's why I object to and want to change today's face values. They guarantee that people whose faces don't fit the norm will be treated unfavourably, often rather patron-izingly. And the number of people with 'don't fit' faces—'not fit for purpose' as the modern phrase would have it—is very large indeed. Not just people with objective disfigurements (estimated at one in 111 people (Changing Faces, 2007)) but many many people who feel in some sense inadequate because of the way they look.

All of us are exposed, to put it as kindly as possible, to unwitting—for the most part, unintentional, I have to assume—facial prejudice. That rankles because, as with all attitudes, they shape people's behaviours and words in their interactions. Worse, I suspect that most people probably don't realize they are doing or saying something which, in a culture with a different set of face values, they might do differently.

At a simple level, it's about how people in the street, strangers, look at me—or don't—because eyes turning away are what I often sense. I doubt they are revolted by my looks—surgery thankfully removed the 'shock factor'—but I think they often look with sympathy, 'poor thing' or with embarrassment that they don't know how to deal with someone like me, not wanting to say the wrong thing or look in the wrong way. Patronization follows the same pattern: 'You are so brave to walk around looking like that. And all that surgery … Marvellous, well done'.

Another expression of today's face values is the 'Don't judge a book by its cover' argument which gets translated as 'Don't worry, James, it's what's inside you that counts'. This is perhaps the clearest statement about our society's aesthetics: my facial scars may be displeasing to the eye but, surely, they cannot hide a beautiful soul and personality.

Another manifestation is sympathetic and sad: with a face like that, you can have little chance of success in life and making relationships will be unlikely ('brave woman' etc.). So people lower their expectations of me and for me. A good friend who is disabled tells the story of how even her mother fell into this when saying about her prospects 'I do hope you'll be able to get a little job somehow'. This is what Susan Daniels, a former Deputy Commissioner of the US Social Security

Administration, famously called 'the soft bigotry of low expectations'. It is unsaid and insidious in how many people with disfigurements (and disabilities) are treated.

Further down the scale of acceptability, today's face values reflect themselves in lousy service in some shops or restaurants where customer staff training has failed to inculcate politeness and in its place comes staring, awkwardness, reluctance to engage or a refusal to serve. At Changing Faces (the UK charity that supports people with facial and body disfigurements), we hear all too often of people who feel they have been refused a job or a promotion because of their facial appearance. Thankfully, in Britain, anti-discrimination legislation is in place to outlaw this but it is very difficult to prove. That means that facial prejudice turns into economic discrimination and disadvantage for many people.

At the extreme, but all too often, people with disfigurements—and their parents—are subjected to ridicule. Children and young people are perhaps most exposed in playgrounds and around schools. But everyone is vulnerable to this. The recent taunts of a group of teenagers still ring in my ears—'Ugh, look at that'. Scarface, Two-Face, Phantom, Pizzaface . . . I have even been called 'Freddie Kruger' (of the horror movie, *Nightmare on Elm Street*) from a scaffolding rig!

However, much as people with disfigurements would like to blame *individuals* for their situation, many now see that these individuals are conditioned by a set of cultural values—and those are very dominant. For the first 18 years of my life, I never questioning my face values, so powerful were they. On the one hand, my good looks were absolutely integral to my self-esteem and my prospects for success in all aspects of my life. And I saw others with good looks too as being more worthy of my liking—indeed, more likely to be likeable.

On the other hand, I imagined disfigurement—ugliness—to be the ultimate downer—a disaster, the worst that could befall anyone. Not that I ever really gave it (disfigurement) more than a second's thought, so oblivious was I. For 18 years, when I saw someone with a face that was a patchwork of scars, spots, or skin blemishes, I automatically judged them by their face. I avoided them, devalued them to a sad, rather tragic person, writing them off as less likely to succeed, difficult to work with, and awkward to socialize with, let alone fall in love with! I would be sorry for them and rather fearful of meeting them again.

Then, as an 18-and-a-half-year old in March 1971, I was given a mirror 3 months after surviving severe burns. My face appeared totally ruined, tarnished. I couldn't stop myself writing myself off. My conditioned reflex told me that, with my horribly scarred face (yes, that's how I described it to myself) I was destined for a life on the margins, in the shadows. It was a deeply depressing thought that threatened to seep into my very core (Partridge, 1990).

What I know from the years of running Changing Faces since 1992 is that, however disfigurement happens, many children, young people, adults, parents and families (are going to) wrestle with exactly that cognitive and emotional agony.

The public behaviour that people have to endure feeds on this negativity. Macgregor famously concluded that people with disfigurements experience 'a marked loss of the civil inattention that most people take for granted' (Macgregor, 1990). And yet, as well as being the centre of attention, they simultaneously experience, if on their own and unempowered, an overwhelming sense of isolation, people turning away, of rejection and discounting.

The time has definitely come to try to change the attitudes that perpetuate this reality.

But Surely we can't Change All This? Are There Any Precedents?

But is that really possible? Isn't it the case that people with disfigurements will just have to learn how to cope, developing a thick skin and some pro-active social skills, probably for ever (or until sci-fi medical science invents a solution)? Could we ever live in a society in which face value judgements towards people with disfigurements were not detrimental, in which disfigurement was not associated with negativity?

Over the last 35 years, I have met countless people—with so-called 'normal' faces and with unusual-looking faces too—who have looked at me askance and said, McEnroe-esque: 'You cannot be serious: changing today's global society's face values is just fantasy thinking'.

I understand these doubters and do not in any way underestimate the enormity of the challenge. But I hold on to three grounds for optimism:

First, let us look at one of the only public attitudes surveys done on the subject (Changing Faces, 2008). Conducted in the UK in January 2008 by Prism (the market research company), it used an Implicit Attitude Test (IAT) methodology (https://implicit.harvard.edu/implicit) and was commissioned by Changing Faces. A sample of 1,000 adults (over 16) was recruited from the Toluna panel (a leading nationally representative panel of web users) structured to ensure minimum numbers from demographic groups.

At first sight—and with due recognition that this IAT methodology has its critics (Gregg, 2008)—the doubters might well be right because the researchers concluded that, from this sample of the population, 9 out of 10 found it very difficult to associate people with facial disfigurements with positive qualities such as being attractive, socially skilled, and likely to succeed and lead happy lives.

However, the crucial point is that they apparently made these judgements whilst not believing they did so. Explicitly, they said that they did not (want to) show such prejudice and bias.

Second, although the scale of the bias against people with disfigurements was stronger than that found in similar surveys conducted in the US on other issues such as race, sexuality, age, and gender, it can be changed. Indeed, since that same test has been on the Changing Faces website, over 3,000 people have taken it—and the bias is 'only' 6 out of 10. In other words, it is possible for people to become more at ease and to shake off their cultural conditioning—perhaps it's as simple as them becoming more familiar with such faces by just visiting a website . . .

Thirdly, we should draw lessons—and hope—from other campaigns for human rights, many of which started life with just as many powerful doubters. In the last 50 years, the whole world has seen a total 'about face' in how people with non-white skins are thought about and treated. In most countries, the racial prejudices and discrimination that used to fetter so many lives are being outlawed and in their place, inclusion and diversity are celebrated. The same is true for women, for gay and lesbian people, for disabled people and for younger and older citizens. In all these cases, our global culture is gradually changing—some countries and societies faster than others inevitably—from a negativity towards openness and welcome.

What this optimism has led me to is the realization that we are dealing with a human rights issue here and nothing less than a human rights campaign will suffice.

We decided at Changing Faces in autumn 2007 to try to initiate such a campaign to challenge and transform public attitudes towards people with facial and other disfigurements. As with all social change campaigns, we needed a banner to attract attention and act as a rallying call to bring supporters together with a unified sense of purpose. After much debate and testing, we decided on 'face equality'—promoting the idea that people should be treated equally and fairly irrespective of their facial appearance. We also analysed why other human rights campaigns had succeeded and identified such factors as determined leadership, mobilized supporters, imaginative campaigning sustained over many years, persistent refusal to tolerate an unjust state of affairs, and, perhaps above all, robust intellectual argument.

Let us look at the argument and then the how the Face Equality campaign has evolved.

Why do People Make These Face Value Judgements?

To embark on a process of change, we need to trace the origins of today's face value judgements and how they affect the way people with disfigurements are treated—and what are the implications for a campaign for changing public attitudes.

First, we need to recognize that faces which are unusual are liable to trigger 'natural' reactions such as an alarm response—fight or flight. Humans, unless given prior warning or explanation, tend to be wary of or be curious about new or different faces. Ugly and all its unpleasant synonyms like grotesque, monstrous, deformed and disfigured are aesthetic judgements that can be applied to a face which is disproportioned in some way and can evoke, as Darwin remarked, 'a reaction of disgust, if not of violent repulsion, horror or fear' (Eco, 2004).

The implications of this hard-wired response are that society's perception of what are 'unusual' facial characteristics needs to be challenged:

- Many more unusual faces should be seen in the public domain so to increase familiarity.
- Far more information about the causes of disfigurement needs to be disseminated.

Second, the cultural forces that shape today's 'face values' are complex to unpick but three dimensions can usefully be elicited:

- The association of 'beauty' and 'success'.
- The association of 'ugliness' to depravity, evil, and villainy.
- The evolution of medicine and surgery.

Beauty and success

There are many analyses available today of our 'beauty culture' but in search of answers I have turned to Umberto Eco, the Italian academic novelist, whose two heavy complementary tomes—*On Beauty* and *On Ugliness*—are hugely enlightening.

The first explores how the idea of beauty has changed over the centuries and between and within different cultures as evidenced in art in all its forms. He attempts to 'identify ... those things pleasing to contemplate independently from the desire we may feel for them' (Eco, 2004, p. 10). The book begins with eleven 'comparative tables' which enable the reader to review the vast diversity of the ideas of Beauty from the works of artists, writers, film-makers, media and advertising—Adonis and Venus, Madonnas (including Madonna), Kings and Queens.

Eco's analysis is deliberately relativistic; he argues persuasively that what is considered beautiful does depend on the culture and the historical period. From Greek mythology onwards, as artistic methods, architecture, media, and fashion have developed so our recognition of what is beautiful has evolved but his is essentially 'a history of a Western idea' (subtitle) because without the art forms to illustrate, there is no analysis.

Although he covers the natural world's beauty, it is man-made beauty that is at the centre of the book—and facial beauty is at its core. And as you scan through the book, that concept has had many dimensions over the years: from the Greek and Roman sculptures through the classical and renaissance eras to pictures of Marilyn Monroe, Audrey Hepburn, Marlon Brando, James Dean, David Beckham, and Lady Diana.

Although it is hard to pin down why certain images were more aesthetically pleasing than others—harmony, proportion, and integrity are suggestions—what makes today's world so extraordinary is that whereas in past eras, beauty was captured in a single sculpture or painting seen by relatively few people, in today's global culture, billions of people can gaze at and worship the same icons. Instant comparisons of someone's eyes, nose, complexion, cheek bones, and jaw angle against the prevailing norm can be—are—made. Researchers have tried to create an amalgam of what is beautiful by morphing the images of many beautiful faces together—but most observers seem to agree that the process removes the beauty. All of that is no problem in itself—beauty is an aesthetic judgement evolving over the centuries, a natural cultural process.

The problem for people with disfigurements or appearance concerns, lies in the adulatory and seemingly widely-accepted hyperbole that surrounds the iconic images (some air-brushed of course in today's magazines). What grates is the simplistic association between them and health, happiness, success in life, wonderful sexually exciting relationships, high income, and celebrity lifestyle. The mass media of cosmetics and fashion advertising, TV, Hollywood and Bollywood films, and many other visual images continuously bombard the senses of the global population with this link—and there seems an insatiable demand for more. Most people are in thrall to it—even though many know, rationally, that the association is nonsense.

The implications for changing public attitudes are that

- The simplistic link between good looks and happiness needs regular debunking.
- The flip-side also needs constant challenging: 'not looking good' does not and should not mean a life with second- or even third-rate prospects.

Ugliness and failure

There are very few books on ugliness—not surprisingly given how unpopular, and therefore unprofitable, it is to be so. Tracing the imagery attached to ugliness back to Greek culture, Eco makes clear that from very early civilization, a strong correlation was made 'between physical ugliness and moral ugliness' (Eco, 2007). Plato in the 4th/5th century BC wrote 'ugliness and discord and disharmony go hand in hand with bad words and bad nature, while the opposite qualities are the sisters of good, virtuous characters and resemble them' (Eco, 2007, p. 33). Greek mythology was challenged by the Christian world in which even evil and ugliness could in some way through prayer and suffering be redeemed. But in the Book of Revelation, the Devil becomes a physical ogre and Hell a place full of ugliness—and those images dominated thinking for generations after the new Bible was written and indeed also in the writings of Mohammed too (Eco, 2007, p. 87).

Through the Middle Ages, the Renaissance, and into the modern era, ugliness appeared in many forms to signify the lowest form of humanity—gargoyles, in satires, in fables (Aesop was apparently a very ugly man), and plays (Shakespeare's witches are 'the hags'), and in paintings and frescoes. Madness, too, and lack of intelligence is also often associated with disfiguration—and the 19th-century obsession with physiognomy brought forth a steady stream of publications about so-called 'criminal types', with measurements of their faces' proportions supposedly linked to stains on their characters.

'From here to the encouragement of the prejudice whereby "ugly people are bad by nature" is but a short step' (Eco, 2007, p. 261)—and that was further facilitated by the link between the unhappiness of ugliness (e.g. in Shelley's *Frankenstein*, 1818) and with the damned (e.g. in Leroux's *Phantom of the Opera*, 1911). Children's stories and fables reinforce this—*Cinderella and the Ugly Sisters, Beauty and the Beast*.

The coming of photography and movies unleashed a further reinforcement with ugliness persistently used to portray an enemy or villain—Bond films are notorious (Dr No, Blofeld, etc.) but many thrillers, dramas, and horror movies use such devices. The horror genre takes it to a higher level with *Dracula, Elm Street,* the dead reincarnated, and many other ghouls. My own 'favourite' is the depiction of the orcs in the children's blockbuster movies about Tolkien's *Lord of the Rings*. Tolkien himself described an orc in one of his *Letters*: '. . . they are (or were) squat, broad, flat-nosed, sallow-skinned, with wide mouths and slant eyes' (Carpenter, 1981). But in the films, they are scarred and disfigured as if from fire and violence.

The implications for changing attitudes are that

- The public need to learn how to think without prejudice and interact normally with people whose faces are unusual.
- All depictions of evil/villainy with scarring and distortion should be challenged.

Evolution of medicine and surgery

From the point of view of people with disfiguring conditions, medical science's progress in saving their lives and improving their aesthetic appearance and functioning is to be applauded greatly. During the 20th century, in plastic surgery, for example, techniques were developed not only to keep patients alive—with severe burns, for example, even with 95% of their body surface affected—but also to reconstruct their faces and bodies. Microsurgery, laser, and other technological developments have made possible free flap transfers, maxillofacial reconstructions, cleft lip and palate repairs which were unheard of even 50 years ago.

The research into face transplantation takes this to a new level although it is already clear from the public appearances of those patients who have taken this leap into the dark, that it cannot remove all disfiguration. Modern plastic surgeons are also increasingly aware that their surgery alone is inadequate and needs to be complemented by excellent psychosocial care.

The irony, however, is that those very same surgical skills have been very successfully applied to the wider population. Cosmetic surgery is now a multi-billion dollar global industry which has promoted itself as close-to-miraculous. The desired harmony, proportion and integrity which goes to make up 'beauty' is now attainable—or so we are led to believe—if one has the money to pay for the cosmetic surgery.

For people with disfigurements and appearance concerns, these developments have some benefits but several unpleasant aspects. First, the claims about cosmetic surgery's methods are less than 100% truthful because all surgery has its aesthetic limits and, of course, nothing can halt the aging process. So, unhappily, many patients—or more correctly, consumers—may be dissatisfied with the results.

Second, the marketing and wider cultural promotion of cosmetic surgery employs all the undermining hyperbole about beauty being the passport to happiness (referred to earlier).

Third, public understanding about the limits of reconstructive surgery remains less than fully informed—and that has the unpleasant consequence that someone with an unusual face is assumed to be only a few operations away from achieving near-perfection—which is usually very far from the truth. Some decide, entirely properly, not to undergo such surgery anyway.

The implications for a social change campaign are:

- The aesthetic limits and risks of modern plastic and cosmetic surgery need to be emphasized so that unrealistic expectations are discouraged.
- People with disfigurements should be offered appropriate psychosocial help to enable them to face a society which still views disfigurement with uncertainty and them as in need of more surgery.

FACE EQUALITY, A CAMPAIGN FOR FAIRNESS AND RESPECT

The Face Equality campaign is in its infancy but over its first 3 years, it can claim to have gathered considerable momentum. The rest of this chapter looks at how, in Britain, Changing Faces has attempted to take it forward, to change public attitudes towards, and ultimately the life prospects of, people with disfigurements.

What is 'face equality'?

Perhaps the easiest way to think about face equality is to realize that when a person with a facial disfigurement meets someone for the first time (and indeed sometimes for quite a few occasions afterwards), s/he is likely to have to make up to 95% of the effort in the interaction because the face-to-face signalling can be confused and the person with the disfigurements has to do and say things to get attention—or rather, to distract attention away and ensure meaningful communication. In a world in which face equality operated, there would be a 50:50 division of effort. This will take years to achieve so the campaign will need to be for 10–20 years or more.

Those who support the campaign—and we aim to win over many people, organizations, politicians, and opinion-formers—are encouraged to adopt the following principles:

- To promote fair and equal treatment for people who have disfigurements to their face or body from any cause.
- To raise public awareness, knowledge, skills, and confidence to enable positive interaction with people with disfigurements.
- To challenge negative attitudes about disfigurement and address issues of disfigurement discrimination and appearance-related bullying.

In practice, we are therefore taking a range of actions designed to steadily and persistently roll the campaign out to the media, schools, employers, lawyers, artists, film-makers, the fashion industry, advertisers, Members of Parliament, and, of course, the public at large.

Importantly, we realize that there is no solid evidence to suggest that public attitudes are malicious. Rather, they are unintentional and unwitting. We therefore intend in the first phase of the campaign to adopt a non-accusatory position seeking to raise awareness and persuade individuals and institutions to change.

One of the best parts of the launch of the campaign in May 2008 was that many organizations in the disfigurement field and from the wider society in the UK gave their whole-hearted support:

The Cleft Lip and Palate Association (CLAPA) fully endorses Changing Faces' Face Equality Campaign. We know there are many, many people with clefts who find it difficult to relate to other people in both social and work situations as a result of looking – and sometimes sounding – different to others. We hope this campaign will increase awareness of facial difference and ensure that familiarity with appearance issues will lead to a far greater level of social acceptance (Gareth Davies, CEO, CLAPA, 2008).

We are conditioned to make rapid assessments of people from their appearance. A person with a facial difference can often be adversely affected by this instinctive reaction. This campaign will help us all to re-assess how we perceive others and therefore the Vitiligo Society fully and wholeheartedly supports this initiative (Jennifer Viles, Vitiligo Society, 2008).

RADAR supports the Face Equality campaign because we want a just and equal society whose strength is human difference. That means rooting out discrimination in all its forms - from insidious prejudice to outright bullying. We wish the campaign every success (Phil Friend OBE, Chair and Liz Sayce, Chief Executive, RADAR (Royal Association for Disability and Rehabilitation, 2008)).

Only the bravest organisations talk about subjects that most people would rather ignore. Changing Faces is one of those organisations. It does a remarkable job raising awareness

of this important issue and challenges negative attitudes to facial disfigurement. We welcome this positive and inspirational campaign which shows that how you look should be
nothing to do with what you can achieve (Nicola Brewer, CEO, Equality and Human Rights
Commission, 2008).

Beyond the UK too, the campaign struck a chord with votes of support from
Stichting Eigen Gezicht in the Netherlands, the Acid Survivors Foundation of
Bangladesh, and the Phoenix Society for Burns Survivors in North America.

In late 2010, we were thrilled to receive this news from the Sunshine Social Welfare
Foundation in Taiwan: 'Face Equality is a powerful concept put forth by Changing
Faces, and it can have an international resonance. We hope that Taiwan can be
among the first to help expand the impact of Face Equality abroad, and hope to have
your approval and support for promoting it in Taiwan'—which we gave willingly.

Progress in the campaign to date

The rationale behind all of this lies in taking forward the suggested 'implications for
campaigning' listed earlier—and to review how the progress of the Face Equality
campaign to date, it is useful to describe some of the activities briefly under those
headings. Much more detail can be gained by visiting the Changing Faces website
(http://www.changingfaces.org.uk).

Judging whether all these interventions are actually shifting public attitudes
is a very tricky question but one which we constantly ask and seek answers to at
micro-level (i.e. on a project by project basis). Macro-level societal change is much
harder to evaluate.

*Many more unusual faces should be seen in the public domain to
increase familiarity*

Changing Faces has taken almost every opportunity over the last few years to put
people with facial disfigurements onto TV screens, into the press and magazines,
but successful as many of these have been in raising awareness, they are likely to be
only limited in their impact, not least because the stereotypical headlines on the
articles, unfortunately and infuriatingly, often discount the very positive stories.

Words and phrases such as 'sufferer', 'victim', 'disfigured for life', 'horribly
scarred', and 'brave' undermine the informing and familiarizing process by reinforcing cultural stigma and negativity. We have now produced guidelines for journalists and TV broadcasters in an attempt to challenge their thinking.

Changing Faces has also had two campaigns of eye-catching posters since 2008
which have been displayed in the London Underground and many billboard poster
sites around London and across the UK. These have shown three adults and four
children with different disfigurements grabbing the public's gaze and challenging
them not to make instant judgements, to find out more and to 'Stand out, show

your support for face equality'. One of the children wrote of the reasons why he got involved with this campaign and what it meant to him—see Appendix.

The making of the children's posters was filmed by a Children's BBC documentary team and the subsequent film, *Billboard Kids*, was shown on BBC 2 to much acclaim in March 2010, showing 'normal' children faced with everyday challenges and taking them in their stride.

Another example of our familiarization efforts was my guest appearance as a newsreader on one of the UK's terrestrial TV channels in November 2009. This was triggered by discussion of media research showing that most TV coverage of disfigurement was either very stereotypical (e.g. drama and films where it was used as a device to identify 'the baddies') or strongly medical in focus (e.g. documentaries about people with rare disfiguring conditions (usually) receiving surgical treatment). There was very little incidental coverage—people with disfigurements as reporters, talk show hosts, soap opera characters . . . or news-readers (Wardle et al., 2009).

The extraordinary media attention that my news reading provoked was significant in itself—60,000 hits on our YouTube site in one day and news coverage all around the world. But, perhaps most important was that virtually nobody objected or switched over to another channel. My performance was apparently so professional that viewers hardly saw that I had an unusual face. Indeed some wrote in to say that after the first news item, they didn't notice—and wanted me and other people with unusual faces to do it more often as it should be routine and non-problematic.

Far more information about the causes of disfigurement needs to be disseminated

Media coverage, the Changing Faces website, and all the links to the many condition-specific support groups in the field are the routine ways in which we are doing this.

But, perhaps more surprisingly, we are having considerable success in reaching employers in the private and public sectors in Britain with 35 major organizations—leaders in the fields of inclusion and diversity—as varied as Marks & Spencer, Barclays, BT, Shell, KPMG, Bradford University, several police forces, and Addenbrookes Hospital (in Cambridge) joining our 'Face Equality at Work' membership scheme. This scheme aims to encourage organizations to think afresh about 'disfigurement' and not as a subject which they think they have covered under their disability or equal opportunities policies. Instead, we offer them a tailored package of help to raise awareness amongst their employees of the scale and causes of disfigurement and, crucially, how to make reasonable adjustments in the way they treat someone with a disfigurement as an employee, colleague or customer. This has undoubtedly enabled many more people to find out about common disfigurements like Bell's palsy, psoriasis, scarring, cleft lip and palate, and cancer treatments.

The employers have chosen different ways to raise awareness of disfigurement such as by holding lunchtime seminars, by handing out leaflets and bookmarks with website details, and by putting the Face Equality posters as screen-savers on all computers. To ensure that awareness of disfigurement is really embedded, Human Resources' departments have reviewed their recruitment policies and customer staff training teams have received training from the Changing Faces Employment team. The Face Equality at Work website is being expanded to allow committed employers to share their experience and we hope that the number of interested organizations will expand considerably in the years to come.

The simplistic link between good looks and happiness needs regular debunking

This is perhaps the most difficult part of today's face values for a disfigurement charity like Changing Faces to challenge—and we have only really made any progress in doing so in our lobbying for effective regulation of cosmetic surgery marketing practice (see later).

We are always looking for opportunities to support projects that counter the orthodoxy such as new children's fiction or film scores. We also make frequent references to the high divorce rates in Hollywood and amongst the so-called beautiful people.

The flip-side also needs constant challenging: 'not looking good' does not and should not mean a life with second-or even third-rate prospects.

There are so many occasions in the media when almost unnoticed and with ease (such as with a single word like 'sufferer' in a press headline), the implication is made that sadness and the second-rate goes hand in hand with disfigurement.

To counter this, our campaign team is constantly looking to challenge such bad practice—and to promote balanced reporting, though guidelines and pressure (see http://www.changingfaces.org.uk for details). We also have teams of 'Face Equality Champions' and media volunteers, people who are well-adjusted to living with the experience of disfigurement, ready to share their story and pick up the cudgels with journalists and editors.

The public need to learn how to think without prejudice and interact normally with people whose faces are unusual

Launching the Face Equality campaign in 2008 was attempted with as much media coverage as possible but, frustratingly, it coincided with several major events which attracted media frenzies—the Burma flooding and the election of Boris Johnson as Mayor of London. Nevertheless the first set of posters, featuring adults with a range of disfigurements, generated considerable attention as they appeared on the streets of London and other UK cities. Each of the posters was designed to challenge how viewers reacted when they met someone whose face was different to the norm: 'Are you the kind of person who doesn't know where to look?' asked a man with neurofibromatosis. 'Are you only comfortable looking here (above the eye-line)?'

asked a woman with facial scars below the eye-line. The third poster showed a man with a cleft lip and palate suggesting where people look when they meet him—straight at his upper lip. All posters encouraged people to go to the website and find out more, including how to interact successfully.

So important do we think this interaction problem is that Changing Faces has a general publicity leaflet (reproduced on the website) one panel of which is dedicated to the social skills required to meet someone with a disfigurement. For example:

- Don't know where to look? Look them in the eye . . . or if that's hard, look at the bridge of the nose—it has the same effect.
- Worried you might be staring? It's ok to be interested in someone's face . . . just be sure you're not *too* interested.
- Don't know what to say? Say hello. Talk about the weather . . . Express interest in something about them . . .
- Don't make 'What happened to you?' the first question . . . Wait until you know them better. . .

Changing Faces is also involved in developing new classroom resources for secondary schools—primarily for students aged 12–14 years—which will enable them to learn about face equality and how they can learn inclusive social skills. Our experience in schools suggests that equal opportunities policies alone will not create an inclusive atmosphere for children with facial disfigurements if staff and other pupils/students are uninformed about disfigurement and socially unskilled or unsure as to how to interact normally with them. It's arguable that such skills should also be taught to—or acquired by—the public at large.

The aesthetic limits and risks of modern plastic and cosmetic surgery need to be emphasized so that unrealistic expectations are discouraged

Changing Faces has been at the forefront of the very public debate about the ethics of face transplantation research since the idea was first mooted in the late 1990s. A full description of our position can be found on our website but in essence, our position is that whilst not in any way against medical science research (such as stem cell research), it is vital for patients and families who are considering such surgery to be very well-informed about its risks and benefits—including about the aesthetic and functional improvement that is likely to be achieved. There is no doubt that such improvement is likely to be considerable but like other reconstructive options, it is not likely to create a 'normal face'—and this has been borne out by media footage of the pioneering patients.

Similarly, we have taken opportunities in public discussions of cosmetic surgery and its regulation to stress that it too has considerable risks and that the aesthetic results may be less than what patients/consumers expect. In Britain, there is ongoing controversy about the advertising and marketing of cosmetic surgery and whether it can be said to be 'legal, decent, honest, and truthful' as is required by the advertising industry's voluntary code of practice. It is encouraging to see that the professional associations of cosmetic surgeons and doctors have produced guidelines in an attempt to stamp out poor practice.

People with disfigurements should be offered appropriate psychosocial help to enable them to face a society which still views disfigurement with uncertainty and them as in need of more surgery

The fact that medicine and surgery cannot remove the aesthetic impact of scars, asymmetry, loss of an eye, skin conditions, and facial paralysis means that patients (and their families) have to learn how to live with their disfigurement in a society which prizes 'good looks' and makes many assumptions about what having a disfigurement is like. Many people who have disfigurements do adjust and live fulfilled, happy lives but there is evidence that a significant proportion find it difficult to adjust, and some never come to terms with 'looking different'.

Health and social care professionals can do much to make the adjustment less daunting—and if they don't, many patients and their families will be inhibited from leading full lives and be less economically active too—possibly making long-lasting demands on the NHS and social services that could be avoided.

Changing Faces has produced a range of advisory guides (including for particular specialties like plastic surgery and dermatology) that describe how their patients' psychosocial adjustment can be bolstered through appropriate psychosocial help for patients such as:

- To acquire positive beliefs about future prospects after a disfigurement.
- To learn good communication skills to manage others' reactions.
- To obtain quality social support from parents, friends and professionals.

Such 'psychosocial help', delivered by and/or supervised by trained psychologists—such as teaching children assertiveness skills to manage the likely bullying they will face—can effectively empower them to live confidently with a disfigurement in today's society.

JUDGING PROGRESS AND PLANNING THE FUTURE OF THE FACE EQUALITY CAMPAIGN

It is extremely difficult to assess after 3 years whether the Face Equality campaign is achieving macro/societal attitudinal change and Changing Faces is seeking robust methods for making such an assessment. We are however encouraged by many micro-level projects and are determined to continue to inform and challenge.

APPENDIX

Changing the way schools face disfigurement

To anyone who looked
at me and thought I'd
never achieve anything
look at me now

Changing *faces*
the way you face
disfigurement

See why Lucas
chose to star in
our face equality
campaign at
www.changingfaces.org.uk

Figure 33.1 Changing Faces Poster. Copyright Changing Faces, with consent for use from the Hayward Family.

Lucas, speaking at the Changing Faces Annual Reception at the Royal Society of Portrait Painters' Exhibition (4 May, 2010), said:

Hello everyone. I'm Lucas and I'm 13. My nose is wider and flatter than most people's. It's something I was born with and the long name for it is frontal-nasal craniofacial dysplasia. I use this name when I want to confuse people!

The first time I realised I had any kind of condition was when I was four, and I went to my local village primary school for the first time. The other children stared and asked questions like 'What's wrong with you?' or 'What happened to you?'.

They didn't understand, and neither did I. It was confusing and scary hearing them say those things, because I didn't understand I looked different. It was shocking to realise I wasn't the same as everyone else. After that, I was bullied for most of my time at primary school.

Boys would punch me and try to wrestle me to the ground and the girls called me cruel names like 'pig nose' or 'elephant man'.

The physical bullying was the worst and most of the time I was in tears and too scared to go into the playground. They were so out of touch in my primary school that the teachers kept me inside until I felt better and told the children to stay away from me, so I ended up on my own. They suggested I see an educational psychologist when it affected my school work. They were thinking I had learning difficulties, but when the report came back from him it showed I was actually very able, but in an oppressive environment.

One day when I was nine years old I'd had enough, so I just got up and went home. That caused a quite a stir . . . and it was soon after that, my parents got in touch with Changing Faces for help and advice. Someone from the charity came to the school to help the teachers and thankfully things got much better from there on.

My next school got it right from the start. They had a meeting with people from Changing Faces and my Mum. They know that looking different is like having something extra to deal with and that it is support that I need to cope with other children's behaviour and reactions. Curiosity about my appearance is now treated appropriate to the manner in which it is asked and I'm pretty happy there.

But it's not just children who react to my appearance in a negative way. Adults do too and as I've grown older I have had to learn how to handle people's reactions so that I can feel good about myself. When I was younger I remember thinking that all adults were angry because of the way they used to look at me. Now, if someone stares too long, or keeps looking back, I often smile and mouth the word 'Hello'.

Strangers tend to have low expectations of me; they assume that because I look different I must have learning difficulties. I still get asked if I need the help sheet by new or supply teachers and some strangers give me nervous sideways glances and speak to me in a way that suggests I might not understand them. Now if I see someone wondering about my IQ, well, generally using an enhanced vocabulary sorts that out for them.

People sometimes ask me when I will have plastic surgery 'to put it right'. It doesn't seem to enter their heads that I might not want any more surgery or that I might be happy with the way I look or that surgery might not actually 'fix it'—which it probably wouldn't. There is more to a person's 'image' than just their physical appearance and surgery is certainly not a solution to other people's attitudes.

But to grow up, constantly being thought of as abnormal when I just simply have an unusual face, does have an effect. I became lonely, self conscious and felt I was worth less than normal looking people. I stopped doing anything at school and was so very sad, I would come home and pretend to my parents that everything was fine and go to my bedroom and cry.

Changing Faces showed me, my family and teachers how to deal with this long term negative pressure and that's why I got involved with the Changing Faces Children's campaign for 'Face Equality' because I want to help other children like me by changing people's beliefs about disfigurement.

It's been a lot of fun so far. The BBC filmed us all at home for a documentary of our involvement but the most exciting bit was when the posters were up in the London Underground and we went on a 'search' to see who's poster was in which station.

It was also really interesting working with the advertising agency because that's what I want to do when I'm older.

The really impressive part of that day's filming, for all of us, was when we came out of one station, just as it was getting dark, and we saw ourselves on this giant illuminated display, it was bigger than a double-decker bus! I never dreamt I would see myself up in lights in the middle of London. We all felt like film stars!

It's exactly that sort of confidence and pride I would like other young people with disfigurements to be able to feel, more of the time.

But it's not always easy to feel like this given people's assumptions about us.

So, if you're looking at me tonight and thinking that I've got a bit of a sad life, I'm not likely to achieve much at school or that I don't have the confidence to make friends, you need to think again.

References

Carpenter, H., (1981). *The Letters of J. R. R. Tolkien.* Boston, MA: Houghton Mifflin.

Changing Faces (2007). *Facts and Figures.* http://www.changingfaces.org.uk/show/feature/search/Facts-and-figures

Changing Faces (2008). *Public Attitudes Survey.* http://www.changingfaces.org.uk/downloads/FE Campaign, Public Attitudes survey.pdf

Eco U. (2004). *On Beauty.* London: Secker and Warburg.

Eco U. (2007). *On Ugliness.* London: Harvill Secker.

Gregg, A. P. (2008). Oracle of the unconscious or deceiver of the unwitting? *The Psychologist,* 21, 762–7.

Macgregor, F. C. (1990). Facial disfigurement: problems and management of social interaction and implications for mental health. *Aesthetic Plastic Surgery,* 14, 249–57.

Partridge, J. (1990). *Changing Faces: the Challenge of Facial Disfigurement.* London: Penguin.

Wardle, C., Boyce, T., & Barron, J. (2009). *Media Coverage and Audience Reception of Disfigurement on Television.* Cardiff: The Healing Foundation and Cardiff University. http://www.cardiff.ac.uk/jomec/resources/09mediacoverageofdisfigurement.pdf

CHAPTER 34

CHANGING PROVISION IN HEALTHCARE SETTINGS IN THE UNITED KINGDOM

JULIA CADOGAN

DESPITE society's burgeoning interest in appearance, health professionals are not always aware of the importance of addressing appearance issues when treating patients who are dealing with the effects of congenital conditions, disease, and injury (Cash & Pruzinsky, 2002). The number of conditions which affect the experience of embodiment and appearance is extensive and includes facial nerve palsies, craniofacial conditions, and dermatological disease such as psoriasis, cancer, rheumatoid arthritis, and traumatic injuries such as burns (see Chapter 27 in this volume). These conditions affect the experience of the body in various ways, such as the ability to smile in facial palsies, movement in arthritis and traumatic injuries, and sensitivity to touch for those affected by psoriasis. In addition, scarring after surgical treatment affects millions of people around the world and, if left untreated, may become raised, dark red, and hardened with the resulting contractures significantly affecting growth and movement. Adjusting to changes to the body which occur as a disease progresses or where, for example, burn scars contract and restrict movement, influence the overall self-perception of appearance. The ways in which appearance-managing behaviours are adopted during adjustment vary significantly between and within individuals and depend on a myriad of intrinsic and extrinsic variables such as resilience and social support. As discussed elsewhere in this handbook, clinicians and researchers recognize the importance of exploring this process of adjustment, learning from those who cope well despite the odds, tracking the progress of affected individuals across the lifespan, and assessing the influence of physiological, developmental, social, cognitive, and neuropsychological factors. The research to date suggests that those who are more robust and resilient are more likely to be able to cope with visible differences and the outcome of treatment (Van Steenbergen et al., 1996; Cooper, 2000). Resilience has been explored by researchers including Rutter (1987) and Cooper (2000) who defined this attribute as 'the ability to develop the self-confidence to withstand the social and psychological pressures' or 'the ability to take the hard knocks, weather the storm and continue to value oneself whatever happens' (Cooper, 2000, p. 31).

Several studies have concluded that the development of a healthy body image in those with disfigurements is more likely where the buffering and resiliency effects of family support, religion, peer support, a sense of humour, coping strategies, and cognitive behavioural skills, such as anxiety management, problem solving, and reframing, are present (Meyerson, 2001; Carr, 2004). The theme of resilience and protective factors is a topic of increasing interest in the appearance arena and runs alongside the discussions about post-traumatic growth (Linley & Joseph, 2004; Berger & Weiss, 2006). However, the study of resilience and protective variables is not a new phenomenon (cf. Rutter, 1985). More recent research includes a longitudinal study of resilience to childhood adversity in a cohort of 1,265 children from birth to 21 years which concluded that important buffers to adversity were 'gender, personality, attachment and peer relationships which act additively in ways which may mitigate or exacerbate the effects of exposure to childhood adversity' (Luthar, 2003, p. 15).

This chapter examines how the provision of care for people affected by appearance concerns, whether or not they have a visible difference, can best optimize adjustment and resilience amongst those affected.

THE PSYCHOLOGICAL CONTEXT

Identifying or being aware of the patient's psychological context is desirable for health service professionals caring for children, young people, and adults who are undergoing appearance-related procedures such as scar-management in burns services, orthodontic treatment in craniofacial services, and mastectomies in cancer services. Exploring the quality of familial relationships and patterns of attachment form part of this backdrop including the importance that the family places on appearance. This latter issue, amongst others, was investigated in a quantitative telephone study conducted by 'Dove' of beauty stereotypes amongst a cohort of

3,300 females from 15–64 years of age in 10 countries. This found that 60% of participants believed that their mothers positively influenced their own feelings about themselves and their beauty. Extrapolating from this, mothers who equate appearance with self-worth are likely to be inadvertently sowing the seeds of body dissatisfaction in their daughters (Etcoff et al., 2006). Therefore, for children and young people with appearance concerns, a familial approach to psychological intervention is important and where the patients are adults, a careful assessment of familial attitudes to appearance during their childhoods informs therapy.

When treating patients with health problems which affect appearance, it is important to take account of psychological health particularly since it is estimated that six million people in the UK have mental health problems or disorders at any one time (Care Quality Commission, 2010). 'People with mental health problems are at a greater risk than the general population of developing a range of serious physical health problems' (Care Quality Commission, 2010, p. 24). It is estimated that this costs the UK £77 billion, mostly in lost productivity (Department of Health, 2009). Although at first sight this may not seem relevant to the topic in hand, the psychological impact of undergoing appearance-changing procedures or acquiring a disfiguring injury or disease is known to affect social confidence (Newell & Marks, 2000) which in turn is likely to influence if and when people return to work.

Where the patient is a child with a condition which affects appearance and his or her carer is experiencing psychological difficulties, this child's postoperative care and subsequent recovery may be detrimentally affected because, for example, carers fail to seek medical treatment or to attend outpatient clinics. This is especially likely in households where there are safeguarding issues, such as neglect or where the mother of a young child is experiencing post-natal depression. 'Depression in the first post-natal year is relatively common and may have a lasting impact on the woman, her baby and other family members' (National Institute for Health and Clinical Excellence, 2007, p. 41). Therefore, identifying parental depression and other factors which may adversely affect children's health and how they cope with appearance concerns and treatment across the lifespan, is important. Equally essential is the routine provision of child protection training to frontline healthcare professionals, particularly for those who are caring for vulnerable groups such as children with burns (National Burn Care Review, 2001; Chester et al., 2006). The effect of abusive relationships on children's psychological health is characterized by dysfunctional attachments and low self-esteem in the short and long term, which in turn have been found to detrimentally affect health behaviours (Ciechanowski et al., 2002; Maunder & Hunter, 2009). For children and adults who have been physically abused and scarred, undergoing medical treatment designed to improve appearance may evoke traumatic memories (Cadogan, 2011), they may also feel repulsed by their bodies and self-conscious (Gilbert & Miles, 2002; Elliott et al., 2005). 'Traumatic reactions or fear of them prevents many women from seeking healthcare and may interfere with their ability to remember information given during healthcare visits' (Elliott et al., 2005, p. 473). In order to ensure these individuals feel more in control of the situation, less distressed, and more likely to attend follow-up appointments, careful sensitive preparation and explanation by health professionals is required.

THE ORGANIZATIONAL CONTEXT

Providing support to people with appearance concerns is challenging for health services, particularly when working in a complicated, hierarchical organization such as the NHS where roles, training, expertise, and experience vary within disciplines and between multi-disciplinary team members. However, studies in healthcare have repeatedly shown that 'better patient care is provided when health professionals work together in multidisciplinary teams (Borrill et al., 2000). An attitudinal shift may be required which enables medical and nursing personnel to feel comfortable about asking patients appearance-related questions. This may be problematic for some due to time pressures, a lack of confidence about coping with a patient's distress, and a lack of emotional awareness and training about the influence of psychological variables on recovery, compliance, and quality of life (Davidson et al., 2001). In addition, the culture of a problem-solving organization such as the NHS, where there is pressure to discharge patients as soon as possible, a lack of privacy and space, and a tendency to regard patients as conditions first and individuals second, works against the ethos of a patient-centred approach (Rumsey et al., 2004). Adopting an emotionally sensitive model of working has to contend with the 'Stagnant Quo' (Smythe, 1984), where change is perceived as threatening by the staff and their own needs for psychological support may be regarded as a sign of weakness or incompetence. Despite this, a survey of 39 health-authorities conducted by Breakwell (1989) concluded that, according to their managers, the roles of 32% of the staff in 10 professional categories included counselling, even when this role had not been included in job descriptions.

COMMUNICATING WITH PATIENTS

Acknowledging that health professionals are more similar than different to patients facilitates dissolution of the 'us' and 'them' culture. This also encourages an exploratory dialogue between medical staff and patients and allows for an honest discussion about risk, expectations of treatment outcomes, and consent. In relation to informed consent, Gorney (in Sarwer et al., 2006) points out that by being empathic and sharing uncertainty of the surgical outcome with the patient, surgeons are less likely to be thought of as omnipotent and infallible. Instead, they are regarded as wishing to establish a participatory decision-making process with patients. He cites examples of conversations with patients to illustrate this point, comparing this statement: 'Here is a list of complications which could occur during surgery. Please read the list and sign it' with: 'I wish I could guarantee you that there will be no problems during or after surgery, but that wouldn't be realistic. Sometimes there are problems that cannot be forseen, and I want you to know about them. Please read about the possible problems and let's talk about them' (Sarwer et al., 2006, p. 323). Here, the attitudinal shift of the surgeon is reflected by the sensitive use of words and the invitation to discuss any concerns resulting in a consultation which is relational and not just task-oriented. Using age-appropriate language with children when discussing treatment is important if the risk of engendering fear and misunderstandings is to be minimized (Levetown, 2008). Since anxiety can be contagious, helping parents and family members to cope with their own anxieties about, for example, skin grafts and lip surgery in a child with a cleft, is essential. *'Half senseless with fear, I craned my neck to look into my parents' faces and when I saw that they, too, were frightened, the bottom fell out of the world'* (Koestler, 1952).

Inpatient Care

For some, being in hospital for a period of time may provide stability, routine, solace, and an opportunity to establish warm relationships with the staff. Where children have endured appearance-altering injuries such as burns, through neglect or deliberate harm, it may be the first time they have lived according to a routine, played with toys, and felt safe and secure with the adults around them. This stability may in turn facilitate cognitive and social development in those children who have been neglected and as the child relaxes and feels more secure, procedural-anxiety and tolerance of physical discomfort may also decrease. Children such as these benefit from the presence of play specialists on the ward (Hubbuck, 2009) whose importance was officially recognized in the National Service Framework (NSF) for Children, Young People and Maternity Services (Department of Health, 2003). Play specialists, nurse counsellors, and psychologists may work alongside each other in helping children to adjust to stressful experiences such as the appearance of a wound or scar using, for example, anxiety management and distraction techniques.

With regard to adolescents in healthcare, their needs are different to those of children and adults. Over the years hospitals have been striving to meet these needs through user participation when designing facilities (Wood et al., 2010), by providing age-appropriate multimedia resources such as computers on wards, by accommodating the need for privacy, and by respecting the emotional distress young people may feel when having to relinquish control and independence. Given the well documented positive correlation between self-worth, self-confidence, and body image amongst teenagers (Prokhorov et al., 1993; Harter, 1999; Lovegrove &

Rumsey, 2005) this distress may be exacerbated, if they also have to contend with disfiguring conditions, injuries, or treatment, particularly when sharing a ward with others. In the case of adults with appearance concerns, they are more likely to live alone than adolescents and may actively resist being discharged from hospital, so sensitive planning is essential (Department of Health, 2010a). Minimizing emotional distress whilst on the ward is aided by the careful planning of the positioning of mirrors on wards, or banishing them altogether, by raising awareness amongst ward staff about the shock which patients may experience when seeing their reflections for the first time and by routinely asking for user feedback about inpatient care:

I did have to go (to the bathroom) so I did go and I opened the door and there was a mirror directly in front of me and it almost gave me a heart attack because it was such a shock to walk in and see my face so, so completely different, I burst into tears' (quote by a male patient who had undergone jaw-surgery in Cadogan & Bennun, 2011).

OUTPATIENT CARE

Primary healthcare services provide much of the long-term care for patients once they are discharged from hospital and return to their communities. At this stage, the sometimes protracted process of physical and psychological rehabilitation and reintegration begins. The need for a raised awareness of appearance concerns is seeping into discussions in the public and political domain in the UK, with a new impetus from politicians to convene meetings with the fashion, magazine, and advertising industries in order to discuss ways of increasing rather than eroding body confidence. Recognizing the importance of body confidence does not only apply to these industries and to hospital-based services it also applies to primary care. Here, the health professionals, particularly GPs, school-health nurses, health visitors, practice nurses, and others, have an important role to play in screening for appearance-concerns, anxieties about appearance-altering treatment, and unrealistic expectations of surgery. This screening would in turn reduce the numbers of inappropriate referrals to the acute sector. This requires incorporating appearance-related questions into consultations, being attuned to the influence of body image on health, and having an understanding that a small and/or concealed physical difference may be as distressing as a larger and/or visible one (Rumsey et al., 2004).

Unsurprisingly, health professionals may be unwilling to explore the psychological health of patients unless access to psychological support is available. In the UK, delivery of healthcare services is shaped, audited, and reviewed in accordance with government directives and standards published by the Department of Health and guided by the National Institute for Health and Clinical Excellence (NICE). The NICE guidelines recommend a stepped care model, collectively known as 'Improving Access to Psychological Therapies programme' (IAPT), whereby identified problems are addressed and treated in primary care by primary care mental health workers using psychological interventions such as cognitive behaviour therapy (CBT) (Beck, 1976).

There is some evidence to suggest that having a practice-based psychology service is less stigmatizing, reveals unmet needs, and provides a service to a broader range of patients than mental health services (Abrahams & Udwin, 2002). In this study, accessibility was thought to explain why more secondary school-aged children and adolescents requested support than previously. Given that adolescents are particularly vulnerable to appearance concerns, having accessible support in the local community from the primary-care practice is more likely to tap into this population (Cash et al., 1986; Prokhorov et al., 1993; Lovegrove & Rumsey, 2005). This is particularly important for adolescents and adults who have experienced traumatic injuries resulting in scarring, self-consciousness, and a reluctance to seek help. In the UK, the remit of primary care will be expanded such that consortia of GP practices will be at the centre of commissioning and delivery of healthcare (Department of Health, 2010b). It is hoped that the increase in acknowledgement of the need for psychological services by the previous government as outlined in *New Horizons: A Shared Vision for Mental Health* (Department of Health, 2009) will continue. As an adjunct, a more contextual model of inequality and prejudice has its place where the 'site of intervention is at the level of the community, through self-help networks and community projects or social and political action that has as it's aim the creation of cultural change' (Roy-Chowdhury, 2010, p. 25).

For all of those whose psychological health is affected by prejudicial cultural attitudes to appearance to look a certain way, this societal change would be welcomed. Service users (Sheldon & Harding, 2010) and those trained in psychological therapies, such as clinical and health psychologists have a role to play in the commissioning of services and in influencing the way health professionals think and deal with body image and appearance issues (Pruzinsky, 2004). '*Ultimately, it is our society that must be rehabilitated and undergo psychological change to reduce its prejudice, foster inclusiveness and increase acceptance*' (Hearst, 2007, p. 111).

The Positioning of Psychological Support

The positioning of psychologists in healthcare settings in the acute sector is such that they are increasingly integrated into at least one specialist multidisciplinary team. These include services caring for patients with diabetes, cancer, cleft lip and palate, burns, rheumatoid arthritis, and renal disease. This enables the psychologist to be proactive and reactive from admission onwards, with a myriad of opportunities to work collegially in various ways. '*When we work cooperatively we accomplish infinitely more than if we work individually. This is the principle of group synergy – that*

*the contribution of the whole group is greater than the sum of its individual members'
contributions'* (West, 2004, p. 7). In addition, the stigma of seeing a member of the
psychology service is attenuated if this provision is woven into routine care and
available when needed. *'If I hadn't have had that access to the psychologist I would
have sought private psychological help but maybe I wouldn't have been as open to doing
it if it hadn't have been there'* (Katie Piper, see later section). This is well illustrated
in cleft and burns services in the UK which will be discussed in the following
sections.

CLEFT SERVICES

Cleft services were reconfigured following recommendations put forward by a
Clinical Standards Advisory Group (CSAG, 1998) for cleft lip and/or palate, with an
emphasis on holistic care provided by a multidisciplinary service which included
the provision of psychological support.

In cleft services, psychologists attend outpatient clinics, visit patients on hospital
wards, see patients in groups or for individual therapy, participate in audit, service
evaluation (Cadogan et al., 2009) and research and meet regularly as a national
special interest group. Through the omnipresence of psychologists, vicarious learning by other team members about psychological aspects of care is possible. The
team may recognize how a psychologist can support them by, for example, helping
patients to cope with surgery and invasive procedures (Haigh et al., 2005) and
ensuring patients do not have unrealistic expectations of surgery (Sarwer et al.,
2006; Cadogan & Bennun, 2011). They may also identify where a mother is finding
it difficult to form an emotional attachment to her baby (Murray et al., 2007) or
highlight situations where the professional's and patient's assessment of appearance and the need for surgery differ significantly (Vargo et al., 2002). Contrastingly,
psychologists may also challenge the medical model and thus be perceived as slowing down treatment and colleagues may need to be supported in recognizing the
extent of the influence of psychosocial and interpersonal factors on recovery
and cooperation with treatment. 'Unlike knowing how to make a better incision,
knowing how to improve our ability to understand another's motivations and
expectations for surgery can benefit our life beyond the operating room or the
office' (Godwyn, in Sarwer et al., 2006, p. 21).

Demonstrating the effectiveness of psychological interventions to the team may
be problematic since psychological well-being is elusive and difficult to quantify,
unlike physical parameters such as the size and depth of a wound or scar. In some
cleft services, awareness-raising is achieved by asking patients and carers to routinely
complete screening questionnaires prior to seeing the team which then informs
the consultation. Psychologists may also ensure that appropriate information is
provided, encourage user participation in the development of information leaflets

and services, and apply evidence-based interventions when working with ward staff who care for patients undergoing appearance-altering surgery. In addition, running parent days and study days for staff such as specialist nurses which address appearance concerns (Clarke & Cooper, 2001) provide opportunities for user participation and collegial forums. The scaffolding for these services is provided by national standards for cleft psychologists and an emphasis on collaborative audit and research between cleft teams and academic researchers.

BURNS SERVICES

Although psychological and physical outcomes for this population are generally encouraging, studies have found that between 20–43% of people experience symptoms of depression between 2–5 years post-injury accompanied by functional impairments (Cronin-Stubbs et al., 2000; Wiechman et al., 2001; Pallua et al., 2003). Since burn injuries are inherently traumatic, individuals often have to deal with post-traumatic stress symptoms and possibly the criminal justice system (in relation to the circumstance surrounding the burn injury) alongside changes in appearance, disabilities, pain, and the presence of pre-existing psychological difficulties (Wisely et al., 2007; Phillips & Rumsey, 2008). In order to cater for the complexity of rehabilitation-needs experienced by patients with these types of injuries and conditions it is important that thorough information and support from the specialist services in the hospital team is passed on to community services (Wisely & Tarrier, 2001).

Once burns patients are discharged, the hospital-based interdisciplinary collaboration between, for example, the psychologist and physiotherapist in helping someone with burn injuries to cope with painful stretches and massage which aim to improve function and appearance of compromised joints and skin, is often not possible due to a lack of resources or lack of specialist skills. A survey of 71 burn-injured patients with appearance concerns (Kleve & Robinson, 1999), for example, found that whilst 66% received psychological support as inpatients, only 4% did so once discharged. For those with appearance concerns with concomitant social anxiety and self-consciousness, the cessation of ongoing and accessible support once at home can result in social isolation, despondency, an exacerbation of post-traumatic stress symptoms, and mental health problems (Partridge, 1990).

The neglect of psychological rehabilitation in the UK for patients with burns was highlighted in the National Burn Care Review (2001) and the importance of redressing this gap was identified: 'An overall strategy of psychological care is necessary that will cover both hospital and community phases of rehabilitation. Ad hoc arrangements will not succeed' (National Burn Care Review 2001, p. 34). This review was followed by the issuing of a document outlining the configuration of staff required for burns centres, units and facilities (National Burn Care Group, 2006) alongside the setting of psychosocial standards based on a tiered system of care provided by the whole team and lead by psychologists. Outreach services support this process through ongoing delivery of medical and psychological care, in conjunction with support and training to schools and health professionals. This care is bolstered by the running of burns camps by UK charities such as Frenchay After Burns (FAB) for patients and their families. An essential component of this input is a focus on the effects which changes in appearance have on individuals and how to support them. An eclectic and integrative model is often required, which is a confluence of preparation, written information, (such as that produced by Changing Faces, the UK based charity) family support, trauma-focused cognitive behaviour therapy, and anxiety management.

'OUTLOOK': A SPECIALIST SERVICE FOR PEOPLE WITH APPEARANCE CONCERNS

The support for those with appearance concerns is also provided by 'Outlook', the sole NHS outpatient service in the UK. This service has demonstrated the effectiveness of its interventions, which are based on 'Social Interaction Skills Training' (SIST, Partridge et al., 1994), and cognitive behaviour therapy (Robinson et al., 1996; Kleve et al., 2002; Maddern et al., 2006). Individual and group interventions are offered across the lifespan, including transition groups for children about to move into secondary school (Maddern & Owen, 2004). Here, the groups aim to help children develop coping strategies if teased, role-play friendship skills, discuss assertiveness and enjoy creating art works together based on the content of the sessions. In the South West of England these art works are on display in hospitals around the region.

A PERSONAL ACCOUNT

By way of illustrating the issues faced by someone who is living with visible scarring, the following sections are excerpts from an interview between Katie Piper, a former model and presenter, and the author.

Katie was the subject of a revenge attack in March 2008, when a man, at the behest of her violent ex-boyfriend, threw sulphuric acid into her face. Both men have since been jailed for life. Katie was left with burns to her chest, upper arms, hands and face, loss of vision in her left eye, as well as oesophageal injuries. Her face was initially treated using a dermal substitute and skin grafts and since this time she has had numerous operations and benefited from the use of a face mask to flatten and soften the scarring. Other treatment included the use of high-pressure water therapy and massage in a rehabilitation clinic in France. A documentary, *My Beautiful Face,* portrays her journey and through the work of her charity, The Katie Piper Foundation, she is aiming to develop rehabilitation services in the UK and to highlight the issues faced by those with disfigurements.

Excerpts from an Interview with Katie Piper, Burns Survivor:

I was very fortunate that there was a psychologist where I was treated. So when I was in a coma my parents benefited from her being there and I know that helped them a lot kind of explained things and feelings. And then when I was an outpatient I came back up to two or three times a week for sessions with the psychologist. I just sort of assumed that was the way it was if you suffered any kind of burns, you had a psychologist on hand, but I have since learned not all units have a psychologist, which personally shocks me. I think psychology is very important and it's great if you've got friends and family you can talk to and obviously you can read things on the internet but I think professional help should at least be offered to everybody and they should have the option to turn it down or to take it. Some people might take it at a later date but I think it should always be there for that person.

I think that psychological support could be expanded to help friends and families, even colleagues. People don't know how to deal with disfigurement and people don't want to offend or hurt people and it is a life-changing thing. Of course I'm a big believer in physio-therapy that's offered at the moment and it's a really good standard, but once you go home it's reliant on you being motivated at a time of depression or being lucky enough to have a family that can afford to be off work to help you with that physio. If you can't reach or if you're depressed, your scar management goes downhill, so I believe in going from hospital to another institution of scar management and rehabilitation as well. The rehabilitation centre would ideally be somewhere rural where it would have physiotherapists and accommodation so you could stay there for a block then go back into society for several months, then come back for another block. Then you could either go to your psychologist or there would be psychological services within the scar management centre.

Continued care is important because I don't think burns are something where it's the acute surgery and then off you go. I think burns affect you in so many ways as so many survivors know. I mean you know I'm two years on and if you can see me now I've got bandages on today and skin grafts because it's continual and that is what needs to be addressed. It is continual and something you have to adjust to. I think people should be given as much support as possible to help them because you can integrate back into society and you can be happy and you can work and find relationships but you do need that support network.

In the French set up you are institutionalised in hospital and then you go to this scar-management centre. I was wearing the plastic mask, there were other people in my classes wearing the mask, I was going to the pool and seeing other people's bodies that were scarred and I wasn't thrown back into society, I was around similar people. Although there was the language barrier, there was still that camaraderie between people. I could see one woman had been there and come back a year on and she'd been wearing the mask and it motivated me to keep wearing it because I could see her results. The morale was good between the patients, you could laugh and joke with people. You didn't feel that you didn't fit in; you didn't have those feelings of not feeling worthy. Everyone was at similar stages and if they weren't, they weren't too far apart, they were enough to encourage each other. And then by the time I was ready to go back into society. I was that little bit further on with that, had a little bit more confidence and it just kind of helped because it made me feel like there was a point and I wasn't starting at the bottom of the pile. I'd made a significant amount of progress. I do think that's important. We hope with the (rehabilitation) centre, not only will it be sort of physiotherapy, but there will be a kind of social network side. We would like to have camouflage make-up lessons, a place where people can come and get their hair done without feeling embarrassed, social activities, also giving people a sense of purpose who were burned years and years ago who could come in and give talks and mentor people. I'd like it to be a community for burns survivors and residential. It is also very important that patients have access to the psychologist, because if you're having rehabilitation, your face is changing all the time, that is something you need to talk to a professional about.

One thing that the clinic helped me realise was I thought nobody would ever want to touch me and touch the burns in case they thought it was contagious or it disgusted them, and I had all these sort of false ideas about that. When I went to the clinic and other people showed me exercises and touched my hands or changed the dressing, and nobody had touched me really, and it was like that kind of helped me in a way. We had a group session of facial exercises for everybody who was facially burned, where you would stretch the face and the muscles for the contractions. And I remember thinking, oh my gosh, I'm sat in a circle in a small room, face to face, I haven't had to do that with anybody but my family and the doctors and that was something new for me. And I remember the first couple of weeks I used to sit and do the facial exercises like this (head down), then after about six weeks I was able to lift up my head and look at everyone else and do it. Those sound like ridiculous things but they were massive hurdles to overcome. And then by a month I was laughing and joking with people in the classes, Yeah, and I don't know, I often think if I hadn't have gone to the scar-management centre, how would I have left the house, how would I have started talking to people again, how would I have been able to go out in the mask and have, you know, eye to eye contact with people? I don't know how, I mean I'm sure I would have somehow done it but I don't actually know how.

We do all care about appearance and I don't think people should be persecuted for that because that is not something to feel guilty about. I think the reason why disfigurement or burns can be taboo or uncomfortable is because we don't see them often and people don't have a great understanding of them. So it's not necessarily people being unkind, it's more ignorance and something you don't see often can be shocking or can make you more curious. So perhaps if it was seen more in the media, but not necessarily portrayed as a victim, but just portrayed as like we see the 'Dove' real women in their underwear, we know women come in different sizes. It's not jaw-droppingly shocking because we know that. But we don't really see people disfigured who look glamorous or in magazines or anything because we just don't. And that's the way society is. So if we're all conditioned in that way then yes, it will always be shocking and yes, we will always be conditioned to think that is unattractive and Cheryl Cole is attractive, because that's just the way we're conditioned.

I've been on the receiving end of two very different reactions and treatments because I've looked two very different ways, but I've also managed to go on a personal journey where I've got to the stage where I'm happy with the way I look. And if I get a bad reaction I can deal with that because I've got acceptance within myself. But I wasn't always at that place and I reacted really badly to people being shocked by my appearance and it really hurt me and I couldn't deal with it. But now that I've kind of had the support, the psychological help, the surgery and got stronger and become empowered, I can now get on with my life because I'm stronger. But it's not, I don't think it's something that if somebody looked at me and said 'Oh you know she had this massive change in appearance and she's ok', and if it happened to them they should be ok like that, because it might sometimes look like that in the media. But my journey was a very long one, with lots of psychological help, lots of steps backwards and it wasn't just overnight. I mean after this surgery I had the other day for my eyes I've got a new scar from the donor site, and I might have new scars as I go on. I think for anybody that is going through the same thing, nobody is invincible, nobody is a hero and it's never going to be plain sailing. Obviously I think my advice to anybody would be to take all the help that is given to you and that's the best way to get through things.

Acknowledgement

I would like to thank Ms Katie Piper for her time and interest in speaking to me about her experiences.

References

Abrahams, S., & Udwin, O. (2002). An evaluation of a primary care-based child clinical psychology service. *Child and Adolescent Mental Health*, 7, 107–13.

Beck, A. T. (1976). *Cognitive Therapy and the Emotional Disorders*. New York: International Universities Press

Berger, R., & Weiss, T. (2006). Posttraumatic Growth in Latina Immigrants. *Journal of Immigrant and Refugee Studies*, 4, 55–72

Borrill, C., West, M., Shapiro, D., & Rees, A. (2000). Team working and effectiveness in the NHS. *British Journal of Health Care Management*, 6, 364–71

Breakwell, G. M., & Alexander-Dunn, C. (1989). Counselling in the non-primary sector of the NHS. A study of DHAs. *Counselling*, 70, 17–25.

Cadogan, J., and Bennun, I. (2011). Face value: an exploration of the psychological impact of orthognathic surgery. *British Journal of Oral and Maxillofacial Surgery*, 49, 376–80.

Cadogan, J. Marsh, C., & Winter, R. (2009). Parents' perceptions of 4D ultra-sound scans following a diagnosis of a cleft lip and/or palate: are they worth it? *British Journal of Midwifery*, 17, 374–80.

Cadogan, J. (2011). The psychological impact of facial burn scars as a result of non-accidental injury in children. *Health Psychology Update*, 20:6–9

Care Quality Commission (2010). *Position Statement and Action Plan for Mental Health*. London: Care Quality Commission.

Carr, A. (2004). *Positive Psychology: The Science of Happiness and Human Strength*. Hove: Brunner-Routledge.

Cash, T. F., & Pruzinsky, T. (2002). *Body Image: A Handbook of Theory, Research and Clinical Practice*. London: The Guildford Press.

Cash, T. S., Winstead, B. A., & Janda, L. H. (1986). The Great American Shape Up. *Psychology Today*, 20, 30–7.

Chester, D. L., Jose, R. M., Aldlyami, E., King, H., & Moiemen, N. S. (2006). Non accidental burns in children: Are we neglecting neglect? *Burns*, 32, 222–8.

Ciechanowski, P. S., Walker, E. A., Katon, W. J., & Russo, J. E. (2002). Attachment Theory: A model for health care utilization and somatization. *Psychosomatic Medicine*, 64, 660–7.

Clarke, A., & Cooper, C. (2001). Psychological rehabilitation after disfiguring injury or disease: investigating the training needs of specialist nurses. *Journal of Advanced Nursing*, 34, 18–26.

Clinical Standards Advisory Group (1998). *Cleft Lip and/or Palate Services*. London: HMSO

Cooper, C. (2000). Face on: discovering resilience to disfigurement. *The New Therapist*, 7, 31–3.

Cronin-Stubbs, D., de Leon, C. F. M., Beckett, L. A., Field, T. S., Glynn, R. J., & Evans, D. A. (2000). Six-year effect of depressive symptoms on the course of physical disability in community-living older adults. *Archives of International Medicine*, 160, 3074–80.

Davidson, L., Connell, M., Staeheli, M., Weingarten, R., Tondora, J., & Evans, A. (2001). Concepts of recovery in behavioural health-history, review of the evidence and critique. [Draft.] Department of Psychiatry, Yale University School of Medicine.

Department of Health (2003). *National Service Framework for Children, Young People and Maternity Services: Standards for Hospital Services*. London: Department of Health

Department of Health (2009). *New Horizons: a Shared Vision for Mental Health*. London: Department of Health.

Department of Health (2010a). Ready to go? *Planning the discharge and the transfer of patients from hospital and intermediate care*. London: Department of Health.

Department of Health (2010b). *Equity and excellence: Liberating the NHS*. London: Department of Health.

National Institute for Health and Clinical Excellence. (2007). *Antenatal and Postnatal Mental Health: Clinical Management and Service Guidance (Clinical Guideline 45)*. London: National Institute for Health and Clinical Excellence.

Elliott, D. E., Bjelajac, P., Fallot, R. D., Markoff, L. S., & Glover-Reed, B. (2005). Trauma-informed or trauma-denied: Principles and implementation of trauma-informed services for women. *Journal of Community Psychology*, 33, 461–77.

Etcoff, N., Orbach, S., Scott, J., & d' Agostino, H. (2006). *Beyond Stereotypes: Rebuilding the Foundation of Beauty Beliefs:* [Findings of the 2005 Dove Global Study.] Dove Campaign for Real Beauty available from http://www.campaignforrealbeauty.com/ (accessed 5 March 2012).

Gilbert, P., & Miles, J. (2002). *Body Shame: Conceptualisation, Research and Treatment*. Hove and New York: Brunner-Routledge.

Haigh, C., Edwards, L., Hearst, D., Cropper, J., & Murray, J. (2005). Faculty for Children and Young People: British Psychological Society Annual Conference 1-3 April 2005.

Harter, S. (1999). *The Construction of Self: A Developmental Perspective*. New York: The Guildford Press

Hearst, D. (2007). Can't they like me as I am? Psychological interventions for children and young people with congenital visible disfigurement. *Developmental Neurorehabilitation*, 10, 105–12.

Hubbuck, C. (2009). *Play for Sick Children*. London: Jessica Kingsley Publishers

Kleve, L., & Robinson, E. (1999). A survey of psychological need amongst adult burn-injured patients. *Burns*, 25, 575–9.

Kleve, L., Rumsey, N., Wynn-Williams, M., & White, P. (2002). The effectiveness of cognitive-behavioural interventions provided at Outlook: A disfigurement support unit. *Journal of Evaluation in Clinical Practice*, 8, 287–95.

Koestler, A. (1952). *Arrow in the Blue*. London: Collins.

Levetown, M. (2008). Communicating with children and families: From everyday interactions to skill in conveying distressing information. *Pediatrics*, 5, 1441–60.

Linley, P. A., & Joseph, S. (2004). Positive change following trauma and adversity: A review. *Journal of Traumatic Stress*, 17, 11–21

Lovegrove, E., & Rumsey, N. (2005). Ignoring it doesn't make it stop: adolescents, appearance and anti-bullying strategies. *Cleft Palate-Craniofacial Journal*, 42, 33–44.

Luthar, S. S. (ed.) (2003). *Resilience and Vulnerability: Adaptation in the Face of Childhood Adversities*. Cambridge: Cambridge University Press.

Maddern, L., & Owen, T. (2004). The Outlook summer group: a social skills workshop for children with a different appearance who are transferring to secondary school. *Clinical Psychology*, 33, 25–9.

Maddern, L. H., Cadogan, J. C., & Emerson, M. P. (2006). 'Outlook': A psychology service for children with a different appearance. *Journal of Clinical Child Psychology and Psychiatry*, 11, 431–43.

Maunder, R. G., & Hunter, J. J. (2009). Assessing patterns of adult attachment in medical patients. *General Hospital Psychiatry*, 31, 123–30.

Meyerson, M. D. (2001). Resiliency and success in adult with Moebius syndrome. *Cleft Palate Craniofacial Journal*, 38, 232–5.

Murray, L, Cooper, P., Creswell, C., Schofield, E., & Sack, C. (2007). The effects of maternal social phobia on mother–infant interactions and infant social responsiveness. *Journal of Child Psychology and Psychiatry*, 48, 45–52.

National Burn Care Group. (2006). Psycho-social rehabilitation after burn injury. Report for the National Burn Care Group. From the Psychosocial Working Party (unpublished).

National Burn Care Review. (2001). *Standards and strategy for burn care: A review of burn care in the British Isles*. London: National Burn Care Review Committee Report.

Newell, R., & Marks, I. (2000). Phobic nature of social difficulty in facially disfigured people. *British Journal of Psychiatry*, 176, 177–81.

Pallua, N., Kunsebeck, H. W., & Noah, E. M. (2003). Psychosocial adjustments 5 years after burn injury. *Burns*, 29, 143–52.

Partridge, J. (1990). *Changing Faces*. London: Penguin.

Partridge, J., Coutinho, W., Robinson, E., & Rumsey, N. (1994). Changing Faces two years on. *Nursing Standard*, 8, 54–8.

Partridge, J., Rumsey, N., Gaskell, S., Castle, R., Phillips, C., Wisely, J., Chute, J., & O'Shaughnessy, J. (2006). *Psycho-social Rehabilitation after burn injury*. London: National Burn Care Group. Psychosocial working party, British Burns Association.

Phillips, C., & Rumsey, N. (2008). Considerations for the provision of psychosocial services for families following paediatric burn injury-A quantitative study. *Burns*, 34, 56–62

Prokhorov, A., Perry, C., Kelder, S., & Kleep, K. (1993). Lifestyle values of adolescents: results from the Minnesota Heart Health Youth Program. *Adolescence*, 28, 637–47.

Pruzinsky, T. (2004). Enhancing quality of life in medical populations: A vision for body image assessment and rehabilitation as standards of care. *Body Image*, 1, 71–81.

Robinson, E., Rumsey, N., & Partridge, J. (1996). An evaluation of the impact of social interaction skills training for facially disfigured people. *British Journal of Plastic Surgery*, 49, 281–9.

Roy-Chowdhury, S. (2010). IAPT and the death of idealism. *Clinical Psychology Forum*, 208, 25–9.

Rumsey, N., Clarke, A., White, P., Wynn-Williams, M., & Garlick, W. (2004). Altered Body Image: Appearance-related concerns of people with visible disfigurements. *Journal of Advanced Nursing*, 48, 443–53.

Rutter, M. (1985). Resilience in the face of adversity: protective factors and resistance to psychiatric disorder. *British Journal of Psychiatry*, 147, 598–611.

Rutter, M. (1987). Psychosocial Resilience and Protective Mechanisms. *American Journal of Orthopsychiatry*, 57, 316–31.

Sandy, J., Williams, A., Mildinhall, S., Murphy, T., Bearn, D., Shaw, B., Sell, D., Devlin, B., & Murray, J. (1998). The Clinical Standards Advisory Group (CSAG) Cleft Lip and Palate Study. *British Journal of Orthodontics*, 25, 21–30.

Sarwer, D. B., Pruzinsky, T. F., Goldwyn, R. M., Persing, J. A., & Whitaker, L. A. (2006). *Psychological aspects of reconstructive and cosmetic plastic surgery.* New York: Lippincott, Williams and Wilkins.

Sheldon, K., & Harding, E. (2010). *Good Practice Guidelines to support the involvement of service users and carers in clinical psychology training.* British Psychological Society, Division of Clinical Psychology.

Smythe, E. (1984). *Surviving Nursing.* New York: Bantam.

Thomas, P., Davison, S., & Rance, C. (eds.) (2001). *Clinical Counselling in Medical Settings.* Hove: Routledge.

Van Steenbergen, E., Litt, M. D and Nanda, R. (1996). Presurgical satisfaction with facial appearance in orthognathic surgery patients. *American Journal of Orthodontics and Dentofacial Orthopaedics*, 109, 653–59

Vargo, J. K., Gladwin, M., & Ngan, P. (2002). Association between ratings of facial attractiveness and patients' motivation for orthognathic surgery. *Orthodontic Craniofacial Research*, 6, 63–71.

West, M. A. (2004). *Effective Teamwork: Practical Lessons from Organizational Research (Psychology of Work and Organizations).* Oxford: BPS Blackwell.

Wiechman, S. A., Ptacek, J. T., Patterson, D. R., Gibran, N. S., Engrav, L. E., & Heimbach, D. M. (2001). Rates, Trends, and Severity of Depression after burn injuries. *Journal of Burn Care & Rehabilitation*, 22, 417–24.

Wisely, J., & Tarrier, N. (2001). A survey of the need for psychological support in a follow-up service for adult burn-injured patients. *Burns*, 27, 801–7

Wisely, J. A., Hoyle, E., Tarrier, N., & Edwards, J. (2007). Where to start? Attempting to meet the psychological needs of burned patients. *Burns*, 33, 736–46

Wood, D., Turner, G., & Straw, F. (2010). *Not just a phase: A Guide to the Participation of Children and Young People in Health Services.* London: Royal College of Paediatrics and Child Health.

CHAPTER 35

INTERVENTIONS FOR FAMILIES AND HEALTHCARE PROFESSIONALS

SUE BROWN

WHEN a baby is born with a visible facial difference, parents and families may have to overcome many challenges. Professionals caring for the child and their family can have an instrumental role in how these challenges are managed. This chapter will identify the nature of some of the challenges and, using an example of a film project, will illustrate how professional interventions can be innovative and benefit from service user involvement.

BACKGROUND

Some visible facial differences can be identified in an unborn baby during the antenatal period by scanning techniques. Other visible facial differences in the baby are only discovered at the time of birth. A facial cleft, for example, occurs in the fetus at about 5–11 weeks of gestation. In the UK, a cleft is often detected during an ultrasound scan at about 20 weeks of gestation (Hodgkinson et al., 2005). There has been much debate amongst parents and health professional about the advantages and disadvantages for parents in knowing about the cleft before the baby's birth.

In cases where the parents find out before birth, it is often argued that this knowledge allows parents time to begin to adjust the child's visible difference before the baby is born (Escalon et al., 2011). However, parents who find out at the time of birth have often said that had they known about the cleft antenatally, they would only have worried throughout the time of the pregnancy and that the pregnancy would have been 'spoiled'. Clinical experience suggests that knowledge before birth tends to result in a more positive birthing experience and early contact with specialist teams can be made. However, timing may not be the most important factor. The way that the news of the baby's cleft is given, the quality and accuracy of the information about the cleft, and the support that is then offered seem, clinically, to be significant factors in parental adjustment. Individual and family factors such as coping style, mood, anxiety, beliefs, meaning, life experiences, and personality are also possible moderators of adjustment.

ADJUSTMENT PROCESSES

Understanding and processing the phenomenon

Congenital facial differences such as clefting are not very common (Hodgkinson et al., 2005). For many parents, families, and some health professionals, the discovery of a visible facial difference is a novel experience. Making an accurate and timely diagnosis means the condition can be described and appropriate terminology applied. This may enable people to link information they have about a phenomenon with what they are seeing in the baby. A diagnosis can also enable specialist help to be accessed and a care plan to be created. Parents and families can begin to process the phenomenon and gather information.

Reactions to the visible facial difference

It can be quite shocking when a baby is discovered to have a visible facial difference. Initial reactions of disgust, horror, anxiety, disbelief, and rejection are common. However, there may also be positive or neutral reactions to the visible difference. When initial reactions are less positive people can experience guilt and may feel ashamed of these reactions. In some cases, the events surrounding the discovery can be psychologically traumatizing and the symptoms of trauma can be enduring.

Loss

Prior to, and during pregnancy, parents 'to be' and family members will have fantasized about their baby. They may have imagined how the baby will look, what the baby will be like, and what kind of life they will have with the baby. When a baby is discovered to have a visible facial difference, this fantasy may have to be abandoned, at least in the short term. Parents and family members may need to grieve for the loss of the imagined baby and it may take them some time and effort to assimilate the new information about the baby's appearance and what will happen as a consequence of the visible facial difference (Despars et al., 2011). Guilt and feelings of shame can occur as people psychologically revisit the fantasy and wish for that baby rather than the one they actually have.

Search for cause and meaning

There is often a desire or a need to have an explanation for why the difference has occurred. In many cases, modern medicine has yet to establish causes for these differences (Hodgkinson et al., 2005).

Many people will attribute blame or cause to factors that have been implicated in other areas of health. They may scrutinize their own behaviour or the behaviour of others in relation to these perceived risk factors and believe that they have found a cause when in fact they may have only have found a coincidence. Clinically people have reported that they blame the difference on smoking, alcohol, recreational drugs, environmental factors, diet, genetics, and stress. This search for explanation is part of normal adjustment but this process can result in increased anxiety, self- or partner blame, or feelings of guilt and shame. A study by Nelson et al. (2009) found that parents of children born with a cleft lip and/or palate who tended to make internal and self-blaming attributions had significantly higher levels of anxiety and perceived stress.

Thoughts about the baby's future

When a discovery of a visible facial difference is made, people also have to make plans for the future. This often involves acquiring information about treatment options for surgery. In some cases there may be an established care pathway for the child that has been well documented and is both clear and predictable. This can help people to feel more secure and may reduce the anxiety associated with uncertainty.

Some parental distress relates to the perceived social stigma of a visible difference. Parents themselves may have previously adhered to negative views of people who look 'different' and may feel guilty about this when their own child has a visible difference. They may have experienced uncomfortable social contact themselves involving others with a visible difference or observed it happening to other people. They may fear stigmatization and have strong desires to protect their child.

As the parents and family imagine the baby becoming a child they may envisage that the visible facial difference will give the child a vulnerability to psychological or social problems. Parents often express fears that their child will be bullied or stigmatized in some way, or that the child's quality of life will be affected. Some parents comment that the gender of their child can make a difference to how worried they feel. This seems to relate to beliefs that a girl's appearance is a more important factor in social success than that of a boy.

Time to adjustment

A qualitative study in Sweden (Johansson et al., 2004), found that parents reported emotional trauma after giving birth to a baby with a cleft but they slowly adjusted to the difference. Stage models described in loss and bereavement work, suggest periods of shock, numbness, disbelief, and anger in reaction to death (Moorey, 1997). Clinically these models can be helpful in normalizing reactions and extreme emotion in relation to the baby's visible difference. However, it is also important to recognize the effects of coping style on this adjustment. Stroebe and Schut (1999) suggest a Dual Processing Model. In this model the person oscillates between two processes. In one they face the grief of giving up the idealized child and in the other they attend, and reinvest in, aspects of their life involving the new baby and the new challenges to be faced. Individual factors such as comorbid anxiety or depression may impact on the process, as could family or systemic factors.

MENTAL HEALTH

There are many challenges and adjustments for parents and families to make with the birth of a new baby. Changing roles, economic pressures, sleep deprivation, and lack of time for oneself are just some of the changes that an individual may perceived as a threat and which they may not feel able to manage (Lazarus, 1966). The impact of these challenges on maternal mental health is evident from research that shows increased risk of maternal anxiety, worry and depression (Heron et al., 2004, Ross & McLean, 2006; Phillips et al., 2009). Much of the literature has focused on maternal well-being but increasingly the prevalence of mental health difficulties in new fathers is being recognized (Paulson et al., 2010). In addition to the distress suffered by the parents who develop mental health problems at this time or whose mental health problems are exacerbated, there are also possible consequences for the baby. When mothers are depressed there is more likelihood of there being insecure or disorganized infant–mother attachment (Martins, 2000). The effect of maternal depression is also being hypothesized as being a causal factor in poorer cognitive outcomes in the child (Sutter-Dallay, 2011). Where mothers experience trauma or loss there is an association with insecure or disorganized attachment in the infant (Wan, 2009).

Maternal anxiety is also known to have an effect on the infant–mother relationship. Figueirdo et al., (2009) reported that maternal anxiety during pregnancy predicted poorer emotional involvement with the infant after birth as well as higher maternal anxiety and depression at 3 months after delivery. Kurth et al. (2010) found that infant crying problems were more commonly reported to, and recorded by, midwives when the mother had physical, psychological, and social problems.

The longer-term effects of these maternal issues on the child in later life is less well supported by research, though clinically well documented. One suggestion is that there will be a poorer ability to form secure and meaningful adult relationships and a continued transmission of attachment problems to future generations (Wan, 2009).

It seems evident that parental mental health problems can impact on the developing child. However, it is not clear whether a baby's visible difference significantly impacts on their parent's mental health and adjustment or if it does, whether this has negative consequences for the child.

Speltz el al. (1997) found that babies with clefts were not at elevated risk of insecure attachments at the end of their first year. However, Despars et al. (2011) found that mothers had higher post-traumatic stress symptoms when their baby had a cleft compared with a normative sample. Mothers with higher ratings were found to have had less secure attachment representations.

PARENT-REPORTED NEEDS

Parental views about what they needed at the time of the discovery of a visible facial difference have been reported in the literature. Kuttenberger et al. (2010) contacted 105 Swiss parents whose child was born with a cleft lip and/or palate. They reported that parents wanted information about surgery, feeding, and the aetiology of clefts.

Broder et al. (1985) concluded that parents wanted counselling to help provide facts about the birth difference, to alleviate guilt, dispel misperceptions, discuss decisions, and facilitate coping. Knapke et al. (2010) surveyed a small number of North American parents about their needs in relation to their child's cleft. Responders wanted better quality and more specific information about their child's cleft and about feeding issues. They said they would like healthcare providers to have more education about cleft lip and palate and wanted to be able to access the internet for reliable information. They also said that it would be helpful if there was consistency of information between providers of healthcare. Johansson et al. (2004) suggested that parental experiences could be used to help educate the public and health professionals about cleft lip and palate and the needs of parents as they adjust.

From this review of the literature, there is evidence that parental anxiety or mood factors before or after birth can impact on the infant's attachment and cognitive development. Having a baby with a visible difference is potentially stressful, upsetting, and traumatizing. In the longer term, parents generally adjust well and do not suffer from clinical depression or anxiety relating to the visible facial difference when the child is older. However, the extent of trauma, anxiety, and mood changes at or around the time of the discovery has not really been researched. Parents identify that they have needs for information and counselling at this time to help them to gain factual knowledge about the difference, the treatment available as well as help to deal with the emotional aspects of such a discovery.

FACILITATING ADJUSTMENT AND PSYCHOLOGICAL WELL-BEING

In a major reconfiguration of cleft lip and palate services in the UK over the past decade, the psychosocial aspects of clefting have been acknowledged and as a consequence many cleft centres routinely offer informational care and counselling to parents and children (CSAG, 1998). These interventions are primarily offered by the cleft specialist nurse, who may refer the parents or children to psychologists, the genetics team, or other members of the cleft team depending on the particular needs of the individuals. Internal audits suggest that parents and children value this service and feel that some of their informational and support needs are being met.

In addition to one-to-one counselling, teams offer other forms of social support to parents and children, for example, in the form of baby and toddler groups where there is the opportunity to meet other parents and their children or antenatal support groups. The Cleft Lip and Palate Association (CLAPA), a UK charity set up to help those affected by clefting, offer supported parental introductions. This enables parents to meet others who have been through the experience who can offer advice and support. Many cleft centres also introduce parents to each other for the same reasons.

As well as this direct information and support to children and families, it is also recognized that part of the role of cleft teams is to aid the development of knowledge of other health, social, and education services about cleft lip and palate. Teams attempt to address systemic factors such as misinformation, late diagnosis, or poor quality disclosure of diagnosis through the provision of written information and teaching sessions.

A SERVICE USER PROJECT

Local evaluations and clinical work suggested that despite high levels of satisfaction with the informational care and support offered to families by the cleft lip and palate team, there were instances of late diagnosis, poor disclosure, and misinformation that caused distress to parents and families. In some instances parents' need for information led them to search the Internet which often resulted in unhelpful material being accessed. The team in Newcastle, UK, had offered a series of teaching sessions in maternity units with a view to increasing awareness about cleft lip and palate and the importance of a timely referral. However, the ongoing occurrence of late diagnoses, late referrals to the team, and negative accounts from parents seemed to suggest that an alternative approach was needed.

An idea was developed to explore the potential benefit of film to address some of these issues. It was proposed that by consulting with parents and families across the geographical region served by a particular team it would be possible to develop themes and topics to be covered that would reflect the informational care and support needs of families.

Film has many potential advantages over other forms of communication; it can be used as an interactive tool, in that people can watch it but also have supported discussion about the content and how the film makes them feel; viewers can choose to stop or restart watching at their own pace. Whilst counselling sessions can be stopped too, they are rarely so flexible that the person can resume at exactly the time they feel ready to begin to engage with the issues again. The message portrayed in the film also promotes consistency to ensure that the same information is given to all people and is not subject to the individual variations that can occur when information and support are given one to one. As with psychological therapy and counselling, film also has the potential to change attitudes and address misperceptions. It can be accessed by a wider number of people than traditional face-to-face contacts. Film also has the advantage of being appealing to people who might opt out of one-to-one counselling for practical reasons such as not being able to get time off work, because they do not recognize the need in themselves or because they feel that the counselling process is stigmatizing or a sign of weakness.

A review of the literature highlights that film has been used successfully to change attitudes and knowledge in a range of health-related areas: HIV-related risk and stigma (Lapinski, 2008); knowledge and psychological effects of overeating (Cottone, 2007); stigmatization of people who are obese (Hennings, 2007); stigmatization of people with schizophrenia by medical students (Altindag, 2006); and stigmatization of people who experience auditory hallucinations (Brown, 2010). Film has also been used successfully to educate health professionals about the psychosocial needs of people with brain tumours and their caregivers (Rabow, 2010).

Initially it was envisaged that only one version of the film was needed. However, after a joint meeting with health professionals and parents it seemed that two films, each with their own emphasis on particular issues were needed.

Parent consultants were recruited to work with the team to develop the scope for the film and to lead five 'Parent Consultation Meetings' across the northern region of the Northern and Yorkshire Cleft Service. These meetings were led by one of the parent consultants, Angela Porritt, using key themes that had been identified from research literature, CLAPA reports, local evaluations, and the clinical experience of cleft team members. They were:

- Experiences of disclosure; how the news of the baby's cleft was given. What effects this had in terms of reaction, recall of information, and parental adjustment.
- Time taken for the parents to be referred to the specialist team: the effects of a delay in this referral taking place, the advantages and disadvantages of the early contact.
- The informational care needs of parents from the time the discovery was made through to the child's early years and the approaches parents took to meet these needs.
- The emotional needs of parents from the time the discovery was made, the approaches parents took to meet these needs, and what helped with this process.

Professional stakeholder views were also sought. A formal meeting with key stakeholders was held and suggestions on what should be included in the film to address health professionals' needs were elicited. Institutions offering training to health professionals likely to be caring for people with a birth difference were contacted to elicit interest and support.

Parental Consultations

At the time of discovery of the cleft

Parents reported positive experiences of discovery and disclosure as well as negative ones. Several parents reported that when the cleft was diagnosed on scan they had a sense that there was something wrong long before the sonographer told them. 'She went really quiet. Like she suddenly started to pay extra attention. She went out of the room and brought someone else with her. After what seemed like ages the more senior one said that the baby had a cleft'.

Another parent reported, 'She [the sonographer] said they had found a problem with the baby. It sounded really serious. I wondered if anything else could be wrong'. Another parents reported, 'The sonographer said she had seen something and that she needed to get someone else. We waited ten minutes with me just lying on the bed. We could hear whispered conversations'. This parent went on to reflect about the worries and upset that she and her partner were feeling at this time.

At the time of birth some parents said there was a delay in them seeing the baby or in the baby being put 'skin to skin'. One dad said, 'we just wanted someone to tell us what was wrong but no one did'. Another father said that when his baby was born, he and his partner knew the baby was going to have a cleft due to antenatal diagnosis so felt well prepared. However, he was really angry when at the baby's birth the midwife covered the baby's mouth with a blanket and told him to look at her eyes. Another dad said, 'when he was born, everyone just went dead silent'. A mum reported how she had been feeling, 'After he was born, I didn't want to speak to anyone, I was so angry that it had happened'.

There were many parental reports of shock and disbelief. 'I was so shocked that I can't remember what was said by the first lady we saw'; 'I felt like I should have been crying'; 'I was just in shock, I couldn't take it in'. 'I was shocked and crying but I was just sitting there'.

Another parent described her reaction, 'When she said "slight problem", my heart was coming out of my chest, I was really emotional, thoughts were whizzing round my head'. Another parent reported that the sonographer became quiet during the scan. The parent said she had a sense that there was something wrong. The sonographer reportedly said, 'I think your baby has got a cleft lip, I need to get a colleague to check with me'. The colleague seemed to come quickly and confirmed the diagnosis. She reported being offered immediate support and being taken to a quiet room where she could talk to a staff member straight away. The parent thought that the sonographer was sensitive and that this approach helped her to take in the news.

There were also reports of the use of outmoded and stigmatizing labels by health professionals. 'Your baby has got a harelip'; 'your baby has got a facial deformity'; 'Your baby has a defect'. But there were also reports of parents not knowing the term 'cleft lip and palate' and having no concept of what a cleft might be. As this parent conveys when her baby was born without an antenatal diagnosis, 'It's got a hole in its head!'.

The magnitude of loss was reported by many parents reflecting in this parent's words, 'In my little world, the day she told me, it was the worst thing'. A dad reported, 'For me it was as if someone had died'.

Some parents reported that the health professionals looking after them became emotional in reaction to the discovery of the cleft. 'The midwife started to cry. We had to say, "it's alright"'. Another parent reported that the doctor seemed anxious.

Informational care needs

Many parents reported a strong need for information. They said that they needed to hear the same information over and over. 'You need to hear it and absorb it, then hear it again'. A dad reflected on common experiences reported at the meetings, 'You go on the internet even though they tell you not to. You look at the worst end of the scale'.

There were strong views expressed about the importance of early contact with the cleft specialist nurse as reflected in this parent's views, 'As soon as the cleft nurse came, I felt in safe hands. She listened to my questions and answered them. Then I would ask the same questions again the next time. She didn't mind that I kept asking over and over again'. Another parent said, 'It was easier to go through the pregnancy as there was so much support'.

In one hospital parents were given a file called the 'Harelip File' which contained leaflets and photographs. Parents reported this was not helpful as they could not relate it to their baby. Another parent commented about a leaflet she had been given at the maternity hospital saying, 'it was about 400 years out of date'.

Many parents reported having been given information that was not correct. This included misinformation about the formation of the cleft, causes of clefting, surgery details, and feeding. On the issue of surgery, some parents were told the baby would be operated on within the week, others were told within a month. Neither reflected current practice.

As one parent summarizes, 'Before the specialist nurse arrived I got all of the wrong information at all of the wrong times'.

Causes

Parents reported that they searched for cause and meaning. One parent reported her worries, 'I thought I was being punished for something'. Another parent told the group, 'I asked the doctor who said he was not really sure about the cause'. In a personal quest for understanding about causation, one parent said, 'I wondered if it was caused by the amniocentesis, lack of folic acid or the flight I went on'. Another parents said she had worried about the glass of wine she had drank when she was pregnant.

In some cases, parents did not worry themselves about their role in causation but did worry about what other people might assume about their role in causation. For example, that they could have caused the cleft through smoking or drinking in pregnancy. One parent recalled being told that the cleft was caused by not taking folic acid during pregnancy. 'I was already feeling horrible, worrying it was something I did or didn't do'.

For parents who had a cleft themselves, there were sometime additional difficulties as this mum conveys, 'I blamed myself, I passed it on. It really helped when professionals said it wasn't my fault'.

At one of the meetings a group suggested that they would have found it helpful if they had been told by 'a very clinical person' that the cleft was not their fault. They thought the person needed to be able to convey experience, confidence and skill to get this message across successfully.

Emotional needs

Parents reported that there was a fine balance to strike for professionals. On the one hand they wanted to know that professionals took the news seriously and understood the significance for the parents. On the other, they wanted professionals to reassure them that the baby's cleft could be repaired and to instil a sense of hope for their child's future. As one parent reported, 'There seemed to be a lack of understanding of my reaction. The doctor seemed flippant to me'. Another parent commented, 'It's important to be allowed to be upset. I felt guilty that I had made a fuss ... that I was some kind of hysterical woman. I needed permission to say how I was feeling'.

Parents reported high levels of worry about how other people would react and what the future would hold for their child. On parent reported, 'When other people got upset, this upset me'. Another commented, 'I felt guilty that I was so upset when in the scheme of things she is fine now'. In relation to the reaction of others, a dad's reactions reflected common views on the perceived need to protect themselves and their child, 'At first I thought it was better that he was a boy, now I realise it doesn't matter'. 'I was worried about how other people might behave, would they stare? I was like a guard dog when we took her out'. A mum said, 'I felt shy and thought everyone was waiting for my reactions when I took her out. I took to saying to people, this is my baby and she has a cleft lip. I didn't feel that I should have to do that though'.

Views about the films

Parents said that the early weeks and months after the discovery of the cleft had been a highly stressful time for them. There was a consensus that film might be a helpful medium to address some of the issues raised in the meetings. In addition to helping professionals know about clefting and the needs of parents and families, it was agreed that film also had potential to help 'new' parents to gain knowledge and understanding of clefting. They said it was important to include the experiences of parents whose children had been though surgery and who were well into their childhood. They also said it would be good to have older children in the film to help parents see that their child can grow and develop just like any other child.

THE NEXT STAGE

A steering group made up of members of the cleft lip and palate team was convened to oversee the production of the films. This included a representative to manage the financial, clinical, and administrative components. Funding was sought from charities and private commercial companies. CLAPA were very supportive of the project and made a significant donation as well as a commitment to promote the films and help with distribution.

The project leaders commissioned a film company to write the scripts for the two films, which were then edited to ensure that the information from the consultation meetings was appropriately addressed.

Parents who had been involved in the consultation meeting were approached to contribute to the film. In the course of hearing about the film being produced, other participants were identified to share their experiences which were also used to illustrate key points made during the parent consultations meetings.

It was decided that the film needed to be a composite of factual and experiential material. Some issues are addressed by professional 'experts' whilst others are addressed by parent 'experts'. The film would be separated into named chapters enabling viewers to select the most relevant parts of the film, parts of the film they felt able to cope with or alternatively, so that sections could be viewed in an order to fit their experience.

To address knowledge and understanding of clefting, the films have an introductory description by a cleft surgeon of the different types of cleft that a baby can have. This includes photographs of babies before and after their primary surgery. A common theme during the consultation process was the often painful speculation parents go through about the aetiology of clefting. Hence, 'up-to-date' information on aetiology is incorporated and permission for the parents to relinquish blame is given by an expert geneticist. Information about parental experiences of finding out about the baby's cleft is addressed though personal accounts that try to reflect the variety of reported experiences gathered during the consultation meetings. Information about the specific feeding needs of babies with palatal clefts is illustrated with coverage of babies feeding. The importance of contact with the cleft specialist nurse for expert feeding advice is stressed.

The care pathway is described to help parents feel more certain about what they can expect in terms of assessment and treatment. The worries that parents reported at the consultation meetings about the reactions of other people to their baby's cleft, the fears they had about bonding with the baby and the concerns about the future for their child as they progress through childhood are also described in the film. It is hoped that by hearing other parents talk through these worries, indirect emotional support can be obtained. Hearing also that many of these anxieties did not come to fruition is also hopefully reassuring for parents and families. Lastly, the films give information about additional support that can be accessed by parents, families, and health professionals.

At the time of writing, the project was nearing completion. The next major challenge is to ensure that the films reach their target audiences. At the beginning of the project it was envisaged that the parent version of the film would be offered to parents and families via the specialist teams and that members of the teams would be present when the film was seen. It was also envisaged that specific parts of the film would be used to enhance the work of the teams and to back up the information that they were giving to families. In the time it took to complete the project, the role of the Internet in people's lives has generally increased. It is often the first place people go to for information and sites such as 'You Tube' and 'Google' have revolutionized the accessibility of personal experiences of birth differences such as cleft lip and palate. In discussion with CLAPA we agreed that a link to the parent film would be made available on the internet through their website but that we would give viewing guidance and contact details for viewers who might need some support after watching the film. The guidance will also stress that the film is intended to enhance the work of the specialist teams and not to act as a replacement of any kind.

CLAPA also agreed to advertise the film on their website and in their newsletters. One of the parents involved in the project very kindly agreed to host the film via the CLAPA link. Those people who do not have ready access to the Internet will be able to obtain a copy of the film by contacting CLAPA or the cleft specialist nurse in their local team. We also hope to set up a way for parents and families to give feedback about the film which will help to identify how the resource could be improved.

It is envisaged that it will be more difficult to target and reach audiences for the professional version of the film. We know from both parent and professional consultations that sonographers, midwives, healthcare assistants, nurses, doctors, and health visitors can sometimes lack experience and knowledge about cleft lip and palate. We also know that the prevalence rates for cleft lip and palate are relatively low and as such may mean that that any given professional may very rarely encounter the phenomenon. Therefore the incentive to learn may be quite low until that encounter occurs, by which time it might be too late for the films to be of benefit to the parents or family. A further problem is the diversity of professional groups that we wish to target and the sheer number of departments and centres we need to reach. Early contact with training and professional organizations indicated an interest and willingness to disseminate the film. Further contact with these organizations is needed to get the film accepted as a training resource. Most cleft teams undertake periodic training sessions within women's health and maternity units. This film can be used to supplement the training and an Internet link is another option to ensure accessibility.

REFERENCES

Altindag, A., Yanik, M., Ucok, A., Alptekin, K., & Ozkan, M. (2006). Effects of an antistigma program on medical students' attitude towards people with schizophrenia. *Psychiatry Clinical Neuroscience*, 60, 283–8.

Broder, H. & Trier, W. C. (1985). Effectiveness of genetic counselling for families with craniofacial anomalies. *The Cleft Palate-Craniofacial Journal*, 22, 157–62.

Brown, S., Evans, Y., Espenschade, K., & O'Connor, M. (2010). An examination of two brief stigma reduction strategies: Filmed personal contact and hallucination stimulations. *Community Mental Health Journal*, 46, 494–8.

Cleft Lip and Palate Association. (2007). *Regionalisation of cleft lip and palate services: has it worked?* London: CLAPA.

Sandy, J., Williams, A., Mildinhall, S., Murphy, T., Bearn, D., Shaw, B., *et al.* (1998) The Clinical Standards Advisory Group (CSAG) Cleft Lip and Palate Study. *British Journal of Orthodontics*, 25, 21–30.

Cottone, E. & Byrd-Bredbenner, C. (2007). Knowledge and psychosocial effects of the super size me on young adults. *Journal of the American Dietetic Association*, 107, 1197–203.

Despars, J., Peter, C., Borghini, A., Pierrehumbert, B., Habersaat, S., Muller-Nix, C., *et al.* (2011). Impact of a cleft lip and/or palate on maternal stress and attachment representations. *The Cleft Palate-Craniofacial Journal*, 48, 419–24.

Escalon, J., Huissoud, C., Bisch, C., Gonnaud, F., Fichez, A., & Rudigoz, R. (2011). Parental impact of 3D/4D ultrasonography in fetal cleft lip and palate. *Gynecology, Obstetrics and Fertility*, 38, 101–4.

Figueiredo, B. & Costa, R. (2009). Mother's stress, mood and emotional involvement with the infant: 3 months before and 3 months after childbirth. *Archives of Women's Mental Health*, 12, 143–53.

Hennings, A., Hilbert, A., Thomas, J., Siegfried, W., & Rief, W. (2007). Reduction of stigma against obese people: effects of an educational film. *Psychotherapy Psychosomatic Medical Psychology*, 57, 359–63.

Heron, J., O'Connor, T., Evans, J., Golding, J., Glover, V. The APSPAC Study Team. (2004). The course of anxiety and depression through pregnancy and the post partum period in a community sample. *Journal of Affective Disorders*, 80, 65–73.

Hodgkinson, P., Brown, S., Duncan, D., Grant, C., McNaughton, A., Thomas, P., & Mattick, C. (2005). Management of children with cleft lip and palate: A review describing the application of a multidisciplinary team working in this condition based upon the experiences of a regional cleft lip and palate centre in the untied Kingdom. *Fetal and Maternal Medicine Review*, 16, 1–27.

Johansson, B. & Ringsberg, K. (2004). Parents' experiences of having a child with cleft lip and palate. *Journal of Advanced Nursing*, 47, 165–73.

Knapke, S., Bender, P., Prows, C., Schultz, J., & Saal, H. (2010). Parental perspectives of children born with cleft lip/and or palate: A qualitative assessment of suggestions for healthcare improvements and interventions. *Cleft Palate-Craniofacial Journal*, 47, 2, 143–50.

Kubler-Ross, E. & Kessler, D. (1997). *Life Lessons: Two Experts on Death and Dying Teach Us About the Mysteries of Life and Living*. New York: Touchstone.

Kurth, E., Spichiger, E., Cignacco, E., Kennedy, H., Glanzmann, R., Schmid, M., *et al.* 2010, Predictors of crying problems in the early postpartum period. *Journal of Obstetrics Gynecology and Neonatal Nursing*, 39, 250–62.

Kuttenberger, J., Ohmer, J., & Polska, E. (2010). Initial counselling for cleft lip and palate: parents' evaluation, needs and expectations. *International Journal of Oral and maxillofacial Surgery*, 39, 214–20.

Lapinski M, Nwulu P. (2008). Can a short film impact HIV-related risk and stigma perceptions? Results from an experiment in Abuja, Nigeria. *Health Community*, 23, 403–12.

Lazarus, R. S. (1966). *Psychological Stress and the Coping Process*. New York: McGraw-Hill

Martins, C. & Gaffan, E. (2000). Effects of early maternal depression on patterns of infant-mother attachment: A meta-analytic investigation. *Journal of Child Psychology and Psychiatry*, 41, 737–46.

Moorey S. (1997). When bad things happen to rational people. In P. Salkovskis (ed.) *Frontiers of Cognitive Therapy. The State of the Art and Beyond*, pp. 450–69. New York: Guildford Publishers.

Neimeyer, R., Baldwin, A., & Gillies, J. (2006). Continuing bonds and reconstructing meaning: mitigating complications in bereavement. *Death Studies*, 30, 714–38.

Nelson, J., O'Leary, C., & Weinman, J. (2009). Causal attributions in parents of babies with a cleft lip and/or palate and their associations with psychological well-being. *Cleft Palate-Craniofacial Journal*, 46, 425–34.

Paulson, J. & Bazemore, S. (2010). Prenatal and postpartum depression in fathers and its association with maternal depression: A meta-analysis. *Journal of the American Medical Association*, 303, 1961–69

Phillips, J., Sharoe, L., Matthey, S., & Charles, M. (2009). Maternally focused worry. *Archives of Women's Mental Health*, 12, 409–418.

Rabow, M., Goodman, S., Chang, S., Berger, M., & Folkman, S. (2010). Filming the family: A documentary film to educate clinicians about family caregivers of patients with brain tumors. *Journal of Cancer Education*, 25, 242–6.

Ross, L.E., McLean, L.M. (2006). Anxiety disorders during pregnancy and the postpartum period: A systematic review. *Journal of Clinical Psychiatry*, 67(8), 1285–98.

Speltz, M., Endriga, M., Fisher, P., & Mason, C. (1997). Early predictors of attachment in infants with cleft lip and/or palate. *Child Development*, 68, 12–25.

Stroebe, M., and Schut, H. (1999). The dual process model of coping with bereavement: Rationale and description. *Death Studies*, 23, 197–224.

Sutter-Dallay, A., Murray, L., Dequae-Merchadou, L., Glatigny-Dallay, E., Bourgeois, M., & Verdoux, H. (2011). A prospective longitudinal study of the impact of early postnatal vs. chronic maternal depressive symptoms on child development. *European Psychiatry*, 2011, 26, 489–9.

Wan, M. & Green, J. (2009). The impact of maternal psychopathology on child-mother attachment. *Archives of Women's Mental Health*, 12, 123–34.

CHAPTER 36

REGULATION OF COSMETIC SURGERY

ALEX CLARKE

We have reached a stage where public expectation, driven by media hype and, dare one say, professional greed, has brought us to a 'perfect storm' in the cosmetic surgical market (British Association of Aesthetic Plastic Surgeons, 2009).

THIS chapter reviews the general principles of regulation and considers in detail the regulatory framework in the UK. Problems inherent in the current arrangements are highlighted and comparisons are made with the situation in France. The current framework of self-regulation by the profession offers little protection to patients in the UK and no protection from cosmetic tourism either to patients travelling abroad for procedures or by incompetent providers travelling briefly to the UK. The cost to the NHS, where patients experience painful or life-threatening complications is a further driver for change. As yet, governments have proved reluctant to legislate for robust regulation of cosmetic procedures, presenting this as the responsibility of the various professional groups. The result is a stand-off in which patients remain vulnerable and the reputation of the profession is damaged.

DEFINITION OF COSMETIC SURGERY

The definition of cosmetic surgery is important because this lies at the heart of the distinction between how cosmetic practice and other medical practice is differentiated. According to the Expert Group on the Regulation of Cosmetic Surgery: Report to the Chief Medical Officer (Department of Health, 2005), cosmetic procedures comprise:

Operations and other procedures that revise or change the appearance, colour, texture, structure or position of bodily features which most would consider otherwise to be within the broad range of 'normal' *for that person* (p. 3).

One problem with this definition is that many people undergoing cosmetic procedures do so because they perceive their appearance to lie outside the norm. Objectively they may appear unremarkable in comparison with a peer group, but the motivation for surgery is subjectively determined, often with reference to an 'ideal' appearance driven by inappropriate comparisons. There is no relationship between the objective appearance and its psychological impact (Moss, 2005; Ong et al., 2007). Therefore the implicit suggestion that cosmetic surgery is a lifestyle choice, thus optional or even trivial, ignores the considerable distress that many people experience in relation to their appearance and the vulnerability of groups that associate a change of appearance with a significant benefit in terms of lifestyle. It is arguable that this group are potentially much more vulnerable and ill equipped to make an informed decision compared with people undertaking procedures which are much better regulated.

This misperception of the nature of cosmetic procedures is arguably prevalent not only in the media and amongst patients but also at the organizational level. Within the UK's NHS, cosmetic procedures are largely unavailable, but in practice, patient requests are often managed through the low-priority treatment pathways set up by most funding bodies. Cook et al. (2003) have described the inconsistencies in how these pathways operate, even where clear assessment frameworks are in place, such as that developed by Clarke et al. (2005). Implicit in these arrangements is the idea that some interventions, such as surgery to treat varicose veins and most cosmetic surgical procedures, are unnecessary or trivial, and can therefore be refused without offering other forms of intervention. Cordeiro et al. (2010) have examined the utility of reconstructive/cosmetic distinctions in decision-making for facial patients, and have demonstrated that patients requesting cosmetic procedures are significantly more distressed in comparison with those who have functional or disease-related conditions which qualify them for reconstructive procedures. Not only are cosmetic surgery guidelines applied inconsistently, but the basis on which treatment is offered is completely counter to the evidence of greatest need. Cordeiro and colleagues argue that it is the underlying perception that cosmetic surgery is 'trivial' that underpins these anomalies. Similarly at the level of government, the idea that cosmetic surgery is unimportant is quite clear. Foad Nahai, President of the International Society of Aesthetic Plastic Surgery (ISAPS) and former President of the American Society for Aesthetic Plastic Surgery (ASAPS), has suggested that

Governments are reluctant to become involved in regulation, as they see this issue as a 'turf battle' between various physician groups and not a public safety or patient safety issue.

However, there is no question that this is a patient safety issue of paramount importance and I take our governments to task for not addressing it (Nahai, 2009).

The lack of research into the patients' expectations and satisfaction with outcome after cosmetic surgery is a further gap which means that treatment decisions and recommendations for good practice are founded on the basis of inaccurate assumptions, the most significant of which is arguably the idea that surgery is simply a lifestyle choice. For some people it may be simply that, but for many it is a last resort made on the basis of significant perceived need and unhappiness, and built on unrealistic expectations of change.

PRINCIPLES OF REGULATION

The general principles of regulation rest on providing information about the procedure and the provider with the goal of allowing the individual to make an informed decision. As defined by the *Expert Group on the Regulation of Cosmetic Surgery: Report to the Chief Medical Officer* (Department of Health, 2005), they place a major responsibility for outcome on the individual seeking surgery: people need to know that treatment will be safe, that the medical and other practitioners who treat them have appropriate qualifications, and that they have information necessary to make informed decisions. But after that, it is up to them to check on their providers: 'Regulation cannot deal with whether or not patients have realistic expectations or are satisfied with the aesthetic outcomes of the procedures they have undergone, or whether or not they have made adequate enquiries on their own behalf in advance' (p. 11).

There is a real question about whether this is an adequate position. Applied to any other form of medical intervention it appears cursory, and there is no mention of the part played by the media in promoting surgery as a panacea for success and happiness. There is a sharp contrast between this definition and the regulatory requirements associated with eliciting informed consent in a research trial, even where the patient is simply completing a questionnaire. Similarly, the idea that the patient needs to do their own research about a procedure is absent in the consent process for any surgical procedures in the NHS.

REGULATION IN THE UK

The tremendous growth in the popularity of cosmetic surgery has been described elsewhere in this book (see Chapter 25), and with this growth in the number of procedures (34,000 carried out by The British Association of Aesthetic Plastic Surgeons (BAAPS) members in 2009) comes a proliferation of providers.

BAAPS estimates that there are in the region of 200,000 providers in the UK operating from 5,000 premises. These vary from accredited surgeons offering high quality services, to Botox® 'parties' run from unlicensed premises such as hotels where alcohol is on offer at the same time.

Attempts to regulate practice have been limited by the debate about where responsibility lies, with the professional bodies such as British Association of Plastic, Reconstructive & Aesthetic Surgeons (BAPRAS) and BAAPS, with the Department of Health (DoH) or with the individual accessing surgery. In England, all health and adult social care is regulated by the Care Quality Commission (CQC), formerly the Health Care Commission (HCC). This means that all hospitals and healthcare providers have a statutory responsibility to deliver care that is safe and of a high standard. Independent hospitals are required to meet the standards for all hospitals. However, because cosmetic procedures are perceived to be purely elective, provided only in the independent sector and are not perceived to be 'therapeutic' healthcare, they do not fit the criteria for organizational regulation via the CQC. This is another example of a problem arising from a fundamental misunderstanding of the nature of cosmetic surgery and the motivation of many of the people to undergo it. While all services offering cosmetic surgery should be registered and inspected, the CQC has no remit to seek out unlicensed clinics, so there is effectively no protection for patients from unscrupulous providers.

Interestingly, a MORI poll commissioned by the Expert Group on the Regulation of Cosmetic Surgery (Department of Health, 2005) demonstrated that people were generally ignorant about the extent of regulation, with 64% believing that cosmetic procedures should be regulated in the same way as other medical and surgical procedures. Whilst 56% of people felt that it was the individual's responsibility to check the qualifications of the surgeon they approached, the remainder felt that this should be done variously by the GP, the hospital or clinic, or British Medical Association (BMA). Nevertheless, cosmetic surgery accounted for 34% of complaints about acute (all private and voluntary healthcare) care to the HCC in 2003/4.

REPORT OF THE EXPERT GROUP ON THE REGULATION OF COSMETIC SURGERY

This report (Department of health, 2005) is worth reviewing in some detail since this made recommendations to the Chief Medical Officer which have been put in place and provide the basis for current practice in the UK.

The Expert Group found evidence that avoidable harm is done to some patients and that procedures were widely advertised and marketed in a way that would be ethically unacceptable if used in relation to other forms of surgery.

The recommendations cover three areas:

- Providers' clinical training, qualifications, and accountability.
- Recommendations about public education and information.
- Recommendations about non-surgical procedures.

RECOMMENDATIONS ABOUT PROVIDERS

Under the provision of the Care Standards Act 2000, standard A4.2, all medical practitioners in private practice have to enrol on the specialist register of the General Medical Council (GMC); however, there is no specific specialist register for cosmetic surgery. This means in effect that people can practise outside the area of competence for which they are registered. It also sets up a barrier to those already in private practice. Surgeons need 5–6 years of experience in the NHS to be eligible for registration, but this prevents the inclusion of surgeons who are trained abroad. Many cosmetic surgeons are experienced surgeons from outside the NHS, and given the shortage of training places in the UK, it is not appropriate to insist on NHS experience for those people who are intending this purely as a means to private practice. Nor is it possible to restrict surgeons in practice because this can be challenged legally as restraint of trade.

To overcome these problems, a provision for surgeons practising before 2002 is in place, and they can be included on the specialist register of GMC where they were already doing cosmetic surgery before April 2002 (when the Act came in), provided they:

- Have completed specialist training.
- Have undertaken training in the areas relevant to the procedures they provide.
- Maintain an accessible register of the patients they have treated.
- Undertake regular patient satisfaction surveys which are available to the registered person and the HCC at least annually.

The Expert Group concluded that these arrangements made it virtually impossible for a person seeking cosmetic surgery to understand or evaluate the precise qualifications and supervisory framework in which their surgeon is practising. They concluded that this was unsatisfactory and recommended that:

- All surgeons for whom these special arrangements apply ensure a strong component of peer review in their independent appraisal and validation processes.
- All doctors and nurses provide all patients with full details of their qualifications and training.
- Training programmes are evolved for all special advisory committees of the relevant medical and surgical specialities.
- HCC looks at whether standards relating to practising surgeons are adequate for contemporary clinical practice.
- All advice to patients be provided by trained nurses or doctors.

However, it is arguable that it is still very difficult for patients to navigate the different qualifications and training described by the plethora of providers, and there is no audit arrangement to establish whether these recommendations have been acted upon.

PUBLIC EDUCATION AND INFORMATION

Information was found by the Expert Group to be generally lacking particularly in relation to risks and how to complain. Risks were often discussed with a patient information team rather than the surgeon and played down. Frequently information was provided by beauty therapists with no medical or nursing qualifications. High-pressure sales techniques and financial incentives were common.

The Expert Group provided minimum recommendations such as: all advertising to include the registration number with the HCC and all information to be provided by either doctors or nurses; all establishments must publish information about consumer rights such as how to complain, details of treatments available and other organizations that provide help; complaints must be recorded and the improvements to the recording and classification of complaints must be made by the GMC to enable comparisons between providers. The GMC should also make information about speciality registration more clearly available to the public on its website. The DoH was required to publish detailed information about accreditation of providers, questions for patients to ask, and what standards of registration and qualifications to expect.

RECOMMENDATIONS ABOUT NON-SURGICAL PROCEDURES

'Cosmetic procedures' as defined by the Expert Group included operations carried out in theatre under general anaesthetic as well as local anaesthetic, Botox®, fillers, and laser (as covered by The Cosmetic Products (Safety) Regulations 2004). It excluded non-structural changes such as ear piercing, tattooing, or other forms of grooming (these being covered by various Local Authority Health and Safety Acts).

Botulinum toxins (Botox®) are regulated and should only be prescribed by a doctor for a named patient. However they are not licensed for cosmetic use and are therefore only used for this purpose on an off-licence basis. This means that in the situations where nurses are delegated to provide treatment they may inadvertently be acting unlawfully. The situation where Botox® 'parties' are arranged, particularly where alcohol is provided at same time, was described by the Expert Group as 'unacceptable'.

Injection of fillers is not regulated. Some are classed as drugs or medical devices. Some are synthetic and others contain human tissue with a potential Creutzfeldt–Jakob disease (CJD) risk.

The recommendations of the Expert Group included:

- Improved adherence to the regulations for botulinum toxins, i.e. prescribed by a doctor for an individual patient and administered by either a nurse or doctor.
- Facilities where botulinum toxins or fillers are provided must be licensed by HCC.
- Cosmetic dentistry should be included under the regulation of the HCC.
- Fillers, whether temporary or permanent, should be better clarified and better information provided to patients.
- All recommendations regarding information about cosmetic procedures, advertising, complaints, etc. to be applied in the same way as for surgical procedures.

The outcomes of the Expert Group recommendations have established more transparency about the provider and the procedures, but the final responsibility remains with the patient who must use these resources to ensure they are properly informed. However, there are still major concerns about the way in which procedures are advertised, the lack of regulation of information on the Internet, and the unrealistic expectations of patients informed by inaccurate media sources. For example, Harvey Markovitch, editor of *Clinical Risk*, suggests that:

There can be no area of medicine where patients in the UK are more in need of protection. We need tight control of advertising of cosmetic surgery – including internet advertising. We need proper regulation of the industry and we need both surgeons and GPs to manage patient expectation (British Association of Aesthetic Plastic Surgeons, 2009).

Even this statement has problems. Despite a GMC recommendation that GPs are informed of any proposed treatment, medical students do not routinely study plastic surgery and many GPs are informed by the same inadequate sources that are used by patients. One of the problems for a clinician is the poor quality of referrals from GPs and psychiatrists who not only lack an understanding of the procedure and its likely outcomes but recommend procedures to patients with no knowledge of the research evidence for effectiveness. Managing the expectations of other health professionals is becoming as important as managing the expectations of patients. It is also clear that many patients prefer to prevent contact between the GP and the surgical provider partly to avoid others knowing that the surgery has taken place, but also because GPs are perceived as unsympathetic to cosmetic surgery requests. For this reason, many surgeons accept referrals and treat patients without informing the GP, despite the fact that they then accept responsibility for the patient's medical outcome whether it is managing a wound infection or a serious medical emergency.

The issue of regulation was examined in a special issue of *Clinical Risk* in November 2009, with a view to further clarification and recommendations. Mercer (2009) discusses the role of the media and calls for tighter regulations in the UK using the comparison of the Food and Drug Administration's role in the US. He advocates selling 'advice, not procedures' (p. 215) and warns that if self regulation fails then, 'like the financial institutions, regulation will eventually be imposed' (p. 215). He further suggests that 'like tobacco, there should be a Europe-wide ban on advertising all cosmetic 'surgical' procedures, including on search engines' (p. 216).

REGULATION OF COSMETIC SURGERY IN FRANCE

In many ways France can be seen as setting the standard in terms of regulation of cosmetic surgery procedures and the minimizing of risk to patients (Fogli, 2009). All forms and methods of publicity and advertising, direct or indirect, in whatever form, including the Internet, are forbidden. There is a clear focus on providing detailed information to patients including a mandatory 'cooling off' period of 15 days, similar to the mandatory period in the UK for financial agreements. One of the common complaints of patients who are dissatisfied with outcome of surgery is that they were 'rushed' into agreeing a date within a short time period. Contrast this with the necessity for patients consenting to participation in a research trial in the UK for whom a mandatory period to think about consent is part and parcel of an ethical consent process.

As a result of these regulations it is reported that there is a reduction in non-qualified surgeons carrying out surgery and far less of a drive to create commercial clinics. However there is a cost in terms of administrative burden for surgeons and there is nothing to stop people outside France advertising their services so there is no protection for patients from cosmetic tourism. Indeed it is arguable that patients are less well protected in that it is difficult for them to find information about reputable as well as disreputable sources.

DRIVERS FOR CHANGE

Cosmetic tourism

The market in international tourism for medical procedures is estimated to be worth between US $20–40 billion and rising (Nahai, 2009). The growth in demand for cosmetic procedures is a problem for the NHS; costs accrue where there is inadequate provision in private clinics for managing complications or where people develop complications after surgery abroad (Jeevan et al., 2008). Approximately 4% of patients undergoing aesthetic procedures will have complications requiring further treatment, and although this is a small percentage, the numbers are increasing proportionally with the growth in demand. In the short term, complications such as postoperative infection may require accident and emergency assessment, treatment with antibiotics, or even hospital admission for sepsis. Longer-term complications such as capsular contracture after breast augmentation often present to the NHS as referrals for reimplantation, and some patients present with high levels of dissatisfaction with private treatment where high expectations have not been met and which is construed as 'surgery which has gone wrong'. The hard line taken by the NHS low-priority treatment panels means that people treated abroad are increasingly barred from accessing remedial surgery in the NHS unless the condition is life threatening. This can result in ethical dilemmas for surgeons who are prevented from offering the highest standard of care, e.g. having to offer mastectomy only without reconstruction where mastectomy is required following free injection of silicone as opposed to a high-risk genetic profile or neoplasm. The high cost for the NHS in providing emergency surgery after cosmetic tourism is an important driver for change.

International guidelines have been produced by the ISAPS and ASAPS (http://www.isaps.org/ethics.php) as an attempt to control cosmetic tourism and these include recommendations that follow-up care should be available in the patient's home town, and advice about restrictions relating to air travel. However, the impetus remains clearly with the patient to check that all these provisions are in place and people are still prepared to ignore the risks where the associated rewards are perceived as high. Indeed there is psychological research evidence to suggest that where risk is perceived to be high, the associated benefits are perceived to be greater (Lloyd et al., 2001); it is therefore arguable that detailed information about complications may serve to encourage patients rather than the converse.

The changing public perception of surgery

The American Society of Plastic Surgeons (ASPS) has suggested that the market for aesthetic surgery has matured and that growth continues in aesthetic medicine and non-invasive approaches (Fogli, 2009). This may reflect a shift away from the value placed on surgery in terms of societal norms. Body size is a good example of the way that cultural ideals are linked with resources: where food is plentiful a thinner body ideal is revered whilst obesity is revered during times of shortage (Rumsey & Harcourt, 2005, p. 5). Similarly tanned skin is revealed when only the rich have access to foreign travel and declines in popularity with the advent of cheap travel. The more accessible cosmetic treatments become, the less the cachet and the higher the opprobrium.

In the UK, the media both promotes and increasingly challenges cosmetic procedures as a lifestyle choice. Programmes such as *Embarrassing Bodies* stimulate a growth in demand for surgery, whilst others such as *How to Look Good Naked* explore alternatives to promoting appearance without cosmetic intervention. It is possible to be lauded for an enhanced appearance and simultaneously castigated, and it remains to be seen whether the international financial recession will be associated with an increase in requests for surgery as people compete for their jobs, or a downturn as people preserve their financial resources.

ALTERNATIVE MANAGEMENT OF APPEARANCE CONCERNS

There is very little research evidence for the benefits of cosmetic procedures in the long term (Cook et al., 2006). Similarly, evidence for benefits of psychological intervention for appearance concerns lacks a strong evidence base but the methodological problems with this work are gradually being recognized and better quality research is being published (Bessell & Moss, 2007). It is increasingly recognized that concern about appearance results in beliefs and behaviours which are very abnormal, lead to great unhappiness and unhealthy life choices. Better understanding of the factors that predict adjustment to appearance concerns will inform psychological interventions which modify the rumination and worry associated with perceived abnormalities of appearance rather than appearance per se. Gradually these approaches may allow people choice; with evidence of effectiveness it is possible that they will become a recommended alternative for people considering surgical solutions, particularly those with very high levels of appearance-related anxiety.

REGULATION BY THE MARKETPLACE

Finally, it is worth considering the scope for regulation via market forces. The drive towards poorly regulated surgeons and cosmetic tourism is largely a financial one. One group of plastic surgeons in London has already moved to undercut their competitors by joining forces to drive down costs via shared infrastructure and bulk ordering of high quality materials. Similarly there are educational programmes in the US which offer reduced rates for people undergoing supervised procedures by surgeons in training. It is arguable that these innovations can be used to drive down costs of better quality care and that this is ultimately a more effective way of regulating the industry.

REFERENCES

Bessell, A. & Moss, T. (2007). Evaluating the effectiveness of psychosocial interventions for individuals with visible differences: A systematic review of the empirical literature. *Body Image*, 4, 227–38.

British Association of Aesthetic Plastic Surgeons. (2009). Cosmetic surgery: a perfect storm. [Press release.] http://www.baaps.org.uk/about-us/press-releases/530-cosmetic-surgery-a-perfect-storm (accessed 8 June 2010).

Clarke, A., Lester, K. J., Withey, S. J., & Butler, P. E. M. (2005). A funding model for a psychological service to plastic and reconstructive surgery in UK practice. *British Journal of Plastic Surgery*, 58, 708–13.

Cook, S. A., Rosser, R., Meah, S., James, M. I., & Salmon, P. (2003). Clinical decision guidelines for NHS cosmetic surgery: analysis of current limitations and recommendations for future development. *British Journal Plastic Surgery*, 56, 448–52.

Cook, S. A., Meah, S., & Salmon P. (2006). Is cosmetic surgery an effective therapeutic intervention? A systematic review of the evidence. *Journal of Plastic & Reconstructive Surgery*, 59, 1133–51.

Cordeiro, C. N., Clarke, A., White, P., Sivakumar, B., Ong, J. L., & Butler, P. E. M. (2010). A quantitative analysis of psychological and emotional health measures in 360 plastic surgery candidates. *Annals of Plastic surgery*, 65(3), 349–53.

Department of Health. (2005). *Expert Group on the Regulation of Cosmetic Surgery: Report to the Chief Medical Officer*. London: Department of Health. http://www.dh.gov.uk/en/Publicationsandstatistics/Publications/PublicationsPolicyAndGuidance/DH_4102046

Fogli, A. (2009). France sets standards for practice of aesthetic surgery. *Clinical Risk*, 15, 224–6.

Jeevan, R. & Armstrong, A. (2008) Cosmetic tourism and the burden on the NHS. *Journal of Plastic & Reconstructive Surgery*, 61, 1423–4.

Lloyd, A., Hayes, P., Bell, P. R. F., & Naylor, A. R. (2001). The role of risk and benefit perception in informed consent for surgery. *Medical Decision Making*, 21(2), 141–9.

Mercer, N. (2009). Clinical risk in aesthetic surgery. *Clinical Risk*, 15, 215–17.

Moss, T. (2005). The relationship between objective and subjective ratings of disfigurement severity, and psychological adjustment. *Body Image*, 2, 151–9.

Nahai, F. (2009) Minimizing risk in aesthetic surgery. *Clinical Risk*, 15, 232–6.

Ong, J. L, Clarke, A., Johnson, M., White, P., Withey, S., & Butler P. E. M. (2007). Does severity predict distress? The relationship between subjective and objective measures of severity in patients treated for facial lipoatrophy. *Body Image*, 4, 239–48.

Rumsey, N. & Harcourt, D. (2005). *The Psychology of Appearance*. Maidenhead: Open University Press.

INTERVENTIONS AT AN INDIVIDUAL OR GROUP LEVEL

....

SCHOOL-BASED INTERVENTIONS TO PROMOTE POSITIVE BODY IMAGE AND THE ACCEPTANCE OF DIVERSITY IN APPEARANCE

....

PHILLIPPA C. DIEDRICHS

EMMA HALLIWELL

THE school setting provides a valuable opportunity to engage young people in interventions that aim to address appearance-related concerns and to promote greater acceptance of diversity in appearance. This setting allows large numbers of young people to be addressed in a relatively short time span using messages that can then be reinforced within peer groups. However, school-based interventions present a number of challenges, particularly in relation to the diverse nature of young people's body image concerns and attitudes. To date, the focus of school-based interventions has tended to be the prevention of negative body image and eating disorders, and encouraging students to be accepting of different body shapes and sizes. The first section of this chapter will present an overview of this research, including an examination of the main theoretical orientations and content utilized in negative body image and eating disorder prevention programmes. It will also review the intervention (e.g. programme content and length) and participant factors (e.g. age, gender, and risk status) that have been found to influence programme success. Examples of effective school-based interventions that have shown particular promise in preventing negative body image and eating disorders will also be presented. The second section of this chapter will explore interventions that have addressed visible difference in the school setting; an important topic that has received much less attention in the literature. This will include a discussion of past and current interventions that have attempted to promote positive attitudes towards people with visible difference among school students, and those that have focused on helping young people with visible difference feel comfortable and well-adjusted in the school setting.

WHY SHOULD WE FOCUS ON APPEARANCE-CONCERNS IN THE SCHOOL SETTING?

Schools, including primary and secondary schools and universities, offer a unique opportunity for health professionals to engage with large groups of young people. The structured environment of schools means that intervention programmes can be easily included within coursework or extracurricular activities. They also provide access to other professionals (e.g. school teachers and faculty) who are expert in working with young people (Yager & O'Dea, 2005). Depending on the age of the young people targeted, school-based interventions have the potential to reach children before their thoughts and opinions about their own and other's appearance become fixed (primary schools), while they experience bodily changes that accompany puberty (secondary school), and at a time when they are most at risk for experiencing negative body image and eating disorders (university) (Smolak et al., 1998b; Levine & Smolak, 2006).

Appearance concerns also play an important role in the schooling experience of many young people. More specifically, young people who experience negative body image are more likely to have impaired performance in the classroom and poor school attendance. One study that examined appearance concerns among young people in the UK found that 31% of teenagers do not engage in classroom debate for fear of drawing attention to their appearance, and 20% report that they stay away from school on days where they lack confidence about their appearance (Lovegrove & Rumsey, 2005). Although some young people with visible differences cope well in the school setting, research suggests that students with visible differences tend to be less popular, have smaller peer groups, and are more likely to experience behavioural and academic problems at school than those without visible differences (Kish & Lansdown, 2000). Changing schools or transitioning from primary to secondary school may be especially challenging for young people with visible differences as they must encounter the reactions of unfamiliar peers and school staff (Rumsey & Harcourt, 2004).

Eating problems and dieting commonly associated with negative body image can also have a detrimental effect on cognitive tasks frequently performed in the classroom. In particular, dieting and restrictive eating are associated with poor attention-span and memory difficulties (Green & Rogers, 1995, 1998). A study of over 1,500 North American university students found that young people with lower grades were more likely to report that body image concerns interfered with their ability to perform academically than those with higher grades (Yanover & Thompson, 2008). Providing further evidence of the centrality of appearance to young people's lives, during a focus group discussion with Australian adolescents, one girl said 'I reckon that if I fitted into size 10 jeans I would be happier. I would rather have that than straight A's.' (Tiggemann et al., 2000, p. 651).

Body image concerns also have a significant impact on the way in which young people interact with their peers at school. For example, 38% of British teenagers studied said that they do not feel at all confident to speak with someone who looks very different from them (Lovegrove & Rumsey, 2005). Another study conducted with 3,500 children from 47 schools across Europe found that physical appearance was the most common reason for making fun of other children, followed by disability and skin colour (British Council, 2008). Migrant students seem to be at particular risk for appearance-related teasing, with 50% of migrant students in the same study reporting that they had been bullied within the last 3 months. Young people with visible differences may also be particularly vulnerable to bullying and appearance-related teasing at school (Maddern & Owen, 2004; Rumsey & Harcourt, 2004).

The high prevalence of appearance-related teasing among school children is concerning in light of the negative impact it has on psychosocial health and well-being. Teasing about appearance is consistently linked to body dissatisfaction, low self-esteem, depression, and thinking about and attempting suicide, regardless of the young person's actual body weight and the presence of a visible difference (Neumark-Sztainer et al., 2002; Eisenberg et al., 2003; Haines et al., 2006). These negative effects hold for adolescent boys and girls across racial and ethnic groups. Furthermore, experiencing weight-related teasing is associated with increases in levels of disordered eating and resistance to engaging in physical activity among adolescents and young adults (Wertheim et al., 2001; Vartanian & Shaprow, 2008). Collectively, this research highlights the importance of developing and implementing effective school-based interventions that promote positive body image and the acceptance of diversity in appearance.

BODY IMAGE AND EATING DISORDER PREVENTION PROGRAMMES IN SCHOOLS

Negative body image and eating disorder school-based prevention programmes originated in the 1980s, in response to the increasing prevalence of body image concerns and eating disorders among young people (Holt & Ricciardelli, 2008). Traditionally, these programmes were didactic and involved the provision of information about the negative consequences of eating disorders, negative body image, and dieting. Early prevention programmes were unfortunately largely ineffective, and more recently there has been a shift towards interactive interventions that adopt a social cognitive model of prevention (Levine & Piran, 2004; Stice & Shaw, 2004).

Social cognitive interventions focus on reducing empirically established socio-cultural, cognitive and behavioural risk factors for the development of negative body image and eating disorders (e.g. body dissatisfaction, internalization of cultural beauty ideals which glorify thinness and muscularity, self-esteem, and healthy weight management behaviours), and intentionally avoid discussions centred around eating disorders (e.g. *Eating Smart, Eating For Me*, by Smolak et al., 1998a). In addition to the social cognitive model, more recent negative body image and eating disorder prevention programmes have adopted developmental, ecological, non-specific vulnerability stressor, and/or feminist-empowerment-relational theoretical orientations (see Levine & Piran, 2004; Levine & Smolak, 2006; for an in depth discussion of these theoretical perspectives).

School-based prevention programmes that adopt a developmental perspective often focus on normalizing bodily changes that occur during puberty. Pubertal development may cause concern for adolescents due to current beauty ideals which emphasize a clear complexion and a slender, toned body shape for women and a slim, muscular build for men (Thompson et al., 2004). These programmes instead focus on healthy growth and development (e.g. *Healthy Buddies* by Stock et al. (2007)). In contrast, an ecological approach to prevention recognizes the need to focus on the environment to promote health and well-being, rather than just focusing on the individual. This approach concentrates on the broader context of young people's lives, and is characterized by prevention programmes that involve parents, school teachers, and communities. They often involve attempts to change school culture in an effort to promote positive body image (e.g. Russell-Mayhew et al., 2007). Prevention programmes that adopt a non-specific vulnerability-to-stressor orientation focus on developing general 'life skills', such as coping skills, stress management, and self-esteem enhancement, with the rationale that these non-specific factors are associated with poor mental health (e.g. *Everybody's Different* by O'Dea & Abraham (2000)). Finally, the feminist-empowerment-relational perspective emphasizes the importance of gender roles and objectification in the development of negative body image and eating disorders. This approach seeks to empower young people to challenge such restrictive social norms (e.g. work with Canadian dance schools (Piran, 1999)).

Reviews of school-based prevention programmes suggest that most interventions draw upon multiple theoretical perspectives (e.g. Holt & Ricciardelli, 2008). Currently there is no consensus as to which theoretical orientation provides the most effective approach to the prevention of negative body image and eating disorders (Stice et al., 2007). Fortunately, however, in recent years there has been progress in determining what type of programme content is most effective.

The content of school-based interventions tends to vary widely, but often includes didactic teaching, audiovisual resources, and small group interactive activities that address established risk factors for the development of negative body image and eating disorders (Stice et al., 2007). As already mentioned, earlier programmes tended to emphasize psychoeducational activities, which aimed to increase knowledge about eating disorders, body image, and nutrition. More recently, however, there has been an increasing emphasis on helping young people to develop skills to resist sociocultural pressures to look a certain way (Stice & Shaw, 2004). Sociocultural resistance activities often focus on media literacy and encourage young people to critically evaluate media images that promote narrow and unrealistic beauty ideals (e.g. *Media Smart* by Wilksch & Wade (2009)). Other prevention programmes incorporate activities targeting healthy-weight control, including learning skills to manage diet and nutrition in a healthy and non-appearance focused manner. Activities to promote body satisfaction, the acceptance of different body shapes and sizes as beautiful, greater self-esteem and coping skills more generally are also frequently incorporated into school-based interventions. Some of these activities have creatively included the use of body image friendly children's books (Dohnt & Tiggemann, 2008), yoga and relaxation techniques (Scime et al., 2006), and theatre and puppetry (Russell-Mayhew et al., 2007; Haines et al., 2008). Finally, dissonance-based activities that engage young people in counter-attitudinal exercises (e.g. role plays, letter writing) that challenge the prevailing thin ideal of beauty have also been included in prevention programmes with young women (e.g. Stice et al., 2000; Becker et al., 2006). In light of the wide ranging and varied content included in school-based programmes, it is important to establish what types of programmes are most effective in preventing negative body image and eating disorders in the school setting, and for what groups of young people they work best.

How successful are these interventions?

Several meta-analyses have evaluated the overall effectiveness of negative body image and eating disorder prevention programmes (e.g. Stice & Shaw, 2004; Fingeret et al., 2006; Stice et al., 2007). There have also been several published reviews of the effectiveness of prevention programmes conducted in school settings specifically (e.g. O'Dea, 2005; Holt & Ricciardelli, 2008; Yager & O'Dea, 2008). Overall, these reviews suggest that while many of the more recent, interactive prevention programmes have been successful in changing young people's attitudes related to body image and disordered eating, few interventions have effectively reduced problematic behaviours.

For example, in the most recent meta-analysis of 58 controlled studies that evaluated eating disorder prevention programmes from 1980–2006 (many of which were conducted in school settings), Stice and colleagues (2007) found that 51% of the interventions significantly reduced at least one risk factor for the development of eating disorders (i.e. internalization of cultural beauty ideals, body dissatisfaction, dieting, and/or negative affect). However, only 29% were successful in reducing disordered eating. In another review, Holt and Ricciardelli (2008) examined the results of 13 published studies that evaluated body image and eating disorder prevention programmes within primary schools in the UK, Canada, Australia, and the US. While the majority of these interventions were successful in improving knowledge about dieting and nutrition, very few were effective in improving self-esteem, body image, and eating problems.

Reviews of school-based prevention programmes have also identified some common methodological limitations within the research. The most rigorous way to evaluate an intervention involves randomly assigning school students to a group that receives the intervention (e.g. media literacy), or to a matched group who receive (1) an alternative intervention (e.g. psycho-education), (2) no intervention, or (3) a placebo task (e.g. an expressive writing activity). This design allows researchers to carefully distinguish between intervention effects and any effects associated with the passage of time, or other non-specific factors (e.g. interacting with a group of students or a programme facilitator). To assess the short- and long-term impact of the intervention, researchers should then assess body image and disordered eating before the intervention is delivered, immediately after the intervention is delivered and again at subsequent follow-up time points. The majority of research in this area, however, has not been so methodologically rigorous. Perhaps this is not surprising, given the challenges of conducting research within schools (e.g. fitting intervention and evaluation activities into already established curricula and crowded class timetables); however, it does prevent strong conclusions being drawn from much of the research.

For example, in Holt & Ricciardelli's (2008) review of primary school targeted interventions, four of the 13 studies reviewed did not have a control group, and none had an alternative intervention or placebo comparison condition. Similarly, the vast majority of studies evaluated in Stice et al.'s (2007) meta-analysis did not include an alternative intervention or placebo condition. Further, although Yager and O'Dea (2008) identified 27 controlled studies that had evaluated the effectiveness of body image and eating disorder prevention programmes targeting university students, 18% of the studies reviewed did not randomly assign students to the study conditions; this means that any observed differences between the conditions could have been attributed to pre-existing differences in the students assigned to each group, rather than intervention effects.

Very few studies have assessed the long-term impact of prevention programmes on students' attitudes and behaviours. In Yager and O'Dea's (2008) review, only 52% of the studies examined included follow-up assessment of intervention effects. Holt and Ricciardelli (2008) also acknowledged that of the prevention studies that do include follow-up measures, very few examine the maintenance of intervention effects more than 12 months later. The lack of follow-up measures means that it is impossible to determine the long-term effectiveness of prevention programmes. Furthermore, it is difficult to determine how transitions to higher levels of education (e.g. primary to secondary) and pubertal development might influence intervention effects (Holt & Ricciardelli, 2008).

While there are methodological limitations to the literature and many programmes have been demonstrated to be ineffective, there are some particularly noteworthy interventions that have been rigorously evaluated, and do demonstrate success in preventing negative body image and disordered eating among school populations. Before providing case examples of some of these successful programmes, we review some of the specific intervention and participant factors that appear to influence the success of prevention programmes.

What factors influence programme success?

Intervention factors

The content and length of prevention programmes, in addition to the type of programme facilitator, have been found to influence the success of school-based interventions. Reviews of programme effectiveness suggest that certain content appears to have a greater impact than others. For example, in Stice et al.'s (2007) meta-analysis of eating disorder prevention programmes, interventions that contained psychoeducational and stress and coping content were less effective than programmes without this type of content. On the other hand, interactive programmes and interventions that included body acceptance content and dissonance-based activities were more effective in reducing internalization of the thin beauty ideal, body dissatisfaction, dieting, negative affect and eating pathology. Similarly, Yager & O'Dea (2005) found that university body image and eating disorder prevention programmes that were didactic, psychoeducational, or cognitive behaviourally oriented were least effective, while, prevention programmes that included media literacy, dissonance-based, and self-esteem boosting activities had more marked positive effects. These findings may be explained by the fact that psychoeducation and activities focused on general coping and stress management do not target empirically established risk factors for negative body image and eating disorders (Stice et al., 2007). Research examining the role of programme length is more ambiguous.

Programme length is a particularly salient issue for school-based interventions, as school curriculums are often crowded, teachers are pressed for time, and it is expensive and labour intensive for specialized interventionists (e.g. psychologists and social workers) to run multiple sessions. Nevertheless, it is often suggested that multi-session interventions may be more effective in reducing problematic attitudes and behaviours, because they give students more time to reflect on the programme content, to apply new skills, and to ask for assistance (Watson & Vaughn, 2006). This may be particularly helpful for young children who have less developed cognitive abilities. In support of this, Stice and Shaw's (2004) meta-analysis of 38 eating disorder prevention programmes from 1980–2004 found that multi-session programmes were associated with greater reductions in body dissatisfaction, dieting and eating pathology than single session interventions. However, in Stice et al.'s (2007) updated meta-analysis, which included a further 13 studies, there was limited support for the benefits of multi-session prevention programmes above and beyond single-session interventions for all risk factors (i.e. internalization of beauty ideals, negative affect, body dissatisfaction, eating pathology), aside from dieting. Further research comparing single and multi-session versions of the same school-based intervention may help to clarify this further.

Another intervention factor that has garnered significant attention in the literature is establishing who are the best people to deliver school-based body image and eating disorder prevention programmes—specialized interventionists, school staff, or peers? School teachers and faculty appear well-placed to deliver interventions due to their regular access to school students and their potential to act as school role models for healthy body image. However, most teachers do not receive appropriate training in body image, eating disorders and nutrition. Indeed, studies have found that teachers cite a lack of training as a barrier to implementing body image and eating disorder prevention strategies in the classroom (see Yager, 2010, for a detailed analysis of issues surrounding teacher training for body image and eating disorder programmes). Other research suggests that some teachers may discriminate against overweight and obese children (Puhl & Brownell, 2006), and that pre-service health and physical education teachers—who may seem like the most appropriate teachers to implement health prevention programmes—report elevated levels of disordered eating and body dissatisfaction themselves, in comparison to pre-service teachers who do not specialize in health (Yager & O'Dea, 2009). It is perhaps not surprising then that Stice et al.'s (2007) meta-analysis found that the most effective eating disorder prevention programmes were delivered by specialized interventionists, rather than endogenous providers, such as teachers.

It is, however, not time- or cost-effective to have specialized external interventionists deliver all school-based prevention programmes. A reliance on people who are external to the school may also undermine ecological approaches to prevention. It is therefore encouraging that researchers have begun to focus on developing effective body image and eating disorder prevention training programmes for teachers (Favaro et al., 2005; McVey et al., 2009). Furthermore, work is underway to develop interventions to reduce body dissatisfaction and disordered eating among pre-service teachers (Yager & O'Dea, in press).

Although much less researched, there is also emerging evidence to suggest that peer-led school-based prevention programmes may also be successful in promoting positive body image and reducing the risk for disordered eating. For example, the *Healthy Buddies* programme, implemented and evaluated in Canada, trained primary school students in grades 4–7 to act as peer teachers, or 'older buddies' to younger students. The older buddies engaged in physical activity sessions and lessons on body image, body acceptance, and nutrition with their younger buddies. While the programme had a limited effect on body image, it did positively influence the children's health-related attitudes and behaviours. More encouragingly, *Reflections: Body Image Program* (Becker & Stice, 2008), a peer-led dissonance-based negative body image and eating disorder prevention programme implemented in sororities in the United States has been demonstrated to be effective in reducing body dissatisfaction and eating pathology among university-age women even at 12 months post intervention (Becker et al., 2006, 2008). Before discussing this programme in more detail, we turn to a review of participant factors that influence the success of school-based prevention programmes.

Participant factors

The age, gender, and risk status of students engaged in school-based prevention programmes may also influence intervention success. Establishing the most appropriate age group to target in body image and eating disorder prevention programmes has been debated in the literature. Some suggest that children in primary school do not have the cognitive abilities to understand and benefit from prevention programmes (Stice & Shaw, 2004; Stice et al., 2007). While others argue that early intervention provides the opportunity to address body image concerns and appearance ideals before children's ideas about appearance become fixed (Smolak et al., 1998b). Furthermore, there is research to suggest that children as young as five years of age are aware of and can be influenced by unrealistic beauty ideals (Dittmar et al., 2006), engage in weight stigma (Penny & Haddock, 2007), and experience body dissatisfaction (Davison & Birch, 2002). Therefore, while the research suggests that current eating disorder prevention programmes have been most effective when participants are over the age of 15 (Stice et al., 2007), it may be unethical to delay prevention efforts until adolescence.

Traditionally, body image and eating disorders were seen as women's health issues. However, as outlined in Chapters 12 and 15, it is now well recognized that young boys and men experience body image concerns and eating disorders (McCabe

& Ricciardelli, 2004). Indeed, a recent survey of young Australians found that body image was reported to be equally concerning for school-aged boys and girls (Mission Australia, 2008). Despite this, school-based eating disorder and body image prevention programmes have overwhelmingly targeted female students. For example, Holt & Ricciardelli's (2008) review of primary school interventions found only five out of 13 prevention programmes included boys, while Yager & O'Dea's (2008) review of 27 university interventions only identified one programme that included young men. To our knowledge, only two programmes have been developed to specifically target adolescent boys' body image (Stanford & McCabe, 2005; McCabe et al., 2010). One study reported small effects, while the other found no effect. Similarly, Stice et al.'s (2007) meta-analysis found that eating disorder prevention programmes were more effective when they targeted girls only, rather than boys or mixed gender groups.

The limited success of current prevention programmes with male populations may be because they have often failed to address and measure aspects of body image that are unique to boys and young men (e.g. concerns about muscularity and body hair) (Tiggemann et al., 2008). Furthermore, research into male body image in general is in its infancy in comparison to research with women. Because of the increasing prevalence of body image concerns among young men, and the fact that most school-based settings are co-educational, there is a continuing need for research into the development and evaluation of body interventions that are appropriate and effective for girls *and* boys.

Prevention programmes can vary along the spectrum of universal, selected, and targeted interventions. Universal programmes address the well-being of large numbers of people, while selective programmes target groups of individuals who may be at risk of developing the focus problem (e.g. eating disorders) due to biological, psychological, or sociocultural factors (e.g. being an adolescent female who lives in a culture that emphasizes beauty) (Levine & Piran, 2004). Targeted interventions on the other hand focus on individuals who already have established precursors of the problem (e.g. are already body dissatisfied and engaging in dieting behaviours), but the problem has not yet fully developed.

Most school-based interventions are selective or targeted, and there is evidence that the risk status of participants influences programme success. Specifically, it appears that targeted programmes are more effective in reducing eating disorder risk factors and pathology than selective programmes (Stice et al., 2007). This may be because the students are already experiencing problems and are therefore more likely to be more motivated to engage in the intervention (Stice & Shaw, 2004). Furthermore, targeted interventions have the benefit of being more cost effective because fewer people and resources are required. However targeted programmes may also be problematic in the school setting, as they single out young people and potentially make already vulnerable students more at risk for being bullied or teased (Holt & Ricciardelli, 2008). It has therefore been suggested that the costs associated with targeted interventions may outweigh the benefits when working in a school setting (Holt & Ricciardelli, 2008).

Examples of effective programmes

The Body Project and Reflections: Body Image Program

Cognitive dissonance-based interventions *The Body Project* (Stice & Presnell, 2007) and *Reflections: Body Image Program* (Becker & Stice, 2008) are among the most successful school-based negative body image and eating disorder prevention programmes to date (see Stice et al., 2008, for a detailed description of the programmes and a review of evidence of their efficacy and effectiveness). Both interventions rely on the social psychology persuasion principle of cognitive dissonance to reduce internalization of the thin ideal for female beauty, an established risk factor for eating disorders (Stice et al., 2008). This is based on the premise that reducing thin ideal internalization will in turn reduce body dissatisfaction, negative affect, and disordered eating.

Cognitive dissonance is the psychological discomfort that occurs when individuals engage in behaviours that are contradictory to their beliefs and attitudes (Festinger, 1957). In order to reduce this discomfort, individuals will often change their beliefs and attitudes to be more consistent with their behaviour. *The Body Project* and *Reflections* capitalize on this by engaging young women in counter-attitudinal intervention and homework activities that challenge the thin ideal of beauty. Examples of these activities include role playing a situation where they discourage a friend from pursuing the thin ideal; engaging in small group discussions about the costs associated with the thin ideal; and writing a letter to a younger girl to convince her of these costs. Theoretically, engaging in these counter-attitudinal activities will lead to cognitive dissonance among these young women and therefore they will reduce their own endorsement and pursuit of the thin ideal in order to reduce the dissonance.

The Body Project (Stice & Presnell, 2007) consists of four 1-hour sessions and is delivered to young women in secondary schools and universities. It has been evaluated in multisite controlled studies in the US, and has consistently been shown to be more effective than an alternative healthy weight intervention, a placebo expressive writing intervention, and assessment-only controls (Stice et al., 2003, 2006, 2009). At-risk and unselected adolescent girls who take part in *The Body Project* are significantly less likely to develop eating disorders, and experience reductions in thin-ideal internalization, body dissatisfaction, negative affect, and psychosocial impairment. These intervention effects have been shown to be maintained at 2, and in some cases 3, years post-intervention. This suggests that *The Body Project* can result in long-term improvements. Furthermore, recent research suggests that *The Body Project* can be successfully implemented by both specialized interventionists and school teachers, although the latter appears to produce smaller effect sizes (Stice et al., 2009).

Reflections: Body Image Program (Becker & Stice, 2008) is a peer-led cognitive dissonance programme that targets university-age women. The programme originated as an adaptation of the early cognitive dissonance eating disorder prevention research (e.g. Stice et al., 2000), and was developed in collaboration with sororities in the US. Reflections consists of two 2-hour sessions that are delivered to programme participants by trained peer leaders. Since its inception in 2002, Reflections has been widely disseminated to sorority members in the US, and has been shown to be effective in reducing body dissatisfaction, thin ideal internalization and dietary restraint up to 1 year post-intervention (Becker et al., 2005, 2006, 2008; Perez et al., 2010). It has also been demonstrated to be more effective than a media literacy intervention. *Reflections* has recently been adapted for delivery and evaluation in British universities (see *The Succeed Body Image Programme*, Becker & Stice, 2011). Further research is necessary to determine if cognitive dissonance programmes may also be effective in preventing negative body image and eating disorders among boys and young men.

Media Smart

Developed in Australia, *Media Smart* (Wilksch & Wade, 2009) consists of eight 50-minute lessons and is a universal prevention programme that targets girls and boys at the beginning of secondary school, regardless of risk status. Based upon earlier media literacy work (e.g. Wade et al., 2003; Wilksch et al., 2006), the programme adopts an interactive style and uses small group work to help young people to build skills to resist appearance-related pressure from the media and advertising industries, and to reduce internalization of the thin and muscular ideals. Activities focus on media literacy, activism, and advocacy; including an exploration of the media's stereotypical portrayal of women and men in advertising, learning about airbrushing, writing protest letters to industry, and role playing strategies to deal with social pressures to look a certain way.

Media Smart has been evaluated in controlled trials with high and low-risk adolescent girls and boys in Australia. Although an earlier trial found that *Media Smart* did not reduce weight and shape concern, dieting, and internalization of media beauty ideals among 15-year-old adolescent girls (Wilksch et al., 2008), more recent trials indicate that *Media Smart* may be an effective intervention for younger girls and boys. These trials have shown that *Media Smart* is effective in reducing 13-year-old girls' and boys' concerns with, and over-evaluation of, body weight and shape, dieting, body dissatisfaction, and depression (Wilksch & Wade, 2009; Wilksch, 2010). These improvements in body image also appear to be maintained at 6 months and 2.5 years post-intervention. So far, the impact of *Media Smart* has only been evaluated when it is delivered by an external interventionist. Further research is necessary to determine if *Media Smart* will also be effective when delivered by school teachers, peers, or other endogenous providers.

SCHOOL PROGRAMMES THAT
ADDRESS VISIBLE DIFFERENCE

Schools are learning and social environments and as such they are also well positioned to support young people with visible differences (Rumsey & Harcourt, 2004). Specifically, they can assist with coping and social skills training among students who have a visible difference, both of which have been shown to improve psychosocial adjustment (Robinson et al., 1996). As the prevalence of visible differences is relatively low, it may be difficult for teachers and schools to receive appropriate training and support in the occasional instances in which they do have a student with visible difference who requires support (Frances, 2000). Further, interventions that focus only on students with visible difference may single out these students from their peers, and potentially reinforce negative stereotypes that they are different to other children.

Another strategy that schools can adopt to address visible differences is to promote an inclusive school environment that is accepting of diversity in appearance. Not only does this strategy avoid problems associated with separating students with visible differences from their peers, but it also has the capacity to address the appearance-related concerns of students with and without visible differences— as these concerns may be derived from the same social norms that emphasize narrowly defined beauty ideals and the importance of looking a certain way (i.e. thin, muscular, clear complexion and a symmetrical face) (Lovegrove & Rumsey, 2005). Despite the potential for school-based interventions to support young people with visible difference and to promote acceptance of diversity in appearance more broadly, typically schools only address these issues if they have a student with a visible difference. Furthermore, there has been very little research that has addressed the development and evaluation of such interventions (Rumsey & Harcourt, 2004). Where this research exists, it tends not to be methodologically rigorous or as advanced as the research investigating negative body image and eating disorders prevention in schools.

Interventions to support children with visible difference in schools

Research suggests that social skills training can assist people with visible differences to better cope with difficult social situations, and in turn can reduce social anxiety and improve psychosocial adjustment (Robinson et al., 1996). Capitalizing on this, Outlook is a hospital-based support unit in South West England that, among other services, provides a social skills training summer programme for adolescents with a visible difference aged 12–13 years (Maddern & Owen, 2004). Based on a cognitive behaviour therapy model, the aim of the Outlook Summer Group programme is to promote the development and practice of social skills that will help young people with visible differences to transition from primary to secondary school. The programme consists of one half day session with six to eight children and a separate session for their parents. The children can then participate in a follow-up session halfway through the first term of secondary school. Sessions typically involve role plays, games and artwork that help young people with visible differences to explore ways to cope with new social experiences, and difficult situations that may occur on the school playground. As yet, it is unknown whether the Outlook Summer Group is effective in helping young people with visible differences better integrate into secondary school. However, Maddern and Owen (2004) conducted a process evaluation of the programme, and found that the majority of the young people and parents sampled reported that they enjoyed taking part and welcomed the opportunity the programme provided to share their experiences with others.

Changing Faces, a UK-based charity that provides support to people with visible differences and their families, has developed a schools service which aims to help young people with visible differences adjust to the school setting. The service encompasses telephone and face to face contact with the young person and/or school staff, postal information, and classroom and teaching modules that offer advice to school staff on topics such as social skills, bullying and building self-esteem. In 2004, the Changing Faces schools service had reached 144 schools in the UK. O'Dell and Prior (2004) surveyed 20 of these schools to explore the school staff's perceptions of the service. The majority of staff, all of whom had had professional contact with a student with a visible difference, reported that the service was helpful. Approximately 50% also reported that the service had positively impacted on their students' adjustment, with the most common improvements being a reduction in bullying and increased self-confidence. Further research with established and validated measures, control comparison groups and follow-up measures is necessary to fully determine the effectiveness of programmes such as the Outlook Summer Group and the Changing Faces schools service in improving the adjustment of young people with visible differences in the school setting.

Interventions to promote acceptance of visible difference in schools

In addition to their school service that focuses on working specifically with young people with visible differences, Changing Faces has also developed a series of education resource packs for schools which target young people with and without visible differences in the school settings. These education packs aim to improve young people's attitudes towards people with visible differences (Changing Faces, 2010).

The packs include lesson plans, Powerpoint presentations, activity sheets, and other resources that teachers can use to promote a school and classroom environment that is inclusive and more accepting of diversity in appearance.

Cline and colleagues (1998) evaluated an early version of the Changing Faces education packs, which at that time included a video, example lesson plans, classroom and library resources, and information on visible differences and relevant organizations. They conducted interviews with 101 school students from five British primary schools and used story and sentence completion tasks to assess the intervention's success in improving students' awareness, acceptance of, and attitudes towards, children and adults with visible difference. Although there were no improvements among students who had received the intervention in comparison to control students on attitudes towards and acceptance of visible difference, the intervention was successful in improving knowledge and understanding about visible differences. A more up-to-date controlled evaluation of the current Changing Faces education resource packs was recently undertaken with 412 students from three secondary schools in the UK (Stock & Whale, 2011). Although reports from both students and teachers indicated that the resources were well received, again there were no significant improvements in students' attitudes towards people with visible differences post-intervention. Pre-intervention attitudes towards people with visible differences within this sample of students, however, were predominantly positive; therefore there may have been little scope for improvement.

FUTURE LESSONS TO BE LEARNT

While this chapter has identified interventions that have shown promise in preventing negative body image and eating disorders, supporting students with visible differences, and in promoting the acceptance of diversity in appearance within schools, it is clear that there is a continuing need for further research in this area. In relation to negative body image and eating disorder prevention programmes, further research and development is needed to address boys' body image concerns within the school setting. Additionally, current programmes tend to adopt multiple theoretical orientations and include a variety of strategies, and few studies have sought to investigate the effectiveness of the individual components of these interventions. Therefore, further research is necessary to establish what components and theoretical orientations are most effective in reducing negative body image and the incidence of eating disorders among young people.

There is also a clear dearth in the literature in relation to the development and evaluation of school-based interventions that address visible difference. As the pressure to fit in with socially prescribed beauty ideals is increasing for young people with and without visible difference, future research may usefully investigate strategies that focus on acceptance of diversity in appearance more broadly in schools;

rather than focusing on either weight and shape or visible difference exclusively. Furthermore, the lessons already learnt in the field of negative body image and eating disorder school-based prevention research (e.g. the programme and participant factors that appear most successful) may provide the starting blocks for the development of school-based interventions that promote positive body image and the acceptance of diversity in appearance more broadly.

REFERENCES

Becker, C. B., & Stice, E. (2008). *Sorority Body Image Program: Group Leader Guide.* New York: Oxford University Press.

Becker, C. B., & Stice, E. (2011). *Succeed Body Image Programme: Manual.* New York: Oxford University Press.

Becker, C. B., Smith, L. M., & Ciao, A. C. (2005). Reducing eating disorder risk factors in sorority members: A randomized trial. *Behavior Therapy,* 36, 245–54.

Becker, C. B., Smith, L. M., & Ciao, A. C. (2006). Peer-facilitated eating disorder prevention: A randomized effectiveness trial of cognitive dissonance and media advocacy. *Journal of Counseling Psychology,* 53, 550–5.

Becker, C. B., Bull, S., Schaumberg, K., Cauble, A., & Franco, A. (2008). Effectiveness of peer-led eating disorders prevention: A replication trial. *Journal of Consulting and Clinical Psychology,* 76, 347–54.

British Council. (2008). *Inclusion and Diversity in Education (INDIE) Research Findings.* http://www.britishcouncil.org/indie-research-findings-full-results.htm

Changing Faces. (2010). Teaching resources available from http://www.changingfaces.org.uk/Education/Teaching-resources

Cline, T., Proto, A., Raval, P., & Paolo, T. D. (1998). The effects of brief exposure and of classroom teaching on attitudes children express towards facial disfigurement in peers. *Educational Research,* 40, 55–68.

Davison, K. K., & Birch, L. L. (2002). Processes linking weight status and self-concept among girls from aged 5 to 7 years. *Developmental Psychology,* 38, 735–48.

Dittmar, H., Halliwell, E., & Ive, S. (2006). Does barbie make girls want to be thin? The effect of experimental exposure to images of dolls on the body image of 5- to 8-year-old girls. *Developmental Psychology,* 42, 283–92.

Dohnt, H. K., & Tiggemann, M. (2008). Promoting positive body image in young girls: An evaluation of 'Shapesville'. *European Eating Disorders Review,* 16, 222–33.

Eisenberg, M., Neumark-Sztainer, D., & Story, M. (2003). Associations of weight-based teasing and emotional well-being among adolescents. *Archives of Pediatric and Adolescent Medicine,* 157, 733–8.

Favaro, A., Zanetti, T., Huon, G., & Santonastaso, P. (2005). Engaging teachers in an eating disorder prevention intervention. *International Journal of Eating Disorders,* 38, 73–7.

Festinger, L. (1957). *A theory of cognitive dissonance.* Palo Alto, CA: Stanford University Press.

Fingeret, M. C., Warren, C. S., & Cepedo-Benito, A. (2006). Eating disorder prevention research: A meta-analysis. *Eating Disorders,* 14, 191–213.

Frances, J. (2000). Providing effective support in school when a child has a disfigured appearance: The work of the Changing Faces school service. *Support for Learning,* 15, 177–82.

Green, M. W., & Rogers, P. J. (1995). Impaired cognitive functioning during spontaneous dieting. *Psychological Medicine,* 25, 1003–10.

Green, M. W., & Rogers, P. J. (1998). Impairments in working memory associated with spontaneous dieting behvaiour. *Psychological Medicine,* 28, 1063–70.

Haines, J., Neumark-Sztainer, D., Eisenberg, M., & Hannan, P. J. (2006). Weight teasing and disordered eating behaviors in adolescents: Longitudinal findings from Project EAT (Eating Among Teens). *Pediatrics,* 117, 209–15.

Haines, J., Neumark-Sztainer, D., & Morris, B. (2008). Theatre as a behavior change strategy: Qualitative findings from a school-based intervention. *Eating Disorders,* 17, 241–54.

Holt, K. E., & Ricciardelli, L. A. (2008). Weight concerns among elementary school children: A review of prevention programs. *Body Image,* 5, 233–43.

Kish, V., & Lansdown, R. (2000). Meeting the psychosocial impact of facial disfigurement: Developing a clinical service for children and families. *Clinical Child Psychology and Psychiatry,* 5, 497–512.

Levine, M. P., & Piran, N. (2004). The role of body image in the prevention of eating disorders. *Body Image,* 1, 57–70.

Levine, M. P., & Smolak, L. (2006). *The prevention of eating problems and eating disorders: Theory, research and practice.* Mahwah, NJ: Lawrence Erlbaum Associates.

Lovegrove, E., & Rumsey, N. (2005). Ignoring it doesn't make it stop: Adolescents, appearance and bullying. *Cleft Palate-Craniofacial Journal,* 42, 33–44.

Maddern, L., & Owen, T. (2004). The Outlook summer group: A social skills workshop for children with a different appearance who are transferring to secondary school. *Clinical Psychology,* 33, 25–9.

McCabe, M. P., & Ricciardelli, L. A. (2004). Body image dissatisfaction among males across the lifespan: A review of past literature. *Journal of Psychosomatic Research,* 56, 675–85.

McCabe, M. P., Ricciardelli, L. A., & Karantzas, G. (2010). Impact of a health body image program among adolescent boys on body image, negative affect, and body change strategies. *Body Image,* 7, 117–23.

McVey, G. L., Gusella, J., Tweed, S., & Ferrari, M. (2009). A controlled evaluation of web-based training for teachers and public health practitioners on the prevention of eating disorders. *Eating Disorders,* 17, 1–26.

Mission Australia. (2008). *National survey of young Australians 2008.* http://www.mission-australia.com.au/document-downloads/doc_details/82-national-survey-of-young-australians-2008-

Neumark-Sztainer, D., Falkner, N., Story, M., Perry, C., Hannan, P. J., & Mulert, S. (2002). Weight-teasing among adolescents: Correlations with weight status and disordered eating behaviors. *International Journal of Obesity,* 26, 123–31.

O'Dea, J. (2005). School-based health education strategies for the improvement of body image and prevention of eating problems: An overview of safe and successful interventions. *Health Education,* 105, 11–33.

O'Dea, J., & Abraham, S. (2000). Improving body image, eating attitudes and behaviours of young male and female adolescents: A new education approach which focuses on self-esteem. *International Journal of Eating Disorders,* 28, 43–57.

O'Dell, L., & Prior, J. (2004). Evaluating a schools' service for children with a facial disfigurement: The views of teaching and support staff. *Support for Learning,* 20, 35–40.

Penny, H., & Haddock, G. (2007). Anti-fat prejudice among children: The 'mere proximity' effect in 5–10 year olds. *Journal of Experimental Social Psychology*, 43, 678–83.

Perez, M., Becker, C. B., & Ramirez, A. (2010). Transportability of an empirically supported dissonance-based prevention program for eating disorders. *Body Image*, 7, 179–86.

Piran, N. (1999). The reduction of preoccupation with body weight and shape in schools: A feminist approach. In N. Piran, M. P. Levine, & C. Steiner-Adair (eds.) *Prevention eating disorders: A handbook of interventions and special challenges*, pp. 148–56. Philadelphia, PA: Brunner/Mazel.

Puhl, R., & Brownell, K. D. (2006). Confronting and coping with stigma: An investigation of overweight and obese adults. *Obesity*, 14, 1802–16.

Robinson, E., Rumsey, N., & Partridge, J. (1996). An evaluation of the impact of social inter-action skills training for facially disfigured people. *British Journal of Plastic Surgery*, 1, 281–89.

Rumsey, N., & Harcourt, D. (2004). Body image and disfigurement: Issues and interven-tions. *Body Image*, 1, 83–97.

Russell-Mayhew, S., Arthur, N., & Ewashen, C. (2007). Targeting students, teachers and parents in a wellness-based prevention programme in schools. *Eating Disorders*, 15, 159–81.

Scime, M., Cook-Cottone, C., Kane, L., & Watson, T. (2006). Group prevention of eating disorders with fifth-grade females: Impact on body dissatisfaction, drive for thinness, and media influence. *Eating Disorders*, 14, 143–55.

Smolak, L., Levine, M. P., & Schermer, F. (1998a). A controlled evaluation of an elementary school primary prevention program for eating disorders. *Journal of Psychosomatic Research*, 44, 339–53.

Smolak, L., Levine, M. P., & Schermer, F. (1998b). Lessons from lessons: An evaluation of an elementary school prevention program. In W. Vandereycken & G. Noordenbos (eds.) *The prevention of eating disorders*, pp. 137–72. New York: New York University Press.

Stanford, J. N., & McCabe, M. P. (2005). Evaluation of a body image prevention programme for adolescent boys. *European Eating Disorders Review*, 13, 360–70.

Stice, E., & Presnell, K. (2007). *The body project: Promoting body acceptance and preventing eating disorders*. New York: Oxford University Press.

Stice, E., & Shaw, H. (2004). Eating disorder prevention programs: A meta-analytic review. *Psychological Bulletin*, 130, 206–27.

Stice, E., Mazotti, L., Weibel, D., & Agras, W. S. (2000). Dissonance prevention program decreases thin-ideal internalization, body dissatisfaction, dieting, negative affect and bulimic symptoms: A preliminary experiment. *International Journal of Eating Disorders*, 27, 206–17.

Stice, E., Trost, A., & Chase, A. (2003). Healthy weight control and dissonance-based eating disorder prevention programs: Results from a controlled trial. *International Journal of Eating Disorders*, 33, 10–21.

Stice, E., Shaw, H., Burton, E., & Wade, E. (2006). Dissonance and healthy weight eating disorder prevention programs: A randomized efficacy trial. *Journal of Consulting and Clinical Psychology*, 74, 263–75.

Stice, E., Shaw, H., & Marti, C. N. (2007). A meta-analytic review of eating disorder preven-tion programs: Encouraging findings. *Annual Review of Clinical Psychology*, 3, 207–31.

Stice, E., Shaw, H., Becker, C. B., & Rohde, P. (2008). Dissonance-based interventions for the prevention of eating disorders: Using persuasion principles to promote health. *Prevention Science*, 9, 114–28.

Stice, E., Rohde, P., Gau, J., & Shaw, H. (2009). An effectiveness trial of a dissonance-based eating disorder prevention program for high-risk adolescent girls. *Journal of Consulting and Clinical Psychology, 77*, 825–34.

Stock, N., & Whale, K. (2011). *An evaluation of a school-based intervention to promote positive attitudes and behaviours towards people with facial disfigurement: Main study report.* Bristol: Centre for Appearance Research.

Stock, S., Miranda, C., Evans, S., Plessis, S., Ridley, J., Yeh, S., *et al.* (2007). Healthy Buddies: A novel, peer-led health promotion program for the prevention of obesity and eating disorders in children in elementary school. *Pediatrics, 120*, e1059–68.

Thompson, J. K., Heinberg, L. J., Altabe, M. N., & Tantleff-Dunn, S. (2004). *Exacting beauty: Theory, assessment and treatment of body image disturbance.* Washington, DC: American Psychological Association.

Tiggemann, M., Gardiner, M., & Slater, A. (2000). "I would rather be size 10 than have straight A's": A focus group study of adolescent girls' wish to be thinner. *Journal of Adolescence, 23*, 645–59.

Tiggemann, M., Martins, Y., & Churchett, L. (2008). Beyond muscles: Unexplored parts of men's body image. *Journal of Health Psychology, 113*, 1163–72.

Vartanian, L. R., & Shaprow, J. G. (2008). Effects of weight stigma on exercise motivation and behaviour. *Journal of Health Psychology, 13*, 131–8.

Wade, T. D., Davidson, S., & O'Dea, J. (2003). A preliminary controlled evaluation of a school-based media literacy program and self-esteem program for reducing eating disorder risk factors. *International Journal of Eating Disorders, 33*, 371–82.

Watson, R., & Vaughn, L. M. (2006). Limiting the effects of the media on body image: Does the length of a media literacy intervention make a difference. *Eating Disorders, 14*, 385–400.

Wertheim, E. H., Koerner, J., & Paxton, S. J. (2001). Longitudinal predictors of restrictive eating and bulimic tendencies in three different age groups of adolescent girls *Journal of Youth and Adolescence, 30*, 69–81.

Wilksch, S. M. (2010). Universal school-based eating disorder prevention: Benefits to both high- and low-risk participants on the core cognitive feature of eating disorders. *Clinical Psychologist, 14*, 62–9.

Wilksch, S. M., & Wade, T. D. (2009). Reduction of shape and weight concern in young adolescents: A 30-month controlled evaluation of a media literacy program. *Journal of the American Academy of Child and Adolescent Psychiatry, 48*, 652–61.

Wilksch, S. M., Tiggemann, M., & Wade, T. D. (2006). Impact of interactive school-based media literacy lessons for reducing internalization of media ideals in young adolescent girls and boys. *International Journal of Eating Disorders, 39*, 385–93.

Wilksch, S. M., Durbridge, M. R., & Wade, T. D. (2008). A preliminary controlled comparison of programs designed to reduce risk of eating disorders targeting perfectionism and media literacy. *Journal of the American Academy of Child and Adolescent Psychiatry, 47*, 939–47.

Yager, Z. (2010). Issues of teacher training for eating disorders and child obesity prevention. In J. O'Dea & M. Eriksen (eds.) *Childhood obesity prevention: International research, controversies and intervention.* Oxford: Oxford University Press.

Yager, Z., & O'Dea, J. (2005). The role of teachers and other educations in the prevention of eating disorders and child obesity: What are the issues? *Eating Disorders, 13*, 261–78.

Yager, Z., & O'Dea, J. (2008). Prevention programs for body image and eating disorders on university campuses: A review of large, controlled interventions. *Health Promotion International,* 23, 173–89.

Yager, Z., & O'Dea, J. (2009). Body image, dieting and disordered eating and activity practices among teacher trainees: Implications for school-based health education and obesity prevention programs. *Health Education Research,* 24, 472–82.

Yager, Z., & O'Dea, J. (2010). A controlled intervention to promote a healthy body image, reduce eating disorder risk and prevent excessive exercise among trainee health education and physical education teachers. *Health Education Research,* 25, 841–52.

Yanover, T., & Thompson, J. K. (2008). Eating problems, body image disturbances, and academic achievement: Preliminary evaluations of the eating and body image disturbances academic interference scale. *International Journal of Eating Disorders,* 41, 184–7.

CHAPTER 38

THERAPEUTIC INTERVENTIONS: EVIDENCE OF EFFECTIVENESS

ELIZABETH JENKINSON

INTRODUCTION

MANY people living with a visible difference seek advice and support from charities, healthcare professionals, and psychologists to manage the physical, emotional, and social challenges they face (Rumsey & Harcourt, 2005). However, few research studies adequately demonstrate the effectiveness of any particular therapeutic approach. Therefore, no evidence-based clinical guidelines for best practice in the delivery of psychological interventions for people with visible differences currently exist.

This chapter aims to provide an overview of the evidence to date which evaluates the effectiveness of therapeutic interventions designed to help people cope with the psychological challenges of a visible difference. It focuses on psychological interventions, rather than those designed to ameliorate physical symptoms. The chapter also considers the evidence across conditions, in accordance with the research evidence that suggests that the aetiology, extent, and severity of a disfigurement are not predictive of adjustment (Moss, 2005).

Firstly, the current provision of therapeutic interventions for adults and children is briefly outlined, followed by a review of the existing evidence base to support the application of these approaches. The chapter closes with a discussion of what needs to change and how change can be achieved when attempting to build the evidence base in the field of appearance research.

CURRENT SERVICE PROVISION

Psychological support is not offered as part of routine care for all patients with disfiguring conditions (see Dropkin, 1989; Hansen & Clarke, 2009) and the support which is available is delivered in a number of settings. Current service provision in the UK includes specialist NHS services, psychology embedded in multidisciplinary teams, and support offered by charities (Hansen & Clarke, 2009) (see Chapter 5). There is also the potential for support and interventions to be delivered in the context of Primary Care, for example, by general practice counsellors, counselling psychologists, clinical psychologists, health psychologists, educational psychologists, and GPs; however, support delivered in these contexts is currently the exception rather than the norm.

Many people who have a visible difference who seek support do so to help with feelings of anxiety and depression and concerns over social situations (Rumsey & Harcourt, 2005). Psychologists and counsellors working with this patient group within the NHS focus predominantly on the use of therapeutic approaches grounded in cognitive behavioural therapy (CBT) in agreement with clinical guidelines for the treatment of depression and anxiety disorders (National Institute for Health and Clinical Excellence (NICE), 2007, 2009). SIST is also utilized by clinicians to help patients deal with the challenges of social situations such as unsolicited questioning, staring and avoidance (Robinson et al., 1996).

Charities also provide independent advice and support for people with visible differences, their families and friends, healthcare professionals, and educators. For example, Changing Faces adopt SIST- and CBT-based approaches, with counsellors and trained charitable sector workers offering self-help literature, in addition to information and counselling on the telephone, via email and/or face-to-face. Their approach assists people with 'interpersonal' challenges, dealing with other people's often negative reactions, and the 'intrapersonal' challenges of living with a visible difference such as low self-esteem, anxiety, and depression (Partridge & Pearson, 2008).

So, with therapeutic approaches such as CBT and SIST being offered, does the current research evidence base support their use for people with visible differences?

ARE INTERVENTIONS EFFECTIVE FOR PEOPLE WITH VISIBLE DIFFERENCES?

Few studies exist which test the effectiveness of therapeutic interventions in reducing distress and increasing social skills and psychological well-being among people with visible differences. As a consequence, there remains little evidence to support the use of any particular approach to intervention or to inform the mode, medium, and setting of delivery.

This section reviews the empirical evidence for CBT, SIST, person-centred counselling, and support groups. It draws on the results of two systematic reviews which have evaluated the empirical quantitative research evidence for the effectiveness of psychological interventions for adults (Bessell & Moss, 2007) and children (Jenkinson et al., in preparation) with visible differences. Both reviews involved extensively searching academic databases and consulting with clinicians to source all relevant studies. Reports were excluded in which interventions for other appearance concerns such as eating disorders and body dysmorphic disorder were tested. All studies were assessed for quality using a hierarchy of evidence, in which randomized controlled trials (RCTs) were considered the gold standard (Centre for Reviews and Dissemination, 2001). Both reviews concluded that there was a lack of good quality evidence to support the use of any particular therapeutic approach, but also suggest that CBT and SIST show promise.

Bessell and Moss's (2007) systematic review of the effectiveness of psychosocial interventions for adults (16 years old and over) with visible differences included 12 papers, with eight detailing interventions with a group of people with the same condition (e.g. vitiligo (Papadopoulos et al., 1999)), one with patients attending a head and neck cancer clinic (Fiegenbaum, 1981), one with patients from two clinics (dermatology and plastics (Newell & Clarke, 2000)) and two with a group of participants with a range of visible differences (Robinson et al., 1996; Kleve et al., 2002). Overall, these studies evaluated four peer support groups, five CBT-based interventions, two SIST interventions, and one person-centred counselling intervention.

Jenkinson's systematic review examined the effectiveness of interventions designed to increase well-being for children and adolescents (5–18 years old) with a range of visible differences (Jenkinson et al., in preparation). Ten studies (nine published papers and one unpublished PhD thesis) were included. Seven assessed the effectiveness of interventions for children and adolescents with burns injuries (Blakeney et al., 1995, 2005; Biggs et al., 1997; Girolami, 2004; Arnoldo et al., 2006; Gaskell 2007; Rimmer et al., 2007), one focused on patients with psoriasis (Scheewe et al., 2001), one on young people with craniofacial conditions (Kapp Simon et al., 2005), and one with a group of children and adolescents with a range of conditions

(Maddern et al., 2006). Two of these studies evaluated CBT-based interventions and eight evaluated interventions grounded in SIST including school re-entry programmes and residential camps.

The evidence that these two reviews offer for broad therapeutic approaches is briefly presented and considered here, alongside more recent research which evaluates new approaches towards helping people with a visible difference who are experiencing distress in relation to their appearance.

Cognitive behavioural therapy

CBT-based approaches to working with people with visible differences focus on helping them to re-evaluate the importance of their appearance as a component of their self-worth (Kleve et al., 2002). CBT is the intervention of choice within the NHS for the treatment of depression, anxiety, and eating disorders in the UK, so CBT-based approaches to the challenges of living with a visible difference sit comfortably alongside current NHS and government approaches to mental healthcare provision (NICE, 2004, 2007, 2009). This approach to working with people with appearance and body image concerns has also been advocated by leading clinicians and researchers in the field of appearance psychology (e.g. Papadopolous, 1999; Newell, 2000; Cash, 2002; Rumsey & Harcourt, 2005; Hansen & Clarke, 2009) and CBT approaches to body image disturbance and appearance concerns for people without visible differences have received support in reviews and meta-analyses (see Jarry & Beradi, 2004; Jarry & Ip, 2005).

However, the popularity and acceptability of this approach with researchers and clinicians working in the field should not be confused with evidence of effectiveness. To date, only a few studies provide good quality evidence to support the use of CBT in helping children and adults cope with the challenges of an altered appearance (Bessell & Moss 2007; Jenkinson et al., 2011).

Face-to-face group and individual CBT interventions

Bessell and Moss (2007) identified two key studies which found individual CBT-based interventions to improve psychosocial well-being with adult patients. Kleve et al. (2002) evaluated sessions provided by Outlook, an NHS outpatients unit in Bristol, UK which specializes in psychological support for patients with a range of visible differences. Sessions were based on CBT and SIST and patient-reported outcome measures showed improvements in anxiety, depression, appearance-related distress, and social anxiety after intervention and at 6-month follow-up. The study could have been improved by including a control group but does provide some evidence that CBT can be effective for people with visible differences.

Papadopoulous et al. (1999) also showed significant gains for people with vitiligo and dermatological conditions attending weekly individual CBT sessions.

Patients showed improvements after intervention on standardized measures of body image dysphoria and automatic thoughts, self-esteem, and dermatology-related quality of life. However, the study findings have limited validity due to factors such as incomplete reporting of descriptive statistics and weak power analysis.

Bessell and Moss (2007) found very limited evidence for the effectiveness of group CBT for adults, with only one study (Fortune et al., 2002, 2004) deemed methodologically sound against the criteria imposed by the authors. This study included patients with psoriasis and assessed the effectiveness of a CBT group intervention in comparison to routine pharmacological treatment. Patients who received the intervention showed improvements in well-being after the intervention in terms of anxiety, depression, life-stress, and a range of illness perceptions. However, no significant changes were found in coping strategies.

Children and adolescents were also shown to benefit from CBT-based interventions in two studies identified by Jenkinson et al. (2011). Maddern et al. (2006) evaluated an outpatient intervention conducted with 19 children and adolescents with craniofacial conditions including cleft lip and palate, dermatological conditions, and limb loss. Four sessions of CBT and problem-solving techniques were led by a psychologist and delivered individually with parental support. Statistically significant reductions in parental reports of anxiety and depression and overall 'problem' scores on the Child Behaviour Checklist (CBCL; Achenbach 1991) were found which were maintained at 6-month follow-up. However, no data were collected from the children themselves, limiting the strength of the conclusions that can be drawn from these findings.

An RCT of a 4–6 week 10-session programme for young people with psoriasis also showed encouraging results (Scheewe et al., 2001). The therapeutic approach was described as 'behavioural therapy' (BT) but the paper also referenced instances of working with patients' cognitions about their appearance and illness beliefs. The intervention group significantly improved in comparison with the control group on measures of self-estimated attractiveness, impairment and self-efficacy but not on measures of anxiety. These improvements were still significant at 1 year follow-up, with the exception of estimated attractiveness.

So, in summary, the picture is promising but the evidence base is limited thus far. Further research is needed in order to offer a definitive recommendation of CBT delivered in a group or individually.

CBT-based self-help manuals and leaflets

Self-help manuals and leaflets can offer an accessible medium to provide information, techniques, and advice to those in need of low levels of psychological support. However, a lack of evidence exists to support their effectiveness in reducing psychological distress related to the experience of living with a visible difference, with only one study (Newell & Clarke, 2000) meeting the criteria necessary for inclusion in systematic reviews.

Adult outpatients with dermatological conditions and conditions associated with eligibility for plastic and reconstructive surgery were sent self-help materials detailing CBT techniques designed to promote coping with anxiety within the context of facial appearance (Newell & Clarke, 2000). The booklets were found to be effective in reducing anxiety and depression and small but significant improvements were found in participants' ability to engage in social situations as assessed by the Social Leisure subscale of the Social Adjustment Questionnaire (SAQ; Marks et al., 1977). Nevertheless, this study had its limitations. The original sample had a male gender bias and there was a high attrition rate. As concluded by Bessell and Moss (2007), the study provides limited evidence for self-help materials which detail CBT techniques but suggests that both CBT and self-help materials require further investigation as appropriate models and as a medium of therapeutic intervention.

Computerized CBT (cCBT)

A new avenue for intervention is computerized CBT (cCBT), which involves the delivery of a programme of CBT sessions via CD-ROM or the Internet. Much like face-to-face delivery, cCBT has been shown to be effective in the treatment of psychological disorders such as anxiety and depression both for adults and young people (see Kaltenthaler et al., 2004; Richardson, 2010) and is recommended by NICE as an effective therapeutic intervention (NICE, 2005). This approach has potential as a novel and accessible approach to offering therapy to people with visible differences.

One recent study provides good quality evidence that cCBT may promote psychological well-being for adults with an altered appearance. Face IT, a cCBT programme for adults with a range of visible differences facilitated by trained healthcare professionals has recently been trialled with success. Six computerized sessions delivered weekly were shown to decrease anxiety and depression and to increase social skills. The programme showed results comparable to a similar intervention delivered face-to-face by highly trained healthcare professionals (Bessell, 2009). Clinicians also reported that an online intervention delivered remotely would help 'immensely' with increasing access to intervention for patients unable to attend appointments face to face (Bessell et al., 2010). Currently no published studies have evaluated the effectiveness of cCBT for people with visible differences when delivered remotely and without support from therapists, although this is planned for Face IT. This is an important step before cCBT could be recommended as a therapeutic tool. For further consideration of online interventions and their development, see Chapter 39.

Third-wave CBT approaches

Third-wave approaches such as Acceptance and Commitment Therapy (ACT), Dialectical Behaviour Therapy (DBT), and Mindfulness are increasingly popular in the field of health and clinical psychology as therapeutic interventions (see Pull, 2009). As second-wave therapies such as CBT and SIST showed promise in the two existing systematic reviews, it seems prudent that the potential of third-wave CBT/BT inspired approaches to alleviate distress should also be investigated within the context of appearance psychology.

Reviews of the effectiveness of these approaches with patients with psychiatric conditions also suggest these approaches may be helpful. Some good quality studies meeting the criteria for inclusion in a recent systematic review and meta-analysis showed positive gains for patients and a moderate effect size for both ACT and DBT interventions (Ost, 2008). However, there was not sufficient evidence to draw firm conclusions about the effectiveness of these approaches and definitively recommend their application.

Social interaction skills training

SIST, school re-entry programmes, and residential camps all aim to skill the participants with coping strategies to engage adeptly with their social world. The underlying premise is that living with a visible difference can present challenges in everyday situations; with social anxiety and avoidance a pervasive issue for many (Rumsey & Harcourt 2005). Training in how to cope with these difficulties is a logical antidote, as summed up by Changing Faces CEO James Partridge, 'Self-confidence grows from learning that, by your behaviour, you can influence how other people respond to you, especially in the first crucial moments of a meeting' (Partridge & Pearson, 2008, p.491)

Group social interaction skills training

Two studies reviewed by Bessell and Moss (2007) evaluated the potential of group social skills training but provide little evidence for their effectiveness.

Fiegenbaum (1981) tested the effectiveness of a 10-week SIST programme for adults with head and neck cancer. Large differences in well-being before and after the intervention were claimed but a small sample size, a lack of reported data, inappropriate statistics, and self-designed outcome measures detract from the validity and credibility of the study.

Robinson et al. (1996) provided limited evidence for the effectiveness of group SIST. Sixty-four adults with a range of visible differences, such as burns, vitiligo, and facial palsies received a 2-day workshop and large improvements were shown after intervention. However, with no control group as a comparison and a lack of multivariate analysis of the dataset, the results must be considered with caution.

The evidence for SIST with children and adolescents is also limited. In a study conducted by Kapp-Simon and colleagues (2005), children with craniofacial conditions received SIST over 12 weeks and social interactions were observed in the school lunchroom before and after the intervention. The study was well-conceived and implemented and a significant increase in observed social interactions was recorded after intervention for those young people in the intervention group. However, the sample size was small (13 in the control group and seven in the intervention group) and measures were observational with no self-report from the children themselves.

School re-entry programmes

School re-entry programmes aim to help young people develop social skills to address the questions and attention they may receive on their return to the classroom, e.g. after sustaining and being treated for an appearance-altering injury or condition (see Frances, 2004). Despite the support they may provide the child, parents, teachers, and classmates, existing quantitative studies have not shown these programmes to be effective. Three studies conducted in the US with children with burns injuries were identified by Jenkinson et al. (in preparation). These showed no differences between control and intervention groups, or changes before and after intervention (Blakeney et al., 1995; Biggs et al., 1997; Girolami, 2004).

Residential camps

The basic tenet of residential camps is to foster the social skills and self-esteem of attendees and to provide peer support, usually over a week-long intensive programme of activities. By practising social interactions with peers in a 'safe' environment, it is hoped that camp goers will gain confidence and skills that have been hard to acquire in settings in which they live. Recent studies evaluating camps for children with burns injuries suggest this approach may be beneficial in optimizing psychological well-being, for at least some attendees.

Specifically, Blakeney et al. (2005) evaluated a 4-day residential school for children and adolescents with burns injuries. They randomized 64, 12–17-year-olds from a waiting list to receive either the social skills programme or routine care. The programme was led by a psychologist and delivered within a group setting. After a year, the intervention group showed significantly greater improvements on internalizing and externalizing subscales of the Child Behaviour Checklist (CBCL, Achenbach 1991) than children receiving routine care. However, the non-intervention group was not comparable to the intervention group in terms of their CBCL scores. Participants in the control group averaged lower baseline scores before treatment, suggesting baseline differences in adjustment to their visible difference and limiting the validity of the findings.

A study by Rimmer et al. (2007) failed to demonstrate benefits for attendees of one camp, but suggested camps may have a cumulative effect, with the authors reporting gains in the self-esteem of Caucasian attendees after year two. Other studies have also suggested that camps may be particularly effective with subgroups of attendees. Arnoldo et al. (2006) showed a week-long residential camp led to improvements in psychosocial functioning for adolescents aged 12 and over and with smaller burns, compared to younger participants with larger burns.

These studies provide some support for the effectiveness of SIST in group and residential settings for children and adolescents with burns injuries, but given a number of limitations highlighted above, research of higher methodological quality is required.

Person-centred therapy

Person-centred therapy is a humanistic approach to psychotherapy or counselling. Therapists help clients find their own solutions to their problems using non-directive, empathic approaches (see Cooper et al., 2010 for a recent review). Only one study included by Bessell and Moss (2007) in their systematic review evaluated the effectiveness of group person-centred therapy for adults with the skin condition vitiligo compared to group CBT and a no-treatment control group (Papadopoulos et al., 2004). Although participants in both intervention groups showed some significant improvements in general health, the study suffered from methodological flaws including inappropriate statistical analysis. Therefore, there is only poor evidence to suggest person-centred therapy works for this population and further investigation of the effectiveness of this approach is required.

Support groups

Support groups enable people with similar conditions and concerns to discuss and share experiences in a safe environment. These are often peer led, with those who have lived the experience facilitating the discussions. Bessell and Moss (2007) identified four studies which evaluated the effectiveness of support group interventions for adults with visible differences but found little good quality evidence on which to base conclusions concerning their effectiveness.

A study of participants with psoriasis (Price et al., 1991) showed significant reductions in anxiety and neuroticism and improved self-esteem both after intervention and at follow-up, providing some evidence of the effectiveness of this approach. The programme included relaxation techniques and hypnosis as well as group discussion and was facilitated by a clinical psychologist; all factors which may have contributed to the positive gains for participants. Two other studies with patients with psoriasis (Bremer-Schulte et al., 1985, Kang Seng & Siew Nee, 1997) also showed some benefit, but due to methodological flaws and poor validity, cannot be considered to provide evidence for the use of this approach. Similarly a study with people with burns injuries (Cooper & Burnside, 1996) offers little evidence despite yielding significant findings. It should be noted, however, that all four studies included feedback from attendees, which showed that participants found the interventions acceptable.

A novel approach to providing peer support is via the use of online discussion forums. These are well utilized by adults and young people with health conditions when seeking social support (Wright & Bell, 2003) and young people have been found to prefer seeking health information and support online instead of face-to-face from healthcare professionals (Gray et al., 2005).

A good example of using this approach to help people with visible differences is I-Face, an online moderated discussion board, developed by Changing Faces and their Youth Council (Partridge & Pearson, 2008) and designed to enable young people with a visible difference to share their experiences. Although currently there is no evidence to support the effectiveness of these approaches in increasing well-being, qualitative studies do suggest that online discussion forums could be a fruitful direction for intervention, particularly for young people with visible differences (Fox, 2008).

Summary of the existing evidence

In summary, there is a lack of good quality evidence to demonstrate the effectiveness of any therapeutic approach in alleviating distress in people with visible differences. However, the lack of evidence of effectiveness does not mean we should conclude that these interventions are ineffective. Undoubtedly the support that is currently on offer is vital to those with pressing needs. However, whilst interventions remain untested or inadequately evaluated, it is impossible to determine the relative effectiveness of interventions for this population, and to unpack which approaches work best for whom, and in what context.

A small number of studies have shown that CBT and SIST can foster positive adjustment. Despite the methodological flaws of some of these studies, both of the systematic reviews cited here concluded that there was some support (albeit low in strength) for the effectiveness of CBT and SIST approaches with people with visible differences. This is an area for ongoing evaluation. Many more high-quality research studies testing these and other existing and novel approaches (such as cCBT) are required to inform evidence-based clinical recommendations for best practice and, ultimately, to best support people coping with the challenges posed by their appearance.

What Needs to Change and How can Change be Achieved?

In order to build an evidence base on which to design, implement, and evaluate effective interventions, what needs to change and how can change be achieved?

A new programme of research at the Centre for Appearance Research in Bristol, UK, aims to identify gaps in the evidence base and develop a consensus about the most appropriate methods of offering and evaluating interventions for people with visible differences. In line with the current evidence available and adapting models of stepped care provision (see Lovell & Richards, 2000; Bower & Gilbody, 2005; NICE guidelines, 2007, 2009) the team has classified different levels of therapeutic intervention in a pyramid reflecting the level of need of the recipients of interventions and offering examples of appropriate interventions; the 'CAR framework of interventions for people with visible differences' (see Fig. 38.1).

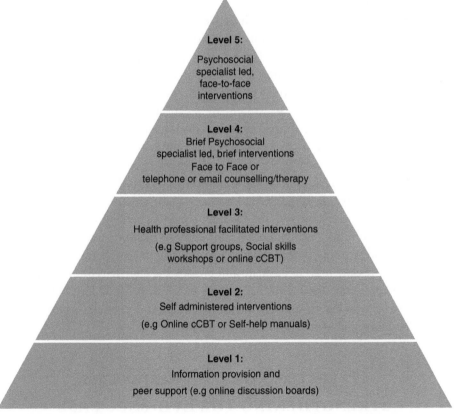

Figure 38.1 CAR framework of interventions for people with visible differences. Adapted from 2007 NICE guidelines for the treatment of anxiety and depression by Jenkinson et al. (2009) on behalf of CAR.

The pyramid illustrates the therapeutic interventions with differing levels of intensity that might be offered to people seeking support via a range of services, such as charities, the NHS and private healthcare providers, schools, and work places. Currently the availability and accessibility of these interventions is limited; however, as an immediate goal, it is suggested that level one interventions (information in leaflets or online) and peer support (face-to-face or online) should be offered to all people with visible differences consulting with healthcare professionals. This may be offered 'in house' or may involve signposting to appropriate organizations. Level two interventions are those designed to 'stand alone'; cCBT programmes and self-help leaflets or manuals. Level three interventions are higher intensity and may involve support groups or cCBT supported by a trained healthcare professional (such as Face IT, see Chapter 39), SIST workshops, camps, or school re-entry programmes. Level four interventions are those designed to meet the needs of the minority requiring more intensive intervention programmes, delivered either face to face, by telephone or email, with level five considered appropriate for people experiencing the highest levels of psychosocial distress and/or with complex case histories or presentations.

In some cases, NHS services such as cleft teams, may offer interventions at various levels of the pyramid within a multidisciplinary service. As suggested by clinicians such as Esther Hansen (see Chapter 5) and following the principles of stratified or multi-access stepped care (see Lovell & Richards, 2000; Bower & Gilbody, 2005), all patients would be offered support at levels 1 and 2 in the first instance, and if appropriate, assessment by a expert in psychosocial care before more intensive therapeutic approaches were considered at Levels 4–5.

One such high-intensity approach has been recently documented by Dr Alex Clarke and colleagues in a manual (Clarke et al., in preparation) drawing on CBT and SIST techniques and the clinical experience of the authors. This is the result of a large programme of work investigating the factors and processes involved in adjustment to a visible difference (see Chapter 9) and focuses on helping patients to manage appearance related cognitions. The manual has not yet been rigorously tested, but draws on the current evidence base. The manual will be available to clinicians in 2013.

There is a pressing need to evaluate and unpack the effective components of the existing and potential therapeutic approaches in this field, at all levels of intervention. However, as previous researchers have found, the task of building up methodologically rigorous evidence in this area is not easy.

Overcoming the Barriers to Strengthening the Evidence base

Despite growing interest in appearance psychology, relatively few studies concerned with understanding the experience of visible difference are published each year.

This could be attributed to this being a diverse population, often hard to access, with a small research community specializing in the field who face challenges around the use of appropriate measurement tools (Rumsey & Harcourt 2005; Bessell & Moss 2007).

The lack of available research funding in this area makes the development of interventions and their evaluation difficult. Recruiting sufficient numbers of participants across a wide geographical area can also prove problematic. In addition, both quantitative and qualitative analysis of data can be challenging and require expertise in research methods, especially when seeking to conduct complex studies such as RCTs. These applied issues can hamper the development of good quality evidence to guide intervention delivery. However, it is important that these concerns are balanced with methodological rigour. Collaborative working partnerships between academics and clinicians can overcome these barriers, with research expertise meeting with clinical experience to facilitate good quality applied research.

As discussed elsewhere in this volume (see Chapters 43 and 50), the field still lacks appropriate measures to assess the psychosocial experience of adults, young people, and children living with visible difference. This presents an additional challenge for those wishing to develop and evaluate the impact of interventions. For example, a recent qualitative study showed parents, teachers and participants at burns camps reported them to be beneficial in terms of raising self-confidence and self-esteem despite statistical analysis showing no significant difference on self-report measures completed before and after camps (Gaskell, 2007). The need to develop and validate appropriate measures of psychological adjustment, well-being, and change is a priority in gaining a better understanding of what comprises effective interventions for this population.

Finally, some additional factors should be considered when gauging the effectiveness of interventions and in planning service provision. Firstly, this chapter has reviewed quantitative studies with little reference to the lived experience of people who have a visible difference. Outcome measures utilized in these studies may miss important aspects of how these interventions are planned, employed, and received, as well as their efficacy. Those commissioning, conducting, and researching interventions should also consider the experience of patients and clinicians alongside measurement of change.

The cost effectiveness of interventions is also key to applying research findings to modern healthcare systems. Interventions should not only be evaluated against a no-intervention control, but also against routine care to gauge whether they represent a valid and effective alternative for service provision.

In summary, in order to develop evidence-based guidelines for best practice in the provision of psychological care for people with visible differences, we need to seek to overcome the barriers to conducting research designed to evaluate therapeutic interventions. Researchers, clinicians, and funders working in academia, health services, and charities must pool their resources and expertise to collaborate in conducting methodologically rigorous applied research to gauge what works when supporting people with visible differences experiencing appearance-related distress.

Conclusions

This chapter provides an overview of existing evidence to support the effectiveness of therapeutic interventions designed to help people cope with the psychological challenges of a visible difference.

There is a need for easy access to evidence-based therapeutic interventions ranging from self-help materials to high-intensity psychological therapies; however, currently little evidence exists to definitively support the use of any particular approach to intervention. Studies found to meet the criteria in two systematic reviews in the field suggest SIST and CBT show promise in helping people with visible differences. However, more methodologically rigorous research studies are needed to test existing and new approaches in order to provide evidence based psychological interventions.

Acknowledgements

The author would like to acknowledge the assistance of Dr Tim Moss, Dr Alyson Bessell, and Dr Heidi Williamson.

References

Achenbach, T. M. (1991). *Integrative Guide to the 1991 CBCL/4–18, YSR, and TRF Profiles.* Burlington, VT: University of Vermont, Department of Psychology.

Arnoldo, B. D., Crump, D. C., Burris, A. M., Hunt, J. L., & Purdue, G. F. (2006). Self-esteem measurement before and after summer burn camp in pediatric burn patients. *Journal of Burn Care and Rehabilitation*, 27, 786–9.

Bessell, A. (2009). Facing up to visible difference: The design and evaluation of a new computer-based psychosocial intervention. Unpublished thesis dissertation. University of the West of England, Bristol, UK.

Bessell, A. & Moss, T. P. (2007). Evaluating the effectiveness of psychosocial interventions for individuals with visible differences: A systematic review of the empirical literature. *Body Image*, 4, 227–38.

Bessell, A., Clarke, A., Moss, T. M, Rumsey, N., & Harcourt, D. (2010). Incorporating user perspectives in the design of an online intervention tool for people with visible differences: Face IT. *Behavioural and Cognitive Psychotherapy*, 38 (5), 577–96.

Biggs, K. S., Heinrich, J. J., Jekel, J. F., & Cuono, C. B. (1997). The burn camp experience: Variables that influence the enhancement of self-esteem. *Journal of Burn Care and Rehabilitation*, 18, 93–8.

Blakeney, P., Thomas, C., Holzer, C., Rose, M. R, Berniger, F., & Meyer, W. J. (2005). Efficacy of a short-term, intensive social skills training program for burned adolescents. *Journal of Burn Care and Rehabilitation*, 26, 546–55.

Blakeney, P., Moore, P., Meyer, W., Bishop, B., Murphy, L., Robson, M., *et al.* (1995). Efficacy of school reentry programs. *Journal of Burn Care and Rehabilitation*, 16, 469–72.

Bower, P. & Gilbody, S. (2005). Stepped care in psychological therapies: access, effectiveness and efficiency. *British Journal of Psychiatry*, 186, 11–17.

Bremer-Schulte, M., Cormane, R. H., Van Dijk, E., & Wuite, J. (1985). Group therapy of psoriasis: Duo formula group treatment (DFGT) as an example. *Journal of the American Academy of Dermatology*, 12, 61–6.

Cash, T. F. (2002). Cognitive behavioural perspectives on body image. In T. F. Cash & T. Pruzinsky (eds.) Body Image: *A handbook of theory, research and clinical practice*, pp. 38–46. London: The Guilford Press.

Centre for Reviews and Dissemination (2001). Undertaking systematic reviews of research effectiveness. *CRD Report Number 4 (2nd ed)* [Online]. http://www.york.ac.uk/inst/crd/SysRev/!SSL!/WebHelp/SysRev3.htm

Clarke, A., Jenkinson, E., Rumsey, N., Newman, S., Newell, R., & Thompson, A. (in preparation). Psychosocial interventions for disfigurement and appearance anxiety: a practical guide.

Cooper, R. & Burnside, I. (1996). Three years of an adult burns support group: An analysis. *Burns*, 22, 65–8.

Cooper, M., Watson, J. C., & Hoeldampf, D. (2010). *Person-centered and experiential therapies work: A review of the research on counseling, psychotherapy and related practices*. Ross-on-Wye: PCCS Books.

Dropkin, M. J. (1989). Coping with disfigurement and dysfunction after head and neck cancer surgery: a conceptual framework. *Seminars in Oncology Nursing*, 5, 213–19.

Fiegenbaum, W. (1981). A social training program for clients with facial disfigurations: A contribution to the rehabilitation of cancer patients. *International Journal of Rehabilitation Research*, 4, 501–9.

Fortune, D. G., Richards, H. L., Griffiths, C. E. M., & Main, C. J. (2004). Targeting cognitive-behaviour therapy to patients' implicit model of psoriasis: Results from a patient preference controlled trial. *British Journal of Clinical Psychology*, 43, 65–82.

Fortune, D. G., Richards, H. L., Kirby, B., Bowcock, S., Main, C. J., & Griffiths, C. E. M. (2002). A cognitive-behavioural symptom management programme as an adjunct in psoriasis therapy. *British Journal of Dermatology*, 146, 458–65.

Fox, F. E. (2008). An exploration of online peer support for young people with chronic skin disorders. Unpublished thesis dissertation. University of the West of England, Bristol, UK.

Frances, J. (2004). *Educating children with a facial disfigurement: creating inclusive school communities*. London: Routledge Falmer.

Gaskell, S. (2007). The challenge of evaluating rehabilitative activity holidays for burn-injured children: Qualitative and quantitative outcome data from a burns camp over a five-year period. *Developmental Neurorehabilitation*, 10(2), 149–60.

Girolami, P. (2004). The impact of a School Reentry Program on the Psychosocial Adjustment of Children with Burn injuries. Unpublished thesis dissertation. Morgantown, West Virginia, USA.

Gray, N. J., Klein, J. D., Noyce, P. R., Sesselberg, T. S., & Cantrill, J. A. (2005). Health information-seeking behaviour in adolescence: the place of the Internet. *Social Science & Medicine*, 60, 1467–78.

Hansen, E. & Clarke, A. (2009). Helping people with an unusual appearance. *The Psychologist*, 21(6), 496–8.

Jarry, J. L. & Berardi, K. (2004). Characteristics and effectiveness of stand-alone body image treatments: A review of the empirical literature. *Body Image*, 1, 319–33.

Jarry, J. L., & Ip, K. (2005). The effectiveness of stand-alone cognitive-behavioural therapy for body image: A meta-analysis. *Body Image*, 2, 317–31.

Jenkinson, E., Bessell, A., Williamson, H. and Dures, E. (2009). *CAR framework of intervention delivery*. Centre for Appearance Research, Bristol.

Jenkinson, E., Moss, T., Byron-Daniel, J., & Naqvi, H. (in preparation.). The effectiveness of psychosocial interventions for children and adolescents who are visibly different: a systematic review of the literature.

Kaltenthaler, E., Parry, G., & Beverley, C. (2004). Computerized cognitive behaviour therapy: A systematic review. *Behavioural and Cognitive Psychotherapy*, 32, 31–55.

Kang Seng, T. & Siew Nee, T. (1997). Group therapy: A useful and supportive treatment for psoriasis. *International Journal of Dermatology*, 36, 110–12.

Kapp-Simon, K. A., McGuire, D. E., Long, B. C., and Simon, D. J. (2005). Addressing quality of life issues in adolescents: Social skills and interventions. *Cleft palate-Craniofacial Journal*, 42(1), 45–50.

Kleve, L., Rumsey, N., Wyn-Williams, M., & White, P. (2002). The effectiveness of cognitive-behavioural interventions provided at Outlook: A disfigurement support unit. *Journal of Evaluation in Clinical Practice*, 8, 387–95.

Lovell, K. & Richards, D. (2000). Multiple Access Points and Levels of Entry (MAPLE): ensuring choice, accessibility and equity for CBT services. *Behavioral and Cognitive Psychotherapy*, 28, 379 –91.

Maddern, L. H., Cadogan., J. C., & Emerson, M. P. (2006). 'Outlook': A Psychological Service for Children with a Different Appearance. *Clinical Child Psychology and Psychiatry*, 11(3), 431–43.

Marks, I. M., Hallam, R. S., Connolly, J., & Philpott, R. (1977). *Nursing in Behavioural Psychotherapy*. London: Royal College of nursing.

Moss, T. (1997). Individual variation in adjusting to visible differences. In R. Lansdown, N. Rumsey, E. Bradbury, & J. Partridge (eds.) Visibly different: *Coping with disfigurement*. London: Butterworth Heinemann.

Moss, T. (2005). The relationships between objective and subjective ratings of disfigurement severity and psychological adjustment. *Body Image*, 2(2), 151–9.

National Institute for Health and Clinical Excellence (2004). *Eating disorders: Core interventions in the treatment and management of anorexia nervosa, bulimia nervosa and related eating disorders* [Online]. http://www.nice.org.uk (accessed 9th October 2010).

National Institute for Health and Clinical Excellence (2005). *Final Appraisal Determination: Computerised cognitive behaviour therapy for depression and anxiety* [Online]. http://www.nice.org.uk (accessed 9th October 2010).

National Institute for Health and Clinical Excellence (2007). Anxiety: management of anxiety (panic disorder, with or without agoraphobia, and generalised anxiety disorder) in adults in primary, secondary and community care (amended) [Online]. http://www.nice.org.uk (accessed 9th October 2010).

National Institute for Health and Clinical Excellence (2009). *Depression: the treatment and management of depression in adults* (update) [Online]. London: NICE. http://www.nice.org.uk (accessed 9th October 2010).

Newell, R. (2000). *Body Image and Disfigurement Care*. London: Routledge.

Newell, R., & Clarke, M. (2000). Evaluation of a self-help leaflet in treatment of social difficulties following facial disfigurement. *International Journal of Nursing Studies*, 37, 381–8.

Ost, L. (2008). Efficacy of third wave of behavioural therapies: A systematic review and meta-analysis. *Behaviour Research and Therapy*, 46, 296–321.

Papadopoulos, L., Bor, R., & Legg, C. (1999). Coping with the disfiguring effects of vitiligo: A preliminary investigation into the effects of cognitive-behavioural therapy. *Journal of Medical Psychology*, 72, 385–96.

Papadopoulos, L., Walker, C., & Anthis, L. (2004). Living with vitiligo: A controlled investigation into the effects of group cognitive-behavioural and person-centred therapies. *Dermatology and Psychosomatics*, 5, 172–7.

Partridge, J. & Pearson, A. (2008). Don't worry it's the inside that counts. *The Psychologist*, 21, 6, 490–1.

Price, M. I., Mottahedin, I., & Mayo, P. R. (1991). Can psychotherapy help patients with psoriasis? *Clinical and Experimental Dermatology*, 16, 114–17.

Pull, C. B. (2009). Current empirical status of acceptance and commitment therapy. *Current Opinion in Psychiatry*, 22(1), 55–60.

Richardson, T., Stallard, P., & Velleman, S. (2010). Computerised cognitive behavioural therapy for the prevention and treatment of depression and anxiety in children and adolescents: a systematic review. *Clinical Child and Family Psychology Review*, 13, 275–90.

Rimmer, R. B., Fornaciari, G. M., Foster, K. N., Bay, C. R., Wadsworth, M. M., Wood, M., et al. (2007). Impact of a pediatric residential burn camp experience on burn survivors' perceptions of self and attitudes regarding the camp community. *Journal of Burn care and Research*, 28, 334–41.

Robinson, E., Rumsey, N., & Partridge, J. (1996). An evaluation of the impact of social integration skills training for facially disfigured people. *British Journal of Plastic Surgery*, 49, 281–9.

Rumsey, N. & Harcourt, D. (2004). Body image and disfigurement: Issues and interventions. *Body Image*, 1, 83–97.

Rumsey, N. & Harcourt, D. (2005). *The Psychology of Appearance*. Maidenhead: Open University Press.

Scheewe, S., Schmidt, S., Peterman, F., Stachow, R., & Warschburger, P. (2001). Long term efficacy of an inpatient rehabilitation with integrated patient education program for children and adolescents with psoriasis. *Dermatology and Psychosomatics*, 2, 16–21.

Wright, K. B., & Bell S. B. (2003). Health-related support groups on the internet: Linking empirical findings to social support and computer-mediated communication theory. *Journal of Health Psychology*, 8(1), 39–54.

CHAPTER 39

COMPUTER-BASED PSYCHOSOCIAL INTERVENTIONS

ALYSON BESSELL

In recent years the use of computer-mediated therapies, including online e-therapy, online support groups, and computer-assisted therapies, has become more and more widespread. The main reason for the increased interest in such techniques is the desire to offer a wide variety of support methods in order to increase access to psychosocial services and increase patient choice (Proudfoot, 2004). The provision of psychological support within healthcare services is currently limited, and even when it is available some people cannot access and do not engage with face-to-face services (Bee, 2008). Therefore it is important to offer alternative models to increase the availability and uptake of psychosocial interventions amongst potential clients and to remove the barriers to support (Proudfoot, 2004). This chapter will start by outlining some of the different models of computer-based interventions currently in use. It will then discuss key issues to be considered when designing and evaluating such interventions using the example of a recently developed online support tool for adults with visible differences, known as Face IT (Bessell et al., 2012).

ONLINE SUPPORT

Many online support groups exist for a wide range of conditions, and visible differences are no exception. Conditions such as psoriasis (The Psoriasis Forum), alopecia (The Alopecia Society), and thyroid eye disease (TED-CT) are already represented on the Internet. Studies into the use of online forums have suggested that people use such resources for a multitude of reasons, including seeking emotional support, seeking information about health and coping, and to disclose personal information (Tichon & Shapiro, 2003). Self-disclosure can be used in a variety of ways: firstly to elicit support from others, secondly to provide support to others, and thirdly, to build group cohesion and cement online relationships (Tichon & Shapiro, 2003). Importantly, self-disclosure seems to provide users with a positive therapeutic effect gained by sharing their experiences (Fox, 2008).

Support groups also offer access to people with similar conditions and allow participants to build their support networks, discuss their concerns, and share experiences. The use of online forums removes some of the difficulties experienced by face-to-face support groups, for example, having enough members together at one time to run face-to-face sessions and geographical location (Sullivan, 2003). Online forums are particularly useful for those in rural areas, those with disabilities, or those without transportation (Sullivan, 2003). They also provide an outlet for those with social anxiety difficulties (Sullivan, 2003), and are especially useful for those who are experiencing social isolation (Weber et al., 2000). The anonymous aspect of online support seems to make them particularly popular and can increase the level of uninhibited discussion experienced by users (Schneider & Tooley, 1986). The format may prove particularly useful for those with appearance concerns, as the absence of the need to reveal their physical appearance makes it easier for them to express themselves (Fox, 2008).

However, research has suggested that some potential participants have low motivation to take part in online groups regularly, possibly due to a lack of personal and immediate contact with others which prolongs the time needed to build a supportive environment online (Winzelburg, 1997). Additionally, although online forums increase self-disclosure (Fox, 2008), the absence of non-verbal communication cues means that messages and support can be misunderstood, potentially leading to a breakdown in effective communication (Joinson, 2001). This is a problem with any form of online communication.

ONLINE THERAPY

Another form of computer-based intervention is online therapy, or e-therapy. This technique is very similar to telephone counselling, but instead of the therapist talking with the client over the telephone, the two exchange emails. The positive aspects of this approach are that the client receives direct support from a qualified practitioner and can engage in a therapeutic relationship with that person, which is often seen as being one of the most important factors for those benefiting from psychological support. Therapy also provides the client with a form of social interaction, which can have the effect of reducing social isolation (Alexy, 2000). However, the therapist will be actively encouraging the client to gain a support network in the real world, in an attempt to address the possible negative impact that the Internet can have on levels of face-to-face social activity.

E-therapy has many advantages over face-to-face counselling. It can be provided from a remote location meaning that it is more suitable for people experiencing social isolation (either geographical or psychosocial) or for those with mobility problems. It can also help to address the lack of service provision for people from rural areas. The research into the efficacy of such techniques is limited to case studies (Zabinski et al., 2001) and small-scale randomized controlled trials (RCTs) (Lange et al., 2001). These studies have found limited effectiveness with similar therapeutic benefits to those gained in face-to-face therapy, including reduced mood disturbance and increased positive coping. Although it is too early to draw any firm conclusions, research has also suggested that e-therapy increases self-efficacy in users, due to client empowerment (Finfgeld, 1999a).

The main problems associated with delivering e-therapy relate to cost-effectiveness in terms of staff time. For individual approaches, the cost per client is far greater than other techniques such as online support groups, where the financial outlay is limited to the maintenance of a website and in some cases, occasional moderation by a facilitator. However, the costs of techniques should be weighed against evidence for their effectiveness in meeting an individual's particular needs at a specific point in time.

COMPUTER-ASSISTED THERAPIES

Cognitive behaviour therapy (CBT) has been adapted for use both on the Internet and via CD-ROMs. The advantage of computerized CBT (cCBT) is that it is a form of self-directed therapy where the therapist provides clients with useful techniques that allow them to help themselves. This means that the technique is easily adapted to the remote setting. The online element of such support means that there is a permanent written resource of information that users can access whenever they wish, an aspect that is not currently available through face-to-face or telephone-based techniques (Winefield, 2006). Psychologists have developed cCBT packages such as Beating the Blues (Proudfoot et al., 2004) and FearFighter (Kenwright et al., 2004). These have been well evaluated, found to be effective for treating both anxiety and depression in patients with mild-to-moderate symptoms, and recommended for use throughout the NHS (National Institute for Health and Clinical Excellence (NICE), 2005). Although the models are CBT-based, aspects of a more person-centred approach, such as positive regard, engagement, and motivation, can be incorporated through the use of video and audio clips (Cavanagh, 2001).

One of the main criticisms of cCBT has been whether or not the lack of a one-to-one therapeutic relationship reduces its effectiveness. The packages are usually self-directed with little or no therapist input. However, the anonymity of such programs can aid the process of exploring problems that may be perceived as embarrassing, such as mental health issues (Cavanagh, 2001). Interestingly many studies have found comparable results to standard CBT (Proudfoot et al., 2004), and some have even found greater improvements (Proudfoot, 2004). Although many packages do involve limited therapist contact, the research papers do not adequately reveal how much therapist contact is used as standard. Therefore it is difficult to assess the extent to which the packages are as effective as a completely stand-alone intervention.

CCBT has been praised for increasing users' self-efficacy by allowing them to work through difficulties on their own (Proudfoot, 2004). It has also been found to be highly cost-effective due to the lack of therapist input and the limited number of sessions (typically eight to 12) involved (NICE, 2005). As with e-therapy, the advantage of cCBT over standard CBT is that it allows individuals with social anxiety, mobility problems, or those from rural areas to seek services without having to travel long distances. Furthermore, the self-directed nature of the technique means that clients can design the intervention around their own difficulties by picking and choosing certain areas to focus upon. CCBT increases client choice by providing alternative methods of seeking support and allows for a more flexible approach to therapy with users being able to access services at any time of the day or night (Department of Health, 2007).

A systematic review of the effectiveness of cCBT concluded that the approach was moderately effective at treating depression and anxiety (Kaltenthaler et al., 2004). The authors indicated that the technique increased treatment choice, availability, and access to services, and was likely to increase compliance. Therefore cCBT was recommended by NICE (2005) to be used to help patients with milder symptoms of anxiety and depression and to relieve the pressure on already overloaded therapy provision within the NHS.

Considerations when Designing and Evaluating Online Psychosocial Interventions

When designing an online tool, it is important to ascertain whether the program allows individuals to receive information quickly and efficiently without the need for extensive training or expert knowledge of technology. It is also important to identify any common errors they might make when using the program. Usability assessment is a process that involves clients, usability experts and software designers using a program as they would in the real-world, in order to identify any aspects that are difficult to use or do not work as intended. This is an important phase of developing any computer-based intervention and many different methods are available (see Olson & Olson, 2003 for an extensive list).

Two of these methods include the use of empirical testing and usability checklists. Empirical testing involves trialling a software interface in controlled conditions under the supervision of a usability expert or researcher (Smilowitz et al., 1994). This process can sometimes be referred to as a 'think aloud' study, where users are asked to provide a running commentary on how they are finding the tool and their experiences of interacting with it. The aim of this approach is to evaluate both the training/educational and graphical aspects of the tool. The facilitator uses open-ended questions to prompt participants to provide detailed feedback if they are finding it difficult to engage with the process, or if they reach the end of a page without commenting. Whilst participants are 'thinking aloud' facilitators take detailed notes on what they are saying and how they are using the tool. Usability checklists consist of a series of questions relating to aspects of a program design and experts or users are asked to rate their satisfaction with each aspect using Likert scales (for an example see Ravden & Johnson, 1989). These checklists can be useful in the later stage of software development to ensure that the requirements of the tool have been met.

Beta-testing is an important part of ensuring that the software tool is fully functional. It takes place in many different ways, but involves a small number of people being given access to the program and asked to identify any problems or usability issues with it (Smilowitz et al., 1994). Unlike 'think-aloud' studies mentioned earlier, this process is less restrictive and allows users free use of a tool often away from the research setting, and in the case of web-based programs, is often conducted in the tester's home. Beta-testing of other similar psychosocial interventions has taken place via focus group-based testing providing qualitative feedback on the program (Bessell et al., 2010) or through piloting the effectiveness of the intervention on a small number of participants (see Proudfoot et al., 2003 for an example).

The key message for any researcher attempting to develop an online intervention is to include potential users at every stage. It is important to start with a needs assessment with both users and health professionals working within the area of interest, and to then ensure that each stage of the development and testing process involves users to ensure the end tool adequately meets their needs.

Graphics and Navigation

When designing an online tool, it is important to ensure that the font type and size make the written information on the website as accessible to all users as possible

(Brewer, 2005), including people with sight difficulties, conditions such as colour blindness, or dyslexia. Font types should be based on bold scripts, such as Arial, and not on scripts with fancy lettering (such as Times New Roman) that can be difficult for people to read. The font should have a minimum size of 12 (Brewer, 2005). If the navigation of a site is too difficult or if information appears cluttered on the screen, the energy required to find or decipher the required information is too great and potential users are likely to look elsewhere (Pirolli & Card, 1999). Kuegler (2000) suggests that if individuals do not find information within three clicks on a website, or at least feel confident that they are close to finding it, they will leave the site.

A growing body of research has indicated the importance of the human element when designing computer programs. In e-therapy, if clients can view a photograph of their therapist, they tend to feel they have more rapport with them (Holmes, 1998). For this reason, it can help to include photos of members of the research or therapy team on the main home page, in order to build rapport and trust, as it gives users the sense that they are viewing a tool with real individual involvement. These small touches may also help to encourage individuals to engage more fully with the program when using it from a remote location and thus help to increase motivation (Holmes, 1998). Other issues associated with motivating clients to remain engaged with computer-based interventions are discussed in the following section.

MOTIVATION AND ENGAGEMENT

Yates (1996) highlighted early on in the history of computer-based interventions that it was imperative that programs should follow the basic principles of behaviour change to enhance motivation and engagement. Tools should provide encouragement and feedback on progress, contain information that promotes self-efficacy, and motivational statements to encourage clients to continue with the intervention even when they are struggling. Yates (1996) advised that clients should be given the opportunity to rehearse material in the program, meaning that they can repeat previous content as often as they wish until they have perfected the techniques.

Computer programs, if used correctly, can generally be more engaging than other types of self-help material such as books, for two main reasons; real-time interaction and simulation of outcome (testing real-world events in a computer simulated environment). For example, within the Face IT program outlined later in this chapter, users are asked to complete a short questionnaire at the end of each session. This enables them to obtain immediate feedback rather than having to score the results themselves or wait for a therapist to do so (as would be the case in a pen and paper version). Furthermore, unlike reading material that can be skipped, computer programs allow the information to be gradually revealed to the user, screen by screen (Yates, 1996), a process known as tunnelling. A useful way of motivating individuals whilst helping them to identify issues and problems as they work through an online program is to allow them to simulate real-world situations and test different outcomes based on different possible responses (Yates, 1996).

ETHICAL CONSIDERATIONS

Specific ethical considerations apply to computer-based interventions (National Institute of Mental Health (NIMH), 2003; BPS, 2007). Finfgeld (1999b) emphasizes the importance of client safety and highlights the need for online programs to be thoroughly tested and for their clinical content to be rigorously scrutinized before users are allowed remote access. This diminishes the risk of participant distress. Testing within the face-to-face environment also allows researchers to identify the kinds of instructions that are most suited to help participants use the program effectively. Technical support issues can also be addressed (Finfgeld, 1999b). Addressing these issues initially in the face-to-face environment makes remote programs more acceptable to clients once interventions are released for online access (Wright & Wright, 1997).

It is also important to properly screen clients before they start using an online program to ensure that only those most suited to specific interactions receive access (Suler, 2000). Those considered unsuitable for online therapy include people experiencing suicidal thoughts (NIMH, 2003) or those with psychiatric, personality or thought disorders (Stofle, 2001). However, Stofle (2001) recommended that online therapy is suitable for use by people experiencing depression and anxiety disorders (including agoraphobia and social phobias).

Sometimes, despite initial screening, participants may become suicidal during the intervention, or experience intense distress. In these instances, it is important to build in mechanisms for detection. Some programs can be designed to alert clinicians when a client's data is demonstrating a problem (Proudfoot, 2004). Simpler ways include ensuring that any assessment or questionnaire data gathered during the program is not completely anonymous (i.e. clients have usernames to make them identifiable to the clinician (Robinson & Serfaty, 2003)) and that clinicians have verified the identity of the users and can contact them if their questionnaire responses are a cause for concern (NIMH, 2003).

Finally, the general ethical considerations of clinician responsibility and integrity need to be addressed. Not only do those administering the intervention need to be fully trained to handle the unique challenges that this technique presents, they also need to have basic psychotherapeutic or counselling training, or a good understanding of the clinical problem the program is designed to address (Griffiths, 2001).

EXAMPLE OF A cCBT TOOL FOR ADULTS WITH VISIBLE DIFFERENCE

Face IT is an online cognitive-behavioural/social skills tool for adults with visible differences (Bessell et al., 2012). Within the field of disfigurement there are very few interventions for those who are coming to terms with living with an altered appearance, and those that do exist are often based in large towns or cities (Bessell & Moss, 2007). Therefore, it was deemed necessary to design an online support tool that could increase access to service provision. This program serves as an example of why it is important to consider the key factors outlined earlier in the design and implementation of an online intervention.

Many of the problems faced by people with a visible difference are related to social situations and interactions. They can experience many forms of social discrimination, hardship, and stigma and common difficulties include staring, name-calling, comments, rejection, and unsolicited questioning about their appearance (Rumsey et al., 2004). These challenges can have a profound impact on psychological well-being and quality of life, often leading to social anxiety, and in some cases social avoidance and isolation.

The process of avoidance occurs because negative reactions from others lead to increased anxiety, which in turn leads to increased awareness of further negative reactions or the tendency to look for such responses (Kent, 2000). Anxiety also increases the individual's sensitivity to any reactions that may be perceived as negative. If the anxiety in such situations is so intense that individuals respond by removing themselves from the anxiety-provoking situation, then they are likely to experience a reduction in anxiety. This means that the avoidant behaviour is reinforced by the reduction in anxiety symptoms, making it more likely that such behaviour will occur again in the future (Newell, 1999). As a result of these various mechanisms, the individuals may impose social isolation upon themselves, as they are unable to deal with the reactions of others (Kent, 2000) (see Chapter 9).

These difficulties suggest that interventions to help those with appearance-related distress associated with having a visible difference should focus on CBT and exposure-based approaches to treatment. A systematic review of current psychosocial interventions for those with appearance-related distress associated with visible differences identified that the CBT and social interaction skills training (SIST) approaches were widely used and there was some evidence that the techniques did reduce psychological distress amongst participants (Bessell & Moss, 2007) (see Chapter 38).

Therefore, it was decided to use these approaches to inform the creation of a new computer-based intervention, Face IT. The program consists of a total of eight sessions covering a range of social skills strategies for overcoming difficulties associated

Session 1: Introduction to visible difference
Session 2: Non-verbal communication
Session 3: Verbal communication
Session 4: Goal setting
Session 5: Cognitive restructuring
Session 6: Social skills & Anxiety management
Session 7: Exposure therapy
Session 8: Summary

Figure 39.1 Face IT program design (see Bessell et al., 2012 for more details).

with having a visible difference, in conjunction with exposure-based techniques for overcoming social anxiety (see Fig. 39.1). Cognitive restructuring was also incorporated to address both individuals' own negative thoughts about their appearance and the negative assumptions they make about the views of others towards their appearance.

The process of designing Face IT involved considering all of the issues outlined earlier (see Bessell, 2009 for more details). Face IT was then evaluated in a RCT of effectiveness against a standard face-to-face intervention and a no-intervention control group. This stage of assessment is vital for any psychosocial intervention to ensure it adequately addresses the needs of the target population. The trial found Face IT to be as effective as face-to-face intervention at reducing appearance-related distress, anxiety, and depression (Bessell et al., 2012).

cCBT for Young People with Visible Differences

The Face IT intervention previously described was designed for use solely by adults with visible differences. However, there is also need for online support amongst teenagers with disfigurements. Researchers at the Centre for Appearance Research at the University of the West of England have therefore developed a new version of the Face IT program targeted specifically at young people, YP Face IT. Young people are a population who have already embraced the online environment, and use it as a means of accessing health information (Schoen et al., 2007). Furthermore, the Internet can minimize the barriers to services that currently exist for many young people (Gray et al., 2005). It is therefore important to ensure that they have a place online where they can access support that is appropriately sourced, rather than seeking out information that may be inappropriate or incorrect.

Research has also suggested that adolescents prefer specific information to generic resources (Gray et al., 2005). Tailoring refers to a process of structuring a software tool so that users receive information and advice that relates specifically to their individuals needs. Tailoring of an online intervention can be achieved through software tunnelling—asking participants screening questions that automatically identify the areas of the program most suitable to their needs. Furthermore, as young people are accustomed to engaging with sophisticated software, it is important that any site for young people contains contemporary graphics and a professional feel to hold their attention, increase their motivation and to encourage engagement with the program.

Incorporating fun technologies, such as computer games may also help to make interventions for young people more engaging. Computer games have been used to treat a wide range of phobias, and have been used in the rehabilitation of patients with burns (Adrianssens et al., 1988). This study involved giving socially withdrawn patients access to role-playing games to help them to re-engage with their social environment. In this way computer games can help to aid social skills training, a potential use within the context of the new intervention program. Since some individuals with visible differences experience difficulties with social interactions, computer games could provide a promising addition to interventions for this group.

SUMMARY AND CONCLUSIONS

This chapter has outlined different models of computer-based interventions, and has considered key design and ethical issues. Researchers must ensure that computer-based interventions are evidence-based, well tested, and meet the needs and requirements of their end-users. Most importantly, researchers and clinicians should remember that the process of developing computer-based interventions is a long one and requires careful consultation with both users and health professionals if it is to be acceptable. The initial evaluation of Face IT suggests it will offer an effective and useful tool for people with visible differences who are currently unable or unwilling to access existing face-to-face psychosocial services, and hopefully this chapter will inspire researchers to develop new models of computer interventions that can complement this tool.

REFERENCES

Adrianssens, P., Eggermont, E., Pyck, K., Boeckx, W., & Gilles, B. (1988). The video invasion of rehabilitation. *Burns*, 14(5), 417–19.

Alexy, E. M. (2000). Computers & caregiving: Reaching out and redesigning interventions for homebound older adults and caregivers. *Holistic Nursing Practice*, 14(4), 60–6.

Bee, P. (2008). Net gains for mental health. *The Times*, 3 March.

Bessell, A. (2009). Facing up to Visible Difference: The Design and Evaluation of a New Computer-Based Psychosocial Intervention. Unpublished thesis dissertation. University of the West of England.

Bessell, A., Brough, V., Clarke, A., Harcourt D., Moss T., & Rumsey, N. (2012). Evaluation of the effectiveness of Face IT, a computer-based psychosocial intervention for disfigurement-related distress. *Psychology, Health and Medicine*, in press.

Bessell, A., Clarke, A., Harcourt, D., Moss, T. P., & Rumsey, N. (2010). Incorporating user perspectives in the design of an online intervention tool for people with visible differences: Face IT. *Behavioural and Cognitive Psychotherapy*, 38, 577–96.

Bessell, A., & Moss, T. (2007). Evaluating the effectiveness of psychosocial interventions for individuals with visible differences: A systematic review of the empirical literature. *Body Image*, 4, 227–38.

Brewer, J. (2005). *How people with disabilities use the web.* [W3C working-group Internal Draft.] http://www.w3.org/WAI/EO/Drafts/PWD-Use-Web/Overview.html.

British Psychological Society. (2007). *Report of the working party on conducting research on the Internet: Guidelines for ethical practice in psychological research online.* Leicester: British Psychological Society.

Cavanagh, K. (2001). Hitting the 'help' key. *The Psychologist*, 14(9), 456.

Department of Health. (2007). *Computer says 'yes' to more accessible therapy.* London: Department of Health.

Finfgeld, D. L. (1999a). Psychotherapy in cyberspace. *Journal of the American Psychiatric Nurses Association*, 5, 105–10.

Finfgeld, D. L. (1999b). Computer-assisted therapy: Harbinger of the 21st Century? *Archives of Psychiatric Nursing*, 13(6), 303–10.

Fox, F. E. (2008). An exploration of online peer support for young people with chronic skin disorders. Unpublished thesis dissertation. University of the West of England.

Gray, N. J., Klein, J. D., Noyce, P. R., Sesselberg, T. S., & Cantrill, J. A. (2005). Health information-seeking behaviour in adolescence: the place of the Internet. *Social Science & Medicine*, 60, 1467–78.

Griffiths, M. (2001). Online therapy: A cause for concern? *The Psychologist*, 14(5), 244–8.

Holmes, L. G. (1998). Delivering mental health services on-line: Current issues. *CyberPsychology and Behavior*, 1(1), 19–24.

Joinson, A. N. (2001). Self-disclosure in computer-mediated communication: The role of self awareness and visual anonymity. *European Journal of Social Psychology*, 31, 177–92.

Kaltenthaler, E., Parry, G., & Beverley, C. (2004). Computerized cognitive behaviour therapy: A systematic review. *Behavioural and Cognitive Psychotherapy*, 32, 31–55.

Kent, G. (2000). Understanding experiences of people with disfigurement: An integration of four models of social and psychological functioning. *Psychology, Health and Medicine*, 5, 117–29.

Kenwright, M., Marks, I. M., Gega, L., & Mataix-Cols, D. (2004). Computer-aided self-help for panic/phobia via Internet at home: A pilot study. *British Journal of Psychiatry*, 184, 448–9.

Kuegler, T. (2000). *Make your site a better information delivery tool.* http://www.clickz.com/showPage.html?page=822901.

Lange, A., Van de Ven, J. P., Schrieken, B., & Emmelkamp, P. M. (2001). Interapy, treatment of posttraumatic stress through the Internet: A controlled trial. *Journal of Behaviour Therapy & Experimental Psychiatry*, 32, 73–90.

National Institute for Health and Clinical Excellence (NICE). (2005). *Final Appraisal Determination: Computerised cognitive behaviour therapy for depression and anxiety (review)*. London: NICE. http://www.nice.org.uk.

National Institute of Mental Health (NIMH). (2003). *Internet-based research interventions: Issues and suggestions chart*. London: National Institute of Mental Health.

Newell, R. J. (1999). Altered body image: a fear-avoidance model of psycho-social difficulties following disfigurement. *Journal of Advanced Nursing*, 30(5), 1230–8.

Olson, G. M., & Olson, J. S. (2003). Human-computer interaction: Psychological aspects of the human use of computing. *Annual Review of Psychology*, 54, 491–516.

Pirolli, P., & Card, S. K. (1999). Information foraging. *Psychological review*, 106, 643–75.

Proudfoot, J. G. (2004). Computer-based treatment of anxiety and depression: Is it feasible? Is it effective? *Neuroscience & Biobehavioral Reviews*, 28, 353–63.

Proudfoot, J., Swain, S., Widmer, S., Watkins, E., Goldberg, D., Marks, I., et al. (2003). The development and beta-test of a computer-therapy program for anxiety and depression: Hurdles and lessons. *Computers in Human Behavior*, 19, 277–89.

Proudfoot, J., Ryden, C., Everitt, B., Shapiro, D., Goldberg, D., Mann, A., et al. (2004). Clinical efficacy of computerised cognitive-behavioural therapy for anxiety and depression in primary care: randomised controlled trial. *British Journal of Psychiatry*, 185, 46–54.

Ravden, A. S., & Johnson, G. (1989). *Evaluating usability of human-computer interfaces: A practical method*. New York: Halsted Press.

Robinson, P., & Serfaty, M. (2003). Computers, email, and therapy in eating disorders. *European Eating Disorders Review*, 11, 210–21.

Rumsey, N., Clarke, A., White, P., Wyn-Williams, M., & Garlick, W. (2004). Altered body image: Auditing the appearance related concerns of people with visible disfigurement. *Journal of Advanced Nursing*, 48(5), 443–53.

Schneider, S. J., & Tooley, J. (1986). Self-help computing conferencing. *Computers and Biomedical Research*, 19, 274–81.

Schoen, C., Davis, K., Scott-Collins, K., Greenberg, L., Des Roches, C., & Abrams, M. (1997). *The commonwealth fund survey of the health of adolescent girls*. New York: The commonwealth fund.

Smilowitz, E. D., Darnell, M. J., & Benson, A. E. (1994). Are we overlooking some usability testing methods? A comparison of lab, beta and forum tests. *Behaviour and Information Technology*, 13, 183–90.

Stofle, G. S. (2001). *Choosing an online therapist*. Harrisburg, PA: White Hat Communications.

Suler, J. R. (2000). Psychotherapy in cyberspace: A 5-dimensional model of online and computer-mediated psychotherapy. *CyberPsychology and Behavior*, 3(2), 151–9.

Sullivan, C. F. (2003). Gendered cybersupport: A thematic analysis of two online cancer support groups. *Journal of Health Psychology*, 8(1), 83–103.

Tichon, J. G., & Shapiro, M. (2003). With a little help from my friends: Children, the Internet and social support. *Journal of technology in Human Services*, 21(4), 73–92.

Weber, B. A., Roberts, B. L., & McDougall, G. J. (2000). Exploring the efficacy of support groups for men with prostate cancer. *Geriatric Nursing*, 21, 250–53.

Winefield, H. R. (2006). Support provision and emotional work in an Internet support group for cancer patients. *Patient Education and Counselling*, 62, 193–7.

Winzelburg, A. (1997). The analysis of an electronic support group for individuals with eating disorders. *Computers in Human Behaviour*, 13, 393–407.

Wright, J. H., & Wright, A. (1997). Computer-assisted psychotherapy. *Journal of psychotherapy Practice and Research*, 6, 315–29.

Yates, F. E. (1996). Developing 'user-persuasive' programs. In F. E. Yates (ed.) Creative Computing in Health and Social Care. Chichester: John Wiley & Sons ltd.

Zabinski, M., Wilfrey, D. E., Puung, M. A., Winzelburg, A. J., Eldridge, K., & Barr, T. C. (2001). An interactive Internet-based intervention for women at risk of eating disorders: A pilot study. *International Journal of Eating Disorders*, 20, 129–37.

CHAPTER 40

USING APPEARANCE CONCERNS TO PROMOTE HEALTH

SARAH GROGAN
DANIEL MASTERSON

APPEARANCE concerns affect a large proportion of the adult population in Western societies (Harris & Carr, 2001; Grogan, 2008), and it has been widely argued that dissatisfaction and anxiety relating to physical appearance have direct impacts on health-related behaviours and well-being in adult men and women. Many authors have suggested that appearance concerns impact on exercise and body building (e.g. Choi, 2000), use of performance-enhancing drugs such as anabolic steroids (e.g. Wright et al., 2000; Grogan et al., 2006a), restrictive dieting and unhealthy eating (e.g. Stice, 2002; Levine & Peran, 2004), and smoking cessation (e.g. Potter et al., 2004; Grogan et al., 2009), and that reducing or raising appearance concerns can be an effective way to promote healthy behaviours.

The aim of this chapter is to bring together recent work from across disciplines (including psychology, gender studies, sociology, and sport and exercise science) to investigate the current evidence base, and to investigate whether appearance concerns can, and should, be used to promote health. Recent evidence relating to studies on exercise, use of performance-enhancing dugs, eating/dieting, smoking, and screening in adults will be reviewed to evaluate the extent of links between appearance concerns and these health-related behaviours. We will then go on to consider whether these links can be used in a positive way to promote health and will also consider some ethical issues relating to raising appearance concerns as a way of promoting health in adults.

Do Appearance Concerns Impact on Health-Related Behaviours?

Dissatisfaction with appearance has been linked with a large number of health behaviours. Before we consider the possible effects of raising or reducing appearance concerns, we need to know whether appearance concerns have a direct impact on health behaviours, and if so, which health-related behaviours are affected.

Exercising

Moderate exercise lowers blood pressure, and improves cardiac function, muscle strength, and aerobic capacity (British Heart Foundation (BHF) 2010). Regular exercise and physical activity prevents disability and improves quality of life, particularly in older adults (Cress et al., 2005) and there is also some evidence that exercise interventions can improve body satisfaction (Campbell & Hausenblas, 2009). However, relatively few adults in the UK engage in the recommended 30 minutes of moderate-intensity physical activity at least 5 days a week, and women tend to exercise less than men (BHF, 2010).

One way to encourage people to exercise might be to focus on potential improvements to muscle tone and the aesthetic aspects of the 'trained' body, and many gyms and sport centres in the UK capitalize on appearance-related motivations by selling exercise programmes as a way to achieve a slender and toned physique, particularly in advertising aimed at women (Choi, 2000). There is some evidence that both men and women exercise in order to look more toned and muscular, and/or to lose weight (e.g. Grogan et al., 2006b) and studies have found that both men and women report being motivated to engage in exercise to change their bodies due to appearance concerns (Grogan & Richards 2002; Grogan, 2008). Kyrejto et al. (2008) found that drive for muscularity scores were linked with a number of health-related behaviours for men and women including exercise participation (resistance training, aerobic training, participation in sport) and diet. They asked both men and women to complete the statement 'To manage my desire to become more muscular I ...' and found that 74.6% of men and 73% of women reported that they exercised to try to change the look of their bodies presenting statements such as 'I work out' or 'I pump iron'. The authors suggest that drive for muscularity (wanting to be more muscular and toned) has the potential to impact positively on health through encouraging engagement in exercise in men and women. In interviews with body builders we have found that appearance concerns were a primary motivator for taking up body building for both women and men (Grogan et al., 2004, 2006a), and many other authors have also suggested that many people deal with appearance concerns and a desire to be bigger or thinner through exercising (Kyrejto et al., 2008) However, none of these studies has looked prospectively at the impact of appearance concerns on exercise participation. This is problematic since people's retrospective accounts may be influenced by their current exercise behaviour and affected by faulty memory as people may reconstruct their reasons for undertaking exercise once they are actually engaged in exercise programmes.

Although being dissatisfied with the way they look can in some cases motivate people to exercise (also see Chapter 22), it may also prevent others engaging in organized sports activities such as joining a gym or exercising at a sports centre. This may be due to concern about revealing their bodies in sports clothes and fitting in with a sport and exercise culture that prescribes a slender and toned body type (Choi, 2000). Some authors have suggested that appearance satisfaction rather than dissatisfaction predicts exercise engagement in men and women (Kruger et al., 2008), so although using appearance concerns to promote exercise may be effective for some people it may demotivate others. Also, it has been suggested that where people are motivated to exercise for appearance reasons, appearance concerns may actually increase as a result of exercise participation (LePage & Crowther, 2010) which may lead to an increase in other unhealthy behaviours such as anabolic steroid use and unhealthy eating (see the following section). Given the lack of prospective research in this area, the potential demotivating effects of a focus on appearance on some people, and the possibility of promoting other unhealthy behaviours through focusing on appearance, the use of appearance concerns as a prime motivator for increasing exercise in general is not indicated at present.

USE OF PERFORMANCE-ENHANCING DRUGS

Although it is difficult to be confident about the exact incidence of performance-enhancing drug use, there is no doubt that this is widespread amongst bodybuilders and weight lifters in the UK, US, Australia, and New Zealand (Cafri et al., 2005; Grogan et al., 2006a). Use of anabolic steroids leads to various health problems including hypertension, kidney and liver problems, and may put users at risk of HIV/AIDS as a result of sharing needles (Lenehan, 2003). In interviews with male and female steroid users, Grogan et al. (2006a) found that one of the key motivating factors for steroid use was feeling insufficiently muscular compared with others at the gym. Health warnings were mistrusted since they did not come from within the steroid-using community. So although appearance concern can motivate healthy exercise (see earlier) it may also motivate steroid use. Kanayama et al. (2003)

present evidence that weight-lifting men who use anabolic steroids were significantly less confident about their appearance prior to taking steroids than a matched group of men who chose not to take steroids. They conclude that use may be most likely to occur in men with low body esteem, implying that steroid use can be predicted from appearance concerns. However, in another interesting study, Litt and Dodge (2008) investigated whether drive for muscularity predicted subsequent use of performance-enhancing drugs and weight-lifting behaviours over a 6-week period in a group of men in a well-controlled prospective study. They found that an attitudinal subscale (items included 'I wish that I were more muscular') did *not* predict self-reports of use of performance-enhancing drugs or weight-lifting behaviour in the following 6 weeks, suggesting that appearance concerns were *not* a reliable indicator of later steroid use. Clearly, data from studies of the relationship between appearance concerns and steroid use is complex and more work is needed in this area. Although interviews and other retrospective evidence suggest that body dissatisfaction may predict later steroid use, we have not been able to find a prospective study that supports this relationship.

EATING

UK and US statistics also show that many women and men eat unhealthily as a way of controlling their weight, including engaging in 'crash' diets (extreme reduction of food intake) and taking unhealthy food supplements and diet pills (Grogan, 2008; Wharton et al., 2008). The UK Eating Disorders Association (BEAT, 2011) also estimates that 1.6 million people in the UK have an eating disorder of some kind. Similar incidence figures are found in other European samples and in the US. Appearance concern has been linked to eating disorders in previous work, and various models of the relationship between body dissatisfaction and eating disorders have been presented and supported (van den Berg et al., 2002). The Dual Pathway Model (Stice, 2001) and Tripartite Model (van den Berg et al., 2002) both predict a direct causal relationship between body dissatisfaction and disordered eating. However, it is debatable whether these patterns can be generalized to eating in non-clinical samples. Also, both models focus on women and on pressures for thinness, making their use problematic for men (who may be under pressure to be muscular rather than thin; Cafri et al., 2005).

In studies where authors have assessed relationships between eating/dieting and body dissatisfaction in non-clinical groups, clear relationships have also emerged. Most researchers find that body dissatisfaction is associated with both dieting and unhealthy eating. For instance, Forrest and Stuhldreher (2007) reported that dissatisfied students reported higher levels of dieting and taking pills to reduce weight, and were more likely to eat meat and less likely to eat fruit than those satisfied with their bodies, linking unhealthy eating with body dissatisfaction. In interviews with women, it has also been found that the main mechanism for dealing with body dissatisfaction is dieting, and that 'crash' dieting is common in women of all ages (Grogan, 2008). There is also good evidence that dieting may be linked to overestimation of body size in women. For instance, Jaworowska and Bazylak (2008) found that women of normal weight were likely to perceive themselves as overweight, and to diet, even when objectively, their weight was within the normal range. Most studies in this area have focused on women, and the incidence of dieting in men is much lower. However, some men obviously do diet and Morgan and Arcelus (2009), in their study of body image and dieting in gay and heterosexual men, found that all participants reported some dissatisfaction and all had considered dieting, although only four of the 15 men (all gay) had actually dieted, with one man losing extreme amounts of weight on a diet of mostly coffee and cigarettes. These kinds of 'crash' diets are obviously not healthy for either men or women. Most participants in a qualitative study of British women (Grogan, 2008) said that they were against what they called 'fad dieting', because such diets were seen to be ineffective in the long term (because they were boring and led to cravings for other foods) and bad for health (because they did not contain necessary nutrients). For instance, one woman said 'I think that fad diets are absolutely stupid. The only way to lose weight is to cut down generally and to exercise' and another 'When I go on one of those silly diets I actually feel tired. I'm obviously not getting enough energy'. However, restriction of food, even when hungry, in order to look slimmer was reported by most of the women in this study.

Quantitative studies in this area are difficult to interpret as they tend to be correlational, measuring appearance concerns and eating at the same time point, which means that we cannot be sure which variable is affecting the other. Studies where body satisfaction has been manipulated and eating has been observed directly have produced conflicting findings. Anschutz et al. (2009) exposed women to 'thin', 'less thin', and body-neutral commercials to try to induce body anxiety and gave women free access to snack foods. It might be expected that women exposed to 'thin' commercials would snack less than those exposed to 'less thin' commercials as they could be expected to become more concerned about their weight through comparing their bodies to those of the thin models. However, the authors found that there were no significant effects of the commercials on body anxiety and that women in the 'less thin' condition ate significantly *less* than those in the 'thin' condition, suggesting that observing 'thin' commercials may be associated with increased (rather than reduced) snack-food intake. The results were not affected by whether the women were dieting or not. In another study, women who were dieting and were given free access to snack foods ate less when exposed to 'thin' commercials than when exposed to 'neutral' commercials (the expected effect if they were more concerned about their bodies), whereas women who were not dieting showed the opposite effect (Anschutz et al., 2008). So it has been suggested both that women may be disinhibited (and eat more) and that they may restrain their eating when observing 'thin' media images, and the link with dieting status is unclear. Clearly there is more work to be done in this area.

Desire to be more muscular has also been linked with consuming protein supplements in men. In Morrison et al.'s (2004) study, drive for muscularity predicted various health-related behaviours, including protein consumption. The authors conclude that a majority of their male participants were dissatisfied with their bodies and wanted to be more muscular (casting doubt on the suggestion that men do not see their bodies in aesthetic terms) and that these attitudes are linked to taking protein supplements. Cahill and Mussap (2007) also found that reduced state body satisfaction was significantly related to men's reported engagement in strategies to increase muscle (which included items such as 'I take food supplements [such as vitamins, protein drinks or diet pills] to increase my muscles'). This effect was mediated by internalization of a muscular/athletic ideal, suggesting that men who value the media-idealized slender and muscular body may be particularly likely to use protein supplements to change the look of their bodies. In Labre's (2005) semi-structured interview study, male students discussed body image with the female author. Men preferred a lean and moderately muscular body and despite expressing overall satisfaction, several participants were limiting carbohydrates and/or fat, and using supplements to try to increase lean muscle.

There is certainly more work needed in this area in terms of understanding the mechanisms linking body dissatisfaction with eating and dieting in non-clinical groups, although there are clearly strong associations between dissatisfaction with weight, 'crash' dieting, and the use of supplements.

SCREENING

Screening for skin and breast cancer through self-examination can be effective in promoting increased survival through enabling earlier treatment (American Cancer Society, 2011; Breakthrough Breast Cancer, 2011). However, only about one-third of women in the West are thought to perform breast self-examination regularly (Chouliara et al., 2004) and only about 9% of people perform skin self-examination with any degree of regularity (Weinstock et al., 2007). One of the factors that might influence likelihood of performing self-examination is body satisfaction. Chait et al. (2009) found that higher scores on the scale measuring satisfaction with different body areas and more positive evaluations of appearance in general were related to having performed skin self-evaluation more frequently in the previous year. Appearance evaluation (a measure of appearance satisfaction) accounted for 6% of the variance in skin self-examination behaviour scores. The authors conclude that an intervention to raise body satisfaction may improve the rates at which skin self-examination was performed. This study is the first to examine this relationship and presents some interesting data with clear health implications, albeit with the usual caveats relating to the limitations of a cross-sectional design and self-report measures. This interesting study suggests that one way forward for research in this area is to see what happens to self-examination behaviours when body satisfaction is improved.

SMOKING

Smoking is linked to shortness of breath, cardiovascular problems, and increased risk of lung cancer (American Lung Association, 2011). In the US and UK the prevalence of tobacco use is highest in young adults and the development of anti-smoking programmes in young people has been identified as a health promotion priority in both countries (ASH 2011; National Institute on Drug Abuse, 2011). There is some evidence that young women may be more likely than young men to use smoking to try to lose weight (Lowry et al., 2002). There is also some evidence that smoking relates to appearance concern in a broader sense than just concern about weight loss. In a US study, Clark et al. (2005) found that 18–24-year-old smokers placed more investment in their appearance, less in their physical fitness, and had greater overweight preoccupation than non-smokers. Grogan et al. (2010) investigated the link between appearance concerns and smoking with 244 17–24-year-olds completing the Multidimensional Body-Self Relations Questionnaire Appearance Sub-Scales (MBSRQ-AS: Cash, 2000). Smokers scored significantly lower than non-smokers on appearance evaluation, and appearance evaluation predicted smoking status in both men and women. Overweight preoccupation, self-classified weight, and appearance orientation did not predict smoking status for either gender. It is concluded that smoking cessation interventions may need to target general concerns about appearance in addition to targeting concerns over weight control.

Correlational studies cannot identify the direction of effect. However, a prospective study by King et al. (2005) provided convincing evidence that body dissatisfaction was predictive of smoking rate at the end of a 12-week randomized smoking cessation trial in women. The authors concluded that a more negative body image predicted more difficulty in quitting smoking. Perception of body size was also an important predictor of smoking outcomes. Women who overestimated their body size were the least likely to quit smoking by the end of treatment based on all outcome assessments. The study used well-validated measures and a relatively large sample of 141 women. However, they were a community sample of sedentary middle aged women so findings may not be generalizable to other groups. Nevertheless, this prospective study that measured appearance concern before smoking cessation suggests that these concerns may predict smoking cessation in women.

How Convincing is the Evidence Base?

Research linking appearance concerns with health-related behaviours varies in quality and very few studies use intervention designs involving manipulation of appearance concerns—arguably the only design that would enable us to be confident about the direction of any relationship. King et al. (2005) have produced evidence that body concerns precede smoking behaviour through their use of a longitudinal design, albeit with the usual caveats about potential influence of a third variable on both appearance concerns and on later smoking. However, Litt and Dodge (2008) failed to show that drive for muscularity attitudes predicted use of performance enhancing drugs in the 6 weeks following body image measurement suggesting that this health-related behaviour is less easy to predict from appearance concerns. The findings of correlational studies are more difficult to interpret with confidence, but cross-sectional studies presented in this review do show associations between appearance satisfaction and other health-related behaviours including use of anabolic steroids (Kanayama et al., 2003), exercise (Kyrejto et al., 2008), skin self-examination (Chait et al., 2009), and eating/dieting (Forrest & Stuldreher 2007; Jaworowska & Bazylak 2008). Notwithstanding the limitations in design, these studies point the way for better controlled studies in these areas to investigate these associations further.

Where Does This Leave Us In Terms of Trying to Promote Health Through Modifying Appearance Concern?

Some authors have argued that raising specific kinds of appearance concerns may impact positively on health behaviours. The best example of this is in work on smoking. Smoking may be linked (especially for women) with weight concern (Potter et al., 2004; King et al., 2005) and fear of gaining weight may discourage people from giving up smoking. However, other appearance-related factors might be expected to act as *disincentives* for smoking. For instance, people may be concerned that smoking will age their skin, especially on the face. Smoking is linked to skin ageing and other negative effects such as yellowing of the teeth (Department of Health, 2010). Grogan et al. (2009) investigated how 87 young men and women smokers and non-smokers (aged 17–24) talked in focus groups about the impact of smoking on appearance. A thematic analysis suggested that women non-smokers were very concerned about skin ageing, and that although smokers believed that smoking made them look 'cool', mature, and sophisticated, they were concerned about skin ageing and would quit if skin ageing and other negative effects on appearance became evident. For instance, one young woman who was a regular smoker said '*It depends if I started to see like real like horrible cat's bum mouth or something like that on me, I'd be more likely to stop'*. One of the main barriers to believing that smoking would affect their appearance was the fact that these young people had not experienced any obvious impacts on their skin so did not believe that skin-ageing was a realistic and self-relevant risk. The authors concluded that facial appearance concerns are relevant to the decision whether to quit smoking, and that smoking-related interventions focusing specifically on appearance were indicated.

One way to highlight the self-relevance of smoking to appearance is to show people realistic images of the possible future effects of smoking on their own faces. This has recently become possible though the development of sophisticated computer techniques such as age-progression software, making it possible to show the differential effects of not smoking versus smoking (Hysert et al., 2003). This is achieved through using wrinkling/ageing algorithms based on photographs of groups of smokers and on published data relating to the specific effects of smoking on the skin. A digital photograph is taken, and the person is shown how his or her face would age with and without smoking. In one of the few controlled studies in this area, Hysert et al.'s (2003) US smokers reported significantly lower intentions to smoke after the intervention.

In a recent British study (Flett et al., 2010; Grogan et al., 2011), women smokers were asked to talk about their experiences of an age-appearance facial morphing anti-smoking intervention. Women were very concerned about the impact of ageing on their faces in general, and in particular the additional impact of smoking on their skin. They reported that seeing their own face aged on the computer screen increased their perceived risk of skin wrinkling, and that they were highly motivated to quit smoking as a result of the intervention. For instance, one young woman said *'It makes it a bit more real when you see things like that rather than someone saying "oh don't smoke, it's bad". Actually seeing this is what you're going to look like'*. Many stated that they would take active steps to quit having seen how they would look if they continued to smoke. For instance, another woman said *'I need to quit smoking 'cause I'm not having wrinkles like that, ok'*. Women were concerned about other people's reactions to them as older smokers with damaged skin, and were shocked at seeing how their faces would age if they continued to smoke. It is concluded that interventions incorporating age-appearance morphing techniques are likely to be effective in helping women to take active steps to quit smoking.

ETHICAL ISSUES IN RAISING APPEARANCE CONCERN TO PROMOTE HEALTH

Raising specific appearance concerns may be an effective way to reduce dangerous health behaviours such as smoking. However, raising appearance concerns may also promote lowered self-esteem which is closely associated with body image

(O'Dea, 2005) and may result in the elevation of other negative health behaviours such as extreme dieting and use of performance-enhancing drugs which are both behaviours associated with self-esteem. So although smoking may be reduced (for instance), other negative health behaviours may be increased unless careful debriefing is carried out to ensure that participants do not become *generally* more concerned about their appearance after the intervention. Also, there is the danger that the promotion of appearance concern in health contexts validates and reinforces the idea that only certain body types and looks are appropriate and socially acceptable. For these reasons (and because the empirical evidence for a direct causal relationship between appearance concern and health behaviours is weak at present) we should be cautious in promoting interventions that raise concern. Any such interventions also need to be administered with care by people who are aware of the possible negative impacts that these can have without additional self-esteem boosting activities and careful debriefing work.

PROMOTING HEALTH THROUGH REDUCING APPEARANCE CONCERN

We should also consider whether it is possible to promote health behaviours through *reducing* appearance concern and promoting positive body image. Having fewer appearance concerns has been linked with a lower likelihood of steroid use, healthier eating, greater ease quitting smoking, and greater likelihood of skin and breast self-examination. Recent research has also shown that interventions such as Media Literacy Training (e.g. Yamimiya et al., 2005), cognitive behavioural therapy (CBT; Jarry & Beraldi, 2004), exposure to feminist ideology and resisting thin-internalization (for women: Peterson et al., 2006), and development of self esteem (O'Dea, 2005), and self-efficacy (Blair et al., 1992) can be effective in promoting positive body-related attitudes and evaluations (Grogan, 2010). There may also be a role for CBT in reducing anxiety associated with body image (Jarry & Beraldi, 2004), and interventions to improve self-esteem may reduce social physique anxiety (O'Dea, 2005).

Relatively few studies have investigated systematically what happens to health behaviours when appearance concerns are reduced in adult samples. One exception is a study by Perkins et al. (2001) where CBT was used to reduce appearance concerns relating to weight gain as part of a smoking cessation programme. In this study an enhanced CBT programme focusing on concerns about weight gain produced significantly higher abstinence rates than a standard CBT programme or a programme focusing on behavioural weight control. Unfortunately weight concerns did not differ significantly between the three groups after the programmes, making these data difficult to interpret, although the change in health behaviour is an important positive finding. It is possible that although these women were still concerned about weight gain they felt more able to control their weight after the enhanced CBT programme. There are very few relevant studies in this area and we need to know more about the direct impact of interventions to reduce appearance concern on the full range of health behaviours. Although it is difficult to predict with confidence how effective any treatment to reduce appearance concern is likely to be in promoting healthy behaviours (because of the problems in study design in research noted earlier), data from correlational studies suggest that there is the potential for improving a variety of health behaviours through promoting appearance satisfaction. Reducing appearance concerns is of course a useful end in its own right, whether or not this impacts directly on health behaviours.

SUMMARY

Evidence reviewed here has suggested that reducing appearance concern may be an effective way to encourage engagement in a range of health-related behaviours including healthy eating and reductions in the use of performance enhancing drugs and smoking. Other work has suggested that raising specific kinds of appearance concerns may be a useful way to encourage people to engage in healthy behaviours such as quitting smoking and engagement in exercise. Further intervention and prospective studies will enable us to find out more about the direction of associations demonstrated by cross-sectional studies in this area. These need to include intervention studies where appearance concern is reduced in a controlled way and health behaviours are recorded directly. Although evidence suggests some important links between appearance concerns and health behaviours, there is still a lot of work to be done to clarify the nature of these associations. We need to know much more about the impacts on health behaviours of changing levels of appearance concerns. And in particular, we need to be sure that interventions developed with the intention to improve health do not impact negatively on other areas of people's lives.

REFERENCES

American Cancer Society. (2011). *Skin Cancer Prevention and Early Detection.* http://www.cancer.org/Cancer/SkinCancer-Melanoma/MoreInformation/SkinCancerPreventionand EarlyDetection/skin-cancer-prevention-and-early-detection-intro (accessed 17 June 2011).

American Lung Association. (2011). *General Smoking Facts.* http://www.lungusa.org/stop-smoking/about-smoking/facts-figures/general-smoking-facts.html (accessed 17 June 2011).

Anschutz, D. J., van Strien, T., & Engels, R. C. M. E. (2008). Exposure to slim images in mass media: television commercials as reminders of restriction in restrained eaters. *Health Psychology,* 27, 401–8.

Anschutz, D. J., Engels, R. C. M. E., Becker, E. S., & Van Strien, T. (2009). The effects of TV commercials using less thin models on young women's mood, body image, and actual food intake, *Body Image*, 6, 270–6.

Action on Smoking and Health. *Facts and Stats*. http://www.ash.org.uk/information/facts-and-stats (accessed 16 June 2011).

BEAT. *About eating disorders*. http://www.b-eat.co.uk/AboutEatingDisorders (accessed 17 June 2011).

Blair, A., Lewis, V., & Booth, D. (1992). Response to leaflets about eating and shape by women concerned about their weight. *Behavioural Psychotherapy*, 20, 279–86.

Breakthrough Breast Cancer. *Breast Awareness: Touch, Look, Check*. http://breakthrough.org.uk/breast_cancer/breast_awareness/index.html (accessed 19 July 2011).

British Heart Foundation. *Get Active For Your Heart*. http://www.bhf.org.uk/keeping_your_heart_healthy/staying_active/get_active_for_your_heart.aspx (accessed 15 July 2010).

Cahill S. & Mussap, A. J. (2007). Emotional reactions following exposure to idealized bodies predict unhealthy body change attitudes and behaviors in women and men. *Journal of Psychosomatic Research*, 62, 631–9.

Cafri, G., Thompson, J. K., Ricciardelli, L., McCabe, M., Smolak, L., & Yesalis, C. (2005). Pursuit of the muscular ideal: physical and psychological consequences and putative risk factors, *Clinical Psychology Review*, 25, 215–39.

Campbell, A. & Hausenblas, H. (2009). Effects of exercise interventions on body mage: A meta-analysis. *Journal of Health Psychology*, 14, 780–93.

Cash, T. (2000). *User's Manual for the Multidimensional Body-Self Relations Questionnaire*. http://bodyimages.com

Chait, S. R., Thompson, J. K., & Jacobsen, P. B. (2009). Relationship of body image to breast and skin self-examination intentions and behaviours, *Body Image*, 1, 60–3.

Choi, P. (2000). *Femininity and the Physically Active Woman*. London: Routledge.

Chouliara, Z., Papadioti-Athanasiou, V., Power, K., & Swanson, V. (2004). Practice and attitudes towards breast self-examination (BES): A cross-cultural comparison between younger women in Scotland and Greece. *Health Care for Women International*, 25, 311–33.

Clark, M. M., Croghan, I. T., Reading, S., Schroeder, D. R., Stoner, S. M., Patten, C. A., & Vickers, K. S. (2005). The relationship of body dissatisfaction to cigarette smoking in college students. *Body Image*, 2, 263–70.

Cress, M. E., Buchner, D. M., Prochaska, T., Rimmer, J., Brown, M., Macera, C., *et al.* (2005). Best practices for physical activity programs and behaviour counseling in older adult populations. *Journal of Ageing and Physical Activity*, 13, 61–74.

Department of Health. (2010). *Give Up To Save Face*. http://www.smokefree.nhs.uk/

Flett, K., Grogan, S., & Clark-Carter, D. (2010). Women smokers' accounts of participating in a facial wrinkling age-progression intervention. Paper presented at Appearance Matters Conference, Bristol, 22–23 June 2010.

Forrest, K. Y. Z. & Stuhldreher, W. L. (2007). Patterns and correlates of body image dissatisfaction and distortion among college students. *American Journal of Health Studies*, 22, 18–25.

Grogan, S. (2008). *Body Image: Understanding Body Dissatisfaction in Men, Women and Children* (2nd edn.). London: Routledge.

Grogan, S. (2010). Gender and body image: Implications for promoting body satisfaction, *Sex Roles*, 63, 757–65.

Grogan, S. & Richards, H. (2002). Body image: Focus groups with boys and men. *Men and Masculinities*, 4, 219–33.

Grogan, S., Evans, R., Wright, S., & Hunter, G. (2004). Femininity and muscularity: Accounts of seven women body builders. *Journal of Gender Studies*, 13, 57–71.

Grogan, S., Shepherd, S., Evans, R., Wright, S., & Hunter, G. (2006a). Experiences of anabolic steroid use; interviews with men and women steroid users. *Journal of Health Psychology*, 11, 849–60.

Grogan, S, Conner, M., & Smithson, H. (2006b). Sexuality and exercise motivations: Are gay men and heterosexual women most likely to be motivated by concern about weight and appearance? *Sex Roles*, 55, 567–72.

Grogan, S., Fry, G., Gough, B., & Conner, M. (2009). Smoking to stay thin or giving up to save face. Young men and women talk about appearance concerns and smoking. *British Journal of Health Psychology*, 14, 175–86.

Grogan, S., Hartley, L., Fry, G, Conner, M & Gough, B. (2010). Appearance concerns and smoking in young men and women: Going beyond weight control, *Drugs: Education, Prevention and Policy*, 3, 261–9.

Grogan, S., Flett, K., Clark-Carter, D., Gough, B., Davey, R., Richardson, D., *et al.* (2011). Women smokers' experiences of an age-appearance anti-smoking intervention: A qualitative study. *British Journal of Health Psychology*, 16, 675–89.

Harris, S. & Carr, A. (2001). Prevalence of concerns about physical appearance in the general population. *British Journal of Plastic Surgery*, 54, 223–6.

Hysert, P. E., Mirand, A. L., Giovino, G. A., Cummings, K. M., & Kuo, C. L. (2003). 'At Face Value': age progression software provides personalized demonstration of the effects of smoking on appearance (Letter). *Tobacco Control*, 12, 238.

Jarry, J. L. & Beraldi, K. (2004). Characteristics and effectiveness of stand-alone body image treatments: a review of the empirical literature, *Body Image: An International Journal of Research*, 1, 319–33.

Jaworowska, A. & Bazylak, C. (2008). An outbreak of body weight dissatisfaction associated with self-perceived BMI and dieting among female pharmacy students. *Biomedicine and Pharmacotherapy*, 9, 679–92.

Kanayama, G., Pope, H. G. Jr, Cohane, G., & Hudson, J. I. (2003). Risk factors for anabolic-adrenergic steroids use among weight lifters: A case-control study. *Drug and Alcohol Dependence*, 71, 77–86.

King, T. K., Matacin, M., White, K. S., & Marcus, B. H. (2005). A prospective examination of body image and smoking in women. *Body Image: An International Journal of Research*, 2, 19–28.

Kruger, J., Lee, C. -D., Ainsworth, B. E., & Macera, C. A. (2008). Body size satisfaction and physical activity levels among men and women, *Obesity*, 16, 1976–9.

Kyrejto, J. W., Mosewich, A. D., Kowalski, K. C., Mack, D. E., & Crocker, P. R. E. (2008). Men's and women's drive for muscularity: gender differences and cognitive and behavioral correlates. *International Journal of Sport and Exercise Psychology*, 6, 69–84.

Labre, M. P. (2005). The male body ideal: perspectives of readers and non-readers of fitness magazines. *Journal of Men's Health and Gender*, 2, 223–9.

Lenehan, P. (2003). *Anabolic Steroids*. London: Taylor and Francis.

Le Page, M. & Crowther, J. (2010). The effects of exercise on body satisfaction and affect. *Body Image*, 7, 124–30.

Levine, M. P. & Piran, N. (2004). The role of body image in the prevention of eating disorders. *Body Image*, 1, 57–70.

Litt, D. & Dodge, T. (2008). A longitudinal investigation of the Drive for Muscularity Scale: Predicting use of performance enhancing substances and weightlifting among males. *Body Image*, 5, 346–51.

Lowry, R., Guluska, D. A., & Fulton, J. E. (2002). Weight management goals and practices among US high school students; Associations with physical activity, diet and smoking. *Journal of Adolescent Health,* 31, 133–44.

Morgan, J. F. & Arcelus, J. (2009). Body image in gay and straight men: A qualitative study. *Eating Disorders Review,* 17, 435–43.

Morrison, T. G., Morrison, M. A., Hopkins, C., & Rowan, E. T. (2004). Muscle mania: Development of a new scale examining the drive for muscularity in Canadian males. *Psychology of Men and Masculinity,* 4, 30–9.

National Institute for Drug Abuse, (2011). *Tobacco/Nicotine.* http://www.nida.nih.gov/DrugPages/Nicotine.html (accessed 17th June 2011).

O'Dea, J. (2005). Body image and nutritional status among adolescents and adults: A review of the literature. *Australian Journal of Eating Disorders,* 52, 56–67.

Perkins, K. A., Marcus, M. D., Levine, M. D., D'Amico, D., Miller, A., Broge, M., *et al.* (2001). Cognitive behavioural therapy to reduce weight concerns improves smoking cessation outcome in weight-concerned women. *Journal of Consulting and Clinical Psychology,* 69, 604–13.

Peterson, R. D., Tantleff-Dunn, S., & Bedwell, J. S. (2006). The effects of exposure to feminist ideology on women's body image. *Body Image: An International Journal of Research,* 3, 237–46.

Potter, B., Pederson, L. L., Chan, S. S. H., Aubut, J. L., & Koval, J. J. (2004). Does a relationship exist between body weight, concerns about weight, and smoking among adolescents? An integration of the literature with an emphasis on gender. *Nicotine and Tobacco Research,* 6, 397–425.

Stice, E. (2001). A prospective test of the dual pathway model of bulimic pathology: Mediating effects of dieting and negative affect. *Journal of Abnormal Psychology,* 110, 124–35.

Stice, E. (2002). Risk and maintenance factors for eating pathology: a meta-analytic review. *Psychological Bulletin,* 128, 825–48.

Van den Berg, P., Thompson, J. K., Obremski-Brandon, K., & Coovert, M. (2002). The tripartite influence model of body image and eating disturbance: A covariance structure modeling investigation testing the mediational role of appearance comparison. *Journal of Psychosomatic Research,* 53, 1007–20.

Weinstock, M. A., Risica, P. M., Martin, R. A., Rawowski, W., Dube, C, Berwick, M., *et al.* (2007). Melanoma early detection with thorough skin self-examination: The 'check it out' randomised trial. *American Journal of Preventive Medicine,* 32, 517–24.

Wharton, C. M., Adams, T., & Hampl, J. S. (2008). Weight loss practices and body weight perceptions among US college studentS. *American College Health,* 56, 579–84.

Wright, S., Grogan, S., & Hunter, G. (2000). Motivations for anabolic steroid use among bodybuilders, *Journal of Health Psychology,* 5, 566–72.

Yamimiya, Y., Cash, T. F., Melnyk, S. E., Posavak, H. D., & Posavac, S. S. (2005). Women's exposure to thin-and-beautiful media images: body image effects of media-ideal internalisation and impact-reduction interventions'. *Body Image,* 2, 74–80.

CHAPTER 41

WHAT NEEDS TO CHANGE AND HOW CAN CHANGE BE ACHIEVED?: SUMMARY AND SYNTHESIS

DIANA HARCOURT

NICHOLA RUMSEY

THE chapters in this section have explored the potential for a broad range of interventions to address appearance-related issues and concerns. We share with the authors the common aims of wanting to provide accessible and effective interventions, shift societal attitudes about the importance placed on appearance, and promote and increase acceptance of diversity.

The number of interventions being developed in this field is increasing rapidly, but ensuring that this enthusiasm and activity by researchers, practitioners, policy-makers, support organizations, and the media results in the maximum benefit for those affected by appearance concerns, without duplicating effort, remains a challenge. The complexities involved in effective and accessible intervention design and delivery cannot be underestimated. This synthesis pulls together some of the many issues raised in this section and discusses the challenges associated with targeting and evaluating interventions effectively, the role of the media in interventions, and the engagement of stakeholders.

Changing individual and societal behaviours, cognitions, and attitudes are mighty tasks and it would be unreasonable to assume that any one intervention could be a universal panacea for current levels of appearance-related concerns and the associated impacts. Until now, we have lacked a clear way of conceptualizing how the various interventions might relate to one another. Several authors in this book (including Julia Cadogan, Elizabeth Jenkinson, and Esther Hansen) have supported a stepped model of care recognizing that individuals' needs differ, with some needing more intense intervention than others, and also recognizing that one person's situation and needs change over time.

Julia Cadogan's interview with Katie Piper illustrates how packages of care and interventions should be tailored to suit an individual's particular needs and objectives. Work by Esther Hanson and others has shown that the key to effective interventions may be to take account of these patient-centred goals, so that people identify for themselves what they consider to constitute a successful outcome. The effectiveness of any individual intervention can then be measured against progress towards these goals. In comparison with a standardized approach that offers the same interventions in a formulaic manner to everyone, interventions driven by patient-centred goals are associated with more positive patient experiences and improved outcomes. However, eliciting patients' goals and expectations can be difficult and health professionals involved in interventions such as the cosmetic surgery services examined in Alex Clarke's chapter are unlikely to have been trained or supported in how to do this effectively. Expectations and goals relating to the aesthetic outcomes of biomedical interventions may well be easier for both patients and health professionals to express than those relating to psychosocial interventions, and ways of eliciting and managing the latter warrant further investigation.

Several chapters in this section highlight the challenges inherent in evaluating the effectiveness of individual, group and societal interventions, particularly in relation to suitable outcome measures, control groups and samples. Randomized controlled trials (RCTs) are still espoused by many as the gold standard of intervention evaluation and, as illustrated in Elizabeth Jenkinson's chapter, their findings are given greater status and significance, particularly in relation to their prominence in systematic reviews, However, they are often not the most appropriate or feasible means of evaluating psychosocial interventions (Mulligan et al., 2005).

Given these challenges and the time and funding needed to develop interventions in the first instance, we grapple regularly with the dilemma of 'how much evaluation is enough?' For example, the Face IT intervention outlined Alyson Bessell in Chapter 39 was developed with the eventual aim of providing online support suitable for self-administration by adults with visible differences. In order to safeguard participants during the development phase, the effectiveness of the intervention was demonstrated in a RCT comparing face-to-face intervention by a specialist with the online Face IT intervention delivered in the presence of a trained therapist, who, in the event, did not intervene and was only present in case of difficulties. The next stage will be to release the intervention to psychosocial specialists who have undergone training in its use, and who will act as gatekeepers, assessing the suitability of recipients and monitoring the impact of the intervention. This whole process has taken place over a period of 5 years, and has required considerable investments of time and financial resources.

Similarly, interventions that have been developed in one country or culture need to be adapted and re-evaluated if they are to be used with a different population. For example, the first step in providing a decision-making aid for women considering breast reconstruction in the UK was to evaluate the feasibility and acceptability of an intervention that had originally been developed in Australia. This work highlighted a number of important changes that would be needed if it was to suit a UK patient group. Likewise, school-based body image interventions may not transfer directly from one country to another. However, these acceptability studies can be costly and time-consuming and, in the meantime, appearance-related concerns and associated risk behaviours continue to rise, and schools and health professionals continue to wait for the intervention to become available. Even the most rigorously evaluated intervention will not meet the needs of all its users. Researchers who are committed to developing effective evidence-based interventions must continually weigh up the demands of thorough evaluation and the pressure from audiences eager for interventions to counter appearance-related distress.

The media's role in relation to appearance concerns is complex. On the one hand, media professionals are berated for promoting unrealistic ideals, but on the other hand, the media also has the potential to be a powerful instrument of intervention, if those same professionals could be persuaded to alter the content and emphasis of their outputs. Those considering the role of the media in relation to any form of intervention need to take account of this complexity and should keep abreast of recent and breaking developments in the various modes of delivery of information in this rapidly evolving field. James Partridge has outlined the use of a range of media in societal campaigns by Changing Faces to foster positive attitudes towards people living with visible differences and to promote greater acceptance of diversity in relation to appearance although the impact of these campaigns is, as yet, unknown. The potential of media that have been relatively underused in the past (e.g. advertising campaigns directly aimed at cinema audiences) and the full capacity of the Internet and 'new media' (e.g. social networking), to promote diversity in appearance rather than narrowing ideals, remain to be fully explored. Societal campaigns need to use these resources effectively and 'go viral' if they are to capitalize on these cost-effective, instant, and global means of communication. But how easy is it to for appearance researchers and practitioners to do this, and to compete with the popularity of messages put out by the media themselves? For example, paparazzi photos of celebrities revealing their 'true' bodies on the beach, in contrast to the usually airbrushed images of perfectly presented physiques, spread quickly but these are typically presented and marketed as a form of entertainment (albeit by shaming individuals and exposing the imperfections of their supposedly admired bodies), rather than used in a positive way to promote natural and more realistic looks.

In recent years we have seen a number of appearance-related public campaigns anchored in the media. For example, in the UK in 2009 Gok Wan fronted a campaign within his TV show *How to Look Good Naked*, calling for body confidence to become a mandatory subject in the UK National Schools Curriculum. This resulted in more than 49,000 signatories to a petition delivered to the Prime Minister, calling for a compulsory hour of body image education for young people each year. This strategy may of course, have been driven by the desire of media professionals to improve the ratings for the TV series, nevertheless, the linking of a celebrity to the campaign will have increased the attention paid to the 'cause', far more so than academics, researchers and practitioners could do alone.

The Face IT intervention outlined by Alyson Bessell is an excellent example of how embracing newly developed modes of delivery can increase opportunities to provide accessible support. The evidence-based approaches used within Face IT have since been adapted to meet the needs of young people with visible differences, in a format that they find appealing and engaging. YP Face IT (Young People's Face IT) has involved young people in its development and evaluation from the outset. The value of user involvement has also been demonstrated in Susan Brown's account of the production of a series of short films about the diagnosis and birth of infants with a cleft. However, the considerable effort, cost, and time involved in developing these products and in regularly reviewing and updating them to ensure any information provided is current, should not be underestimated.

As well as promoting the benefits of interventions, we need to carefully consider any potential pitfalls associated with them. For example, Phillippa Diedrichs and Emma Halliwell highlight the need to ensure that school-based interventions aiming to improve body satisfaction and promote acceptance of diversity do not unwittingly single out or focus attention upon young people because of their size or visible difference. Likewise, those designing societal interventions need to be wary not to stigmatize particular individuals within the broader population, nor to alienate segments of the audience by insinuating (perhaps in a somewhat accusatory way) that they hold negative attitudes and/or behave unhelpfully towards those whose appearance does not meet societal ideals. Whole-school approaches, involving pupils of all ages, teachers, support staff, and parents have been endorsed as a way of normalizing the consideration of appearance issues. Applying this principle to create 'whole-society' interventions that avoid focusing on a particular subgroup would be a monumental task involving a basic shift in cultural attitudes, but the lure of establishing a society in which appearance is no longer lauded over other attributes which contribute more effectively to psychological well-being, is fundamentally appealing.

The complexities involved in successful attitude change have long been challenging for psychologists of all persuasions. Whilst interventions might be effective in changing beliefs and the degree of internalization of appearance ideals, this does not necessarily equate to lasting changes in behaviour. In other words the intention–behaviour gap that has been the bane of the working lives of those looking to promote health is also an issue for those working in the field of appearance.

So far, this synthesis has focused on interventions designed to improve body satisfaction, adjustment to an altered appearance, and/or to challenge societal attitudes. Sarah Grogan and Daniel Masterson's chapter demonstrates how appearance concerns might be used as a motivator to engage people in interventions to promote health. In keeping with the positive approaches adopted by other successful health promoting interventions, they highlight how raising self-esteem through improved body image may lead to the take-up of favourable health behaviours. However, drawing on appearance-related concerns to promote positive health behaviours can reinforce unhelpful appearance stereotypes. For example, emphasizing the effect of tanning on the onset and progress of wrinkles in order to encourage people to avoid sun exposure could inadvertently promote negative attitudes towards ageing. Yet again, the challenges of successfully walking the tightrope between positive results and detrimental outcomes are evident.

Finally, it is important to consider the stakeholders involved in the provision of appearance-related interventions. The prime stakeholders should surely be people who are expected to use and benefit from these interventions. In recent years, there has been a steadily increasing acceptance of the need to engage and involve service users in all stages of research and intervention development, and this is considered in depth by Amanda Bates, in Section 4. As we saw in Section 1, the provision of healthcare (including the range and availability of interventions) is also politically driven, so there is also an imperative to engage policy-makers and funders as they are key stakeholders in implementation. Some initiatives, for example, the integration of psychologists as core members of care teams for people affected by cleft in the UK, have been very successful. Achieving change in other areas, including burns care, has been more challenging. An awareness of the relevant gatekeepers and their particular agendas is crucial, as is making the most of opportunities as they arise (e.g. the current interest amongst Members of Parliament in the UK in relation to body image in young people) as these are pivotal to the success or otherwise of attempts to inform and shape policy and care provision.

However, not everyone is motivated to engage with the issues raised in this section and there could be resistance from some stakeholders towards the proposals being made. For example, why would the media want to change their coverage of appearance issues if they are currently meeting their objectives of generating audiences and advertising revenue? Similarly, why would cosmetic surgery companies endorse campaigns for realistic images in the media if this reduced the demand for their services? And why would surgeons who have devoted their careers to studying and training in appearance-altering surgical techniques want to embrace an alternative approach towards addressing appearance-related concerns? This last question has been eloquently answered by Esther Hansen and Peter Butler (see Chapter 5) who are advocates for the benefits of surgical and psychological services working in tandem within a plastic and reconstructive unit. However, combined services like this are not standard practice, and bold, innovative attempts to persuade key stakeholders to change their practices are urgently needed.

In summary, this section has highlighted the complexities associated with intervention design, evaluation, and delivery. Many questions remain, including whether interventions are suitable and effective for people of different ethnicities, how to facilitate effective participant involvement in the development of interventions, and the most appropriate research methods to establish the efficacy of interventions. These are considered further in the following section, which examines issues in appearance research.

REFERENCE

Mulligan, K., Newman, S. P, Taal, E., Hazes, M., Rasker, J. J. & OMERACT 7 Special Interest Group (2005). The design and evaluation of psychoeducational/self-management interventions. *The Journal of Rheumatology*, 32(12), 2470–4.

SECTION 4

RESEARCH ISSUES

CHAPTER 42

RESEARCH ISSUES: OVERVIEW

DIANA HARCOURT

NICHOLA RUMSEY

THE chapters in Section 4 focus on issues pertaining to the design and conduct of the research that has underpinned the development of the psychology of appearance as an applied and academic subject in recent years.

Firstly, Ross Krawczyk, Jessie Menzel, and Kevin Thompson present an overview of the multiple dimensions of body image and the broad range of measures available to assess affect, cognitions, and behavioural aspects. They remind us of the demanding process of scale development and the challenges facing researchers conducting quantitative and experimental research. They include a call for the development of consensus measures with good psychometric properties as a means to develop research further. This is a useful and practical guide to one of the many styles of research conducted in this field. The following chapters demonstrate issues relevant to alternative methods and, although we cannot cover every possible approach within the confines of the space available here, we hope that this section will encourage new and established researchers alike to review the current methods and consider alternative or complementary approaches in the future.

Many researchers, including some of the contributors to this volume, have highlighted a need for larger sample sizes and more representative research. Martin Persson's chapter offers a response to these calls, and uses a population-based study in Sweden to show how very large-scale datasets can identify areas for further research and address questions that would otherwise be difficult and costly to investigate.

For some time now, the relative merits of qualitative versus quantitative methods have been discussed as much within appearance research as they have within other areas of psychology. Emma Dures draws a line under the debate about the supremacy of one approach over another and argues eloquently and coherently for the use of mixed methods in appearance-related research. However, this approach is not embraced by everyone, and Emma examines the perspectives of both the proponents and detractors.

Neil Coulson then offers a very useful guide for researchers who are contemplating the world of online research, and considers the benefits, opportunities, and challenges presented by the growing use of the Internet. Diana Harcourt's chapter also considers the potential expansion of new technologies and web-based research alongside the possibilities offered by alternative methods including arts-based approaches. Her chapter suggests that the use of a broader range of methods could be interesting and advantageous for researchers, and would offer alternative means by which people can be engaged with, and participate in, appearance research.

Participant involvement is the crux of Amanda Bates's chapter. She draws on her personal experience of being a research participant, a person living with a visible difference, and a researcher to offer a thought-provoking and practical guide to participant involvement in appearance research. The promotion of participants' voices in research more generally has come increasingly into the spotlight in recent years and patient and public involvement (PPI) is now a key requirement for funders of research. Questions relating to plans for PPI are routinely included on application forms for research funding, and increasingly, this has become one of the criteria against which funding applications are judged. Clearly, recognition of the advantages of involving individuals in research through means other than merely as participants has gained momentum and PPI is a key issue for researchers to embrace going forward. The summary and synthesis of this section considers the opportunities presented by advances in PPI and the use of alternative research methods.

CHAPTER 43

METHODOLOGICAL ISSUES IN THE STUDY OF BODY IMAGE AND APPEARANCE

ROSS KRAWCZYK

JESSIE MENZEL

J. KEVIN THOMPSON

DEFINING BODY IMAGE AND RELATED CONSTRUCTS

CURRENTLY several measures exist that tap into people's perceptions of their bodies and physical appearance. The sheer number and variety of these measures is a testament to the complex and varied nature of physical appearance and body image as constructs. Cash and Pruzinsky (2002) have made the point that body image cannot be captured using one term alone and that body image transcends merely our mind's eye picture of the body. In support of the broad nature of this construct, research in the field of body image has operationalized body image in more than 16 different terms (Thompson et al., 1999). These facets include, but are not limited to, weight satisfaction, body satisfaction, appearance evaluation, body schema, body checking, size perception and accuracy, and body distortion—all of which contain either a perceptual, affective, cognitive, or behavioural component (Thompson et al., 1999). More succinctly, body image can thus be defined as a person's thoughts, perceptions, and feelings regarding the body (Grogan, 2008).

While the measurement of body image theoretically extends to internal, competence-based aspects of the body (e.g. proprioceptive awareness, strength), the vast majority of measures are concerned with self-perceived physical appearance. The currently available measures of physical appearance-related body image cover the many facets and dimensions just described. The four major types of measures used to assess and define body image include global satisfaction measures, affective measures, measures of cognitions, and behavioural measures.

Global and site-specific satisfaction

Perhaps the most commonly used measures are those that assess a person's overall evaluation of his or her body—a dimension typically labelled as satisfaction (Thompson et al., 1999). Satisfaction can be defined as a liking or favourable opinion and can be applied towards the body as a whole (i.e. global satisfaction), or site-specific components of physical appearance, such as body parts (e.g. waist, arms), weight, or shape.

One technique for assessing body satisfaction is to calculate the discrepancy between a person's ideal physical appearance and his or her actual physical appearance. This actual versus ideal discrepancy can be defined in several ways—for height, weight, or overall shape. For example, to determine a person's weight satisfaction, one might find the difference between the person's actual (observed weight) and his or her ideal. Figural rating scales can also be used to obtain actual versus ideal discrepancies. Participants are presented with a series of figure drawings that vary based on one physical attribute (e.g. height, muscularity, shape, etc.) and select the one that best represents their current appearance and the figure that best represents their ideal appearance. Figural scales are useful because they can allow the researcher to control for variation among one physical attribute and allow for easy quantification of the actual versus ideal discrepancy. Newer figure rating scales, such as the Body Image Assessment Scale (Gardner et al., 2009) and the Photographic Figure Rating Scale (Swami et al., 2008) have made use of anthropomorphic measurements to increase the accuracy in representing body types.

Questionnaires also exist which measure various facets of body satisfaction, both general and site specific. These questionnaires, which typically employ Likert scales, allow researchers to assess several characteristics of body satisfaction or several body sites at a time. Measures of overall satisfaction with appearance typically assess the extent to which a person feels physically attractive and/or likes his or her 'looks'. For example, an item from the Appearance Evaluation subscale of the Multi-Dimensional Body-Self Relations Questionnaire (MBSRQ), a popular measure of body satisfaction, states 'I like my looks just the way they are' (Brown et al., 1990). The Body Areas Satisfaction subscale from the MBSRQ, on the other hand, assesses satisfaction with specific areas of the body (e.g. face, torso, arms) (Brown et al., 1990). Two other questionnaire measures assess clinically significant body dissatisfaction, defined as overvaluation of weight and shape with regard to a person's sense of self. These measures are the Weight Concern and Shape Concern subscales of the Eating Disorder Examination, questionnaire version (Fairburn & Beglin, 1994).

Affective measures

The affective component of body image refers to the feelings or emotions (e.g. anxiety and distress) experienced as the result of satisfaction/dissatisfaction with the body. Another affective component also includes shame felt as the result of failing to live up to the physical appearance of one's culture (McKinley & Hyde, 1996). Again, these emotions can be associated with global appearance or with specific body sites, as is often experienced in body dysmorphic disorder (BDD). Reed and colleagues' (1991) Physical Appearance State and Trait Anxiety Scale (PASTAS) measures feelings of nervousness, tension, and anxiety associated with 16 specific aspects of physical appearance. Conversely, the Situational Inventory of Body Image Dysphoria (SIBID; Cash, 2002) measures distress and other emotions associated with social and interpersonal situations.

Cognitive measures

The cognitions (thoughts, beliefs, and schemas) that maintain self-perceived physical appearance have been receiving increasing attention in body image research. These measures focus on the conclusions or attributions that individuals make as the result of evaluation of their own appearance or the beliefs that form as the result of cultural messages about beauty. One popular measure in this area is the Sociocultural Attitudes Towards Appearance Questionnaire (SATAQ-III) which measures the extent to which individuals 'buy-into' the cultural standards of thinness conveyed by the popular media in Western culture (Thompson et al., 2004). Other measures assess specific cognitive distortions related to dissatisfaction or disturbance in self-perceived physical appearance. For example, the Assessment of Body Image Cognitive Distortions (Jakatdar et al., 2006) asks people to respond to statements like 'Imagine you're invited to a party on the beach. Would you think that because of something about your appearance you probably won't fit in or enjoy participating?'

Behavioural measures

Attitudes, emotions, and thoughts regarding physical appearance can also manifest as behaviour. Increasing attention has been brought of late to these behaviours that reflect the way a person feels about his or her physical appearance. For example, a person who is dissatisfied may engage in behaviours aimed at altering their appearance (e.g. restrained eating to lose weight, obtaining cosmetic surgery, or wearing loose or concealing clothing). Others who experience a high degree of anxiety regarding physical appearance may avoid mirrors or wearing certain clothes in public situations (e.g. swimsuits). These avoidance behaviours have been captured by Engle et al.'s (2008) Body Image Avoidance Scale. Still others may engage in excessive checking behaviours which may indicate over-evaluation of physical appearance (e.g. pinching body fat, weighing multiple times a day). These behaviours have been assessed using the Body Checking Questionnaire (Reas et al., 2006) and the Body Image Compulsive Actions Scale (Engle et al., 2008).

SCALE DEVELOPMENT

There are a fairly large number of established, empirically supported scales that target various aspects of body image, but frequently researchers must modify existing scales or create new ones in order to study their construct of interest. Developing new scales in any area is a demanding process in which the developer must attend to a great number of issues. The new scale should clearly focus on one of the previously discussed domains (global satisfaction, affective, cognitive, and behavioural) and once this has been chosen, both reliability and validity must be established in order to create a useful and high quality scale. Also, the construct of interest and target population must be carefully considered and defined. Developing new scales in the area of body image assessment is no exception to these standards. However, there are several issues that are especially relevant to measuring body image that warrant discussion.

First, measures of body image constructs must often be created separately for women and men due to differences in appearance ideals (Cafri et al., 2002; McCabe & Ricciardelli, 2004; Thompson, 2004). For example, an important factor in studying women's body image is the drive for thinness, the desire for a cultural appearance ideal that involves having very little body fat. Among men, the drive for thinness is less important. Instead, men tend to focus on the drive for muscularity, an appearance ideal involving large size, leanness, and heavy musculature. If a researcher wanted to assess appearance satisfaction among both men and women, the drive for thinness would be a key variable of study among the women in the study but not as relevant among the men. Therefore, any scale designed to measure appearance satisfaction would have to take this difference into account. For this reason, measurement tools must often be adapted, modified, or created separately for women and men.

A second issue when designing new measurement tools is that a scale must target a specific construct within the realm of body image (Thompson, 2004). All too often, people discuss body image as a single construct when in reality it is multifaceted (Cash, 2002). In recent years, those studying body image have created a number of empirically supported assessment tools that focus on specific constructs within the area of body image (see earlier and Cash & Grasso, 2005), but more work is needed. Researchers must design and use scales that define and target specific, individual facets of body image. In order for this to be accomplished, one must first carefully define the construct of interest by reviewing past research and choosing an agreed upon (or at least empirically supported) definition. Only by looking at past work can convergent and divergent validity be assessed. If the scale being designed is the first to measure the specific construct, then research is needed to provide a clear definition of the construct and support the necessity of the new scale. It is also possible that a scale measures multiple dimensions of body image. If so, these dimensions need to be well differentiated into separate factors and factor analytic procedures should be conducted to confirm the hypothesized structure of the scale. Regardless of the new scale having a single or multiple factors, it should target specific, well-defined, individual constructs within the realm of body image.

A third consideration in scale development that is especially relevant to the area of body image is the distinction between state and trait measurements (Cash & Pruzinsky, 2002; Thompson, 2004, 2009; Tiggemann, 2005). State measurements focus on constructs that change relatively quickly over time while trait constructs are thought to be much more stable. When conducting research, it is often important to make a distinction between these two, especially when timing may play a role in the results. This issue is particularly important in the area of appearance and body image assessment because it is quite common to study the effects of specific stimuli or manipulations in an experimental or longitudinal design. The distinction between state and trait constructs is also an important one for the interpretation of results and in forming new theory. For example, in the classic 'swimsuit study' (Fredrickson et al., 1998), a primary construct of interest was self-objectification (Fredrickson & Roberts, 1997), which can be conceptualized as either a state or trait construct. In this example, the researchers clearly explained the nature of state and trait self-objectification, chose to measure trait self-objectification because it matched their research design, and finally chose a trait self-objectification scale that accomplished their measurement goal. By doing so, they provided a solid conceptual base for the interpretation of their results and increased the meaningfulness of their study. Similar care to choose a state or trait construct will enhance future research.

Finally, it is of great importance to consider the target population when constructing a new scale. Many aspects of a scale, including individual item meanings and overall factor structure, can change depending on the participant's demographic characteristics. A researcher may obtain drastically different results when collecting data from various populations of study (specific samples that have been found to be highly relevant to appearance and body image research are discussed in a later section). While it is expected that overall means will differ between samples, this issue is relevant to scale construction because an instrument may be psychometrically sound with some populations and not with others. For example, an instrument may be designed to measure body satisfaction and it may accomplish this by assessing thoughts about leanness, muscularity, and height. The psychometrics of this scale are likely to be good with men, but poor with women simply because the scale is assessing issues that are more salient to men. If the target population is adult women or adolescent boys, for example, then the questions and overall content must match the target construct as it manifests in these groups. Despite these differences between populations, a psychometrically sound, valid instrument must be created. This can be accomplished by reviewing past research, identifying constructs that are most relevant to various populations, using this information to guide scale construction, and assessing both reliability and validity within the population of interest.

Populations of Study

Specifying and selecting an appropriate population of study is vital in many areas of research, but it is especially so in the field of body image. A target population is usually chosen along with the research question and hypothesis. For example, a researcher may decide to study a hypothesized decline in appearance satisfaction among adolescents in the United States. The population of interest is all adolescents in the US and a sample must be chosen to represent this population. If the research question was more specific, then the researcher would have to target the specific population by getting a representative sample. Choosing a population and sample of study is often a balancing act in which a researcher must consider the phenomena of interest, how well these phenomena are represented in the potential target population, how the phenomena may differ between groups within the population, and how well results of the study using a specific sample will generalize to the population. In studying appearance and body image, there are several demographic variables that are of particular importance.

The first and perhaps most obvious issue of selecting a sample is the question of studying males, females, or both. This issue is especially relevant to appearance and body image research because many constructs differ greatly between males and females. Not only do males and females differ in physical appearance, but they also tend to value different aspects of their appearance; for example the differentiation in cultural appearance ideals leading to the drive for muscularity among men and the drive for thinness among women (Cafri et al., 2002; McCabe & Ricciardelli, 2004; Thompson, 2004). Any study examining cultural appearance ideals would have to take this difference into account or have potentially erroneous results. For example, if a researcher lumped men and women together in a sample for analysis, they would be able to compute a mean drive for thinness and drive for muscularity score. However, both of these scores would be meaningless as the means would potentially include a group of people who scored high and another who scored low for each construct. A better way of conducting this study would be to compute the means for men and women separately. Generally, males and females should be studied separately because of differing physical appearance and cultural appearance ideals.

A second important variable to consider when selecting a population/sample is the age of participants. Severe body image dissatisfaction is not a phenomenon that begins in adulthood. Adolescents and children as young as 8 years of age express dissatisfaction with their appearance (Gardner, 2002; Smolak & Thompson, 2009). Because body image constructs exist across many ages, researchers must use strategies and measurement tools that are age appropriate. While an adult is probably able to accurately self-report their emotions regarding their appearance, a young child is much less likely to be able to do so. To conduct research with these populations, specialized measures need to be chosen, created, or adapted. Another challenge is that it cannot be assumed that appearance and body image constructs manifest themselves in the same way for adults, adolescents, and children. Therefore, researchers need to address these potential differences empirically and not make assumptions. Also, caution is needed when comparing groups because inequality of ages across groups could influence results. Finally, age can have a large influence on longitudinal studies in this area—this issue will be discussed later.

A third important consideration relating to various populations of study is the racial and ethnic composition of the population. There is evidence that various races and cultures have differing appearance ideals and values placed on specific aspects of appearance and body image. For example, it appears that African American culture is more accepting of a wider range of body weights and shapes (Celio et al., 2002) when compared to European Americans. It has also been reported that Latina women tend to have greater weight-related satisfaction than their European American counterparts, but this effect disappears as the Latina women become more acculturated in the US (Altabe & O'Garo, 2002). Additionally, we recently found that symptoms of body dysmorphic disorder were significantly lower among African American women when compared to all other racial and ethnic groups while no significant differences were found between groups of men (Boroughs et al., 2010). While more research is needed to find evidence of similarities or differences among ethnic and racial groups on body image, it is clear that racial and ethnic composition of samples can play an important role in many appearance and body image issues. For this reason, researchers need to consider the racial and ethnic composition of their sample and test for potential differences between these groups. Also, differing appearance ideals may lead some measurement tools to be reliable and valid for some groups but not others. Researchers need to be cognizant of these methodological issues related to race and ethnicity to ensure that their research is as accurate and representative as possible.

Finally, a relatively new and emerging line of research has examined appearance and body image differences between heterosexual and LGBT populations (see Chapter 16). Overall, significant differences have been found for many important constructs. For example, Hospers and Jansen (2005) found that homosexual males were at a higher risk for eating disorders than heterosexual males. They also found that body dissatisfaction and self-esteem played a vital role in the relationship between homosexuality and eating disorders. It appears that homosexual men are more likely to experience greater peer pressure regarding their appearance. Boroughs et al. (2010) found significant differences in symptomatology of body dysmorphic disorder between sexual orientation groups and genders. Sexual minority women experienced the highest symptomatology, followed by heterosexual women and sexual minority men who did not differ, followed by heterosexual men who experienced the lowest symptomatology. Further evidence regarding lesbian women has shown inconsistency, sometimes finding that lesbians are at lower risk for body image and appearance dissatisfaction and sometimes finding no differences with heterosexual women (Rothblum, 2002). Overall, the research in this area has been somewhat inconsistent, leaving a great deal of room for future research to improve upon past methodology and clarify the relationship between gender, sexuality, and body image. Because of this mixed past evidence, it is necessary for researchers to take the potential differences between the LGBT and heterosexual populations into account when constructing scales, designing studies, and interpreting results.

In summary, there are several important considerations relating to differences among demographic groups that researchers might take into account when doing research in the area of appearance and body image. Care must be taken to choose measurement tools that match the target population (Thompson, 2004). Once chosen, reliability and validity need to be assessed for the current sample rather than simply relying on past work. Finally, researchers must consider diversity of the target population in terms of gender, age, race, culture, sexuality, and any other relevant demographic characteristic. Doing these things will greatly improve future research in this area.

SPECIFIC RESEARCH DESIGNS

There are also important methodological issues relating to research designs, specifically longitudinal studies, correlational studies, and true experiments, which need to be considered carefully. This section will focus on each of these in turn.

Longitudinal studies

Perhaps the most important consideration when conducting longitudinal research in the realm of body image is the effect of age (see also Chapter 43). Beyond targeting specific, study appropriate age groups, age plays a vital role in all longitudinal work. The key factor in these studies is the passage of time; the advancing age of the participants. In the realm of body image, this consideration is particularly important because of the drastic and rapid physical changes that can occur at certain times in life, such as puberty. For example, if a longitudinal study takes place over 4 years, it may measure participants from ages 13–17 or from ages 17–21. It is reasonable to think that the participants in the study looking at ages 13–17 will show greater change because of the developmental changes of puberty. A person's appearance will likely undergo great change from ages 13–17. They will probably also have major emotional, cognitive, and behavioural changes. Comparatively, the changes between ages 17–21 are likely to be smaller. For this reason, we can conclude two things about the study of appearance and body image. First, longitudinal work is a vital methodology in this field. Second, the psychometrics of instruments need to be evaluated at all time points because potential changes in appearance and body image may invalidate some measurement tools. This issue can largely be addressed by assessing the reliability at each time point and by using multiple measures of body image constructs in order to assess validity.

Another important consideration is the influence of cohort effects—important changes in society or culture that affect people at a specific point in time. This issue is important for both comparing past studies and for interpreting results of longitudinal studies. When comparing past studies that were performed at different times, it is important to consider potential factors that could differentially influence the results. Of such factors, one of the largest in recent society is the invention and popularization of the Internet. Because of this, if one were to study any socially influenced phenomenon, then some of the contributing factors would probably be quite different if the study were performed in the 1980s, 1990s, or 2000s. For example, pro-anorexia websites have become a focus of some research in the area of eating disorders (Norris et al., 2006). If researchers were examining the social influences on the desire to be thin in 2010, then these websites would be likely to be of importance. However, this would not be the case for the same research performed before the Internet was widely available. Similarly, if a longitudinal study spans an important social or cultural development, then this must be taken into account. Failure to do so may result in poor interpretation of results, perhaps misattributing results to sample changes when the true cause is a change in society. This issue is relevant to all longitudinal work, but is especially so in the area of appearance and body image. For instance media changes rapidly in both content and method of distribution, meaning cohort effects are especially likely. Another reason for the relevance to the area of body image is that the general population appears to be becoming less satisfied with their appearance over time, with dislike of overall appearance and of specific body sites increasing significantly from the 1970s to the 1980s and again to the 1990s (Cash, 1997). This relatively rapid and recent change highlights the necessity of taking societal changes and cohort effects into account when conducting longitudinal and prospective research about appearance or body image (Thompson, 2009).

Correlational and cross-sectional studies

Correlational and cross-sectional investigations are diverse in methodology and scope. They can be as simple as measuring the association between two variables among a small sample, and as complex as multiway, multivariate comparison while statistically controlling for numerous variables across many large samples. Regardless of scope or methodology, there are issues with these types of studies when applied to the study of appearance and body image.

The problem of 'proxy' variables (Kramer et al., 2001) is quite prominent in appearance and body image research (Thompson, 2009). This problem can occur when one variable is found to be a strong predictor of a second variable using a correlational design. Naturally, a researcher will conclude that the first variable predicts the second and draws theoretical conclusions. The problem arises when in reality the first variable is highly correlated with a third variable that is the true best predictor, both statistically and theoretically. For example, a researcher may conduct a study and find that number of hours of television watched is negatively correlated with appearance satisfaction. They then conclude that more time watching television predicts lower appearance satisfaction. However, it is quite possible that the hours of television watched is highly correlated with the internalization of appearance ideals and that this internalization is what is truly driving the effect of lowered appearance satisfaction. The hours of television were simply a 'proxy' for the true predictor. This problem can occur in any research where a causal relationship cannot be established (i.e. in any non-experimental design). It occurs most often when researchers use only a single measure to assess a single variable within a topic area. In the previous example, if internalization was not measured then erroneous conclusions may have been drawn. This issue is particularly important to the area of appearance and body image because researchers frequently use only a single measure of body image. Once multiple measures of the same or similar constructs are used, it enables researchers to use more thorough and complex statistical procedures to disentangle the complicated relationships among variables. This can also enable greater emphasis to be placed on identifying moderators and mediators. Overall, researchers in this area need to use multiple appearance and body image measures to avoid proxy problems and more accurately identify relationships between variables.

A second major limitation when using correlational designs in the field of body image and appearance is the relative lack of standardized measures. Being a relatively young field, many researchers have created their own measures and instruments to assess various constructs. While these are frequently high quality instruments with sound psychometrics, this practice does lead to a great diversity of measurement tools. This creates problems when comparing studies and performing meta-analyses. As stated by Cash (2002), the field is in need of psychometrically sound measurement tools that are designed with a specific purpose. That means that they are designed to measure a specific construct and are validated with the intended populations of use. These measures may then be used by multiple researchers across many studies. This will allow direct comparison of studies and prevent researchers from needing to create and validate new measures for each study. While this issue has been partly addressed (see some measurement tools discussed in the first section of this chapter), much work still needs to be done.

Experimental methodology

Experimental methodology is quite common in the study of appearance and body image. In order to be considered a true experiment, a study must have both random assignment to conditions and manipulation of an independent variable. This makes studying several topics difficult in the area of appearance and body image because many important constructs cannot be randomly assigned or experimentally manipulated. Therefore, they cannot be tested as causal factors. However, many types of body image research are appropriately studied with true experiments. These studies typically involve exposure to an appearance or body image related stimulus followed by measurement of an outcome variable. These outcome variables are quite diverse and can be attitudes, cognitions, emotions, or behaviours. As with all experimental methodologies, these studies tend to be very high in internal validity, but some challenges arise when attempting to design an experiment that represents reality. The artificial nature of a tightly controlled lab setting simply cannot perfectly reflect phenomena as they exist in the real world. Similar challenges face researchers when they attempt to interpret the results of experiments and generalize them to real world settings.

One of the most common topics in the area of appearance and body image studied with experimental methodology is the influence of cultural appearance ideals and the media. Many true experiments have exposed participants to various forms of media or to situations that remind the participant of cultural appearance ideals. These typically find that this exposure is related to a variety of outcomes such as body dissatisfaction, disordered eating, weight/shape control, and endorsement of unrealistic cultural appearance ideals (Levine & Murnen, 2009). Although this is one of the more common research topics and designs in this field, it faces significant challenges relating to the experimental manipulation of the independent variable. Specifically, it is crucial to have a manipulation check to ensure that the participant is attending to the media exposure during the study since they could be paying close attention or they could be ignoring the stimuli, paying attention to something else entirely. This is a particularly important issue in the area of appearance and body image because the potential effect of the experimental manipulation may be due to a participant trait variable, such as internalization of the media's messages (Heinberg & Thompson, 1995). If the participant does not attend to the stimuli, then it is possible that this schema will not be primed, and the result will be a non-significant finding. A manipulation check should be a relatively brief questionnaire, post-exposure, asking participants questions regarding some details of the exposure stimuli.

Another problem with conducting true experiments in this way is that passive exposure to appearance ideals in the media does not reflect all real-world situations. In our daily lives, media exposure does not take place in a controlled laboratory environment. In the real world, exposure to media can take many forms in many different situations such as surfing the Internet, reading a magazine in a waiting room, seeing a billboard while driving, etc. These examples are all quite different to viewing an idealized image in a laboratory setting, which may compromise the generalizability of findings (external validity). Also, media exposure in daily life is often accompanied by discussion, comments, or varied reactions by others. While conducting a true experiment will always come with a cost to external validity, this can be minimized if researchers are aware of this issue and attempt to represent reality with their experimental manipulation. Some work in this area has already attempted to address this limitation by using novel experimental manipulations (Thompson, 2009). This trend should continue in order to advance the field in new and meaningful ways.

Another challenge faced by many experiments in the social sciences, but especially in this area, is concealing the true nature of study. Participants' responses and actions cannot be trusted when interpreting results if they were aware of the purpose of the study. One can imagine how this could easily occur in a simple experiment about media exposure and body image. A participant comes into a study, signs consent forms, views some advertisements featuring unrealistic appearance ideals, is asked about their body shame and body dissatisfaction, and is debriefed.

It seems quite likely that, given this scenario, the participant would be aware of the purpose of the study, which could influence their responses (demand characteristics). Perhaps the participant would exaggerate their reported shame and dissatisfaction to conform to what they believe to be the purpose of the study. Perhaps knowledge of the purpose of the study would protect them from the negative influence of the media exposure. If this occurs, these responses cannot be interpreted as meaningful. This limitation can and should be avoided through thoughtful study design and pilot testing.

Overall, experimental methodology is particularly powerful with distinct advantages and disadvantages. It is quite good for examining directional and causal relationships between specific variables and is the only way that causal conclusions can be drawn. These types of studies are vital to any area because we can learn things from them that we cannot gain from other types of methodology such as prospective, longitudinal, and correlational work. However, true experiments come with important limitations and considerations that must be addressed in order for these methods to contribute to the field as effectively as possible.

CONCLUSIONS

In this chapter, we offered an overview of the different dimensions of body image, followed by an examination of key issues related to measurement and research designs. It is important to be as precise as possible when considering the different dimensions of body image and the measures that purport to assess these constructs. Consideration of the appropriateness of certain measures for a specific sample characteristic, including age, gender, and ethnicity is essential. Various research designs entail unique challenges for the body image researcher. These issues are highlighted in the hope of guiding researchers in the formation of a methodologically sound investigation.

REFERENCES

Altabe, M. & O'Garo, K. N. (2002). Hispanic body images. In T. Cash & T. Pruzinsky (eds.) *Body image: A handbook of theory, research, and clinical practice*, pp. 250–6. New York: Guilford Press.

American Psychiatric Association. (2000). *Diagnostic and statistical manual of mental disorders (4th ed., Text Revision)*. Washington, DC: American Psychiatric Association.

Boroughs, M. S., Krawczyk, R., & Thompson, J. K. (2010). Body dysmorphic disorder among diverse racial/ethnic and sexual orientation groups: Prevalence estimates and associated factors. *Sex Roles*, 63, 725–37.

Brown, T. A., Cash, T. F., & Mikulka, P. J. (1990). Attitudinal body image assessment: Factor analysis of the Body-Self Relations Questionnaire. *Journal of Personality Assessment*, 55, 135–44.

Cafri, G., Strauss, J., & Thompson, J. K. (2002). Male body image: Satisfaction and its relationship to well-being using the Somatomorphic Matrix. *International Journal of Men's Health*, 1, 215–31.

Cash, T. (1997). *The body image workbook: An 8-step program for learning to like your looks.* Oakland, CA: New Harbinger.

Cash, T. & Grasso, K. (2005). The norms and stability of new measures of the multidimensional body image construct. *Body Image*, 2, 199–203.

Cash, T. & Pruzinsky, T. (eds.) (2002). *Body image: A handbook of theory, research, and clinical practice.* New York: Guilford Publications, Inc.

Celio, A., Zabinski, M., & Wilfley, D. (2002). African American body images. In: T. Cash & T. Pruzinsky (eds.) *Body image: A handbook of theory, research, and clinical practice*, pp. 234–42. New York: Guilford Press.

Fairburn, C. G. & Beglin, S. J. (1994). Assessment of eating disorders: Interview or self-report questionnaire? *International Journal of Eating Disorders*, 16, 363–70.

Fredrickson, B. & Roberts, T. (1997). Objectification theory: Toward understanding women's lived experiences and mental health risks. Psychology of Women Quarterly, 21, 173–206.

Fredrickson, B., Roberts, T., Noll, S., Quinn, D., & Twenge, J. (1998). That swimsuit becomes you: Sex differences in self-objectification, restrained eating, and math performance. Journal of Personality and Social Psychology, 75, 269–84.

Gardner, R. M. (2002). Body image assessment of children. In: T. Cash T. & Pruzinsky (eds.). *Body image: A handbook of theory, research, and clinical practice*, pp. 127–34. New York: Guilford Press

Gardner, R. M., Jappe, L. M., & Gardner, L. (2009). Development and validation of a new figural drawing scale for body image assessment: The BIAS-BD. *Journal of Clinical Psychology*, 65, 113–22.

Grogan, S. (2008). *Body image: Understanding body dissatisfaction in men, women and children* (2nd edn.). New York: Routledge/Taylor & Francis Group.

Heinberg, L. & Thompson, J. K. (1995). Body image and televised images of thinness and attractiveness: A controlled laboratory investigation. *Journal of Social and Clinical Psychology*, 14, 325–38.

Hospers, H. J. & Janse, A. (2005). Why homosexuality is a risk factor for eating disorders in males. Journal of Social and Clinical Psychology, 24, 1188–201.

Jakatdar, T. A., Cash, T. F., & Engle, E. K. (2006). Body-image thought processes: The development and initial validation of the Assessment of Body-Image Cognitive Distortions. *Body Image*, 3, 325–33.

Kramer, H. C., Stice, E., Kazdin, A., Offord, D., & Kupfer, D. (2001). How do risk factors work together: Mediators, moderators and independent, overlapping and proxy risk factors. *American Journal of Psychiatry*, 158, 843–56.

Levine, M. P. & Murnen, S. K. (2009). 'Everybody knows that mass media are/are not [pick one] a cause of eating disorder': A critical review of evidence for a causal link between media, negative body image, and disordered eating in females. *Journal of Social and Clinical Psychology*, 28, 9–42.

McCabe M. P. & Ricciardelli, L. A. (2004). Weight and shape concerns of boys and men. In J. K. Thompson (ed.) *Handbook of eating disorders and obesity*, pp. 606–34. New York: Wiley.

McKinley, N. & Hyde, J. (1996). The Objectified Body Consciousness Scale: Development and validation. *Psychology of Women Quarterly*, 20, 181–215.

Norris, M., Boydell, K., Pinhas, L., & Katzman, D. (2006). Ana and the internet: a review of pro-anorexia websites. *Eating Disorders*, 39, 443–7.

Reas, D. L., White, M. A., & Grilo, C. M. (2006). Body Checking Questionnaire: Psychometric properties and clinical correlates in obese men and women with binge eating disorder. *International Journal of Eating Disorders*, 39, 326–31.

Reed, D., Thompson, J. K., Brannick, M. T., & Sacco, W. P. (1991). Development and validation of the Physical Appearance State and Trait Anxiety Scale (PASTAS). *Journal of Anxiety Disorders*, 5, 323–32.

Rothblum, E. (2002). Gay and lesbian body images. In T. Cash & T. Pruzinsky (eds.). *Body image: A handbook of theory, research, and clinical practice*, pp. 210–18. New York: Guilford Press.

Smolak, L. & Thompson, J. K. (2009). *Body image, eating disorders, and obesity in youth* (2nd edn.). Washington, DC: American Psychological Association.

Swami, V., Salem, N., Furnham, A., & Tovee, M. J. (2008). Initial examination of the validity and reliability of the female photographic figure rating scale for body image assessment. *Personality and Individual Differences*, 44, 1752–61.

Thompson, J. K. (2004). The (mis)measurement of body image: Ten strategies to improve assessment for applied and research purposes. *Body Image*, 1, 7–14.

Thompson, J. K. (2009). Special issue: Commentary. *Journal of Social and Clinical Psychology*, 28, 127–32.

Thompson, J. K., Heinberg, L. J., Altabe, M. N., & Tantleff-Dunn, S. (1999). *Exacting beauty: Theory, assessment, and treatment of body image disturbance*. Washington, DC: American Psychological Association.

Thompson, J. K., van den Berg, P., Roehrig, M., Guarda, A., & Heinberg, L. J. (2004). The Sociocultural Attitudes Towards Appearance Questionnaire-3 (SATAQ-3): Development and validation. *International Journal of Eating Disorders*, 35, 293–304.

Tiggemann, M. (2005). The state of body image research in clinical and social psychology. *Journal of Social and Clinical Psychology*, 24, 1202–10.

CHAPTER 44

USING RETROSPECTIVE APPROACHES IN THE STUDY OF DISFIGUREMENT

MARTIN PERSSON

Conducting research in the field of appearance psychology presents many challenges to researchers, including the large range of conditions resulting in physical differences and in many instances the relatively small numbers of people with each variant of each condition, who are often geographically dispersed and who may or may not be actively engaged with treatment. As medical treatment focuses predominantly on functional and aesthetic aspects of conditions resulting in physical difference there may be many people living with psychological and social challenges that have not been recognized as part of their healthcare needs.

How can researchers rise to the challenge of recruiting large, representative samples in order to assess if there are social and psychological challenges associated with a particular condition? The preferred methodology would be to establish a large-scale prospective cohort study. However, these studies require extensive funding and major commitment from participants and researchers over many years, and are therefore rare. An alternative is to consider the possibility of using a retrospective approach, using information that has been documented for purposes other than research (Hess, 2004). This allows the researcher to capitalize on a wealth of information that has already been obtained, without generating an additional burden for the research participant. Although the data set is unlikely to include all the measures that the researcher might consider ideal, this approach has the potential to provide information that can alert researchers to hitherto unrecognized issues and can be used to support the need for further investigation in relevant areas. Retrospective population studies can also provide relatively large samples of people with different medical conditions and this can be particularly helpful in relation to people with rare diseases who are difficult to access in other types of research.

There are different types of retrospective studies, each with their own advantages or disadvantages. One type is the case series study. In this approach, medical records and/or case reports of people with a particular (usually rare) condition are examined in order to gather evidence or understanding about one or more aspects of the condition. For example; at the Stockholm Craniofacial Centre, they reviewed 80 records of consecutive children born with cleft lip and palate between 2005–2007 to categorize the type and intensity of speech and language intervention in order to examine their current service provision (Westberg & Lohmander, 2011). The information gained can offer the researcher sufficient evidence and insight to decide whether a subsequent prospective study would be appropriate (Grisso, 1993). If the aim is to examine numerous case reports or medical records and to involve several researchers in this process, it is advantageous to design a case report form (CRF) to facilitate a standardized approach to collecting the required information (Jansen et al., 2005). There are some drawbacks to the case series approach. As with all retrospective studies, the researcher is dependent on the detail and accuracy of previously recorded data. There is also the possibility of selection bias as the researcher has no control over the original 'sample'. In addition, there will be no control group against which to make comparisons (Hess, 2004).

The case–control study, as the name implies, has the advantage of providing the researcher with retrospective data from a target group and a 'control' or comparison group within the study design. This means that it is possible to make some methodological assumptions about the data generated. One assumption is that the medical condition of interest or the exposure to a specific incident is the only, or the major difference between the case and control group. For example, a case–control study was used by the author to compare the educational outcomes in secondary school between individuals with cleft and the rest of the population. (The results are discussed in more detail later in this chapter.) The second assumption is that if the medical condition or the exposure to a specific event does not cause the outcome that is examined, it means that the medical condition has no influence on the outcome, or that the exposure to a specific event is equally distributed between the case and control group. In our example, it would mean that there were no differences in educational outcomes between individuals with cleft and the general population. The third assumption is if there is a difference due to the medical condition or the specific event of interest in the case group versus the control group, then the difference should denote an increased risk of this outcome. Going back to the example, our case–control study showed that individuals with cleft had significant deficits in their educational outcome in comparison to the general population (Persson et al., 2010). The study therefore showed that individuals with cleft have an increased risk for negative educational outcome when compared to the general population.

In a retrospective case–control study, it is possible to obtain results sooner than is possible in a prospective study, and the process is considerably less expensive than a prospective study (Schulz and Grimes, 2002). There are disadvantages too, of course. The researcher is once again dependent on the quality of the recorded data and although in theory, all cases in the population should be included in the proposed study, there is still the possibility of selection bias (Persson et al., 2010). It is often harder to delineate the target group or to generate precise incidence rates. It is also at best, difficult and at worst, impossible, to control for confounding factors (Lewallen & Courtright, 1998). Therefore, it is rarely possible to establish any cause and effect relationships based upon the outcomes of case–control studies.

When using this approach, it is important to clearly define the eligibility criteria for the cases to be included in the study. This might, for example, include particular clinical symptoms, age range, diagnostic methods, and geographical location or treatment centre (Lewallen & Courtright, 1998; Schulz & Grimes, 2002). If you are not using a whole population register that will offer you a population control group then it is important to define an appropriate control group within the study—one which is similar to the cases in all aspects except for the target medical condition or event, including socioeconomic status, educational level, and age, for example, since the control group can often be the weakest link in a case–control study (Grimes & Schulz, 2002). Then the controls should be matched with the cases on the basis of such characteristics. It is, however, possible to 'over-match' so it becomes impossible to find enough suitable controls (Lewallen & Courtright, 1998). In some case–control studies, the researchers supplement data derived from a register or other records by approaching the cases and controls about a target variable either using interviews or questionnaires. This may introduce an element of recall bias to the data, for example, cases may have more detailed memories about a particular event of interest than the controls, or vice versa—particularly when the event is sensitive (Grimes & Schulz, 2002). A Swedish study looked at two independent epidemiological studies about the association of induced abortion and breast cancer. One of the studies gathered the information about induced abortion from the 'cases' with breast cancer and from the healthy controls through interviews. The other study used an approach that linked the cases and controls to a register that had information about induced abortions. The two studies covered the same period, therefore the cases and controls where the same in both studies. In comparing the

two studies, it became apparent that the healthy controls when interviewed demonstrated a significant bias in underreporting induced abortion (Lindefors-Harris
et al., 1991).

In order to explain in more detail the process of conducting a case–control study,
a study of young people born with cleft will be used as an example (Persson et al.,
2007). Previous research had established that in addition to the burden of treatment for functional deficits (in speech and hearing, for example) and, in cases of a
cleft affecting the lip, differences in appearance in the mouth and nasal areas, people affected by a cleft are likely to have to cope with social and psychological sequa-
lae. This may affect their self-perceptions (e.g. body image) and social functioning.
At the time of this study, however, it was not clear whether a cleft was also associated with differences in other physical attributes such as height and weight. Some
previous research addressing the issue of physical development in individuals with
cleft has indicated that there may be an increased risk for impeded growth (Bowers
et al., 1987; Felix-Schollaart et al., 1992; Cunningham and Jerome, 1997; Becker
et al., 1998; Lipman et al., 1999) while other research has indicated no influence
(Ranalli & Mazaheri, 1975; Day, 1985; Lee et al., 1997; Nackashi et al., 1998). The
samples in these previous studies were small, and the results were difficult to compare due to differing proportions of males and females included in the samples,
and/or the wide disparity in the age of participants in the various studies.

Accordingly, in order to assess the issues of physical growth in individuals with
cleft, a case–control study was designed. For this purpose, medical data were
obtained from the Swedish National Service enrolment register for the years 1991–
1997. This is a military record administered by the Swedish National Service
Administration. Permission to use the register was obtained from The National
Board of Health and Welfare and all data about patients were rendered unidentifi-
able, so we (the researchers) could not identify any individual when conducting the
analysis. In Sweden at that time military enrolment was mandatory for all men
around the age of 19 years. Those who were not required to participate in military
enrolment had either a severe handicap or a chronic disease that was documented
medically and which was judged to permit exemption from all forms of military
service. From this register we obtained a sample of 335 individuals with cleft lip
with or without cleft palate (CL±P) and 88 individuals with cleft palate (CP) only
that were compared against a sample of 272,879 men. By using this approach, we
had access to all the individuals with cleft together with a large control group. In
essence we conducted a population-based study since it involved all the individuals
who participated in the military enrolment for the defined time period.

When collecting data in this type of study it is imperative to be consistent in
the way information is collected for both the cases and controls. In our study, the
following variables were collected for both groups using specific cut-off points for
the data analyses; a body weight of less than 60kg (132 pounds)—the average body
weight of a Swedish male at the time of military enrolment is 72.3kg (159.1 pounds);

a height of less than 170.0cm (5 feet 7 inches)—the average height is 179.8cm (5 feet 11 inches); a body mass index (BMI) of less than 19 (a BMI between 18–19 is considered 'thin' and below 18 is 'undernourished')—a normal BMI is in the range of 20–24 and the average BMI for the Swedish male at military enrolment is 22.4.

We examined the data for males with cleft lip and palate (CL+P) and for males with cleft palate only (CP). It would have been advantageous to have been able to separate the group with CL±P into cleft lip only and cleft lip and palate only. This was not possible due to the design of the register and this clearly highlights some of the disadvantages inherent in retrospective studies in that the researcher is completely dependent on the quality of collected data in the register used.

When analysing data derived from population based case-control studies, the most common approach is to generate an odds ratio (OR) that reflects the odds of the outcome in cases compared with the odds of the outcome in controls (Grimes & Schulz, 2008; Hartung & Touchette, 2009). The odds ratio of 1 indicates that the outcome is equal for the cases and controls, while an odds ratio of less than 1 indicates that the outcome (e.g. a particular height) is less likely to occur in the cases than in the controls and an odds ratio higher than 1 indicates that the outcome is more likely to occur in the cases than the controls (Hess, 2004). As mentioned previously, confounding is a particular issue that needs to be considered in interpreting the results of case–control studies. In some studies it is possible to control for this, for example, by using carefully prescribed eligibility criteria. It is also possible to address the confounding issue during the analysis. The most frequently used techniques are logistic regression or stratification of the data using the Mantel–Haenszel approach (Schulz & Grimes, 2002).

In our study, the variables were divided into intervals. In each of these, comparisons were made between groups by means of the Mantel–Haenszel technique. The results are presented as odds ratios with 95% confidence intervals (95% CI) estimated by a test-based method (Miettinen, 1974). The results clearly indicated that for the group with CL±P, the odds ratio for weighing less than 60kg was significantly increased: 1.74 (95% CI 1.28–2.37). The same phenomenon was observed in the group with CP, the corresponding odds ratio being 2.13 (95% CI 1.18–3.83). The group with CL±P showed no significant deviation in height, the odds ratio for being less than 170cm was 1.21 (95% CI 0.77–1.89). While in the group with CP there was a significant difference compared with the control group, the corresponding odds ratio being 2.25 (95% CI 1.09–4.50). There was a significant difference between the group with CL±P and the controls in relation to BMI. The odds ratio for having a BMI below 19 was 1.55 (95% CI 1.12–2.12), but in the group with CP there was no significant difference, the odds ratio being 1.71 (95% CI 0.90–3.18) compared with the control group. As the CL±P group weighed significantly less, but there was no significant deviation in height, their BMI is lower since it is calculated on a height/weight ratio. The group with CP had significant differences in both height and weight, hence no difference in BMI.

In summary, the case–control study we conducted generated data that enabled us to suggest that there is a long-term consequence of having a cleft on physical development and it appears that these young men are less likely to reach the general norm for male body dimensions. From an appearance research perspective, this outcome is of great interest, especially when considering the implications in the context of current findings relating to male body image. This research clearly indicates that most men have a preference for being muscular and at the same time for being leaner (Mishkind et al., 1986; Pope et al., 2000; Tiggemann et al., 2008). In addition, studies have shown that the majority of men express a preference for being taller (Tiggemann et al., 2008). If men are dissatisfied with their bodies, there are associated psychosocial risks, including depression and low self esteem. A variety of risk behaviours may also ensue, such as using steroids or engaging in disordered eating (Olivardia et al., 2004). The implication is that for males with a cleft, in addition to coping with the functional and aesthetic deficits resulting from their condition and the associated burden of treatment, this study also indicates that they are at risk of being considerably thinner and/or shorter than the average male. Thus they may feel they cannot live up to current stereotypes associated with the desirability of height and muscularity (Pope et al., 2000; Tiggemann et al., 2008). These findings indicate that further research is necessary to examine if males born with a cleft are at greater risk of experiencing negative impacts on their psychological well-being.

From a methodological perspective, this study had advantages and disadvantages that are typical of case–control studies. Among the strengths are the representativeness and size of the sample of young male adults with cleft and the equally representative and very large control group of the rest of the Swedish male population. Both groups were medically fit enough be enlisted in the military and the data were all derived from a specific time period. The study did not generate any burden to the participants and was relatively inexpensive to conduct, yet it contributed the important finding that males with cleft are impeded in their physical development as young adults. The disadvantage of the study design is that we had to rely on the classification of cleft type used in the register, and the data cannot explain the mechanisms causing the deficits in physical development in the young male adults with cleft. Furthermore, we could only look at outcomes for males since military enlistment is not mandatory for Swedish women.

In conclusion, despite some limitations, well-designed retrospective studies can generate important new insights in the field of appearance and can be used to generate hypotheses that can be further examined in prospective studies.

REFERENCES

Becker, M., Svensson, H., & Kallen, B. (1998). Birth weight, body length, and cranial circumference in newborns with cleft lip or palate. *The Cleft Palate-Craniofacial Journal*, 35(3), 255–61.

Bowers, E. J., Mayro, R. F., Whitaker, L. A., Pasquariello, P. S., LaRossa, D., & Randall, P. (1987). General body growth in children with clefts of the lip, palate, and craniofacial structure. *Scandinavian Journal of Plastic and Reconstructive Surgery and Hand Surgery*, 21(1), 7–14.

Cunningham, M. L., & Jerome, J. T. (1997). Linear growth characteristics of children with cleft lip and palate. *Journal of Pediatrics*, 131(5), 707–11.

Day, D. W. (1985). Accurate diagnosis and assessment of growth in patients with orofacial clefting. *Birth Defects Original Articles Series*, 21(2), 1–14.

Felix-Schollaart, B., Hoeksma, J. B., & Prahl-Andersen, B. (1992). Growth comparison between children with cleft lip and/or palate and controls. *The Cleft Palate-Craniofacial Journal*, 29(5), 475–80.

Grimes, D. A., & Schulz, K. F. (2002). An overview of clinical research: the lay of the land. *Lancet*, 359(9300), 57–61.

Grimes, D. A., & Schulz, K. F. (2008). Making sense of odds and odds ratios. *Obstetrics and Gynecology*, 111(2 Pt 1), 423–6.

Grisso, J. A. (1993). Making comparisons. *Lancet*, 342(8864), 157–60.

Hartung, D. M., & Touchette, D. (2009). Overview of clinical research design. *American Journal of Health System Pharmacy*, 66(4), 398–408.

Hess, D. R. (2004). Retrospective studies and chart reviews. *Respiratory Care*, 49(10), 1171–4.

Jansen, A. C., van Aalst-Cohen, E. S., Hutten, B. A., Buller, H. R., Kastelein, J. J., & Prins, M. H. (2005). Guidelines were developed for data collection from medical records for use in retrospective analyses. *Journal of Clinical Epidemiology*, 58(3), 269–74.

Lee, J., Nunn, J., & Wright, C. (1997). Height and weight achievement in cleft lip and palate. *Archives of Disease in Childhood*, 76(1), 70–2.

Lewallen, S., & Courtright, P. (1998). Epidemiology in practice: case-control studies. *Community Eye Health*, 11(28), 57–8.

Lindefors-Harris, B. M., Eklund, G., Adami, H. O., & Meirik, O. (1991) Response bias in a case-control study: analysis utilizing comparative data concerning legal abortions from two independent Swedish studies. *American Journal of Epidemiology*, 134(9), 1003–8.

Lipman, T. H., Rezvani, I., Mitra, A., & Mastropieri, C. J. (1999). Assessment of stature in children with orofacial clefting. *MCN. The American Journal of Maternal Child Nursing*, 24(5), 252–6.

Miettinen, O. (1974). Simple interval estimation of risk ratios. *American Journal of Epidemiology*, 100, 515–16.

Mishkind, M. E., Rodin, J., Silberstein, L. R., & Striegelmoore, R. H. (1986). The embodiment of masculinity—cultural, psychological, and behavioral dimensions. *American Behavioral Scientist*, 29(5), 545–62.

Nackashi, J. A., Rosenbloom, A. L., Marks, R., Williams, W. N., Seagle, M. B., & Frolova, L. E. (1998). Stature of Russian children with isolated cleft lip and palate. *The Cleft Palate-Craniofacial Journal*, 35(6), 500–2.

Olivardia, R., Pope, H. G., Borowiecki, J. J., & Cohane, G. H. (2004). Biceps and body image: The relationship between muscularity and self-esteem, depression, and eating disorder symptoms. *Psychology of Men and Masculinity*, 5, 112–20.

Persson, M., Becker, M., & Svensson, H. (2007). Physical characteristics of young men with cleft lip, with or without cleft palate, and cleft palate only. *Scandinavian Journal of Plastic and Reconstructive Surgery and Hand Surgery*, 41, 6–9.

Persson, M., Becker, M., & Svensson, H. (2010). Academic Achievement in individuals with cleft—a population-based register study. *The Cleft Palate-Craniofacial Journal,* Dec 23. [Epub ahead of print].

Pope, H. G., Gruber, A. J., Mangweth, B., Bureau, B., deCol, C., Jouvent, R., *et al.* (2000). Body image perception among men in three countries. *American Journal of Psychiatry,* 157(8), 1297–301.

Ranalli, D. N., & Mazaheri, M. (1975). Height-weight growth of cleft children, birth to six years. *Cleft Palate Journal,* 12, 400–4.

Schulz, K. F., Grimes, D. A. (2002). Case-control studies: research in reverse. *Lancet,* 359(9304), 431–4.

Tiggemann, M., Martins, Y., & Churchett, L. (2008). Beyond muscles: unexplored parts of men's body image. *Journal of Health Psychology,* 13(8), 1163–72.

Westberg, L. R., & Lohmander, A. (2011). Early speech intervention in children born with cleft lip and palate: a review of records at Stockholm Craniofacial Center. Craniofacial Society of Great Britain and Ireland—Annual Scientific Conference; 13–15 April 2011; University of York, York, UK.

CHAPTER 45

MIXED METHODS: THE BEST OF BOTH WORLDS?

EMMA DURES

MIXED methods research designs have become increasing popular in the field of health sciences, including the psychology of appearance. While proponents claim the approach offers flexibility and the 'best of both worlds', detractors are concerned that such research is undertaken without sufficient understanding or recognition of the underlying philosophies associated with different methodological traditions and that the quality of the research is compromised as a result. The aim of this chapter is to set out key arguments in support of mixed methods and to show how the approach is often well suited to the multidimensionality and complexity of appearance-related research.

A DEFINITION OF MIXED METHODS

There is much discussion about what constitutes a mixed methods approach, but defining characteristics include: quantitative and qualitative methods within the same project; a design that clearly specifies the sequencing and priority given to the quantitative and qualitative elements of data collection and analysis; and an explicit account of how the quantitative and the qualitative aspects of the research relate to each other (Denscombe, 2008). A mixed methods approach should recognize the importance of traditional quantitative and qualitative research while acknowledging that different research questions relate to different units of study, requiring different data collection methods and producing different types of data (Moore, 2003). Qualitative elements of the research ask 'what' and 'how' in order to explore deeply, gain insights, and understand underlying issues. Quantitative elements ask 'how many' and 'how strong' in order to measure, predict, and correlate. Shared qualitative and quantitative aims include looking at relationships and examining links of the phenomena under investigation. Mixed methods designs have been described as both an intellectual and practical synthesis based on qualitative and quantitative research with the potential to generate the most informative, balanced, and useful results (Johnson et al., 2007). However, the legitimacy of mixed methods is potentially undermined by a failure to appreciate epistemological issues and provide justification for, and transparency of, the mixed methods design (O'Cathain et al., 2008). One reason for this could be the continued dominance of the quantitative versus qualitative paradigm debate despite the potential advantages of using both approaches together.

THE TRADITIONAL QUANTITATIVE VERSUS QUALITATIVE PARADIGM DIVIDE

The concept of the paradigm encapsulates researchers' beliefs about their set of practices, their efforts to create knowledge, and definitions of their scientific discipline. Paradigms inform researchers about what is important, legitimate, and reasonable (Patton, 1980). Traditionally there has been an understanding that qualitative and quantitative approaches to research represent incompatible paradigms through which to study the social world, because they are underpinned by fundamentally different assumptions about the nature of reality (ontology) and ways of knowing and understanding (epistemology). At the most basic level those who work within a quantitative framework assert that reality is universal, objective, and quantifiable, while those who adopt a qualitative stance argue that reality is socially constructed by and between the persons who experience it. Distinctions that epitomize their incompatibility include: the use of words and pictures in qualitative data versus the use of numbers in quantitative data; the qualitative focus on meanings versus the quantitative focus on behaviour; the adoption or rejection of natural science as a model; an inductive versus a deductive approach; and the identification of cultural patterns versus the seeking of scientific laws (Hammersley, 1992). Consequently, quantitative researchers coming from the perspective of statistical generalization have seen qualitative findings as too context specific and based on unrepresentative samples which make their claims unwarranted. Meanwhile qualitative researchers view quantitative research as overly simplistic, de-contextualized, reductionist in terms of its generalizations, and inadequate for capturing the meanings and experiences of the individual (Brannen, 2004).

This traditional divide between perspectives and the idea that uncoupling methods from their philosophical frameworks and using them independently is poor practice (Darlaston-Jones, 2007) can create a sense that researchers should define themselves as either quantitative or qualitative practitioners. This can be reinforced when university faculties, journals, and funding bodies have a strong preference for a given approach (Green & Preston, 2005).

ARGUMENTS IN SUPPORT OF MIXED METHODS

To a very large extent, the paradigm wars can be considered over and peace can be regarded as having broken out (Bryman, 2006, p. 113).

One line of argument developed by those wishing to emerge from this long-running debate rests on whether qualitative/quantitative differences are as distinct as the literature has suggested (Schwandt, 2000). While stressing that most social scientists do not entirely reject qualitative/quantitative dichotomies, Morgan (2007) has conceptualized points of connection rather than incompatibility. He has taken three seemingly essential differences: induction–deduction, subjectivity–objectivity, and context–generality. He has then offered the terms 'abduction', 'intersubjectivity', and 'transferability' to bridge the respective dichotomies. Abductive reasoning moves back and forth between induction and deduction. This more iterative process is often a fairer reflection of research in practice. It can also be the case that inductive enquiry associated with qualitative research and hypothetic-deduction associated with quantitative research are reversed, with both approaches using both forms of logic. Intersubjectivity emphasizes the process of communicating shared meaning in research and acknowledges that complete subjectivity or complete objectivity are abstract and impossible notions. The emphasis on the utility of research findings to influence practice in health-related fields makes communication, dissemination, and an awareness of research from other perspectives important. Transferability proposes that findings need not be so unique that they have no implications beyond the research context or so generalized that they would apply across the board in any setting. The idea that qualitative research lacks the power of quantitative research to generalize refers only to statistical inference. Qualitative findings may be generalized in a different sense, such as at an abstract level where they are considered in relation to their theoretical application (Ritchie & Lewis, 2003).

  Alongside rethinking conceptual distinctions, there is the practical issue of finding ways to do research that can capture the dualisms inherent in the lived experience, such as the public versus the private, the sociocultural collective versus the individual, and structure versus agency. Mason (2006) highlighted the need for an approach that can accommodate the multidimensionality of everyday lives, which are lived on both micro- and macro-scales. The key argument is that the functional issue of appropriately matching methods to research topics is more important than adhering to methodological orthodoxy. Research strategies should be devised that are best suited to a particular purpose rather than being only tied to a philosophical position (Brannen, 2005). Basing the research design on the research question rather than the other way round is well suited to investigating appearance because working towards a fuller understanding requires research at different levels (e.g. intra-individual through to population) and across disciplines (e.g. psychology, sociology, epidemiology). For example, body image can be conceptualized as the mental picture people have of their physical self, and the mental picture they believe others have of them (Cash, 2001). It includes perceptions of, and attitudes to, their appearance, attractiveness, state of health, and sexuality (White, 2000). It also incorporates a sense of how their body image influences interactions, and other people's reactions to them (Cash & Fleming, 2002); making it a major factor in social and interpersonal relationships (Luskin Biordi et al., 2006). Mixed methods can facilitate wide ranging questions and multidisciplinary collaboration by encouraging the fusion of a range of approaches and expertise.

THE PHILOSOPHY OF MIXED METHODS

An awareness of basic philosophical assumptions even if they are not a central aspect of one's work is seen as a requisite of good research and overlooking them is a charge that has been levelled at mixed methods designs (Nygren & Blom, 2002). One reason for this is likely to be the traditional concern of epistemology with what 'ought to' rather than what 'is' and the process of working 'top-down' from a theoretical framework rather than 'bottom-up' by empirical investigation (Becker, 1996). This way of designing research does not always resonate with researchers whose activities often reflect some accommodation of the realities of social life that cannot be fully accounted for or explained by referring to philosophical positions. However, the philosophy of pragmatism is highly compatible with research in practice and often said to underpin mixed methods.

The pragmatism typically associated with mixed methods emerged from the work of John Dewey, William James, and George Herbert Mead. Pragmatists consider practical consequences, functional knowledge, and the impact of research on practice to be essential components of meaning and truth (Maxcy, 2003). A pragmatic approach does not ignore the relevance of epistemology but it does reject the top-down privileging of ontological assumptions at the expense of conducting useful research (Morgan, 2007). Given the position that truth is what works at the time, rather than belief in any one system of reality, there is no need for a strict dualism between the mind and a reality completely independent of the mind. Instead researchers may use both quantitative and qualitative data because together they provide the best understanding of the research problem. The important point is to establish a purpose and rationale for why quantitative and qualitative data need to be mixed (Creswell, 2003). Pragmatism can be seen as a philosophical response to research purists and as a method of inquiry.

APPEARANCE RESEARCH IN PRACTICE

Appearance research encompasses the generation of knowledge, the development and testing of theory, and putting theory into practice to help manage appearance concerns and alleviate distress. Collecting primary data to achieve the former and evaluating interventions to achieve the latter often occurs in complex 'real world' contexts (Robson, 1999). In practice this can mean conducting research with clinical populations in dynamic settings, such as hospitals; answering questions identified by a range of people, such as service users and healthcare professionals; focusing on solving complex problems and taking action; being limited by the time and cost constraints of funders; and tailoring the work toward client or stakeholder needs rather than academic peers. The flexibility and breadth of mixed methods designs are suited to these values and priorities.

Mixed methods have been used in exploratory fieldwork studies and surveys, evaluation research, and instrument development (O'Cathain, 2009). It is not possible to cover the range of mixed methods designs here but Creswell (2003) outlines key considerations that apply more generally:

- Are the different elements to be implemented concurrently or sequentially?
- Is priority to be given to the qualitative or quantitative data sets, or shared equally?
- Will integration of the qualitative and quantitative elements take place at the point of data collection, analysis, interpretation, or a combination?

How researchers respond to these issues will depend on their research questions, but they should be explicitly addressed. Examples of commonly used designs include:

- A sequential explanatory framework, conducted in two phases with the collection and analysis of quantitative data followed by the collection and analysis of qualitative data (e.g. Ivankova et al., 2006; Bessell, 2009). Typically, the qualitative findings help with interpretation of the quantitative results by enabling more detailed examination of what they might mean and unearthing the individual meanings and experiences 'behind' the numbers.
- A sequential exploratory framework is similar to the explanatory one, but the collection and analysis of qualitative data is followed by the collection and analysis of quantitative data (e.g. Mendlinger & Cwikel, 2008; Dures, 2010; Bessell et al., 2010). This design is particularly suited to investigation of a new phenomenon and the development of emergent theory, for example, when the inductive qualitative findings inform the subsequent deductive quantitative component. It can be used to examine the distribution of a phenomenon identified in a small sample within a larger population.

- A concurrent triangulation strategy, which involves the use of different methods to confirm, cross-validate, or corroborate findings, based on the idea that the weakness inherent in one approach is counterbalanced by the strengths of the other (e.g. Magee et al., 2007; Kennett et al., 2008; Reisner et al., 2010).

For the evaluation of interventions, including randomized and non-randomized designs, guidance from the UK's Medical Research Council advocates the inclusion of nested qualitative studies within largely quantitative designs. The qualitative element, often in the form of in-depth interviews or focus groups, can capture processes of change and unanticipated consequences of the intervention. These data can be helpful looked at alongside the quantitative outcome measures that show the size of effect the intervention has had. Together the data sets can inform theory and the measures to be included in future research. There have been calls to improve measurement and instrument development in appearance research (Thompson, 2004; see also Chapter 43). According to the US Food and Drug Administration advice on patient-reported outcome measures, measurement should not rely solely on quantitative psychometric evaluation. For example, content validity should be established through interviews and focus groups to ensure that all the concepts important to the target population are included. Cognitive interviewing should then be used to ascertain participants' understanding of the instrument content. Criterion validity, test–retest reliability, and sensitivity to change of the instrument can then be evaluated using statistical methods. The use of mixed methods in this way will enhance the reliability and validity of new instruments.

CONCLUSIONS

A mixed methods approach is appealing to increasing numbers of researchers, frustrated by the limitations of working within a solely quantitative or qualitative paradigm. Appearance-related research is often a real-world endeavour requiring answers to questions at a variety of levels and from a variety of disciplinary perspectives. The flexible, pragmatic adoption of mixed methods designs enables researchers to be responsive to a range of practical and ethical issues that can arise when working in this field. However, it is important to justify and explain the approach as the value of mixed methods research is diminished if it is not grounded in a clear purpose and the sequencing and mixing are not clearly specified.

REFERENCES

Becker, H. (1996). The epistemology of qualitative research. In R. Jessor, A. Colby, & R. Shweder (eds.) *Essays on Ethnography and Human Development: Context and Meaning in Social Inquiry*, pp. 53–72. Chicago, IL: University of Chicago Press.

Bessell, A. (2009). Facing up to Visible Difference: The Design and Evaluation of a New Computer-Based Psychosocial Intervention. Unpublished thesis dissertation. University of the West of England.

Bessell, A., Clarke, A., Harcourt, D., Moss, T., & Rumsey, N. (2010). Incorporating user perspectives in the design of an online intervention tool for people with visible differences: Face IT. *Behavioural and Cognitive Psychotherapy*, 38(5), 577–96.

Brannen, J. (2004). Working qualitatively and quantitatively. In C. Seale, G. Gobo, J. Gubrium, & D. Silverman (eds.) *Qualitative Research Practice*, pp. 312–26. London: Sage Publications.

Brannen, J. (2005). Mixed methods research: A discussion paper. ESRC National Centre for Research Methods website: http://www.ncrm.ac.uk/publications/methodsreview/ MethodsReviewPaperNCRM-005.pdf

Bryman, A. (2006). Paradigm peace and the implications for quality. *International Journal of Social Research Methodology*, 9(2), 111–26.

Cash, T. (2001). *The Body Image Workbook*. Oakland, CA: New Harbinger Publications.

Cash, T. & Fleming, E. (2002). The impact of body-image experiences: Development of the body image quality of life inventory. *International Journal of Eating Disorders*, 31, 455–60.

Creswell, J. (2003). *Research Design: Qualitative, Quantitative and Mixed Methods Approaches*. London: Sage Publications.

Darlaston-Jones, D. (2007). Making connections: The relationship between epistemology and research methods. *The Australian Community Psychologist*, 19(1), 19–27.

Denscombe, M. (2008). Communities of practice: A research paradigm for the mixed methods approach. *Journal of Mixed Methods Research*, 2(3), 270–83.

Food and Drug Administration. http://www.fda.gov/Drugs/GuidanceComplianceRegulatory-Information/Guidances/ (accessed 11 April 2012).

Dures, E., Rumsey, N., Morris, M., & Gleeson, K. (2010). Mixed methods in health psychology: Theoretical and practical considerations of the third paradigm. *Journal of Health Psychology*, 16(2), 332–41.

Green, A. & Preston, J. (2005). Editorial: Speaking in tongues—Diversity in mixed methods research. *International Journal of Social Research Methodology*, 8(3), 167–71.

Hammersley, M. (1992). Deconstructing the qualitative-quantitative divide. In Brannen, J. (Ed.) *Mixing Methods: Qualitative and Quantitative Research*, pp. 39–55. Aldershot: Ashgate.

Ivankova, N., Creswell, J., & Stick, S. (2006). Using mixed methods sequential explanatory design: From theory to practice. Field Methods, 18(1), 13–20.

Johnson, R., Onwuegbuzie, A., & Turner, L. (2007). Toward a definition of mixed methods research. *Journal of Mixed Methods Research*, 1(2), 112–33.

Kennett, D., O'Haga, F., & Cezer, D. (2008). Learned resourcefulness and long term benefits of a chronic pain management program. *Journal of Mixed Methods Research*, 2(4), 317–39.

Luskin Biordi, D., Warner, A., & Knapik, G. (2006). Body image. In Lubkin, I. & Larsen, P. (eds.) *Chronic Illness: Impact and Interventions* (6th edn.), pp. 181–98. Canada: Jones and Bartlett.

Magee, H., Heron, P., Cartwright, J., & Askham, J. (2007). *Information for people living with conditions that affect their appearance: Summary and recommendations*. Oxford: Picker Institute Europe.

Mandel, A. R. & Keller, S. M. (1986). Stress management in rehabilitation. *Archives of Physical Medicine & Rehabilitation*, 67(6), 375–9.

Mason, J. (2006). Mixing methods in a qualitatively driven way. *Qualitative Research*, 6(1), 9–25.

Maxcy, S. (2003). Pragmatic Threads in mixed methods research in the social sciences: The search for multiple modes of inquiry and the end of the philosophy of formalism.

In A. Tashakorri, A. & Teddlie, C. (eds.) *Handbook of Mixed Methods in Social & Behavioral Research*, pp. 51–90. Thousand Oaks, CA: Sage.

Medical Research Council. http://www.mrc.ac.uk/complexinterventionsguidance

Mendlinger, S. & Cwikel, J. (2008). Spiraling between qualitative and quantitative data on women's health behaviours: A double helix model for mixed methods. *Qualitative Health Research*, 18(2), 280–93.

Moore, K., Van Haitsma, K., Curyto, K., & Saperstein, A. (2003). A pragmatic environmental psychology: A meta-theoretical inquiry into the work of M. Powell Lawton. *Journal of Environmental Psychology*, 23(4), 471–82.

Morgan, D. (2007). Paradigms Lost and Pragmatism Regained: Methodological implications of combining qualitative and quantitative methods. *Journal of Mixed Methods*, 1(1), 48–76.

Nygren, L. & Blom, B. (2002). Qualitative inquiry and evaluation in the beginning of a third decade. *Qualitative Social Work*, 1(3), 285–9.

O'Cathain, A. (2009). Editorial: Mixed methods research in the health sciences—A quiet revolution. *Journal of Mixed Methods*, 3(1), 1–6.

O'Cathain, A., Murphy, E., & Nicholl, J. (2008). The quality of mixed methods studies in health services research. *Journal of Health Services Research and Policy*, 13(2), 92–8.

Patton, M. (1980). Strategic themes in qualitative inquiry. In M. Patton (Ed.) *Qualitative Evaluation and Research Methods* (2nd edn.), pp. 35–91. London: Sage Publications.

Ritchie, J. & Lewis, J. (2003). *Qualitative Research in Practice: A Guide for Social Science Students and Researchers.* London: Sage.

Reisner, S., Perkovich, B., & Mimiaga, M. (2010). A mixed methods study of the sexual health needs of New England transmen who have sex with nontransgender men. *AIDS Patient Care and STDs*, 24(8), 1–13.

Robson, C. (1999). *Approaches to Social Research in Real World Research.* Malden, MA: Blackwell Publishing,

Schwandt, T. (2000). Three epistemological stances for qualitative inquiry. In N. Denzin & Y. Lincoln (eds.) *Handbook of Qualitative Research* (2nd edn.), pp. 189–213. Thousand Oaks, CA: Sage.

Thompson, J. (2004). The (mis) measurement of body image: Ten strategies to improve assessment for applied and research purposes. *Body Image*, 1, 7–14.

White, C. (2000). Body image dimensions and cancer: A heuristic cognitive behavioural model. *Psycho-Oncology*, 9, 183–92.

CHAPTER 46

METHODOLOGICAL CHOICES: ONLINE RESEARCH

NEIL S. COULSON

INTRODUCTION

IN recent years we have witnessed an exponential growth in Internet access with recent estimates indicating Internet usage is somewhere in the region of 7,000,000,000 which represents a 28.7% worldwide population penetration (Internet World Statistics [IWS], 2011). Indeed, since 2000 there has been a 444.8% increase in the number of people using the Internet worldwide. However, the proportion of the population who use the Internet varies by region with the highest figures (77.4%) seen in North America, followed by Oceania/Australia (61.3%), Europe (58.4%), with the lowest usage reported in Africa (10.9%). The use of the Internet also appears to be related to a number of sociodemographic factors, for example, age, location, marital status, and education. For example, within the UK (Office for National Statistics, 2011), over 60% of adults over 65 years of age had never accessed the Internet, compared with only 1% of those aged 16–24 years. Similarly, whilst the vast majority (97%) of adults educated to degree level had accessed the Internet, only 45% without any formal qualifications had done so.

The Internet has many potential applications within the appearance-related domain. For example, it may be used as a means for therapeutic intervention, to set up and manage patient support groups, promote training and education, as well as facilitating appearance-related research. It is the last of these which will be the focus for discussion in this chapter. The aim of this chapter is to consider common methodological choices and issues which may arise when undertaking online appearance-related research.

TYPES OF ONLINE RESEARCH

There are a number of different types of online research methodologies which may lend themselves to appearance-related research and new innovations in technology mean that the potential research tools we can use are constantly expanding (see Chapter 47). However, in this chapter I will focus on three commonly used online methodologies and reflect on some of the advantages and disadvantages surrounding their use.

Email/web-based surveys

A popular type of online research is the use of surveys either through interactive interviews or through the self-completion of a range of measures. Such online surveys can be a very convenient research tool, not least because all the data can be downloaded directly into a database thereby making analysis possible almost immediately. Using email to administer an online survey can be helpful, particularly if it is sent to a predetermined group with a known number of recipients, thus making the calculation of a response rate easier. Other types of online survey recruitment may limit the extent to which the researcher, however, can determine the response rate, particularly if the survey has been posted to a public website or discussion group. Nevertheless, uploading a survey to a public website can be a useful recruitment strategy as was found by Young et al. (2004). In their study of factors related to breast augmentation, a 177-item survey was uploaded to a public website for a period of 6 months. During this time, the survey was completed by 4011 women, including 2273 who had received breast implants and 1738 who were considering augmentation. Online surveys also have the advantage of looking identical (subject to the browser being used) to participants. It can be designed to be attractive, easy to use and navigate, and 'progress bars' can be included to encourage participants to complete the full survey. However, using online surveys can be challenging especially if the researcher wishes to create the survey from scratch using HTML (HyperText Markup Language), but, a number of software companies now offer relatively easy to use packages which take care of all your design needs (e.g. SurveyMonkey, Qualtrics).

Online focus groups

The focus group is a well-known tool for researchers with an emphasis on interaction and the opportunity to explore what people feel or think about an issue and why. However, face-to-face focus groups may be problematic for a variety of reasons including personal organization, access to transport, other time commitments, as well as having the confidence necessary to meet new people in a potentially unfamiliar location. This latter concern may be especially problematic for individuals with a visible difference (Wahl et al., 2002). More recently, we have seen examples of online focus groups being used in appearance-related research (e.g. Fox et al., 2007) yet their use as a data collection tool is still regarded as somewhat novel but is growing in popularity.

Online focus groups can be set up in a variety of ways and whilst traditional face to face groups also have flexibility in how they are run, the issue of timing is more crucial in the online setting. For example, an online focus group can be set up in real-time, that is to say, it operates synchronously with all participants being online at the same time. Those who have used synchronous or real-time exchanges have often concluded that these types of group interaction are characterized by immediacy and dynamism (O'Connor & Madge, 2003) and this can contribute to a greater expression of emotion. However, synchronous online focus groups are not without their potential difficulties. For example, although all participants have, in theory, an equal opportunity to participate in the discussion, the participant who has more advanced typing skills is the one with the power and potential to say the most. Moreover, the pressure to type and send responses may limit the extent to which a participant considers and deliberates about their response. The danger is that such responses may not be reflective and some argue, could increase their superficiality (Gaiser, 1997). An additional consideration surrounds the challenges of being a moderator of a synchronous group. As Fox et al. (2007, p. 542) reflect, 'moderating synchronous focus groups requires relatively fast typing skills and some experience with the style of real-time discussion'. However, it is not just typing skill which is being tested in this format it is also the skill of understanding the complexities of online real-time discussion. For example, in her study of young people with skin problems participating in a real-time focus group, Fiona Fox reports the challenge of interpreting silences which can be difficult. The skill rests in knowing whether participants are thinking, typing, or choosing not to answer or respond to a question (Fox et al., 2007).

Conversely, the focus group can be set up asynchronously with participants not required to be online at the same time. Typical examples of asynchronous online focus groups include discussion forums and bulletin boards where messages are posted in a folder and viewed by other participants and responded to. This may be helpful if the study is more international in focus and participants live in different time zones. Moreover, it could be helpful for those participants who are slow typists and may also allow more reflective and detailed responses. However, some authors actually debate whether this truly constitutes a focus group (e.g. Bloor et al., 2001).

Using email posts and archives

In recent years we have seen a growing number of studies which have derived their data from emails and archives, such as discussion forums. Email messages and archives can provide the researcher with a rich source of data which reflect naturally occurring conversations between individuals. From a purely practical perspective, this source of data lends itself well to qualitative analysis, not least because it is pre-transcribed and can, in many instances, be easily imported into qualitative computer software packages. However, there are a number of other potential advantages to this form of online research.

One of the most striking advantages is the fact that this particular methodology provides access to a potentially sizeable and diverse sample. This may be especially beneficial when researchers are trying to access those individuals who may not engage with more traditional face-to-face research, such as interviews or surveys. The observational nature of the research may also be a potential advantage in that the researcher is not visible to those whose communication is being studied and this may limit the extent to which the data are distorted or influenced. It could therefore be argued that the data generated are more naturalistic and not researcher led. For example, Suzuki and Calzo (2004) recognized the fact that young people may not interact with or disclose their worries to health professionals or other adults and so examined the content of questions posted to a teen bulletin board. Their results revealed a broad range of anxieties and worries, including those related to changing body image.

In addition, this type of online methodology may be especially helpful when we are researching a topic which is highly personal and/or sensitive. For example, Langer and Beckman (2005) conducted a qualitative analysis of a Danish online discussion forum which was concerned with a range of cosmetic surgery issues. In particular, they were interested in exploring the different types of information being sought, views towards a range of cosmetic surgical procedures, and reasons for considering a cosmetic procedure as well as the decision-making process. Their results demonstrated that much could be learnt about this very personal issue and a deeper understanding of it was obtained. Interestingly, they noted that members of the forum commonly shared very personal experiences and reflections of their cosmetic surgery, often posting lengthy and detailed personal narratives. Indeed, they found that approximately 87% of all postings included personal experiences and stories. This example highlights the great potential to explore personal/sensitive issues through accessing rich and naturalistic data.

However, this type of online research methodology is not without potential disadvantages. For example, one common criticism surrounds the extent to which data derived from online discussion is limited by the socio-demographic characteristics of Internet users (see 'Issues in sampling and potential bias' section). This potential bias may limit the extent to which research conducted using this online method is representative of the phenomenon under investigation. Furthermore, within online groups members vary in the extent to which they participate.

Some people 'lurk' and do not disclose their own thoughts and views on a particular topic. Again, this raises issues about the representative nature of the data. Groups may also vary in how they are set up and whether they are moderated (either by a peer or a professional) and this can influence how the group evolves and potentially, the nature and content of the online discussion.

Key Issues in Online Research

Issues in sampling and potential bias

One common concern about the use of online methods is that studies of this type may suffer from sampling bias. In particular, it has been argued that online methods will lead to a non-representative sample as a result of the characteristics of Internet access and use (Kraut et al., 1998; Krantz & Dalal, 2000). As noted earlier, the number of people with access to the Internet is growing and thus this 'problem' is potentially declining. Nevertheless, there is often still concern surrounding the potential for sampling bias as a result of convenience sampling, however, with larger samples it is argued that this problem diminishes. An alternative to convenience sampling is through invited participation into a study and this has been a popular approach, though potentially low response rates may be associated with this method. Additionally, the method of recruitment may be an important consideration as a growing body of studies suggest that the lowest response rates may be seen when an unsolicited email invitation is used.

Credibility and validity of data collection

An important consideration when thinking about undertaking appearance-related research online is whether potential participants will complete material in the same way as they would using traditional methods, such as face-to-face or mail surveys. The completion of a measure could be affected by the layout on a webpage. However, this may be a difficult issue to address given the range of different types of web browsers available. That said, one could similarly argue that there is no way of knowing whether paper-based versions of particular measures differ from study to study.

When considering conducting online research one needs to be mindful of characteristics of participants which might be relevant to the data collection process. For example, their language skills or differing cultural interpretations of material presented online may be important, especially if a survey is distributed internationally. Furthermore, the issue of participant engagement can be a challenging one, especially since the anonymity and 'distance' between the researcher and participant may mean that they feel less accountable. However, opinion is divided on this issue and some researchers argue that this 'distance' may in fact lead participants to offer a more truthful and open account of their views and experiences (Gosling et al., 2004).

It is also worth reflecting on the actual process of completing an online survey. Respondents may rush their responses, miss out items or skip questions. However, this can be dealt with by creating surveys which alert the participant to any missing items. There is also the potential for participants to make repeat submissions, which is something that is unlikely in traditional research methods, especially in face-to-face research. In addition, a number of researchers have expressed concern over the extent to which participants in online research studies may misrepresent themselves. Again, the jury is out on the extent to which this problem is particular to online research as little empirical data is available. However, some encouraging results were published by Buchanan et al. (2005) which found that only one participant from a sample of 1199 needed to have their data deleted due to fraudulent responses.

The final issue considered here is the extent to which online measures are reliable and valid. There is some evidence of variation in the distribution of scores generated according to whether the data was collected online or through traditional methods. Some authors have argued that measures which are completed online may lead to higher scores, compared with the norms created by measures completed using traditional methods. Indeed, this has been found in measures of anxiety, depression, neuroticism and openness, mood regulation and negative affect (George et al., 1992; Davis, 1999; Joinson, 1999; Schulenberg & Yutrzenka, 1999; Johnson, 2000; Fouladi et al., 2002). It would seem that this may be a potentially important issue especially if clinical cut-off points are to be re-drawn using online data collection methods.

Ethical issues

Broadly speaking, the ethical issues raised by online research are similar to those raised by traditional or offline research methodologies and include issues of informed consent, confidentiality, and the security of the site. Additional and often more complex ethical issues may be raised in relation to research which is more opportunistic, for example, the analysis of the content of online discussion forums or chat rooms. Each of these broad categories is considered in turn as follows.

Planned research

Where the online research is planned, websites and forums may be set up for the purpose of data collection. In such instances, researchers are able to engage with potential participants in a way which serves to facilitate the gaining of informed consent and assures participants an appropriate level of confidentiality and anonymity by making any messages or responses private. It is relatively straightforward to email potential participants information sheets and consent forms or upload them onto a website. Participants can return, via email, their consent form or can indicate their consent by 'ticking' a mandatory response box on an online survey. Regardless of which specific type of informed consent is used, the participant should be offered the contact details of the researcher in case any queries or difficulties arise.

Online forums can be password protected thereby preventing responses being located through search engines. In addition, researchers can close and remove the material once the study has been completed.

Opportunistic research

In cases where online material is being used for research purposes when it was not generated originally for that purpose, then the ethical issues raised are often more complex. This is seen especially in work which examines material generated in online discussion forums, archives, and chat rooms. Is it ethically permissible to analyse messages posted to an appearance-related online discussion forum? The answer to this, it can be argued, rests on the distinction between 'public' and 'private' space. Where discussion is private and no observation is expected, then informed consent should be sought. However, informed consent could be waived when the communication is more public and a certain level of public visibility is implied. The extent to which online discussion can be considered 'public' or 'private' is complex. Some researchers consider messages posted to online forums and chat rooms to be public (Salem et al., 1997; Sharf, 1997; Finn, 1999), whereas others argue that individuals participating in online discussion forums or chat rooms do not necessarily assume their communication to be public (Eysenbach & Wyatt, 2002). Furthermore, it may also be possible that members might perceive their communication to be public within the group but private to others (e.g. researchers) outside the group (Herring, 1996).

In order to address this issue, Eysenbach and Till (2002) suggest that if some form of registration is required to gain access to the online material, then this can be regarded as a more private site. Conversely, when material can be accessed without any registration or subscription, then this can be regarded as publicly available. This is not to say that any material which requires registration can never be studied, but that informed consent should then be sought either from the individuals themselves or perhaps through a gatekeeper, such as an online forum moderator.

Another ethical issue arising from this particular type of online research is the potential breach of confidentiality of group members, as it is important for researchers to protect their participants from unintentional harm or exposure. A number of precautions can be taken to ensure the anonymity of participants when analysing messages posted to online forums. For example, if verbatim quotes from the messages are to be used, researchers should remove all personally identifiable information from the message. This may include names, pseudonyms, or geographical location of the members, and the name of the selected online forum (Sixsmith & Murray, 2001; Kraut et al., 2004; British Psychological Society, 2007). Although some researchers argue that removal of all personally identifiable information would lead to the omission of valuable data that may be crucial to the aims of the research, upholding the confidentiality of the participant should be prioritized over the concern of information loss.

CONCLUSION

Using the Internet to undertake online appearance-related research carries with it a number of advantages that need to be carefully considered alongside any disadvantages arising from the specific methodology. Issues of convenience and access need to be considered in relation to issues of sampling, data collection, and ethics.

REFERENCES

Bloor, M., Frankland, J., Thomas, M., & Robson, K. (2001). *Focus groups in social research.* London: Sage.

British Psychological Society (2007). *Conducting research on the Internet: Guidelines for ethical practice in psychological research online.* Leicester: British Psychological Society.

Buchanan, T. & Smith, J. (1999). Using the Internet for psychological research: Personality testing on the World Wide Web. *British Journal of Psychology,* 90, 125–44.

Buchanan, T., Ali, T., Heffernan, T., Ling, J., Parrott, A., Rodgers, J., *et al.* (2005). Non-equivalence of online and paper-and-pencil psychological tests: The case of the Prospective Memory Questionnaire. *Behaviour Research Methods, Instruments and Computers,* 37(1), 148–54.

Davis, R. (1999). Web-based administration of a personality questionnaire: Comparison with traditional methods. *Behaviour Research Methods, Instruments and Computers,* 31, 572–7.

Eysenbach, G., & Till, J. E. (2001). Ethical issues in qualitative research on internet communities. *British medical journal,* 323, 1103–5.

Eysenbach, G. & Wyatt, J. (2002). Using the Internet for surveys and health research. *Journal of Medical Internet Research,* 4(2), e13.

Finn, J. (1999). An exploration of helping processes in an online self-help group focusing on issues of disability. *Health and Social Work,* 24, 220–31.

Fouladi, R., McCarthy, C., & Moller, N. (2002). Paper and pencil or online? Evaluating mode effects on measures of emotional functioning and attachment. *Assessment,* 9, 204–15.

Fox, F. E., Morris, M., & Rusmey, N. (2007). Doing synchronous online focus groups with young people: Methodological reflections. *Qualitative Health Research,* 17(4), 539–47.

Gaiser, T. (1997). Conducting online focus groups: A methodological discussion. *Social Science Computer Review,* 15(2), 135–44.

George, C. E., Lankford, J. S., & Wilson, S. E. (1992). The effects of computerized versus paper-and-pencil administration on measures of negative affect. *Computers in Human Behaviour,* 8, 203–9.

Gosling, S. D., Vazire, S., Srivastava, S., & John, O. P. (2004). Should we trust web-based studies? A comparative analysis of six preconceptions about Internet questionnaires. *American Psychologist,* 59(2), 93–104.

Herring, S. (1996) *Computer mediated Communication: Linguistic, Social and Cross-Cultural Perspectives.* Amsterdam: John Benjamins

Internet World Statistics (2011). Available online at http://www.internetworldstats.com (accessed 10 January 2011).

Johnson, J. (2000). Predicting observers' ratings of the Big Five from the CPI, HPI and NEO-PI-R: A comparative validity study. *European Journal of Personality,* 14, 1–19.

Joinson, A. (1999). Anonymity, disinhibition and social desirability on the Internet. Behaviour research methods, *Instruments and Computers,* 31, 433–8.

Krantz, J. & Dalal, R. (2000). Validity of web-based psychological research. In M. H. Birnhaum (ed.) Psychological Experiments on the Internet, pp. 35–60. San Diego, CA: Academic Press.

Kraut, R., Patterson, V., Lundmark, M., Kiesler, T., Mukho-padhyay, T., & Scherlis, W. (1988). Internet paradox: A social technology that reduces social involvement and psychological well-being? *American Psychologist,* 53, 1017–31.

Kraut, R., Olson, J., Banaji, M., Bruckman, A., Cohen, J., & Couper, M. (2004). Psychological research online. *American Psychologist,* 59, 105–17.

Langer, R. & Beckman, S.C. (2005). Sensitive research topics: netnography revisited. *Qualitative Market Research: An International Journal,* 8(2), 189–203.

O'Connor, H. & Madge, C. (2003). Focus groups in cyberspace: Using the Internet for qualitative research. *Qualitative Market Research: An International Journal,* 6(2), 133–43.

Office for National Statistics (2011). *ONS Opinions Survey.* http://www.statistics.gov.uk (accessed 10 January 2011).

Salem, A. D., Bogat, G. A., & Reid, C. (1997). Manual help goes on-line. *Journal of Community Psychology,* 25, 189–207.

Schulenberg, S.E. & Yutrzednka, B.A. (1999). The equivalence of computerized and paper-and-pencil psychological instruments: Implications for measures of negative affect. *Behaviour Research Methods, Instruments and Computers,* 31(2), 315–21.

Sharf, B. F. (1997). Communicating breast cancer on-line: Support and empowerment on the Internet. *Women and Health,* 26, 65–84.

Sixsmith, J. & Murray, C.D. (2001). Ethical issues in the documentary data analysis of internet posts and archives. *Qualitative Health Research,* 11, 423–32.

Suzuki, L. K. & Calzo, J. P. (2004). The search for peer advice in cyberspace: An examination of online teen bulletin boards about health and sexuality. *Journal of Applied Developmental Psychology,* 25, 685–98.

Wahl, A. K., Gjengedal, E., & Hanestad, B. R. (2002). The bodily suffering of living with severe psoriasis: In-depth interviews with 22 hospitalized patients with psoriasis. *Qualitative Health Research,* 12, 250–61.

Young, V. L., Watson, M. E., Boswell, C. B. & Centeno, R. F. (2004). Initial results from an online breast augmentation survey. *Aesthetic Surgery Journal,* 24(2), 117–35.

CHAPTER 47

USING NOVEL METHODS IN APPEARANCE RESEARCH

DIANA HARCOURT

THE growth of the body of research into the psychology of appearance in recent years has been based primarily on well-established methods, notably semi-structured, face-to-face interviews, standardized questionnaires, and experimental studies. Yet alongside these traditional methods there has also been some, albeit relatively limited, use of alternative or novel approaches towards study design, data collection, analysis, and participant engagement.

This chapter uses a selection of methods to examine the benefits and challenges of using novel approaches in appearance research. Where possible, examples are used from within the existing appearance literature. However, since this chapter also aims to highlight the potential use of methods that have received little attention in this field, it also draws on a broader range of research. The opportunity to expand the range of research methods being used in appearance research is highlighted.

DEVELOPING NOVEL METHODS

The development of alternative methods involves thinking 'outside the box' of more traditional approaches, and offers the potential of novel and ground-breaking research. Most writing on the development of innovative methods refers to the use of new technology and qualitative methods. For example, Holloway & Todres (2007) suggest three areas for the development of qualitative research: the integration of art and science, collaboration with researchers and others from different disciplines, and the development of alternative means of dissemination. These suggestions could apply equally well to quantitative research and, as Taylor and Coffey (2009) highlight, to a more effective use of mixed methods. Readers are directed to Emma Dures's chapter in this volume for a detailed consideration of the use of mixed methods in appearance research. This chapter focuses on the possible use of new technology, visual methods, and arts-based research.

USING NEW TECHNOLOGY

Emerging trends and technological developments present opportunities for new means of engaging participants, and may encourage the recruitment of groups who are typically hard to reach or are a challenge to engage in appearance research, for example, young men.

Cyberspace has presented an opportunity for researchers to expand their range of tools to include email, websites, bulletin boards, and blogs (Hookway, 2008). Studies analysing the use of online support groups and discussion boards for people with eating disorders (Winzelberg, 1997) and cancer (Seale et al., 2006) have shown that participants do discuss personal appearance-related issues in these settings. Singleton et al. (2010) found that men were willing to discuss their experiences of living with gynecomastia (pronounced breast tissue in men) online, demonstrating how sensitive topics that can prove difficult to research through face-to-face interviews, can be explored through online methods that participants may perceive as relatively anonymous and less threatening. A thematic analysis of messages on an Australian fashion magazine's online discussion forum in response to a newspaper report on the size of models depicted in the media (Fletcher & Diedrichs, 2010) demonstrates how online research can enable a timely investigation in response to a topical issue. Neil Coulson's chapter in this book (see Chapter 46) explores the use of online research in detail, specifically the analysis of online forums and message boards.

The use of web-logs ('blogs') within any area of research is relatively new. Whilst preparing this chapter, a literature search failed to identify any published appearance-research based on their use, yet a search of readily accessible blogs confirmed that entries revealing attitudes towards appearance and body image issues are rife. Blog entries can be compared with diary studies since both are means of eliciting an individual's thoughts and experiences, posts (entries) are archived chronologically and are therefore a potential resource for longitudinal research. However, blogs are written with an audience in mind whereas diary entries are typically private (unless the diary has been established explicitly for the purpose of the research) (Hookway, 2008).

Hookway suggests that blogs offer advantages over diaries in terms of providing instant, low-cost, naturalistic data without the need for transcription or travel by either the researcher or participant, and bloggers may not be self-conscious of what they write, which could be advantageous when researching thoughts and feelings about appearance. However, the analysis of unsolicited blogs may mean that the researcher's aims are not met. Solicited 'research-driven' blogs, on the other hand, are responses to the researcher's request for data, but posts may be prone to impression management and the participant's willingness to please. Hookway (2008) gives a detailed, practical guide to blog research and the ethical dilemmas (particularly around informed consent) that this can present.

Text messaging (SMS) presents an alternative means of communicating with participants, and may be particularly appealing in research with young people for whom texting is an everyday activity. A study of 16–24-year-olds' perspectives on health found that more than 97% were willing to provide their phone number for research purposes (Haller et al., 2006).

Successful use of SMS and online diaries in research into sensitive topics such as sexual behaviour (Lim et al., 2010) found they were popular with participants who considered them more private than paper diaries. Whilst SMS seems to have been little used within appearance research, its potential to obtain time-specific body satisfaction ratings or to remind participants to complete diary entries could be explored further.

Recently, debate about the possible use of Twitter within research (see Sutton, 2010) either by analysing unsolicited posts, or sending a tweet seeking responses to a specific research question, has raised the additional issue that details of those who post comments on Twitter are unknown, which may prove difficult when trying to publish the resulting data in some journals.

Advantages and limitations of online methods

One of the advantages of online methods is that they may facilitate the inclusion of people who might otherwise be unable to participate due to issues around time commitment, transport, and distance. Tates et al., (2009) reported the benefits of online focus groups in research with young people undergoing cancer treatment, whilst Williamson et al. (2010) used an innovative combination of both online data collection and photography to overcome the challenges of access and recruitment with this hard to reach group. Online data collection has the potential of a global participant pool, and may thereby broaden samples within appearance research beyond the current tendency to be largely UK, US, or Australian-focused. These methods may also appeal to people whose lack of confidence in face-to-face settings such as individual or group interviews, may deter them from engaging in such situations. This may be particularly pertinent for those whose concern about their appearance results in distress and anxiety around meeting others (Fox et al., 2007). Also, the lack of face-to-face contact may facilitate discussion about sensitive topics, such as how participants feel about their bodies.

However, online research excludes those who lack access or confidence in the use of online communications, and concerns have been expressed that computer-based research and interventions effectively collude with people who try to avoid face-to-face contact with others as a means of managing high levels of appearance-related anxiety. An alternative view is that the use of methods that are acceptable to people with very high levels of concern enables their voices to be heard when a reliance on face-to-face methods may not. Whilst it's harder for a researcher using online methods to detect non-verbal information, including signs of distress, if they do not see the participant (Tates et al., 2009), this is no different to other, more established research methods such as postal questionnaires or telephone interviews. Some research has suggested that telephone interviews are as effective as face-to-face interviews and, within an appearance context, Egan et al.'s (2011) study of positive experiences associated with having a visible difference concluded that data obtained during telephone interviews were as rich and informative as that from individual and group face-to-face interviews.

The particular issues of conducting appearance research in an 'appearance-less' medium are explored by Fox et al. (2007) who used synchronous online focus groups to explore young people's experiences of living with a chronic skin condition. Fox et al. (2007) provide a practical guide and reflection on the benefits and challenges of using real-time online exchanges between participants (as opposed to the asynchronous communications more typically analysed through discussion forums and message boards). They conclude that synchronous online focus groups are advantageous since the immediacy of responses reflects the normal interaction between individuals and facilitates expression of emotions, using a medium that is familiar to young people.

Keeping abreast of technological developments will be key in the development of new methods. For example, what are the possibilities for using computer tablets such as iPads in research? Likewise, advances in computer generation may offer opportunities that as yet we cannot envisage. The role of avatars has already been considered in appearance research and some researchers (e.g. Bond et al., 2010) have used computer games to examine body dissatisfaction. Their role within future research could be both enlightening and engaging. Alternatively, is there a danger of placing too much reliance on technologies that will transpire to be short-lived 'fads'?

Arts-Based Research and Visual Methods

The phrase 'arts-based research' encompasses a broad range of methods including photography, drawing, graffiti boards, collages, sculpture, storytelling, and theatrical performance, all of which can help to engage participants in a manner that written or verbal data collection may not. Whilst methods such as drawing and photography are more accepted methods and are likely to be considered within visual methods research, other methods (e.g. puppetry, scrapbooking) are less well established and rarely used (Coad, 2007).

Visual methods research has expanded and developed greatly in recent years. Photography, video recordings, and drawings have all been used in a variety of contexts, for example, to elicit health-related stories (Hanna & Jacobs, 1993; Radley & Taylor, 2003; Guillemin, 2004). It is intuitively appealing to consider their use in appearance research since we are, after all, interested in an essentially visual topic. Quantitative measures and qualitative research (such as questionnaires and interviews) rely on numerical and verbal data whilst visual data has a closer affinity with the original topic under investigation. The term 'visual methods' covers a wide range of options—the focus here is on photography, video, drawings, and scrapbooks as exemplars.

Photography

An advantage of studies in which participants produce photographs that are used as a prompt and a focus for an interview about their experiences, is that participants have control over the extent and timing of their involvement, and how they choose to represent their experiences. Interviews conducted in conjunction with photographs can yield richer, more detailed information than that generated by word-only interviews. Some women in a study of cancer patients' experiences of a changing appearance during chemotherapy treatment (Frith & Harcourt, 2007) described how engaging with the photography had been beneficial and distracted them from the rigours of their disease and its treatment. This study typically involved participant engagement for 6 months or more, and whilst this enabled the dynamic nature of appearance change to be explored, these more interactive and ongoing studies will not appeal to everyone, especially whilst also managing the demands of treatment for a serious health condition. There could be benefits in offering participants a range of ways in which they could take part in a programme of research.

Video

A small number of appearance-related studies have focused on the making of participant-created videos. When asked to document their life through video, adolescents categorized as being obese included the psychosocial impact of name-calling, feelings of isolation, and their resentment towards supposedly attractive celebrities through a medium that was then used to raise awareness amongst health professionals (Rich et al., 2002). The use of novel methods to facilitate novel innovative dissemination is discussed later in this chapter.

Drawings

Drawings have been used effectively within a broad range of research, including perceptions and experiences of spinal cord injury (Cross et al., 2006), breast cancer (Harrow et al., 2008), and menopause (Guillemin, 2004), all of which can impact on appearance, although this was not the primary focus of these studies. Drawings have a long history in disciplines such as anthropology (Guillemin, 2004) and in research with children, but their potential use within appearance research has received little, if any, attention. Whilst some studies (e.g. Reynolds et al., 2007) have quantitatively assessed drawings alongside standardized measures of psychological functioning to ascertain the impact of a health condition, most arts-based research takes a qualitative approach. Typically, participants are interviewed on the topic in question, and then asked to create a picture that represents their experiences of that issue and to describe the drawing and their reasons for it (e.g. their choice of colour, size, composition). According to Bricher (1999), good quality conversations occur alongside other activities, so a discussion about appearance concerns might be facilitated by an arts-based activity such as drawing.

Scrapbooking

Ongoing research within the Centre for Appearance Research is exploring the use of scrapbooking as a means of actively involving young people in a programme of research exploring their experiences of their appearance. This novel approach, which has not previously been used in this field, involves participants creating a scrapbook or album by collating personally meaningful memorabilia such as photographs, artwork, tickets, invitations, greetings cards, letters, quotes, and certificates, which depict their unique experiences and act as a focus for a semi-structured interview. These albums can be seen as a form of extended diary, in that entries are not restricted to written data, and can be considered more dynamic, and potentially fun, engaging, and accessible for participants. Whilst interviews at a later date can benefit from having the participant's album as a focus and a prompt for discussion, it is important to bear in mind that albums can evoke powerful memories. If these revolve around sensitive experiences, for example, those associated with a visible difference, the researcher must be prepared for the possibility that interviews will be emotionally charged and must have appropriate support available, both for participants and themselves.

Drama

Gray et al. (2001) reflect on the use of dramatic representations of experiences of living with breast cancer, which were developed on the basis of interviews with breast cancer patients. These have been presented to audiences of health professionals and members of the public, from whom data have been gathered in relation to their responses to the performance and the issues it raises. Recently, Y Touring (http://www.ytouring.org.uk), a theatre company within Central YMCA in the UK that produces theatre, new media, and drama workshops to facilitate discussion of sensitive and difficult health topics, has created a performance on the issues of cosmetic surgery and body image which have acted as prompts for focus group discussions with school children. This approach can act as a means of data collection, and also dissemination, public engagement, and education.

Advantages and limitations of arts-based methods and visual methods

Arts-based methods present some interesting challenges for researchers. One of their attractions is that they may make participation more appealing and engaging for people who might not otherwise take part in research, especially young people (Coad, 2007). However, others might find the notion of engaging in arts-based work off-putting, for fear of being judged on their artistic ability or not considering themselves 'arty'. Being asked to create an arts-based image whilst the researcher is present (e.g. Cross et al., 2006; Harrow et al., 2008) could be particularly unappealing for some potential participants. The importance of developing a good rapport before asking participants to create a visual image (Harrow et al., 2008) and throughout ongoing photography research (Frith & Harcourt, 2007) has been highlighted.

For some researchers, artwork is merely a 'way in' to engage the participant and is not, in itself, a form of data. Others include analysis of the images themselves, but the participant's true meaning of their artwork or visual data can only be ascertained and understood by analysing their verbal explanation alongside the images (Cross et al., 2006). Guillemin (2004) suggests that drawings are best used as an adjunct to other approaches, for example, alongside other methods within longitudinal research in order to explore how participants see changes to their body over time, such as before and after appearance-altering surgery.

Visual methods also raise important ethical considerations, including the identification and informed consent of non-participants captured in photographs (see Frith & Harcourt, 2007). Clark et al. (2010) have considered the ethical issues of image-based research at length, including how aspects other than facial features (e.g. unusual jewellery, the background captured in photographs, the composition of drawings) can identify those depicted in the images they create.

NOVEL METHODS OF DISSEMINATION

An exciting aspect of novel methods is that they offer an opportunity for alternative means of dissemination, including exhibitions, performances, and the inclusion of participants' photography and art work within standard conference presentations. These may be powerful and thought-provoking, either as an alternative or a complement to traditional dissemination activities such as publishing in peer-reviewed journals. They may also help to convey research findings to those who are unlikely to access academic journals or conference presentations, and may also overcome barriers due to language comprehension or communication difficulties. However, issues around confidentiality and anonymity of participants need careful consideration. For example, images used in dissemination activities may be 'pixellated' in order to obscure facial images and prevent participants being identified, but they may still be identifiable.

COMBINING NOVEL WITH ESTABLISHED METHODS

The potential use of established methods which have been under-utilized within appearance research should not be overlooked, either alone or in conjunction with novel methods. For example:

Diaries (either structured or unstructured, free responses) offer the potential to explore changes in response to body image and appearance over time and through material that is likely to have greater meaning and validity for participants than data obtained through standardized measures (Furness & Garrud, 2010). Whilst diaries can be advantageous, they require ongoing commitment from participants which could become burdensome and may bias a sample in favour of those more confident with written media. Furthermore, the process of diary-keeping may act as a form of intervention, akin to expressive writing, by encouraging participants to reflect on their thoughts about their appearance—an issue raised by Furness & Garrud (2010) in a longitudinal, prospective study that used free response diaries to explore cancer patients' adaptation to facial surgery.

Vignettes have had relatively little use in appearance research. Jenkinson et al. (2010) used hypothetical vignettes of patient scenarios in order to explore general practitioners' likelihood of referring a patient with a visible difference for psychological support. Manipulating information within the various vignettes demonstrated that perceived distress, visibility and severity of the disfigurement influenced health professionals' decision making—a finding that may not have been elicited without the use of the vignettes.

Q-Methodology is an interesting approach that can combine the use of both qualitative and quantitative data. Walsh (2010) explored people's understandings of visible difference, in a Q-study that required participants to sort statements about disfigurement that had been generated through a series of focus group discussions.

Experimental studies are already using many different novel designs. For example, the success of Dittmar et al.'s (2009) work on the impact of the media on body image has been due to the careful and rigorous design of studies that effectively mask participants' awareness of the purpose of the study and lessen the likelihood of socially desirable responses. For this same reason, some researchers (e.g. Grandfield et al., 2005; O'Connor, 2011) have used Implicit Association Tests (IATs) aiming to explore subconscious attitudes towards appearance and body image.

Further work could also look to expand the combined use of psychological and physiological methods and extend the use of novel appearance-related stimuli (e.g. footage of television programmes, media advertising campaigns) to facilitate discussion within focus group studies.

Broadening the array of methods in appearance research also presents more options for triangulation. For example, Furness and Garrud (2010) triangulated their data collected through diaries with previous interview studies involving patients with facial cancer, whilst Williamson et al.'s (2010) study of young people's experiences of changes to appearance during cancer treatment triangulated findings from a photography-based study with an online survey.

Novel Methods and user
Involvement in Research

The case for an increased role for user involvement in research (i.e. those who have direct experience of the topic under investigation) is addressed in Amanda Bates's chapter in this volume (Chapter 48). Appropriate and effective means of facilitating user involvement could include the use of novel methods. For example, rigorous means of eliciting the priorities of users and patients in agenda setting have been established (see The James Lind Alliance, http://www. lindalliance.org). Broerse (2010) reports the benefits of a mixed methods approach towards agenda setting involving burns survivors. Whilst burns survivors in this study highlighted the need for psychosocial research, health professionals focused on prioritizing biomedical topics. This approach demonstrated the conflicting priorities of clinicians and patients, and enabled patients' voices to be heard within the agenda-setting discussions. However, there is still some way to go to persuade all stakeholders of the importance and value of involving participants in this way.

Ongoing Issues

Whilst work on the development of novel methods continues, a number of questions remain unanswered. For example, to what extent do these innovative methods actually extend our knowledge of the psychology of appearance? Do they provide different results? Do they address novel questions, and provide alternative or entirely novel findings, or is their contribution in the engagement of participants who might not otherwise be involved? Could they deter some people, who might find traditional methods more appealing and 'safe'? Do they increase the likelihood of typically under-represented groups taking part in research, or are some groups still overlooked or alienated by the research process? Do they further increase the likelihood that people from 'traditional' participant groups (e.g. white, middle class, with an interest in appearance) will become involved?

Researchers still need to explore whether alternative methods might increase participation in appearance research by hard-to-reach groups. For example, black and minority ethnic (BME) groups continue to be under-represented, despite attempts to broaden recruitment in areas with large BME populations. Whilst some studies specifically focused on appearance issues amongst BME groups have been carried out (e.g. Thompson et al.'s 2010 study of South Asian's experiences of vitiligo), they have usually been conducted in English. A focus group study by Hughes et al. (2009) used facilitators who were fluent in Bengali, Gujarati, Punjabi, or Urdu so that non-English speaking South Asians, or those who preferred not to be interviewed in English, could take part in a study that explored views about disfigurement.

Innovative working and novel methods can develop through cross-disciplinary research (Holloway & Todres, 2007). For example, working with health economists has become increasingly common amongst those developing and evaluating interventions to support people with appearance concerns. Novel methods offer greater potential for real connections and cross-disciplinary appearance work (e.g. between psychologists, sociologists, allied health professionals, artists, health economists, historians, anthropologists, gerontologists, IT specialists, counsellors, media specialists and policy-makers) that could result in coherent and comprehensive research which appeals to a wider audience.

Conclusion

Whilst this chapter offers only a snapshot of novel methods within appearance research, there is still potential for the creation of new and alternative methods, and for the ongoing development and refinement of the approaches outlined. This will require a good level of reflection on what they can offer and ways of overcoming the challenges they present. Developments in this field have the potential not only to advance knowledge and understanding in appearance research, but also to contribute to the research methods literature more broadly.

Regardless of the method used, the value and quality of any particular study is dependent on the researcher's ability and the rigour with which the study is conducted. The impact of research will continue to be determined by the extent to which the methods used are the best fit to the questions being asked, the intended audience, and the aims of the research. Finally, whilst the use of novel methods presents some interesting challenges for researchers, it may also raise challenging questions for gatekeepers, funders, those giving ethics approval, editors, and journal reviewers. Researchers using novel methods must always be prepared to explain and justify their choice of approach to those who may not be aware of these approaches or experienced in their use.

REFERENCES

Bagnoli, A. (2009). Beyond the standard interview: the use of graphic elicitiation and arts-based methods. *Qualitative Research*, 9(5), 547–70.

Bond, R., Dittmar, H., & Moorehouse, A. (2010). Computer games and body dissatisfaction in young men, oral presentation at Apperance Matters 4, June 2010, Bristol.

Bricher, G. (1999). Children and qualitative research methods: a review of the literature related to interview and interpretive processes. *Nurse Researcher*, 6(4), 65–77.

Broerse, J. E. W., Zweekhorst, M. B. M., van Rensen, A. J. M. L. & de Haan, M. J. M. (2010). Involving burn survivors in agenda setting on burn research: an added value? *Burns*, 36, 217–31.

Clark, A., Prosser, J. & Wiles, R. (2010). Ethical images in image-based research. *Arts & Health*, 2(1), 81–93.

Coad, J. (2007). Using art-based techniques in engaging children and young people in health care consultations and/or research. *Journal of Research in Nursing*, 12(5), 487–97.

Cross, K., Kabel, A., & Lysack, C. (2006). Images of self and spinal cord injury: exploring drawing as a visual method in disability research. Visual Studies, 21(2), 183–93.

Dittmar, H., Halliwell, E., & Stirling, E. (2009). Understanding the impact of thin media models on women's body-focused affect: the roles of thin-ideal internalization and weight-related self-discrepancy activation in experimental exposure effects. *Journal of Social and Clinical Psychology*, 28(1), 43–72.

Egan, K., Harcourt, D., Rumsey, N., & The Appearance Research Collaboration. (2011). A qualitative study of the experiences of people who identify themselves as having adjusted positively to a visible difference. *Journal of Health Psychology*, 16, 739–49.

Fletcher, R. & Diedrichs, P. C. (2010). 'Does one size fit all?' fashion consumer opinions on average size models in the media, oral presentation at the Appearance Matters 4 conference, June 2010, Bristol.

Fox, F. E., Morris, M., & Rumsey, N. (2007). Doing synchronous online focus groups with young people: methodological reflections. *Qualitative Health Research*, 17, 539–47.

Fox, F. E., Rumsey, N., & Morris, M. (2007). 'Ur skin is the thing that everyone sees and you cant change it!': Exploring the appearance-related concerns of young people with psoriasis. *Developmental Neurorehabilitation*, 10(2), 133–41.

Frith, H. & Harcourt, D. (2007). Using photographs to capture women's experiences of chemotherapy: reflecting on the method. *Qualitative Health Research*, 17(10), 1340–50.

Furness, P. J. & Garrud, P. (2010). Adaptation after facial surgery: using the diary as a research tool. *Qualitative Health Research*, 20, 262–72.

Grandfield, T. A., Thompson, A. R., & Turpin, G. (2005). An attitudinal study of responses to a range of dermatological conditions using the Implicit Association Test. *Journal of Health Psychology*, 10, 821–9.

Gray, R. E., Sinding, C., & Fitch, M. I. (2001). Ross E. Gray, Christina Sinding, and Margaret I. Fitch navigating the social context of metastatic breast cancer: Reflections on a project linking research to drama. *Health*, 5, 233–48.

Guillemin, M. (2004). Understanding illness: using drawings as a research method. *Qualitative Health Research*, 14, 272–89.

Haller, D., Sanci, L., Sawyer, S., Coffey, C., & Patton, G. (2006). R U OK 2 TXT research? Feasibility of text message communication in primary care research. *Australian Family Physician*, 35(3), 175–6.

Hanna, K. M. & Jacobs, P. (1993). The use of photography to explore the meaning of health among adolescents with cancer. *Issues in Comprehensive Pediatric Nursing*, 16(3), 155–64.

Harrow, A., Wells, M., Humphris, G., Taylor, C., & Williams, B. (2008). 'Seeing is believing, and believing is seeing': An exploration of the meaning and impact of women's mental images of their breast cancer and their potential origins. *Patient Education & Counselling*, 73, 339–46.

Holloway, I. & Todres, L. (2007). Thinking differently: challenges in qualitative research. *International journal of qualitative studies on Health and Well-being*, 2, 12–18.

Holt, A. (2010). Using the telephone for narrative interviewing: a research note. *Qualitative Research*, 10, 113–21.

Hookway, N. (2008). 'Entering the blogosphere': some strategies for using blogs in social research. *Qualitative Research*, 8, 91–113.

Hughes, J., Naqvi, H., Saul, K., Williamson, H., Johnson, M. R. D., Rumsey, N., & *et al.* (2009). South Asian community views about individuals with disfigurement. *Diversity in Health and Care*, 6, 241–53.

Jenkins, N., Bloor, M., Fischer, J., Berney, L., & Neale, J. (2010). Putting it in context: the use of vignettes in qualitative interviews. *Qualitative Research*, 10(2), 175–98.

Jenkinson, E., Moss, T., & Rumsey, N. (2010). Primary care decision making regarding referral to psychological services: the role of visibility and severity of a patients' disfigure-ment, poster presentation at the Appearance Matters 4 conference, June 2010, Bristol.

Lim, M., Sacks-Davis, R., Aitken, C. K., Hocking, J. S. & Hellard, M. E. (2010). Randomised controlled trial of paper, online and SMS diaries for collecting sexual behaviour informa-tion from young people. *Journal of Epidemiology and Community Health*, 64, 885–9.

O'Connor, D. B., Hurling, R., Hendrickx, H., Osborne, G., Hall, J., Walklet, E., et al. (2011). Effects of written emotional disclosure on implicit self-esteem and body image. *British Journal of Health Psychology*, 16, 488–501.

Radley, A. & Taylor, D. (2003). Images of recovery: a photo-elicitation study on the hospital ward. *Qualitative Health Research*, 13, 77–99.

Reynolds, L., Broadbent, E., Ellis, C. J., Gamble, G., & Petrie, K. J. (2007). Patient drawings illustrate psychological and functional status in heart failure. *Journal of Psychosomatic Research*, 63, 525–32.

Rich, M., Patashnick, J., Huecker, D., & Ludwig, D. (2002). Living with obesity: visual narrative of overweight adolescents. *Journal of Adolescent Health*, 30(2), 100.

Seale, C., Ziebland, S., & Charteris-Black, J. (2006). Gender, cancer experience and internet use: a comparative keyword analysis of interviews and online cancer support groups. *Social Science and Medicine*, 62, 2577–90.

Singleton, P., Fawkner, H., White, A., & Foster, S. (2010). The road to surgery for gynecomastia: what can health professionals learn from men's experiences? Oral presentation at Appearance Matters 4 conference, June 2010, Bristol.

Tates, K., Zwaanswijk, M., Otten, R., van Dulmen, S., Hoogerbrugge, P. M., Kamps, W. A., *et al.* (2009). Online focus groups as a tool to collect data in hard-to-include populations: examples from paediatric oncology. *BMC Medical Research Methodology*, 9, 15.

Sutton, J. (2010). Pleased to tweet you. *The Psychologist*, 23(9), 730–1.

Taylor, C. & Coffey, A. (2009). Editorial—special issue: qualitative research and methodological innovation. *Qualitative Research*, 9(5), 523–6.

Thompson, A. R., Clarke, S. A., Newell, R., & The Appearance Research Collaboration (ARC) (2010). British South Asian Experiences of living with vitiligo: visible difference, culture & ethnicity. Presented at Appearance Matters 4, July 2010, Bristol.

Walsh, E. (2010). People's understandings of difference in appearance: a Q methodology study, Oral presentation at Appearance Matters 4 conference, June 2010, Bristol.

Williamson, H., Harcourt, D., Halliwell, E., Frith, H., & Wallace, M. (2010). Adolescents' and parents' experiences of managing the psychosocial impact of appearance change during cancer treatment. *Journal of Pediatric Oncology Nursing*, 27(3), 168–75.

Winzelberg, A. (1997). The analysis of an electronic support group for individuals with eating disorders. *Computers in Human Behaviour*, 13(3), 393–407.

CHAPTER 48

PROMOTING PARTICIPATION AND INVOLVEMENT IN APPEARANCE RESEARCH

AMANDA BATES

INTRODUCTION

THE consideration of how best to promote participant voices in appearance research is timely in view of the increasing emphasis on public involvement in research more generally. Public involvement, which is also known as user involvement, is the engagement of patients and the public in the research process, for example, in research design and in the dissemination of findings (Hanley et al., 2003). The growing importance of public involvement is reflected in the stipulation of such involvement by some funding bodies (Boote et al., 2009).

The public involvement literature employs different language, for example, the terms 'service user', 'consumer', and 'patient' are often used interchangeably. However, each has different connotations, and people may well prefer certain terms to others (Herxheimer & Goodare 1999). According to Hanley et al. (2003), the term 'public' includes patients and potential patients, informal carers, parents/guardians, disabled people, organizations representing those who use services, people who use health and social services, and members of the public who may receive health promotion programmes and/or social services. Therefore, the term 'public' will be used in this chapter to describe people who may be involved in research; this choice of term seems particularly appropriate to appearance research because we all have an appearance, and as such, any of us may be affected by appearance concerns.

This chapter will consider participation in appearance research on a continuum, from the beginning of a research idea, through to the dissemination of results. The opportunities and challenges in participation and public involvement in appearance research will be considered, and the reader will be offered strategies for involving the public throughout the research process. As someone with a visible difference who is familiar with research, I will also describe my personal experiences of participation and involvement in appearance research.

As a starting point, it seems imperative to consider how to encourage public engagement and interest in appearance research at a general level, which may in turn foster participation and involvement in specific research initiatives.

PUBLIC ENGAGEMENT

Researchers working in the field of appearance have recognized the importance and value of communicating the broad focus of their research efforts to the public in innovative ways. Payne and Dawson (2008) discussed how the Centre for Appearance Research collaborated with a Science Communication Unit to engage lay audiences with appearance and body image issues at a Bristol media centre by using an installation of mirrors and asking the question 'What do you see when you look in the mirror?'. Cardboard tags attached to mannequins were provided for the public to write their answers on. Similarly, Clarke et al. (2006) described a public engagement exercise in which public opinion about face transplantation was ascertained at a Royal Society Summer Science Exhibition.

Engagement activities may be a powerful way of increasing public understanding of the experience of visible difference and the consequences of appearance concerns. People who have appearance concerns may more readily see how their contribution to research might make a difference, for example, to improve quality of care, treatment, and service delivery. Hopefully, efforts to engage lay audiences with appearance research will continue and will further break down barriers to research participation and involvement; bridging the divide between researchers and the researched is essential, as well as being morally and ethically right (Wright et al., 2007) (see Webb and Poliakoff (2008) for a useful discussion about public engagement in psychological research).

PARTICIPATION IN RESEARCH:
A PERSONAL PERSPECTIVE

As someone with a visible difference, I have often been invited to take part in research, and my experiences have certainly varied. At a personal level, I have felt much more able to articulate and express my thoughts and ideas in a qualitative research setting as opposed to (for example) a questionnaire. This is my own personal preference, however, and the appropriate methodology naturally depends upon the research question being asked. However, discussing feelings about my different appearance, associated treatment, and past experiences can be emotive, and therefore it has always been important to me that the researcher and I establish a rapport prior to the interview. There are two personal experiences of research participation I would like to describe in order to highlight some issues which arose for me as a participant in appearance research.

In my teens, I took part in a research project in which I was initially approached by a researcher via my multidisciplinary cleft team. I was quite naive about research at the time, and was concerned that not taking part would compromise my treatment, so I agreed to participate. I was asked by the researcher to choose five personal photographs from my own collection which were significant to me in the context of having a visible difference. The researcher came to my home, looked at the photographs, and asked me a series of questions. I was reassured that I would be given feedback about the research, but unfortunately I never heard anything from the researcher again. As a result, I felt very used and let down, particularly as I had shared incredibly personal information and images. Consequently I did not take part in research again for some time.

A few years later I was interviewed by a researcher who was interested in my life history in the context of having a visible difference. This process was much more empowering; the researcher took time and effort to put me at ease, and I felt in control of the situation. The interview helped me shape my thoughts about my personal history, and highlighted issues that I had never expressed before. It was a liberating experience which gave me permission and the opportunity to talk about issues not generally discussed at a day-to-day level. I think I was also amazed that anyone was interested in my experiences! As part of the de-briefing after the interview, the researcher offered me information about different support organizations, which was incredibly useful. A few months later, I was sent the transcript of our interview and was invited to make any comments I wished. I was also sent a copy of the researcher's final thesis. I really enjoyed reading this and was able to clearly see how my contribution formed part of the research process from beginning to end. The researcher's approach to the interview enabled me to feel comfortable and in control of the process. This positive experience reignited my interest in appearance research.

These two instances illustrate how researchers' different approaches to participants can either enhance or discourage participation, and a researcher's choice of methods can also impede or improve access to participant voices.

Methodological Considerations

Appearance research has at its disposal a wealth of methods to access and promote participant voices in research and appearance researchers have thought creatively about the use of novel methods, in order to investigate appearance related topics effectively and represent participant views. For example, Frith and Harcourt (2005) described the use of photography to explore women's experiences of chemotherapy following a diagnosis of breast cancer. Fox et al. (2007) conducted online focus groups with young people who had chronic skin conditions, and Furness and Garrud (2010) studied adaption after facial surgery using diaries as a research tool.

In a discussion of methodologies which facilitate the participant's voice in research, Gilbert (2004) cited the following techniques: narrative research, photography and pictorial representation to construct stories, artwork, poetry, writing, and biographical and autobiographical accounts. Vivid personal accounts of having a visible difference are also evident in the literature, for example, Partridge (1990), and Grealy (1994) (see also Chapter 47).

Whereas quantitative research has a tradition of using standardized measures which may fail to tap individual experience, qualitative research has been shown to improve access to participant voices, and the detailed reporting of participant views, leading to the refinement and development of methodology. For example, as a result of an issue being spontaneously raised by three participants, Yearsley (2005) generated a further interview item in her research about the attitudes of people with visible differences toward facial transplantation. The appearance-related concerns of young people were investigated by Lovegrove and Rumsey (2005) who used action research methodology to develop a questionnaire to ascertain attitudes towards appearance, and to devise ways for coping with appearance based bullying. Further, Edwards et al. (2005) conducted in-depth interviews with young people with visible differences (who were referred to as 'expert informants' in the project), and used grounded theory to develop two Quality of Life modules which aimed to assess the effectiveness of psychosocial and surgical interventions.

Personal experience suggests that whether a researcher chooses quantitative or qualitative methodology, a researcher's approach to facilitating participation and feeding back study findings can have lasting consequences.

PUBLIC INVOLVEMENT IN RESEARCH:
ISSUES FOR CONSIDERATION

INVOLVE, (the national advisory group which supports greater public involvement in NHS, public health, and social care research in the UK), defines involvement as 'an active partnership between the public and researchers in the research process, rather than the use of people as the "subjects" of research' (INVOLVE, 2004).

There are many ways in which the public can be involved in research, for example, compiling a research agenda, suggesting outcome measures, developing questionnaire and interview items, advising on recruitment to studies, commenting on a lay summary or helping to write it, analysing data, attending conferences, and disseminating findings (Broerse et al., 2010). Different models of public involvement have been proposed, with some viewing it as a hierarchy (e.g. Arnstein's (1969) ladder of citizen participation in the US), depending upon how much control is assumed by the professional/researcher. A more recent UK model is INVOLVE's (2004) continuum which conceptualizes three levels of involvement; consultation (e.g. asking the public for their views), collaboration (denoting a more ongoing and active partnership with the public), and user-controlled research (in which the power and decision making lies with service users). The public can also design and carry out research. The level of involvement should be appropriate to the research aims, and different levels of involvement may be appropriate and relevant at different points in the research process (Wright et al., 2010). When involving the public, researchers should work with people who are potential end users of the results and outcomes of the research project (Hanley et al., 2003).

As highlighted by Beresford (2005), and Mercer (2002), there are some areas of health research in which public involvement has long been established, for example, in cancer and mental health. However, public involvement in appearance research is far less developed (although as noted by Chambers et al. (2004), involvement is not always reported in journal articles). Appearance researchers therefore have a positive opportunity to reflect upon, and learn from, developments in other fields which aim to encourage increased public involvement in research.

INVOLVING THE PUBLIC IN SETTING
RESEARCH AGENDAS

It has been argued that public involvement is ethical because research topics which are the most relevant and important to the public can be identified and targeted, thus avoiding unnecessary investment of funds and resources on peripheral issues (Boote et al., 2002). Boote et al. (2009) also highlighted that it should be possible for people to be involved in research which may have an impact on their health, particularly as taxpayers contribute to publicly funded research. The public are in a key position to bring their valuable experiences, knowledge, and insights to the research process, thus potentially improving the relevance of the research to the end users (Beresford 2005).

Broerse et al. (2010) compared the research priorities of health professionals and burn survivors, and found that although their priorities largely overlapped, they differed in their top four respective topics. The biggest research priority for burn survivors was the itching and oedema from scars and donor sites, whereas the top priority for professionals were the mechanisms involved in wound healing and scar development. Interestingly, psychosocial issues were highly prioritized by burn survivors (the third and fourth topics identified), but were 13th on the professionals' prioritization list. Although the authors commented on the meaningful dialogue which took place between service users and professionals, service users stated that their satisfaction with the process partly depended upon whether their identified priorities would result in tangible research (Broerse et al., 2010). This highlights the importance of managing people's expectations from the start, and identifying optimal ways of maintaining an ongoing dialogue with the public about research (Boote et al., 2002).

INVOLVING THE PUBLIC IN RESEARCH DESIGN

To facilitate successful public involvement, people's input should be sought at the very start of the research process, and involving the public in the design stage of research offers the potential to influence all aspects of a study (Staniszewska et al., 2007). As Hewlett et al. (2006) highlighted, early involvement may lead to a change of aims and methods.

The public could play a role in the design of questionnaires which aim to measure (for example) the psychosocial impact of an appearance altering condition, and the public could also be involved in setting the agenda for the topics for systematic reviews (Smith et al., 2009). Research has also involved the public in the analysis of research data (Staley 2009) and it is a misconception that public involvement is the preserve of qualitative research. For example, Hanley et al. (2001) surveyed over 100 clinical trial coordinating centres in the UK about the extent and nature of public involvement in randomized controlled trials. Respondents indicated a range of roles for the public including the development of protocols, the refining of patient information, and taking an active role in steering groups. These roles were felt by respondents to facilitate more relevant and user friendly trials.

FUNDING FOR PUBLIC INVOLVEMENT AT THE DESIGN STAGE

Involving the public in the design phase of research has cost implications (Boote et al., 2009), and these may preclude some researchers from initiating early public involvement. Some organizations do, however, make funds available to researchers who wish to involve the public in the design phase of their research. For example, some National Institute for Health Research (NIHR) Research Design Services in the UK offer grants for public involvement (Boote et al., 2009), and some Universities also operate similar schemes (such as the Credit Union at the University of the West of England, Bristol, in the UK). Although the pots of money available are typically small, they are an excellent opportunity to fund an important step in the research process.

USER-CONTROLLED RESEARCH

Examples of user-controlled research in the field of appearance are very few. This notable gap paves the way for the public to not only identify research topics, but to also carry out the research themselves, and subsequently analyse and disseminate the results. As highlighted by INVOLVE (2004), however, user-controlled research does not necessarily mean that service users carry out each step of the research; 'professional' researchers can also play a part (INVOLVE 2004).

PUBLIC INVOLVEMENT IN DISSEMINATION

At the end of the research, the public are often well placed to disseminate results in a user friendly fashion (rather than through the traditional format of formal conference papers or journal articles targeted at professional groups) through local support groups/organizations (Hanley et al., 2003), effectively closing the research loop. Other possibilities include the writing or editing of lay summaries of research, co-presenting at conferences and being involved in the writing of formal reports and academic papers (Hewlett et al., 2006).

ETHICAL CONSIDERATIONS

Unlike participation in research, ethical consent is not needed for public involvement in the UK (see INVOLVE and National Research Ethics Service (NRES) joint statement (2009)), and this principle applies to adults and young people/children alike.

However, involving the public may well highlight ethical issues (Smith et al., 2008). For example, if children and young people are to be involved in the research process, a Criminal Records Bureau (CRB) check is appropriate. Therefore, although ethical consent is not needed for public involvement, ethical considerations are still applicable (Wright et al., 2010), as highlighted by my own experiences of public involvement.

Involvement in Research: A Personal Perspective

As someone with a visible difference who has been invited to contribute to research design in the past, I had many questions and concerns prior to agreeing to being involved. For example, would my involvement affect the service or treatment I received? Who else would be involved (professionals and/or service users), and would they be known to me already? This question would be particularly relevant if the person conducting the research was also involved in my treatment and/or care. Might I have been in hospital or clinic with others who were involved with the project? I wanted to know what was required of me, how much time I would need to allocate to the project, whether and how much I would be paid, and/or would my expenses be paid? I was concerned that I would not understand medical terminology/jargon, and would appear incompetent. I was also worried that if I disagreed with the researchers or clinicians then my input into the project might no longer be welcome. I wondered what training or support I might receive, and who I should contact with concerns or questions. I wondered what I might learn, and whether I could list my involvement role on my CV. I was very concerned as to whether my contribution would actually make a difference to the research, how that difference would be demonstrated, and who would feedback to me. Personally, I was also very aware of the researcher's use of language. For example, if I was asked to contribute to a study on facial deformity/abnormality (terms which I view as unhelpful and negative (see Rumsey and Harcourt (2005) for a fuller discussion), I would question the researcher's familiarity with the potential sensitivities around appearance research, although my involvement in this situation could be an opportunity to educate the researcher!

Hewlett et al. (2006) highlighted a number of related issues in their discussion of patient research partners (patients who collaborate with researchers) in rheumatology research. Some partners were concerned that other patients might believe that they had received preferential treatment because of their involvement with the research (in which the professor also happened to be their clinician). Emotional reactions can also be provoked by an invitation to be involved in research, with some people questioning whether they are worthy or able enough to take part (Smith et al., 2009). Although not all prospective candidates for involvement will have as many questions as I did, these issues highlight the need for researchers to be mindful of sensitivities and good practice in public involvement.

CHALLENGES IN PUBLIC INVOLVEMENT

The challenges inherent in public involvement are clearly evident in the literature. A common concern voiced by researchers is that members of the public who are involved in research are not necessarily representative (Boote el al. 2009). However, one or two researchers are not representative of all researchers either! The aim of involvement is to elicit multiple perspectives rather than to gain a definitive user representative view (Bradburn & Maher 2005). In a similar vein, professionals may believe that the public do not have an understanding of research, and that they are biased about health topics thus posing problems for the neutrality of academia, and the progression of knowledge (Boote et al., 2009). As highlighted by Smith et al. (2008), members of the public bring different perspectives and interests to research in the same way that researchers and professionals do, and negotiations to agree the end product may well be illuminating.

The time and cost implications of public involvement have been noted by many authors (e.g. Hanley et al. (2003)), but as Corneli et al. (2007) demonstrated, the additional cost of funding public involvement amounted to less than 5% of their research budget for 1 year. As discussed, there are also small grants available in the UK for public involvement at the design stage.

In their review of patient research partners collaborating with professionals, Hewlett et al. (2006) noted communication challenges, such as professionals having 'corridor meetings', and access to email, phone, and conferences, all of which potentially exclude research partners. These challenges were met by having one-to-one meetings to discuss the role of a partner, offering information on public involvement, and arranging access to a desk, phone, stationery, and library facilities, including email.

The dynamics of an advisory group which involves members of the public may need careful monitoring. For example, members may hold very different viewpoints or become distressed if others downplay an issue which is important to them. They may also feel intimidated if one member is particularly articulate or forthright or if they feel that their peer had coped more positively than they did. In this situation, having discussed the matter with the person affected, it may be necessary for researchers to meet separately with one or two individuals in order to prevent any further distress, and to ensure individual views are heard.

As previously highlighted, some language used to describe a visible difference can be unhelpful and negative (Strauss 2001), so it is important for researchers to be mindful of this when involving the public in any aspect of the research process. Initially professionals can also experience difficulties when trying to alter their language to make it more appropriate and accessible to members of the public (Rhodes et al., 2002).

Staley et al. (2009) noted that some people recount negative experiences of involvement and can feel burdened and overloaded, which is why it is extremely important for researchers to follow good practice guidance and carefully monitor and be flexible in their approach to involvement activity. For example, some people involved in appearance research may need to help them understand aspects of the research process or may be undergoing treatment which may limit their time and opportunity for involvement. This can usually be overcome by offering a choice of modes of involvement.

One of the challenges is finding people who might like to be involved and avoiding the temptation to approach only those who are articulate and easily accessible. With reference to public involvement in cancer research, Stevens et al. (2003) referred to their attempts to maximize inclusion by trying to access seldom heard voices. For example, isolated members of the public, older people or those people affected by a rare condition, or a short-term condition may not be given the opportunity to become involved in research. Similarly, Rhodes et al. (2001, 2002) highlighted that disabled people, and those from ethnic minorities, are often excluded from public involvement. It should also not be assumed that children, young people, or older people are unable to be involved in research (see Kirby, 2004; Dewar 2005); however, imaginative and novel methods may be necessary to engage them. Stevens et al. (2003) utilized local radio and newspapers, and placed information about the study in GP surgeries, libraries, supermarkets, and in the Citizens Advice Bureau to facilitate access to seldom heard voices. Clinicians also approached patients and carers in clinic. Researchers can also contact user organizations, hospitals, local GP practices, support groups, or go online to access people who may be interested (Rhodes et al., 2002). In addition, some service user organizations may already have structures in place for handling approaches from researchers (Entwistle et al., 1998), or may have service user panels/councils set up comprising people who have already displayed an interest in research.

Professionals may feel threatened by the presence and input from the public (Thompson et al., 2009), and may also feel a lack of autonomy, and a decreased ownership of the research (Boote et al., 2002). Some professionals may find it challenging to view the public as research contributors and colleagues, as opposed to patients (Hewlett et al., 2006). It is clear that a cultural shift is needed in order to facilitate successful involvement and an avoidance of the potential tokenism highlighted by Hewlett et al. (2006). This major shift may take some time to develop as researchers adapt to a new way of working (Thompson et al., 2009).

GOOD PRACTICE IN PUBLIC INVOLVEMENT

For those wishing to learn more, there is some excellent literature available on good practice in public involvement (e.g. INVOLVE has a range of publications which can be downloaded from their website, http://www.invo.org.uk). The following principles of good practice are widely agreed by organizations promoting public involvement. Time and resources are essential for public involvement (Boote et al., 2006), and it is important to build realistic estimates of these into any funding application; naturally, it takes time to build relationships with people. Being clear with potential public partners about what is required of them during the research project from the outset and managing their expectations will enable people to make informed decisions about whether or not they wish to be involved (Boote et al., 2002). Pre-empting any concerns and identifying any training or support needs are also important (Boote et al., 2009). For example, if people have contributed to a research bid, they should be made aware that the research will not necessarily be funded (Staniszewska et al., 2007). It may also be beneficial to draw up a role description in conjunction with those who would like to be involved, and to offer people a named contact during the research process (Hewlett et al., 2006).

The ability to refund people's expenses is good practice, and researchers should also consider paying people for their time and expertise (INVOLVE 2010). However, welfare benefits can be affected by payment, hence the importance of early investigation of this issue (Smith et al., 2009). Other incentives, aside from paying people directly, may include offering gift vouchers or other rewards. For example, in research involving young people with visible differences, Coad et al. (2010) offered a variety of incentives including certificates of attendance for young people, and the opportunity to attend university lectures.

Ascertaining and meeting people's access requirements is also important (Hewlett et al., 2006). Someone with appearance concerns may also have access needs (e.g. the need for large print, an induction loop) which should be identified and addressed. People may wish to contribute to research in a variety of ways, for example, via email or phone, as opposed to attending meetings. If people do attend meetings, jargon should be avoided, and it might be useful to provide meeting attendees with a glossary of research terms or a 'jargon buster' prior to the meeting (Hewlett et al., 2006). It is essential that meetings are chaired effectively to allow everyone the opportunity to voice their opinion, and TwoCan Associates on behalf of the UK Clinical Research Collaboration (UKCRC) and National Cancer Research Institute (NCRI) (2010) has published useful guidance for chairpersons working in public involvement. Hewlett et al. (2006) also highlighted the pivotal role of the Principal Investigator in research meetings as s/he sets the standard and etiquette for those attending the meetings. Having just one member of the public on an advisory/ steering group may feel intimidating and tokenistic (Rhodes et al., 2002), so it is good practice to involve at least two people.

MEASURING THE IMPACT OF PUBLIC INVOLVEMENT

Measuring and assessing the impact of public involvement is a topical issue, and has led to the identification of assessment criteria by some authors working in the field.

For example, the public involvement literature, and Wright et al.'s (2010) direct experience of involvement formed a basis for appraisal guidelines to assess the quality and impact of public involvement in research (Wright et al., 2010). Criteria included 'Is the nature of training provided appropriate?', and 'Has there been any attempt to involve users in the dissemination of findings?'. Based on formal consensus methods (an expert workshop and a two-round postal Delphi process), Barber et al. (2007) also described principles and indicators of successful public involvement in NHS research, for example. 'Ensure that researchers have the necessary skills to involve consumers in the research process'. Further, Staley (2009) reported on the impact of public involvement in NHS, public health, and social care research. Researchers and members of the public involved in research cited the factors contributing to whether or not involvement influenced the project, including continuous and long-term involvement in a research project, and training and support for the public (Staley, 2009).

CONCLUSION

As someone with a personal experience of a visible difference, I strongly believe the promotion of participant voices and the involvement of the public in appearance research is an important priority. It has been hugely encouraging to see how the research landscape has begun to shift and recognize the intensely valuable contribution that the public can make to the research process. Researchers should be encouraged to move away from an ad hoc single study approach to involvement (Stevens et al., 2003), and consider appropriate long-term strategies for public involvement within appearance research.

Although participation and involvement in research can present challenges, the right approach built upon good practice can also reap many rewards. There is an increasing commitment by researchers in the field of appearance to promote the voices of those who either participate or are involved in the research process. It is now time to translate this commitment into overarching and meaningful strategies which enhance the voices of those that appearance research seeks to benefit.

REFERENCES

Arnstein, S. R. (1969). A ladder of citizen participation. *Journal of the American Institute of Planners,* 35(4), 216–24.

Barber, R., Boote, J. D., & Cooper, C. L. (2007). Involving consumers successfully in NHS research: a national survey. *Health Expectations,* 10, 380–91.

Beresford, P. (2005). Developing the theoretical basis for service user/survivor-led research and equal involvement in research. *Epidemiologia e Psichiatria Sociale,* 14(1), 4–9.

Boote, J., Baird, W., & Beecroft, C. (2009). Public involvement at the design stage of primary health research: a narrative review of case examples. *Health Policy,* 95, 10–23.

Boote, J., Barber, R., & Cooper, C. (2006). Principles and indicators of successful consumer involvement in NHS research: Results of a Delphi study and subgroup analysis. *Health Policy*, 75, 280–97.

Boote, J., Telford, R., & Cooper, C. (2002). Consumer involvement in health research: a review and research agenda. *Health Policy*, 61, 213–36.

Bradburn, J. & Maher, J. (2005). User and carer participation in research in palliative care. *Palliative Medicine*, 19, 91–2.

Broerse, J. E. W., Zweekhorst, M. B. M., van Rensen, A. J. M. L., & de Haan, M. J. M. (2010). Involving burn survivors in agenda setting on burn research: an added value? *Burns*, 36, 217–31.

Clarke, A., Simmons, J., White, P., Withey, S., & Butler, P. E. (2006). Attitudes to face transplantation: results of a public engagement exercise at the Royal Society Summer Science Exhibition. *Journal of Burn Care & Research*, 27(3), 394–8.

Chambers, R., O'Brien, L., Linnell, S., & Sharp, S. (2004). Why don't health researchers report consumer involvement? *Quality in Primary Care*, 12, 151–7.

Coad, J., Bates, A., & Williamson, H. (2010). Looking forward and thinking together—User involvement in Practice in Appearance related projects. Workshop presented at Appearance Matters 4 conference, Bristol, UK, June 2010.

Corneli, A. L., Piwoz, E. G., Bentley, M. E., Moses, A., Nkhoma, J. R., Tohill, B. C., *et al.* (2007). Involving communities in the design of clinical trial protocols: the BAN Study in Lilongwe, Malawi. *Contemporary Clinical Trials*, 28(1), 59–67.

Dewar, B. J. (2005). Beyond tokenistic involvement of older people in research—a framework for future development and understanding. *Journal of Clinical Nursing*, 14, 48–53.

Edwards, T. C., Patrick, D. L., Topolski, T. D., Aspinall, C. L., Mouradian, W. E., & Speltz, M. L. (2005). Approaches to craniofacial-specific quality of life assessment in adolescents. *Cleft Palate Craniofacial Journal*, 42(1), 19–24.

Entwistle, V. A., Renfrew, M. J., Yearley, S., Forrester, J., & Lamont, T. (1998). Lay perspectives: advantages for health research. *British Medical Journal*, 316, 463–6.

Fox, F., Morris, M., & Rumsey, N. (2007). Doing synchronous online focus groups with young people: Methodological reflections. *Qualitative Health Research*, 17(4), 539–47.

Frith, H. & Harcourt, D. (2005). Picture this: Using photography to explore women's experiences of chemotherapy. *Health Psychology Update*, 14(3), 2–9.

Furness, P. J. & Garrud, P. (2010). Adaptation after facial surgery: using the diary as a research tool. *Qualitative Health Research*, 20(2), 262–72.

Gilbert, T. (2004). Involving people with learning disabilities in research: issues and possibilities. *Health and Social Care in the Community*, 12(4), 298–308.

Grealy, L. (1994). *In the mind's eye: an autobiography of a face*. London: Arrow

Hanley, B., Truesdale, A., King, A., Elbourne, D., & Chalmers, I. (2001). Involving consumers in designing, conducting and interpreting randomised controlled trials: questionnaire survey. *British Medical Journal*, 322, 519–23.

Hanley, B., Bradburn, J., Barnes, M., Evans, C., Goodare, H., Kelson, M., *et al.* (2003). *Involving the public in NHS, public health and social care research: Briefing notes for researchers* (2nd edn.). Eastleigh: INVOLVE.

Herxheimer, A. & Goodare, H. (1999). Who are you, and who are we? Looking through some key words. *Health Expectations*, 2, 3–6.

Hewlett, S., de Wit, M., Richards, P., Quest, E., Hughes, R., Heiberg, T., *et al.* (2006). Patients and professionals as research partners: challenges, practicalities, and benefits. *Arthritis & Rheumatism*, 55(4), 676–80.

INVOLVE (2004). http://www.invo.org.uk (accessed 17 August 2010).

INVOLVE/NRES (2009). *Patient and public involvement in research and research ethics committee review.* http://www.invo.org.uk/pdfs/INVOLVE_NRESfinalStatement310309.pdf

INVOLVE (2010). *Payment for involvement: A guide for making payments to members of the public actively involved in NHS, public health and social care research.* Eastleigh: INVOLVE.

Kirby, P. (2004). *A guide to actively involving young people in research: for researchers, research commissioners, and managers.* Eastleigh: INVOLVE.

Lovegrove, E. & Rumsey, N. (2005). Ignoring it doesn't make it stop: adolescents, appearance and bullying. *Cleft Palate Craniofacial Journal*, 42(1), 33–44.

Mercer, M. (2002). Emancipatory disability research. In C. Barnes, M. Oliver, & L. Barton (eds.) Disability Studies Today, pp. 228–49. Cambridge: Polity.

Partridge, J. (1990). *Changing Faces.* London: Penguin.

Payne, E. & Dawson, E. (2008). Mirror, Mirror on the wall: a novel way of engaging lay audiences in thought and discussion about body image and appearance issues. *Health Psychology Update*, 17(2), 16–18.

Rhodes P., Nocon A., Wright J., & Harrison, S. (2001). Involving patients in research: setting up a service users' advisory group. *Journal of Management in Medicine*, 15 (2), 167–71.

Rhodes, P., Nocon, A., Booth, M., Chowdrey, M. Y., Fabian, A., Lambert, N., *et al.* (2002). A service users' research advisory group from the perspectives of both service users and researchers. *Health and Social Care in the Community*, 10(5), 402–9.

Rumsey, N. & Harcourt, D. (2005). *The Psychology of Appearance.* Berkshire: Open University Press.

Smith, E., Donovan, S., Manthorpe, J., Manthorpe, J., Brearley, S., Sitzia, J., *et al.* (2009). Getting ready for user involvement in a systematic review. *Health Expectations*, 12, 197–208.

Smith, E., Ross, F., Donovan, S., Manthorpe, J., Brearley, S., Sitzia, J., *et al.* (2008). Service user involvement in nursing, midwifery and health visiting research: A review of evidence and practice. *International Journal of Nursing Studies*, 45(2), 298–315.

Staley, K. (2009). *Exploring Impact: Public involvement in NHS, public health and social care research.* Eastleigh: INVOLVE.

Staniszewska, S., Jones, N., Newburn, M., & Marshall, S. (2007). User involvement in the development of a research bid: barriers, enablers and impacts. *Health Expectations*, 10, 173–83.

Stevens, T., Wilde, D., Hunt, J., & Ahmedzai, S. (2003). Overcoming the challenges to consumer involvement in cancer research. *Health Expectations*, 6, 81–8.

Strauss, R. P. (2001). 'Only skin deep': health, resilience and craniofacial care. *Cleft Palate-Craniofacial Journal*, 38, 226–30.

Thompson, J., Barber, R., & Ward, P.R. (2009). Health researchers' attitudes towards public involvement in health research. *Health Expectations*, 12, 209–20.

TwoCan Associates for the UKCRC, & NCRI (2010). *Patient and public involvement (PPI) in research groups—Guidance for Chairs.*

Webb, T. L and Poliakoff, E. (2008). Public engagement. *The Psychologist*, 21(8), 680–1.

Wright, D., Corner, J. L., Hopkinson, J., & Foster, C. (2007). The case for user involvement in research: the research priorities of cancer patients. *Breast Cancer Research,* 9(Suppl. 2), S3.

Wright, D., Foster, C., Amir, Z., Elliott, J., & Wilson, R. (2010). Critical appraisal guidelines for assessing the quality and impact of user involvement in research. *Health Expectations,* 13, 359–68.

Yearsley, N. (2005). Facial Transplantation: Beliefs Held by Individuals with a Visible Difference. Unpublished Dissertation; University of Bath, UK.

CHAPTER 49

RESEARCH ISSUES: SUMMARY AND SYNTHESIS

NICHOLA RUMSEY

DIANA HARCOURT

THE contributors to Section 4 have drawn on their own experiences and expertise to consider current issues in appearance research and have offered a range of suggestions and valuable guidance to new and established researchers in this field.

We are moving from a time during which research questions were formulated primarily by clinicians and academics, through current times in which researchers are increasingly involving the public in shaping the focus of research, to a new era in which the public are involved at all stages of the research process. In addition to the compelling moral and ethical imperatives of including the public in research, systematic patient and public involvement (PPI) is now becoming a requirement by governments and the majority of funding bodies. Amanda Bates' consideration of how to promote participants' voices in appearance research is stimulating and timely.

Effective public engagement requires a considerable investment of effort and time on all sides, and is not something to be undertaken lightly. Some researchers still see involvement at all stages of research as 'one step too far'—after all, research is daunting and demanding as it is, with the challenges associated with funding, ethical and research design approvals, ongoing research governance, and pressure to publish. However, others, for whom PPI is now routine, see it as providing an essential grounding in applied research, and report that the experience becomes second nature and less onerous as researchers become more adept at providing for the needs of their PPI representatives over time. Amanda's reflection that she prefers qualitative research methods is a reminder that participants should ideally be provided with options for their mode of participation and highlights the benefits of considering mixed and possibly novel methodologies.

Appearance is a popular choice amongst undergraduate and postgraduate students of psychology and other disciplines including medicine, nursing, and public health who are seeking a topic for their dissertation research, further highlighting its personal relevance to this population. The most popular methodology for 'entry level' research in this field is the administration of standardized measures to explore relationships between existing constructs. Indeed, most of the published research papers in this field report data collected in this way. In their chapter, Ross Krawczyk and colleagues have made the case for the further development and use of scales which are specific to the particular domain of body image being measured, and to the gender, developmental stage, sexual orientation, and ethnic and cultural background of participants. Yet there are tensions inherent in this proliferation of measures too. Standardized tools with acceptable psychometric properties are time consuming to develop, and this work occupies a great deal of research time and funding in this area. As more and more constructs are identified, the more confusing and fragmented the field appears, particularly for newcomers, and the harder it is to make direct comparisons between various studies. The potential load on participants of measuring the different constructs can be considerable. While undergraduates may complete questionnaires willingly (particularly when this effort is rewarded with course credits), the experience may not be rewarding for others. Amanda's comments about her experience of completing a variety of questionnaires and the disconnection between the questions and her own experience are thought provoking and highlight the benefit and importance of including those affected by appearance-related issues in the development of measures from the outset. Researchers should certainly consider the appeal and relevance of their chosen methods of data collection for participants.

Martin Persson has drawn our attention to the potential use of population-based studies. Sometimes, the influence that a piece of research has on policy and provision of care is limited because it has used a small sample size, yet researchers struggle (both logistically and in relation to budgetary and time constraints) with obtaining larger samples. Data derived from enormous samples through population studies, such as those which have been the focus of Martin's work, are only available in a minority of countries. However, researchers who are able to access these databases can make use of information which has already been collected, in a very cost-effective way. Providing that the measures used by the original developers are fit for purpose, findings from these population-based approaches have enormous potential to guide future research agendas—Martin's findings that 16-year-old males born with a cleft palate are of shorter stature, lighter weight, and with less physical strength than their peers is currently the topic of considerable interest in the field of cleft research.

Emma Dures has pointed out that appearance research is very much a 'real-world' endeavour, requiring answers to questions at a variety of levels and from a range of perspectives. Having used mixed methods at The Centre for Appearance Research for a number of years, we take no convincing of the benefits of this approach, however, Emma's points about the ways in which methods can and should be combined are worthy of careful consideration by those who would perhaps define themselves as an advocate of purely qualitative or quantitative approaches.

Alongside the increasing use of mixed methods has been a rise in the development and use of innovative methods in appearance research, many of which are capitalizing on the opportunities presented by developments in new technology and the availability of the Internet. Some of these new and alternative methods raise interesting ethical dilemmas which will continue to stretch the thinking of researchers. Clearly the potential use and benefits of online methods will continue to expand. Web-based data collection, for example, offers the potential for huge sample sizes to be recruited cost-effectively and over a relatively short space of time. Phillippa Diedrichs and colleagues recently designed a web-based study consisting of a standardized measure and a series of open-ended questions relating to body confidence, which accompanied a primetime TV series broadcast in the UK over 6 consecutive weeks in early 2011. More than 77,000 participants completed the survey during this period, far exceeding expectations and resulting in the largest survey into appearance-related issues in the UK (Diedrichs et al. in preparation). A survey of this size without the use of online data collection would be unfeasible. The exciting alternatives that are now available in the armoury of research methods at our disposal are likely to be particularly appealing to some participants. They can be considered as 'stand alone' methods, or could work well in combination with more established techniques.

In summary, the chapters in this section have illustrated the breadth of established and innovative methods suited to appearance research. Looking ahead, important issues facing researchers in this field will include how best to involve people affected by appearance-related issues at every stage of the research process, the development of innovative ways to recruit and engage participants, maximizing the use of population-based data and developments in online technology, and the most effective means of disseminating the results of research, including how best to raise the awareness of key stakeholders in policy and practice.

REFERENCE

Diedrichs, P. C., Rumsey, N., Halliwell, E. & Paraskeva, N. (in preparation). Body image in Britain: The prevalence of appearance concerns among 77630 adults.

SECTION 5

WHERE DO WE GO FROM HERE?

CHAPTER 50

THE PSYCHOLOGY OF APPEARANCE: THE FUTURE

NICHOLA RUMSEY
DIANA HARCOURT

COMPELLING evidence now supports the view that interest in appearance has never been higher and, whilst many people are content with their looks, levels of appearance concerns are escalating. These are not benign concerns—the chapters in this book demonstrate the huge strides made in providing data to show that they are detrimental to well-being and social functioning, and that they contribute to a variety of health risk behaviours. These effects hold true for people with and without visible differences, and for people who are considered good looking as well as those who consider themselves to be further from current societal ideals. However, an improved understanding of the linkages between the factors that contribute to levels of appearance-related concern and their consequences is only one step in the process.

Despite the clear consensus amongst researchers that current appearance ideals and the 'beauty myths' associated with them are damaging to many, the challenge of bringing about change is enormous. The myths are fuelled by the might of the media and global industries with a vested interest in maintaining levels of appearance-related concern and distress. So, where and how do we go forward from here? How can change be achieved and what should we be aiming to achieve in the short and longer term? In this final section we highlight what we believe are the key issues and priorities for research and practice in the future.

How Best to Progress Understanding Through Research

One of the phrases used most consistently by contributors to this volume and others working in this field is 'more research is needed'. In the recent past, appearance was often considered a superficial and unimportant topic in psychology (Rumsey & Harcourt, 2005), and therefore rarely included in general psychology textbooks. We hope that readers of this volume have either had their existing commitment to research in this area reinforced, or that they have been convinced of the need to understand and influence attitudes towards appearance and the current levels of concern.

Collectively, the authors in this book have compiled an agenda for future research which could keep aspiring, early career, and more established researchers busy for a lifetime, if only the funding and infrastructure for research in this field were available. Our experience suggests that growing numbers of psychology undergraduates and postgraduates are drawn to the field of appearance, yet funding opportunities to do this work are few and the numbers of established researchers working in the field is relatively small. We keep an ongoing list of priority areas, research questions, and possible projects and have learned over the years to be opportunistic in matching pockets of funding, projects, and available people—it would be fair to say that we are never short of projects and people, but funding remains a constant challenge.

Prominent on the agenda emerging from this book is the urgent need to examine experiences across the lifespan since although childhood, adolescence, and early adulthood have been the focus for the majority of research to date, appearance concerns are clearly not the preserve of the young. A detailed understanding of the nature and impact of appearance concerns for males of all ages and the role of ethnicity and culture have also been neglected issues to date, as have any implications of these for the development of appropriate support and intervention.

As generations of young people who have lived within an appearance-obsessed society become parents, there is a growing imperative to research the role of family and friendships in reinforcing or ameliorating appearance concerns. More studies are needed concerning intimate relationships too. Initial research suggests these may be protective when well established and stable, yet changes to aspects of appearance that are particularly associated with intimacy (such as those resulting from breast cancer treatment, or from genital surgery) can put pressure on even the most supportive relationships when body image, confidence, and feelings of femininity or masculinity are affected. Appearance concerns can also lead to, or exacerbate, fears of becoming involved in a close relationship with a potential partner, for people with and without visible differences.

On the basis of our experience of running a research centre which includes specialists in disfigurement and appearance issues in the broader population, we commend
to readers the benefits of merging these two fields, and of considering everyone,
regardless of whether or not they have a visible 'difference' as falling on the same
broad continuum of adjustment and distress. Colleagues from these two camps have
gained much from each other in terms of an understanding of the cognitive processes
involved in adjustment, the filters people use to process information from their social
environments, and in relation to the development of interventions to promote
increasing acceptance of diversity in appearance, both within the self and in relation
to others. This broader approach promotes a view of people with disfigurements as
just that—people first, who happen to have a disfigurement—rather than a population apart ('disfigured people'). It helps us to understand that other developmental
processes and life events will affect individuals' adjustment to looking different from
others and also reminds us that although a disfigurement may be the reason that
brings them on to the radar of researchers and clinicians, other appearance concerns
(e.g. weight and shape) may trump the disfigurement and be the cause of distress.

In relation to new and breaking developments in the field, the burgeoning interest in the role of genetics and personality in appearance-related adjustment are
worthy of mention. Work in these areas has the potential to shed light on a variety
of predispositions which may contribute to more comprehensive explanations of
individual differences in vulnerability and resilience including, for example, the
role played by temperament (e.g. neuroticism) or attributional style (optimism/
pessimism). The developing field of neurocognitive psychology may add to our
understanding of the ways in which congenital conditions may affect social functioning in ways other than through an altered appearance. For example, there are
early indications that additional complications of some syndromes involving a cleft
lip and/or palate may include neurocognitive deficits which may compromise the
ability to read and process nonverbal signals from others. Future agendas within
appearance research will also be influenced by more general trends in researchers'
host disciplines. Since we completed our last book (Rumsey & Harcourt, 2005),
positive psychology has become more widely established, and many researchers in
the field of appearance have embraced the study of positive adjustment in addition
to the more established tradition of focusing on problems and difficulties.

What is the future for theory in the field of appearance? As discussed in the summary and synthesis of Section 2, researchers have identified a plethora of constructs,
many of which provide small pieces in the overall jigsaw of appearance-related
adjustment and distress. However, the 'list' of constructs (together with their
accompanying measures) and of subspecialisms within the ever-broadening
umbrella of appearance-related research is now so long that it has justified the
recent compilation of an 'encyclopaedia' (Cash, 2012). This complexity is baffling
to many newcomers to the field, and even amongst established researchers there is
a growing sense of fragmentation of knowledge. The process of isolating individual

contributory factors to adjustment could continue indefinitely, so, just how far is it useful to drill down? We believe it is important to keep an applied focus in mind and to continue down this line only when the results are likely to have clinical or practical implications. We believe that researchers should draw breath at this point and look for agreement on key issues, broad constructs, and processes and on the measures that can most appropriately be used to assess these. A consensus of this sort has the potential to galvanize the combined efforts of this research community by increasing the sense of shared purpose within the community, and by offering new entrants and more established researchers a common framework within which the complexity and multiplicity of antecedents and consequences of adjustment can more easily be understood. Where possible and appropriate, we should involve people affected by appearance concerns in this process, as this would be particularly helpful in ensuring the ecological validity of the framework and may enable researchers to establish a shared agenda for priority areas for research.

If the research community continues down the current route, those committed to using their work to change policy and practice should bear in mind the tendency for the eyes of clinicians, the public, and policy-makers to glaze over when research-ers present diagrams involving multiple boxes and arrows, or when we use jargon and excessive detail to discuss the minutiae involved in adjustment. If we are not careful, those with the potential to influence change are sent running for the hills. With a common framework, the research community could unite in talking with confidence and clarity about broad constructs and processes and in this way, greatly increase our potential to influence change. Although the thought of achieving this sort of consensus approach brings the analogy of 'herding cats' to mind, it can be done! The ARC model (Rumsey et al., under review), discussed in Section 1 is an example of how several researchers and clinicians with their own areas of specialism can agree a common framework and explain the evidence base for the application of research findings in an accessible way. A very current example of the process of agreeing such a framework is exemplified by the collective efforts of the psycholo-gists appointed to teams specializing in the care of people affected by a cleft in the UK, and who have been required to achieve a consensus on mandatory audit mea-sures and key developmental points at which to collect this data in order to contrib-ute to national databases. This group has agonized for many years over how to achieve agreement about both audit and research. Now, with the impending launch (in 2012) of a UK birth cohort study involving all new babies with a cleft and their families (http://www.thehealingfoundation.org), minds have been focused, and significant progress has been made towards establishing a broad framework within which to conceptualize adjustment, thus making the task of identifying contribu-tory factors and developmental key-stages much more straightforward. A model in which all the psychologists collect key measures, and also retain the flexibility to pursue their own particular research interests, whilst clearly locating these sub-group activities within the overall framework, is emerging.

When thinking about how we can best progress understanding through research, we should be thinking more broadly and creatively about the methods we use and, where possible, offer participants a choice of methods or ways in which they can take part and engage in research agendas. Several chapters in this book have demonstrated ways of putting patients in the driving seat (or at least as co-pilots, not just passengers) and we encourage readers to take these issues on board, regardless of their particular methodological, epistemological or theoretical viewpoint.

Academic researchers also need to think 'outside the box' in efforts to provide clinicians with tools and measures that can be used in practice rather than to remain in the wings, ham-strung by conventional 'rules and regulations' relating to measurement. For example, in relation to the imperative to develop ways of screening the suitability of patients for cosmetic surgery and other appearance-altering procedures (see Chapter 25), we maintain that it is preferable to develop and evaluate a brief, user-friendly screening instrument which has been informed by research and clinical experience than to insist that a weighty battery of standardized measures (unusable in busy clinics and unwelcome by prospective patients) is the only valid method of assessment. Researchers should also support and encourage clinicians to evaluate their work effectively, and may best achieve this by promoting the advantages offered by including practitioner researchers in healthcare teams. Our colleague Alex Clarke (see Chapter 36) has led the way in demonstrating what can be achieved with a combination of excellent research and clinical skills, but would also testify to the challenges of trying to maintain and fund this dual role in times of economic and institutional upheaval.

How Best to Achieve Change

Having established that both further research and societal change are needed, how should we focus our efforts to reduce appearance related dissatisfaction and distress at an individual level, and promote acceptance and a celebration of diversity in appearance at a societal level?

The tiered model of interventions introduced by Elizabeth Jenkinson in Chapter 38 is a very practical framework to support those faced with the challenges of living with a visible difference which could also be used to classify interventions relating to mainstream body image in the general population, and be expanded to include interventions at a societal/population level to change or challenge societal messages (e.g. poster campaigns, changes to media content) at level zero (see Fig. 50.1). The Centre for Appearance Research (CAR) framework also encourages coherence vertically, in that the same evidence based approaches (e.g. challenging appearance-related beliefs; improving confidence in social situations) can be used in the most intense one-to-one interventions at Level 5 and also operationalized in different ways at lower levels. Developing the framework to incorporate mainstream body

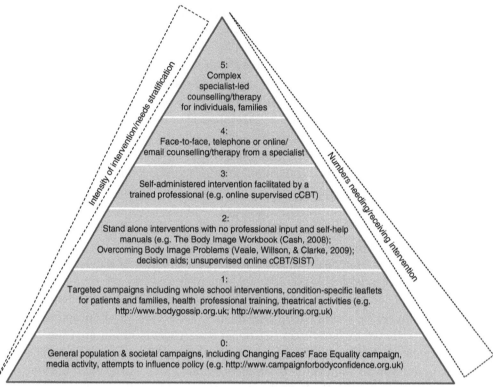

Figure 50.1 The CAR framework of appearance-related interventions.

image and societal interventions in this way supports our view, outlined above, that individuals' appearance concerns are most usefully considered along a continuum rather than segregated according to whether or not they are related to having a visible difference.

Individual interventions

Our current, limited evidence base at the level of interventions aimed at individuals, points to the efficacy of approaches based on cognitive behavioural therapy (CBT) and incorporating appropriate social skills training. Third-generation techniques may also hold promise, and we should continue to be aware of interventions being developed in other fields that may have potential benefits within the appearance arena. And, rather than seeking a 'gold standard' intervention that would suit everyone, we should be open to a variety of approaches as recipients' needs vary between individuals and over time, and responses to the same intervention approach will also vary. Specialists delivering interventions or supporting self-help interventions may benefit from the guidance available from the manual developed by the Appearance Research Collaboration (see Clarke et al., 2011) and online interventions such as Face IT outlined in Chapter 39.

The adoption of the CAR framework may offer research and healthcare teams alike a structure within which all members can conceptualize the tasks involved in addressing needs, and understand the potential of their own contribution to changing attitudes towards appearance and ameliorating appearance-related distress. However, it also raises the question of how best to identify those who are likely to benefit from the various levels of interventions. When assessing individual needs and the most appropriate way of providing support, it is important to bear in mind that people seeking intervention may often have complex needs that are not solely appearance-related. For example, at Level 5 in this framework, a person affected by burns injuries may benefit from support in relation to post traumatic stress, the impact their injury has had on the family and mental health issues, as well as appearance-related concerns. For some, additional appearance-related interventions that are unique to a specific condition (for example the particular demands of managing burns scarring) may also be appropriate and could be administered at Levels 1, 2, 3, 4, or 5 depending on the degree of distress being experienced. Societal interventions (Level 0) to promote understanding and acceptance of visible differences and to promote diversity in appearance may help to promote feelings of acceptance and integration.

Many professionals (including those in health and educational settings) and parents/carers are very aware of the challenges and issues experienced by those for whom they are responsible, but many others remain unaware that appearance concerns are causing distress. This was acutely evident to us when we were recruiting participants through general medical practices for a study into adjustment to visible differences. We were assured by several family practitioners that their patients were not troubled by appearance issues and they were subsequently surprised to find that not only were their patients keen to take part in the study, but also that a sizeable proportion reported significant concerns. There is clearly still a need for effective education and training, and also rigorously evaluated screening tools that are not unduly onerous, either for the affected person, or for health professionals and those potentially providing support. Appropriately raising awareness of signs and symptoms of appearance concerns (without simultaneously encouraging the view that everyone who does not meet societal ideals must be troubled), and then providing the means to support people in this work (for example, through training or signposting to appropriate and accessible resources), and specialist training (e.g. in relation to the aims and approach of each intervention, together with experience of working with each particular target client group) for those working at the higher levels of the framework are ongoing challenges. Without this, health professionals are unlikely to raise these issues with patients and their appearance-related needs will remain unaddressed. Even if these needs are recognized, professionals may avoid the issue rather than run the gauntlet of opening a can of worms that they feel unprepared for, or lack confidence in dealing with. Konradsen et al. (2009) talked about 'the silencing of disfigurement' by health professionals working with head and neck cancer patients—we suspect there is a broader 'silencing of appearance' by health professionals, and others, more generally.

Health professionals must also be encouraged to shoulder some of the burden of responsibility for changing broader attitudes towards appearance. They and others in positions of influence, including teachers and people working in the media, for example, should carefully consider their use of language, and ensure that they do not inadvertently fuel existing 'beauty myths' and individual insecurities. This requires them to examine their own values and assumptions about appearance. It would be beneficial to increase awareness of the breadth of appearance issues as part of medical, media, and educational training.

Societal approaches

The pervasiveness of appearance-related distress amongst people of all ages makes it clear that interventions focussed on ameliorating the concerns of individuals are not sufficient. Attitude change is notoriously difficult, but this challenge cannot be shirked, and efforts to intervene at group and societal levels need to be doubled and redoubled.

The media and advertising industries have a key role to play in this regard. The agendas of the majority of media professionals, even those who genuinely seek to promote the voice of those affected by appearance concerns, are to attract and entertain as large an audience as possible, together with generating income from advertising revenues. This potentially clashes with researchers' and clinicians' agendas and can make working with the media difficult, but impenetrable as the world of the media professionals may appear, we ignore its power at our peril—and when the agendas of researchers and producers have converged (albeit tenuously), we have experienced this power through the medium of huge numbers of respondents to surveys in a short timescale, offering us an otherwise unobtainable dataset which has proven invaluable when arguing for resources to develop interventions.

A broader (and more typical) spectrum of appearance is needed in all aspects of the media in order to promote diversity in appearance. In recent years, the number of documentaries about people living with disfigurement has increased dramatically but the focus of many of these is on entertainment and the shock factor. We do not yet understand what impact media portrayals of people with disfigurement have on viewers, with or without a visible difference themselves. Are they challenging or reinforcing stereotypes? Are they satisfying viewers' curiosity and tendency toward voyeurism in the comfort of their own home, negating the tendency to stare when encountering a person with a particular condition in real life? Or will this media exposure heighten unwanted attention in real life?

Wardle and Boyce (2009) recommended that people with rare and unusual conditions, and those further from current appearance ideals (whether or not by virtue of a visible difference) should appear regularly in both key and supporting roles both on and off camera rather than appearing only as a focus for scrutiny. A recent study of viewers' reactions to James Partridge presenting the lunchtime news bulletin on a UK terrestrial TV station for 1 week in November 2009 (see Chapter 33) found that whilst viewers supported attempts to raise the profile of people with disfigurements in the media, they emphasized that this should not take priority over ability (Venus and Harcourt, submitted). The media has also been recommended as a means of naturally introducing children to diversity of appearance. For example, Cerrie Burnell (a successful actress and TV presenter who was born without a right hand and forearm) was appointed as a presenter on children's TV programmes by virtue of her aptitude, not her appearance. However, her visible difference prompted comment amongst parents, some of whom thought her appearance was inappropriate and upsetting for children, although children themselves seemed unaffected. More research is needed to understand better the spectrum of responses and how best to influence them. This example also reminds us of the need to consider the influence that parents have on young people's attitudes towards appearance and the need for multiple approaches in the bid to achieve change.

The debates about the influence and potential of the media do not relate only to the medium of television. The potential to promote positive body image and acceptance of diversity through all aspects of traditional and emerging new media could be investigated further. The print media are also full of words and images promoting unrealistic appearance ideals. Even forms of communication without visual images, such as radio (through presenters' discourse, the topics of phone-ins and news items) and novels portray and promote appearance ideals. Occasionally, programmes and news items challenge current appearance ideals and practices, but the 'background script' contributes to their perpetuation and to the promotion of celebrity culture. For example, as we write this chapter the TV, Internet, radio, and print media are discussing celebrities' hair transplants, dieting, and dental braces.

Are advertisers peddling unrealistic dreams and promoting unrealistic ideals, preying on the vulnerable and fuelling expectations that are unachievable? It is an irrefutable fact that it is in the interests of advertisers to reinforce stereotypes in order to sell their 'appearance-enhancing' and 'anti-ageing products'. The adverts imply that their products will halt or delay the ageing process (at considerable expense to the consumer) and yet, the effects of ageing are inexorable. An acceptance of this fact by consumers would be more adaptive than the unrealistic expectations that beauty products can help them defy the combined forces of nature and gravity. Advertisers are also inventive—new areas of the body are regularly identified as needing improvement (with associated products being offered as a solution to the 'problem'). For example, we have recently noticed an emerging imperative for women to have 'beautiful underarms'—it is no longer sufficient to be hair-free, advertisements for deodorants now promote a new message that underarm skin must have particular properties to be attractive too! Providers of cosmetic procedures are also innovative, providing an ever increasing array of injections and surgical procedures to 'correct abnormalities' in appearance and in so doing, improve the well-being and quality of life of people purchasing the procedures.

These advertisements for lotions, potions, and cosmetic procedures prey on those who are vulnerable—those who believe, either temporarily (perhaps because their confidence has been shaken by stress of a life event), or more habitually, that they will be more fulfilled and have a better life if they change the way they look. Relying on these superficial solutions is not conducive to long term well-being or self-esteem, so if a person believes their happiness is contingent on good looks and youth, and if the opinions of others are all important, they will inevitably be disappointed. It's a somewhat sobering thought that just a very small percentage of the budgets spent on advertising these beauty products could fund a sizeable body of research and intervention delivery.

Chapter 33 in Section 3 discusses public campaigns to change attitudes towards people with disfigurement. The impact of these is not yet known. People who have been personally affected can be particularly powerful advocates of change, but again, one person's solution to a particular problem (e.g. how to recover from and live with a visible difference) will not fit all. While for some segments of the intended audiences, the messages may achieve their intended purpose, for others, they may hit the wrong buttons. The impact of these messages both on others affected by similar conditions and on broader audiences should be evaluated. Partnerships between researchers and lay led organizations are needed (e.g. to evaluate attitude change campaigns). Building these relationships takes time, commitment, good communication skills, and the building and maintaining of trust, particularly in relation to the agendas of each party—what will happen if an evaluation demonstrates an intervention doesn't work, for example? Of course, these pressures are not unique to appearance, nor to public campaigns, but they are nevertheless worthy of careful attention.

Consideration should also be given to the broader impact on viewers of the images and messages used in fund raising campaigns by a range of charities. These messages can never be neutral. Every week, soulful close-up images of doe-eyed children in resource-poor countries with unrepaired cleft lips and sad expressions appear in British newspapers, designed to tear at the heart strings and to persuade people to donate to the cause. Likewise, some cancer charities rely on images of women and young people with chemotherapy-induced alopecia within their fund raising activities. There is no denying the effectiveness of these campaigns in an environment where competition for donations is intense. Campaigners, researchers, and fund-raisers are emotionally charged and invested in their own particular theories about what needs to be achieved and how to achieve it. The short- and longer-term responses of viewers to these images, messages, and campaigns have yet to be evaluated and it may be that some reinforce rather than change unhelpful stereotypes. Ideally, researchers and those making the effort to raise money, educate, or challenge societal attitudes should walk hand-in-hand through the maze that is attitude change going forward.

Within Level 1 of the CAR framework in Fig. 50. 1, there appears to be promise in the results of some interventions that have been used to tackle the attitudes and beliefs of whole communities, such as schools or universities. Once again, we are advocates of interventions that focus on increasing acceptance and appreciation of diversity in appearance across the board, as we believe it is more helpful to achieve change through interventions which normalize appearance concerns rather than highlight the differences between groups (e.g. in relation to people with disfigurement, or who are very large). Although many interventions target pupils and students within a particular institution, we should also bear in mind that children and students can go on to influence the views of parents, other family members, and friends who were not exposed to the intervention directly. Peer-assisted learning has been used effectively within schools in other subject areas (e.g. in relation to promoting anti-smoking campaigns) and we should consider how we can use these principles more widely. Teachers, tutors, and head-teachers are gatekeepers to messages about appearance, and effort is needed to develop packages of training for them.

In addition to ongoing research into the most effective ways of reducing distress and promoting appearance-related attitude change in educational settings, a key challenge is how to influence the inclusion of appropriate material in an already packed timetable. In the UK, the curriculum for PSHE (Personal, Health & Social Education) would seem the obvious home for this material, but teachers have many other compulsory topics to cover and convincing them of the need to incorporate the content needed to achieve change will be difficult. A better strategy may be to weave material relating to appearance more broadly across the curriculum (e.g. within history, art, or design and technology). The TV presenter Gok Wan has campaigned for 1 hour per year to be added to the national curriculum in the UK, but current evidence (see Chapter 37) suggests it is unlikely that this would be enough to make changes to young people's body image and attitudes towards appearance. Should we be pragmatic and take whatever sessions are offered by any one institution, or hold out and lobby for a more comprehensive approach? If 1 hour is the only available option, what should be included to make best use of the opportunity?

Despite the obvious challenges inherent in societal interventions, our experience is that the public at large will be receptive. Interest in this field is evidenced by the growing numbers that attend talks and public engagement events, such as Science Festivals, Science Cafes, and educational activities, and we often find that a sizeable number of people want to stay on after such events to share their own concerns and thoughts on the issues that have been raised. Funds to support this public engagement work seem to be more accessible than in the past but achieving them is a very competitive process. As well as opportunities to disseminate research findings, these events provide a context for gathering views on research agendas and promoting positive attitudes towards appearance. Ways of maintaining effective and ongoing public engagement, for example through web-based and permanent interactive exhibits in museums and science centres, in addition to one-off events, warrant further consideration and are a current focus within CAR.

As noted in Chapter 18 there is a growing momentum for change in Australia and several countries in Europe. As we write, the signs that policy-makers are taking appearance issues onboard are promising. Body image researchers from CAR are now working with national and international organizations that are keen to deliver interventions to promote diversity of body shapes, increase body satisfaction, and reduce appearance concerns. These various parties are also leading members of the Campaign for Body Conference (http://www.campaignforbodyconfidence. wordpress.com), supported by a newly established All Party Parliamentary Group on Body Image. This level of support at parliamentary level enables the government to be lobbied and questioned, and parliamentary enquiries to be set up thereby putting body image firmly on the political agenda. The challenge is to ensure that this enthusiasm and motivation to raise the profile of this agenda continues and that it encompasses all aspects of appearance, not only weight and shape.

MAKING BEST USE OF ECONOMIC
AND POLITICAL CLIMATES

The broader utility of the framework in Fig. 50.1 and the feasibility of the campaigns outlined earlier will be affected by the prevailing economic and political environment of host nations. Several contributors to this volume have highlighted how agendas and systems within different countries and cultures vary greatly and we acknowledge that the majority of our suggestions for change are relevant to countries which are relatively resource-rich. However, all of the contributors have written their chapters at a time of economic recession and in the midst of increasing pressure on the funding of research, education, and healthcare—circumstances in which appearance issues might be seen, by some, as frivolous.

A recurring theme throughout this book is the need for strong collaboration and synergy between clinicians, researchers, and other stakeholders including funding bodies, lay-led organizations, and policy-makers. The effort involved in establishing and maintaining the collaborations necessary to achieve large sample sizes, prospective, longitudinal studies, and in delivering multicentre research is considerable, and the paperwork and systems involved in research governance (particularly in healthcare settings) can feel increasingly burdensome and time-consuming. Tough decisions are being made by research funders about where their priorities should lie, and the competition amongst researchers for limited resources is increasing year on year. In such difficult circumstances, it is particularly important for researchers to demonstrate the relevance of their work to current policy. For example, recent proposals for the UK government's long-term vision for public health (Department of Health, 2010) specifically acknowledged the role of body confidence in influencing health behaviours, thereby presenting opportunities for researchers and clinicians with interests in this area.

Increasingly, economic and political pressures are determining who has access to which interventions (e.g. surgical or psychosocial), yet the basis on which local and national priorities are determined is often opaque. Researchers and clinicians must engage with policy-makers in order to understand and influence their agendas. If policy-makers remain unimpressed by research evidence that interventions are beneficial, and by the moral imperative that to deny someone access to a beneficial intervention is unethical, then we must also collaborate with health economists to demonstrate that our interventions are also cost-effective.

Concluding Remarks

In this book, we and the contributing authors have drawn attention to the levels and impacts of distress and dissatisfaction with appearance, but also to factors contributing to more positive outcomes. These issues are not trivial. Without intervention, people with appearance concerns will continue to raise generations who strive to meet increasingly unachievable appearance ideals as they believe their lives will be better as a consequence and who experience anxiety and distress when they, inevitably, fall short of these ideals. The call for change is not about the protagonists being spoilsports. Rather, it is a call to arms to rein in concern about appearance to a level where people can enjoy making the most of their looks if they choose to, without distress, and without fear of being negatively judged or censored by their peers and by society.

References

Cash, T. F. (2008). *The Body Image Workbook: An 8-step Program for Learning to Like Your Looks, 2nd Edition*. Oakland: New Harbinger Publications.

Cash, T. F. (Ed). (2012). *Encyclopedia of Body Image and Human Appearance*. New York: Academic Press.

Clarke, A., Rumsey, N., Newman, S., Thompson, A., Jenkinson, E. on behalf of the Appearance Research Collaboration (in press). *Psychosocial Interventions for Disfigurement and Appearance Anxiety: a Practical Guide*, Oxford: Wiley.

Department of Health (2010). Healthy Lives, Healthy People: White Paper, Our Strategy for Public Health in England, London: Department of Health.

Konradsen, H, Kirkevold, M, & Zoffmann V. (2009). Surgical facial cancer treatment: the silencing of disfigurement in nurse-patient interactions. *Journal of Advanced Nursing*, 8, 65: 2409–18.

Rumsey, N. & Harcourt, D. (2005). *The Psychology of Appearance,* Buckingham: Open University Press.

Rumsey, N., Charlton, R., Clarke, A., Harcourt, D., James, H., Jenkinson, E., et al. (under review). Factors associated with distress and positive adjustment in people with disfigurement: evidence from a large multi-centred study.

Veale, D., Willson, R. & Clarke, A. (2009). *Overcoming Body Image Problems including Body Dysmorphic Disorder: A Self-Help Guide Using Cognitive Behavioural Techniques,* London: Constable Robinson.

Venus, L., & Harcourt, D. (submitted). Public responses to disfigurement in the media.

Wardle, C., & Boyce, T. (2009). *Media Coverage and Audience Reception of Disfigurement on Television.* Cardiff: The Healing Foundation and Cardiff University.

Author index

SUBJECT INDEX